MW00388369

THE LUTHERAN DIFFERENCE

500TH ANNIVERSARY OF THE REFORMATION

The Lutheran Difference

An Explanation & Comparison of Christian Beliefs

General Editor
Edward A. Engelbrecht

Contributing Editors
Robert C. Baker • John P. Hellwege Jr.
Rachel C. Hoyer • Charles P. Schaum

Writers
Armand J. Boehme • William M. Cwirla
Alfonso Espinosa • Korey Maas • Thomas Manteufel
Angus Menuge • Michael Middendorf
Steven P. Mueller • Patra Pfotenhauer
Robert Rossow • Gregory Seltz • Bret Taylor

CONCORDIA PUBLISHING HOUSE • SAINT LOUIS

Copyright © 2014 Concordia Publishing House
3558 S. Jefferson Ave., St. Louis, MO 63118-3968
1-800-325-3040 • www.cph.org

First edition copyright 2010.

Text derived from *The Lutheran Difference* Bible study series.

Manufactured in the United States of America

Library of Congress Cataloging-in-Publication Data

The Lutheran difference.
p. cm.
Edited by Edward A. Engelbrecht
Includes index.
ISBN 978-0-7586-2670-7
1. Lutheran Church—Doctrines. 2. Lutheran Church—Missouri Synod—Doctrines. 3. Lutheran Church—Apologetic works. 4. Lutheran Church—Missouri Synod—Apologetic works. I. Engelbrecht, Edward. II. Title.

BX8065.3.L86 2010
230'.41—dc22 2010029475

2 3 4 5 6 7 8 9 10 23 22 21 20 19 18 17

Contents

List of Comparisons

Preface to the Reformation Anniversary Edition

"I thought she was going to kiss me," said my teenage son after we visited a Roman Catholic mass.

In the midst of the service, the congregation paused for the Greeting of the Peace and, unlike my son's experience at our home church, he noticed that couples around the sanctuary were actually kissing one another on the lips rather than just shaking hands. When a middle-aged woman turned to greet him, he experienced a moment's panic. However, she simply extended her hand and wished him God's peace—what a relief! Only afterward did he recognize that the persons kissing one another were married couples, and that everyone else was just shaking hands.

Visiting other churches is a remarkable learning experience; it can not only relieve a person from misunderstandings, but also amplify the sense of just how differently Christians may believe and practice their faith. To prepare this Reformation anniversary edition of *The Lutheran Difference*, I led my family on a pilgrimage to other churches in our area and then discussed with them the differences we experienced. (It only seemed fair to actually visit other Christians before writing about them; it's amazing how much you learn from talking with people directly, listening to them, and setting aside your assumptions.) My wife and I were so grateful for the kind welcome we received at each church and for the fact that the Scripture and the Gospel were likewise proclaimed. In this preface, I will share a few of our experiences.

Denominations and Change

A church's teaching remains the most important factor in affecting whether a person will join or leave (Barna Group, "Three Major Faith and Culture Trends for 2014," online article). Yet those studying the sociology of American churches are also concluding that differences between denominations are declining. They believe that segments of American churches are becoming more and more like one another.

For example, after surveying churches for core beliefs, the Barna Group concluded that the differences between Roman Catholics and mainline Protestants are growing smaller and are almost negligible. On a different note, as our family visited a variety of liturgical churches, we were also struck by the number of common elements in the services, and even common texts and tunes as denominational hymnals influenced one another. Also, the organ prelude at the Catholic basilica was by J. S. Bach—a serious Lutheran; several of the Protestant churches sang the same popular Christian song that we heard broadcast on a local Christian radio station. However, one experience revealed a shocking difference. When attending an Episcopal service, we listened as the priest and the congregation recited together the Apostles' Creed and the Lord's Prayer. To our surprise, persons seated around us substituted the word "God" for "Father" and "God's only Son" for "His only Son," etc., avoiding the use of any masculine references to God. Even as conservative liturgical trends and Christian radio might influence congregational practices, liberal theology might chip away at core texts of the faith.

Although researchers suggest that what a church believes is the most important factor in whether or not people attend and stay there, I would suggest that practice is at least as important as doctrine. Doctrine and practice, of course, intertwine. But what churches profess and what they practice can also be quite different. I find that the laity especially identify churches by their practices while remaining less conscious of differences in belief. People will say things like, "Roman Catholics kneel when they pray; Protestants don't." This is not true, of course, but is easily concluded if you have limited experiences with other Christians. Musical choice is a huge factor in congregational practice. As we visited other churches, we most often heard them sing to piano and organ, guitar and drums. Yet the Coptic Christians used a small set of cymbals and a triangle to accompany their chants, which sounded so incredibly Near Eastern to our American ears. And sometimes Christians do the same or similar things for very different reasons. The Pentecostals were kicking off their shoes so they could more easily dance; the Copts kicked off their shoes to go to the Sacrament (shoes in Near Eastern culture are considered unclean; cf. Exodus 3:5!).

In 2001, the Barna Group noticed a trend toward similarities among Pentecostal, Charismatic, and nondenominational Christians who increasingly share similar beliefs. They also noted that people are picking and choosing what they want to believe, leading to "an age of theological anarchy" as broader influences reach individual members ("Religious Beliefs Vary Widely by Denomination," Barna Group, June 25, 2001 online article).

Among advocates of church growth, other factors are increasingly more important than one's denominational heritage. For example, Dr. Timothy Keller, founder and senior pastor of Redeemer Presbyterian Church in Manhattan, writes in "Leadership and Church Size Dynamics" that the differences between how large and small churches work may be much greater than differences between denominations (2010 online article, www.sermoncentral.com). He suggests that when a church staff member moves from a small church to a large church, the change may feel like entering a different denomination.

In contrast, the Barna Group concluded that people's expectations and experiences are very similar no matter what kind of church they attend or how large the congregation is. They are looking to connect with God, transform their lives, gain spiritual insights, feel cared for, and help those less fortunate than themselves (See "What People Experience in Churches," Barna Group, January 9, 2012 online article). Such sociological approaches search for the views of individuals rather than focus on their affiliation with a denomination; these short surveys likely homogenize the views they explore.

Denominational Distinctives

Despite the surveys and observations of sociologists, churches are retaining their denominational or tradition-specific differences. For example, we witnessed the following on our visits:

The Armenian Apostolic Orthodox had their Badarak service—in Armenian, no less!

The Baptists carried their Bibles to church and had an altar call.

The Coptic Orthodox prayed in English, Coptic, and Arabic, requesting the blessings of the saints more than anyone else we visited. The men sat on one side and the women on the other.

The Episcopalians used the Book of Common Prayer and accommodated various theologies.

The Lutherans calmly preached Law and Gospel and had the shortest Greeting of Peace among the Protestants.

The megachurch did everything pop-culture big and had a group dancing to a Michael Jackson song (I am not kidding!).

The Methodists just prayed to experience the love of Jesus and the Holy Spirit. The pastor began his sermon by decrying the social gospel, which influenced them deeply.

The Pentecostals worshiped ecstatically, danced, and spoke in tongues. Their worship leader was rockstar talented.

The Presbyterians prayed for their hearts to ascend to heaven and commune with Jesus' presence there.

The Roman Catholics said mass in a grand setting, prayed to the saints, and even chanted a little bit in Latin.

The fact that many of the large Protestant churches were using big screens to display lyrics for their songs did not blunt their differences in belief and emphasis. The fact that all the liturgical churches had some form of the Greeting of the Peace hardly made them all the same, as my son is sure to tell you. Although North American denominations may grow more alike in some respects, anyone visiting them or interacting with their members will need some account of how and why Christians are different, which is why *The Lutheran Difference* became such a popular Bible Study series and a book.

500 Years of Reformation and Counting

Without question, congregations and denominations of the twenty-first century are different from those of the sixteenth century when the Reformation was so needed. The ecumenical movement during the twentieth century increased dialogue among Christians worldwide. Vatican II (1962–65) brought substantive changes to Roman Catholic practice and attitudes, which is evident when you visit their services. Such changes have led some to wonder whether the Reformation still matters 500 years later.

The Reformation still matters for many of the same reasons it did so many years ago, in particular because there is an ever-pressing need to keep the Gospel of forgiveness and new life in Christ at the center of the Christian faith. The experience of ancient Israel should inspire Lutheran vigilance. Throughout biblical history, we see how Israel experienced reform only to fall back into beliefs and practices that drew them away from the Lord. God's people needed ongoing reform as the biblical books of Samuel, Kings, and Chronicles powerfully attest. Although I may write with joy that our family repeatedly heard other Christians confess their faith in Christ as the Savior from sin whenever we visited other denominations, I may also attest that the message of Christ was not always central. Churches are always tempted to make other things—authority, healing, prosperity, popularity, relevance, unity, emotion, or tradition—the center of their mission and message. The Reformation cuts through all these and lays the focus upon Christ and reconciliation through Him as the mission of the Church. What hinders reconciliation to the Lord requires reform, no matter how dear it may be to our prevailing culture.

Conclusion

As you study this Reformation anniversary edition, pray for personal reform as well as ongoing reformation for your church. Through faith, hope, and love, the Lord dearly wants to transform our lives and our life together so that the Gospel prevails and prospers among us (1 Corinthians 13:13). Love and celebrate your church as you listen to and interact with other Christians. Lutherans have so much to share with the world in 2017 and beyond.

Preface to the First Edition

On Believing and Living as a Lutheran Christian

> I ask that men make no reference to my name; let them call themselves Christians, not Lutherans. . . . But if you are convinced that Luther's teaching is in accord with the gospel . . . then you should not discard Luther so completely, lest with him you discard also his teaching, which you nevertheless recognize as Christ's teaching. You should rather say: Whether Luther is a rascal or a saint I do not care; his teaching is not his, but Christ's.
>
> —Martin Luther, 1522 (AE 45:70–71; 36:265)

In an age that encourages nondenominationalism, using the name "Lutheran" may seem out of place. Some might even charge that it is wrong or sinful to use the name. But to my thinking, it is important to say clearly what you believe about Jesus Christ and His Word. The name "Lutheran" is shorthand for getting to those facts. It simply means, "I agree with Luther," whose teaching has been well-known for nearly five hundred years.

Calling yourself "nondenominational" became popular in the late twentieth century. But the idea stems from nineteenth-century movements that encouraged people to call themselves simply "Christians" in the hope of uniting all of Christendom. Those efforts failed and actually resulted in an increased number of denominations!

Ironically, nondenominationalism is likewise causing an increase in the number of denominations. Ed Stetzer, director of Lifeway Research, notes that as today's nondenominational churches grow, they form memberships and associations that have many of the characteristics of existing denominations (e.g., the Willow Creek Association, the Association of Related Churches, and the Acts 29 Network).[1] Stetzer also points out that nondenominational churches may undergo rapid changes in doctrine, noting an example of a megachurch in Tulsa, Oklahoma, that quickly turned from charismatic beliefs to unitarian beliefs. While emerging

1 "Life in Those Old Bones: If You're Interested in Doing Mission, There Could Hardly Be a Better Tool than Denominations," *Christianity Today* (June 2010): 24–29.

denominations are going through these changes, liberal denominations and organizations that formed from mergers in the twentieth century are now going bust. With all these changes, people today want the facts about Christianity, and they want to know why those facts matter. That is what this book is all about.

From Series to Book

This book began as a popular Bible Study series. We originally planned to cover some basic topics of Christian doctrine but found that people were so excited about the content and presentation that we extended the number to eighteen booklets. In this new work, we gather together all the rich content of the series, order it around the Nicene Creed, and present it in one accessible volume so readers can access the facts they need based on actual church documents compared with the teachings of Scripture.

As Lutherans interact with other Christians, they often find themselves struggling to explain their beliefs and practices. Although many Lutherans have learned the "what" of the doctrines of the Church, they do not always have a full scriptural foundation to share the "why." When confronted with different doctrines or denominations, they sometimes cannot clearly state their faith—much less understand the differences.

Because of insecurities about explaining particular doctrines or practices, some Lutherans may avoid opportunities to share what they have learned from Christ and His Word. *The Lutheran Difference* identifies how Lutherans differ from other Christians and shows from the Bible why Lutherans differ. Such information will prepare Lutherans to share their faith clearly; it will help non-Lutherans understand the Lutheran difference.

Lutheran Focus

The first church built on the basis of Luther's teaching from Scripture provides a powerful illustration of the Lutheran difference: the Castle Church at Torgau, Germany. The Reformation stands at the end of the medieval or Gothic period, when most churches were ornately decorated as though the designers were trying to fill every surface with illustration or ornament. The churches often had numerous altars dedicated to a variety of saints. The Baroque era follows the Reformation with a similar florid style. These styles give the eye and mind little rest. In stark contrast, iconoclasts of the sixteenth century hacked away the medieval designs, destroyed the imagery, and tore out the organs. They went from one extreme to the other.

Amid these extremes, Luther gave instructions for the design of the Torgau church. The ornamentation is focused on the pulpit and the altar from which one learns of Christ in the words of Scripture and in the blessed Sacrament of His body and blood. The eye and mind can focus and rest on Christ and His Word. The design is brilliant in simplicity and emphasis. This became characteristic of Lutheran devotion and art.

Lutherans Confess Christ

All who worship the Holy Trinity and trust in Jesus Christ for the forgiveness of sins are regarded by Lutherans as fellow Christians, despite denominational (or nondenominational!) differences. This is an exciting time to be Lutheran, given the remarkable growth of our churches in South American and Africa and the growing strength of traditional Lutheran bodies in the International Lutheran Council, which formed at a 1993 meeting in Antigua, Guatemala. Philip Jenkins, who is the Edwin Earle Sparks Professor of History and Religious Studies at Pennsylvania State University, has noted this rapidly increasing number of new Lutherans in *The Next Christendom: The Coming of Global Christianity.* Jenkins highlighted changes in East Africa, where Lutheran groups have grown by 9 to 15 percent each year.[2] How exciting to see these new Lutherans boldly confessing Christ!

Lutheran churches first described themselves as *evangelisch* or "evangelical churches" (literally, "Gospel churches"). Opponents of these churches called them "Lutheran" after Dr. Martin Luther, the sixteenth-century German Church reformer. The general populace began to use the name too. It became so common and widespread that our churches have used the name *Lutheran* ever since. However, Lutherans are not disciples of Dr. Martin Luther, but disciples of Jesus Christ. They are, as Dr. Gene Edward Veith puts it, "the first evangelicals."[3] They proudly accept the name *Lutheran* because they agree with Dr. Luther's teaching from the Bible, as summarized in Luther's Small Catechism (1529), which is the most widely and continuously used summary of Christian teaching since the ancient creeds.

In Christ,
Rev. Edward A. Engelbrecht, STM
Senior Editor of Professional and Academic Books and Bible Resources
Concordia Publishing House

2 Revised and expanded edition (Oxford: Oxford University Press, 2007), 242–43.

3 *The Spirituality of the Cross*, rev. ed. (St. Louis: Concordia, 2010), 18–20.

Abbreviations

AC	Augsburg Confession
AE	*Luther's Works, American Edition*. Volumes 1–30: Edited by Jaroslav Pelikan. St. Louis: Concordia, 1955–76. Volumes 31–55: Edited by Helmut Lehmann. Philadelphia/Minneapolis: Muhlenberg/Fortress, 1957–86.
Ap	Apology of the Augsburg Confession
CCC2	Catechism of the Catholic Church. 2nd edition. Libreria Editrice Vaticana, 2000.
Concordia	*Concordia: The Lutheran Confessions*. 2nd ed. Edited by Paul T. McCain et al. St. Louis: Concordia, 2006.
ESV	English Standard Version of the Bible
FC Ep	Formula of Concord, Epitome
FC SD	Formula of Concord, Solid Declaration
KJV	King James Version of the Bible
LC	Large Catechism
LCMS	The Lutheran Church—Missouri Synod
LSB	*Lutheran Service Book*. The Commission on Worship of The Lutheran Church—Missouri Synod. St. Louis: Concordia, 2006.
NIV	New International Version of the Bible
SA	Smalcald Articles
SC	Small Catechism
Tr	Treatise on the Power and Primacy of the Pope
WA	*D. Martin Luthers Werke: Kritische Gesamtausgabe*. 73 vols. in 85. Weimar: H. Böhlau, 1883–.

Overview of Christian Denominations

The following outline of Christian history will help you understand where the different denominations come from and how they are related to one another. This outline may be used in connection with the "Comparisons" sections found throughout the book. Statements of belief for the different churches are drawn from their official confessional writings.

This outline and the "Comparisons" sections are based on documents such as the *Canons and Decrees of the Council of Trent* and *The Westminster Confession of Faith*. How can these older texts still characterize today's denominations? First, many of these documents have not been repealed and therefore remain in force. They define the long-standing doctrinal positions of today's churches. Second, many of these documents have served as conversation partners for the Book of Concord, the doctrinal confessions of the Lutheran Church. Awareness of such conversations helps Lutherans better understand their own beliefs.

The documents quoted in the "Comparisons" sections may cause people to wrestle with possible differences between personal beliefs and the publicly stated beliefs of their church body. Yet God calls His people to believe the Gospel and His truth revealed in Scripture. That remains the final standard of all comparisons shown here.

The Great Schism

Eastern Orthodox: On July 16, 1054, Cardinal Humbert entered the Cathedral of the Holy Wisdom in Constantinople just before the worship service. He stepped to the altar and left a letter condemning Michael Cerularius, patriarch of Constantinople. Cerularius responded by condemning the letter and its authors. In that moment, Christian churches of the East and the West were severed from each other. Their disagreements centered on what kind of bread could be used in the Lord's Supper and the addition of the *filioque* statement to the Nicene Creed. This addition says the Holy Spirit proceeds from the Father "and the Son."

The Reformation

Lutheran: On June 15, 1520, Pope Leo X wrote a letter condemning Dr. Martin Luther for his Ninety-five Theses. Luther's theses had challenged the sale of indulgences, a fund-raising effort to pay for the building of St. Peter's Basilica in Rome. Luther's challenge struck directly at the papal teaching concerning the authority of Scripture, the nature of the sacraments, the suppression of the Gospel in favor of church regulations, and the papal claim that doctrines absent from Scripture remain necessary for salvation. The pope's letter charged Luther with heresy and threatened to excommunicate him if he did not retract his writings within sixty days. Luther replied by publicly burning the letter. Leo excommunicated him on January 3, 1521, and condemned all who agreed with Luther or supported his cause.

Reformed: In 1522 the preaching of Ulrich Zwingli in Zurich, Switzerland, convinced people to break their traditional Lenten fast. Also, Zwingli preached that priests should be allowed to marry. Zwingli claimed that Word and Sacraments have a mere symbolic value. He said that God uses only the direct action of the Holy Spirit in the heart and divine providence. When local friars challenged these departures from medieval church practice, the Zurich Council supported Zwingli that the Bible should guide Christian doctrine and practice. Zwingli influenced Reformed churches in Switzerland and laid the foundation for John Calvin. Calvin and other Reformed theologians admitted that Word and Sacraments are more than just symbols, but they still differed greatly from Lutherans on the Lord's Supper and predestination. Churches of the Reformed tradition include Presbyterians and Episcopalians.

Anabaptist: In January 1525, Conrad Grebel, a follower of Ulrich Zwingli, rebaptized Georg Blaurock. Blaurock began rebaptizing others and founded the Swiss Brethren. Their insistence on adult believers' Baptism distinguished them from other churches of the Reformation. Anabaptists attracted social extremists who advocated violence in the cause of Christ, complete pacifism, or communal living. Mennonite, Brethren, and Amish churches descend from this movement.

The Counter-Reformation

Roman Catholic: When people call the medieval church "Roman Catholic," they make a common historical mistake. Roman Catholicism as we know it emerged after the Reformation. As early as 1518, Luther and other reformers had appealed to the pope and requested a council to settle the issue of indulgences. Their requests were hindered or denied for a variety of theological and political reasons. Finally, on December 13, 1545, thirty-four leaders from the churches who opposed the Reformation gathered at the invitation of Pope Paul III. They began the Council of Trent (1545–63), which established the doctrine and practice of Roman Catholicism.

Post-Reformation Movements

Baptist: In 1608 or 1609, John Smyth, a former pastor of the Church of England, baptized himself by pouring water over his head. In Holland, because of English persecution during the reign of James I, he formed a congregation of English Separatists who opposed the rule of bishops and infant Baptism. This marked the start of the English Baptist churches, which remain divided doctrinally over the "no-will" predestination theology of John Calvin (Particular Baptists) and the "free-will" theology of Jacob Arminius (General Baptists). Arminius influenced the Wesleys (see below). In the 1800s, the Restoration Movement of Alexander Campbell, a former Presbyterian minister, adopted many Baptist teachings. These churches include the Disciples of Christ (Christian Churches) and the Churches of Christ.

Wesleyan: In 1729, John and Charles Wesley gathered with three other men to study Scripture, receive Communion, and discipline one another according to the "method" laid down in the Bible. Later, John Wesley's preaching caused religious revivals in England and North America. As among the Baptists, both Calvin and Arminius have left their legacies among Methodists, Wesleyans, Nazarenes, and Pentecostals that form the Wesleyan family of churches.

Liberal: In 1799, Friedrich Schleiermacher published *Addresses on Religion* in an attempt to make Christianity appealing to people influenced by rationalism. He argued that religion is not a body of doctrines, provable truths, or a system of ethics, but it belongs to the realm of feelings. His ideas did not lead to the formation of a new denomination, but they did deeply influence Christian thinking. Denominations most thoroughly affected by liberalism are the United Church of Christ, Disciples of Christ, and Unitarianism.

Overview of the Lutheran Confessions

For nearly five hundred years, Lutherans have used the eight documents and the three creeds gathered into the Book of Concord, popularly known as "the Lutheran Confessions," as a public witness and testimony of what the Bible teaches. These statements of faith provide clear, unambiguous, and certain witness to the Christian faith. Throughout *The Lutheran Difference*, reference is made to these documents. The following provides a brief introduction and historical context for the documents. For more information, see *Concordia: The Lutheran Confessions*, 2nd ed. (St. Louis: Concordia, 2006).

The Creeds

Historic Christianity confesses the faith through the words of three ancient creeds: the Apostles' (the baptismal creed), the Nicene (confesses the equality of the persons of the Trinity), and the Athanasian (confesses the teaching of the Trinity and the person and work of Jesus Christ). Lutherans speak these creeds in their worship and use these texts to frame their discussion of the faith. The inclusion of these three ancient creeds in the Book of Concord demonstrates that Lutherans are not a sect but confess the orthodox Christian faith.

The Augsburg Confession of 1530

Holy Roman Emperor Charles V invited the Lutheran princes and theologians to a gathering in the German city of Augsburg to discuss settling the religious controversy arising from Dr. Martin Luther's writings. The resolution was considered necessary to ensure the Lutheran princes would help with the military effort to keep the Turks out of Europe. Philip Melanchthon, a lay associate of Dr. Luther, wrote the Augsburg Confession to clarify what the Lutherans believed. Melanchthon summarized Lutheran teaching from the Bible, addressed the controversies of the day, and identified the abuses that the Lutherans corrected. This confession remains a standard of Lutheran teaching.

Apology of the Augsburg Confession

Published in 1531, the Apology (or defense) was also written by Philip Melanchthon. It was prepared as a response to the Romanist theologians Confutation (or reply) to the Augsburg Confession. The Apology defends the Lutheran position as defined in the Augsburg Confession and further explains Lutheran beliefs.

The Smalcald Articles

On June 4, 1536, Pope Paul III announced that a council of the church would be held in Mantua in 1537 to address the issues raised by the Protestants. The elector (or prince) or Saxony asked Luther to prepare some articles for discussion at this council. Although they were never used at the council, Lutherans recognized the value of these talking points as statements of belief on which they would stand fast. The articles also identify areas of churchly practice in which compromise might be possible.

The Treatise on the Power and Primacy of the Pope

Philip Melanchthon also prepared this document, which was originally presented as a treatise at the same gathering at which the Smalcald Articles first appeared. It is actually an appendix to the Augsburg Confession, and it states the Lutheran perspective on the office of the pope.

Small Catechism and Large Catechism

Luther wrote his Small Catechism, or little manual for Christian instruction, in 1528. His intention was to give heads of households, normally fathers, a booklet for teaching the basics of the Christian faith to all those under their care. The Large Catechism is actually a collection of sermons preached by Luther in 1528. These sermons were edited into book form and expand the topics of the Small Catechism. Both Luther's Small and Large Catechisms were first published in 1529 and have been used by the Lutheran Church in the instruction of youth and adults for nearly five hundred years.

Formula of Concord

Following Luther's death in 1546, confusion disrupted the Lutheran churches. Some wished to compromise on matters of doctrine in order to attain greater peace and unity with Calvinists and Roman Catholics.

Others claimed to be true Lutherans but strayed from Luther's teaching. In 1576, Elector August of Saxony called a conference to clarify the issues. The result was the Formula of Concord (*concord* means "harmony"), published in 1580. The Solid Declaration is the unabridged version; the Epitome is an abridged version intended for congregational study.

General Lutheran Facts

Although all Christian churches use Holy Scripture, Lutherans emphasize that Scripture is the final and only certain judge of doctrine and practice (*sola scriptura*)—not human traditions, reason, or churchly authority.

Lutherans confess the three ecumenical creeds (Apostles', Nicene, and Athanasian) as correct summaries of biblical teaching.

Lutherans form the largest family of Protestants, numbering more than sixty million worldwide.

Today, Lutheran churches are growing fastest in Ethiopia, Tanzania, and Papua New Guinea.

Among Protestant denominations, Lutherans tend to have greater unity. For example, there are fourteen Lutheran denominations in North America. In contrast, other denominational families (Reformed, Anabaptist, Baptist, etc.) have at least twice that number.

I Believe According to the Scriptures

TOPIC ONE

God's Word[1]

Engaging This Topic

"If there is only one Bible, why are there so many different denominations?"
"Why do churches agree on some points and disagree on others?"
"Which interpretation of this Bible verse is correct?"

We rely on assumptions to interpret, or understand, any form of writing. The same is true for the Bible. We use what we already believe to help us understand God's Word. For example, if we believe our God can and does accomplish miracles in the created world, we accept the biblical stories of Jonah and Lazarus as historically true. However, if we believe God cannot or does not work this way, we may assume these accounts to be fictional stories created by authors trying to prove some spiritual point. If we hold that Jesus is both fully divine and fully human, we accept His death on the cross as the sacrificial atonement for our sins. On the other hand, if we believe that Christ was simply a remarkable human being, we may suppose this teaching to have been developed by pious Christians in order to preserve the collective memory of the Master.

Lutherans maintain assumptions in interpreting the Holy Scriptures. In the Scriptures, Christ points to the truthfulness, reliability, and perfection of God's Word (see Matthew 4:4; 5:17; Mark 12:24–27; Luke 4:21; 24:27, 44; John 5:39; 10:35; 17:17). Because the Holy Spirit gives faith in Christ as our Savior, and because He directs us to God's Word, Lutherans seek to

1 This chapter adapted from *The Lutheran Difference: God's Word*, written by Michael Middendorf, with contributions by Robert C. Baker. Copyright © 2004 Concordia Publishing House.

interpret the Bible with humility, relying on the guidance and direction of the Holy Spirit as He leads us to Christ.

Lutheran assumptions in biblical interpretation can be summarized as follows:

1. God's Word, because it is His Word, is without error (John 10:35; 17:17, 2 Timothy 3:16–17; 2 Peter 1:21). This means that the Bible cannot lie or deceive (Psalm 19:7; 119:7; John 10:35; 17:17; Romans 3:4; 2 Timothy 3:16–17; 2 Peter 1:21) and that God's Word is the only rule for faith and life (Psalm 119:105; 1 Corinthians 4:6; Galatians 1:6–9).

2. Christ is the heart and center of God's Word (John 5:39; Acts 10:43). This means the doctrine of justification by God's grace through faith in Christ is the chief doctrine of the Scriptures (John 3:16–17; Galatians 4:4–5; Hebrews 2:14–17; 1 Timothy 1:15). Also, Christians should carefully distinguish Law and Gospel (John 1:17; 2 Corinthians 3:6).

3. The Holy Spirit helps us to understand God's Word (Psalm 119:73; John 14:26; 1 Corinthians 2:14). This means difficult passages of Scripture are to be interpreted by other, clearer passages (Acts 17:11). Also, as we read Scripture, in humility we derive the plain meaning of words from their literal sense, unless clearly directed otherwise by context (2 Timothy 3:15).

Sometimes it is difficult to understand why, if everyone is using the same Bible, there are different teachings among denominations. The differences do not reside in the written text, that is, the shapes formed by ink on paper. Rather, the differences lie primarily in the assumptions made by the readers. *The Lutheran Difference* will compare and contrast the Lutheran assumptions of biblical interpretation with those of other church bodies and with your own personal assumptions.

Lutheran Facts

Lutherans believe the Bible is God's inspired and inerrant (without error) Word. The Book of Concord refers to the "unchanging" and "infallible" truth of God's Word, which "cannot and will not fail us" (Preface to the Book of Concord 20; FC Ep XI 14; *Concordia*, pp. 9, 499). In his Large Catechism, Luther confesses: "God's Word cannot err" (LC IV 57; *Concordia*, p. 429). He urges us to believe the Scriptures, because "they will not lie to you" (LC V 76; *Concordia*, p. 439).

The Word of God permeates Lutheran worship services. The liturgy is full of direct quotations from Scripture. Hymns, if not quoting the Bible directly, paraphrase passages and themes. Sermons are based on specific texts of God's Word.

Lutherans also emphasize teaching God's Word to children and adults. Memorization of Bible passages is emphasized in Lutheran schools, Sunday schools, adult Bible studies, and at home.

Lutherans believe that God's Word exposes the deepest thoughts and desires of the human heart (Hebrews 4:12). At the same time, it powerfully gives new birth through the Gospel (1 Peter 1:23). Because of this, Lutherans believe that God's Word of Gospel is a Means of Grace.

And God Said . . .

> Marcellus: "Shall I strike at it with my [long, heavy sword]?"
> Horatio: "Do, if it will not stand."
> Bernardo: " 'Tis here!"
> Horatio: " 'Tis here!"
> Marcellus: " 'Tis gone!"
> —William Shakespeare, *Hamlet*, Act 1, Scene 1

The ghost of Hamlet's father disappears at will and reappears, only to have his son avenge his murder. Like the ghost, the gods of most religions seem interested in humanity only when it suits their own purposes. Selfish and self-serving, they enter and exit the stage of human history at their convenience.

Is there a God? How do we know? How can we know what God is like? How does God relate to people in general and to me specifically? Questions such as these are at the heart of almost every religion, including Christianity. The answers to these questions also form the heart and basis of our lives.

We often hear: "Actions speak louder than words," but do they really? Consider your own interactions with family members, co-workers, or friends. Do you learn more about people from what they say or by what they do? Now consider your own words and actions. Do they always agree? In the case of the God of the Scriptures, His words often speak louder than, or at least as loud as, His actions.

God Speaks

If God had not spoken to us through Scripture, would we know there is a God? The apostle Paul tells us in Romans 1:19–20 that God's existence, eternal power, and divine nature are clearly seen in the creation around us. Thus even though God does not speak in words that we hear with our ears, the heavens and skies declare God's glory (Psalm 19:1–4). Both of these passages emphasize that the natural world reveals that there must be a God—and every human being is exposed to this reality. But we have more than just visual clues in nature to tell us that there is a God.

Already in Genesis 1, God spoke. In fact, on each day of creation Scripture records that "God said," and then things actually came into being (Genesis 1:1–3). And this pattern continues through the remainder of Genesis 1. Right from the beginning, God is revealed as the God who speaks words. And His words powerfully accomplish what He says.

We communicate with those around us in a number of ways—by what we say and don't say and by what we do and don't do. It has been said, "It is better to keep your mouth closed and let people think you are a fool than to open it and remove all doubt." According to this proverb, the very act of speaking is an act of self-revelation!

Self-revelation through speech takes on two main forms: human and divine. Our inadequacies and our inconsistencies may remain hidden if we remain silent, but when we speak they become all too apparent. When God speaks, however, His words reveal to us more and more of His wisdom and goodness. In fact, it is only through God's Word (the Bible) that we are able to know God personally and hear His plan of salvation. According to John 17:3, our salvation and the promise of eternal life are ours only by knowing (being in relationship with) the true God and His Son, Jesus Christ.

According to the Scriptures, God's existence, along with His power and majesty, are revealed in nature (natural revelation or natural knowledge of God). However, Christians acknowledge that God more specifically reveals to us additional information about Himself in the Bible. For example, in Malachi 3:6 God reveals His unchanging nature; in Leviticus 19:2 He asserts His holiness; and Psalm 90:2 asserts God's eternal or everlasting nature. God declares that He is a "jealous God" in Exodus 20:5, a statement that comes toward the beginning of the Ten Commandments (Exodus 20:3–17). While such a declaration may seem out of synch with our understanding of jealousy as a sin, the term in this context means "zealous." As the people of Israel stand before God at Mount Sinai, the scene is reminiscent of a wedding ceremony uniting God and His people. God desires Israel for Himself and does not want to "share her" with other gods (Exodus 20:4–5). Thus He will be "jealous" and will punish those who break their commitment to Him. However, God's "mercy triumphs over judgment" (James 2:13), and in Exodus 20:6 He reveals that His "steadfast love" (Gospel) extends far beyond the bounds of His punishment (Law).

Even though God has revealed Himself to us in the Scriptures, we are unable to comprehend some of God's ways and thoughts (Isaiah 55:8–9). While we cannot fathom why some people suffer and others succeed, we can trust God's wisdom, knowledge, judgments, and paths (Romans 11:33–36). The doctrine of the "sufficiency of Scripture" asserts that God has revealed all that we need to know for our salvation, not that God reveals everything to us. These are reasons to have awe and respect for God and to praise Him for His glory.

Words are often necessary to explain actions, and, in the same way, actions can explain words. How do God's words and actions come together as one? In Jesus Christ, we have God's final and ultimate word: the fulfillment of the promised Word (John 1), who shares with us God's words of life (John 5:39). In 2 Corinthians 1:18–20, Paul addresses his plans for visiting the Christians in Corinth. In that context, he makes a profound theological statement: "As surely as God is faithful" (v. 18), Paul says, God's promises are all fulfilled or answered "Yes!"—and they are done so in Jesus Christ. Jesus was brought to the Corinthians through the proclamation of Paul, Silas, and Timothy. In response, the Corinthians are called to say "Amen" to the glory of God (v. 20). All of us have heard the same affirmative Word. All God's promises have been fulfilled for us in Christ, and we are called to give the same "Amen" response. In 2 Corinthians 4:6, Paul reminds us that even as God's speaking at creation was followed by action, so God's speaking is fulfilled when His Word shines the light of Jesus Christ into our hearts.

Where Do We Look?

Consider the many ways people search for God, for meaning in life, and for spiritual truth. Some believe that they can find God by looking within themselves or that human reason or experience can provide answers to questions of ultimate importance. But our reason or experience cannot answer the important questions about God. Instead, the Bible is our only authoritative source for such knowledge. There God comes near and speaks about Himself in His own words. In Romans 10:8, Paul quotes Deuteronomy 30:14 to assert that God had spoken to the Israelites in His Word through Moses. The Old Testament prophets use the phrase "The word of the Lord came" more than seventy times to point out that God's Word came to them, not vice versa. Finally, God has come to reveal Himself in the person of Jesus Christ (Hebrews 1:1–2).

For those who chase after material possessions and earthly things as the zenith of human existence, Jesus tells us in Matthew 4:4 that we are to live on "every word that comes from the mouth of God" (see also Deuteronomy 8:3; John 4:34). In Romans 10:14–17, Paul clearly states that God continues speaking to His people through the oral proclamation of His Word. The apostle concludes that people cannot believe or be saved unless they hear the message "through the word of Christ" (Romans 10:17). When "the word of faith" is proclaimed, God still draws near to people in order to save them through the message of Christ's death and resurrection. We live on God's Word and in His Word as well.

The People's Voice

People often try to describe and characterize God or to say what God would or would not do. Many have concluded there is no hell, that God is love and welcomes everyone, and that He would never send anybody to hell even if it did exist. As a result, people do not usually think of God as a judge or view Jesus as having wrath (see, for example, Revelation 6:16–17). On the other hand, the "particularity of the Gospel" (see especially John 14:6; Acts 4:12) is also a scandal to those who accept any and all religions as valid approaches to God. When we hear such unbiblical statements about God, we gently yet firmly read or recite specific Scripture passages. God's own words carry more "authority" with people than trying to summarize the Bible's or the church's teaching. But to take such an approach means we must know the Scriptures well.

Finally, in contrast with God's words, let's take a look at our own words and what they may reveal to others. Are your words and actions consistent? The apostle James points out that "we all stumble in many ways" (3:2). As James proceeds to use various analogies to illustrate how we are unable to tame our tongue or to control the damage it causes (vv. 3–9), this is, in one sense, condemning Law. On the other hand, this is good third use of the Law, reminding us to match our actions and words. After hearing the gracious words of God spoken to us, we praise God with our lips and use our mouths to speak to others about His mercy.

Comparisons

Eastern Orthodox: "The most ancient and original instrument for spreading divine revelation is holy tradition. From Adam to Moses there were no sacred books. Our Lord Jesus Christ Himself delivered His divine doctrine and ordinances to His Disciples by word and example, but not by writing. The same method was followed by the Apostles also at first, when they spread abroad the faith and established the Church of Christ. The necessity of tradition is further evident from this, that books can be available only to a small part of mankind, but tradition to all" (*The Longer Catechism of the Eastern Church*, question 21).

Lutheran: "We believe, teach, and confess that the only rule and norm according to which all teachings, together with ‹all› teachers, should be evaluated and judged [2 Timothy 3:15–17] are the prophetic and apostolic Scriptures of the Old and New Testament alone. For it is written in Psalm 119:105, 'Your word is a lamp to my feet and a light to my path.' St. Paul has written, 'even if we or an angel from heaven should preach to you a gospel contrary to the one we preached to you, let him be accursed' (Galatians 1:8)" (FC Summary 1; *Concordia*, p. 473).

Reformed/Presbyterian: "Although the light of nature, and the works of creation and providence, do so far manifest the goodness, wisdom and power of God, as to leave men inexcusable; yet are they not sufficient to give that knowledge of God, and of His will, which is necessary unto salvation; therefore it pleased the Lord, at sundry times, and in divers manners, to reveal Himself, and to declare that His will unto His Church; and afterwards, for the better preserving and propagating of the truth, and for the more sure establishment and comfort of the Church against the corruption of the flesh, and the malice of Satan and of the world, to commit the same wholly unto writing; which maketh the holy Scripture to be most necessary; those former ways of God's revealing His will unto His people being now ceased" (*The Westminster Confession of Faith*, chapter 1).

Roman Catholic: "The sacred and holy, oecumenical and general Synod of Trent—lawfully assembled in the Holy Ghost, the same Legates of the Apostolic See presiding therein . . . receives and venerates with an equal affection of piety, and reverence, all the books both of the Old and of the New Testament—seeing that one God is the author of both—as also the said traditions . . . preserved in the Catholic Church by a continuous succession" (*Canons and Decrees of the Council of Trent*, Session 24, Decree concerning the Canonical Scriptures; cf. CCC2, Part 1, article 3).

Baptist: "We believe that the Holy Bible was written by men divinely inspired, and is a perfect treasure of heavenly instruction; that it has God for its author, salvation for its end, and truth without any mixture of error for its matter; that it reveals the principles by which God will judge us; and therefore is, and shall remain to the end of the world, the true center of Christian union, and the supreme standard by which all human conduct, creeds, and opinions should be tried" (*New Hampshire Baptist Confession*, article 1).

Wesleyan/Methodist: "The Holy Scriptures contain all things necessary to salvation; so that whatsoever is not read therein, nor may be proved thereby, is not to be required of any man that it should be believed as an article of faith, or be thought requisite or necessary to salvation" (*Methodist Articles of Religion*, article 5).

Liberal Protestant: "The facts of history have shown that Paul was in error in his teaching in 1 Thessalonians about the coming of the Lord in the clouds of heaven. It is a palpable infidelity to truth to affirm that this teaching was true; it is a double error to transfer it to the present time and reaffirm it for our own day. Some portions of his teachings about marriage and spiritual gifts, however adapted to meet the needs of the Corinthians, are impossible of reaffirmation today. Whether the preacher in the pulpit passes these things over in silence and limits himself to the things that have attested themselves as true by the test of human experience, as may often be his wisest course or the teacher finds it necessary to deal with them explicitly, honestly, and frankly, as he must if they come up for consideration at all, both the preaching and the teaching will be made more effective religiously and morally than when it is assumed that all the views of the New Testament writers are equally valuable" (Ernest DeWitt Burton in *A Guide to the Study of the Christian Religion*, ed. Gerald Birney Smith [Chicago: University of Chicago Press, 1916], pp. 236–37).

Point to Remember

Long ago, at many times and in many ways, God spoke to our fathers by the prophets, but in these last days He has spoken to us by His Son. *Hebrews 1:1–2*

Now That's Inspired!

What with the introduction of machines and of sudden inventions, millionaires cannot be helped. We might as well make the most of it.
—Gerard Stanley Lee, *Inspired Millionaires*

The year was 1908. The United States was recovering from a sharp economic downturn. Many working-class people saw the rich as immoral. Others like Gerard Lee saw the rich as a source for general public improvement. This debate continues to the present. Money certainly inspires some wealthy people to bend the rules, yet it can also inspire and enable others to aid society. Money often remains the goal of those who complain about the rich. For others whose focus is not money, inspiration toward action can come from another source. The promise of better benefits or shorter working hours may motivate someone to change jobs. The desire for a better appearance may encourage a dieter to remain faithful to the diet plan. Thoughts of sunny, windswept beaches may compel a family to save a few extra dollars each week for that much-needed vacation.

Someone may leave a concert, lecture, movie, or even worship service and say, "That was truly inspiring!" After looking at a beautiful sunset or mountain, someone may say, "That really inspires me!" These common uses of the word *inspire* mean "to animate, arouse, affect with feeling or thought, uplift," and so on. But that is not what we mean when we use the term *inspired* to describe the Scriptures.

Unlike powerful people, God does not need any external "inspiration" to put His plan of salvation into action. God is the sole source of His speaking and acting; yet He has done much more than "inspire" His people with a "good story." Scripture describes itself as "breathed out by God" (2 Timothy 3:16), from which the Church gets the term *inspired*. The doctrine of inspiration examines the question "Is the Bible man's words or God's Word?" Let's look at some statements that try to answer this question.

1. God dictated His Word. Each author's own personality was not involved.

2. God worked through the abilities, personalities, backgrounds, and training of various authors to speak His Word to people.

3. The words written in the Bible are the "words" of God.

4. God gave the authors thoughts; the authors put them in their own words.

5. The Bible merely *contains* the Word of God. Some words are God's; some are simply human.

6. God revealed the basic Gospel message to the authors of Scripture. When they address other topics, they are giving their own thoughts and opinions.

7. The words in the Bible are basically human words, containing the personal biases and prejudices of the authors.

8. The Bible contains God's Word to the people and churches of those days. God's Word does not apply in the same way today.

9. The Bible is God's words to the churches of today, and His words should all be applied literally.

10. The Bible gives specific directions from God to His people in the days they originally addressed. The teachings, doctrines, and principles still apply, but the applications in our day may differ.

Some of these statements may be disputable, but statements 2, 3, and 10 are true; the rest are false. Statements 6 and 7 reveal what has been called "Gospel reductionism" or reducing the inspired Scriptures to the motivational content of the Gospel message. Statement 9 falls flat because most churches do not encourage handling deadly snakes (Isaiah 11:8), nor do they require women to cover their heads in worship despite the clear instructions in 1 Corinthians 11:1–16. However, as statement 10 points out, the principle of "headship" (properly understood) is still relevant.

So is the Bible the words of man and/or God's Word? Ultimately, the Church has concluded that the answer is "both/and." Logically, it seems impossible for words to be both from men and from God. As a result, the Church calls this a "mystery" and a miracle of God that cannot be completely explained to our human reason. But when discussing this issue, theologians typically use the term *inspiration*.

Divine Author/Human Authors

In our quest to answer the question "Is the Bible man's word or God's word?" we turn to Scripture. In 2 Timothy 3:14–17, Paul says:

> But as for you, continue in what you have learned and have firmly believed, knowing from whom you learned it and how from childhood you have been acquainted with the sacred writings, which are able to make you wise for salvation through faith in Christ Jesus. All Scripture is breathed out by God and profitable for teaching, for reproof, for correction, and for training in righteousness, that the man of God may be competent, equipped for every good work.

Here, when Paul says "all Scripture," he refers specifically to the Old Testament since the New Testament was likely not yet completed and collected in Paul's day. But what he says about it is important: "All Scripture is breathed out by God." The phrase "breathed out by God" in verse 16 has also been translated "inspired" because the word for "breath" or "wind" in Greek and Hebrew is the same as the word used for "spirit" and the Holy "Spirit." A connection with the Holy Spirit and inspiration is at least implied here by Paul. God *breathed* or *spirited* the Scriptures. The use of the word *all* is also significant. When used in reference to inspiration, it means everything in the written Scriptures comes fully from the breath of God; nothing is excluded.

We can look to the apostle Peter for further explanation: "Knowing this first of all, that no prophecy of Scripture comes from someone's own interpretation. For no prophecy was ever produced by the will of man, but men spoke from God as they were carried along by the Holy Spirit" (2 Peter 1:20–21). As did Paul, when Peter talks about *Scripture*, he refers to the entire Old Testament. But what does Peter mean by the phrase "prophecy of Scripture"? People usually understand *prophecy* to mean "predicting the future." However, the word *prophecy* in the Scriptures is much broader. It means speaking and applying God's will in a variety of settings. Consider these examples.

1. Moses was the greatest prophet of the Old Testament.
2. In the Hebrew Bible, Moses' writings are followed by the Former Prophets (Joshua through Kings) and then the Latter Prophets (Amos, Hosea, Micah, Isaiah, and so on).
3. The prophets use the majority of their words to speak of the past and the present, not simply the future.

Prophecy is speaking for God and is God speaking. Notice again the exclusive terminology of Peter's statement ("no prophecy") for explaining plenary inspiration. This excludes either the view that the Scriptures are merely a human product (see statement 7 above) or what is called the "dictation theory" (see statement 1 above). The latter implies the authors were passive and uninvolved; it makes them seem robotic, automatic, or mechanical. The origin of Scripture is clearly God, but at the same time "men spoke from God." Here is also a clear reference to the Holy Spirit carrying along those who "spoke from God."

The Old Testament prophets use the phrase "Thus says the Lord" or something very similar more than 350 times! Why is this significant? By saying "Thus says the Lord," the Old Testament prophets assert that the message they speak is directly from the Lord and spoken in His behalf, as described also by the apostle Peter. The words of the prophets are the Lord's words! The prophets often spoke of the Word of the Lord coming to them and becoming a part of them. They then "had to" proclaim what the Lord revealed to them.

How did this process of inspiration work with specific Old Testament prophets and prophecy? Let's look at several examples from the prophet Jeremiah.

Jeremiah 1:9: "Then the LORD put out His hand and touched my mouth. And the LORD said to me, 'Behold, I have put My words in your mouth.'" Here the prophet declares that the Lord put His words into Jeremiah's mouth.

Jeremiah 26:2: "Thus says the LORD: Stand in the court of the LORD's house, and speak to all the cities of Judah that come to worship in the house of the LORD all the words that I command you to speak to them; do not hold back a word." God commands Jeremiah to speak everything He had revealed to him.

Jeremiah 20:9: "If I say, 'I will not mention Him, or speak any more in His name,' there is in my heart as it were a burning fire shut up in my bones, and I am weary with holding it in, and I cannot." This passage reveals that even when Jeremiah tried to hold in God's Word, he could not.

Jeremiah 15:16: "Your words were found, and I ate them, and Your words became to me a joy and the delight of my heart, for I am called by Your name, O LORD, God of hosts." As opposed to trying to hold God's words in, when Jeremiah received or "ate" the Word of the Lord, it was a great joy. This passage reveals how the Lord's words became a part of the prophet who "ingested" them.

Similar language is used in Ezekiel 2:9–3:4:

> And when I looked, behold, a hand was stretched out to me, and behold, a scroll of a book was in it. And He spread it before me. And it had writing on the front and on the back, and there were written on it words of lamentation and mourning and woe. And He said to me, "Son of man, eat whatever you find here. Eat this scroll, and go, speak to the house of Israel." So I opened my mouth, and He gave me this scroll to eat. And He said to me, "Son of man, feed your belly with this scroll that I give you and fill your stomach with it." Then I ate it, and it was in my mouth as sweet as honey. And He said to me, "Son of man, go to the house of Israel and speak with My words to them."

Notice again how God's words to Ezekiel are received, eaten, and then proclaimed.

We can also look to Isaiah's vision of the Lord:

> In the year that King Uzziah died I saw the Lord sitting upon a throne, high and lifted up; and the train of His robe filled the temple. Above Him stood the seraphim. Each had six wings: with two he covered his face, and with two he covered his feet, and with two he flew. And one called to another and said: "Holy, holy, holy is the LORD of hosts; the whole earth is full of His glory!" And the foundations of

> the thresholds shook at the voice of Him who called, and the house was filled with smoke. And I said: "Woe is me! For I am lost; for I am a man of unclean lips, and I dwell in the midst of a people of unclean lips; for my eyes have seen the King, the LORD of hosts!" Then one of the seraphim flew to me, having in his hand a burning coal that he had taken with tongs from the altar. And he touched my mouth and said: "Behold, this has touched your lips; your guilt is taken away, and your sin atoned for." And I heard the voice of the Lord saying, "Whom shall I send, and who will go for us?" Then I said, "Here am I! Send me." And He said, "Go, and say to this people: 'Keep on hearing, but do not understand; keep on seeing, but do not perceive.'" (Isaiah 6:1–9)

Isaiah's call is "inspiring" just like those cited by Peter, Paul, and Jeremiah. After seeing God on His throne, Isaiah laments his unclean lips. After his mouth is touched with a coal from the altar, he is cleansed from sin. Then Isaiah is able to speak the Word of the Lord.

All these Old Testament passages establish that Scripture—the written Word—is God-inspired. But the phrase "thus says the LORD" doesn't appear often in the New Testament. Instead, God gives us other clues that the New Testament books are His Word. Consider the following:

1. "It is the Spirit who gives life; the flesh is no help at all. The words that I have spoken to you are spirit and life" (John 6:63). When Jesus speaks, His words are from the Spirit of God (compare 2 Peter 1:20–21). They also have the power to give life.

2. "For I received from the Lord what I also delivered to you, that the Lord Jesus on the night when He was betrayed took bread . . ." (1 Corinthians 11:23) and "For I delivered to you as of first importance what I also received: that Christ died for our sins in accordance with the Scriptures" (1 Corinthians 15:3). In these passages, Paul says he received "from the Lord" and "delivered to you." These are technical rabbinic words for accurately and authoritatively receiving words directly or indirectly from the source and then faithfully passing them on just as received. Thus Paul states that he is writing the Word of the Lord.

3. "Paul, an apostle—not from men nor through man, but through Jesus Christ and God the Father, who raised Him from the dead—and all the brothers who are with me, To the churches of Galatia" (Galatians 1:1–2) and "For I would have you know, brothers, that the gospel that was preached by me is not man's gospel. For I did not receive it from any man, nor was I taught it, but I received it through a revelation of Jesus Christ" (Galatians 1:11–12). The apostle Paul based the

authenticity of his Gospel message on the fact that it came by direct revelation from the Lord Jesus.

4. "And we also thank God constantly for this, that when you received the word of God, which you heard from us, you accepted it not as the word of men but as what it really is, the word of God, which is at work in you believers" (1 Thessalonians 2:13). When Paul taught in Thessalonica, the believers there did not simply receive his words. Rather, they comprehended that Paul truly spoke the Word of God to them.

5. "Or was it from you that the word of God came? Or are you the only ones it has reached? If anyone thinks that he is a prophet, or spiritual, he should acknowledge that the things I am writing to you are a command of the Lord. If anyone does not recognize this, he is not recognized" (1 Corinthians 14:36–38). In this passage, Paul explicitly asserts that he is writing the Lord's command, not merely his own.

6. "For the Scripture says, 'You shall not muzzle an ox when it treads out the grain,' and, 'The laborer deserves his wages'" (1 Timothy 5:18). This passage quotes Deuteronomy 25:4 and then the words of Jesus recorded in Luke 10:7. Both quotations are introduced with the phrase "For the Scripture says." This reveals that as Paul wrote to Timothy (around AD 65) Jesus' words were already considered equal with the Old Testament Word of God.

7. "And count the patience of our Lord as salvation, just as our beloved brother Paul also wrote to you according to the wisdom given him, as he does in all his letters when he speaks in them of these matters. There are some things in them that are hard to understand, which the ignorant and unstable twist to their own destruction, as they do the other Scriptures" (2 Peter 3:15–16). Peter's letter, written about the same time Paul wrote to Timothy, acknowledges that Paul's writings were being collected, studied, misunderstood, and distorted shortly after they were written. Even more important, the end of verse 16 explicitly groups Paul's writings together with "the other Scriptures." This places his letters on the same level as Jesus' words and the Old Testament.

8. "These things I have spoken to you while I am still with you. But the Helper, the Holy Spirit, whom the Father will send in My name, He will teach you all things and bring to your remembrance all that I have said to you" (John 14:25–26) and "I still have many things to say to you, but you cannot bear them now. When the Spirit of truth comes, He will guide you into all the truth, for He will not speak on His own authority, but whatever He hears He will speak, and He will declare to

you the things that are to come. He will glorify Me, for He will take what is Mine and declare it to you. All that the Father has is Mine; therefore I said that He will take what is Mine and declare it to you" (John 16:12–15). In these passages from John's Gospel, Jesus establishes another link between the Holy Spirit and the Word of the Lord. In John 14, the Holy Spirit teaches the disciples all things and reminds them of everything Jesus said. This explains how we received accurate and reliable written Gospels through the disciples Matthew and John. In addition, Mark's Gospel is traditionally linked with the disciple Peter. Luke also received his information from those "who from the beginning were eyewitnesses and ministers of the word" (Luke 1:2). However, this is not to be limited merely to direct quotations from Jesus in "red-letter" Bibles. It includes all the words of the Lord. In John 16, the Spirit guides people into all truth by hearing from Jesus and then speaking His Word and will to us.

A Great and Holy Helper

The apostle Paul makes a clear distinction about our ability to understand God's Word:

> For who knows a person's thoughts except the spirit of that person, which is in him? So also no one comprehends the thoughts of God except the Spirit of God. Now we have received not the spirit of the world, but the Spirit who is from God, that we might understand the things freely given us by God. And we impart this in words not taught by human wisdom but taught by the Spirit, interpreting spiritual truths to those who are spiritual. The natural person does not accept the things of the Spirit of God, for they are folly to him, and he is not able to understand them because they are spiritually discerned. The spiritual person judges all things, but is himself to be judged by no one. "For who has understood the mind of the Lord so as to instruct Him?" But we have the mind of Christ. (1 Corinthians 2:11–16)

Paul asserts that it is only by receiving the Holy Spirit, who is freely given from God (v. 12), that we are able to understand the spiritual truths of God's spiritual words. Notice that the uses of "spiritual," the references to things that are "spiritually discerned," and the description of a "spiritual" person all are related to the Holy Spirit. In our day, the word *spiritual* tends to have a much broader meaning than in this passage where it is a direct link to the Holy Spirit. The Holy Spirit produced the Scriptures, but His work did not stop there. The Holy Spirit enables people to understand the truths of the Scriptures and even to know the mind of the Lord Christ (v. 16). In addition, Luke notes that Jesus had to open the minds of the first disciples before they could understand that the spiritual truth of the Old Testament is that it foretold the Gospel message (Luke 24:45).

We need the Spirit before we can understand the Word of God. Yet Jesus says His words are "Spirit and are life" (John 6:63). So which comes to us first: the Word or the Spirit? This is not like the brain teaser "Which came first, the chicken or the egg?" The point is that we should not separate the Spirit from the Word. They come together as "Spirit-filled" words. The passage from 1 Corinthians above reasserts the link between Jesus' words, the Holy Spirit who enables us to comprehend them, and the life given by the Spirit through those words.

Every Good Work

The main purpose of Scripture in our lives is laid out in Paul's second letter to Timothy:

> But as for you, continue in what you have learned and have firmly believed, knowing from whom you learned it and how from childhood you have been acquainted with the sacred writings, which are able to make you wise for salvation through faith in Christ Jesus. All Scripture is breathed out by God and profitable for teaching, for reproof, for correction, and for training in righteousness, that the man of God may be competent, equipped for every good work. (3:14–17)

Although its main task is "to make you wise for salvation through faith in Christ Jesus" (v. 15), the God-breathed Scriptures also strive to equip God's people for doing good works (v. 17; see also Ephesians 2:10; the third use of the Law). The Scriptures do this by identifying which works are good in God's eyes. In addition, by teaching, rebuking, correcting, and training, the Scriptures steer us away from evil and toward good. Yet the Gospel is the primary focus, which provides the proper motivation for what follows.

Look and listen for "inspired" words from God in your daily life. Any contact we have with the inspired Word of God from Scripture would qualify, whether it comes by directly reading the Bible, by hearing it read, or as it is used by other sources. Insofar as a pastor, teacher, book, song, or billboard quotes the Scriptures, those words are inspired since they repeat inspired words. However, this does not make the entirety of a sermon or hymn or song inspired.

Comparisons

Verbal inspiration: The Holy Spirit led the prophets, evangelists, and apostles to write the books of the Bible. He guided their writing, inspiring their very words while working through their particular styles of expression. Therefore, the Bible's words are God's Word. Conservative Christian churches hold this view. Many also maintain that the original writings of the Bible were without error (the doctrine of inerrancy) but that some mistakes entered the text as the scribes copied, edited, or translated the Scriptures over the centuries.

Partial inspiration: Christians affected by theological liberalism hold different views of the inspiration of the Bible. For example, some would assert that the Bible is God's Word but that the authors erred in some factual details. Others would say that the Bible *contains* God's Word and that the Spirit leads people today to determine which parts of the Bible God wants them to follow. Still others would say that the Bible is one testimony to God's Word, along with writings used in other religions.

Inspired translations: Some churches hold that God inspired certain translations of the Bible. For example, the Eastern Orthodox Church holds that God inspired the Greek Septuagint translation of the Old Testament. Some English-speaking Protestants hold that God inspired the King James translation of the Bible.

Point to Remember

But the Helper, the Holy Spirit, whom the Father will send in My name, He will teach you all things and bring to your remembrance all that I have said to you. *John 14:26*

God's Pen Is Mightier Than All!

Every man will read a book with more pleasure or even with more ease, if it is written in fairer characters.

—Epictetus, *Discourses*

The early second-century Stoic philosopher Epictetus believed that happiness was attainable only by living virtuously and taming one's passions. His *Discourses*, possibly penned by Arrian, his disciple, praise the power of the human soul and the authority of human reason. Affected by ill health and misfortune throughout most of his life, Epictetus nevertheless sought well-being from within.

Epictetus's pen has played a formative role in the study of philosophy. For some, his writings have encouraged self-denial and close introspection in order to obtain contentment. But do Epictetus's words continue to have the power and authority they once did? Or have they, like the works of so many other philosophers, been relegated to the dusty shelves of history?

"The pen is mightier than the sword." We understand this phrase to mean that written words are often more powerful than military might. Many times in history the power of words has stood up against and even defeated the power of the sword. The Reformation is clearly one of these cases since the printing press aided in the effort. One could say the writings of Dr. Luther, particularly the Ninety-five Theses, overpowered the strength of the Holy Roman emperor. The Declaration of Independence is another example where the strength of words provided the motivation to overcome superior military might.

God's Word was probably originally written with a sharpened piece of reed or perhaps some type of quill. But we can say God "penned" His Word to us through various authors. So which is mightier, the penned Word of God or the sword? In Ephesians 6:17 Paul calls God's Word "the sword of the Spirit." If the sword of the Spirit is God's Word, they are, at least in that analogy, one and the same. Thus God's Word is the instrument of His Spirit and it wields considerable power.

Power and Authority

It is because the Scriptures are the inspired Word of God that they have power and authority. Genesis 1 revealed the power and authority of God's Word. God "said" and created all that exists (see, for example, Genesis 1:3). Jeremiah tells us the Lord's Word is like fire and a hammer that breaks rocks to pieces (23:29). In Jeremiah, we see the Law at work, bringing low and breaking down sinful hearts. Isaiah compares the Word of the Lord to rain or snow: "For as the rain and the snow come down from heaven and do not return there but water the earth, making it bring forth and sprout, giving seed to the sower and bread to the eater, so shall My word be that goes out from My mouth; it shall not return to Me empty, but it shall accomplish that which I purpose, and shall succeed in the thing for which I sent it" (55:10–11). Rain and snow come from the skies and produce fruitful, beneficial results. So it is with the Lord's Word from heaven. It accomplishes the Lord's powerful purpose in sending it.

Jesus uses an analogy similar to that found in Isaiah 55 when He speaks the parable of the sower. In Luke, we read that the Word of God is like a seed that can produce amazingly abundant fruit (Luke 8:8). Here the analogy is to the growth and spread of God's kingdom through the ministry of Jesus' Word.

Hebrews 4:12 speaks of the Word of God as a two-edged sword. It is described as living, active, sharp, and penetrating. It also judges. God's Word cuts through everything else and gets to the heart of the matter!

The power of God's Word is proclaimed in both Law and Gospel. In John 12:48 Jesus says His Word will condemn those who reject both Him and His Word on the Last Day. This is the powerful Law. In fact, the Greek word translated as *power* in Romans 1:16 is *dunamis*, from which we also form *dynamite* and *dynamic*. There Paul stresses that the ultimate power of God is His power to save through the good news of the Gospel. This is an important passage to consider. We usually think of power and authority in terms of the Law because it forces, compels, and pushes down. But, as in the analogies of rain and seed, the power of God's Word is the ultimate positive power. It gives life, produces fruit, nourishes, sustains, and saves.

Seed That Lasts

The apostle Peter writes:

> You have been born again, not of perishable seed but of imperishable, through the living and abiding word of God; for "All flesh is like grass and all its glory like the flower of grass. The grass withers, and the flower falls, but the word of the Lord remains forever." And this word is the good news that was preached to you. So put away all malice and all deceit and hypocrisy and envy and all slander. Like newborn infants, long for the pure spiritual milk, that by it you may grow up into salvation—if indeed you have tasted that the Lord is good. (1 Peter 1:23–2:3)

This passage says a number of things that relate the Word of God to our own lives. First, life apart from God perishes (v. 23). Peter also quotes Isaiah 40, which speaks of all humans and all human glory as flowers and grass. None of these last; all wither and fade. God's Word, on the other hand, stands forever. Therefore, it powerfully gives imperishable life.

Second, phrases such as "born again" (1:23) and "newborn infants" (2:2) are probably references to Baptism. The Greek word *baptizein* simply means "to wash." The bath or act of washing corresponds with the Greek word *baptisma*. There are many references in the Scriptures to Baptism in which that specific word is not present (e.g., John 3:3, 5; Ephesians 5:26). According to 1 Peter 1:25, God's Word is proclaimed. But when God's proclaimed Word is combined with water, it produces Christian Baptism. Martin Luther's explanation of Holy Baptism in the Small Catechism agrees with Scripture (cf. *Concordia*, pp. 339–40).

Third, in the original Greek language, 1 Peter 2:2 calls us to desire the "pure spiritual milk of God's Word." Why are we to "crave" it? What does it seek to accomplish in our lives? The "natural" hunger of a baby is for milk; the "supernatural" hunger of a born-again (1 Peter 1:23) believer is for God's Word. It not only gives imperishable life, it also nourishes that life and enables it to grow (2:2). According to 1 Peter 3:21, Baptism, the water and the Word, saves. But the Word then also enables us to grow up in that salvation (2:2). Some scholars also see a reference to the Lord's Supper in 2:3 where the Lord's goodness is tasted.

Well-Armed

One of Paul's analogies for the Christian life is to describe us as soldiers of the cross in Ephesians 6:10–17:

> Finally, be strong in the Lord and in the strength of His might. Put on the whole armor of God, that you may be able to stand against the schemes of the devil. For we do not wrestle against flesh and blood, but against the rulers, against the authorities, against the cosmic powers over this present darkness, against the spiritual forces of evil in the heavenly places. Therefore take up the whole armor of God, that you may be able to withstand in the evil day, and having done all, to stand firm. Stand therefore, having fastened on the belt of truth, and having put on the breastplate of righteousness, and, as shoes for your feet, having put on the readiness given by the gospel of peace. In all circumstances take up the shield of faith, with which you can extinguish all the flaming darts of the evil one; and take the helmet of salvation, and the sword of the Spirit, which is the word of God.

Paul lists the opponents aligned against the believer: the devil's schemes, rulers, authorities and powers of this dark world, and the spiritual forces of evil. With those foes against us, we surely need defensive armor: the breastplate of righteousness, the shield of faith, the helmet of salvation. We are defended by the armor of truth, righteousness, faith, and salvation. But defense isn't enough. Our main offensive weapon, described by Paul as "the sword of the Spirit" is the Word of God. God stands us up in the faith and equips us so that we are enabled to stay standing (vv. 13–14).

As the Christian reaches out with the sword of the Spirit, the world is often offended by the Law. Its assertion of an overarching, universal morality is offensive to many in our postmodern world. Recall the passage from Hebrews: "For the word of God is living and active, sharper than any two-edged sword, piercing to the division of soul and of spirit, of joints and of marrow, and discerning the thoughts and intentions of the heart" (4:12). The exclusive claims of the Gospel (see John 14:6; Acts 4:12) are also offensive to many in our day who see spiritual truth and legitimacy in almost any and every form of religion. If others are offended by Christianity, it should be God's message of Law and Gospel that offends them, rather than the conduct or abrasiveness of Christians. Ephesians 6:15 says that in addition to our armor, we are also equipped with the readiness that comes from the Gospel of peace.

Comparisons

Eastern Orthodox: "We undoubtingly confess, as sure truth, that the Catholic Church cannot sin, nor err, nor utter falsehood in place of truth; for the Holy Ghost, ever working through His faithful ministers the fathers and doctors of the Church, preserves her from all error" (Missive of the Eastern Patriarchs on the Orthodox Faith, article 12, quoted in *The Longer Catechism of the Eastern Church*, answer 271).

Lutheran: "In this way the distinction between the Holy Scriptures of the Old and of the New Testament and all other writings is preserved. The Holy Scriptures alone remain the judge, rule, and norm. According to them—as the only touchstone—all teachings shall and must be discerned and judged to see whether they are good or evil [1 Thessalonians 5:21–22], right or wrong" (FC Ep Summary 7; *Concordia*, p. 474).

Reformed/Presbyterian: "We may be moved and induced by the testimony of the Church to a high and reverent esteem of the holy Scripture; and the heavenliness of the matter, the efficacy of the doctrine, the majesty of the style, the consent of all the parts, the scope of the whole (which is to give all glory to God), the full discovery it makes of the only way of man's salvation, the many other incomparable excellencies, and the entire perfection thereof, are arguments whereby it doth abundantly evidence itself to be the Word of God; yet, notwithstanding, our full persuasion and assurance of the infallible truth, and divine authority thereof, is from the inward Word of the Holy Spirit, bearing witness by and with the Word in our hearts" (*The Westminster Confession of Faith*, chapter 1.5).

Roman Catholic: "The Roman Pontiff, when he speaks *ex cathedra* . . . is possessed of that infallibility with which the divine Redeemer wills that His Church should be endowed for defining doctrine regarding faith or morals" (First Vatican Council, *Pastor aeternus*, ch. 4, July 18, 1870; cf. CCC2 para. 891).

Conservative Protestant: These groups generally agree that the Holy Scriptures are authoritative in all areas of faith and life, and they derive their doctrine and practice from their respective understandings of the Bible.

Liberal Protestant: These denominations vary in submission to the authority of God's Word depending on their beliefs about its accuracy and inspiration. Viewpoints may range from seeing the Bible as a mere historical book irrelevant to modern theology and morality to regarding only the teachings about Christ as inspired and authentic.

Point to Remember

And beginning with Moses and all the Prophets, He interpreted to them in all the Scriptures the things concerning Himself. *Luke 24:27*

You Have My Word on It!

I shall return.

—General Douglas MacArthur, March 20, 1942

Douglas MacArthur's military career was filled with many "firsts." He was first in his class throughout his education. He was nominated twice for a Congressional Medal of Honor in World War I. He finally received the Medal of Honor in World War II, the first recipient whose father had also received that medal. These "firsts" gave a special quality to MacArthur's words. When the Japanese had overrun his forces in the Philippines and Bataan, when hope seemed lost and he was in retreat, MacArthur promised to return and win the fight. From October 1944 to July 1945, he delivered on that promise and later signed the treaty to end the war on September 2, 1945.

How many times have you heard or said, "You have my word on it"? Sometimes a friend or colleague gives us his "word on it," but his word proves to be untrue. That can change our image of the person. And when circumstances make us unable to keep our word, we are disappointed in ourselves. Keeping your word—or relying on someone else to keep his or her word—is a large part of our daily lives. But how we have looked at *truth* has changed over the years. The following offers a brief, historical review to set the stage for this section.

History progressed through the Middle Ages into the Renaissance, which heralded a "rebirth" of classical learning. The Renaissance began around 1450 and continued through the time of the Reformation (1500s). The Thirty Years' War (1618–48) brought the politically "established" churches into disrepute and helped to create a climate of personalized religion known as Pietism. This same climate of individualism helped to popularize the Age of Rationalism that followed. The height of this time was the Enlightenment (1700s). Human reason and the modern scientific method governed public life, learning, and policy, which limited religion to private life. Later reactions that included Romanticism provided a role for human emotion and aesthetics to accompany and guide intellect (1760–1914). Many leading figures believed that human reason, aesthetics, and emotion could solve all problems and serve as the ultimate authority.

These developments had a dark side. It is true that mankind has always experienced violence and oppression in society. Rationalism and Romanticism tried to offer ways to put violence, oppression, war, poverty, and so on in the past. However, these modern movements could not account for the source of reason, the source of morality, and other aspects of life that give society its order and its moral compass. Socialism, Nihilism, and Communism arose as radical alternatives. Society had little place for God and the sanctity of human life. Many began to suspect that the world is fundamentally irrational, and the adherents of this perspective would be energized by the works of Charles Darwin and Herbert Spencer. Not only did these and other figures have profound effects on education, health care, and social policy in Europe and North America, but they also provided ideas that many world leaders would use to justify entering into World War I and that Adolf Hitler would use to conceive his "final solution."

Rationalism has undergone many challenges during the twentieth century in science, politics, and religion. Romanticism and Rationalism collapsed after the First World War, while Socialism and Communism have spread their influence. Especially following the social upheavals of the 1960s, scholars and media figures often speak of our culture today with the term *postmodern*. Postmodernism tends to reject absolute truth because it sees absolutes as a means to enforce power. Postmodernism allows multiple "truths" to compete and coexist in the sciences, politics, the humanities, and religion. Nevertheless, it concedes that relationships of community and power define human society. Postmodernism can quickly turn "coexistence" into a "corrective" reversal of power where the former "victim" dominates the former "oppressor."

Even the hard sciences have to concede different ways of looking at reality. The Age of Reason brought Newton's laws of physics in the 1600s. The twentieth century brought two additional perspectives. Einstein's theories of relativity explained the large-scale behavior of the universe and unlocked black holes and hydrogen bombs. Max Planck's theories of quantum mechanics explained the chaotic world of subatomic particles. None of these three perspectives can be harmonized. In the same way, popular morality (e.g., situational ethics and gender issues), politics (e.g., "spin" or "might makes right"), and religion (e.g., New Age) have all embraced the idea that different perspectives can be right in their own way.

So, as Pilate asked, what is *truth*? Jesus said to the Father, "Your word is truth" (John 17:17). That statement can be a particular challenge for those in a postmodern culture to accept.

One Book, Many Books

Christians speak of the Bible as God's Word of truth. However, we often view the Bible as if it were one book. Actually, the Bible is a collection or library of sixty-six different documents written over a period of more than a thousand years by at least thirty different human authors. How did these documents "become" the Bible? The technical term for this issue is "the canon." *Canon* is a Greek word for a "reed" or "straight rod." It came to be used like we use the term "measuring stick." As a result, when the word *canon* is used of the Holy Scriptures, it expresses that these documents are the authoritative "measuring stick" for what we believe about God, the world, and ourselves.

Who decided that the sixty-six books in the canon were the divinely revealed "Truth" of God? The Old Testament books were regarded as authoritative as soon as they were given through Moses and the other authors. As a result, in practical use and understanding, an Old Testament canon existed throughout the history of Israel, beginning with Moses. However, the specific thirty-nine books in our Old Testament were not identified as such until around the time of Christ. A similar situation occurred with the twenty-seven documents we speak of as the New Testament. The early Church immediately used the words of Jesus and Paul and regarded them as authoritative (review "Now That's Inspired!" beginning on p. 10). However, it was not until the late fourth century that the twenty-seven documents in the Bible were specifically listed as the New Testament canon.

It may seem troublesome at first to acknowledge that God never gave a specific list for the Old or New Testament; neither is the formation of the canon a scientifically verifiable process. Rather, in regard to establishing both the Old and New Testament collections, the circumstances were similar. There was an ongoing, nearly unanimous acceptance of most of the books as the divinely inspired Word of God. A few books that were questioned by some (e.g., Esther, Daniel, Revelation) gradually came to be included and then universally recognized by the Church. At the same time, books about which there was dispute and uncertainty (e.g., Ecclesiasticus, the *Shepherd of Hermas*) were excluded. Ultimately, the acceptance of sixty-six documents as the Bible is a matter of faith in the God who gave them, who preserved them for us, who handed them down to us, and who continues to speak His Word of truth through them today.

The following verses tell us a great deal about the truth of God's Word.

Psalm 12:6: "The words of the LORD are pure words, like silver refined in a furnace on the ground, purified seven times." God's words are flawless and pure, like metal that is perfectly refined.

Psalm 119:86, 89: "All Your commandments are sure; [the insolent] persecute me with falsehood; help me! . . . Forever, O LORD, Your word is firmly fixed in the heavens." Psalm 119 asserts again and again that the Lord's words, commands, precepts, and laws are true, trustworthy, and eternal. This applies to the Law and its commands, which come from God and do assert an absolute morality of right and wrong. However, the Hebrew word *Torah*, which is translated as *law*, has a broader meaning ("instruction" or "revelation") that also encompasses the Gospel. (See Psalm 119:138, 151, 160 for more examples.)

2 Samuel 22:31: "This God—His way is perfect; the word of the LORD proves true; He is a shield for all those who take refuge in Him." God's Word is flawless; His ways are perfect. The Gospel content of the second half of the verse proclaims that this perfect God is our shield and refuge.

John 10:35: "Scripture cannot be broken." Once God has spoken, His Word stands.

John 17:17: "Sanctify them in the truth; Your word is truth." Jesus identifies or equates God's Word and truth.

These verses give clear indication that God's Word is truth. But some would argue that other parts of the Bible contradict this. Think about the prophet Jonah. He was sent by the Lord to announce that in forty days Nineveh would be destroyed (Jonah 3:3–4). However, that did not happen (3:10). Was Jonah's prophecy, and therefore God's Word, untrue? We find the answer in Jeremiah 18:7–10: "If at any time I declare concerning a nation or a kingdom, that I will pluck up and break down and destroy it, and if that nation, concerning which I have spoken, turns from its evil, I will relent of the disaster that I intended to do to it. And if at any time I declare concerning a nation or a kingdom that I will build and plant it, and if it does evil in My sight, not listening to My voice, then I will relent of the good that I had intended to do to it." This is called the contingency of prophecy. Lutherans have a good insight into these situations with the paradox between God speaking Law and speaking Gospel. The Jeremiah passage spells out in more detail how God is consistent in applying Law or Gospel depending on the circumstances. In Jonah, the Ninevites responded to the proclamation of the Law with repentance, and God relented, as He promises in Jeremiah 18. However, Jeremiah also reminds us that those who receive God's grace and then turn away will rightly receive the condemnation of His Law. The marvelous assurance in all this is James 2:13: God's "mercy triumphs over judgment." God's desire to save us through the Gospel is greater than His just determination to punish sinners. Both are true, however.

If God's Word is truth, how does this relate to what Jesus says about Himself in John 14:6: "I am the way, and the truth, and the life. No one comes to the Father except through Me"? If God's Word is truth and Jesus is truth, then it may be proper to equate Jesus with God's Word.

True to the Text

What is the purpose or role of God's truthful Word in our lives? "Sanctify them in the truth; Your word is truth" (John 17:17). Jesus calls on His Father to sanctify Jesus' followers by the truth. The verb *sanctify* means to "make holy" or to "set apart." In John 17:19, Jesus hallows or sets Himself apart to accomplish His mission in order that He may make us truly holy: "And for their sake I consecrate Myself, that they also may be sanctified in truth." (See also 1 Corinthians 1:30.) In John 17:17, the point is that God makes us holy; we cannot do it ourselves. This "making us holy" is related directly to the truth, which is equated to the Father's Word. The primacy of the Gospel is once again stressed. The truth of God's Word is that He desires to make us holy as He is holy.

How does holiness fit into God's Word being truth? What does it reveal about the nature and purpose of God speaking to us? Two passages in Leviticus reveal God's relationship to His Old Testament people: "Keep My statutes and do them; I am the Lord who sanctifies you" (20:8) and "For I am the Lord who brought you up out of the land of Egypt to be your God. You shall therefore be holy, for I am holy" (11:45). As we read in John—that it is God who makes us holy, not we ourselves—so we see from Leviticus that the same was true in the Old Testament. God's people were not supposed to try to become holy by keeping the Law; neither were they able to do so. Rather, Leviticus 20:8 states that the Lord made them holy or sanctified them just as Jesus says in John 17:17! Leviticus 11:45 points out that the people's motivation for trying to live holy lives was a response to the Gospel of the exodus and a desire to be like the God who had already saved them and made them holy.

So God's Word is held up as the truth for God's people, but as sinful human beings, we sometimes have difficulty leaving it at that. The tendency of the Pharisees and the teachers of the Law was to equate their oral traditions with the Word of God. In Matthew 15:6, Jesus condemns them for setting aside or even nullifying the Word of God for the sake of their tradition. Throughout its history, certain segments of the Church have also exhibited a tendency to elevate tradition to the level of God's Word or even higher. This creates disharmony among members and confuses the unbelieving world. Martin Luther fought the traditions of papal power by asserting "Scripture alone" as the sole source of authority in the Church. We must be careful to speak with the authority of God's Word where God's Word speaks but also make clear when that is not the case.

Certain Truth

In our life today, the truth of God's Word is openly and frequently challenged. The creation account (Genesis 1–2), Noah's ark and the flood (Genesis 6–9), the sun standing still in Joshua 10, and the miracles present in Jesus' ministry and throughout the Scriptures are often dismissed by nonbelievers as good stories, but not *truth*. The Christian may respond that such events are supernatural since God's intervention is directly involved. As a result, those events are logically contrary to the normal workings of nature and its laws. While it is impossible to prove such events, it is also impossible to disprove them. If God and the supernatural are excluded at the outset, some other explanation must be made (e.g., naturalistic evolution, the early Church made up the miracles, and so on). A Christian's response will vary according to the circumstances. However, the Christian faith is just that: faith, which the writer to the Hebrews defines as "the assurance of things hoped for, the conviction of things not seen. . . . By faith we understand that the universe was created by the word of God" (11:1, 3).

Jesus says to the Father, "Your word is truth" (John 17:17). What is the difference between God's Word being *true* and God's Word being *truth*? In our day of competing truths or even a rejection of the existence of absolute truth in any form, it is vital that we look to the Scriptures. The conviction that the Scriptures are true or inerrant is properly a conviction of faith, as noted earlier. Any society with no absolute truths is headed toward chaos.

Civilization must have some overarching, moral truths. Even if these are not directly from or based upon Scripture, they can make decent order in a society (see Romans 2:12–16). This recognizes that there are other human sources of truth. For example, we have learned much about ourselves and the world around us through the fields of psychology, biology, anthropology, and so forth. Many of the "truths" discovered in these areas have supplemented the truths of the Scriptures, rather than competing against them. But the Scriptures do not simply assert themselves to be one truth among many other truths. They claim to be *the* Truth with a capital *T*. They reveal the truth about the one true God and His relationship with humanity.

Comparisons

Many philosophical ideas in our society compete for our attention and acceptance. In addition to rationalism and postmodernism (discussed earlier), other "-isms" jockey for position when we study the absolute and changeless truths of the Bible. Often Bible readers are not even aware that such ideas influence and color their interpretation of God's Word.

Rationalism: "We can figure that out." This philosophy rejects religious faith or dogma in determining truth, and relies solely on human reason and analysis. Secular humanism (which deifies the human person, human society and its achievements) and atheism (which denies that God exists) are philosophically related to rationalism.

Relativism: "Everything is relative." There is no absolute reference for the values human beings place in their beliefs or behaviors. As a philosophical theory, relativism has two inherent problems: it is itself either relativistic (that is, subject to change) or absolutist (by claiming there are no absolutes).

Moral relativism: "There are no moral absolutes." Morals arise from society's agreed-upon customs, traditions, or etiquette. In contrast, *moral absolutists* believe that timeless norms are not culture-bound but are derived from natural law, human nature, religious sources, or a combination of these.

Subjectivism: "Perception creates reality." There is no true reality apart from our perception. Objectivists, however, argue that there is an underlying reality to all things existing independently of our perception. Subjectivism tends also to conflict with everyday human experience.

Pragmatism: "Whatever works is right." This notably American philosophical system sets goals as standards of reality and judges concepts by how well they help achieve those goals. Although this system is helpful in many situations, pragmatism's chief weaknesses lie in determining the inherent value of the desired goals and deciding who or what makes those determinations.

Point to Remember

But this I confess to you, that according to the Way, which they call a sect, I worship the God of our fathers, believing everything laid down by the Law and written in the Prophets. *Acts 24:14*

The Word and the Word Made Flesh

Lord, keep us steadfast in Your Word;
Curb those who by deceit or sword
Would wrest the kingdom from Your Son
And bring to naught all He has done.
—Martin Luther (*LSB* 655:1)

To Martin Luther the primary focus of the Scriptures was God's grace, mercy, and forgiveness through Jesus Christ. The Bible served as a sort of manger, Luther said, in which the Christ Child was laid. Throughout his often tumultuous life, Luther would go to that manger to encounter his Savior. There a little Child could give him something the grown-up world could not: comfort and hope in the midst of every trouble.

Earlier we said "Actions speak louder than words." With God there is no dichotomy between the two. God speaks and it happens. God promises and He fulfills. But there is even more here. The Scriptures teach that God's Word became a person in Jesus of Nazareth. Scripture speaks of this as the doctrine of the incarnation, from the Latin word meaning "in-fleshed."

Getting to the Point

Jesus says some very interesting things about the Scriptures, the written Word of God. Let's look at several passages in which Jesus discusses the focal point of the Old Testament Scriptures.

John 5:39–40: "You search the Scriptures because you think that in them you have eternal life; and it is they that bear witness about Me, yet you refuse to come to Me that you may have life." The Old Testament Scriptures testify to Jesus. Note that Jesus does not contradict the conclusion that, at the same time, the Scriptures also point the way to eternal life.

John 5:46–47: "For if you believed Moses, you would believe Me; for he wrote of Me. But if you do not believe his writings, how will you believe My words?" Jesus asserts that Moses "wrote about Me." Believing in Moses (i.e., Genesis through Deuteronomy) would mean believing in Jesus as well.

Luke 24:44–47: "Then He said to them, 'These are My words that I spoke to you while I was still with you, that everything written about Me in the Law of Moses and the Prophets and the Psalms must be fulfilled.' Then He opened their minds to understand the Scriptures, and said to them, 'Thus it is written, that the Christ should suffer and on the third day rise from the dead, and that repentance and forgiveness of sins should be proclaimed in His name to all nations, beginning from Jerusalem." Everything the Old Testament said about the coming Messiah, or Christ, has been fulfilled in the suffering, death, and resurrection of Jesus. Jesus opened the minds of His disciples so they could see that He was the fulfillment of all that had been prophesied.

Other passages in the New Testament make a similar point about Jesus. The first chapter of the letter to the Hebrews begins by asserting that Jesus, God's Son, is the final and ultimate way in which God has spoken to His people. First Peter 1:10–12 points out that the Old Testament writers wrote about and eagerly anticipated the salvation that has now come through the suffering and glory of Christ. While they did not fathom the exact when or how of the fulfillment, the Spirit of Christ was, nevertheless, pointing them ahead to Jesus.

In the Gospels, we read Jesus' own words: "It is the Spirit who gives life; the flesh is no help at all. The words that I have spoken to you are spirit and life" (John 6:63; compare Deuteronomy 8:3). Later in that same chapter, Peter affirms: "You have the words of eternal life, and we have believed, and have come to know, that You are the Holy One of God" (6:68–69).

However, the relationship between Jesus and the Word of God is even more complete. How did God create all that exists? "God said" (Genesis 1:3), and all that exists came into being by God speaking His Word. John's Gospel restates the message of Genesis 1: "In the beginning was the Word, and the Word was with God, and the Word was God. He was in the beginning with God. All things were made through Him, and without Him was not any thing made that was made" (John 1:1–3). John identifies the Word as being present and active "in the beginning." In fact, says John, the Word *was* God, and all things were created through that Word. Then John makes a most remarkable statement: "And the Word became flesh and dwelt among us, and we have seen His glory, glory as of the only Son from the Father, full of grace and truth" (1:14). This verse declares the incarnation in its most straightforward language. The Word became flesh in Jesus, the babe, the Son of Mary. The Word was God (John 1:1), and the Word-God became human flesh (1:14). This is the joyful message of Jesus' conception and birth revealed in a dream to Joseph (Matthew 1:20–21) and to the Virgin Mary by the angel Gabriel (Luke 1:35) and fulfilled the night the angels sang above the Bethlehem hills (Luke 2:1–14).

John also begins his first letter with what was "from the beginning," that is, Jesus Christ.

> That which was from the beginning, which we have heard, which we have seen with our eyes, which we looked upon and have touched with our hands, concerning the word of life—the life was made manifest, and we have seen it, and testify to it and proclaim to you the eternal life, which was with the Father and was made manifest to us—that which we have seen and heard we proclaim also to you, so that you too may have fellowship with us; and indeed our fellowship is with the Father and with His Son Jesus Christ. And we are writing these things so that our joy may be complete. (1 John 1:1–4)

John again identifies Jesus as the Word of life who was from all eternity. In Jesus, the Word became flesh, a physical human being. As John and the other disciples heard, saw, looked at, and touched the human body of Jesus, they encountered "the Word of life" in the flesh. The purpose of the incarnation was to bring us into fellowship with the Father through the Son, and ultimately into fellowship with one another (1 John 1:3). Sharing this message so that others have fellowship with us makes our joy complete (v. 4).

Finally, in Revelation 19:11–16 John describes his vision of an individual on a white horse:

> Then I saw heaven opened, and behold, a white horse! The one sitting on it is called Faithful and True, and in righteousness He judges and makes war. His eyes are like a flame of fire, and on His head are many diadems, and He has a name written that no one knows but Himself. He is clothed in a robe dipped in blood, and the name by which He is called is The Word of God. And the armies of heaven, arrayed in fine linen, white and pure, were following Him on white horses. From His mouth comes a sharp sword with which to strike down the nations, and He will rule them with a rod of iron. He will tread the winepress

> of the fury of the wrath of God the Almighty. On His robe and on His thigh He has a name written, King of kings and Lord of lords.

The same author who wrote the Gospel and 1 John again pictures Jesus for us, but this time in the apocalyptic imagery of Revelation. Jesus is called "Faithful and True" (19:11; see also John 14:6). He judges and makes war (v. 11). He is dressed in a robe dipped in blood (v. 13). He has a sword coming from His mouth (v. 15; see also Revelation 1:16; Ephesians 6:13). On His robe and thigh is written the name "King of Kings and Lord of Lords" (v. 16). The end of verse 13 specifically identifies His name as "the Word of God" (see also John 1:1, 14).

Finding the Center

According to the number of words in the King James Version of the Bible, 76 percent of God's words to us are in what we call the Old Testament. What impact does this statistic have on you? Consider what Paul says in 2 Timothy 3:16–17: "All Scripture is breathed out by God and profitable for teaching, for reproof, for correction, and for training in righteousness, that the man of God may be competent, equipped for every good work." As New Testament Christians, we often neglect the Old Testament in our devotions, our discussions, and our worship. Instead, we should eagerly "study the Scriptures" (John 5:39) as "the whole counsel of God" (Acts 20:27).

If Jesus is the center of the Scriptures, what does this mean for how we read, interpret, understand, and apply the Old Testament Word of God? We now read the Old Testament through the events of the birth, life, ministry, death, resurrection, ascension, reign, and promised return of Jesus Christ. We view those Scriptures as fulfilled in Christ, but we also can see more in the Old Testament now that the bud of God's plan of salvation has fully flowered (see 1 Peter 1:10–12). For example, one can perceive the three persons of the Trinity at work in Genesis 1:1–3. The Father created (v. 1); the Son was the Word (v. 3); the Spirit was hovering (v. 2). Hosea 11:1 can simply be a statement about the exodus of God's people from Egypt, but now, in the fullness of time, it is more completely embodied in Jesus' return from Egypt as described in Matthew 2:14–15, 19–21. God's Old Testament people came out of Egypt, passed through the waters of the Red Sea, and spent forty years in the wilderness. In Matthew's Gospel, Jesus comes out of Egypt, passes through the waters of His Baptism, and spends forty days in the wilderness (Matthew 2–4). "My God, my God, why have You forsaken me?" (Psalm 22:1) is David's desperate cry; it is fully and absolutely experienced by Jesus on the cross (Mark 15:34). These are just a few of the many examples of how the Old Testament points to Jesus as the fulfillment of Scripture.

As we look toward the end of the world, what does Jesus say about our response to those awesome and sometimes frightening events? As recorded in Luke's Gospel, our Savior says: "And then they will see the Son of Man coming in a cloud with power and great glory. Now when these things begin to take place, straighten up and raise your heads, because your redemption is drawing near" (21:27–28) and "Truly, I say to you, this generation will not pass away until all has taken place. Heaven and earth will pass away, but My words will not pass away" (21:32–33). Here Jesus assures us that when the world as we know it comes to an end, He is coming to take us home, and our redemption is drawing near (v. 28). If all else fails and falls apart, including the heavens and earth as we know them, His Word will never pass away (v. 33). Recall 1 Peter, which quotes Isaiah 40: " 'The grass withers and the flower falls, but the word of the Lord stands forever.' And this word is the good news that was preached to you" (1:24b–25). This is the God-breathed Word of God that speaks to us today.

Growing in the Gift

In "God's Pen Is Mightier Than All!" (see p. 19), we read 1 Peter 2:2, which states: "Like newborn infants, long for pure spiritual milk, that by it you may grow up into salvation—if indeed you have tasted that the Lord is good." Salvation is a gift, yet it is also something we can "grow up into" according to Peter. How is this true? A baby is born alive and is no more or less alive as he or she grows from infancy through adulthood. In a similar manner, we are born again in Baptism through the power of God's enduring Word (1 Peter 1:23; 3:21). We are alive in relationship with God and cannot become any "more" alive. But, just as a child grows, so we can grow up in our knowledge and our living out of the salvation God has bestowed upon us.

How can you personally resolve to grow up in your salvation by continuing to crave the pure, spiritual milk of God's Word? Consider these ideas: start a new Bible class; join an existing Bible class; read through the Bible in a year; listen to the Bible regularly on tape or CD. This is not a legalistic "thou shalt" exercise, but a response to tasting the goodness of God's Word and simply wanting more! This desire or craving is motivated by God's Spirit and strives to allow God to draw us ever closer to Him as we are exposed to His holy and precious Word. "God's Word is our great heritage And shall be ours forever; To spread its light from age to age Shall be our chief endeavor. Through life it guides our way, In death it is our stay.

Lord, grant, while worlds endure, We keep its teachings pure Throughout all generations" (*LSB* 582).

Comparisons

Eastern Orthodox: "Why, then, was holy Scripture given? To this end, that divine revelation might be preserved more exactly and unchangeably" (*The Longer Catechism of the Eastern Church*, question 22).

Lutheran: "Out of His immense goodness and mercy, God provides for the public preaching of His divine eternal Law and His wonderful plan for our redemption, that of the holy, only saving Gospel of His eternal Son, our only Savior and Redeemer, Jesus Christ. By this preaching He gathers an eternal Church for Himself from the human race and works in people's hearts true repentance, knowledge of sins, and true faith in God's Son, Jesus Christ. By this means, and in no other way (i.e., through His holy Word, when people hear it preached or read it, and through the holy Sacraments when they are used according to His Word), God desires to call people to eternal salvation. He desires to draw them to Himself and convert, regenerate, and sanctify them" (FC SD II 50; *Concordia*, p. 529).

Reformed/Presbyterian: "The whole counsel of God, concerning all things necessary for His own glory, man's salvation, faith, and life, is either expressly set down in Scripture, or by good and necessary consequence may be deduced from Scripture: unto which nothing at any time is to be added, whether by new revelations of the Spirit, or traditions of men. Nevertheless we acknowledge the inward illumination of the Spirit of God to be necessary for the saving understanding of such things as are revealed in the Word" (*The Westminster Confession of Faith*, chapter 1.6).

Roman Catholic: "Furthermore, in order to restrain petulant spirits, it [this Council] decrees, that no one, relying on his own skill, shall—in matters of faith, and of morals pertaining to the edification of Christian doctrine—wresting the sacred Scripture to his own senses, presume to interpret the said sacred Scripture contrary to that sense which holy mother Church—whose it is to judge of the true sense and interpretation of the Holy Scripture—hath held and doth hold" (*Canons and Decrees of the Council of Trent*, Session 24, Decree concerning the Canonical Scriptures; cf. CCC2 para. 113).

Baptist: "We believe that, in order to be saved, sinners must be regenerated, or born again; that regeneration consists in giving a holy disposition to the mind; that it is effected in a manner above our comprehension by the power of the Holy Spirit, in connection with divine truth, so as to secure our voluntary obedience to the Gospel; and that its proper evidence appears in the holy fruits of repentance, and faith, and newness of life" (*New Hampshire Baptist Confession*, article 7).

Wesleyan/Methodist: "The Holy Scriptures contain all things necessary to salvation; so that whatsoever is not read therein, nor may be proved thereby, is not to be required of any man that it should be believed as an article of faith, or be thought requisite or necessary to salvation" (*Methodist Articles of Religion*, article 5).

Liberal Protestant: "If the source of our sin is located in a non-psychological 'nature' which we inherit, we shall, of course, interpret the work of Christ in terms of His 'natures,' divine and human. But if we think of sin concretely and refer it to its psychological causes, we shall interpret salvation in terms of conscious experience. We shall then not ask concerning the 'nature' of Jesus, but rather concerning His religious consciousness and life. We shall emphasize His God-consciousness and His ability to create in His disciples a trust in God which gives spiritual insight and moral power" (Gerald Birney Smith, ed., *A Guide to the Study of the Christian Religion* [Chicago: University of Chicago Press, 1916], pp. 531–32).

Point to Remember

From childhood you have been acquainted with the sacred writings, which are able to make you wise for salvation through faith in Christ Jesus. *2 Timothy 3:15*

Lutheran Summary of God's Word

Augsburg Confession Conclusion 5

We have mentioned only those things we thought it was necessary to talk about so that it would be understood that in doctrine and ceremonies we have received nothing contrary to Scripture or the Church universal. It is clear that we have been very careful to make sure no new ungodly doctrine creeps into our churches. (*Concordia*, p. 63)

Apology of the Augsburg Confession IV 5

All Scripture ought to be distributed into these two principal topics: the Law and the promises. For in some places Scripture presents the Law, and in others the promises about Christ. In other words, in the Old Testament, Scripture promises that Christ will come, and it offers, for His sake, the forgiveness of sins, justification, and life eternal. Or in the Gospel, in the New Testament, Christ Himself (since He has appeared) promises the forgiveness of sins, justification, and life eternal. (*Concordia*, p. 83)

Small Catechism: The Third Commandment

You shall sanctify the holy day. *What does this mean?* Answer: We should fear and love God so that we may not despise preaching and His Word, but hold it sacred, and gladly hear and learn it. (*Concordia*, p. 319. See also LC I 91–93, *Concordia*, p. 369.)

Small Catechism: The First Petition

Hallowed be Thy name. *What does this mean?* Answer: God's name is indeed holy in itself. But we pray in this petition that it may become holy among us also. *How is this done?* Answer: When the Word of God is taught in its truth and purity and we as the children of God also lead holy lives in accordance with it. To this end help us, dear Father in heaven. But anyone who teaches and lives other than by what God's Word teaches profanes the name of God among us. From this preserve us, heavenly Father. (*Concordia*, p. 332. See also the Second and Third Petitions, *Concordia*, pp. 333–34; and LC V 76, *Concordia*, p. 439.)

Formula of Concord Epitome Summary 1

We believe, teach, and confess that the only rule and norm according to which all teachings, together with ‹all› teachers, should be evaluated and judged [2 Timothy 3:15–17] are the prophetic and apostolic Scriptures of the Old and of the New Testament alone. For it is written in Psalm 119:105, "Your Word is a lamp to my feet and a light to my path." St. Paul has written, "even if we or an angel from heaven should preach to you a gospel contrary to the one we preached to you, let him be accursed" (Galatians 1:8). (*Concordia*, p. 473)

Formula of Concord Epitome Summary 7

In this way the distinction between the Holy Scriptures of the Old and of the New Testament and all other writings is preserved. The Holy Scriptures alone remain the judge, rule, and norm. According to them—as the only touchstone—all teachings shall and must be discerned and judged to see whether they are good or evil [1 Thessalonians 5:21–22], right or wrong. (*Concordia*, p. 474)

Formula of Concord Solid Declaration Summary 3

1. First, ‹we receive and embrace with our whole heart› are the prophetic and apostolic Scriptures of the Old and New Testaments as the pure, clear fountain of Israel. They are the only true standard or norm by which all teachers and doctrines are to be judged. (*Concordia*, p. 508)

Formula of Concord Solid Declaration XI 12

Against this false delusion and thought we should set up the following clear argument, which is sure and cannot fail: All Scripture is inspired by God. It is not for self-confidence and lack of repentance, but "for reproof, for correction, and for training in righteousness" (2 Timothy 3:16). Also, everything in God's Word has been written for us, not so that we should be driven to despair by it, but so that "through the encouragement of the Scriptures we might have hope" (Romans 15:4). (*Concordia*, p. 604)

TOPIC TWO

Law and Gospel[1]

Engaging This Topic

"I just don't get it."
"What's that?"
"You Lutherans say you believe in the Ten Commandments,
but you worship on Sunday, not the Jewish Sabbath."
"But Jesus is our Sabbath rest."
"So, the Third Commandment no longer applies?"

With characteristic boldness Martin Luther once defined the content of the Christian faith by saying, "The proper subject of theology is man guilty of sin and condemned, and God the Justifier and Savior of man the sinner."[2] Although brief and provocative, it is not a rash statement. Luther, who was by vocation a professor of the Bible, understood well that theology—words *about* God—has its only sure foundation in Scripture, the Word *of* God. As Luther's years of study continually made evident, the great subject of Scripture itself is man as sinner and God as Savior.

By his own admission, however, Luther did not always understand the content of Scripture. As a young monk he was acutely aware of what it had to say about his own sin and well-deserved condemnation, but he knew little of its comforting doctrine of God the Justifier and Savior. This he came to know only once he had learned to distinguish between Scripture's two main themes. As Luther stated, "When I discovered the proper distinction—namely, that the law is one thing and the gospel is another—I made myself free."[3]

For Luther, a proper distinction between Law and Gospel opened the door to a right understanding of God's Word and, therefore, a right understanding of God's will for humankind and our salvation. Throughout its

1 This chapter adapted from *The Lutheran Difference: Law and Gospel*, written by Korey Maas, with contributions by Robert C. Baker. Copyright © 2005 Concordia Publishing House.

2 AE 12:311.

3 AE 54:443.

history, the Lutheran Church has continued to maintain that rightly distinguishing between Law and Gospel is absolutely necessary in this regard. The Law shows us God's will and reveals our sin; the Gospel proclaims our salvation in Christ. To confuse these two doctrines is to remain confused about ourselves and about our God. To misunderstand them is to misunderstand the reason for the incarnation, life, death, and resurrection of Christ. In short, Law and Gospel are the means by which we can rightly understand the whole of the Christian faith.

This is, of course, not an easy task. Luther himself realized that no one can perfect the art of properly distinguishing between these two biblical doctrines. But in light of their great importance, he also encouraged Christians to exercise daily in this task. "He who masters the art of exact distinction between the law and the Gospel should be called a real theologian," he said, speaking equally of pastors, professors, and parishioners.

Lutheran Facts

Although all Christian churches use Holy Scripture, Lutherans emphasize that Scripture is the final and only certain judge of doctrine and practice (*sola scriptura*)—not human traditions, reason, or churchly authority.

Lutherans also confess the three ecumenical creeds (Apostles', Nicene, and Athanasian) because they correctly summarize biblical teaching.

Lutherans find that distinguishing Law and Gospel is a key interpretive principle in understanding the Bible. As John tells us in his Gospel: "For the law was given through Moses; grace and truth came through Jesus Christ" (1:17). (See also 2 Corinthians 3:6). This distinction between Law and Gospel is particularly helpful when we look at how sinners are justified before God by His grace through faith in Christ: "For God so loved the world, that He gave His only Son, that whoever believes in Him should not perish but have eternal life. For God did not send His Son into the world to condemn the world, but in order that the world might be saved through Him" (John 3:16–17; see also Galatians 4:4–5; Hebrews 2:14–17; 1 Timothy 1:15.)

Lutherans believe that the proper application of Law and Gospel is imperative, so that sinners are brought to repentance through the condemnation of the Law and are justified through faith in the promises of the Gospel.

The confusion of Law and Gospel leaves one between Scylla and Charybdis: either self-righteous or with weakened faith. Such confusion confirms unrepentant sinners in their sinful thoughts, words, and deeds, and starves repentant sinners of God's free forgiveness through Christ's life, death, and resurrection.

God's Word: The Law

In a madhouse there exists no law.
—John Clare

If we are in a great hurry, we may not appreciate traffic laws. If we are buying a home or opening a business, we may dislike existing zoning laws. Rules and regulations can sometimes seem highly inconvenient. Most people, however, recognize their importance. In fact, every society in the world has some form of law, some code of right and wrong. Without laws the world would become a madhouse.

Why is it that we are annoyed by certain laws? Most often, it's simply because they prevent us from doing what we want to do. But this is precisely their goal. In the same way, God, knowing all too well our sinful nature, has lovingly give us His divine Law to prevent us from succumbing to sin and being driven even further from Him.

Holy Legality

God's Law, like God Himself, is holy, righteous, and good. Although it threatens and accuses sinners, the Law does so as part of God's plan to reveal our sin and our consequent need for salvation. He Himself has mercifully provided this salvation in the person of Christ, who both fulfilled the Law and suffered its condemnation on our behalf.

Exhorting the Christians of Ephesus to live a holy and God-pleasing life, Paul distinguishes between those who are wise and unwise. The wise, he explains, are those who "understand what the will of the Lord is" (Ephesians 5:17). We can look to Psalm 40 to see how the Old Testament writers described the Law: "I delight to do Your will, O my God; Your law is within my heart" (v. 8). The psalmist, clearly one of the wise referred to by Paul, proclaims that he earnestly desires to do the will of God. He goes on to say that he knows God's will because he knows God's Law. The Law of God does indeed express His will for our life. For this reason, the Lutheran Confessions can refer to the Law quite simply as "God's unchangeable will" (FC Ep VI 7; *Concordia*, p. 487). Not only does the Law teach "what is right and pleasing to God," but it also "rebukes everything that is sin and contrary to God's will" (FC Ep V 3; *Concordia*, p. 484). Because the Law expresses nothing less than the will of a holy, righteous, and good God, Paul can also explain that the Law itself is "holy and righteous and good" (Romans 7:12).

Because the Law expresses God's holy and perfect will for His creation, He desires that all clearly know what this will is. To this end He gave the written Law to His Old Testament people (see Exodus 31:18). Moses received the summary of God's Law, the Ten Commandments, on two stone tablets.

Not all people are descended from Israel, however. Not all have been taught the Ten Commandments as Israel was commanded to teach her children. Are some, then, without the Law? This is the question Paul answers in the opening chapters of Romans. While admitting that the Gentiles "do not have the law"—that is, the written Law given to Israel—Paul explains that "they show that the work of the law is written on their hearts" (2:15). In fact, this "natural" law was given to all people even before the "revealed" Law of the Commandments. Thus the confessors write that those before Moses (even those before the fall into sin) "had God's Law written into their hearts, because they were created in God's image" (FC Ep VI 2; *Concordia*, p. 486). To be sure, sinful human nature prevents a perfect understanding of this natural law, but it does not prevent all understanding. For this reason Paul can explain that the Gentiles are without excuse, because, as the reformers wrote: "Mankind's reason or natural intellect does still have a dim spark of the knowledge that there is a God. It also knows about the doctrine of the Law" (FC SD II 9; *Concordia*, p. 521).

While Scripture is clear that all know the Law, it is also perfectly clear that none keep the Law. The author of Ecclesiastes announces that there is no one "who does good and never sins" (7:20). John explains the relationship between sin and the Law, stating that "everyone who makes a practice of sinning also practices lawlessness; sin is lawlessness" (1 John 3:4). In agreement with John, the Lutheran Confessions bluntly state: "Sin is everything that is contrary to God's Law" (FC SD VI 13; *Concordia*, p. 559). Lest people be tempted to think lightly of sin, to downplay their own sinfulness by believing they keep *most* of the Law, sinning only occasionally or breaking only minor points of the Law, James takes pains to explain the folly of this thinking. With a sweeping condemnation he declares that "whoever keeps the whole law but fails in one point has become accountable for all of it" (2:10). In this light, it is perfectly understandable that the confessors would note that "all Scripture, all the Church cries out that the Law cannot be satisfied" (Ap V [III] 45 [166]; *Concordia*, p. 108).

So if it's impossible for us to keep the Law, what is its purpose? Paul tells us in 1 Timothy 1:8–11:

> Now we know that the law is good, if one uses it lawfully, understanding this, that the law is not laid down for the just but for the lawless and disobedient, for the ungodly and sinners, for the unholy and profane, for those who strike their fathers and mothers, for murderers, the sexually immoral, men who practice homosexuality, enslavers, liars, perjurers, and whatever else is contrary to sound doctrine,

> in accordance with the gospel of the glory of the blessed God with which I have been entrusted.

The Law of God is not static. God Himself uses it to produce certain effects. In fact, the Law can be put to several uses.[4] In his letter to Timothy, while noting that care must be taken to use the Law properly, Paul gives some indication of one of its uses. He says it was made "for the lawless and disobedient, for the ungodly and sinners, for the unholy and profane" (1 Timothy 1:9). The Law and its threat of punishment are to prevent these people from doing what their sinful nature would otherwise compel them to do. This is referred to as the first use of the Law. Luther states in the Confessions: "We hold that the Law was given by God, first, to restrain sin by threats and the dread of punishment" (SA III II 1; *Concordia*, p. 271). Likewise, the confessors note that the Law was given "(1) that by the Law outward discipline might be maintained against wild, disobedient people" (FC Ep VI 1; *Concordia*, p. 486).

The Law is meant not only to prevent sin, but it also reveals sin. Paul says that it is *only* through the Law that sin is revealed. He confesses: "If it had not been for the law, I would not have known sin" (Romans 7:7). Paul does not merely comment on his own experience; expressing the same thought elsewhere, he notes that "through the law comes knowledge of sin" (Romans 3:20). Because it is only by means of the Law that we become conscious of sin, this second use of the Law is what the Confessions call its chief use: "the chief office or force of the Law is to reveal original sin with all its fruits. It shows us how very low our nature has fallen" (SA III II 4; *Concordia*, p. 271).

There are serious consequences for breaking God's Law. In addition to revealing man's sin, the second use of the Law also reveals the consequences of sin. It reveals that the holy and sinless God—who also created His people to be holy and sinless—does not at all take sin lightly. He Himself announces, "Cursed be anyone who does not confirm the words of this law by doing them" (Deuteronomy 27:26). The ultimate consequence of this curse, Paul explains, is death, both temporal and eternal. It is in the light of such scriptural testimony that the authors of the Lutheran Confessions acknowledge that the Law "threatens its transgressors with God's wrath and temporal and eternal punishments" (FC SD V 17; *Concordia*, p. 555). Even more strongly, they write that we are "accused or condemned by God's Law. So we are by nature the children of wrath, death,

---

4 The Lutheran Confessions denote three uses of the Law [see FC Ep VI 1; *Concordia*, p. 486]. Two of these apply to all people, while the third applies only to those who have first been called and redeemed by the Gospel. We'll look at this third use in "Law, Gospel, and Sanctification," p. 77.)

and damnation, unless we are delivered from them by Christ's merit" (FC SD I 6; *Concordia*, p. 512).

The Law of God may be used in different ways. There is one thing, however, for which the Law is not to be used. Paul, a former proponent of the Law, makes this point again and again in his letters to the early Christian churches. "Now it is evident that no one is justified before God by the law" (Galatians 3:11), he writes. He goes even further, stating bluntly that "you are severed from Christ, you who would be justified by the law" (Galatians 5:4). This is obviously no small point. Although the Law expresses God's will; although it is holy, righteous, and good; and although it has many uses, it cannot effect salvation. Paul goes so far as to say that those who try to use it for this end have instead forfeited salvation. The confessors could therefore reach no conclusion other than that "it is clear that we are not justified by the Law. Otherwise, why would we need Christ or the Gospel . . . ?" (Ap V [III] 136 [257]; *Concordia*, p. 120).

Crime and Punishment

If our civil laws can at times seem burdensome, the divine Law of God can seem even more so! No one escapes its jurisdiction. No one escapes accusation for breaking this Law. And, if we were left to our own devices, no one would escape its penalties.

It is impossible to be nonchalant when meditating on the Law of God. It not only commands and prohibits, but it also points out our failure to obey and the dire consequences that follow. If your meditation on the Law produces "true terrors, contrition, and sorrow," then you have properly understood it (FC SD II 54; *Concordia*, p. 530; see SA III II 4; *Concordia*, p. 271). It is time to hear the Gospel!

Paul had reminded his readers in Galatia of God's Old Testament announcement of a curse on all those who do not fulfill the Law (3:10). He also reminds them of another biblical curse: "Cursed is everyone who is hanged on a tree" (Galatians 3:13). This, says Paul, applies even to Jesus Himself, who hung on the cross. But how could the sinless Christ who fulfilled the Law be cursed? Paul explains that He became "a curse for us," in our place (Galatians 3:13). He who fulfilled the Law received the punishment deserved by those who have not fulfilled it. Thanks be to God! Those condemned by the Law have been redeemed from its curse.

Utter Silence

Paul informs us that the Law speaks "so that every mouth may be stopped, and the whole world may be held accountable to God" (Romans

3:19)—*every* mouth, the *whole* world. Although every society throughout the world has some form of law, not all people recognize the Law of the God who created this world.

As you encounter those who do not know or do not believe the Bible, consider how you might begin to discuss both Law and Gospel with them. Many do not know the Ten Commandments. Others may know them and reject them. Yet all people recognize and live their lives according to some form of law, some understanding of right and wrong. Conversation with unbelievers might begin with an attempt to understand the nature of the "law" they follow. On the basis of their explanation, you might emphasize the common ground between what they believe, what all people believe, and what is stated in the Commandments. You might then point out that these commonalities suggest a common source—God Himself. Furthermore, you might ask what happens when they do not fulfill their own "law." You could point out that the inability to keep even those laws which we acknowledge is an indication that there is something fundamentally wrong with mankind. Our inability to keep the Law reveals our need for the Gospel.

Comparisons

Eastern Orthodox: "What is necessary in order to please God and to save one's own soul? In the first place, a knowledge of the true God, and a right faith in Him; in the second place, a life according to faith, and good works" (*The Longer Catechism of the Eastern Church*, question 3).

Lutheran: "We believe, teach, and confess that the Law is properly a divine doctrine [Romans 7:12]. It teaches what is right and pleasing to God, and it rebukes everything that is sin and contrary to God's will. For this reason, then, everything that rebukes sin is, and belongs to, the preaching of the Law" (FC Ep V 3–4; *Concordia*, p. 484).

Reformed/Presbyterian: "God gave to Adam a law, as a covenant of works, by which He bound him and all his posterity to personal, entire, exact, and perpetual obedience; promised life upon the fulfilling, and threatened death upon the breach of it; and endued him with power and ability to keep it. . . . Although true believers be not under the law as a covenant of works, to be thereby justified or condemned; yet is it of great use to them, as well as to others" (*The Westminster Confession of Faith*, chapter 19.1, 6).

Roman Catholic: "The holy Synod declares first, that, for the correct and sound understanding of the doctrine of Justification, it is necessary that each one recognize and confess, that, whereas all men had lost their innocence in the prevarication of Adam . . . free-will, attenuated as it was in its powers, and bent down, was by no means extinguished in them" (*Canons and Decrees of the Council of Trent*, Session 6, Decree on Justification; cf. CCC2 paras. 143, 154–55).

Baptist: "We believe that man was created in holiness, under the law of his Maker; but by voluntary transgression fell from that holy and happy state; in consequence of which all mankind are now sinners, not by constraint, but choice; being by nature utterly void of that holiness required by the law of God, positively inclined to evil; and therefore under just condemnation to eternal ruin, without defense or excuse" (*New Hampshire Baptist Confession*, article 3).

Wesleyan/Methodist: "Although the law given from God by Moses, as touching ceremonies and rites, does not bind Christians, nor ought the civil precepts thereof of necessity be received in any commonwealth, yet, notwithstanding, no Christian whatsoever is free from the obedience of the commandments which are called moral" (*Methodist Articles of Religion*, article 6).

Liberal: "We cannot define Christian ethics in terms of a church-controlled society. Neither can we regard Christian duty as identical with biblical precepts. . . . Christian ethics should be defined as the determination of the duties of a modern Christian living in the modern world. To define it in terms of an ethical system belonging to another age is to fail to make Christianity ethical" (Gerald Birney Smith, ed., *A Guide to the Study of the Christian Religion* [Chicago: University of Chicago Press, 1916], p. 570).

Point to Remember

I delight to do Your will, O my God; Your law is within my heart.
Psalm 40:8

God's Word: The Gospel

> Ill news hath wings, and with the wind doth go,
> Comfort's a cripple and comes ever slow.
> —Michael Drayton

War, famine, crime, scandal—such is the stuff of headlines. It grabs our attention; it sells newspapers. And it depresses us. There is, to be sure, a desperate shortage of good news in our daily news—so much so that we are frequently skeptical of good news. In moments of cynicism we may even be tempted to label it sentimentalism rather than proper news.

What was the last bit of good news you read in the newspaper, saw on television, or heard on the radio? What was the last bit of good news that had relevance for your own life? While it may seem challenging to find good, current news that has immediate and personal relevance, the death and resurrection of Christ—"old news" for more than 2,000 years—remains the best news. No matter how many times this news is heard, it never loses its personal relevance.

Power Points

The Christian faith and life are set on the foundation of the Gospel of Jesus Christ. This Gospel is the central doctrine of Christian theology, that which distinguishes the Christian faith from all other religions and philosophies. It is, in short, the peculiar good news of Christ's death and resurrection for the free forgiveness of sins.

Paul refers to the Gospel as "the power of God for salvation to everyone who believes" (Romans 1:16). Even in such a short phrase he manages to highlight the manner in which the Gospel differs from the Law. Two differences can be noted here. First, the Gospel is not about doing what is commanded; it is about believing what is promised. And most important, unlike the Law, which cannot justify, Paul specifically states that the Gospel is "for salvation." These significant differences are concisely expressed in the Apology of the Augsburg Confession: "The Gospel (which is properly the promise of forgiveness of sins and of justification for Christ's sake) proclaims the righteousness of faith in Christ. The Law does not teach this" (Ap IV [II] 43; *Concordia*, p. 88).

In the passage discussed above, Paul mentions righteousness being "revealed" with the Gospel. In his letters to the Ephesians and the Corinthians, he sheds some light on why the Gospel must be revealed.

> In all circumstances take up the shield of faith, with which you can extinguish all the flaming darts of the evil one. (Ephesians 6:16)

> In their case the god of this world has blinded the minds of the unbelievers, to keep them from seeing the light of the gospel of the glory of Christ, who is the image of God. (2 Corinthians 4:4)

The apostle Paul requests the prayers of the Ephesians so that his proclamation of the Gospel may be made clearly and boldly. Significantly, he refers to the Gospel as a "mystery" (see Ephesians 3). Unlike the Law, which is written on the hearts of all people, the Gospel cannot be known by natural human reason. In this light, Paul's request is quite urgent: unless the Gospel that has been revealed *to* him is subsequently revealed *by* him in his preaching, people will remain in their sins. What is more, because reason cannot comprehend it, the Gospel will not be believed unless this belief is effected by God Himself. This is indicated when Paul notes that unbelievers are "blinded" and are kept "from seeing the light of the gospel" (2 Corinthians 4:4). For this reason, while noting that the human mind has some knowledge of the Law, the Lutheran Confessions explain that "it is so ignorant, blind, and perverted that even when the most ingenious and learned people on earth read or hear the Gospel of God's Son and the promise of eternal salvation, they cannot by their own powers perceive, apprehend, understand, or believe and regard it as true" (FC SD II 9, *Concordia*, pp. 521–22).

Scripture declares that God's Law is universal; it is given to all people. But for whom is the Gospel *revealed*? Timothy, who is himself a young preacher of the Gospel, is told that Christ "gave Himself as a ransom for all" (1 Timothy 2:6) because He "desires all people to be saved" (1 Timothy 2:4). This bit of information is particularly relevant for those appointed to the task of proclaiming God's Word. Christ did not die only for some; nor is God stingy with His Good News. Christ's death covered the sins of all people; He therefore desires His Gospel of forgiveness to be preached to all people. The apostle Peter agrees with Paul, assuring his readers that God is "not wishing that any should perish" (2 Peter 3:9). In agreement with both Peter and Paul, the Formula of Concord insists that "Christ calls all sinners to Himself and promises them rest. He is eager ‹seriously wills› that all people should come to Him" (FC Ep XI 8; *Concordia*, p. 498). Likewise, the Formula rejects the notion that "God is unwilling that everyone should be saved. But some—without regard to their sins, from God's mere counsel, purpose, and will—are chosen for condemnation so that they cannot be saved" (FC Ep XI 19; *Concordia*, p. 500).

For fuller descriptions of the Gospel's purpose, we can turn to Mark, 2 Corinthians, and Romans. Mark begins his life of the Savior by calling it "the gospel of Jesus Christ" (1:1). Paul, writing to the Corinthian church, mentions that he has preached "the gospel of Christ" (2 Corinthians 2:12). In the same manner, when he refers to the Gospel in his Letter to the

Romans, he calls it "the ministry of the gospel of Christ" (15:19). As most Christians have learned, the word *Gospel* simply and literally means "Good News." But the apostles and evangelists do not have just any good news to share; it is very specific news. It is the Good News about Christ, it is His Gospel. Thus the reformers state that "the Gospel presents Christ to us" (Ap XIIA [V] 76; *Concordia*, p. 168) and further clarify that "the Gospel is such a preaching as shows and gives nothing else than grace and forgiveness in Christ" (FC SD V 12; *Concordia*, p. 555). No matter how good the news, if it is not about Jesus, it is not the Gospel of the Scripture. As its authors emphasize time and again, Jesus stands at the beginning, center, and end of the Christian Gospel.

Sadly, many people and many religions preach about Christ without in fact preaching the Gospel. In the early days of the Church, as in our own day, there were those who not only misunderstood the Gospel but who also misapplied it. In an attempt to prevent this, Paul writes to the Corinthians, reminding them of the Gospel as he had purely preached it: "Now I would remind you, brothers, of the gospel I preached to you, which you received, in which you stand, and by which you are being saved, if you hold fast to the word I preached to you—unless you believed in vain. For I delivered to you as of first importance what I also received: that Christ died for our sins in accordance with the Scriptures, that He was buried, that He was raised on the third day in accordance with the Scriptures" (1 Corinthians 15:1–4). Here Paul highlights three important events: Christ's death for our sins, His burial, and His resurrection on the third day. Even more succinctly, Paul had reminded them earlier that when he was with them he endeavored to preach nothing "except Jesus Christ and Him crucified" (1 Corinthians 2:2). Christ's death and resurrection is the only basis on which the forgiveness of sins and eternal life rests. As such, it is the only basis on which the Gospel can be proclaimed. Christ's death and resurrection for our salvation *is* the Gospel. As the Lutheran Confessions state: "This is the very voice unique to the Gospel, namely, that for Christ's sake, and not for the sake of our works, we obtain the forgiveness of sins through faith" (Ap V [III] 153 [274]; *Concordia*, p. 123).

Not only do the writings of Paul purely set forth the Gospel message, but they also offer strong warnings against being deceived by false gospels and those who preach them. The apostle harshly rebukes the Galatians for "turning to a different gospel—not that there is another one" (1:6–7). But he saves his strongest words for those who were guilty of misleading them, those trying to "distort the gospel of Christ" (1:7). With righteous anger Paul prays that such men be eternally condemned (1:8). Although it may sound extreme, Paul's reaction is by no means an overreaction. He is well aware of what is at stake. The context of his letter makes clear that some in

Galatia were preaching works as if they were necessary for salvation. No, says Paul; to mingle Law and Gospel is to pervert the Gospel and thereby endanger salvation.

This confusion of Law and Gospel may have begun in Paul's time, but it certainly didn't end there. It was also very much at the heart of the debates of the Reformation. The reformers, therefore, had to clarify that "the Gospel is not a preaching of repentance or rebuke. But it is properly nothing other than a preaching of consolation and a joyful message that does not rebuke or terrify. The Gospel comforts consciences against the terrors of the Law, points only to Christ's merit, and raises them up again by the lovely preaching of God's grace and favor, gained through Christ's merit" (FC Ep V 7; *Concordia*, p. 485).

Living by Faith

In the same way that many people faithfully read the morning paper or turn on the evening news, Christians are eager to hear important news that affects their lives. There is none more important or more relevant than the good news of Christ Himself.

What does that mean for the worship life of a Christian? As Paul notes, the Gospel is a mystery; it is not self-evident. Furthermore, because of our sinful nature, we may misunderstand or even be tempted to reject the Gospel after having received it. But God Himself stirs up and strengthens our faith. This faith, Paul writes, comes by hearing the Word of the Gospel itself (Romans 10:17). For this reason Christians eagerly take advantage of opportunities to have their forgiveness announced and their faith strengthened where and when the Good News is preached.

Frequent study of God's Word and of sound Christian doctrine also keep us from being swept along by the tide of popular preaching and writing that portrays Christianity in a light not dissimilar to many self-help groups. The Gospel, properly speaking, is like no other teaching. As we continue to study God's Word, we become equipped not only to recognize the Gospel and to distinguish it from contrary messages, but also to refute false teachings that may otherwise endanger our faith and salvation.

Communicating the Message

In our sinful world, where good news is so infrequently heard, it is easy to become skeptical about such news or cynical about its content. But our Lord assures us that His Gospel is no sentimental story; it is true, faithfully reported, and eternally relevant. It is good news indeed.

Although it may seem strange to us, there are many who find the Gospel too good to be true. *Free* forgiveness, they say; I don't have to do *anything*? There is, however, nothing that is too good to be true. Truth is not a matter of good or bad; quite simply, something is either true or it is not. The New Testament authors go to great lengths to verify the truth of the news they preach. Explaining the Gospel to the Corinthians, Paul specifically mentions that the resurrected Christ had been seen by hundreds of people, most of whom were still alive to be consulted (1 Corinthians 15:1–8). The news of Jesus' death and resurrection is indeed true; happily, this true news is also good news.

While some unbelievers think the Gospel is too good to be true, others say the importance of Jesus is found in His moral example, and they dismiss Him as the one who both fulfilled the Law and suffered its consequences in our stead. To be sure, the sinless life of Jesus does provide a perfect moral example, and Scripture does encourage us to imitate this example. As we are all too aware, however, a perfect example is an example to which we cannot live up. Our gross lack of perfection is, in fact, what prompted Christ's incarnation, death, and resurrection—not merely to provide us with an example, but to redeem us. This redemption through Christ is the very Gospel itself.

Comparisons

Eastern Orthodox: "What was Christ's doctrine? The Gospel of the kingdom of God, or, in other words, the doctrine of salvation and eternal happiness, the same that is now taught in the Orthodox Church (Mark 1:14–15). How have we salvation by Christ's doctrine? When we receive it with all our heart, and walk according to it. For, as the lying words of the devil, received by our first parents, became in them the seed of sin and death; so, on the contrary the true Word of Christ, heartily received by Christians, becomes in them the seed of a holy and immortal life (1 Peter 1:23). How have we salvation by Christ's life? When we imitate it. For He says, 'If anyone serves Me, let him follow Me; and where I am, there shall also My servant be' (John 12:26)" (*The Longer Catechism of the Eastern Church*, questions 196–98).

Lutheran: "But the Gospel is properly the kind of teaching that shows what a person who has not kept the Law (and therefore is condemned by it) is to believe. It teaches that Christ has paid for and made satisfaction for all sins [Romans 5:9]. Christ has gained and acquired for an individual—without any of his own merit—forgiveness of sins, righteousness that avails before God, and eternal life [Romans 5:10]" (FC Ep V 5; *Concordia*, p. 484).

Reformed/Presbyterian: "Elect infants, dying in infancy, are regenerated and saved by Christ through the Spirit, who works when, and where, and how He pleases. So also are all other elect persons, who are incapable of being outwardly called by the ministry of the Word. . . . God did, from all eternity, decree to justify all the elect, and Christ did, in the fullness of time, die for their sins, and rise again for their justification: nevertheless, they are not justified until the Holy Spirit doth, in due time, actually apply Christ unto them" (*The Westminster Confession of Faith*, chapters 10.3 and 11.4).

Roman Catholic: "The Synod furthermore declares that . . . the beginning of the said Justification is to be derived from the prevenient grace of God, through Jesus Christ . . . that so they, who by sins were alienated from God, may be disposed through His quickening and assisting grace, to convert themselves to their own justification, by freely assenting to and cooperating with that said grace" (*Canons and Decrees of the Council of Trent*, Session 6, chapter 5; cf. CCC2 para. 2001).

Wesleyan/Methodist: "The condition of man after the fall of Adam is such that he cannot turn and prepare himself, by his own natural strength and works, to faith and calling upon God; wherefore we have not power to do good works, pleasant and acceptable to God, without the grace of God by Christ preventing us, that we may have a good will, and working with us, when we have that good will" (*Methodist Articles of Religion*, article 8).

Baptist: "We believe that the blessings of salvation are made free to all by the Gospel; that it is the immediate duty of all to accept them by a cordial, penitent, and obedient faith; and that nothing prevents the salvation of the greatest sinner on earth but his own inherent depravity and voluntary rejection of the Gospel; which rejection involves him in an aggravated condemnation" (*New Hampshire Baptist Confession*, article 6).

Liberal: "Theologically, the content of Christology is to be found by asking two questions: 'From what do men need to be saved?' and 'How is Jesus related to man's salvation?' If the source of our sin is located in a non-psychological 'nature' which we inherit, we shall, of course, interpret the work of Christ in terms of His 'natures,' divine and human. But if we think of sin concretely and refer it to its psychological causes, we shall interpret salvation in terms of conscious experience. We shall then not ask concerning the 'nature' of Jesus, but rather concerning His religious consciousness and life. We shall emphasize His God-consciousness and His ability to create in His disciples a trust in God, which gives spiritual insight and moral power. As Schleiermacher declared, the important thing about Jesus is His *God-consciousness*" (Gerald Birney Smith, ed., *A Guide to the Study of the Christian Religion* [Chicago: University of Chicago Press, 1916], pp. 531–32).

Point to Remember

I am not ashamed of the gospel, for it is the power of God for salvation to everyone who believes, to the Jew first and also to the Greek. *Romans 1:16*

Distinguishing Law and Gospel

"Say It Loud—I'm Black and I'm Proud"
—James Brown hit single, 1968

In our society, the majority idea that people have different worth simply based on stereotypes has done much harm to all people. This behavior is based on the practice of false discrimination. We still hear a lot about false discrimination. Employers, for example, announce that they do not discriminate on the basis of age, race, sex, or other criteria. Reputations can be ruined by the mere accusation of discrimination. But there is a difference between false discrimination and making valid judgments based on fact instead of fiction or stereotypes. When based on the facts, discriminating, which simply means "making distinctions," is often a useful—even necessary!—skill. Despite the negative connotations the word may have in certain situations, we all must discriminate among sets of facts.

Under certain circumstances, discrimination is even to be encouraged. The artist's eyes are able to discriminate hundreds of colors from one another. This allows him to use the full spectrum of color in his paintings. The young child is taught to discriminate between appropriate and inappropriate behaviors. This skill, part of social awareness, is honed as the child matures. These are both positive examples of discrimination. And the dictionary lists the positive definition as primary: making distinctions, using good judgment. In this section, we will concern ourselves with the primary definition here. *Discriminating*—making distinctions or using good judgment—is of great importance when we are talking about God's Law and His Gospel.

Handle with Care

In the previous sections, we looked at the natures and uses of both Law and Gospel. Now it becomes important to further clarify their proper distinction. This distinction is not arbitrary or invented; it is revealed in Scripture itself as the means by which all of God's Word is to be rightly understood and interpreted. Properly understanding God's Word, the Christian will properly understand God's will for his or her salvation.

Let's look again to Paul's instructions to young Timothy for an example of this "proper understanding." Paul reminds Timothy that he is appointed a preacher of both Law and Gospel, and that the Law is good—"if one uses it lawfully" (1 Timothy 1:8). Timothy is to know that the Law can be used improperly and with harmful results. In the same manner, Paul exhorts Timothy to be one who is "rightly handling" (2 Timothy 2:15) the Word of God. Again, an incorrect use of God's Word may confuse and even lead astray those who hear its proclamation. Paul gives good pastoral advice. Knowing the power and effects of both the Law and the Gospel, Paul is concerned that Timothy rightly divide and properly proclaim each, neither confusing nor mingling them together. Paul's concern is highlighted in the Lutheran Confessions, which observe that if Law and Gospel are "mixed with each other" then "Christ's merit is hidden and troubled consciences are robbed of comfort" (FC SD V 1; *Concordia*, p. 552). Therefore the confessors also state: "We believe, teach, and confess that the distinction between the Law and the Gospel is to be kept in the Church with great diligence as a particularly brilliant light. By this distinction, according to the admonition of St. Paul, God's Word is rightly divided [2 Timothy 2:15]" (FC Ep V 2; *Concordia*, p. 484). Here we see the good kind of discrimination at work.

In his second Epistle to the Corinthians, Paul makes a clear distinction between what he calls "the letter" and "the Spirit" (3:6) of the Law. He gives his readers a clue regarding the nature of the former by indicating that it came with letters engraved on stones, a reference to the two tables of the Law given to Moses (3:7). In verse 17 Paul further explains that the Lord Himself is the Spirit. The letter came with Moses, the Spirit with Christ. But Paul not only distinguishes between their names and origins; he also notes their radically different effects. He tells the Corinthians that "the letter kills, but the Spirit gives life" (3:6). This is certainly true. As noted earlier, the chief use of the Law accuses us, condemns us, and announces the deadly consequences of our failure to obey God's commands. But the proper function of the Gospel is to reveal Christ and the eternal life that He has won for us. The distinctly different effects of the Law and of the Gospel are also noted in the confessional writings of the Lutheran Church. They confess that "whenever the Law alone exercises its office, without the Gospel being added, there is nothing but death and hell" (SA III III 7;

Concordia, p. 273). But when the Gospel is revealed—whether in Word or Sacrament—"it works forgiveness of sins, delivers from death and the devil, and gives eternal salvation" (SC IV; *Concordia*, p. 339).

When he writes to the Galatians, Paul also makes a distinction between two things found in Scripture. He here refers to them as the Law and the promises. As he explains their differences, he notes that the Law was "added because of transgressions" (3:19) and that it cannot impart life. By way of contrast, he notes that the Christian's inheritance "comes by promise" (3:18) so that this promise "might be given to those who believe" (3:22) This promise is clearly the Gospel promise of salvation, a promise received by Abraham in the Old Testament and later fulfilled with Christ's coming in the New Testament. Paul's distinction is maintained by the Lutheran confessors, who note that "all Scripture ought to be distributed into these two principal topics: the Law and the promises" (Ap IV [II] 5; *Concordia*, p. 83). The Law and the promises, though different, are certainly not unrelated. Paul strongly insists that the Law is not opposed to the promises of God. Rather, he says, "The law was our guardian until Christ came" (Galatians 3:24). The authors of the Formula of Concord explain how the Law prepares sinners for and leads them to Christ and His Gospel: "(a) Through the preaching of the Law and its threats in the ministry of the New Testament the hearts of impenitent people may be terrified, and (b) they may be brought to a knowledge of their sins and to repentance. This must not be done in such a way that they lose heart and despair in this process. . . . People must be comforted and strengthened again by the preaching of the Holy Gospel about Christ" (FC SD V 24–25; *Concordia*, p. 557).

It is not infrequently heard that the Old Testament is Law while the New Testament is Gospel. This is understandable. The first four books of the New Testament are referred to as the Gospels; likewise, many New Testament figures (including Jesus Himself) use the word *Law* as a sort of shorthand in reference to either the books of Moses or the entire Old Testament. But the New Testament is not without the Law; nor is the Old Testament without the Gospel. Consider, for example, the following passages:

Exodus 20:1–3: "And God spoke all these words, saying, 'I am the LORD your God, who brought you out of the land of Egypt, out of the house of slavery. You shall have no other gods before Me.'" The chapter continues with the rest of the Ten Commandments through verse 17.

Isaiah 53:5–6: "But He was wounded for our transgressions; He was crushed for our iniquities; upon Him was the chastisement that brought us peace, and with His stripes we are healed. All we like sheep have gone astray; we have turned—every one—to his own way; and the LORD has laid on Him the iniquity of us all." Read the rest of Isaiah 53 for a full description of Christ's life and death and purpose: clear Gospel.

Romans 2:1, 5–9: "Therefore you have no excuse, O man, every one of you who judges. For in passing judgment on another you condemn yourself, because you, the judge, practice the very same things. . . . But because of your hard and impenitent heart you are storing up wrath for yourself on the day of wrath when God's righteous judgment will be revealed. He will render to each one according to his works: to those who by patience in well-doing seek for glory and honor and immortality, He will give eternal life; but for those who are self-seeking and do not obey the truth, but obey unrighteousness, there will be wrath and fury. There will be tribulation and distress for every human being who does evil, the Jew first and also the Greek." The heading for this section of Romans 2 is "God's Righteous Judgment"—pretty harsh words of Law are spoken here.

Ephesians 1:2–8: "Grace to you and peace from God our Father and the Lord Jesus Christ. Blessed be the God and Father of our Lord Jesus Christ, who has blessed us in Christ with every spiritual blessing in the heavenly places, even as He chose us in Him before the foundation of the world, that we should be holy and blameless before Him. In love He predestined us for adoption as sons through Jesus Christ, according to the purpose of His will, to the praise of His glorious grace, with which He has blessed us in the Beloved. In Him we have redemption through His blood, the forgiveness of our trespasses, according to the riches of His grace, which He lavished upon us, in all wisdom and insight." Here Paul is jubilant in his description of our redemption through Christ. This is a joyful depiction of Gospel.

Four passages from Scripture. Two Old Testament, two New Testament. Two Law, two Gospel. Law and Gospel each clearly in the Old Testament and each clearly in the New Testament. The confessors, especially eager to highlight the Gospel's Old Testament presence, make note of this when they write that "in some places Scripture presents the Law, and in others the promises about Christ. In other words, in the Old Testament, Scripture promises that Christ will come, and it offers, for His sake, the forgiveness of sins, justification, and life eternal. Or in the Gospel, in the New Testament, Christ Himself (since He has appeared) promises the forgiveness of sins, justification, and life eternal" (Ap IV [II] 5; *Concordia*, p. 83).

Jesus pointed to the presence of the Gospel in the Old Testament as He read the Scriptures in the synagogue:

> And He came to Nazareth, where He had been brought up. And as was His custom, He went to the synagogue on the Sabbath day, and He stood up to read. And the scroll of the prophet Isaiah was given to Him. He unrolled the scroll and found the place where it was written, 'The Spirit of the Lord is upon Me, because He has anointed Me to proclaim good news to the poor. He has sent Me to proclaim liberty to the captives and recovering of sight to the blind, to set at liberty those who are oppressed, to proclaim the year of the Lord's favor.' And He rolled up the scroll and gave it back to the attendant and sat down. And the eyes of all in the synagogue were fixed on Him. And He began to say to them, 'Today this Scripture has been fulfilled in your hearing.'" (Luke 4:16–21)

Jesus shocked His audience in Nazareth. Reading from the prophet Isaiah, He concluded by announcing that Isaiah's Gospel promise was being fulfilled in their very presence. In terms unmistakable to His hearers, He announced that He was the Anointed One (i.e., the Messiah, the Christ) mentioned by the prophet. He was the one with whom the Good News arrived.

This announcement was not lost on Jesus' disciples. Peter, in the Book of Acts, tells his audience that it was not Isaiah alone who foretold the coming of Christ; rather, "to Him all the prophets bear witness" (10:43). This revelation is quite significant. Not only can the whole of Scripture be divided into Law and Gospel, but also the whole of Scripture is about Jesus Himself. Not only are Law and Gospel the keys to rightly understanding the written Word of God, but they are also the keys to understanding the incarnate Word of God and His divine work. The Lutheran Confessions describe this work by saying that the Law is "an alien work of Christ. Passing through this teaching, Christ arrives at His proper office, that is, to preach grace, console, and give life, which is properly the preaching of the Gospel" (FC Ep V 10; *Concordia*, p. 485).

Paul very clearly and succinctly summarizes the great emphases of Scripture. Men are sinners, but "Christ Jesus came into the world to save sinners" (1 Timothy 1:15). Sin leads to death, but "the free gift of God is eternal life" (Romans 6:23). Sin and salvation, life and death—from Genesis to Revelation the Scriptures consistently highlight this dialectic of Law and Gospel. One exhorts, the other comforts; one chastises, the other consoles; one condemns, the other saves. These dual emphases are illustrated and proclaimed throughout the great sweep of Old Testament history, in the preaching of Christ, in the sermons of Acts, in the Letters of Paul and the other New Testament authors. From this witness of the whole of Scripture—and even in such brief verses as those shown here—the reformers were led rightly to believe that "whenever the Law and works are mentioned, we must know that Christ cannot be excluded as Mediator" (Ap V [III] 251 [372]; *Concordia*, p. 138).

The author of Hebrews can help us confirm the necessity of properly distinguishing between the Law and the Gospel: "And without faith it is impossible to please Him, for whoever would draw near to God must believe that He exists and that He rewards those who seek Him" (11:6). There are some who believe the Bible to be a sort of guidebook to holy living, that is, a book that describes and prescribes what people must do to live a holy life. This is not entirely incorrect; the Law found in Scripture certainly tells us how we are to live. But the author of Hebrews reminds us that, even if we were to expend all of our energy in the observation of the Law, we would remain unable to please God without faith. Thus the confessors write that "these two things should always be understood in the preaching of the Law. First, the Law cannot be obeyed unless we have been reborn through faith in Christ, just as Christ says in John 15:5, 'Apart from Me you can do nothing.' Second, some outward works can certainly be done. But this general judgment, which interprets the whole Law, must be retained. 'Without faith it is impossible to please [God]' (Hebrews 11:6)" (Ap V [III] 135 [256], *Concordia*, p. 120). As the Letter to the Hebrews gloriously explains, this faith that is God-pleasing is faith in God's own promises, His Gospel. To read the Bible simply as a book of laws is therefore to misread it. It is also—and most important—a book of promises.

Divine Discernment

Discrimination between different foods and medicines is not merely an intellectual exercise. It can be, in some situations, a matter of life and death. So it is with those desiring to be fed with and healed by God's Holy Word.

Many people, even many Christians, do not properly understand the distinction between Law and Gospel. Not recognizing the difference between the two, many outside of the Church regard Christianity as a religion of rules and regulations, of doom and gloom. Even more distressing, there are those within the Church who remain burdened with a sense of guilt or anxiety because they know they do not measure up to the demanding biblical standard of holiness. Properly understanding the distinction between Law and Gospel, the Christian will realize that this guilt is produced by the Law. He or she will also know—and be greatly comforted to know!—that the message of the Gospel is that our guilt has been removed. Despite any feelings to the contrary, our Lord sees us as perfectly holy, our sins having been covered by the death of His only Son.

A proper understanding of the distinction between Law and Gospel will affect the way in which you daily read and study the Bible. Many people simply open the Bible and begin reading at random. Some read the Bible merely as literature. Others scan the text of Scripture looking for answers to particular questions. Reading God's Word is always to be encouraged. But reading God's Word with an awareness of its two major themes will provide a depth of understanding that many miss. Being aware of the nature and purpose of the Law, readers will gain a deeper understanding of their own nature: creatures made in the image of God but, having fallen into sin, separated from God and standing under His judgment. Being aware of the nature and purpose of the Gospel, readers will gain a deeper understanding of God's own nature: loving, merciful, and forgiving, willing to sacrifice His own Son so that we might once again be united with Him.

Test Your Skills

We do hear a lot about discrimination. But perhaps not enough! Paul warns us that God's Word must be correctly handled; he informs us that the Law is good—but only if used properly. In humble thanksgiving for this precious gift of God's Word, the Christian responds with the desire to use this gift faithfully and properly, distinguishing carefully between Law and Gospel.

We've heard the oversimplified comment that the Old Testament contains the Law while the New Testament contains the Gospel. As it stands, this comment is not false. The Old Testament does "contain" the Law and the New Testament does "contain" the Gospel. When stated in this simplified manner, however, the impression may be given that these are the only contents of each. Review the passages on pages 56–57 that show clearly both Law and Gospel in the Old Testament and the New Testament. Were there no Gospel before Christ's incarnation, then Old Testament believers would have been denied salvation. Paul declares, "No one is justified before God by the law" (Galatians 3:11). The author of Hebrews, however, clearly indicates that Old Testament believers will dwell with God in heaven:

> By faith Abraham obeyed when he was called to go out to a place that he was to receive as an inheritance. And he went out, not knowing where he was going. By faith he went to live in the land of promise, as in a foreign land, living in tents with Isaac and Jacob, heirs with him of the same promise. For he was looking forward to the city that has foundations, whose designer and builder is God. By faith Sarah herself received power to conceive, even when she was past the age, since she considered Him faithful who had promised. Therefore from one man, and him as good as dead, were born descendants as many as the stars of heaven and as many as the innumerable grains of sand by the seashore. These all died in faith, not having received the

things promised, but having seen them and greeted them from afar, and having acknowledged that they were strangers and exiles on the earth. For people who speak thus make it clear that they are seeking a homeland. If they had been thinking of that land from which they had gone out, they would have had opportunity to return. But as it is, they desire a better country, that is, a heavenly one. Therefore God is not ashamed to be called their God, for He has prepared for them a city. (Hebrews 11:8–16)

Comparisons

The following table shows Bible passages sorted into their relation to Law and Gospel, which will provide examples to improve your ability to sort the content into Law, Gospel, or a few special cases.

SCRIPTURE	LAW	GOSPEL	BOTH	OTHER
Exod. 20:3	As the First Commandment, this passage is clearly Law.			
John 3:16		This verse, of course, is "the Gospel in a nutshell."		
Lev. 11:7–8				As ceremonial law, Old Testament food restrictions have been abrogated (abolished) through the coming of Christ (see Matthew 5:17; Acts 10:9–16).
Job 19:25–27		Job's expression of expectant hope in his living Redeemer, and his own bodily resurrection, is Gospel.		
Isa. 9:6–7		Fulfilled in Christ, Isaiah's ancient prophecy is Gospel.		

SCRIPTURE	LAW	GOSPEL	BOTH	OTHER
Mark 16:16			The gift of faith and the promises of Holy Baptism are Gospel. Rejecting God's saving gifts and promises through unbelief places one under the Law's condemnation.	
Luke 22:19–20		The institution of the Lord's Supper, whereby Christ grants us the forgiveness of sins through His broken body and poured-out blood, is Gospel.		
Eph. 2:8–10			That which God provides us because of Christ, namely, His unmerited grace and the gift of faith to receive it, is Gospel. God's condemnation of our self-righteous works, as well as the works performed after we have come to faith, are Law.	
Col. 3:1–4			Paul faithfully presents the Gospel (see also 2:9–15) as the motivation for the Christian's thankful obedience to the Law.	
1 Tim. 5:23	While Paul's Holy Spirit-inspired words appear to be "sanctified advice," properly speaking they are still Law.			
Heb. 13:1	The writer's appeal to fraternal charity is Law.			

Point to Remember

The letter kills, but the Spirit gives life. *2 Corinthians 3:6*

Applying Law and Gospel

Careless talk costs lives.
—World War II security slogan

In the context of war, saying the wrong thing to the wrong person at the wrong time can be a deadly mistake. But even off the battlefield, our words can have serious and unintentional consequences if we do not choose and speak them carefully. Sometimes we say too much, sometimes too little. Sometimes we say the wrong thing; sometimes we speak at the wrong time. Many such misunderstandings are of minor importance; in fact, as an essential part of any situation comedy, they are often a source of amusement. When the words are God's own, however, misunderstanding becomes much more serious.

Completing the Task

It is of great importance that Christians properly understand Law and Gospel. It is of equal importance, especially if we are to make disciples of all nations, that Christians be able to articulate and correctly apply God's Word of Law and Gospel. In order to do so, it is necessary to understand not only the nature and purpose of each but also the effects—intentional and unintentional—that each may have upon their hearers.

Despite unending hardship and persecution, the apostle Paul remained well aware of his task as an apostle. It was nothing other than "to testify to the gospel of the grace of God" (Acts 20:24). Given the persecution he suffered, Paul could have made his life infinitely more comfortable if he had simply refused to give such testimony. Or he could have given a less controversial testimony. He did not, however, because he knew that saving faith is founded upon no testimony other than that of God's gracious Gospel. And, as he explains in his Epistle to the Romans, "faith comes from hearing" (10:17). For this reason the authors of the Lutheran Confessions note that faithful proclamation of the Gospel is the means by which Christ "gathers an eternal Church for Himself . . . . By this means, and in no other way (i.e., through His holy Word, when people hear it preached or read it, and through the holy Sacraments when they are used according to His Word), God desires to call people to eternal salvation" (FC SD II 50; *Concordia*, p. 529).

Apostles are one thing—it's their job to proclaim the Gospel—but what about the rest of us? Why is it necessary that all God's servants faithfully proclaim the Law as well as the Gospel? Although the proclamation of the Gospel is the means by which Christ calls men to salvation, this does not mean that there is no necessity of also applying the Law. Although He Himself would fulfill the Law in His atoning death, Jesus tells His audience: "Whoever relaxes one of the least of these commandments and teaches others to do the same will be called least in the kingdom of heaven" (Matthew 5:19). For this reason it is vitally important that we know what God's commandments are, that we know His Law. This is also essential because if we do not know the Law we will remain unaware of our sin and our consequent need for salvation. As the psalmist asks, "Who can discern his errors?" (19:12).

Unless God's Law itself reveals our sin and accuses us of it, we will remain ignorant of our need for the Gospel. Both Law and Gospel must therefore be applied to Christians and non-Christians alike. The truth of this and the reasons for doing so are emphasized in the reformers' confession that "these two doctrines, we believe and confess, should always be diligently taught in God's Church forever, even to the end of the world. They must be taught with the proper distinction." The reasons are so that "(a) through the preaching of the Law and its threats in the ministry of the New Testament the hearts of impenitent people may be terrified, and (b) they may be brought to a knowledge of their sins and to repentance" and so that they "be comforted and strengthened again by the preaching of the Holy Gospel about Christ" (FC SD V 24–25; *Concordia*, p. 557).

The Book of Acts, describing the early growth of the Christian faith, contains a large number of evangelistic sermons. Two examples of such sermons illustrate the manner in which Law and Gospel were applied by early Christian preachers. In chapter 2, Peter recalls the events of Christ's life, death, and resurrection. As he does so, he applies the Law by emphasizing that Christ's death was effected "by the hands of lawless men" (v. 23), including his hearers. But when the Law had done its work, when his audience was "cut to the heart" (v. 37), Peter is quick to apply the Gospel. He encourages them to receive Baptism "in the name of Jesus Christ for the forgiveness of your sins" (v. 38), and he assures them that the Gospel promises have been made even for them and for their children (v. 39). Peter also applies Law and Gospel in his sermon of chapter 3. He accuses his audience of having "denied the Holy and Righteous One" (v. 14) and of having "killed the Author of life" (v. 15). But having done so, he also assures them that, with repentance, God will "send the Christ appointed for you, Jesus" (v. 20). He concludes by announcing again that Jesus was raised and sent "to you first, to bless you" (v. 26). These sermons illustrate well the faithful application of both Law and Gospel. They also illustrate the emphasis of the Lutheran Confessions that "the two doctrines belong together and should also be taught next to each other, but in a definite order and with a proper distinction" (FC SD V 15; *Concordia*, p. 555). Peter preaches both. Distinguishing between the two, he first preaches the Law to effect repentance. After the Law has done its work, he then applies the Gospel to comfort and console with the Good News of salvation.

Let's look at two other examples of Law and Gospel from Scripture:

> And behold, a man came up to Him, saying, "Teacher, what good deed must I do to have eternal life?" And He said to him, "Why do you ask Me about what is good? There is only one who is good. If you would enter life, keep the commandments." He said to Him, "Which ones?" And Jesus said, "You shall not murder, You shall not commit adultery, You shall not steal, You shall not bear false witness, Honor your father and mother, and, You shall love your neighbor as yourself." The young man said to Him, "All these I have kept. What do I still lack?" Jesus said to him, "If you would be perfect, go, sell what you possess and give to the poor, and you will have treasure in heaven; and come, follow Me." When the young man heard this he went away sorrowful, for he had great possessions. And Jesus said to His disciples, "Truly, I say to you, only with difficulty will a rich person enter the kingdom of heaven. Again I tell you, it is easier for a camel to go through the eye of a needle than for a rich person to enter the kingdom of God." When the disciples heard this, they were greatly astonished, saying, "Who then can be saved?" But Jesus looked at them and said, "With man this is impossible, but with God all things are possible." (Matthew 19:16–26)

And our second example:

> About midnight Paul and Silas were praying and singing hymns to God, and the prisoners were listening to them, and suddenly there was a great earthquake, so that the foundations of the prison were shaken. And immediately all the doors were opened, and everyone's bonds were unfastened. When the jailer woke and saw that the prison doors were open, he drew his sword and was about to kill himself, supposing that the prisoners had escaped. But Paul cried with a loud voice, "Do not harm yourself, for we are all here." And the jailer called for lights and rushed in, and trembling with fear he fell down before Paul and Silas. Then he brought them out and said, "Sirs, what must I do to be saved?" And they said, "Believe in the Lord Jesus, and you will be saved, you and your household." And they spoke the word of

> the Lord to him and to all who were in his house. And he took them the same hour of the night and washed their wounds; and he was baptized at once, he and all his family. (Acts 16:25–33)

In each of these passages essentially the same question is asked. Although the way in which the question is phrased betrays something of the mind-set of those who ask, each asks about the way of salvation. The answers received by these two men, though, are startlingly different and may at first cause some confusion. The jailer is given what is perhaps the expected answer: "Believe in the Lord Jesus, and you will be saved" (Acts 16:31). This is the Gospel answer: faith alone, believing in Christ and His promise, effects salvation. The young man in Matthew, however, is told to "keep the commandments" (Matthew 19:17). When he claims to have done so, Jesus tells him to sell everything he has. We then read that the young man "went away sorrowful" (v. 22). What accounts for these different answers? Did Jesus really mean to suggest that obeying the Law or selling our possessions is necessary for salvation? Absolutely not! Rather, Law and Gospel are applied as they are appropriate. The jailer was at the point of despair; he had drawn his sword to kill himself; he fell trembling before Paul and Silas. The night's terrifying events had displayed God's mighty power and left him in desperate need of consolation. By way of contrast, the rich young man approached Jesus proudly and completely unaware of his own sinfulness. He was in need of hearing the Law and being made aware of his inability to earn his own salvation.

The manner in which Jesus and Paul apply Law and Gospel illustrates the powerful effects of each—and the vital need for not only distinguishing between the two but also knowing when each needs to be applied. As Luther often wrote: "The Law is to be preached to secure sinners, the Gospel to terrified sinners." This is because "the Law always accuses and terrifies consciences" (Ap IV [II] 38; *Concordia*, p. 87), preparing them for that which will "console, and give life, which is properly the preaching of the Gospel" (FC Ep V 10; *Concordia*, p. 485).

The Gospel is effectively applied to sinners not only in the preaching of God's Word but also in the administration of Baptism in the name of His Son. As Paul explains to the Galatians, all who have been baptized into Christ become "heirs according to promise" (3:29). Here again Paul uses the word *promise* as a synonym for the Gospel itself. He also speaks to Titus of our having become heirs on account of this washing and rebirth. Through this application of water and the Word of the Gospel, he writes, Jesus saved us. (See Titus 3:4–7.) The Gospel benefits of Baptism are extolled in the Small Catechism, which explains that "it works forgiveness of sins, delivers from death and the devil, and gives eternal salvation to all who believe this, as the words and promises of God declare" (SC IV; *Concordia*, p. 339).

As the Gospel is revealed and applied in the Sacrament of Baptism, so it is in the Sacrament of Holy Communion. On the night of its institution, Jesus explained the great benefit of this Sacrament. Taking the cup, He told His disciples they were about to receive "My blood of the covenant, which is poured out for many for the forgiveness of sins" (Matthew 26:28). This forgiveness of sins is the essence of the Gospel. It is for this reason that the Lutheran Confessions can boldly state that "the entire Gospel and the article of the Creed—I believe in . . . the holy Christian Church, . . . the forgiveness of sin, and so on—are embodied by the Word in this Sacrament and presented to us" (LC V 32; *Concordia*, p. 435). Preaching, Baptism, the Lord's Supper—the Lord has left His Church many and various means by which the Good News of His salvation is to be applied to sinners seeking consolation. In humble thanksgiving we receive these gifts for our benefit.

So what is the relationship between the Gospel and the Church? "Cleansing," "washing," and "making holy" all describe the work of the Gospel, the benefits received from Christ's having given Himself up for us. It is, in fact, this work of the Gospel that both brings the Church into existence and preserves her until the Lord's return. Therefore the Church is urged to purely and continually preach and teach the Gospel of Jesus Christ. Jesus Himself declares that this is the only means by which we remain a part of His Church: "If you abide in My word, you are truly My disciples" (John 8:31). At the same time, the Church is jealously to guard the pure doctrine of the Gospel, watching out for those who "create obstacles contrary to the doctrine that you have been taught" (Romans 16:17). On the basis of its central place in the Church, the authors of the Lutheran Confessions note that the Gospel is the means by which the Church can be both recognized and defined. "We know," they write, "that Christ's Church is with those who teach Christ's Gospel" (Ap V [III] 279 [400]; *Concordia*, p. 143). This, they further explain, relates not only to the preaching of the Gospel but also to its application in the Sacraments: "The Church is the congregation of saints [Psalm 149:1] in which the Gospel is purely taught and the Sacraments are correctly administered" (AC VII 1–2; *Concordia*, p. 34).

Aptly Applied

God's Word is powerful. His Word of Law and His Word of Gospel, however, each produce very different results. For this reason it is important that each is applied properly, at the right time, in the right amount, and in the right order.

It is comforting to know that God Himself has appointed and ordained ministers of His Word and Sacrament. We are often unable to discern our own sinfulness. We are also frequently tempted to downplay the consequences of what we may consider to be insignificant faults. That we might never delude ourselves or become self-righteous, God Himself has ordained men to proclaim and to apply the Law, to reveal and announce on the basis of His Word that we are—even if it is not obvious—sinful and deserving of God's wrath. But we may give thanks that this is not the only task for which God has appointed His ministers. They are also to proclaim the Gospel. Although we are often unaware of our sins, we can become equally forgetful regarding the forgiveness of our sins. For this reason pastors are charged with the task of faithfully and constantly preaching this forgiveness in biblical sermons and applying this forgiveness in the administration of the Sacraments.

Christians hear Law and Gospel proclaimed by their pastor. They, in turn, communicate Law and Gospel in conversations with their friends and neighbors. As this section illustrates, however, Law and Gospel are not to be applied randomly or without thought. Consideration must be given to the purpose and effects of each, as well as to the circumstances particular to the hearer. Because the Law is meant to reveal sin and the Gospel to forgive sin, it will be important to apply the one before the other. At times there may even be circumstances under which there is no necessity of proclaiming the Law. Those already conscious of and burdened by their sin will find relief only in the words of God's sure promise of forgiveness for the sake of Christ.

A Faith-Filled Response

Our God is a gracious God. Not only has He revealed Himself in Scripture, but He has appointed pastors to proclaim His Word faithfully. Through them He applies His Gospel not only by means of the spoken Word but also through the means of Baptism and Holy Communion. A gracious God indeed!

Christians often hear it said—even by fellow Christians—that attendance at services of Word and Sacrament is unnecessary. "After all, I can get the same thing from reading my Bible at home," comes the reply. It is certainly true that God's Word contains all that is necessary for salvation. However, there is great benefit in hearing this Word *proclaimed*. For this reason the preaching office was ordained by Christ Himself. Through the work of this office, Law and Gospel are distinguished and applied to the Church and her members. What is more, this written and proclaimed Word is not the only benefit God would have His people receive. As a reading of God's Word makes clear, Jesus also instituted the Sacraments by which His Gospel is applied. We come into God's house not because we are coerced by necessity, but because we are eager to receive all of the good gifts made available for the strengthening and preserving of our faith.

Because the Gospel is indeed applied in the Sacrament of the Altar, Luther arranged brief questions and answers as an aid to those preparing for its reception (see "Christian Questions with Their Answers," *LSB*, pp. 329–30). In a biblical, pastoral manner, Luther first appeals to the Law. "Do you believe that you are a sinner?" he asks. "How do you know this?" "What have you deserved from God because of your sins?" As the answers to these questions make clear, it is the Law, summarized in the Ten Commandments, that reveals our sin, its consequences, and our need for the Gospel. This Gospel is then extolled in brief questions regarding Christ's death for the forgiveness of sins and, finally, with respect to the Sacrament itself. Contemplation of these questions and their answers is an ideal way to spend a few moments, either before worship begins or while you await your turn to approach the altar.

Comparisons

Eastern Orthodox: "What must we join with prayer in order to be grounded in the hope of salvation and blessedness? Our own exertions for the attainment of blessedness (Luke 6:46; Matthew 7:21). What doctrine may we take as our guide in these exertions? The doctrine of our Lord Jesus Christ, which is briefly set forth in His Beatitudes, or sentences on blessedness" (*The Longer Catechism of the Eastern Church*, questions 435–36).

Lutheran: "We believe, teach, and confess that the distinction between the Law and the Gospel is to be kept in the Church with great diligence as a particularly brilliant light. By this distinction, according to the admonition of St. Paul, God's Word is rightly divided [2 Timothy 2:15]" (FC Ep V 2; *Concordia*, p. 484).

Reformed/Presbyterian: "They whom God has accepted in His Beloved, effectually called and sanctified by His Spirit, can neither totally nor finally fall away from the state of grace; but shall certainly persevere therein to the end, and be eternally saved. . . . Nevertheless they may . . . fall into grievous sins; and for a time continue therein; whereby they incur God's displeasure, and grieve His Holy Spirit; come to be deprived of some measure of their graces and comforts; have their hearts hardened, and their consciences wounded; hurt and scandalize others, and bring temporal judgments upon themselves" (*The Westminster Confession of Faith*, chapter 17.1, 3).

Roman Catholic: "If anyone says, that the man who is justified and howsoever perfect, is not bound to observe the commandments of God and of the Church, but only to believe; as if indeed the Gospel were a bare and absolute promise of eternal life, without the condition of observing the commandments; let him be anathema. If anyone says, that Jesus Christ was given by God to men as a Redeemer in whom to trust, and not also as a Legislator whom to obey; let him be anathema." (*Canons and Decrees of the Council of Trent*, Session 6, On Justification, canons 20–21; cf. CCC2 paras. 1965–86).

Baptist: "We believe that the Law of God is the eternal and unchangeable rule of His moral government; that it is holy, just, and good; and that the inability which the Scriptures ascribe to fallen men to fulfill its precepts arises entirely from their love of sin; to deliver them from which, and to restore them through a Mediator to unfeigned obedience to the holy Law, is one great end of the Gospel, and of the means of grace connected with the establishment of the visible Church" (*New Hampshire Baptist Confession*, article 12).

Wesleyan/Methodist: "Original sin stands not in the following of Adam (as the Pelagians do vainly talk), but it is the corruption of the nature of every man, that naturally is engendered of the offspring of Adam, whereby man is very far gone from original righteousness, and of his own nature inclined to evil, and that continually" (*Methodist Articles of Religion*, article 7).

Liberal: "Today we are coming more and more to think of religion as a normal and natural experience. Those who confuse experience with its doctrinal interpretation are greatly perplexed by this tendency, for it seems like abandoning fundamental realities of Christianity. But the history of religion has made us aware that, so far as the supernaturalistic details of a doctrine of salvation are concerned, these appear in various forms in pagan religions as well as in Christianity. . . . The distinctive qualities of Christian salvation must be looked for in the kind of moral and religious character produced by Christian faith" (Gerald Birney Smith, ed., *A Guide to the Study of the Christian Religion* [Chicago: University of Chicago Press, 1916], p. 523).

Point to Remember

But I do not account my life of any value nor as precious to myself, if only I may finish my course and the ministry that I received from the Lord Jesus, to testify to the gospel of the grace of God. *Acts 20:24*

Law, Gospel, and Justification

Though justice be thy plea, consider this,
That in the course of justice none of us
Should see salvation.
—Portia, in Shakespeare's *The Merchant of Venice*

"I was perfectly justified!" Such is often the cry of those seeking to escape punishment. The claim—in the courtroom as well as in popular use—is a legal claim, an appeal to the laws of the state or to commonly accepted ideas of right and wrong. A lawyer, for example, may argue that his client committed no murder; rather, it was "justifiable homicide." That is, it was legal homicide, an act not condemned by the law. Quite frequently we attempt to justify our actions by appealing to the law. That is, though we understand why others think we have committed some wrong, we argue that technically—according to the letter of the law—we are innocent.

Just an Observation

Although we may often think of *justify* and *justification* as technical theological language, they are in fact derived from the courtroom. They are legal terms. It is not surprising, then, that even in their theological use they have some relation to the Law. What may be surprising is the way in which the Bible speaks of justification in relation to the Law.

Although discussed in section 1, the Law's inability to justify deserves mention again. In Galatians 2:15–16 (only two verses!) Paul says three times that justification is impossible according to the Law. He obviously does not want this point to be missed. And just to make sure it is not, he emphasizes this even more strongly again in the fifth chapter, saying that "You are severed from Christ, you who would be justified by the law; you have fallen away from grace" (v. 4). This is no small matter. The Law of God is good and holy, but by it we cannot be made holy. Paul makes this point so strongly and so often that it could not be ignored by the Lutheran reformers. They wrote that "by their own strength, people cannot fulfill God's Law. They are all under sin, subject to eternal wrath and death. Because of this, we cannot be freed by the Law from sin and be justified" (Ap IV 40; *Concordia*, p. 87). But this does not mean that the Law has no place in God's plan for our salvation.

Although the Law is powerless to justify, the New Testament is also clear that the Law plays an important role in preparing people for the free gift of justification. Paul takes pains to insist that the Law is not opposed to the promises of God. What, then, is their relationship? Paul explains that "the law was our guardian until Christ came, in order that we might be justified by faith" (Galatians 3:24). Justification is by faith, not Law. But it was the Law that led us to Christ, in whom we place our faith. How did it do this? The accusations of the Law lead sinners to repentance. Concerning this the Lutheran Confessions state that "*to repent* means nothing other than to truly acknowledge sins, to be heartily sorry for them, and to stop doing them. This knowledge comes from the Law" (FC SD V 8–9; *Concordia*, p. 554). By this function of the Law man is prepared to receive the Gospel. Being made aware of his sins, man is made aware of his need for forgiveness. Thus the Law is sometimes referred to as God's "alien" work, while the Gospel is called His "proper" work. The confessors make this distinction when discussing the relationship between the Law, the Gospel, and justification: "He must do the work of another (reprove), in order that He may ‹afterward› do His own work, which is to comfort and to preach grace" (FC SD V 11; *Concordia*, pp. 554–55).

What, then, is the relationship between Jesus and the Law? All men are born under the Law. Jesus, being true man as well as true God, was not exempted from this condition of birth. Paul makes note of this when he mentions that the Son of God was "born of woman, born under the law" (Galatians 4:4). But, as he goes on to explain, Jesus was born this way for a particular purpose. He was born under the Law "to redeem those who were under the law" (v. 5). What exactly does the apostle mean by this? Remembering the chief purpose of the Law—to reveal man's sin and to accuse him of his sinfulness—it would not be wrong to say that the Law announces a curse on us. It announces that we who have not fulfilled the Law deservedly face death and condemnation. The good news is that we do not face these consequences. Paul explains the reason for this. "Christ redeemed us from the curse of the law by becoming a curse for us" (Galatians 3:13). Not only was Christ born *like* us, born under Law, but He was also born *for* us, to suffer in our place the curse that had been pronounced on us. Therefore, commenting on Galatians 3:13, the Confessions state that "the Law condemns all people. But Christ—without sin—has borne the punishment of sin. He has been made a victim for us and has removed that right of the Law to accuse and condemn those who believe in Him" (Ap V [III] 58 [179]; *Concordia*, p. 109).

Christ's relationship to the Law—being born under it and having suffered its curse—radically affects the relationship between Christians and the Law. Although the Law formerly accused us, or, as Paul says, "stood against us with its legal demands," its power to do so has now been nullified. Having both fulfilled the Law and suffered under it, our Lord canceled "the record of debt" (Colossians 2:14). With Christ's very body the Law was taken away and nailed to the cross. We can therefore joyfully confess with

Paul that "Christ is the end of the law" (Romans 10:4). We can joyfully confess with the reformers that "since they [Christians] are counted righteous, the Law cannot accuse or condemn them, even though they have not actually satisfied the Law" (Ap V [III] 58 [179]; *Concordia*, p. 109). That final clause is important. We have not actually satisfied the Law. Our relation to the Law has not changed because of something we have done. It is only on account of Christ and His saving work that the Law no longer accuses or condemns. It is only on account of the Gospel that the curse of the Law has been removed.

Jesus' relationship to the Law is intimately entwined with His relationship to the Gospel. While Paul tells the Romans that his Gospel is none other than "the preaching of Jesus Christ" (16:25), he also explains to the Corinthians that the Gospel saves (1 Corinthians 15:2). As he outlines the content of this saving Gospel message, he cannot but mention the central event of the Gospel, that "Christ died for our sins" (v. 3). That is, Christ died because we had broken the Law; Christ suffered the ultimate penalty of the Law's curse. It might be said in a sense that Jesus' relation to the Law *is* the Gospel. The news that He suffered the Law's penalty in our place *is* the good news. This is the point Luther makes as he confesses the doctrine of justification in his famous explanation of the Creed's Second Article: "I believe that Jesus Christ . . . is my Lord. He has redeemed me, a lost and condemned creature, purchased and won me from all sins, from death, and from the power of the devil. He did this not with gold or silver, but with His holy, precious blood and with His innocent suffering and death" (SC II; *Concordia*, p. 329).

If, then, we were all born under the Law, what is our relationship with the Gospel? Paul informed the Colossians that, on account of Christ's death, they have been reconciled to God and can now stand "holy and blameless and above reproach before Him" (1:22). They are told simply that this is "the hope of the gospel" (1:23). Indeed it is! Once being alienated, now being reconciled; once being evil, now being holy; once enemies, now free from accusation—these are the amazing effects of the Gospel of Jesus Christ. These are benefits not to be squandered. Paul therefore urges his audience to continue in their faith, to remain "stable and steadfast, not shifting from the hope of the gospel that you heard" (1:23). Paul's exhortation to the Colossians remains relevant for each of us today. Having been redeemed from the Law and reconciled by the Gospel, let us continue joyfully and thankfully in the faith that lays hold of such good news. We can do so with the assurance that it is God's own Spirit who has "called me by the Gospel, enlightened me with His gifts, sanctified and kept me in the true faith" (SC II; *Concordia*, p. 330).

Sons and Heirs

Thanks be to God, we have no need of appealing to the Law. Thanks be to God, we have been redeemed from the Law! Jesus Himself suffered what we lawfully deserved, giving us instead a free and unearned pardon.

As you consider Jesus' relationship with the Law, what comfort can you take in the circumstances of His birth, life, and death? Christians familiar with both the Scriptures and their own behavior will be acutely aware of their inability to keep the Law. This should never lead one to despair of salvation, however. The good news of the Gospel is that Jesus Himself was born under the Law, that He perfectly fulfilled the Law's demands in His earthly life, and that He suffered the condemnation of the Law in His atoning death. These things He did in our place, for our sake. This is the Christian's great comfort: all that we cannot do, Christ has done for us.

How can we, like the Colossians, "continue in the faith, stable and steadfast" (1:23)? Just as we have been saved through faith in the Gospel of Jesus Christ, so, too, does the ministry of the Gospel continue to strengthen and preserve our faith. This, in fact, is the reason behind the writing of so many of Paul's New Testament Letters. He knows that his audience has received salvation by grace through faith in Christ. In many cases it was Paul himself who first proclaimed the Gospel of Christ to them. Yet he writes to remind them of this Gospel, to comfort, to encourage, and to strengthen the faith of those who already believe. These same benefits are received when we read the Scriptures or hear them proclaimed. Likewise, we receive these benefits through the administration of the Gospel by means of the Sacraments. So long as we remain in this world, afflicted by sin and our lingering sinful nature, we will eagerly seek to make use of these gracious gifts of God.

All about Christ

The Christian can indeed proclaim, "I was perfectly justified!" This claim can be made confidently even in the court of God Himself. But it is not made with an appeal to the Law. The Christian instead appeals to Christ, whose perfect life and perfect death are the basis for our perfect justification.

All of this is indeed comforting good news. But the question remains: How do we respond to a friend who believes that both believing the Gospel and obeying the Law are necessary for salvation? How do we clarify the distinctive purposes of Law and Gospel? As the Scriptures and the Lutheran Confessions frequently make clear, the mingling of Law and Gospel is a dangerous and harmful thing. One way in which they are mingled or confused is by appointing to one the work of the other. To be sure, as we will review in the next section, Christians do follow the Law of God; but this in no way affects the justification that has been freely received by faith in the Gospel of Christ. Perhaps the best response to those who believe that keeping the Law is necessary for salvation is to review with them the numerous passages in which Paul declares that the Law cannot justify. Galatians 5:4 is a particularly strong statement on this matter: "You are severed from Christ, you who would be justified by the law; you have fallen away from grace." Galatians 3:3 is also relevant; here the Galatians are asked, "Are you so foolish? Having begun by the Spirit, are you now being perfected by the flesh?"

Comparisons

CHURCH BODY	ORIGINAL SIN	LAW'S PURPOSE	GOSPEL'S PURPOSE	SALVATION
Eastern Orthodox	Stained soul; will able to cooperate with grace.	Show God's will for our lives.	Provide empowering grace, yielding obedience.	Ultimately depends on the Christian's obedience.
Lutheran	Thoroughly corrupted soul; will turned completely against God.	Point out our sin, restrain evil, and show God's will for our lives.	Provide forgiving grace through Word and Sacrament.	Assured to all who believe in Christ's perfect obedience and sacrifice.
Reformed/ Presbyterian	Thoroughly corrupted soul; will turned completely against God.	Point out our sin, restrain evil, and show God's will for our lives.	Provide forgiving grace, symbolized by Word and Sacrament.	Never sure, as it is given only to the elect, those whom God has pre-chosen.
Roman Catholic	Corrupted soul; will able to cooperate with grace.	Show God's will for our lives.	Provide empowering grace, yielding obedience.	Ultimately depends on the Christian's obedience.
Baptist	Thoroughly corrupted soul; will greatly impaired.	Show God's will for our lives.	Provide grace so that will chooses salvation.	Ultimately depends on the Christian's decision.

CHURCH BODY	ORIGINAL SIN	LAW'S PURPOSE	GOSPEL'S PURPOSE	SALVATION
WESLEYAN/ METHODIST	Thoroughly corrupted soul; will greatly impaired.	Show God's will for our lives.	Provide grace so that will chooses salvation.	Ultimately depends on the Christian's decision.
LIBERAL	Primarily a psychological experience.	Man-made for life in community.	Model of Jesus' ethical life.	Pertains only to betterment of this life.

Point to Remember

For by grace you have been saved through faith. And this is not your own doing; it is the gift of God, not a result of works, so that no one may boast. *Ephesians 2:8–9*

Law, Gospel, and Sanctification

Is that which is holy loved by the gods because it is holy,
or is it holy because it is loved by the gods?
—Plato

Even the pagan philosopher Plato was greatly concerned with the issue of holiness. In our modern society, however, *holy* has become a four-letter word in more than the literal sense. Although we are inundated with aids and advice for self-help and self-improvement, holiness, it seems, is not something to which our world aspires. To the contrary, being "holier than thou" is an accusation with which no one wants to be charged.

A Faith That Works

Sanctification is perhaps one of the most frequently misunderstood, and therefore most hotly debated, topics in the Christian Church. As with the interpretation of Scripture and the doctrine of justification, to arrive at a correct understanding of sanctification it is necessary to properly understand and consistently maintain the biblical distinction between Law and Gospel.

James famously declares that "faith apart from works is dead" (2:26). He offers a clear reminder that faith is not the end of Christian life, but its beginning. This does not at all imply that deeds must be added to faith in order to effect our salvation. It does mean, however, that our saving faith is also a sanctifying faith. The faith by which we lay hold of the Gospel promise is also a faith that prompts us to do those works that please God. Indeed, it is only this saving faith that allows us to perform God-pleasing works, works that God Himself has revealed in His Law. Paul explains this while clearly distinguishing between justification and sanctification. Justification, he says, "is the gift of God, not a result of works" (Ephesians 2:8–9). And yet, once being justified, we are freed "for good works, which God prepared beforehand, that we should walk in them" (2:10). The Lutheran reformers likewise distinguish between Law and Gospel, justification and sanctification, when they write that "though people who are truly believing ‹in Christ› and truly converted to God have been freed and exempted from the curse and coercion of the Law, they are still not without the Law on this account. They have been redeemed by God's Son in order that they should exercise themselves in the Law day and night ([Psalm 1:2;] Psalm 119)" (FC Ep VI 2; *Concordia*, p. 486).

This point is further clarified in Paul's Letter to the church at Rome. Because the Law reveals sin and condemns sin, those who live under the Law are also slaves to sin. But the Christian lives under grace. Paul is quick to point out, however, that our freedom from the Law has not given us a license to sin. Freedom from the Law does not mean complete freedom; the Christian remains a slave, not to sin and the Law, but now to righteousness. It is only as holy slaves to righteousness that we have been freed to obey that which is holy and righteous. While the Law always accuses, in Christ we have been freed to obey and it no longer condemns us. Indeed, those who have been made slaves to righteousness by the working of God's Spirit will eagerly and inevitably walk in the ways of God's holy Law. The Confessions thus explain that "when we have received the Holy Spirit through faith, the fulfilling of the Law necessarily follows" (Ap XX 92; *Concordia*, p. 201).

But how do we distinguish between works that are truly good and other forms of obedience? In Matthew 15, the vocabulary used by the Pharisees offers a striking contrast to that used by Jesus. The Pharisees asked Jesus accusingly, "Why do Your disciples break the tradition of the elders?" (Matthew 15:2). Jesus replied by asking why the Pharisees break "the commandment of God" (v. 3). Indeed, He says, they break God's command for the sake of tradition. By doing so they have become guilty of nullifying God's Word for the sake of human traditions. Some human traditions may certainly be useful and good. But they do not have the status of commandments, and they must never supplant God's commandments. The New Testament refers quite harshly to those who suggest otherwise, calling them insincere "liars" (1 Timothy 4:2) who follow "deceitful spirits and teachings of demons" (v. 1). The authors of the Lutheran Confessions warn against such teachings by explaining that the "doctrine of the Law is needed by believers in order that they may not make up a holiness and devotion of their own. Using God's Spirit as an excuse, they must not set up a self-chosen worship, without God's Word and command" (FC SD VI 20; *Concordia*, p. 560). Our sanctification is not a matter of self-chosen good works; rather, it is a matter of those works to which God Himself exhorts us and which His Holy Spirit works in us to fulfill.

Psalm 119 is a beautiful meditation on the Law of God. In it the psalmist expresses his love of God's Law and his desire to walk in its ways. Given our understanding of the first and second uses of the Law, this may at first seem strange. Surely no one delights in the coercion, accusation, and condemnation that result from the first two uses. The psalmist understands, however, that the Law has yet another use. The Formula of Concord notes this third use in saying that "God's Law is useful (1) because external discipline and decency are maintained by it against wild, disobedient people; (2) likewise, through the Law people are brought to a knowledge of their sins; and also (3) when people have been born anew by God's Spirit . . . they live and walk in the Law" (FC SD VI 1; *Concordia*, pp. 557–58). As a revelation of the will of God—a lamp and a light (Psalm 119:105)—it serves as a guide for those who have been redeemed and thus freed to live their lives in accordance with God's will. While it is impossible to please God without faith, the Law teaches those who do have faith how they might by their actions please God in their daily lives. This third use of the Law is therefore an exclusively Christian use of the Law. It is proclaimed to those who have been justified by Christ's Gospel in order that they might know how to "live under Him in His kingdom, and serve Him in everlasting righteousness, innocence, and blessedness" (SC II; *Concordia*, p. 329).

We have been justified by Christ. How, then, have we been sanctified, that is, set apart for a sacred purpose? In discussing sanctification, Paul uses the language of "putting off" and "putting on." Much like the manner in which we change clothes, he says, we have also taken off our old selves and put on new selves. This new self, Paul says, is "being renewed in knowledge after the image of its creator" (Colossians 3:10). Using a different metaphor, Peter speaks of the Christian "being built up as a spiritual house" (1 Peter 2:5). Significantly, both Peter and Paul speak of these processes in passive terms: "being renewed" and "being built." The process of becoming a "holy priesthood" is not something in which the Christian endeavors alone. To the contrary, it is something that God Himself effects; He renews, He builds—He makes holy, that is, *sanctifies*, according to His will. Indeed, we could not even make a beginning if God Himself were not active in this process. As the reformers wrote: "The Law indeed says it is God's will and command that we should walk in a new life [Romans 6:4]. But it does not give the power and ability to begin and do it. The Holy Spirit renews the heart. He is given and received, not through the Law, but through the preaching of the Gospel (Galatians 3:14)" (FC SD VI 11; *Concordia*, p. 559). For this reason they even distinguish between man's own works done in obedience to the Law and those that result from the Spirit's working in man. They write: "When a person is born anew by God's Spirit . . . and led by Christ's Spirit, he lives according to God's unchangeable will revealed in the Law. Since he is born anew, he does everything from a free, cheerful spirit. These works are not properly called 'works of the Law,' but works and 'fruit of the Spirit' [Galatians 5:22]" (FC SD VI 17; *Concordia*, p. 560).

Scripture consistently affirms that, even after his conversion, man neither keeps the Law nor becomes sanctified without God Himself working in and through him. Thus even Jesus Himself prays to His Father that He may "sanctify them in the truth" (John 17:17). Likewise, Paul assures the Philippians that the God who justified them will also sanctify them; he writes that "He who began a good work in you will bring it to completion" (1:6). And again he assures them that "it is God who works in you, both to will and to work for His good pleasure" (2:13). Although the work of God in sanctification is sometimes overlooked in contemporary Christianity, it was not neglected by the authors of the Lutheran Confessions. Recognizing that "the Law cannot be kept without Christ; likewise, the Law cannot be kept without the Holy Spirit" (Ap V [III] 5 [126]; *Concordia*, pp. 102–3), they were led to joyfully confess that it is the Holy Spirit who "has called me by the Gospel, enlightened me with His gifts, sanctified and kept me in the true faith" (SC II; *Concordia*, p. 330).

Paul's confession to the Romans about sanctification is powerful:

> For I know that nothing good dwells in me, that is, in my flesh. For I have the desire to do what is right, but not the ability to carry it out. For I do not do the good I want, but the evil I do not want is what I keep on doing. Now if I do what I do not want, it is no longer I who do it, but sin that dwells within me. So I find it to be a law that when I want to do right, evil lies close at hand. For I delight in the law of God, in my inner being, but I see in my members another law waging war against the law of my mind and making me captive to the law of sin that dwells in my members. (Romans 7:18–23)

Paul desires to do the will of God, yet he is unable to do so. He agrees with the Law, but his sinful nature will not allow him to fulfill it. He therefore reminds the Philippians that even he cannot say "that I have already obtained this or am already perfect" (3:12). Because sin still clings to even those redeemed by Christ, the sanctified life is not a life of perfection. That is, sanctification will never be completed this side of heaven. The reformers thus confess that "believers are not renewed in this life perfectly or completely. Their sin is covered by Christ's perfect obedience . . . . Nevertheless, the old Adam still clings to them in their nature and all its inward and outward powers" (FC SD VI 7; *Concordia*, p. 559). They likewise condemn the opinion that "a Christian who is truly regenerated by God's Spirit can perfectly keep and fulfill God's Law in this life" (FC Ep XII 25; *Concordia*, p. 502). Although we are assured by the Gospel that God Himself has *declared* us perfectly holy and sees us as such, we will not be *made* so until our bodies are transformed in His heavenly presence.

Be clear on this: A misunderstanding of sanctification, because it is a misunderstanding of Law and Gospel, is no small matter. Calling them foolish and bewitched, Paul strongly chastises the Galatians for such a misunderstanding. He asks them bluntly: "Having begun by the Spirit, are you now being perfected by the flesh?" (3:3). Or, put another way, he asks if they began with the Gospel only to turn then to the Law. The folly of doing so is pointed out by indicating that the Holy Spirit does not work among them because they obey the Law, but only on the basis of their faith. Taking up the practical example of circumcision, the apostle again warns against trusting in one's ability to obey the Law. The Christian, while continuously being sanctified by the Holy Spirit, will never take confidence in his or her ability to fulfill the Law. Rather, we say with Paul: "But far be it from me to boast except in the cross of our Lord Jesus Christ" (Galatians 6:14). It is in the Gospel of the cross that our justification has been announced and our sanctification begun.

Saint and Sinner

Holiness is by no means something to be avoided, neither in conversation nor in life. It is commanded by our holy God Himself. And yet, as we must confess, we are incapable of making ourselves holy.

Because we are incapable of effecting our own salvation, it is a great consolation to know that we are not responsible for it. The same is no less true of sanctification. Although we have put off the old self and put on a new, even this new self remains unable to fulfill the Law. It is greatly comforting to know, then, that we are not left to fulfill the Law of our own power. Instead, Christ prays that the Father Himself sanctify us by means of His Word (John 17:17). The apostles Peter and Paul also assure us that another is at work in us, renewing us and building us into a holy—that is, a sanctified—priesthood. Our sinfulness, therefore, is no cause for despair. It is cause for us ever more thankfully to take hold of God's promises, the promise of what He has done on the cross and the promise of what He continues to do in our daily lives.

Christians who honestly assess their life and works are forced to confess that they are not perfect, that their actions are not in accordance with the Law, and that they even do many things contrary to their own desires. Although this continuing sinfulness is cause for great sorrow, it is some small comfort to know that our struggle against sin is not unique; even Paul was not free from sin. But Paul's lifelong battle with the flesh provides comfort not only because "misery loves company," but because he offers an exemplary illustration of how the Christian is to respond to his or her own sinfulness. Like Paul, we will freely and humbly acknowledge and confess our sin, give constant thanks for Christ's free justification, and pray for the Holy Spirit's ongoing work of sanctification.

Christ in Action

"Holy, holy, holy" the Church sings in the Sanctus. It is a description of our God, but it also describes God's desire for His people. He so desires our holiness that He not only declares us holy for the sake of His Son, Jesus Christ, but also, through the working of His Holy Spirit, He Himself acts to make us holy.

The claim that God justifies man while man sanctifies himself is often made in an attempt to simplify the distinction between the doctrines of justification and sanctification. However, this is an *over*simplification that inadvertently subverts the work of the triune God. God alone is responsible for *declaring* us holy. But He is not complacent in the process of our *being made* holy. The indwelling of His Holy Spirit stirs up in the Christian a new love of the Law and a desire to keep the Law. But if it were not for the continual working of this Spirit within us, we would remain helpless to work out our sanctification. God, in His great mercy, has not redeemed us only to leave us to our own devices. Instead, through the means by which He first called us to Himself, He continues to work in us, renew us, and transform us into the holy people we were first created to be.

There are some who do not believe in a third use of the Law. Some also believe that, since Christ has cancelled the written code, even the second use of the Law, which acts as a mirror to show us our sins, need not be preached to Christians. Christ did indeed fulfill the Law and nullify its accusatory power. Yet as even a cursory reading of the New Testament Letters reveals, the earliest Christian authors did not shy away from proclaiming the Law to their (Christian!) audiences. The first Letter to the

Corinthians illustrates this well. Although Paul rebukes the Corinthians for numerous sins, he never insinuates or implies that they are less than redeemed brothers and sisters in Christ. Paul understood that Christians remain, in the words of Luther, "at the same time saint and sinner." Through the preaching of the Law, we, too, are reminded of our sinfulness. Being thus reminded, we are encouraged to cling ever more dearly to the sure promise of the Gospel, the power of God for our salvation—and for our continual sanctification.

Comparisons

Progressive sanctification: Some church bodies today teach that sanctification, God's process whereby He effectively makes us holy, is progressive. The Lutheran Church teaches that sanctification may vary at different times in a person's life (see Romans 7:14–19; Galatians 2:11; 5:17; 1 John 1:8).

Possibility of sanctification: Lutheran Christians, along with Presbyterians and some Evangelicals, teach that perfect sanctification in this life, due to the persistent effects of the devil, the world, and our sinful flesh, is impossible, and that Christians claiming to be sinless have, under the influence of Satan, deceived themselves (see 1 John 1:8, 10; John 8:44). Other church bodies, particularly the Eastern Orthodox and Roman Catholic churches, teach that perfect sanctification is difficult to obtain, but it can be done—the saints, for example. Still others, particularly from the Wesleyan family of church bodies, including the Methodists, Pentecostals, and Holiness groups, teach that perfect sanctification is attainable in this life by any Christian earnestly seeking it.

Requirement of sanctification: Correlative with their doctrine of purgatory, the Roman Catholic Church insists that perfect sanctification is required before enjoying the beatific vision of God. Upon death, the saints, due to their achievement of perfect holiness, enter immediately into heaven. Those not achieving full sanctification in this life are "purged" (hence, "purgatory") of their sins after death for an indeterminate time until they are able to enter God's presence.

Point to Remember

We were buried therefore with Him by baptism into death. *Romans 6:4*

Lutheran Summary of Law and Gospel

Augsburg Confession IV

Our churches teach that people cannot be justified before God by their own strength, merits, or works. People are freely justified for Christ's sake, through faith, when they believe that they are received into favor and that their sins are forgiven for Christ's sake. By His death, Christ made satisfaction for our sins. God counts this faith for righteousness in His sight (Romans 3 and 4 [3:21–26; 4:5]). (*Concordia*, p. 33)

Apology of the Augsburg Confession IV 5–6

All Scripture ought to be distributed into these two principal topics: the Law and the promises. For in some places Scripture presents the Law, and in others the promises about Christ. In other words, in the Old Testament, Scripture promises that Christ will come, and it offers, for His sake, the forgiveness of sins, justification, and life eternal. Or in the Gospel, in the New Testament, Christ Himself (since He has appeared) promises the forgiveness of sins, justification, and life eternal. Furthermore, in this discussion, by *Law* we mean the Ten Commandments, wherever they are read in the Scriptures. (*Concordia*, p. 83)

Apology of the Augsburg Confession IV 43–44

Since justification is gained through the free promise, it follows that we cannot justify ourselves. Otherwise, why would there be a need to promise? Since the promise can only be received by faith, the Gospel (which is properly the promise of the forgiveness of sins and of justification for Christ's sake) proclaims the righteousness of faith in Christ. The Law does not teach this, nor is this the righteousness of the Law. For the Law demands our works and our perfection. But, for Christ's sake, the Gospel freely offers reconciliation to us, who have been vanquished by sin and death. This is received not by works, but by faith alone. (*Concordia*, p. 88)

Formula of Concord Epitome V 7

The Law and the Gospel are also contrasted with each other. Likewise also, Moses himself as a teacher of the Law and Christ as a preacher of the Gospel are contrasted with each other [John 1:17]. In these cases we believe, teach, and confess that the Gospel is not a preaching of repentance or rebuke. But it is properly nothing other than a preaching of consolation and a joyful message that does not rebuke or terrify. The Gospel comforts consciences against the terrors of the Law, points only to Christ's merit, and raises them up again by the lovely preaching of God's grace and favor, gained through Christ's merit. (*Concordia*, p. 485; FC Ep V is devoted entirely to the discussion of Law and Gospel)

Formula of Concord Solid Declaration V 1

The distinction between the Law and the Gospel is a particularly brilliant light. It serves the purpose of rightly dividing God's Word [2 Timothy 2:15] and properly explaining and understanding the Scriptures of the holy prophets and apostles. We must guard this distinction with special care, so that these two doctrines may not be mixed with each other, or a law be made out of the Gospel. When that happens, Christ's merit is hidden and troubled consciences are robbed of comfort, which they otherwise have in the Holy Gospel when it is preached genuinely and purely. For by the Gospel they can support themselves in their most difficult trials against the Law's terrors. (*Concordia*, p. 552; FC SD V is devoted entirely to the discussion of Law and Gospel)

I Believe in One God, Father, Almighty

TOPIC THREE

God the Father[1]

Engaging This Topic

"I can't get through the day without talking with my Father in heaven."

"I used to believe in God and pray the Lord's Prayer each day."

"Why did you stop?"

"Are you kidding? With all the evil in this world, how could I say, 'Our Father who art in heaven'? If God cares about us, He sure has a strange way of showing it. I feel like an orphan."

More than 90 percent of U.S. citizens and more than 80 percent of Canadian citizens believe in God. These poll results offer encouragement for those who believe in the importance of religion and its influence on the family and society. But mere belief in God does not make people good or guarantee a good conscience.

Such poll results offer little comfort when we know that some who say "yes" to belief in God also engage in the worst forms of behavior. We must ask ourselves what we and our neighbors should believe about God and how we should live in view of that belief. In other words, we need to know what's true about God.

Changing Views of God

Beliefs about who God is and what He does have changed throughout the centuries. Many ancient documents describe not just one God but many gods. These gods were usually associated with natural forces or processes such as the weather and the changing of the seasons. They behaved like humans with superhuman powers, acting on lust, greed, envy, and pride.

1 This chapter adapted from *The Lutheran Difference: God the Father*, written by Bret Taylor, with contributions by Edward Engelbrecht. Copyright © 2004 Concordia Publishing House.

The ancient documents reveal the fear people experienced because of their belief that an inability to please these gods would result in punishment.

Around 2100 BC, a man in Mesopotamia (modern Iraq) began making new claims about the divine. He declared that God spoke to him and had revealed that there were no other gods besides Him. The man learned that though God does punish, He punishes fairly and not on a whim. More important, this one God loved people and desired to bless them. The man's name was Abraham (Genesis 12:1–25:11). His understanding of God has become the basis of most modern beliefs about God. Jews, Christians, and Muslims consider Abraham one of God's true prophets.

What Abraham believed about God had little immediate impact on beliefs among the ancients. Most people continued to fear that there were many gods who needed to be appeased. However, two moments in history show that Abraham's knowledge about God was becoming understood by others also. In approximately 1365 BC, the Egyptian Pharaoh Akhenaton did away with all but one of the Egyptian gods. However, his religious reform caused great upheaval in Egyptian society and did not last very long. Nearly a thousand years later, the three great Greek philosophers—Socrates, Plato, and Aristotle—criticized the idea that there were many gods and the belief that the gods behaved shamefully like human beings. They concluded that there must be only one divine being, the source of all that was good. While most Greeks continued to sacrifice to their many gods, Aristotle's most famous student, Alexander the Great (356–323 BC), spread his teacher's views abroad, preparing the way for a lasting change in religious belief.

The Unique Teaching of Jesus

Another great change in beliefs about God did not come through a sage philosopher or a powerful ruler. It came through a humble descendant of Abraham, a common laborer named Jesus of Nazareth. When Jesus was about thirty years old, He began traveling around Galilee, preaching about God from the Hebrew Scriptures, which we know today as the Old Testament. Many people came to hear Jesus preach. Many experienced miraculous healings.

Although Jesus based His teaching about God on the Hebrew Scriptures, He brought a unique emphasis and made a shocking claim. He emphasized that God wanted to be understood as Father. And Jesus claimed that He had a unique relationship with God—that He was in fact the Son of God come down from heaven (see John 14–17).

Jesus' unique emphasis on the Fatherhood of God and His own divine Sonship eventually led to His arrest by the Jewish temple guard and His execution by the Roman governor, Pontius Pilate. These groups feared that Jesus would lead an uprising of the common people, which would challenge their authority.

But Jesus' disciples viewed His teaching and execution in a completely different way. They insisted that Jesus had come not to overthrow the worldly authorities, but to establish a spiritual kingdom of righteousness and peace. They asserted that the miracles of Jesus did not end with His death, but that the heavenly Father raised Jesus from the dead to demonstrate the truth of His message about God and the spiritual kingdom (Acts 2:22–41). Instead of taking up arms, the disciples took to the streets, preaching the Fatherhood of God and the uniqueness of Jesus, His Son. Jesus' teaching spread rapidly, first among the Jewish people, then among the Gentiles.

Our Father

The early Christians saw in the history of religions a unique, even miraculous, place for their message. The truth that there was only one God had been preserved among the forebears of Jesus for more than two thousand years. Among the Gentiles, the Greek philosophers spread the idea that there was only one god, preparing the way for the Gospel of Jesus. By the end of the first century the Christian message had traveled throughout the Roman Empire.

Today, the words of Jesus' prayer, "Our Father who art in heaven . . ." are among the most frequently quoted words in human history, recited daily by Christians for two thousand years. Christianity has become the world's largest religion (about two billion professing to follow Christ). The unique teachings and emphases of Jesus have not only taught the world about the Fatherhood of God but also have encouraged our modern ideas about justice, freedom, and mercy, because these are characteristics of our Father in heaven.

Lutheran Facts

Dr. Martin Luther encouraged Christians to recite daily Jesus' prayer, "Our Father who art in heaven . . ."

Lutherans regard themselves as children of God, adopted by the heavenly Father through the Sacrament of Holy Baptism. Lutherans present their children for Baptism already as infants, believing that people of all ages can have a blessed relationship with the heavenly Father.

Lutherans hold to the ancient Christian creeds (Apostles', Nicene, and Athanasian), which summarize biblical teaching about who God is and distinguish the persons of the Godhead: Father, Son, and Holy Spirit.

Lutherans recite the creeds during worship. The Nicene Creed is usually recited at Communion services. The Athanasian Creed is recited on Trinity Sunday. Other services typically use the Apostles' Creed.

The Lord Is One!

> The one who calls God "Father" immediately knows [about] and contemplates the Son.
>
> —Athanasius, *Contra Arianos* 1.33

"I believe in God, the Father Almighty," Christians assert. Since the earliest times of the Christian Church, people have confessed this simple, yet important, statement of faith. Actually, this statement of faith goes back thousands of years earlier to one just as powerful: "The Lord our God, the Lord is one" (Deuteronomy 6:4). What do we mean by this? Who is God and what is He like? We live in a world that is filled with information at our fingertips, yet knowing God seems beyond us. There is no Web page that gives us the nitty-gritty about God, no toll-free telephone number to call and ask Him our questions. What are we to do? How do we come to know God and His will?

The doctrine of God the Father and His attributes is not often questioned within the Christian Church. Lutheran Christians confess that there is a great God who loves people of all races and nations. The Almighty has paved the way for us to receive from Him much more than we can ever imagine! Article I of the Augsburg Confession states: "God is one divine essence who is eternal, without a body, without parts, of infinite power, wisdom, and goodness" (*Concordia*, p. 31). Most of the teachings that challenge this doctrine are from non-Christian or pagan religions.

Many in our world decide that the best "god" they can have is themselves. Their search ends with what they feel and desire, seeking to go no further than their own perceived needs. Making ourselves "gods" is not a new trend in the realm of human existence. The first sin was a direct result of wanting to be like God (see Genesis 3:4–7).

What is your view of God? What are the main attributes that come to your mind when you think about Him? Many people associate God with love, perfection, and eternity; others think of Him as wrathful. Without a solid understanding of God and His qualities, it is easy to fall into the trap of making God the way we want Him to be. A god that is the invention of our own ideas and ideologies is no God at all!

The Attributes of God

Scripture has much to say about the attributes of God. Deuteronomy 6:4 says, "Hear, O Israel: The LORD our God, the LORD is one." The message is quite clear: there is one God. This is monotheism. The New Testament echoes this statement, saying there is "one Lord, one faith, one baptism, one God and Father of all, who is over all and through all and in all" (Ephesians 4:5–6). This removes the possibilities of multiple gods (polytheism) or the existence of everything as god (pantheism).

Exodus 20:5 tells us that God is "a jealous God," while in 1 John 4:8 we read that "God is love." What happens if we deny either of these attributes of God? God demands complete obedience and is not willing to share the stage with anyone else ("jealous"), but He is also perfect love at the same time. If we deny either of these attributes, we end up with less than a full picture of God. If God is only love, there is no need for redemption, since God would not judge against anyone. If God is only wrathful and demanding, redemption is pointless because we can never measure up in His eyes.

According to James 1:17 and Malachi 3:6, God does not change. The God we read about in Genesis 1:1 is the same in Revelation 22:21. Since He never changes, we know that His promises and blessings to us will never change either.

In Exodus 3:5–6 and 33:18–23; Judges 6:22–23; 1 Kings 19:11–13; and Isaiah 6:5–7, we read about Moses, Gideon, Elijah, and Isaiah each having a personal encounter with the almighty God. Their common responses show us still more attributes of God. Each man is unable to face God. They cover themselves or hide their faces and are in deep fear for their lives. God's holiness and perfection are more than sinful humans can stand. Romans 3:23 reminds us that "all have sinned and fall short of the glory of God."

After Daniel was rescued from the lions, King Darius issued a decree that wonderfully tells of God's nature and being:

> Then King Darius wrote to all the peoples, nations, and languages that dwell in all the earth: "Peace be multiplied to you. I make a decree, that in all my royal dominion people are to tremble and fear before the God of Daniel, for He is the living God, enduring forever; His kingdom shall never be destroyed, and His dominion shall be to the end. He delivers and rescues; He works signs and wonders in heaven and on earth, He who has saved Daniel from the power of the lions." (Daniel 6:25–27)

King Darius was not necessarily a believer. He speaks based on what he has observed with regard to God's rescue of Daniel. Darius has come to realize that there is a higher authority than himself on this earth.

God even gives us His own name, Yahweh or "I AM" (Exodus 3:14). This name reflects God's eternal nature. "I AM" has been and will always be! When talking with a group of Jews, Jesus used this name to refer to Himself and to clearly define His divine nature: "Truly, truly, I say to you, before Abraham was, I am" (John 8:58). But the people were ready to stone Jesus because they considered this to be heresy.

The One and Only

Many in today's world say that we all worship the same God whose various names arose merely from cultural differences. While some claim that Allah, Shiva, and Buddha are the same God we hear of in the Holy Scriptures, Yahweh is clear that He is the only God. When the people of Israel began to worship other gods (Baal, Asherah, and so on), Yahweh made it very clear that He was the only God worthy of worship (see 1 Kings 18:16–39).

How, then, do we understand who God is? John records in his Gospel that Philip had the same concern, asking Jesus to "show us the Father" (John 14:8). Jesus' response to His followers and to us is that to know God, we must look at Jesus and His works and words (see John 14:9–11). He is the incarnate God come to earth to live among us (John 1:14). Through Him and His death and resurrection we are able to see God's demand for perfection and His eternal love at the same time.

Many people shape God according to their own thoughts and ideas. But if we "create" God according to our own thoughts and design, we have stripped God of His divine nature and turned Him into an idol. He does not have to answer to us or explain His thoughts and actions. Out of His eternal love, He comes down to us and builds a relationship with us. It is *all* about Him, not about us!

Confession and Culture

As you listen to the radio, watch TV, or read magazines, notice how other people view God. Western culture has become ambiguous about who God truly is. But we confess in the Athanasian Creed: "And yet there are not three Lords, but one Lord" (*Concordia*, p. 17). There is only one God. The Father is the First Person of the Godhead, equal in glory to the other persons and also coeternal in majesty. The Father is uncreated, incomprehensible, eternal, and almighty.

Comparisons

The word *creed* comes from the Latin *credo*, meaning "I believe." Creeds are summary confessions of faith used by the vast majority of Christians. They developed at a time when most people could not read, so they needed a memorable rule of faith. The use of a creed is rooted in the recitation of the *Shema* in ancient Judaism. Part of Jewish daily prayer, the *Shema* (Hebrew for "hear") is drawn from Deuteronomy 6:4–9, 11, 13–21 and Numbers 15:37–41. It served as a summary of biblical teaching and was probably recited by Jesus and the apostles. (See Mark 12:28–31, where Jesus recites a portion of the *Shema* to answer a teacher of the law.)

After Jesus ascended into heaven, the earliest Christians began using summaries of Christian teaching (e.g., see 1 Corinthians 15:3–5). These summaries developed into the creeds listed below.

Apostles' Creed: A summary that began to take shape already at the time of the apostles. This creed developed from a series of questions asked of a person at the time of Baptism. History shows that congregations in Rome were using a form of this creed already in the second century, but the wording did not receive its standard form until much later. Most churches from the Western (Latin) tradition still use the Apostles' Creed for instruction and as a confession of faith in worship.

Nicene Creed: A summary of Christian teaching adopted by congregations of the Roman Empire at the Council of Nicaea in 325. The Council of Constantinople expanded the creed in 381 to help settle other Christological controversies of the fourth century. Today, Eastern Orthodox churches and most churches from the Western (Latin) tradition confess the Nicene Creed in worship, especially during a Communion service. In the Middle Ages the Western churches added the *filioque* statement (see the Glossary, p. 683) and other minor changes, such as changing "we believe" to "I believe."

Athanasian Creed: This longer creed addresses the Christological controversies of the fourth and fifth centuries. Although named for Athanasius (ca. 296–373), the bishop of Alexandria who vigorously opposed Arianism, he did not write this creed, since it emerged much later. Many churches of the Western (Latin) tradition use the Athanasian Creed. Lutheran congregations typically recite it on Trinity Sunday. The creed has been included in Eastern Orthodox services, minus the *filioque* statement (see the Glossary, p. 306).

No creed but the Bible: Congregations of the Restoration movement rejected the use of creeds early in the nineteenth century. They taught that creeds divided Christians from one another and that agreement on the Bible as God's Word was a sufficient basis for unity. Christian Churches, Disciples of Christ, and Churches of Christ descend from this movement.

Liturgical churches (Eastern Orthodox, Lutheran, Reformed, Roman Catholic, and some Wesleyans) regularly recite a creed during their worship services. Many nonliturgical churches accept the teachings of the creeds but do not use them in their worship services.

Point to Remember

God said to Moses, "I AM WHO I AM." And He said, "Say this to the people of Israel, 'I AM has sent me to you.'" *Exodus 3:14*

God of Promise

> The complete novelty and uniqueness of Abba as an address to God in the prayers of Jesus shows that it expresses the heart of Jesus' relationship to God. He spoke to God as a child to its father; confidently and securely, and yet at the same time reverently and obediently.
> —Joachim Jeremias (*Prayers of Jesus*, pp. 62–63)

Few words are as powerful as the word *Dad*, whether we are hearing it or saying it. There is such a bond of connection and love in that single word. Moses and other ancient prophets hid from the almighty God, the Perfect and Holy One, because of their fear and sinfulness. Yet this very God grants us a relationship with Him in which we can call Him *Father*. This is a truth beyond our understanding.

It is interesting that for many people entering the United States through Ellis Island, the only documentation they had of their identity was their baptismal certificate. Just as this allowed many people into a new world with new opportunities, it also identifies us as children of the Almighty with eternal opportunities. Through Baptism, God, our heavenly *Dad*, makes us a member of His family.

By our sinful nature and actions we have removed ourselves from God's family and our inheritance. We have isolated ourselves from His love and pushed Him out of our lives. But through Christ, God restores to us that relationship of Father and child. He freely gives us the greatest gift a child could receive: salvation and eternal life. Now we can call Him *Father* and be assured of His love and grace throughout this life and into the next.

Think about the fondest memories you have of your earthly father or other male role model. In what way did he help shape your understanding of God as Father? The relationship God desires with us is one of closeness and intimacy. It is amazing that the eternal and perfect God would want to be close to us sinful humans! Throughout time, God has given His people physical signs of this relationship. In the Old Testament He enacted the covenant of circumcision to be a seal of His love to His people. Today He gives us Baptism as that seal of His love. He comes to us and offers Himself as Father; we cannot approach Him on our own. Because of sin, earthly fathers fail and let us down, but God, who is perfect, never will.

The Family of God

Sometimes the easiest way to identify ourselves to others is through family relationships: "I'm John's son" or "Jack is my uncle—my dad's brother." We can use this same method to identify our relationship with God. The prophet Isaiah and the apostles Paul and John clearly describe that God has called us as His children (see Isaiah 63:16; 2 Corinthians 6:18; 1 John 3:1). He is the one who approaches us with His love. Thus we can say, "I'm a child of God!"

Paul reminds us that before we knew God, we "were enslaved to those that by nature are not gods" (Galatians 4:8). But though we were by nature slaves to sin and death (see Romans 3:23; 7:14–15), by grace through faith the heavenly Father gives us a future as His heirs (Galatians 4:6–7). We have been promised the kingdom of God. Paul writes to the Romans: "For you did not receive the spirit of slavery to fall back into fear, but you have received the Spirit of adoption as sons, by whom we cry, 'Abba! Father!' The Spirit Himself bears witness with our spirit that we are children of God, and if children, then heirs—heirs of God and fellow heirs with Christ" (8:15–17). The term *Abba* used here is an Aramaic term for "Daddy." It implies the intimate relationship between a father and his child.

To be an heir, you must be born into that relationship or adopted or included in the will. Jesus told Nicodemus that he needed to be "born again" to see God's kingdom (John 3:3). Then He explains that we are "born" into His family through "water and the Spirit" (John 3:5). God has placed faith in our hearts through Baptism. We are "born again" into His family through this act of grace and mercy from God.

Now that we are His children, we can approach God in a special way. In Matthew 6:9, Jesus instructs us, "Pray then like this: 'Our Father in heaven, hallowed be Your name.' " Martin Luther explains the introduction to the

Lord's Prayer in his Small Catechism in this way: "God would tenderly encourage us to believe that He is our true Father and that we are His true children, so that we may ask Him confidently and with all assurance, as dear children ask their dear father" (SC III; *Concordia*, p. 331).

Instead of fearing and dreading God, we can approach God in prayer with confidence and love. Imagine that your child approached you and asked for the car keys. Which request would you listen to: "O Head of this house, you alone have the keys to the car. I humbly beseech thee to share them with me . . ." or "Daddy, could I please use the car?" Certainly, God is deserving of high and holy praise, but He also wants us to approach Him in love and intimacy.

We also carry a great responsibility as members of God's family to share God's forgiveness with others (see Matthew 6:14–15). When we speak to others about God's love and grace, we represent our Father to them.

Heirs of the Promise

Through His covenant of circumcision with Abraham (see Genesis 17:1–13), God promised that He would be Abraham's God and the God of his descendants. He also said He would give Abraham the Promised Land. This is an everlasting covenant.

God gives New Testament believers a substitute for circumcision—Baptism. Paul tells us that through Baptism we "put on Christ" (Galatians 3:27). Paul also says that we are the descendants of Abraham through faith in Christ (v. 29). All members of God's family are equally valued. God sent His Son, Jesus, to die for people of all races, nationalities, and status (v. 28).

One of Jesus' most familiar parables regarding our relationship with God is the parable of the prodigal son (Luke 15:11–32). The father demonstrates an accepting and loving attitude toward his sons, no matter what they do or say to him. His sacrificial love reflects God's love for us. The father gives everything to his sons, even if they turn on him or are disrespectful. God's love is like this. He comes to sinful humans who ignore, hate, or disrespect Him, yet He loves them enough to sacrifice His own Son.

Comparisons

Eastern Orthodox: "[Why] are children baptized? For the faith of their parents and sponsors, who are also bound to teach them the faith so soon as they are of sufficient age to learn" (*The Longer Catechism of the Eastern Church*, question 292).

Lutheran: "Our works, indeed, do nothing for salvation. Baptism, however, is not our work, but God's. . . . Baptism is nothing other than water and God's Word in and with each other [Ephesians 5:26]. That is, when the Word is added to the water, Baptism is valid, even though faith is lacking. For my faith does not make Baptism, but receives it" (LC IV 35, 53; *Concordia*, pp. 426, 428).

Reformed: "Baptism is a sacrament of the New Testament, ordained by Jesus Christ, not only for the solemn admission of the party baptized into the visible Church, but also to be unto him a sign and seal of the covenant of grace, of his ingrafting into Christ" (*The Westminster Confession of Faith*, chapter 28.1).

Anabaptist: "Concerning baptism we confess that penitent believers, who, through faith, regeneration, and the renewing of the Holy Ghost, are made one with God, and are written in heaven, must, upon such Scriptural confession of faith, and renewing of life, be baptized with water, in the most worthy name of the Father, and of the Son, and of the Holy Ghost" (*The Dordrecht Confession*, article 7).

Roman Catholic: "For, in those who are born again, there is nothing that God hates; because there is no condemnation to those who are truly buried together with Christ by baptism into death; who walk not according to the flesh, but, putting off the old man, and putting on the new who is created according to God, are made innocent, immaculate, pure, harmless, and beloved of God, heirs indeed of God, but joint heirs with Christ" (*Canons and Decrees of the Council of Trent*, Session 5, Concerning Original Sin; cf. CCC2 para. 270).

Baptist: "We believe that Christian Baptism is the immersion in water of a believer, into the name of the Father, and Son, and Holy Ghost; to show forth, in a solemn and beautiful emblem, our faith in the crucified, buried, and risen Saviour, with its effect in our death to sin and resurrection to a new life" (*New Hampshire Baptist Confession*, article 14).

Wesleyan: "Baptism is not only a sign of profession, and mark of difference, whereby Christians are distinguished from others that are not baptized; but it is also a sign of regeneration, or the new birth. The baptism of young children is to be retained in the Church" (*Methodist Articles of Religion*, article 17).

Liberal: "Religion is concerned to affirm the possibility of a vital spiritual relationship in which the soul of man feels that it has a rightful home in the universe. . . . If we are to be true to the demands of actual religious experience, we should give our primary attention to the identification of what is of value for our faith rather than to the attempt to vindicate non-natural [divine] origins. . . . We feel that religious faith is better if we deny that baptism supernaturally effects a change in character" (Gerald Birney Smith, ed., *Guide to the Study of the Christian Religion* [Chicago: University of Chicago Press, 1916], pp. 515, 553).

Point to Remember

In Christ Jesus you are all sons of God through faith. For as many of you as were baptized into Christ have put on Christ. *Galatians 3:26–27*

Our Maker

From a part of [God] was born the body of the universe, and out of this body were born the gods, the earth, and men.
—*Rig-Veda* X.90.1–5, Hindu text

Many religions have taught that a divine being made the world. Yet their followers did not come to know God with the intimacy confessed by Christ and the early Christians.

In the art world, one of the ways to determine if a painting is genuine is to examine the signature of the artist. Without verification of that signature, the painting may be a forgery, and the true artist's name and reputation would be tarnished.

In many ways this is what seems to be happening to God's work of art, His creation. Since we live in an information age, we seek the truth about how our world came into existence and how it works. We know the exact angle necessary for light to strike the rain to form a rainbow. We can identify the single gene or segment of DNA that causes a certain medical condition. Yet examining these individual pieces of data can quickly and easily consume us so that we ignore the Author and Creator.

This leads our society to view the chief work of art in God's creation—humanity—as no different from the rest of the world. We see that society views people based only on their worth and value from a societal point of view, not the unique, individually loved creation that God intended each person to be. But all the works of God's hands are shaped in love and grace. Humanity is His authentic signature telling the world that He is the Creator of His work of art. Consider Luther's explanation of the First Article of the Apostles' Creed: "I believe that God has made me and all creatures. He has given me my body and soul, eyes, ears, and all my limbs, my reason, and all my senses" (SC II; *Concordia*, p. 328).

Because of our sinful nature, we try to explain God out of our understanding of creation. We take credit for those things we think will give us status or glory, and we credit "chance" or "circumstances" for those we are unable to rationalize. By grace God forgives our selfishness and our self-centered approach to life. He has given us "eyes of faith" to see His power in His creation and to give Him glory. Think about a time when you were overcome by awe in God's creation. Did it deepen your understanding that God is behind these experiences? Only through faith can we connect these experiences to God.

Why are people so eager to substitute a loving God as Creator with luck or chance? Fallen human nature is eager to remove God from His control over the world. If God is not in control, then we are! This perspective results in an upheaval of God's plans and design. If creation is the result of random chance, we are not bound to care for it. If humans are no different from any other form of matter, we can discard them when they no longer serve our needs.

Father, Creator

How do we come to know that God is Creator? His creation "speaks" on His behalf: "The heavens declare the glory of God, and the sky above proclaims His handiwork. Day to day pours out speech, and night to night reveals knowledge. There is no speech, nor are there words, whose voice is not heard. Their voice goes out through all the earth, and their words to the end of the world" (Psalm 19:1–4). And in Romans we read: "For His invisible attributes, namely, His eternal power and divine nature, have been clearly perceived, ever since the creation of the world, in the things that have been made. So they are without excuse" (1:20). All people possess a "natural knowledge of God," knowing that God exists, that He is powerful, and that He is the Creator.

Romans 8:19–22 tells us that creation is also "talking" of other things. Creation is caught in the effects of sin. Sin has corrupted the creation as originally designed, so it also eagerly awaits the second coming of Christ when it, too, will be renewed.

The Scriptures show that God is in control of nature: He drove back the sea so the Israelites could escape the Egyptians (Exodus 14:21–22). He made the sun stand still at Gibeon so the Israelites could conquer the Amorites (Joshua 10:12–14). Jesus calmed the waves and the winds when

His disciples thought they would surely drown (Matthew 8:23–27). God has total control of the "laws of nature." The God who made the oceans, sun, and wind can cause them to change and do as He commands. He does this for His people. Faith accepts these gracious acts as evidence of His love and favor.

So we know that God made and controls all of His creation, but is all creation "equal"? The psalmist writes:

> For You formed my inward parts; You knitted me together in my mother's womb. I praise You, for I am fearfully and wonderfully made. Wonderful are Your works; my soul knows it very well. My frame was not hidden from You, when I was being made in secret, intricately woven in the depths of the earth. Your eyes saw my unformed substance; in Your book were written, every one of them, the days that were formed for me, when as yet there was none of them. (Psalm 139:13–16)

The prophet Jeremiah echoes this (1:4–5). And Paul takes it a step further in 1 Corinthians 8:6: "For us there is one God, the Father, from whom are all things and for whom we exist, and one Lord, Jesus Christ, through whom are all things and through whom we exist." God has specially made humans. He "knit" and "formed" us in our mothers. Because we are specially made by God, we have value beyond measure. God also gave humans life. Although animals and plants also have life, perhaps even "spirit" (see Ecclesiastes 3:18–21), they were not created in God's image as were Adam and Eve (Genesis 1:27).

We also hear of a *new creation*, the Christian! Even though we are sinful and deserve punishment, God makes us new in Christ. We represent God's love and mercy toward humankind; therefore, we can tell others of the wonderful love God has shown to us. (See 2 Corinthians 5:17; Ephesians 1:4–6 and 2:10.)

Since we are a new creation, we now view the rest of God's creation differently, especially people. James 1:27 and 1 John 3:11–16 are two places in Scripture that describe for us how we can respect created life. These verses remind us that we should value all people, especially those who are in need or distress. We serve the Creator by serving those He created.

Faith and Facts

The controversy between evolution and creation has left its mark on the soul of society. The fight between "faith" and "fact" rages on. While we know that God is Creator, and that He has given us some details as to His creation, many questions remain. According to Genesis 1, we know that God created all things by His Word. We also know that He completed His creation in six 24-hour days, and that everything produces according to its own kind. But we do not know many other details. For example, we do not know exactly how long ago God created the world. And yet we do know that God was at the center of these acts and that He alone is to be given credit!

The value of human life has been diminishing ever since Cain murdered Abel. From a worldly perspective, a person's value is connected to his or her perceived worth. Isaiah 43:1 and Matthew 18:10–14 describe the value God places on each individual. What are we worth in God's eyes? We are more precious to Him than we can ever know. Not only does He call us by name, but He is also willing to sacrifice His own Son to bring us into His family.

Eventually, this matter depends on what a person believes about the Scriptures. Are they merely a collection of men's thoughts and ideas, or are they truly the Word of God? Second Peter 1:20–21 tell us that "no prophecy of Scripture comes from someone's own interpretation. For no prophecy was ever produced by the will of man, but men spoke from God as they were carried along by the Holy Spirit." And 1 Corinthians 1:20–25 reminds us that the world will view us as foolish because we believe these things. We hear that all Scripture is "God-breathed," or inspired (see 2 Timothy 3:16). These are not just words from men, but are God's own words. And yet they (and we) will sound foolish to the world. We will be considered ignorant because we believe such things. God promises us His grace and peace even when others consider us foolish.

Comparisons

Six-day creation: Traditionally, Christians have believed that God created all things in six days, as described in Genesis 1–2. They have maintained that existing species may be altered by selective breeding or mutation, but that no new species have arisen. Most conservative church bodies view God the Father as a personal and intimate Creator.

Creation through evolution: Charles Darwin's (1809–82) theory of evolution has sparked much controversy among theologians. More liberal denominations have supported the view that God created all things through a process of evolution over millions or billions of years.

Strict separation of theology and science: Some liberal theologians do not believe that theology should even address questions about the origin of the universe. "Such questions as the origin and age of the earth and of the solar system; the origin and age of man and the lower forms of life; the origin and distribution of races of men, of languages, and of species of animals are now dealt with as purely scientific questions. The answers to them in nowise belong to or affect religion" (Gerald Birney Smith, ed., *Guide to the Study of the Christian Religion* [Chicago: University of Chicago Press, 1916], p. 449).

Point to Remember

The Lord God formed the man from the dust of the ground and breathed into his nostrils the breath of life, and the man became a living creature. *Genesis 2:7*

Our Provider

All I have needed Thy hand hath provided;
Great is Thy faithfulness, Lord, unto me!
—Thomas O. Chisholm (1866–1960)

The story is told of a young boy opening his Christmas stocking. He took out several pieces of candy and stuffed them into his mouth. Then, turning to his sister, he asked, "Haywh, shis, cawn I haff anuffr piesh?"

Here is the true nature of humankind shown for all to see. Already blessed with so much, we demand more and try to stuff ourselves full of our own desires. Because of our sinful nature, we believe that we have "earned" all that we have and all that we have accomplished. We watch our stock portfolios, work those overtime hours, and seek that bigger car or house. We fail to realize that, of ourselves, we are nothing and cannot take credit for anything. Contentment, if not dead, is surely on life support. Eventually, sin is the force that motivates us to replace God with ourselves or something else. We are materialistic because we do not trust God's promises to care for us.

Yet God comes to us and blesses us. He gives us gifts that we take for granted: life, family, vocation, and faith. Although we don't recognize or admit that all things come from Him, He still blesses us. As Luther reminds us in his explanation of the First Article of the Apostles' Creed: God gives "me clothing and shoes, meat and drink, house and home, wife and children, fields, cattle, and all my goods. He provides me richly and daily with all that I need to support this body and life" (SC II; *Concordia*, p. 328).

Christians have received the great message of God's love in Christ Jesus and the peace and joy that message brings. By grace God has given us all things, and through His Son's death, He forgives us for our prideful and arrogant ways. We are able to look at our surroundings and realize that everything we have is a gift from God. We are blessed to be a blessing to others.

Good Gifts

Who is responsible for all "good gifts"? God is to be given credit for all blessings we receive, both spiritual and physical, as we read in Psalm 111: "He provides food for those who fear Him; He remembers His covenant forever. He has shown His people the power of His works, in giving them the inheritance of the nations. The works of His hands are faithful and just; all His precepts are trustworthy; they are established forever and ever, to be performed with faithfulness and uprightness" (vv. 5–8). James repeats this point: "Every good gift and every perfect gift is from above, coming down from the Father of lights with whom there is no variation or shadow due to change" (1:17). We have been blessed with many accounts in Scripture of God providing for His people, for example, Exodus 16:2–3, 13–17; 17:5–6; 1 Kings 17:7–16; and Matthew 14:13–21. God, who is spiritual, still cares for our physical needs. Since He created us with certain needs, He provides for us. God is willing and able to overcome any problem for His people.

Some Christians believe that God blesses only those who follow Him. But Jesus tells us that God "makes His sun rise on the evil and on the good, and sends rain on the just and on the unjust" (Matthew 5:45). God provides for all people of the earth, those who believe and those who don't. Luther writes: "God gives daily bread, even without our prayer, to all wicked people; but we pray in this petition that He would lead us to realize this and to receive our daily bread with thanksgiving" (SC III; *Concordia*, p. 335).

Although Christians have this knowledge of God's provision, they often worry and doubt. But God promises to provide for us in every situation. We are His special creation, and He desires to take care of us. As Jesus reminds us, our Father takes care of the birds of the air, the lilies and grass of the field, and we are move valuable than they (Matthew 6:25–30). Our Father will provide.

Scripture also speaks to those who have a lot of worldly possessions and money. In Matthew 6:19–24 Jesus helps us evaluate how we view our material possessions by telling us we cannot serve two masters—God and money. Jesus calls us to set our priorities correctly. We are told that storing up treasures on earth must not be our top priority. Instead, we must look for spiritual treasures. Paul tells us in 1 Timothy 6:17–19 to share that which God has given and to become rich in deeds.

In Matthew 6:9–13 Jesus tells us how we should pray for daily bread. But what is daily bread? In his explanation of the Fourth Petition, Luther defines daily bread as "everything that belongs to the support and needs of the body, such as food, drink, clothing, shoes, house, home . . ." (SC III; *Concordia*, p. 335). We are to focus on spiritual matters first. God will take care of our physical needs in His own way.

Stewardship

We often speak of *stewardship* with regard to God's gifts to us. This involves much more than money. We look at our priorities in our whole life: time, talent, and treasures. Luke records the story of the widow's offering (21:1–4). God sees the motivation behind our offering. Sacrificial offering is pleasing to God, while outwardly large gifts may not be. (See also the story of Cain and Abel in Genesis 4; and the story of Ananias and Sapphira in Acts 5:1–11.) God seeks an attitude of service and love more than money.

Contentment is addressed in many places in Scripture. Paul tells the Philippians he has "learned in whatever situation I am to be content" (4:11). He tells Timothy that "if we have food and clothing, with these we will be content" (1 Timothy 6:8). And the Hebrews are reminded that they are to "be content with what you have" (13:5). Contentment comes from a knowledge that everything is God's and that we are receiving His grace. It also comes from placing priority on God and spiritual matters, not on earthly things.

Surely if anyone had a reason to complain about his condition, it was Job. A brief scan of the first few chapters of the Book of Job reveals that he lost his home, children, industry, and health, and still he praised God! When we think of Job, it's usually to recount these awful losses. But we would do well to remember his incredible faith: "Job arose and tore his robe and shaved his head and fell on the ground and worshiped. And he said, 'Naked I came from my mother's womb, and naked shall I return. The Lord gave, and the Lord has taken away; blessed be the name of the Lord.' In all this Job did not sin or charge God with wrong" (Job 1:20–22). And when his wife told him to "curse God and die," Job retorted: "Shall we receive good from God, and shall we not receive evil?" (2:9–10). James 5:10–11 tells us of Job's perseverance, not patience. How does a view like Job's—that all is from God—help when things are taken away from us? If we realize that all is God's, we do not feel that we have been robbed—it wasn't ours to begin with! Job's story enables us to see that though everything is taken away, our faith may remain! Job was angry and questioned God. Yet in his despair over earthly life and the fairness of God, he continued to testify about his faith (e.g., Job 19:25–27). We never know how we will handle difficulties and loss, but with God's grace and mercy, our faith can stand firm.

Comparisons

Christianity has always taught that God provides for the life of all people as well as salvation in Christ. Martin Luther placed special emphasis on the continual and intimate care God shows in sustaining His creation. Some modern movements have challenged this Christian teaching and Luther's emphasis.

Martin Luther: "[God] provides me richly and daily with all that I need to support this body and life. He protects me from all danger and guards and preserves me from all evil. He does all this out of pure, fatherly, divine goodness and mercy" (SC II; *Concordia*, p. 328).

Deist: The Deist movement (seventeenth century) viewed God as a "divine watchmaker." In this view God "wound up" the universe and then let it go. He is not intimately involved in His creation, but has left it to run by natural laws. Deistic views remain popular among scientists and agnostics.

Liberal: Theological liberalism questions the possibility of miracles. As a consequence it also undermines the biblical teaching of providence, teaching that God does not immediately and intimately intervene for the good of His creation. "Christian theology has summed up the content of religious faith in its doctrine that man's fate in the universe is in the control of a morally perfect God, who shapes events according to the demands of absolute righteousness. . . . Perhaps no greater service could be rendered today than to persuade men of the positive significance of a *questioning* faith. It may be religiously more fruitful than the kind of faith which believes itself to be in possession of final doctrines" (Gerald Birney Smith, ed., *Guide to the Study of the Christian Religion* [Chicago: University of Chicago Press, 1916], pp. 513, 518).

Point to Remember

Seek first the kingdom of God and His righteousness, and all these things will be added to you. *Matthew 6:33*

Our Preserver and Protector

> May the strength of God pilot us. May the power of God preserve us.
> May the wisdom of God instruct us. May the hand of God protect us.
> May the way of God direct us. May the shield of God defend us.
> —St. Patrick of Ireland

There are certain events that will be with us forever: Pearl Harbor, President Kennedy's assassination, the *Challenger* explosion, September 11. In one way or another, these have shaken us to the core. We clearly hear the questions that are asked of God, maybe because we are doing the asking. "Where are You, God? Are You watching out for us? Will You keep us safe?"

These questions point to a fundamental need for safety in human existence. When situations make us feel insecure, we are eager to ask for God and His protecting hand. And yet, does God promise that we will always be safe on this earth? What do we mean when we say that God is our protector? As we look at God's Word, we see that protection and safety of His people is a popular and strong message, but maybe not in the way the world understands it. We see with eyes of faith that God's protection is clear and present, but we must also realize that we do not understand God's ways or timing. He is God, and we aren't!

Through God's grace and love He daily watches over us and keeps us from the devil, demonstrating this in Christ's victory over death. This gives us the ability to recognize God's grace and mercy in our lives and to share that knowledge in and through any circumstance. It gives us assurance that God is watching over us and will call us to be with Him in eternal safety. He keeps His people healthy and happy, but mostly God protects our faith from the devil's temptations and plots.

In Luther's explanation of the Seventh Petition of the Lord's Prayer, he writes: "We pray in this petition, as in a summary, that our Father in heaven would deliver us from all kinds of evil, of body and soul, property and honor. And finally, when our last hour shall come, we pray that He would grant us a blessed end and graciously take us from this vale of tears to Himself into heaven" (SC III; *Concordia*, p. 338).

A Caring Father

God is very clear about His protection and care for His people. In Matthew 28:19–20, Jesus promises to be with us to the end of the age. In John 10:27–29 He says he will care for us as a shepherd for his sheep.

There are many examples of God's protection for His people. Daniel 3:8–27 tells us of Shadrach, Meshach, and Abednego in the fiery furnace. Daniel 6:1–23 is the story of Daniel and the lions' den. Acts 12:1–11 recounts Peter's rescue from prison by an angel of the Lord. Acts 16:22–34 is about Paul and Silas in prison and the conversion of the Philippian jailer. All these stories show clearly that God can do miraculous things to save His people and protect them. Each of these stories also shows people who were in "trouble" because of their faith and obedience to God. Does God always rescue His people? The fact that there are martyrs would suggest that His plan for some people is that they come to their eternal home through these means.

David experienced tough times. A simple shepherd, he was thrust into the political and frenzied world of King Saul, who didn't appreciate the fact that David was better suited to be king. Later, Absalom, David's own son, attempted to overthrow him in a violent coup, but ended up hanging in a tree. Despite these upheavals, David finds strength and peace from the knowledge that God is with him. In 2 Samuel 22:1–7, 26–32, David recognized that God is the one who saved him from his enemies and preserved his kingdom. At least three times in this section of Scripture, David refers to God as his "Rock." This depicts the stability and firmness that David received from knowing God's protection.

The psalms are full of beautiful and strong words regarding God's preservation and protection of His people. One of the best known is Psalm 46, with its message of hope and security. Even though the world is crumbling around us, God is in control! "Be still [calm down!], and know that I am God" (v. 10). This fills us with confidence and security that our lives are in His hands.

Does God promise us an easy life on this earth? Does He say that only positive things will happen to us because we are His people? No. In Matthew 5:10–12, 44; 2 Timothy 3:12–13; and 1 Peter 1:6–7, God tells us clearly that as believers we should be ready for persecution. Many people believe that in today's society there is no persecution of Christians. Yet more people have died for their faith in the last hundred years than at any other time in history (e.g., the persecution of the Armenians during World War I, the suppression of Christianity under Nazism and Communism, the violence against Christians carried out by Hindus and Muslims in Asia and Africa). God warns us to expect persecution. His promises to be with us and care for us are not overturned by suffering. Instead, they become real and beautiful to hear.

God promises hope in these difficult times. Romans 5:3–5; James 1:2–4; and Revelation 7:13–17 share this great message of hope with us. In these passages we are told that through trials we receive many blessings as well: hope, endurance, faith, and eternal life. We are blessed either way.

Our Refuge

Scripture often describes God as a "refuge" (e.g., Deuteronomy 33:27; Psalm 5:11–12; Joel 3:16). A refuge is a place that offers security from the evils outside. Think of an armed castle, complete with moat. That's the kind of protection we have through our heavenly Father. God gives us the comfort to face the day-to-day trials because we know we are safe in His arms.

Often, even people of God cannot see past the problems of this world to find God's protection. They feel that things are too tough or aren't going the way they would like, so they fling God aside and try going their own way. Numbers 14:1–4 gives an account of what the children of Israel first thought when they heard the report of the Promised Land. They grumbled against Moses and Aaron and said they'd be better off back in Egypt—where, if you'll recall, they were slaves! The story of Caleb and Joshua and the other ten spies reflects the conflict inside the believer's heart and soul. We know that God has given us His promises, but the reality of the world in front of us often makes us doubt. When things happen to us, we see the "giants" that confront us and forget God's plan of mercy and grace.

Many times we need someone to look at a situation, reflect on God's providence, and speak clearly that God is in control. Most of the Israelites saw no way to defeat the Canaanites. Yet Caleb and Joshua were able to rely on God, not human wisdom. They gave an assessment based on true teaching about God and based on the confidence that comes from faith. Today we also need people who are equipped to speak about God's grace and mercy in order to strengthen and guide us in difficult situations. In addition to support from fellow Christians, God specifically has called pastors, teachers, and others in full-time ministry to be "Calebs" for us today. We thank God for servants who speak up for God in any and all situations!

Not only can we misunderstand God's plan, but we are often also unaware of His timing. We want protection now! We do not realize that God's plans are not always our own. The raising of Lazarus is a prime example of God working in His time, not the time frame of humans. (See John 11:17–44.) Jesus delayed going to Lazarus to show His glory to those who needed to see it. Through Lazarus's death we have come to understand that Jesus is the "resurrection and the life." The response of Mary and Martha is typical of ours: they wanted Jesus to come immediately, not when He felt it was time. They did not understand that God can work even in our darkest times. He gives us opportunities to trust Him more.

Comparisons

The word *vocation* ("calling") is used in a variety of ways. The different uses of the word stem from different traditions in Western Christendom.

Medieval: The word *vocation* was used mainly to describe God's calling of servants in the Church. A *clerical vocation* meant a parish pastor. A *religious vocation* meant a person who lived as a monk or nun in isolation from broader society. (*Vocation* could describe the fixed states in which people labored in medieval society: serfs, lords, and so on.) A sharp contrast was made between those called to serve God in the Church and all other workers. This view of vocation was important for later Roman Catholicism.

Lutheran: Martin Luther applied the word *vocation* not only to clergy but also to all workers. He emphasized that God commanded, blessed, and worked through all types of legitimate labor. The heavenly Father called people to different types of work so that they might bless one another.

Calvinist: John Calvin largely accepted Luther's view of vocation but added that labor should lead to profit as a mark of God's blessing. Later, some Calvinists came to view profit as a mark of election to salvation.

Anabaptist: Menno Simons and Jacob Hutter were influenced by Luther's view on vocation, but they taught that Christians could not legitimately serve in government. They also emphasized communal sharing of profit.

Modern: Since the Enlightenment, the tendency has been to separate vocation from God's call to work. Christianity taught people to live in service to God and His goals. In contrast, modern movements have taught people to live their lives for personal goals, state goals, or collective social goals. Vocation has come to mean one's career with no reference to God's calling.

Point to Remember

God is our refuge and strength, a very present help in trouble. Therefore we will not fear. *Psalm 46:1–2*

The Mission of God

Through the Church, the heavenly Father enlists the services of all Christians in various ways. Some will witness while they remain in their particular calling; others have decided to make witnessing their profession by becoming pastors and career missionaries. In all of these ways, the Gospel proclamation, handed down first to the apostles, continues to reach out to people, confronting them and calling them to Christ.

God's mission, the *missio Dei*, is never separate from the Church's activity. God voluntarily binds Himself to His Word and works through it as the Church administers it to the world. God's mission leads the Church's mission and remains bound to it.

Scholars have suggested many other terms and concepts to replace "mission." Remarkably, none have managed to push it aside. "Mission" has embedded itself in the life and language of the Church for centuries. Both Roman Catholic and Protestant Christians have used it since the sixteenth century. In addition to this historic argument, one should point out that the English term "mission" is anticipated by the Greek word *apostellō* in the New Testament (John 17:18; 20:21). God the Father sent Christ. Christ the crucified and risen Lord sends out His disciples, and after their death the Church continues that call of the Lord by sending Christians into all parts of the world. In this way, the Church calls herself "apostolic" because of the mission she does.

Preaching the Gospel is the central activity of mission. The Great Commission texts, in particular, clearly oblige the Church to proclaim the Gospel to all nations (Matthew 28:18–20; Mark 13:10; 16:15–16; Luke 24:46–48). Within that proclamation or preaching activity, we should include also a broader array of communicating the Gospel—namely, private witness, the non-oral forms such as the lifestyle of believers, and the use of symbols. Our concentration on preaching activity gives stems from Paul's preaching activities (Romans 16:25; 1 Corinthians 1:21; 2 Timothy 4:17), whereas the broader use of the word "mission" allows for the type of informal proclamation that goes on between Christians and their non-Christian family members, friends, and neighbors.

The Kingdom of God

Frequently, Scripture points to the kingdom of God that the ministry of Jesus Christ and the continued preaching of the Gospel bring into this world. The kingdom began with the activity of preaching by John the Baptist and continued with Jesus Himself before it moved to His disciples. Everyone who hears the news of the coming kingdom is received into it through conversion by coming to faith in Christ (Matthew 4:17). For this reason, the kingdom of God is established through the Gospel and faith. It is by definition a spiritual entity that stands apart from all worldly attempts to promote it through power and force (John 18:36).

The famous Lutheran hymn writer Philip Nicolai (1556–1608), for example, wrote *Commentaries on the Kingdom of Christ* (*Commentarii de regno Christi*, 1597). Nicolai and all Orthodox theologians underscored God's universal salvific will as one that seeks to embrace all nations. They saw that claim inherent in the Gospel itself. Thus the Gospel must be proclaimed and heard by all, as the Jesuit missionaries at that time were already proclaiming the Gospel in parts of India and China. Although Nicolai and the Lutheran Orthodox theologians were not engaged in mission directly themselves, they recognized that the kingdom of God was expanded also through the preaching and teaching of other Christian missionaries.

Martin Luther frequently embraces the "kingdom of God" in his theology. The Large Catechism contains a mission prayer under the Second Petition: "Thy kingdom come." Luther observes that though God's kingdom comes without our prayer, we should pray that it may also come to us through the preaching of the Word and the Holy Spirit. This is an important point, because Luther thereby underscores the divine and spiritual dimension of the kingdom. God the Father furthers it through His means, the Word.

Today, the "kingdom of God" theology is receiving renewed attention. In 1980, the World Mission Conference in Melbourne convened under the theme of the Second Petition of the Lord's Prayer, "Thy kingdom come." The kingdom of God inaugurates itself in this world with transforming powers that change society and rectify problems in this world. Unfortunately, in the minds of some, the kingdom of God gets promoted not so much through the Word of God in the contrite hearts of those plagued by personal guilt and sin, but instead by the mission of the Church when she corrects the social plights and abject conditions of suffering humanity. As much as Lutherans would like to affirm the Gospel's transforming power of changing social structures and concerns, the Gospel serves chiefly as the vehicle of restoring the relationship between God and the sinner through the atoning sacrifice of Jesus Christ.

Mission as Conversion

Another important mission concept connected with the "kingdom of God" is that of conversion (Matthew 3:2; 4:17; Acts 2:38). The call to "convert" implies literally a change of mind and heart as one encounters the Gospel. The Gospel does not make any exceptions here, such as accepting a greater tolerance for religious pluralism; it calls every person to repentance and faith in Christ, to become a member of the heavenly Father's family.

Scripture summons everyone to turn away from every other religious affiliation to an exclusive faith in Christ alone (Mark 1:4; Luke 24:47). Thus the call to repent and believe in Christ embodies the quintessence of mission. More positively, conversion signifies a turn to the joyous news of salvation and the beginning of a new life in Christ enacted through the Holy Spirit.

In communities where the social network of family and kinships are greatly respected, single conversions typically have the potential of alienating and separating families from one another. For this reason, Christian Keysser (1877–1961), a Lutheran missionary to Papua New Guinea, debated the benefits and liabilities of baptizing single individuals against the consent and agreement of the family. Yet conversion signifies a transition from old allegiances to new ones; it places one into the body of Christ and a new circle of people. It creates a community of those who share a common faith in their Lord and anxiously await His return. That switch, however, is never clear-cut. A tension between the "old" and the "new" world continues to exist. New converts must readjust their former family relationships. Thus every converted Christian will struggle with his past, even if it implies that a new life has begun that sets itself apart from this world (John 15:18–25).

Mission as Church Planting

Next to the goal of conversion, every missionary enterprise must confront the task of planting churches. Matters such as setting up a constitution, electing elders, nominating treasurers, or opening bank accounts fulfill the goal of church planting. Theologically speaking, however, a church must be considered planted once faith comes about and the believers meet together to be nurtured and strengthened through the Gospel. That agrees with the Lutheran definition of the Church as "the assembly of saints in which the gospel is taught purely and the sacraments are administered rightly." The Third Article of the Apostles' Creed, too, confesses the Church as "the holy, catholic Church, the communion of saints." When we apply these definitions to the overall goals of church planting, we must draw the distinction between those goals that speak of the true essence of a church and our human goals set in terms of ecclesiastical structure and organization.

Our theological definition of the Church as the "communion of saints" includes the important aspect of "community." While each individual goes through repentance and believes on his own, the goal of church planting includes the notion of community and a sense of belonging to a larger fellowship (Romans 12; 1 Corinthians 12). Church planting helps individual believers to see themselves as part of a worshiping community where faith is strengthened and nurtured. The congregation is the household of God, our Father.

THE SPREAD OF LUTHERAN MISSION WORK THROUGHOUT THE WORLD (SEE FOLLOWING MAP)

At the close of the Reformation, the famous Lutheran preacher and hymn writer Philip Nicolai wrote *A Commentary on the Reign of Christ* (1597). Nicolai's work provided a geographical survey of regions reached by the Gospel. He stirred Lutherans to increase foreign mission work.

Lutheran mission work spread in three basic ways: (1) publications of Gospel literature; (2) missionaries sent by Lutheran rulers, churches, and mission societies; and (3) Lutheran congregations established by immigrants. The map on the next two pages highlights five centuries of work by Lutheran missionaries—only a sampling—which we hope will stir you to support further mission work.

1523—Luther writes *Jesus Christ Was a Jew by Birth* as a missionary tract; in 1529, he publishes the Small Catechism to support the instruction of converts to Christianity.

1557—Primus Truber translates and publishes the Gospels, the Catechism, and other resources for the Croats and the Wends.

1558—Estonian, Latvian, and Livonian Lutheran peasants are resettled in Russia.

1559—Swedish King Gustav Wasa begins and supports mission work among the Lapplanders.

1634—Peter Heyling begins mission work in Egypt and Ethiopia.

1648—John Campanius translates the Catechism for the Delaware Indians.

1706—Bartholomäus Ziegenbalg and Heinrich Plütschau begin mission work in Tranquebar (Tharangambadi), India.

1721—Hans Egede serves as missionary to the Eskimos in Greenland.

1742—Johann Philipp Fabricius begins mission work with the Tamil in Madras (Chennai), India.

1749—German Lutheran immigrants land at Halifax, Nova Scotia.

1762—Christian Frederick Schwartz conducts mission work at Trichinopoly (Tiruchirapalli) and, later, Tanjore (Thanjavur), India.

1839—August L. C. Kavel and congregation arrive in Adelaide, Australia.

1844—John Ludwig Krapf begins mission work in Zanzibar, Tanzania.

1845—August Crämer founds missionary colony in Frankenmuth, MI, to work with American Indians.

1851—Theodor Fliedner and four deaconesses begin relief work among Arab people in Jerusalem.

1854—The mission ship "Candace" (Hermannsberger Mission) reaches Port Natal (Durban), South Africa.

1861—St Martin's Church organized in Cape Town, South Africa.

1864—Ludwig I. Nommensen begins mission work with the Bataks of Indonesia.

1866—John Engh and Nils Nilsen begin mission work in Madagascar.

1877—Synodical Conference begins mission work among African Americans.

1883—Daniel Landsmann begins mission work among the Jews in New York.

1886—Johan Flierl begins mission work in New Guinea. Missionary Union of Sweden begins work in Congo, Africa.

1887—Theodore Schmidt organizes congregation in Valdivia, Chile.
H. J. B. Gellmuyden serves a congregation in Buenos Aires, Argentina.

1892—James A. B. Sherer begins mission work in Japan.

1894—K. G. T. Naether begins mission work in Krishnagiri, India.
T. F. Mohn starts a mission station in Ambur, India.

1901—Christian J. Broders and then William Mahler organize mission work in Brazil.

1913—Edward L. Arndt begins mission work in Hankow, China.

1936—Henry Nau and Jonathan Udo Ekong begin mission work in Calabar Province, Nigeria.

1947—Alvaro Carino and Herman Mayer begin mission work in Manila, Philippines.
Lutheran World Federation (LWF) organized in Lund, Sweden.

1948—Willard Burce and Otto Hintze begin mission work in New Guinea.

1950—LCMS Texas District sends pastors to Mexico City.

1952—Taiwan Lutheran Mission organized.

1956—The Bleckmar Mission (Hannover) begins work among Indians living in South Africa.
The Norwegian Lutheran Mission founds its radio mission, Norea Mediemisjion.

1958—Lutheran mission work organized in South Korea.

1965—Lutheran Bible Translators (originally, "Messengers of Christ") send Don and Mary Murray to the Philippines.

The Cold War (1948–91) interfered with the development of new mission work. Since the collapse of communism, Lutheran mission work has begun anew in parts of Eastern Europe and Asia (e.g., Kyrgyzstan, 1998), as well as in Côte d'Ivoire and Guinea in Africa. In 1993, the International Lutheran Council (ILC) was organized at Antigua, Guatemala, and is strengthening the bonds of confessional Lutheran Churches worldwide.

As Scripture and the Nicene Creed teach, Jesus Christ "will come again with glory . . . whose kingdom will have no end." Therefore, we boldly pray the words of Luther's mission hymn, "O let the people praise Thy worth, In all good works increasing; The land shall plenteous fruit bring forth, Thy Word is rich in blessing. May God the Father, God the Son, And God the Spirit bless us! Let all the world praise Him alone, Let solemn awe possess us. Now let our hearts say, 'Amen!'" (*LSB* 823:3).

ARCTIC
OCEAN
Arctic Circle
1721
1749
1845
1883
1648
PACIFIC
ATLANTIC
1877
Tropic of Cancer
Tropic of Cancer
1950
Equator
Equator
OCEAN
Tropic of Capricorn
1901
1887
1887

ARCTIC
OCEAN
1559
1558
1998
1851
1958
1892
PACIFIC
1913
1952
Tropic of Cancer
1894
1742
1762
1706
1947
1965
OCEAN
1634
INDIAN
Equator
1864
1886
1948
1844
1866
Tropic of Capricorn
1956
1854
1861
OCEAN
1839

Lutheran Summary of God the Father

Athanasian Creed

Whoever desires to be saved must, above all, hold the catholic faith.

Whoever does not keep it whole and undefiled will without doubt perish eternally.

And the catholic faith is this,

that we worship one God in Trinity and Trinity in unity, neither confusing the persons nor dividing the substance.

For the Father is one person, the Son is another, and the Holy Spirit is another.

But the Godhead of the Father and of the Son and of the Holy Spirit is one: the glory equal, the majesty coeternal.

Such as the Father is, such is the Son, and such is the Holy Spirit:

the Father uncreated, the Son uncreated, the Holy Spirit uncreated;

the Father infinite, the Son infinite, the Holy Spirit infinite;

the Father eternal, the Son eternal, the Holy Spirit eternal.

And yet there are not three Eternals, but one Eternal.

just as there are not three Uncreated or three Infinites, but one Uncreated and one Infinite.

In the same way, the Father is almighty, the Son almighty, the Holy Spirit almighty;

and yet there are not three Almighties but one Almighty.

So the Father is God, the Son is God, the Holy Spirit is God;

and yet there are not three Gods, but one God.

So the Father is Lord, the Son is Lord, the Holy Spirit is Lord;

and yet there are not three Lords, but one Lord.

Just as we are compelled by the Christian truth to acknowledge each distinct person as God and Lord,

so also are we prohibited by the catholic religion to say that there are three Gods or three Lords.

The Father is not made nor created nor begotten by anyone. The Son is neither made nor created, but begotten of the Father alone.

The Holy Spirit is of the Father and of the Son, neither made nor created nor begotten but proceeding.

Thus, there is one Father, not three Fathers; one Son, not three Sons; one Holy Spirit, not three Holy Spirits.

And in this Trinity none is before or after another; none is greater or less than another;

but the whole three persons are coeternal with each other and coequal so that in all things, as has been stated above, the Trinity in Unity and Unity in Trinity is to be worshiped.

Therefore, whoever desires to be saved must think thus about the Trinity.

But it is also necessary for everlasting salvation that one faithfully believe the incarnation of our Lord Jesus Christ.

Therefore, it is the right faith that we believe and confess that our Lord Jesus Christ, the Son of God, is at the same time both God and man;

He is God, begotten from the substance of the Father before all ages; and He is man, born from the substance of His mother in this age;

perfect God and perfect man, composed of a rational soul and human flesh;

equal to the Father with respect to His divinity, less than the Father with respect to His humanity.

Although He is God and man, He is not two, but one Christ:

one, however, not by the conversion of the divinity into flesh but by the assumption of the humanity into God;

one altogether, not by confusion of substance, but by unity of person.

For as the rational soul and flesh is one man, so God and man is one Christ,

who suffered for our salvation, descended into hell, rose again on the third day from the dead,

ascended into heaven, and is seated at the right hand of the Father, from whence He will come to judge the living and the dead.

At His coming all people will rise again with their bodies and will give an account of their own deeds.

And those who have done good will enter into eternal life, and those who have done evil into eternal fire.

This is the catholic faith; whoever does not believe it faithfully and firmly cannot be saved. (*Concordia*, pp. 17–18)

Augsburg Confession I

Our churches teach with common consent that the decree of the Council of Nicaea about the unity of the divine essence and the three persons is true. It is to be believed without any doubt. God is one divine essence who is eternal, without a body, without parts, of infinite power, wisdom, and goodness. He is the maker and preserver of all things, visible and invisible [Nehemiah 9:6]. Yet there are three persons, the Father, the Son, and the Holy Spirit [Matthew 28:19]. These three persons are of the same essence and power. Our churches use the term *person* as the Fathers have used it. We use it to signify, not a part or quality in another, but that which subsists of itself.

Our churches condemn all heresies [Titus 3:10–11] that arose against this article, such as the Manichaeans, who assumed that there are two "principles," one Good and the other Evil. They also condemn the Valentinians,

Arians, Eunomians, Muslims, and all heresies such as these. Our churches also condemn the Samosatenes, old and new, who contend that God is but one person. Through sophistry they impiously argue that the Word and the Holy Spirit are not distinct persons. They say that *Word* signifies a spoken word, and *Spirit* signifies motion created in things. (*Concordia*, p. 31)

Large Catechism I 16

So we learn from this article that none of us owns for himself, nor can preserve, his life nor anything that is here listed or can be listed. This is true no matter how small and unimportant a thing it might be. For all is included in the word *Creator*. (*Concordia*, p. 400)

TOPIC FOUR

Creation[1]

Engaging This Topic

> "We believe that God created everything in six 24-hour days."
> "You've got to be kidding! So you don't believe in evolution?"
> "Microevolution, yes; macroevolution, no."
> "And you maintain that that position, in view of modern science, is tenable?"

It may come as a surprise, but when the Bible uses the word *doctrines* (teachings) in the plural, the word is presented negatively as coming from men (Matthew 15:9; Mark 7:7; Colossians 2:22) or from demons (1 Timothy 4:1). Christian doctrine, however, is one. It is one teaching that comes from God, and each component of that teaching plays an integral role in conveying a singular message. Take out one component, like creation, and the whole is adversely affected. Conversely, if we faithfully confess each component of Christian teaching, then the integrity of Christian doctrine is preserved. What does the Gospel of Jesus Christ—His life, death, and resurrection for the salvation of all people—have to do with all this? The Gospel of Jesus Christ—who He truly is and why He came into the world—makes sense only within the biblical worldview that espouses a belief in a divine Creator and His creation.

God's purpose in creation (the reason He made us) is that He is pleased to love and to give.[2] *Creator* and *creation* describe God's love for all He has made. The creation is God's arena for giving His gifts of love, especially the gift of His Son. The Scriptures show us why we ought to view our Creator and His creation in this way.

In *The Science of God*, British biochemist, historian, and Christian theologian Alister E. McGrath lists several popular uses of the word *nature*.

---

1 This chapter adapted from *The Lutheran Difference: Creation* by Alfonso O. Espinosa, edited by Robert C. Baker. Copyright © 2007 Concordia Publishing House.

2 See William C. Weinrich, "Creation *ex Nihilo*: The Way of God," *Logia* 4, no. 2 (Eastertide 1995): 39.

McGrath points out that the numerous definitions of nature are not only different but also inconsistent. However, where they are homogeneous is in their denial of a biblical worldview of our Creator and His creation. God created the world to love and to give. We know this with certainty through God's loving and giving of His divine-human Son, Jesus Christ, our Savior. By holding on to the singular doctrine recorded in Holy Scripture, which includes the teaching about God, our Creator and His creation, we hold on to Christ (John 5:39).

Lutheran Facts

Until the twentieth century, Lutherans, along with most Christians, believed and taught that God created the universe in six 24-hour days. This was Luther's view (AE 1:5, 42, 44). In his 1535 lectures on Genesis, Luther insisted that Moses' record of creation was to be taken literally, even if respected Church fathers such as Augustine advocated for an allegorical approach (AE 1:5).

Luther was not unaware of Greek and Roman writers such as Epicurus (341–270 BC) or Lucretius (94–39 BC). Lucretius argued that the fear of death could be conquered by viewing it simply as the cessation of bodily life in a godless, eternal universe. Ironically, this is essentially the view of Darwinian evolution. In these matters, Luther preferred to follow the Holy Spirit-inspired Moses (AE 1:6, 185).

Some contemporary Lutherans, along with many Roman Catholic Church theologians and many mainline Protestant groups, advocate for theistic evolution (simply, that God used evolution as a mechanism to create species). Others find intelligent design compatible with the Scriptures. However, while being informed of competing views and even engaging in the debate, Lutherans trust in the simple Bible account of creation recorded in Genesis and affirmed by the Lord Jesus Himself.

For Luther, the Word of creation is the Word of the incarnation: our Savior, Jesus Christ. Thus, for Luther and his doctrinal heirs, creation and redemption are both vital and inseparable (AE 1:16–20).

Creator and Creation

> Materialism is absolute, for we cannot allow a Divine Foot in the door.
>
> —Richard Lewontin, "Billions and Billions of Demons"

> Yet man, this part of Thy creation, desires to praise Thee.
>
> —St. Augustine, *Confessions*, Book One

There are two radically divergent views about our origins. One is purely materialistic, maintaining that the physical universe is all that exists. The other view is theistic, holding that there is something beyond the physical universe, something spiritual. While affirming the created material world, the Bible also expresses this latter, divine truth.

The doctrine of creation is an integral part of Christian faith. We cannot say, "I believe in Jesus Christ, but I reject what the Bible teaches about the Creator and creation." Life's most basic questions include: Who am I? Where did I come from? Why am I here? Our identity, origins, and purpose form our perception about our lives and the world in which we live. For the Christian, the doctrine of creation provides the theological foundation upon which rests the whole teaching of Scripture. Some Christians fail to see this, thinking that they can believe in Jesus Christ and reject not only what He said about creation but also the integral role creation plays in the whole corpus of Christian teaching. Ultimately, how one views the Creator and His creation either magnifies or diminishes what one believes about Jesus Christ.

At times, we can speak out of both sides of our mouth. One moment we confess the Apostles' Creed, and in the next we refer to "Mother Nature." Perhaps some people, including unbelievers, tend to personify nature because they know in their hearts that there is a Creator (Romans 1:19–21). Corrupted by sin, the human mind transfers the "natural knowledge" of God to created things (v. 23) or even to imaginary entities such as "Mother Nature." While people reveal their confusion about creation by using this term, we are given an opportunity to speak about the true Creator, Father God, when we hear it.

The Distinction between the Creator and Creation

"In the beginning, God created the heavens and the earth" (Genesis 1:1). In the beginning, only God existed—nothing and no one else. God is the sole Creator or Builder of the entire universe: "the builder of all things is

God" (Hebrews 3:4). The Son of God (the pre-incarnate Christ) as well as the Holy Spirit were also present and active in creation: "He is the image of the invisible God, the firstborn of all creation. For by Him all things were created, in heaven and on earth, visible and invisible, whether thrones or dominions or rulers or authorities—all things were created through Him and for Him" (Colossians 1:15–16). These passages are clear: God created all things.

Some people have a difficult time distinguishing between the Creator and His creation. They want to apply the law of cause and effect to everything that exists, including God. However, creation had a beginning; God did not. "Before the mountains were brought forth, or ever You had formed the earth and the world, from everlasting to everlasting You are God" (Psalm 90:2). The expression "everlasting to everlasting" is another way of expressing that God is *eternal*. That is, He is not confined to time. When God created "all things," that included time, which is inextricably tied to space. God is from eternity, the state of perpetual existence.

In 2 Timothy 1:9, Paul says God gave us "His own purpose and grace . . . in Christ Jesus before the ages began." And Paul greets Titus: "Paul, a servant of God and an apostle of Jesus Christ, for the sake of the faith of God's elect and their knowledge of the truth, which accords with godliness, in hope of eternal life, which God, who never lies, promised before the ages began" (1:1–2). Notice how God's Word speaks of that which was before time. God proposed to save us by His grace in Christ through faith in Him, and to give us eternal life.

God is the "first" and the "last," the "Alpha and the Omega," the one "who is and who was and who is to come, the Almighty," "the beginning and the end" (Revelation 1:8; 21:6; 22:13). There is none like God. Only He—Father, Son, and Holy Spirit—existed prior to the creation of time, matter, and space.

The basic cosmological argument for the existence of God goes like this:

1. Whatever begins to exist has a cause.
2. The universe began to exist.
3. Therefore, the universe has a cause.

The Scriptures show that the first premise does not apply to God, because God never *began* to exist; He has always existed.

Suppose that someone claimed that there was another god who created God (or that there was an infinite regress of gods). The God of the Bible, that is, the one true Creator and God, refutes the notion of the existence of other gods: "I am the LORD, and there is no other, besides Me there is no God" (Isaiah 45:5). Thus, in truth, Allah, Krishna, Hera, Baal, or other deities man has worshiped throughout the ages or continues to worship, do not exist. Behind the worship of false gods, however, lurk real demons, who encourage such false worship (1 Corinthians 10:20–21).

God's Purpose for Creation

Holy Scripture teaches that there are clear distinctions between the Creator and His creation. God is both eternal (beyond time) and infinite (beyond limitation), while His creation is temporal (bound to time) and finite (limited). However, this does not tell us *why* God created the heavens and the earth. Luther provides an answer in his explanation of the First Article of the Apostles' Creed: "He does all this [creating] out of pure, fatherly, divine goodness and mercy" (SC II; *Concordia*, p. 328).

There is a goal or purpose for all things. We read in Proverbs: "The Lord has made everything for its purpose, even the wicked for the day of trouble" (16:4). And Paul reiterates to the Romans: "And we know that for those who love God all things work together for good, for those who are called according to His purpose" (8:28). How does knowing that God has a *good* purpose for His creation impact our faith? We have reason to take comfort, because these verses assure us that our lives have meaning according to God's good purposes for us in Christ.

But what is God's purpose for His creation? According to Psalm 104:27–28, God's purpose for His creation is to give it "good" things. The most important thing for the creation to do is to receive good things from God.

We know from Matthew 5:44–45 that the heavenly Father cares for both good and evil people, the righteous and unrighteous. We also know that we are to love our enemies, that is, those who do evil against us. Indeed, verse 45 teaches us about the love mentioned in verse 44: it is a love based on *action*, as in giving without discrimination. If your enemy is hungry, feed him (Romans 12:20). This should be both comforting and liberating. Too often we feel restricted about our ability to love because of the hard feelings and emotions we carry inside. This giving, however, is not based on emotion. We are to be imitators of God (Ephesians 5:1). We are to do as He does, and we see His love through His giving. The triune God is all-knowing (omniscient), all-powerful (omnipotent), and present everywhere (omnipresent). He does that which is in accordance with His divine will. However, He is also good and loving, actively showing His goodness and love to His creation. The chief and foremost example of His love is the suffering and death of His Son, Jesus Christ, for the sins of the whole world.

Creation as God's Gift

Clearly, God made us because He is pleased to give and to love. "Creator" and "creation" describe God's love for all that He has made. Creation is God's arena for giving His gifts of love, especially the gift of His Son.

> So Paul, standing in the midst of the Areopagus, said: "Men of Athens, I perceive that in every way you are very religious. For as I passed along and observed the objects of your worship, I found also an altar with this inscription, 'To the unknown god.' What therefore you worship as unknown, this I proclaim to you. The God who made the world and everything in it, being Lord of heaven and earth, does not live in temples made by man, nor is He served by human hands, as though He needed anything, since He Himself gives to all mankind life and breath and everything. . . . Being then God's offspring, we ought not to think that the divine being is like gold or silver or stone, an image formed by the art and imagination of man. The times of ignorance God overlooked, but now He commands all people everywhere to repent, because He has fixed a day on which He will judge the world in righteousness by a man whom He has appointed; and of this He has given assurance to all by raising Him from the dead." (Acts 17:22–25, 29–31)

The teaching that Jesus Christ is the world's only Savior does not conflict with the "natural knowledge of God." Jesus is the world's only Savior from sin and our only Mediator with God. Unbelievers may acknowledge a supreme being because the Law is written on their hearts and verified through the observation of nature (natural law and human reason). However, through the Gospel alone we learn that the all-knowing, all-powerful Creator is our good and gracious heavenly Father who gives us His good gifts through His Son, Jesus Christ. We, like Paul, can share our faith with others who may believe in a supreme being but who do not yet confess Jesus as their Savior.

Having given us new birth in Baptism, God our Father, by His grace, has given us an eternal inheritance and connected us to the death and resurrection of His Son, Jesus Christ. Even when we suffer earthly trials of various kinds, we know that our Father is allowing us to be purified and our faith to be proven genuine. Nevertheless, our Father will meet every need and graciously give us "all things." (See Romans 8:32 and 1 Peter 1:3–7.)

Point to Remember

> Do you thus repay the Lord, you foolish and senseless people? Is not He your father, who created you, who made you and established you? *Deuteronomy 32:6*

Creation Out of Nothing

> The accuracy of the declaration that God created the cosmos out of "nothing" depends on which definition of nothing the statement implies.
>
> —Hugh Ross, *The Genesis Question*

> When John says, "All things were made by Him," he is refuting the Stoic notion which imagines that matter was not created.
>
> —Philip Melanchthon, *Loci Communes*

The Bible clearly teaches that God made all things and that nothing existed before God made it. But what do we mean by "nothing," and why does it matter? Picture yourself opening up a cookie jar. Upon lifting the lid you discover that it is empty. In exasperation, you might exclaim, "Nothing!"

Why is the concept of *absolute* nothingness (no dimensions, no matter, no energy, no space, no time, no color, and so on) so difficult to imagine? As human creatures, we experience everything through our physical senses: sight, hearing, touch, taste, and smell. Hence, it is difficult to conceive of existence apart not only from the use of our senses but also the need for them. To imagine God only, apart from time, matter, and space, is likewise to conceive of our own nonexistence. This is difficult. In these matters, we must simply take God at His Word, which says, "In the beginning."

Perhaps some people find the concept of an *eternal*, *uncreated* universe (such as is expressed in pantheism, Hinduism, or the New Age movement) so appealing because believing in *something* eternal, even an uncreated universe, provides some degree of comfort if the alternative is *nothing* eternal. However, as Christians, our only sure and everlasting comfort is found in an eternal, uncreated God who shows His unfathomable love for His creation, especially through the sending of His one and only Son, both uncreated according to His divinity and created according to His humanity.

Bible Words for "Creation"

Scripture uses different words to describe the doctrine of creation. Taken in isolation, the importance of these words describing God's work might be overlooked. However, when the words are carefully examined, we see a glorious picture of God's almighty power and personal touch.

Jeremiah saw the potter "making" (ESV) or "shaping" (NIV) a clay pot (18:4). In Hebrew, this word is *asah*, which means "to fashion" or "to shape." As the potter does with the clay, God reshapes or reforms Israel. However, *asah* also shows God as the Creator, who creates in an orderly way and who begins His creation with only His Word. According to Psalm 136:5, God made (*asah*) the heavens "by understanding." God prepares, fits, and adapts characteristics that display His supreme ability and wisdom.

"Then the LORD God formed the man of dust from the ground and breathed into his nostrils the breath of life, and the man became a living creature" (Genesis 2:7; see also v. 19). Another creation word, *yatsar*, is translated as "formed" (ESV and NIV). Isaiah 43:1 uses this word as well: "But now thus says the LORD, He who created you, O Jacob, He who formed you, O Israel: 'Fear not, for I have redeemed you; I have called you by name, you are Mine.'" *Yatsar* shows the superiority and higher wisdom of the Creator over His creation. It also communicates that His creation is totally dependent on Him. God is the Creator of His people.

In Hebrew, another word for "formed" (ESV) and "created" (NIV) is *qanah*: "For You formed my inward parts; You knitted me together in my mother's womb" (Psalm 139:13). This brings creation close to home, so to speak, by making creation very personal. Why is this aspect important to the doctrine of creation? Belonging to God should give us a sense of His vested interest in and care for us. He "formed" (ESV) and "created" (NIV) our inmost being, or inner parts. This shows God's immediate and immanent care for and knowledge of each person who has ever been created or conceived. This is important in our appreciation of the doctrine of creation because the Creator identifies with His creation in the most personal and intimate way.

God's creation is described as having been "set in place" (Psalm 8:3 ESV and NIV) and "fashioned" (Psalm 119:73 ESV) or "formed" (NIV). When things are fashioned or formed and set in place, they are designed. These verses reveal not only the careful forethought, planning, and execution of the moon and the stars in the sky but also of each human creature.

"By faith we understand that the universe was created by the word of God, so that what is seen was not made out of things that are visible" (Hebrews 11:3). In Greek, "created" (ESV) or "formed" (NIV) is *katartidzein*, which means "to order, to make, or to form into a proper state." Again, we have a strong description of intelligent design. This verse affirms God's creation of the universe out of nothing and teaches us that what we see does not come from what is visible (so much for naturalism, the idea that everything has come from natural causes).

The Word That Makes Christianity Unique: *Bara'*

Many of the words we've studied thus far demonstrate the special care, wisdom, and design the Creator puts into His amazing creation. However, one particular Hebrew word truly makes the Christian faith unique: *bara'*. Occurring forty-nine times in the Old Testament, *bara'* presents the creative work of God as separate from anything already made from existing material.

Genesis 1:1 tells us "in the beginning, God created the heavens and the earth." In Hebrew, *bara'* is the word for "created." The verb depicts God bringing into existence that which never existed before—at the beginning of everything, including time. What is significant about the first verse of the Bible containing the word *bara'*? It is the first verb and the second word of the Bible (in Hebrew). *Bara'* establishes our dependence upon God. To Him alone be the power and glory! As for trying to speak about "before" the beginning, Luther quotes St. Augustine: "God was making hell ready for those who pried into meddlesome questions" (AE 1:10). Luther is humorously earnest in his rejection of sinful human pride that seeks to know what is God's alone to know. Also, it is interesting to note that modern science affirms that creation has a beginning. The law of entropy (the second law of thermodynamics), along with the scientific discoveries of an expanding universe and the background radiation of the universe, suggest that the universe is *not* eternal and that it had a *beginning.*

Let's look a little further in Genesis: "So God created the great sea creatures and every living creature that moves, with which the waters swarm, according to their kinds, and every winged bird according to its kind. And God saw that it was good. . . . So God created man in His own image, in the image of God He created him; male and female He created them" (1:21, 27). *Bara'* is used in connection with animals and with man. Interestingly, *bara'* occurs *three times* in Genesis 1:27! Does it surprise you that the Bible uses *bara'* for man? *Bara'* indicates that God created sea life, birds, and humankind as unique and distinct creatures. This rules out macroevolution (the "evolution" of one species into a totally separate species), including the theory that nonhuman primates (or a common ancestor shared by modern apes and man) are man's ancestors. Here it should be noted that Darwinian evolution is dependent upon millions or billions of years of evolution in order for the theory to be plausible. While we easily witness microevolution (genetic adaptation within species), we do not witness macroevolution.

"Lift up your eyes on high and see: who created these? He who brings out their host by number, calling them all by name, by the greatness of His might, and because He is strong in power not one is missing. . . . Have you not known? Have you not heard? The LORD is the everlasting God, the Creator of the ends of the earth. He does not faint or grow weary; His understanding is unsearchable" (Isaiah 40:26, 28). *Bara'* appears in both of these verses ("created" and "Creator") and fits well with the other descriptions of God's greatness. As the chapter continues, the prophet extols God's strength and power as the eternal Creator of all things. It is this all-powerful and loving God that has compassion on us in our weaknesses and who gives us the strength that we need to do those things He has called us to do.

"Create in me a clean heart, O God, and renew a right spirit within me" (Psalm 51:10). The psalmist prays that God will create (*bara'*) in him a pure heart. Like the heavens and the earth, other creatures, and human beings, God alone creates our conversion. How can we apply this truth to the false claim that we must do something in order to receive salvation? David also prays for God to create (*bara'*) a clean heart within him. Since God cleanses our sinful consciences through the blood of His Son, there is nothing anyone else can contribute to our salvation.

Christian Faith Depends on Almighty God Alone!

The belief that there is only one source or generator of power is called *monergism*. In Christianity, we know this one Source as God! In creation and in re-creation He requires no assistance or cooperation on our part (*synergism*).

So far we've discussed how the Bible uses words relating to God as the sole Creator and re-Creator of all that exists. What are the practical results of a monergistic faith? All of this is yet another way of expressing that we are saved by "grace alone" (*sola gratia*). We read in John 6 that we come to Christ because we are "given" to Him by the Father (vv. 37, 39), because the Father "draws" us (v. 44), and because the Father "grants" (ESV) or "enables" (NIV) us to come to Him. The foundation of our salvation is grace alone (*sola gratia*)—it is God's free gift of His undeserved mercy in Christ Jesus, which we receive through faith. As Paul tells the church at Ephesus: "For by grace you have been saved through faith. And this is not your own doing; it is the gift of God, not a result of works, so that no one may boast. For we are His workmanship, created in Christ Jesus for good works, which God prepared beforehand, that we should walk in them"

(Ephesians 2:8–10). The faith given us is not from ourselves. Our new lives are created "in Christ Jesus." Faith, the proper and vital response of the Christian, is receptivity to God's grace in Christ. We are called to be served by God and to receive His service.

Because of this faith, one thing is necessary or needful, as the story of Martha and Mary illustrates: "Mary . . . sat at the Lord's feet and listened to His teaching" (Luke 10:39). Like Mary, the one thing necessary for us is to receive Christ through His Word—the Gospel of the free forgiveness of our sins through faith in Him.

Comparisons

Eastern Orthodox: "What is expressed by the words of the Creed, *Maker of heaven and earth, and of all things visible and invisible?* This: that all was made by God, and that nothing can be without God. Are not these words taken from holy Scripture? They are. The book of Genesis begins thus: *In the beginning God created the heaven and the earth.* The Apostle Paul, speaking of Jesus Christ, the Son of God, says: *By him were all things created, that are in heaven, and that are in earth, visible and invisible, whether they be thrones, or dominions, or principalities, or powers: all things were created by him, and for him.* Colossians 1:16" (*The Longer Catechism of the Eastern Church*, questions 97–98).

Lutheran: "Our churches teach with common consent that the decree of the Council of Nicaea about the unity of the divine essence and the three persons is true. It is to be believed without any doubt. God is one divine essence who is eternal, without a body, without parts, of infinite power, wisdom, and goodness. He is the maker and preserver of all things, visible and invisible [Nehemiah 9:6]" (AC I 1–2; *Concordia*, p. 31).

Reformed/Presbyterian: "It pleased God the Father, Son, and Holy Ghost, for the manifestation of the glory of His eternal power, wisdom, and goodness, in the beginning, to create or make of nothing, the world, and all things therein whether visible or invisible, in the space of six days; and all very good" (*The Westminster Confession of Faith* [1647], chapter 4.1).

Roman Catholic: "This one only true God, of his own goodness and almighty power, not for the increase or acquirement of his own happiness, but to manifest his perfection by the blessings which he bestows on creatures, and with absolute freedom of counsel, created out of nothing, from the very first beginning of time, both the spiritual and the corporeal creature, to wit, the angelical and the mundane, and afterwards the human creature, as partaking, in a sense, of both, consisting of spirit and of body" (*Dogmatic Decrees of the Vatican Council*, 1870, chapter 1; cf. CCC2 paras. 279–324).

Baptist: "We believe that there is one, and only one, living and true God, an infinite, intelligent Spirit, whose name is JEHOVAH, the Maker and Supreme Ruler of Heaven and earth. . . . that in the unity of the Godhead there are three persons, the Father, the Son, and the Holy Ghost" (*New Hampshire Baptist Confession* [1833], article 2).

Wesleyan/Methodist: "There is but one living and true God, everlasting, without body or parts, of infinite power, wisdom, and goodness; the maker and preserver of all things, both visible and invisible. And in unity of this Godhead there are three persons, of one substance, power, and eternity—the Father, the Son, and the Holy Ghost" (*Methodist Articles of Religion* [1784], article 1).

Liberal: "Thus the conflict between science and religion, which had grown out of this attempt to discredit modern science by an appeal to the supposedly inspired science of Scripture, drew to a close at the opening of the twentieth century. It was settled, not by the overthrow of either, but by the emancipation of both from unnatural alliances and unwarranted pretensions. Science achieved its freedom and the recognition of its value to religion in all enlightened religious circles. The way was prepared for the rational and scientific treatment of all questions between science and religion. This has become the distinguishing mark of modern Christianity" (Errett Gates in *A Guide to the Study of the Christian Religion*, ed. Gerald Birney Smith [Chicago: University of Chicago Press, 1916], pp. 448, 450).

Point to Remember

Let them praise the name of the Lord! For He commanded and they were created. *Psalm 148:5*

Creation in Six Days

> Taking the most obvious meaning of the language, the Scriptures teach in Genesis that our universe was created fully functioning in six 24-hour days.
>
> —Jeremy L. Walter, *In Six Days* (ed. John F. Ashton)

> If, then, we do not understand the nature of the days . . . let us confess our lack of understanding rather than distort the words, contrary to their context, into a foreign meaning.
>
> —Martin Luther, *Lectures on Genesis* (AE 1:5)

Often, intellectual objections to a six 24-hour day creation are sophisticated fronts for spiritual and moral problems. On the other hand, there is no doubt that among Christian teachings, a six 24-hour day creation is one of the most controversial. We must ask, "What does the Bible actually mean by these six days?"

If God has a precise meaning for the word *day* in connection to creation, can He not also give us ways to study that and the faith to accept this meaning without changing it? While words such as *day* may have multiple meanings, there are interpretive clues within a text (context) that point to a particular meaning. It is of paramount importance that we read God's Word according to what God intends for us to understand; otherwise we abandon what is true and replace it with falsehood.

For Lutherans, a principle of biblical interpretation is to treat the biblical text literally, that is, as it reads, unless the context clearly indicates otherwise. Lutherans do not deny that there are a variety of human authors, writing styles, and types of literature. The Scriptures contain prose, poetry, and parables, for example. Nevertheless, we pray for the Holy Spirit's guidance as we seek to understand the meaning of any given text—indeed, any given word—of Scripture so that we comprehend what God wants for us to understand and believe.

What's in a Day?

God's Word uses the word *day* in three different ways. The first way *day* (Hebrew: *yom*) is used in Scripture refers to "daytime" or "daylight." "God called the light Day, and the darkness He called Night. And there was evening and there was morning, the first day" (Genesis 1:5). People use this meaning of *day* on a regular basis. For example, "I want to finish this project while it is still day."

The second use of the word *day* is seen in Genesis 2:4: "In the day that the Lord God made" is similar to our expression: "in my grandfather's day" or "back in the day." This use of *day* means a longer period of time over several days, weeks, months, or years. It often refers to another period, generation, or era. This is a figurative use of the word *day*.

The third use of the word *day* is actually the most common. In fact, when the word *day* is used in the Bible, a 24-hour day is meant more than 90 percent of the time. "And after fasting forty days and forty nights, He [Jesus] was hungry" (Matthew 4:2). In this passage, *day* means one of the forty literal 24-hour days that Jesus spent in the wilderness. "The Son of Man must be delivered into the hands of sinful men and be crucified and on the third day rise" (Luke 24:7). Here, *day* means the third 24-hour day, that is, that Jesus rose on Sunday, the first day of the week. If we changed the meaning of the word *day* in these verses, the entire message would be distorted and become nonsensical. The reason for this is that *day* has a precise, intended meaning that makes sense of the overall communication.

Why We Confess Twenty-four Hours

The Bible uses the word *day* in different ways. To discover what *day* means in Genesis 1, we must use an important principle of biblical interpretation: Scripture interprets Scripture.

Perhaps the strongest reason for accepting creation days as 24-hour days is that this is the most common meaning of the word *day* in the Bible. Common-use or agreed-to meanings of words are vital for successful human communication; without a common-use meaning of the words we use, we have no reference point for understanding what is being said.

In Genesis 1:5, 8, 13, 19, 23, 31 and 2:2–3, Moses enumerates the days: the first day, the second day, and so on. We use similar language to refer to days until Christmas, days spent on vacation, and the like. Of course, counting days is common. When we count days, we most always do so in terms of literal 24-hour days. For example, children often count days until Christmas. A child would never count such days in terms of periods of daylight or epochs. Married adults may count the days until their wedding anniversary. Connecting such counted days to the concept of a seven-day week further reinforces the notion that one is referring to literal 24-hour days.

In the passages above, the Lord describes each creation day with the phrase "and there was evening and there was morning." This phrase, "there was evening and there was morning," is a textual clue that literal 24-hour days are meant in this passage. For example, suppose a friend were to say, "I spent *the day* at the ballpark," and was asked, "Well, what did you do?" If the friend responded, "Well, *in the morning* I toured the facilities and *in the evening* I watched the game," more than a 24-hour period of time, that is, a literal day, could hardly be meant.

Let's compare two passages from Genesis:

> And God set them in the expanse of the heavens to give light on the earth, to rule over the day and over the night, and to separate the light from the darkness. And God saw that it was good. And there was evening and there was morning, the fourth day. (1:17–19)

> These are the generations of the heavens and the earth when they were created, in the day that the LORD God made the earth and the heavens. (2:4)

How does the use of *day* in verse 18, in the sense of daylight, affirm the definition of *day* in verse 19 as a literal 24-hour day? How does a figurative use of *day* in 2:4 serve as a signal or qualifier that we are no longer using the common definition? If we resort to a less common meaning of a word, then the other words surrounding the word under consideration provide contextual clues for the new meaning. This is exactly what happens in Genesis 2:4. Not only is the enumeration no longer applied to *day*, but we have just been informed in chapter 1 that the creation took place over several days, but this creation is reduced to *day* in this context. These clues make it clear that we're dealing with a new definition and one that is obviously less common thus far in the text.

God provides a powerful explanation of the days of creation in Exodus.

> Remember the Sabbath day, to keep it holy. Six days you shall labor, and do all your work, but the seventh day is a Sabbath to the LORD your God. On it you shall not do any work, you, or your son, or your daughter, your male servant, or your female servant, or your livestock, or the sojourner who is within your gates. For in six days the LORD made heaven and earth, the sea, and all that is in them, and rested on the seventh day. Therefore the LORD blessed the Sabbath day and made it holy. (Exodus 20:8–11)

> You shall keep the Sabbath, because it is holy for you. Everyone who profanes it shall be put to death. Whoever does any work on it, that soul shall be cut off from among his people. Six days shall work be done, but the seventh day is a Sabbath of solemn rest, holy to the LORD. Whoever does any work on the Sabbath day shall be put to death. Therefore the people of Israel shall keep the Sabbath, observing the Sabbath throughout their generations, as a covenant forever. It is a sign forever between Me and the people of Israel that in six days the LORD made heaven and earth, and on the seventh day He rested and was refreshed. (Exodus 31:14–17)

In these passages, the six days of physical labor are directly compared to the six days of creation. The Sabbath day is compared to the seventh day when God rested. The days being compared to the creation days are clearly 24-hour days.

Consider Psalm 90:4 and 2 Peter 3:8:

> For a thousand years in Your sight are but as yesterday when it is past, or as a watch in the night. (Psalm 90:4)

> But do not overlook this one fact, beloved, that with the Lord one day is as a thousand years, and a thousand years as one day. (2 Peter 3:8).

Some Christians appeal to these verses as proof that the days of creation were not literally 24-hour days. However, these verses do not pertain to creation, because they are teaching about God Himself. God is beyond the confinements of time, and to try to apply any limitation to Him is pointless.

The scientific community has begun to acknowledge that the universe had a beginning, which the Bible has attested for thousands of years. Ironically, what *is* evolving is better science! For the Christian, what is the relationship between the Bible and science? As Lutherans, we thank God for science and use and enjoy it as a great gift from God to do us good. Nevertheless, we do not use contemporary science, modern psychology, or current sociological trends or tastes to interpret or reinterpret Scripture. We most certainly do not claim that the Holy Spirit is revealing something different from the plain meaning of God's written Word. It is helpful to remember that science is evolving over time as God allows us to increase our knowledge of creation. While some current scientific facts may remain fixed, others may quickly be discredited as our knowledge of the created world increases and our theories improve.

The Vital Order of the Days

The order in which God created the universe is not incidental to the doctrine of creation. While evolutionists may view the biblical account with great skepticism, unfounded criticism is often short-sighted and inattentive to the nuances of the biblical text.

For example, in Psalm 104:24 and Job 38–39, Scripture presents God making the universe with wisdom, that is, according to a divine plan. While Psalm 104:24 extols God's wisdom in creating the universe, Job 38–39 shows the meticulous detail and design of creation. Notice the details in Job's account. They reinforce that we are to go into the world celebrating the extraordinary design of God's creation. Later, we will review that the fall of man caused negative consequences not only for humankind but also for the rest of creation. This fact, however, does not make God's very good creation into something evil. God's design and wisdom are still evident. Let us rejoice in this truth!

"And God set them in the expanse of the heavens to give light on the earth" (Genesis 1:17). Lutheran theologians have interpreted this verse to mean either that God created the sun, moon, and stars on Day 4 or that on this day they were formed out of the light created on Day 1. Lutherans such as theologian Philip Melanchthon affirm that God created the universe out of nothing and that He is not bound to its "laws." His student Martin Chemnitz clearly states that humans do not have the ability to settle these types of issues and must rely on the truthfulness of God's Word. If someone attacks an issue that by definition cannot be settled, that argument is a straw man. The point regarding the order of the days is to show God's intentional, historical act of creation in a manner that accurately reveals the way in which He conducted His creating. With wisdom and power He brought clarity and order from chaos for the blessing and benefit of His creatures.

Comparisons

The following are some ways people have tried to make sense of the days of creation.

Day-Age Theory: Each day in the creation week is an epoch of time that may contain millions or billions of years. Christians supporting this view often cite Psalm 90:4 and 2 Peter 3:8 out of context for support.

Gap Theory: This view accepts six 24-hour days of creation but also maintains that a primordial earth, different than our current, ordered earth, may have been "without form and void" for millions or billions of years before the "Spirit of God was hovering over the face of the waters" (Genesis 1:2). Proponents of this view maintain that Genesis 1:2 expresses an unknown, huge "gap" of time.

Revelatory Theory: The days of creation are not real 24-hour days, but days of spiritual visions given to the prophet who recorded this account, or perhaps it is a revelation seen only by angels.

Phenomenological Theory: Progressive creation views the days of creation as the observation of a theoretical man standing on the surface of the earth during the appearance of the things mentioned in Genesis. That is, creation is described from a human's perspective, not as an actual or scientific account of how the earth or universe came to be.

Genesis as Myth Theory: The historical-critical method renders the days of creation as pure myth. The days of creation communicate religious truths to people, but they do not reflect actual space-time history. In this view, Adam and Eve serve as symbols or archetypes, but were not actual, historical people.

Point to Remember

Ah, Lord God! It is You who have made the heavens and the earth by Your great power and by Your outstretched arm! Nothing is too hard for You. *Jeremiah 32:17*

Creation That Is Orderly and Distinct

If our Creator specifically designed men and women for each other, then any other arrangement is a perversion of our design.
—Bruce Malone, *Search for the Truth*

In the absence of God everything becomes relative.
—William Lane Craig, *Hard Questions, Real Answers*

Biology professor Carolus Linnaeus, the son of a Swedish Lutheran pastor, is famous for developing a system of taxonomic classifications, which are still in use today: kingdom, phylum, class, order, family, genus, and species. As humans, we are described as

Species	*sapiens*
Genus	*Homo sapiens*
Family	Hominid (great apes)
Order	Primate (first-rank)
Class	Mammal (milk-giving)
Phylum	Chordate; subphylum Vertebrate
Kingdom	Animal

Long before Linnaeus, however, God made distinctions within His creation. According to His wisdom, His creation was and is orderly and distinct. The phrases "according to its kind," "according to their own kinds," and "according to their kinds" appear in the account of the creation of both plant and animal life (see Genesis 1:11–12, 21, 24–25).

No "missing link" (transitional form) between a common ape-human ancestor and a human being has ever been found. We easily recognize that species are *constant*. Fish beget fish, birds beget birds, and human beings beget human beings. What does this observable feature of creation say about its Creator? God is a God of order and design. His intention and will was and is to apply distinctions to plant life, animals, and humans. Although sometimes there are only miniscule differences between created species, the constancy of species within their own "kind" is amazing and expresses God's divine stamp upon nature.

Created but Different

The Hebrew word for "soul" or "living" is *nephesh*. While the Bible speaks of both man and animals having *nephesh*, we see some important differences between them in Genesis 1:26–29 and Ecclesiastes 12:7, where *nephesh*, or "living," appears before "creatures," "creature," and "being." The important distinction between animal and human life is, of course, that humans were created in God's image (Genesis 1:26–29). We lost God's image as a result of the first sin, which brought about both temporal and spiritual death. Our sin brought God's condemnation, death, and decay into the order of other creatures and the rest of creation as well. Even those who do not trust in Christ, or who do not believe in God, can observe this. When a person who trusts in the merits of Christ dies, his or her soul (Hebrew: *ruach* or "spirit") goes to be with God its Creator (Ecclesiastes 12:7).

A special creature stands out in Psalm 104: the Leviathan. "Here is the sea, great and wide, which teems with creatures innumerable, living things both small and great. There go the ships, and Leviathan, which you formed to play in it" (vv. 25–26). Some believe that the Leviathan was a great alligator or other familiar creature. We don't know exactly what it was. Although the word *dinosaur* was coined in 1842 by Richard Owen, the exceptional descriptions of this creature in Job 41 are reminiscent of what we might expect in terms of a dinosaur.

Let's look at the description of some other animals in Genesis: "And God said, 'Let the earth bring forth living creatures according to their kinds—livestock and creeping things and beasts of the earth according to their kinds.' And it was so. And God made the beasts of the earth according to their kinds and the livestock according to their kinds, and everything that creeps on the ground according to its kind. And God saw that it was good" (1:24–25). What kinds of animals come to mind as you read this description? In Job 40:15–24, the great creature described there is the Behemoth. Like the Leviathan, we don't know exactly what this creature was, but the descriptions of it in Job 40 are reminiscent of other prehistoric creatures whose skeletal remains have been found.

God used the "earth" and the "dust from the ground" to create both animals and man (see Genesis 1:24; 2:7). However, God breathed into the nostrils of the man, formed from the dust of the ground, the breath of life. Unlike the other creatures, God gave man dominion (stewardship) over the creation that He had made. When man sinned, his created nature, including his dominion over creation, was affected. All beasts do not obey us as they did Adam. We are intelligent, but we don't always think clearly or rightly. We do not always conceive and give birth, and we pass on to our children disease and death. While we continue to possess these concreated gifts, they do not exist in a state of perfection because in the fall humankind lost the image of God, that is, original righteousness. However, through the Gospel in Word and Sacrament, God is restoring in us His image, that is, the image of His Son.

Sometime between Days 1 and 6 of creation, God created purely spiritual beings called angels. (See Colossians 1:16; Job 38:4–7; Hebrews 1:14.) Angels are "ministering *spirits*" (Hebrews 1:14). According to this verse, their special role is to serve those who will inherit salvation. There are many differences between angels and human beings. But we do best to avoid unbiblical concepts about angels, including prayer to or the worship of angels, or the belief that believers (consisting of body and soul) are transformed into angels in heaven when they die.

Male and Female

In Matthew 19, Jesus affirms traditional marriage—the lifelong, one-flesh union of one man and one woman. The complementary distinction of "male and female" (Genesis 1:27) was designed by God because the two "shall become one flesh" (Genesis 2:24).

Bara' (creation from nothing) is used three times in Genesis 1:27, the third time to describe God's creation of man as male and female. God's command to Adam and Eve (and to all married couples) is "Be fruitful and multiply" (Genesis 1:28). Marriage is between a man and a woman, who are commanded by God to have children. But since the first sin, this command has been constantly challenged by the devil and our sinful nature. The Lutheran Confessions point out:

> The adversaries object to these arguments. They say that in the beginning, the commandment [Latin: *mandatum*] was given to populate the earth. Now that the earth has been populated, marriage is not commanded. See how wisely they judge! Human nature is so formed by God's Word that it is fruitful not only in the beginning of creation,

> but as long as this nature of our bodies exists. Humanity is fruitful just as the earth becomes fruitful by the Word, 'Let the earth sprout vegetation, plants yielding seed' (Genesis 1:11). Because of this ordinance, the earth not only started to produce plants in the beginning, but as long as this natural order exists, the fields are covered every year. Therefore, just as human laws cannot change the nature of the earth, so, without God's special work, neither vows nor a human law can change a human being's nature.[3]
>
> Another reason for marriage is addressed in Genesis 2:18–22:
>
> Then the LORD God said, "It is not good that the man should be alone; I will make him a helper fit for him." Now out of the ground the LORD God had formed every beast of the field and every bird of the heavens and brought them to the man to see what he would call them. And whatever the man called every living creature, that was its name. The man gave names to all livestock and to the birds of the heavens and to every beast of the field. But for Adam there was not found a helper fit for him. So the LORD God caused a deep sleep to fall upon the man, and while he slept took one of his ribs and closed up its place with flesh. And the rib that the LORD God had taken from the man he made into a woman and brought her to the man.

The "problem" was Adam's loneliness. So God created "a helper fit for him," which implies a counterpart, a perfect match to make him whole. God took a rib or a part of his flesh, and from this He made the woman. Notice also that the man is asleep; he did not invent marriage. The choice for his wife is entirely a gift from God. Even today, marriage is still a gift from God between man and woman, not a changeable human work.

After the fall into sin, procreating children and companionship are not the only reasons for marriage. As we read in 1 Corinthians 7, marriage curbs or controls "the temptation to sexual immorality" (v. 2). When the married couple comes together, they protect each other from Satan's temptation (v. 5). By instituting marriage, God is countering sexual immorality.

Bridegroom and Bride

When we consider that marriage counters immorality, we realize that it is not simply a benefit for the married couple. Traditional marriage also benefits society. We see in Proverbs that children benefit from the respective service of parents of both sexes. Society benefits from stable, lifelong marriages in which children are raised in loving and law-abiding homes. A stable home is the foundation of a stable society. (See Proverbs 1:8–9; 2:20–22; 6:20–35.)

---

3 Ap XXIII 8; *Concordia*, p. 211.

When a Christian husband and wife are faithful in marriage, they are a living illustration of the relationship between Christ and His Bride, the Church (Ephesians 5:22–33). The woman is compared to the Church. The man is compared to Christ. Through their faithful witness, a husband and wife demonstrate to the world in word and deed the virtues of sacrifice, commitment, submission, and forgiveness.

Submission and sacrifice become mere empty words if they are temporary or mere pretense. The Lord tells us that marriage is a lifelong union of husband and wife. (See Matthew 19:4–9; Malachi 2:13–16.)

Occasionally, government actions or laws go against Scripture (e.g., abortion on demand, gay "marriage"). How do Christians obey both the civil government as God's institution and God as He has spoken in His Word? The government is established by God for our good. If the government does evil against others, then the Christian must seek to counter and correct this. In Acts 4, Peter and John were commanded to stop speaking and teaching about Christ, but they disobeyed and remained obedient to God. In Exodus 1, the midwives disobeyed the king and continued to assist the Israelite women without harming the baby boys as they were born. In Daniel 3, Shadrach, Meshach, and Abednego disobeyed the king and refused to worship his golden image. In Daniel 6, Daniel ignored the king's edict to pray only to him. In Revelation 13, it is clear that the saints would not worship the beast in possession of worldly authority. In this same way, we should defend what marriage is and reject what it is not according to God's good creation. Everything contrary to this reality should be resisted; governmental authority does not automatically make what is immoral permissible for Christians.

Comparisons

Our Creator instructs us on how to live in relation to Himself and the rest of His creation. His instruction is known through His Word. The Word of God, the Bible, is the basis for Christian ethics (what we understand to be right and wrong). There are, however, many competing ethical systems in our world today:

Relativism: Right and wrong is based on a person's preference. What is right for one person may not be right for another, and so forth. There are no absolutes, though such a claim is itself absolute. Ultimately, this position is self-contradictory.

Utilitarianism: What is right is based on what will do the least harm while promoting the greatest good for the most people. The big question is who or what determines what the "greatest good" is. "Right" becomes a matter of public opinion, and an entire society may approve of what is immoral or evil.

Situationism: There is only one law: the law of love. What is right is doing the most loving thing in a given situation. The problem comes in knowing how to make this determination. What if, in a given situation, two people disagree about what is the most loving thing to do?

Naturalism: Moral standards are attempts to apply religious values to human behavior. Since everything comes from purely natural causes, all morality is contrived. However, this view accepts agreed-to moral standards for the sake of societal peace and the avoidance of unnecessary violence and destruction.

Absolutism: There is an objective moral standard that communicates moral absolutes. For the Christian, this standard is the Holy Bible, the Word of God. For example, the Ten Commandments are moral absolutes that reveal the Creator's holiness, so that "right" and "wrong" are unchanging as God is unchanging. "Conflicting absolutism" is the view that, by virtue of sin entering into the world, there are times when, no matter which way we turn in a situation, we will experience the pain of living in a fallen world. This reality makes the Gospel of Jesus Christ all the more precious to the sinner confronted by his or her limitations. What is maintained, however, is that, because of the Creator, there are moral absolutes.

Point to Remember

He answered, "Have you not read that He who created them from the beginning made them male and female, and said, 'Therefore a man shall leave his father and his mother and hold fast to his wife, and the two shall become one flesh'?" *Matthew 19:4–5*

Creation Fallen from the Creator

> In a universe of blind physical forces and genetic replication, some people are going to get hurt.
>
> —Richard Dawkins, *River Out of Eden*

> "[The chance that higher life forms might have emerged through evolutionary processes is comparable with the chance that] a tornado sweeping through a junkyard might assemble a Boeing 747 from the materials therein."
>
> —Sir Fred Hoyle, "Hoyle on Evolution," *Nature*

God declared His creation to be very good (Genesis 1:31). However, after this declaration, something happened to affect it in a very serious way.

Adam and Eve's sin had drastic consequences not only for them but also for the rest of creation. After the fall, God cursed His creation because of their rebellion.

> The Lord God said to the serpent, "Because you have done this, cursed are you above all livestock and above all beasts of the field; on your belly you shall go, and dust you shall eat all the days of your life. I will put enmity between you and the woman, and between your offspring and her offspring; He shall bruise your head, and you shall bruise his heel." To the woman He said, "I will surely multiply your pain in childbearing; in pain you shall bring forth children. Your desire shall be for your husband, and he shall rule over you." And to Adam He said, "Because you have listened to the voice of your wife and have eaten of the tree of which I commanded you, 'You shall not eat of it,' cursed is the ground because of you; in pain you shall eat of it all the days of your life; thorns and thistles it shall bring forth for you; and you shall eat the plants of the field. By the sweat of your face you shall eat bread, till you return to the ground, for out of it you were taken; for you are dust, and to dust you shall return." (Genesis 3:14–19)

This passage shows us both the cause and effect of sin in the created order. Scripture makes clear that on the Last Day God will purify forever the heavens and the earth by fire, even as He temporarily purified the earth by the flood. (See Romans 8:20–21; 2 Peter 3:5–7.)

It is hard to reconcile God declaring His creation "very good" and our experience of the sin-damaged world in which we live. But Scripture tells us not to become overly attached to this world, which is passing. Paul's counsel is to live as if we are not "engrossed in" the things of the world (1 Corinthians 7:29–31 NIV). Paul is not in any way contradicting the loving service we are to give to our spouses or the pleasure we derive from receiving God's gifts. The point is that we must not be shortsighted, forgetting that these things are temporary and that we are called to prepare for the eternal things. John says categorically: "Do not love the world or the things in the world. If anyone loves the world, the love of the Father is not in him. For all that is in the world—the desires of the flesh and the desires of the eyes and the pride in possessions—is not from the Father but is from the world. And the world is passing away along with its desires, but whoever does the will of God abides forever" (1 John 2:15–17). Do not put the passing things ahead of the eternal things!

When Sin Entered into the World

At its root, sin is pride: the idolatry of self instead of the worship of the Creator. (See Isaiah 14:12–15; Ezekiel 28:14–17; Matthew 15:17; 1 John 3:4.) Lucifer's heart was filled with pride, which led to his fall (see Proverbs 16:18). Likewise, out of our hearts comes prideful sin that demonstrates itself in our thinking, feeling, speaking, and acting. Only God through His grace can cleanse us from our sin and purify our guilty consciences. He cleanses our guilty hearts and forgives our prideful desires through the blood of His one and only Son, Jesus Christ.

God warned Adam about eating any fruit of the tree of the knowledge of good and evil (Genesis 2:16–17). Obviously, Adam conveyed that command to Eve (Genesis 3:4–6). The devil tempted Eve with the lie that she could become "like God" (that is, the devil tempted her based on his original evil desire revealed in Isaiah 14). Yet, Eve (and Adam) had already been created "in the image of God." What more could there be except to take God's place? That sin of pride was in Eve's heart, and in Adam's, who accompanied her and committed the same sin.

But God's nature is love (1 John 4:16). Created in God's image and possessing original righteousness, Adam and Eve had total freedom to love God. In their rebellion of unbelief, however, they *chose* not to love God. They disobeyed Him. How is love tied to obedience? First John 5:3 tells us: "For this is the love of God, that we keep His commandments. And His commandments are not burdensome." Love serves the other. As creatures, Adam and Eve refused their service of love by disobeying God's express command and words: "You shall not eat."

The ground was cursed because of Adam's sin (Genesis 6:17). Later, after Adam's death, Genesis 6:5 states that "every intention of the thoughts of his [man's] heart was only evil continually." This condition grieved the Lord, who decided to blot people and animals from the earth. This occurred not because of anything inherently wrong with the earth, but because of humankind's rebellion.

Jeremiah 17:9 tells us: "The heart is deceitful above all things, and desperately sick; who can understand it?" But God has a solution for this heart problem: "I will give you a new heart, and a new spirit I will put within you. And I will remove the heart of stone from your flesh and give you a heart of flesh" (Ezekiel 36:26). God's solution is to give us a new heart. It is important to note that God is not going to fix the old heart, but completely replace it with a new heart. God does this through His Word, specifically the Gospel of Jesus Christ, which is applied to us through preaching, reading, and sharing the message of the cross and through the Sacraments. "Baptism, which corresponds to this, now saves you, not as a removal of dirt from the body but as an appeal to God for a good conscience, through the resurrection of Jesus Christ" (1 Peter 3:21). Adam and Eve trusted in the first Gospel, God's promise of the One who would be victorious over their enemy, Satan (Genesis 3:15). We know that God fulfilled that promise in the person of Jesus Christ. We now trust in the promise of life won through Jesus' death and resurrection.

The Ways People Turn from God

"You shall have no other gods before Me" (Exodus 20:3). The Israelites violated the First Commandment and committed gross idolatry (Exodus 32:1–10). God's reaction to this was burning wrath and the intention to consume all of them with fire. In this case, the people worshiped and served the creature rather than the Creator. Ultimately, all worship of false gods is "communion" with demons (1 Corinthians 10:20–21).

Rejecting the Creator while glorifying the creature is a sign of sin and rebellion. In fact, one of the leading contemporary examples of this is Darwinian evolution. It perpetuates the pattern of creature over Creator as natural selection replaces special creation.

Through modern genetics and the study of DNA (deoxyribonucleic acid), "neo-Darwinism" has been able to answer a question Darwinism could not: How are certain traits inherited? Classical Darwinism was unable to answer how traits were inherited among species. Through the study of DNA, we now know on a chemical basis how traits are passed down through the generations. However, neo-Darwinism is still dependent upon the theory that vast amounts of time are needed for macroevolution to occur. In six thousand years of human writing, no one has recorded a concrete example of macroevolution.

Idols Do Not Live!

In the Old Testament, we learn that King Ahab had brought trouble upon Israel and his father's house because he abandoned the commandments of God. Four hundred and fifty false prophets gathered against Elijah and called on Baal to light their altar on fire. Baal's response was complete silence—no response. Idols have no breath in them. God's response to Elijah's call was a fire that "consumed the burnt offering and the wood and the stones and the dust, and licked up the water that was in the trench" (1 Kings 18:38). There was no question He was the true God and Baal was nothing. Baal could not provide for the people because Baal did not really exist. Life must come from life. In Jesus is life. "Whoever has the Son has life; whoever does not have the Son of God does not have life" (1 John 5:12).

Comparisons

Here are additional arguments against Darwinian evolution:

The Anthropic Principle (the design of the universe is fine-tuned for life on earth): Guillermo Gonzales and Jay Wesley Richards, in *The Privileged Planet* (Regnery, 2004), and Hugh Ross, in *The Creator and the Cosmos* (NavPress, 2001), show the just-right nature of all conditions in the universe for making earth habitable. The expansion rate of the universe, the velocity of light, the average distance between stars, and so much more, all show design (see Psalm 19:1; Romans 1:20).

Irreducible complexity (complex biological systems cannot be reduced): Michael J. Behe, in *Darwin's Black Box* (Free Press, 1996), argues that design is not mystical but can be logically deduced from the physical structure of a system. He also notes that both Darwinists and non-Darwinists agree that aspects of biology appear designed. Irreducible complexity shows that life must begin as life and that there must be an intelligent cause.

Specified complexity (we can recognize design in complex systems): In several of his works, William A. Dembski argues that intelligent design is identifiable (see, for example, *The Design Revolution*, InterVarsity, 2004). The logical possibilities for causality are limited: necessity (the result is contingent, caused by the law of gravity, for example); chance (even if something appears complex, it may have been caused by accident); and design (if something is not necessary and is not accidental, it must be *specified*). Specified complexity is seen when chance does not sufficiently explain the emergence of multipart, tightly integrated complex biological systems apart from design.

Point to Remember

> For His invisible attributes, namely, His eternal power and divine nature, have been clearly perceived, ever since the creation of the world, in the things that have been made. So they are without excuse. *Romans 1:20*

Creation and the Gospel

> In the beginning were the particles and the impersonal laws of physics. And the particles somehow became complex living stuff; And the stuff imagined God; But then discovered evolution.
>
> —Phillip E. Johnson, *The Right Questions*

> In the beginning was the Word . . . . All things were made through Him, and without Him was not any thing made that was made. In Him was life, and the life was the light of men.
>
> —John 1:1, 3–4

If life comes from life, then the life we continue to see all around us, as well as the new life conceived in the womb, is coming from life! "Creation" is too often spoken of as an ancient event, as if it has ceased. It hasn't! Creation is *ongoing*, and in more ways than one!

God's creation and His providence (or preservation of His creation) are connected. How is this evidenced both by divine revelation and through the natural law, which is expressed in creation? Psalm 104 describes a present, continuous, and ongoing creation. It gloriously praises God's ongoing work of providence, that is, God's divine care for all that He has created. In Acts 17:27–28, Paul quotes ancient poets such as Epimenides, Aratus, and Cleanthes, who, either through the Law written in their hearts or by observation of the created order, taught about a single creator who preserved his creation. This does not mean, however, that these poets intimately knew the one, true God, who can be known, believed in, and worshiped only through faith in His Son, Jesus Christ. Paul is simply using the reputable teaching of known Greek philosophers to appeal to the Athenians and to "win their ears" for a clear presentation of the Gospel. Later (v. 32), some obviously heard more about Jesus.

Colossians 1:15–17 puts God's creation and God's preservation side by side: "He [Christ] is the image of the invisible God, the firstborn of all creation. For by Him all things were created, in heaven and on earth, visible and invisible, whether thrones or dominions or rulers or authorities—all things were created through Him and for Him. And He is before all things, and in Him all things hold together." Creation is clearly indicated in verse 16. In verse 17, preservation is expressed in the words "in Him all things hold together." Both are absolutely necessary for life, since life cannot begin or continue without them.

God's Providence Shows His Love and Mercy

> You are the Lord, You alone. You have made heaven, the heaven of heavens, with all their host, the earth and all that is on it, the seas and all that is in them; and You preserve all of them; and the host of heaven worships You. (Nehemiah 9:6)

> He [Christ] is the radiance of the glory of God and the exact imprint of His nature, and He upholds the universe by the word of His power. After making purification for sins, He sat down at the right hand of the Majesty on high. (Hebrews 1:3)

These passages extol God's continuing work in and for His creation through His Son, Jesus Christ. Knowing that God and Christ are always working to preserve and protect God's creation should assist Christians in seeing more clearly their vocations as the earth's stewards (see Genesis 1:28–29; 2:15). Enabled and renewed by the Gospel, we can work to preserve and protect the earth.

God prepares rain for the earth, and He makes grass grow on the hills. God gives food to the animals. God gives all people the sun and the rain. If God cares for the birds of the air, He will also care for us, especially since we are more valuable to Him than they. All things will be added to us as we seek first the kingdom of God and His righteousness. (See Psalm 147:8–9; Matthew 5:45; 6:25–33.)

The extent to which God extends His creative Word and providential care even to the unborn is related by the psalmist: "Your eyes saw my unformed substance; in Your book were written, every one of them, the days that were formed for me, when as yet there was none of them" (Psalm 139:16). God's creation of every child is amazing. It is characterized by meticulous care and detailed design. For God to give such attention to the unborn proves the intrinsic worth of each child. If an unborn child is this important to God, how much more should we invest in their care and protection! To this we add God's unfathomable love for each human creature, which was expressed totally and fully in the sending of His one and only Son, Jesus, to the cross for the sins of the whole world (John 3:16–17).

We should never forget that Jesus died and rose again for the sins of each member of the human family, the born and the unborn.

Christ Is Making All Things New

Jesus identifies Himself by pointing to His and His Father's ongoing work (John 5:17). The ongoing work of the Holy Trinity—the Father, the Son, and the Holy Spirit—in the created order rules out the "watchmaker god" of Deism, which theorizes that God stepped away from His creation after making it, allowing it to "run" on its own. The Trinity's continuous involvement in creation also rules out the god of theistic evolution, who is employed for sentimental reasons.

Part of Christ's ongoing work for us is to intercede for us before our Father in heaven (Romans 8:34). On the glorious Last Day, when He returns, what will He do for us? John paints a beautiful picture of life in heaven when Christ returns (see Revelation 21:1–5). The new heaven and the new earth will be without defect. Our physical bodies having been raised in perfection, we will enjoy life forever with God and with Christ and all those who have trusted in Him. God will wipe every tear from our eyes, because "the former things have passed away" (v. 4).

Another part of Christ's ongoing work for us is making us His "new" creations in Baptism. (See John 3:5–7; Romans 6:4; 2 Corinthians 5:17.) In Baptism, God gives us new, spiritual birth by water and the Spirit. In Christ, we are a new creation that walks in newness of life.

God grants faith through the hearing of the Gospel of Christ crucified and resurrected for the forgiveness of our sins. Faith comes from hearing the Word of Christ (Romans 10:17), that is, the Gospel of God reconciling the world through Jesus' life, death, and resurrection. The word is Christ's Word, which is spoken by His ambassadors. Christ makes His appeal through them. When a person listens to such a messenger, he is actually listening to Christ. While all people are given the opportunity to be the "salt" and "light" of the world and to share the Gospel with others, Christians should support the "ministry of reconciliation" (2 Corinthians 5:18).

In the Sacrament of the Altar, our Savior feeds us with His body and blood. Christ uses this Sacrament to continue His work of forgiving our sins and re-creating us in His image. In the Lord's Supper, we participate in the body and blood of Christ (1 Corinthians 10:16). In this Sacrament, we are to recognize Christ's body in the bread (11:29) and blood in the wine (real presence). We confess that Christ applies His saving work, the forgiveness of sins, life, and salvation, as well as imparts His image to us through this Sacrament and through the Gospel and Baptism.

Creation Vital to the Gospel

Ultimately, false teaching about how the universe came to be undermines the Gospel of Jesus Christ. The theory of evolution attacks the very need for the divine, invisible God. Darwinism implicitly denies the divinity of Christ—and ultimately our salvation through Him.

It is impossible—according to philosophical materialism—that Christ could be any more than a mere man. But if Christ is no more than a man, what of the Gospel? If Christ were a mere man and not also the divine Son of God, then He would have neither the power nor the authority to save us. To deny Christ's divinity is to empty the Gospel of its power.

Creation and redemption stand or fall together. If the Creator is denied, the true Christ will also be denied. In His place appears a pseudo-gospel that is either moralistic or sentimental. Christ becomes merely a great leader, teacher, or revolutionary, or one whom we should pity because of His crucifixion upon the cross.

The prophet Jeremiah confesses God's amazing creation and also His saving work of rescuing the Israelites from Egyptian bondage (32:17–27). Like Jeremiah, we confess both God's creation and His salvation through His Son, Jesus Christ, who rescued us from the bondage of our sins. The integrity of the Christian faith is tied to the scriptural account of creation, which is verified by our Savior in the Bible and expressed in the ancient Christian creeds.

Comparisons

There are many worldviews that confuse the creation and thereby reject the Gospel of Jesus Christ:

Atheism (along with Darwinism, Naturalism, and Materialism): God is denied altogether. The Gospel of Jesus Christ is irrelevant.

Agnosticism: There is no way to know with certainty whether or not God exists. The Gospel is indefinitely put off.

Polytheism: There are many gods. Since the Gospel of Jesus Christ is exclusive, it is resented.

Panentheism: God is always changing as the world changes. The Gospel is inflexible.

Finite Godism: God is not identified with the world, but He is finite and limited. The Gospel of Jesus Christ is unreliable.

Pantheism: God is the world and is therefore not personal. The Gospel is nonsensical.

Deism: God does not interact with the world, is impersonal, and doesn't perform miracles. The Gospel of Jesus Christ is contradictory.

Monism: All reality is one ("God" is too limiting a concept). The Gospel is meaningless.

Monotheism: There is one personal God who created all things. The Gospel of Jesus Christ is either accepted or denied depending on the type of monotheism.

Christianity: God is the Almighty Creator who has uniquely revealed Himself through His one and only Son, Jesus Christ. The Gospel is the only way the one true God—Father, Son, and Holy Spirit—saves us from sin, death, and the power of the devil.

Point to Remember

> [Christ] is the image of the invisible God, the firstborn of all creation. For by Him all things were created, in heaven and on earth, visible and invisible, whether thrones or dominions or rulers or authorities—all things were created through Him and for Him. *Colossians 1:15–16*

Lutheran Summary of Creation

Augsburg Confession I 2

God is one divine essence who is eternal, without a body, without parts, of infinite power, wisdom, and goodness. He is the maker and preserver of all things, visible and invisible [Nehemiah 9:6]. (*Concordia*, p. 31)

Augsburg Confession XIX

Our churches teach that although God creates and preserves nature, the cause of sin is located in the will of the wicked, that is, the devil and ungodly people. Without God's help, this will turns itself away from God, as Christ says, "When he lies, he speaks out of his own character" (John 8:44). (*Concordia*, p. 41)

Augsburg Confession XXVII 19–21

God's commandment is this, "Because of the temptation to sexual immorality, each man should have his own wife" (1 Corinthians 7:2). It is not just a command given by God. God has created and ordained marriage for those who are not given an exception to natural order by God's special work. This is what is taught according to the text in Genesis 2:18, "It is not good that the man should be alone." Therefore, those who obey this command and ordinance of God do not sin. (*Concordia*, p. 54)

Apology of the Augsburg Confession XXIII (XI) 7

First, Genesis 1:28 teaches that people were created to be fruitful, and that one sex should desire the other in a proper way. We are not speaking about lustful desire, which is sin, but about that appetite that was in nature in its perfection. They call this physical love. This love of one sex for the other is truly a divine ordinance. (*Concordia*, p. 211)

Small Catechism: The First Article

Creation

I believe in God, the Father Almighty, maker of heaven and earth.

What does this mean? Answer: I believe that God has made me and all creatures. He has given me my body and soul, eyes, ears, and all my limbs, my reason, and all my senses, and still preserves them. In addition, He has given me clothing and shoes, meat and drink, house and home, wife and children, fields, cattle, and all my goods. He provides me richly and daily with all that I need to support this body and life. He protects me from all danger and guards me and preserves me from all evil. He does all this out of pure, fatherly, divine goodness and mercy, without any merit or worthiness in me. For all this I ought to thank Him, praise Him, serve Him, and obey Him. This is most certainly true. (*Concordia*, p. 328)

Large Catechism II 11

It is as if you were to ask a little child, "My dear, what sort of a God do you have? What do you know about Him?" The child could say, "This is my God: first, the Father, who has created heaven and earth. Besides this One only, I regard nothing else as God. For there is no one else who could create heaven and earth." (*Concordia*, p. 399)

Large Catechism II 21

We would not act as though others must fear and serve us, as is the practice of the wretched, perverse world. The world is drowned in blindness and abuses all the good things and God's gifts only for its own pride, greed, lust, and luxury. It never once thinks about God, so as to thank Him or acknowledge Him as Lord and Creator. (*Concordia*, p. 400)

Formula of Concord Epitome I 4

God created the body and soul of Adam and Eve before the fall. But He also created our bodies and souls after the fall. Even though they are corrupt, God still acknowledges them as His work, it is written in Job 10:8, "Your hands fashioned and made me." (*Concordia*, p. 475)

Formula of Concord Epitome I 6

In the same way, Christ redeemed human nature as His work, sanctifies it, raises it from the dead, and gloriously adorns it as His work. (*Concordia*, p. 475)

Formula of Concord Epitome I 25

The distinction between God's work and that of the devil is made in the clearest way by these terms. For the devil can create no substance, but can only, in an accidental way—with God's consent—corrupt the substance created by God. (*Concordia*, p. 477)

Formula of Concord Solid Declaration VI 10

We must also explain clearly what the Gospel does, produces, and works toward the new obedience of believers. We must also explain the Law's office in this matter, regarding believers' good works. (*Concordia*, p. 559)

Formula of Concord Solid Declaration VIII 85

But from the moment when deity and humanity were united in one Person, the Man, Mary's Son, is and is called almighty, eternal God, who has eternal dominion, who has created all things and preserves them "through the communication of attributes" . . . , because He is one Person with the Godhead and is also very God. (*Concordia*, p. 595)

TOPIC FIVE

Angels and Demons[1]

Engaging This Topic

"You believe in angels? You've got to be kidding!"
"The Bible teaches that there *are* angels . . . and demons."
"So you believe in harps, wings, pitchforks, and pointy tails?"
"Well, not exactly."

When you hear the word *angel*, what image comes to mind? Clarence from the movie *It's a Wonderful Life*? Tess from *Touched by an Angel*?

On the other hand, what comes to mind when you hear the words *demon* or *devil*? When you think about angels and demons, do you think of those comical creatures sitting on someone's shoulders—an angel in a white gown and wings and a demon with a pitchfork and pointy tail, each sitting on a shoulder? Some media blur the lines between angels and demons with conflicted figures like vampires and werewolves.

For many people, popular films, books, comic books, and other media are their only sources of information about angels and demons—if they believe in these creatures at all. Angels often appear on screen savers, book covers, and wall calendars as pastel-colored feminine virtues or chubby, winged infants, while demons may be pale, sinister schemers, skulking black mists, or twisted, monstrous creatures. But these are inaccurate portrayals of angels and demons.

In contrast, this chapter will share the truth about angels and demons using God's errorless Word. What the Bible says about angels, demons, and other related topics is vitally important to Lutherans because what God says about these matters can be trusted. As God's people, we want to grow in our understanding of what God has revealed in the Scriptures, so that we believe in what God teaches us about angels and demons and can share this knowledge with others.

1 This chapter adapted from *The Lutheran Difference: Angels and Demons*, written by Armand J. Boehme, with contributions by Robert C. Baker. Copyright © 2006 Concordia Publishing House.

Lutheran Facts

The Lutheran Church accepts the Holy Scriptures as God's errorless Word. Because the writers of that Word, under the inspiration of the Holy Spirit, wrote about bodiless spiritual entities created by God, Lutherans believe in angels. Good angels are spiritual beings that serve primarily as messengers and as ministering spirits both to God and to believers. *Angel* in Latin and Greek means "messenger," which corresponds to the Hebrew word that we see, for example, in the name *Malachi*, "my messenger." Lutherans also believe in evil angels or demons.

Jesus' coming was foretold by angels; His conception, birth, and resurrection were announced by them. Jesus received angelic ministrations after His desert temptation and following His garden agony. He frequently encountered demon-possessed persons whom He released from satanic activity and control. Jesus preached about angels and demons. The apostles also encountered both angels and demons in their ministries. Frequently, the Bible records angels assuming bodily (corporeal) form, taking on the appearance of human men to deliver a special message from God.

Throughout the ages, the Church's creeds and her liturgies and prayers have affirmed the Bible's teaching of the existence of angels and demons. Lutherans believe that angels serve God and human beings and pray for believers. However, on the basis of Scripture, Lutherans do not condone the human worship of angels or prayers made to them. These they reserve for God alone.

Angels and Their Beginning

"I'm an angel."

—Irish folk-rock drummer Caroline Corr

Claiming to be a (mostly) good or innocent person is acceptable in today's culture, even if the closest point of reference is a pure, holy spiritual being without any faults whatsoever. Such claims are prevalent especially in the public square. There, opinions about spiritual matters (and not simply God or Jesus) are so diverse that it staggers the mind. So we should not be surprised about the many opinions on angels and demons. Religious opinion is everywhere in this setting; religious fact is hard to find.

Diverse opinions about spiritual matters, including God, Jesus, angels, and demons, arise because people rely on their own human reason or experience as the sources of authority instead of God's Word. Human reason, unaided by faith, is totally blind to the truth of spiritual matters. It creates for itself a self-made and self-serving religion. For example, some believe that angels and demons either do not exist or, if they do, they are harmless (angels) or will only hurt the other guy (demons).

The Creation of Angels

Although the Bible mentions angels in almost three hundred passages, no one passage tells us about their creation. While Genesis 1 is silent about their creation, John 1:1–5 informs us that before God created the universe, nothing existed besides Him. Also, Genesis 2:2–3 shows that God rested from all His creative work on the seventh day. From these two passages, we learn that God created angelic beings sometime during the six days when He created "all things visible and invisible," as we confess in the Nicene Creed. If those who doubt that God created angels at all find no mention of them in Genesis 1, they should look at passages where Jesus, God in human flesh, confirms their existence (see Matthew 22:30; 25:31; Luke 16:22).

Psalm 148 begins with the Hebrew word *Hallelujah*, meaning, "Praise the Lord." This psalm depicts all of God's creation singing a great hymn of praise to its Creator, God. Note how "angels" and "hosts" (v. 2) are included with "heavens" and "heights" (v. 1), "sun," "moon," and "stars" (v. 3)—indeed, with everything else that God created. The implication is clear: God created angels.

Colossians 1:15–17 affirms what we learned from John 1:1–5, namely, that the pre-incarnate Son of God, along with the Father and the Holy Spirit, was active in creating all that was made. This includes angels. Nehemiah 9:6 teaches that God created the host of heaven, which worships Him. Angels are called "the host of heaven" (1 Kings 22:19) or the "heavenly host" (Luke 2:13). Therefore, part of angelic activity is to worship the triune God—Father, Son, and Holy Spirit.

In one of his table talks, Martin Luther said that he thought God did not describe the creation of invisible angels because God did not want people to speculate about it. In Acts 23:8 Paul says that the Jewish sect called the Sadducees denied both the bodily resurrection of the dead and the existence of angels. Some people today also doubt their existence. But denying angels' existence breaks the First Commandment, because such denial exalts human reason above God; the Second Commandment, because it besmirches the holiness of God's Word and calls Christ a liar; the Third Commandment, because it contravenes God's Word, the exact opposite of holding it sacred and gladly hearing and learning it; and the

Eighth Commandment, because it doubts God's Word and accuses God of being untruthful.

As Christians, we confess our belief in God's creation of the angels in the First Article of the Nicene Creed when we say God is "maker of . . . all things visible and invisible" (*Concordia*, p. 16), including angelic beings. The Creed reflects not only the scriptural truth concerning God's creation of the angels, but also the source of our forgiveness of sins, including the sin of disbelief in angels, which is found in the Second Article: "And in one Lord Jesus Christ . . . who for us men and for our salvation" (*Concordia*, p. 16).

What Does *Angel* Mean?

The term *angel* does not designate the nature or essence of angels but rather their office as God's ambassadors or messengers. The Greek word for *angel* (*angelos*) is also used for human messengers such as John the Baptist (Matthew 11:10).

We see angels as messengers of God throughout Scripture. The angel Gabriel told the Virgin Mary that she would conceive and give birth to the Messiah, the "Son of God" (Luke 1:35), whom God had promised in the Old Testament Scriptures. Following Jesus' crucifixion and burial, the angel's message to the women at the tomb was that Jesus had risen as He said and that they should announce this fact to His disciples (Matthew 28:6–7).

Isaiah 6:1–8 offers a beautiful portrait of Confession and Absolution. Seeing God in His temple, the prophet Isaiah is moved to confess his guilt in God's awesome and holy presence. Through the actions of the angel, God broke the barrier between Himself and Isaiah and forgave Isaiah's sin. The seraph, a type of winged angel, took a burning coal from the altar of sacrifice, pointing to the atonement secured by the shedding of blood. The angel's message of reconciliation ("Behold, this has touched your lips; your guilt is taken away, and your sin atoned for" [Isaiah 6:7]) brought God's forgiveness personally to Isaiah. This Absolution moved the prophet and enabled him to powerfully preach to God's people concerning the coming Christ (Isaiah 7:14).

Creaturely Actions

As created beings, angels do what all of God's creatures do—worship God. In Revelation 5:11–12, we see an angel reject John's worship of him and point to his own common servanthood with John and the prophets. He clearly exhorted John to "worship God" (Revelation 22:8–9). Angels are not to be worshiped because they are created beings just like humans, though without physical bodies. Worshiping God alone is what all of God's creatures do.

The First Commandment (Deuteronomy 5:7) forbids the worship of anyone or any thing other than the triune God. While portraits, paintings, statues, and special days such as St. Michael and All Angels remind us of God's special messengers, we should never worship or pray to angel. Since all people are sinners whether they worship angels or not, we all need God's grace and forgiveness in Christ. That grace enables us to join the angelic choirs of heaven in singing their songs of praise to Father, Son, and Holy Spirit.

Comparisons

Eastern Orthodox: "What are the *angels*? Incorporeal spirits, having intelligence, will, and power. What means the name *angel*? It means a *messenger.* Why are they so called? Because God sends them to announce his will. Thus, for instance, Gabriel was sent to announce to the Most Holy Virgin Mary the conception of the Saviour" (*The Longer Catechism of the Eastern Church*, questions 99–102).

Lutheran: "The angels in heaven pray for us, as does Christ Himself [Romans 8:34]. So do the saints on earth and perhaps also in heaven [Revelation 6:9–10]. It does not follow, though, that we should invoke and adore the angels and saints [Revelation 22:8–9]. . . . Nor should we divide different kinds of help among them, ascribing to each one a particular form of assistance, as the papists teach and do. This is idolatry. Such honor belongs to God alone" (SA II 26; *Concordia*, p. 267).

Reformed/Presbyterian: "Religious worship is to be given to God, the Father, Son, and Holy Ghost; and to him alone: not to angels, saints, or any other creature: and, since the fall, not without a Mediator; nor in the mediation of any other but of Christ alone" (*The Westminster Confession of Faith*, chapter 21.2).

Roman Catholic: "This one only true God . . . created out of nothing, from the very first beginning of time, both the spiritual and the corporeal creature, to wit, the angelical and the mundane, and afterwards the human creature, as partaking, in a sense, of both, consisting of spirit and of body" (*Dogmatic Decrees of the Vatican Council* [Vatican I], III 1; cf. CCC2 paras. 311, 328–36).

Baptist: "*Of the angels.* The angels were created by God to glorify him, and obey his commandments. Those who have kept their first estate he employs in ministering blessings to the heirs of salvation, and in executing his judgments upon the world" (*Confession of the Free Will Baptists*, IV 2).

Liberal: "The development of modern Christianity has been characterized by an increasing tendency to appeal to reason as a criterion of the truth . . . no element of religious faith or practice has escaped its influence . . . . It is not enough that a belief, ceremony, or institution have the sanction of authority or custom; it must secure the sanction of reason by proving its truth or its worth" (Errett Gates, in *A Guide to the Study of the Christian Religion*, ed. Gerald Birney Smith [Chicago: University of Chicago Press, 1916], p. 434).

Point to Remember

But the angel said to the women, "Do not be afraid, for I know that you seek Jesus who was crucified. He is not here, for He has risen, as He said. Come, see the place where He lay." *Matthew 28:5–6*

Who and What Are Angels?

An angel is a spiritual creature without a body created by God for the service of Christendom and the Church.
—Martin Luther

Some Christians believe that human beings turn into angels when they die. This is not true. As we learned earlier, God created angelic beings sometime during the six days of creation. While the Bible does not give the account of the creation of angels, in two passages it does describe the creation of male and female (Genesis 1:26–27; 2:7–24). Humans, comprised of both a soul and a body, are an entirely separate order of created beings. They do not transform into angels at death.

Perhaps some people do not understand, or do not believe in, the Bible's teaching about the bodily resurrection of the dead. Others may misunderstand Matthew 22:30, where Jesus states believers are "like angels in heaven," such as, in heaven males and females do not marry (as angels are unmarried). Some may misread that text, missing the word *like*, and think that believers become angels when they die and go to heaven. More comforting than the misguided notion that believers become angels when they die is the scriptural truth that at death the souls of believers join the angels and saints with God and Christ in heaven and look forward to the bodily resurrection of the dead.

Invisible but Present

What is the nature of God's angels, and whom do they serve? How would you describe this to someone who is not a Christian? Angels are spiritual creatures—creatures without physical, touchable, seeable bodies (Luke 24:39). While they do not occupy space and are not present in all places at the same time (omnipresent), they nevertheless may be at a particular place (e.g., Peter was visited by an angel in prison in Acts 12:7). Angels are "ministering spirits" (Hebrews 1:14) who serve "those who are to inherit salvation" because they are believers. This is one of the links between angels and the saving Gospel. God's good angels serve Christians—those saved by God's grace in Christ and who shall inherit eternal life and salvation.

In the Scriptures, angels frequently appear to believers when God wants to share a message. Genesis 19:1 tells us that angels can assume bodily form, for these angels were seen by Lot and by many other men in town who wanted to have sex with them (Genesis 19:5). In Luke 1:11–12, God's Word tells us that an angel of the Lord appeared to Zechariah in the temple and that Zechariah saw the angel.

God's Word also tells us that the angels in their assumed physical bodies "reached out their hands and brought Lot into the house with them and shut the door" (Genesis 19:10). The angels also took the hands of Lot, his wife, and his daughters and pulled them out of Sodom so they would not be destroyed there (vv. 15–16). Thus, though they do not possess physical bodies, God can provide angels with the ability to act as if they had bodies, including the physical attributes of dimension, touch, and strength.

God's angels are "mighty ones" (Psalm 103:20; 2 Thessalonians 1:7). However, God's Word does not say that angels are almighty in the same way that God is almighty. Whatever God-given gifts and abilities they possess, angels remain created beings subject to God. They are subordinate to God's power and Christ's rule (1 Peter 3:22).

While angels are able to do many things that human beings cannot do, there are things that humans can do that angels are unable to do as purely spiritual beings. For example, Jesus says that angels do not experience marriage (Matthew 22:30), because they are spiritual creatures without bodies. Lacking the physical bodies of human beings, angels cannot procreate. Hence, unlike human beings, all the angels that exist now were created sometime within the six days of creation. Since human beings do not become angels when they die, and since angels do not have little angel children, their numbers do not increase.

This verse also puts to rest the speculation some have concerning Genesis 6:2: "The sons of God saw that the daughters of men were attractive. And they took as their wives any they chose." Some believe on the basis of this verse that angels (a faulty interpretation of the phrase "sons of God") married human beings and had half-angel, half-human children or even giants. The context rules out this faulty interpretation, for it speaks only of human beings. Genesis 6:1 speaks of "man" and "daughters." The idea that angels married human women and had giant children with them is fiction.

Some friends or loved ones may tell us that they have had an experience with an angel. As Lutheran Christians, we want to be sensitive to those people. On one hand, we do not want to deny that such experiences can occur even today. (This is not Christianity, but rationalism, which completely denies the supernatural; see Hebrews 13:2.) We should exercise caution in this matter, since Satan can appear as an "angel of light" (2 Corinthians 11:14). Instead of searching for angels and placing our hopes on them, we should look to Jesus, "the founder and perfecter of our faith" (Hebrews 12:2), who in His flesh exercises power and dominion over angels (1 Peter 3:22).

A Unique Angel

In the Old Testament, we read about a unique angel called "the angel of the Lord." His uniqueness is seen in what he accepts from human beings that other angels do not accept. This raises the question as to whether this angel is something more than an angel. Where Scripture refers to "the" Angel of the Lord (not just "an" angel of the Lord) and especially where this Angel has an extended interaction with people, many interpreters have suggested that this Angel is the pre-incarnate Christ, the Second Person of the Holy Trinity. Although some debate exists concerning a few passages, the majority of the passages are clear on the issue, as we shall see in the following example.

The Angel of the Lord is also called "the Lord" (Judges 6:14, 16, 23). Gideon is told he will not die even though he has seen the Lord face-to-face. Unless special dispensation is granted, no sinful human being can see God face-to-face and live (Exodus 33:20–23). What the Angel accepts from Gideon is divine worship in the form of a sacrifice (Judges 6:18–21).

The name of the Angel of the Lord is "wonderful" (Judges 13:18). Having seen the Angel of the Lord, Manoah said, "We shall surely die, for we have seen God!" (Judges 13:22). Manoah's wife assured him that would not be the case since the Angel had accepted their sacrifice and had made them a special promise. Angels are created beings, are not to be worshiped (Revelation 22:9), and sacrifices are not to be made to them. Therefore, since this Angel accepts the worship and sacrifice of Gideon, Manoah, and his wife, He must be God. Otherwise, the First Commandment is being broken.

Choir Practice

Although human beings do not become angels when they die, believing human beings have a close association with angels. That association finds expression here on earth in the Divine Service. Worship services are, in essence, choir practice for eternity.

On the basis of 1 Corinthians 11:10 and 1 Timothy 5:21, Lutheran theologians such as Heinrich Schmid and R. C. H. Lenski have said that God's angels worship with us here on earth. Better put, in our Sunday Divine Services, we join with the angels in their heavenly worship. This is also implied in the Christian liturgy when the pastor prays, "Therefore with angels and archangels and with all the company of heaven we laud and magnify your glorious name, evermore praising you and saying, 'Holy, holy, holy Lord God of Sabaoth; heav'n and earth are full of Thy glory'" (*LSB*, p. 195).

Luke 15:10 tells us that the angels rejoice when even one sinner repents of his sins. Whenever we confess our sins and receive the forgiveness of our sins through Christ's Gospel, there is great joy among the heavenly host. It is true that we should be sorry when confessing our sins either privately or publicly, but then in Absolution we should be joyful in the full confidence that because of Christ's death and resurrection our sins have been fully atoned for. We are forgiven!

Angelic Hymns

The Bible records the actual hymns sung by angels on earth and in heaven. They correspond to those sung in the Lutheran liturgy.

> "Glory to God in the highest, and on earth peace among those with whom He is pleased!" (Luke 2:14)

> "Holy, holy, holy is the Lord of hosts; the whole earth is full of His glory!" (Isaiah 6:3)

"Amen! Blessing and glory and wisdom and thanksgiving and honor and power and might be to our God forever and ever! Amen." (Revelation 7:12)

Point to Remember

"Holy, holy, holy, is the Lord God Almighty, who was and is and is to come!" *Revelation 4:8*

Ranks and Number of Angels

The helmed Cherubim,
And sworded Seraphim,
Are seen in glittering ranks with wings display'd.
—John Milton (1608–74), *Hymn on the Nativity*

Martin Luther once suggested that there were ten trillion angels, one thousand for each and every person on earth. Other Christians have debated the number of angels that could sit on the head of a pin. Ultimately, we do not know the exact number of angels that exist because Scripture does not tell us. Also, the discussion about the number of angels that could stand on the head of a pin would be futile because angels are spiritual creatures that occupy no physical space except when God wills it.

Name, Rank, and Serial Number

In several places, the Bible gives us an indication of the number of angels:

The ten thousands of holy ones. (Deuteronomy 33:2)

Is there any number to His armies? (Job 25:3)

The chariots of God are twice ten thousand, thousands upon thousands. (Psalm 68:17)

A thousand thousands served Him, and ten thousand times ten thousand stood before Him. (Daniel 7:10)

But you have come . . . to innumerable angels in festal gathering. (Hebrews 12:22)

> And I heard . . . the voice of many angels, numbering myriads of myriads and thousands of thousands. (Revelation 5:11)

When the soldiers came to arrest Jesus in Gethsemane, one of His disciples drew his sword and cut off a servant's ear. Jesus told him to put his sword away and said, "Do you think that I cannot appeal to My Father, and He will at once send Me more than twelve legions of angels?" (Matthew 26:53). In Jesus' day, the word *legion* designated a Roman military grouping of about six thousand soldiers. Thus Jesus is noting that His Father could summon to His aid more than seventy-two thousand angels. This speaks not only to the immense number of angels but also to the intimate relationship that Jesus, God's only-begotten Son, enjoys with His Father. We can be confident that the angels are large in number, even if we cannot count them.

Some Christians have thought that there are as many as twenty-seven ranks or divisions of angels. They cite Romans 8:38–39; Ephesians 1:21; 3:10; Colossians 1:16; and 1 Peter 3:22. Some early Church Fathers, and even some Lutheran theologians, also believed this. While the word *angel* appears in Romans 8:38–39 and *angels* appears in 1 Peter 3:22, the other terms in these passages could refer either to (a) angels as a whole, (b) fallen angels, or (c) earthly powers active against Christ's Church. (In Ephesians 1:21, Paul uses the phrase "rule and authority and power and dominion" to refer to "spiritual forces of *evil* in the heavenly realms" without implying that ranks exist among demons.) Thus these passages are perhaps best interpreted as referring to all angels, not different ranks of angels.

The only clear ranking of angels that the Bible speaks about is the distinction between "angels" and "archangels." Daniel 10:13 and 12:1 describe Michael as "one of the chief princes" or as "the great prince." First Thessalonians 4:16 speaks about an "archangel," which Jude 9 identifies as Michael. From these verses, we can conclude that Michael is the only archangel.

We meet a specific kind of angel in Isaiah 6:2–6. This is the only passage in the Bible mentioning a type of angel called seraphim. Here they are standing above God, who is seated on His heavenly throne. The seraphim possess—according to this text—faces, feet, and six wings each. One of the seraphim acts in response to Isaiah's statement about his sin. Acting like a priest in the Old Testament, the angel uses tongs to remove a hot coal from the incense altar and, unlike a human priest, touches it to Isaiah's lips. The Absolution is clear: "Your guilt is taken away, and your sin atoned for" (v. 7).

In Genesis 3:24, we meet another kind of angel: the cherubim. This occurs after the fall in the Garden of Eden. While in popular art cherubs are often depicted as chubby babies with wings, the first ones we meet in the

Bible are fearsome spiritual creatures brandishing flaming swords. Artistic depictions of cherubim appeared in the tabernacle of the Israelites and later the Jerusalem temple. Apparently, while the seraphim possess three pairs of wings, the cherubim possess only one pair. (See Exodus 25:19–22; 26:31; 36:8.) Cherubim and seraphim are specific names for certain types of angels, not angelic ranks, as some have supposed.

The Throne of God

The God of Abraham, Isaac, and Jacob is King of kings and Lord of lords. It is only fitting, then, that He should have a throne. Several Bible passages describe God's throne, the mercy seat (cover) on the ark of the covenant, and the golden cherubim.

> So the people sent to Shiloh and brought from there the ark of the covenant of the LORD of hosts, who is enthroned on the cherubim. And the two sons of Eli, Hophni and Phinehas, were there with the ark of the covenant of God. (1 Samuel 4:4).

> And Hezekiah prayed before the LORD and said: "O LORD, the God of Israel, enthroned above the cherubim, You are the God, You alone, of all the kingdoms of the earth; You have made heaven and earth." (2 Kings 19:15)

> Give ear, O Shepherd of Israel, You who lead Joseph like a flock! You who are enthroned upon the cherubim, shine forth. (Psalm 80:1)

> The LORD reigns; let the peoples tremble! He sits enthroned upon the cherubim; let the earth quake! (Psalm 99:1)

All these verses speak of God being enthroned above the cherubim. This designation reflects the design of the top of the ark of the covenant. It was above the ark's mercy seat and in between the two cherubim that God would come to meet and speak with His people (Exodus 25:22). The mercy seat was an earthly symbol of God's gracious and merciful presence in the midst of His people. It was also a symbol of God's heavenly throne and of God's kingly rule over His people. God's heavenly throne, seen in Isaiah 6, is surrounded by angels. So the symbol of His throne here on earth, the mercy seat, is surrounded by angels as well.

So God is enthroned above the cherubim. But what do they do? Genesis 3:24 tells us that the cherubim with their flaming swords prevented sinners from entering the Garden of Eden after the fall, thus keeping impenitent sinners from having an eternal sinful existence resulting from eating the fruit of the tree of life. These cherubim exhibited God's wrath over sin. In

2 Samuel 22:11 and Psalm 18:10, we see God depicted as riding on a cherub. The image of God riding on cherubim reveals God acting according to Law and Gospel to bless believers and punish sinners. That image also recalls the ark, a visible manifestation of God's gracious presence. There His enthronement between the two cherubim above the atonement cover, or mercy seat, of the ark provided the corporate forgiveness for Israel.

We're in Heaven

Not only were artistic representations of cherubim prominent in the tabernacle of the Israelites, they also figured in the Jerusalem temple. These representations were highly significant of an unseen spiritual reality rarely seen by the human eye. In addition to the golden cherubim on the mercy seat of the ark of the covenant and woven into the curtain separating the Most Holy Place from the Holy Place, Solomon's temple had additional representations of these angelic creatures. On either side of the ark, Solomon placed two large cherubim crafted of olive wood (each was fifteen feet tall and each had a fifteen-foot wingspan). Cherubim were also carved into the temple walls and on the temple doors, and they graced the portable bronze carts used by the priests for ceremonial washing. As these angels truly surround God's heavenly throne, so they were visible around His spiritual throne and seat of mercy here on earth. The tabernacle and the temple signified God's gracious and merciful presence in the midst of His people. (See 1 Kings 6:23–35; 7:29–36; 2 Chronicles 3:14.)

In Ezekiel 9:3; 10:1–22; and 11:22–23, we see the cherubim that surround God's throne. Their presence around the throne of God is symbolized by the cherubim seen in the temple and tabernacle. Ezekiel is commanded by God to record the fact that God's presence and glory left the temple because of the idolatry and sin of the Israelites. As Hebrews 9:5 notes, these angels are "cherubim of glory." Their presence either in reality or in symbolic form reflected the presence of God and of His glory. When God's glory departed the Jerusalem temple, so did the living cherubim (Ezekiel 10:18–19; 11:22–23). Truly God's people could see the cherubim carved in the temple walls and conclude that if God's angels are here, then God is here also, and therefore I must be in the presence of God. Significantly, cherubim appear in Ezekiel's idealized temple (Ezekiel 41:18–25) to which God's glory returns (Ezekiel 43).

"The cherubim shall spread out their wings above, overshadowing the mercy seat with their wings, their faces one to another; toward the mercy seat shall the faces of the cherubim be" (Exodus 25:20). The cherubim constantly gaze at the mercy seat of the ark of the covenant. This is God's throne and the place of His gracious and merciful presence on earth. The blood sprinkled there atoned for the sins of the people (Leviticus 16:6, 11, 14–17). The cherubim look at blood sprinkled by the Jewish high priest once a year, which looks forward in time to another, final sacrifice and another High Priest. Indeed, as Paul says, Jesus, our Savior, is God's mercy seat (Greek: *hilasterion*; Romans 3:25), the full manifestation of God's presence and the only place from whence we receive the full forgiveness of sins, pardon, peace, and eternal life. The eyes of the cherubim, and our eyes, are turned to God's mercy seat, God's throne of grace, Jesus, our Lord. There we contemplate in deepest humility and adoration God's unfathomable love in Christ for sinners like you and me.

Point to Remember

> Then I looked, and I heard around the throne and the living creatures and the elders the voice of many angels, numbering myriads of myriads and thousands of thousands. *Revelation 5:11*

Good and Evil Angels (Demons)

> Hell is paved with good intentions.
> —Bernard of Clairvaux, as recorded by Francis de Sales

This proverb and its variants express human frustration about how our attempts to do good things often go awry. It also suggests that there is lurking evil in those seen as good. For hundreds of years this proverb has warned us about hasty, ill-thought, or superficial "good" intentions, desires, and actions that ultimately add to the misery instead of helping the situation.

During the last two hundred years, people added "the road to . . ." at the beginning of the proverb to soften the blow and to encourage forethought and planning. More recently, from comedy films to horror novels, stories about taking the wrong road out of haste, ignorance, or some other character flaw have dotted the landscape of popular culture. Most of us can recall taking a wrong road, whether on a literal journey or as a bad choice, and ending up in the wrong place or with the wrong outcome. Most of the time our stories have either a happy ending or at least an avoidance of total loss. However, sometimes travelers are not able to get back on the right road. Sometimes children and adults make fatal mistakes that we see on the evening news. A wrong road can lead to a place of great danger.

Which Road?

God's created angels faced a fork in the road. Everything was going fine until that point.

Genesis 28:11–13 and John 1:50–51 both indicate that angels pass between heaven and earth as if they were ascending and descending a ladder or a stairway. Keep in mind that angels are illocal; as spiritual beings they do not usually occupy space. The revealed image of a ladder or stairway helps the finite human mind grasp the enormous difference between angelic travel and our own. Psalm 103:20–21 tells us that besides offering Him prayer and praise, angels also do the Lord's bidding according to His Word. This includes God's will both in heaven and upon earth. Good angels are God's ministers of both service and protection, which will be detailed more fully in another section.

Genesis 1:31 tells us that God pronounced "very good" on all He had made. That includes the angels He created sometime during the six days. They were holy and sinless as was the whole of God's creation. Yet God created angels with such freedom that they could choose to disobey, which some of them did. Sin was not yet present in the Garden of Eden, Satan and the evil angels had not fallen, and Adam and Eve had not yet been tempted. That changes with Genesis 3:1: "Now the serpent was more crafty than any other beast of the field that the Lord God had made. He said to the woman, 'Did God actually say, "You shall not eat of any tree in the garden"?'" While Scripture does not tell us the exact time when some of the angels fell, it is possible that their fall occurred through this very act of violating God's created order through Eve's temptation. Or their fall could have been prior to it.

Christians traditionally have interpreted several passages to provide insights into the fall of the devil, known also as Lucifer and Satan. Isaiah 14:12–15 describes the fall of the king of Babylon, who also represents the devil. The Hebrew "Day Star" in verse 12 likely refers to Venus, which reflects sunlight at dawn to appear as the "morning star." A traditional Latin rendering for Venus is "Lucifer," light-bearer, which appears in the Vulgate (Jerome's translation of the Holy Scriptures). Lucifer is a false sun as the devil is a false god. The only true Morning Star is Christ (Revelation 22:16). Note in this passage the extreme pride of ascending above the "stars," which are traditionally interpreted as angels (v. 13); setting up a "throne" (v. 13); and becoming like the "Most High" (v. 14). The ultimate result of the devil's gargantuan pride, however, is Sheol, the underworld or hell (v. 15). In Ezekiel 28:12–19, the king of Tyre personifies the devil, who is depicted as a cherub in the Garden of Eden until "unrighteousness was found" in him (v. 15). In Ezekiel 31:1–17, the pharaoh of Egypt is depicted as a mighty cedar tree, felled in Eden and taken down to Sheol (vv. 16–17) with other cedars. This passage alludes to the devil's fall and the fall of the evil angels. It mentions Eden as well.

In Jude 6 and Revelation 12, we read about the wrong road taken by some of God's angels. Of those angels who followed the devil's rebellion, losing their positions of authority in God's realm, some were taken prisoner and will be held in hell until the Last Day (Jude 6). Others roam the earth. Louis Brighton writes:

> Here in Rev[elation] 12:4 the casting of the stars out of heaven to the earth dramatically portrays the dragon pulling other angels with him in his rebellion against God. A third of the stars were involved with the dragon in this rebellion. Whether one takes 'the third' as a literal number or as a symbolical number, it suggests not a majority, but a sizable minority of the angelic host. This is the only reference in the Bible which suggests the number of angels that the dragon took with him in his opposition to God.[2]

Prior to Christ's ascent into heaven, the devil and his evil angels were allowed into God's presence in heaven. Where are they now? We read in Job 1:7 and 2:1–2, 7 that even following their fall, the devil and evil angels had access to God's throne. Mark 5:12–13 and Matthew 12:43–44 show incidents of demonic possession during Jesus' earthly ministry, but they also show that of those evil angels, or demons, who were not bound in hell immediately after their fall (Jude 6), the remainder are loose on earth and are set in violent opposition to God, His creation, and His people.

In the Lord's Prayer, we ask that God deliver us from evil. How is this accomplished? The Lord's Prayer is itself part of the Christian's arsenal against the devil and his evil forces (the prayer is God's Word). In it we petition our loving heavenly Father for deliverance from evil. In his Large Catechism, Luther writes concerning this petition:

> Therefore, we finally sum it all up and say, 'Dear Father, grant that we be rid of all these disasters.' But there is also included in this petition whatever evil may happen to us under the devil's kingdom: poverty, shame, death, and, in short, all the agonizing misery and heartache of which there is such an unnumbered multitude on the earth. . . . So there is nothing for us to do upon earth but to pray against this archenemy without stopping. For unless God preserved us, we would not be safe from this enemy even for an hour.[3]

---

2 *Revelation*, Concordia Commentary (St. Louis: Concordia, 1999), 329.

3 LC III 114–16; *Concordia*, p. 422.

The Right Road

The above passages show that God's angels were faced with the decision to either go off on the wrong road with Satan or stay on the right road with God, their Creator. The following passages strongly emphasize this truth.

In Matthew 18:10, Jesus says that while they minister on earth, God's good angels "always see the face of My Father who is in heaven." Since sinful human beings cannot bear to see even a small manifestation of God's or Christ's glory (Matthew 17:6), this emphasizes the fact that the angels who did not fall with Lucifer are holy and do God's will. They perpetually enjoy the beatific vision of God, or eternal happiness, which we believers will enjoy only in heaven.

First Timothy 5:21 tells us that though the Scriptures do not detail in what their election consists, God's good angels that remained faithful after the angelic rebellion are now confirmed in their goodness and holiness. This means that the good angels can no longer sin, nor can they fall. They are God's own forever. This is a source of great comfort to us Christians, because it means that these servants of God always mean to do His good and gracious will for us and that they will never do us any harm. "Are they not all ministering spirits sent out to serve for the sake of those who are to inherit salvation?" (Hebrews 1:14).

The Wrong Road

The good angels remained on the right road, but some angels did not, including Satan. The world has never been the same since.

John 8:44 tells us that Satan did not continue to stand or abide in the truth. He turned away from God and His truth to a lie, and thus became thoroughly corrupted and thoroughly evil. In his instruction to Timothy concerning the qualifications for bishops or pastors, Paul mentions that the devil's original sin was pride or conceit (1 Timothy 3:6).

The rejection or suppression of God's truth (Romans 1:18) manifests itself in ungodliness. Pride rejects God's order and His Word (v. 20), which leads to sin. The evil results of pride were first demonstrated in Eden by the devil, then by Eve and Adam, and now by every human creature. Our only hope is our precious Savior, who came to destroy the devil's work (Hebrews 2:14–15; 1 John 3:8).

As noted earlier, some of the rebellious angels were confined in hell following their rebellion (2 Peter 2:4). Because they took the wrong road of rebelling against God, the ultimate destination of the devil and all his evil angels is the eternal fire of hell, from which there will be no escape (Matthew 25:41). However, those human beings who believe and are baptized shall be saved (Mark 16:16) and shall be among that great multitude in heaven crying out, "Salvation belongs to our God who sits on the throne, and to the Lamb!" (Revelation 7:10).

Comparisons

Many philosophical ideas compete for our attention when we discuss biblical concepts like angels and demons. Often Bible readers are not even aware that such ideas influence and color their interpretation of God's Word.

Rationalism: "We can figure that out." Rationalism rejects religious faith or dogma in determining truth and relies solely on human reason and analysis. Secular Humanism (which deifies the human person, human society, and its achievements) and atheism (which denies that God exists) are philosophically related to Rationalism. Rationalists would deny the existence of angels and demons because the concept of invisible, bodiless beings is irrational. Rationalists see God, angels, and demons as merely an expression of human culture and deep-seated needs.

Relativism: "Everything is relative." There is no absolute reference for the values human beings place in their beliefs or behaviors. As a philosophical theory, relativism has two inherent problems: either it is itself relativistic (that is, subject to change) or absolutist (by claiming there are no absolutes). Relativists would allow for multiple and competing authorities or sources of information about angels and demons besides the Bible.

Subjectivism: "Perception creates reality." There is no true reality apart from our perception. Objectivists, however, argue that there is an underlying reality to all things existing independently of our perception. Subjectivists would tend to base what they believe about angels and demons not on external sources of authority, but on their own personal experience or feelings.

Point to Remember

> In the presence of God and of Christ Jesus and of the elect angels, I charge you to keep these rules without prejudging, doing nothing from partiality. *1 Timothy 5:21*

What Do Evil Angels Do?

The devil made me do it.
—Comedian Clerow "Flip" Wilson (1933–98)

Human interest in the devil—and evil in general—sometimes takes a comedic twist. We see that here in the popular catchphrase coined by the late Flip Wilson. However, in reality there is nothing funny about the devil. He is very real. Demons are very real. Demonic possession is very real. And perhaps this is one of the devil's better tricks. By dulling our senses to the real danger he and his minions pose, we may be more willing to take the bait.

Why do some people downplay the danger associated with following one's horoscope, experimenting with witchcraft or Wicca, participating in pagan religious rites, or playing with a Ouija board? Sometimes the devil uses nonsense to snare people by diverting their hopes and their focus away from God, the true source of all good things. For example, the name "Ouija" is a combination of the French and German words for "yes," *oui* and *ja*. Yet the act of asking a plastic pointer to spell out answers instead of praying to God is idolatry; it is sin. Even though astrology and tarot cards are no longer considered to be a science, people still follow horoscopes or tarot readings to find answers instead of looking to God and His Word.

Witchcraft, Wicca, and neopagan rituals are a deeper step into idolatry. Wicca is a largely feminist, environmentalist re-imagining of older occult themes. For example, Old English *wicca* meant a male sorcerer; *wicce* (pronounced almost like *witchy*) was a female. Terms such as *Wiccan*, *wizard*, *warlock*, and so forth have different meanings and contexts today than they had in medieval times. The affinity of Wicca with rural English and Celtic mythology says more about historical social tensions than so-called "magick." It also shows that people frustrated with their conditions sometimes turn to cults that draw them in and control them by promising an alternative means to power, and, in some cases, an outlet for deviant sexuality. These movements, artificial and poorly based on ancient knowledge as they may be, nevertheless represent a deliberate rejection of God and Judeo-Christian influence in society.

In *The Screwtape Letters*, C. S. Lewis warns Christians against undue fascination with the devil and things demonic. The fascination with evil is undoubtedly the result of the allure of power, which appeals to sinful pride. Conceit was the devil's original sin (1 Timothy 3:6). Those who rely on horoscopes, experiment with the occult, participate in non-Christian worship, or play with an Ouija board delude themselves into thinking that such activities produce no ill effects. These practices violate the First and Second Commandments and are pathways for demonic influence and control.

The Results of Their Revolt

The fall of Satan and the evil angels had consequences for the human race. The evil angels seek to draw as many of us as possible into their rejection of our heavenly Father's Word and His grace.

Let's look at the steps taken by the devil in tempting Eve and Adam, and the relationship between temptation and God's Word.

1. Satan subverts God's order by speaking first with Eve instead of her husband (Genesis 3:1; God will speak first with Adam [v. 9], whom He created first).
2. Satan causes Eve to doubt God's Word (Genesis 3:1).
3. Her faith weakened by unbelief, Eve becomes confused about what God actually said, mixing truth with error (Genesis 3:3).
4. Satan lies (Genesis 3:4) about God's Word and thus commits murder, because Eve and Adam will first die spiritually, then physically.
5. Satan appeals to Eve's sinful pride, because she wants to be like God (Genesis 3:6).

In Luke 8:12, Jesus notes that the devil desires to come and snatch God's Word out of human hearts by doubt and deceit. Thus human beings do not believe the salvation God's Word reveals and are lost in their sin. The devil "cannot allow anyone to teach or to believe rightly" (LC III 62, see also 63–64; *Concordia*, pp. 415–16). The devil attempts to replace God's truthful Word with the doctrines of demons that deceive, lie, and teach contrary to God's Word, as well as "the commandments of men" (Matthew 15:9; see also Colossians 2:18–23), which, while sounding pious, are contrary to God's truthful Word (see 1 Timothy 4:1–3).

What has the devil's rebellion and the revolt of the evil angels brought into this world? By participating in the devil's rebellion, the serpent was cursed. In the midst of the curse, we hear the first Gospel promise: "I will put enmity between you and the woman, and between your offspring and her offspring; He shall bruise your head, and you shall bruise His heel" (Genesis 3:15). The woman's pain in childbearing was increased, and while equal to her husband, she would resent his headship and seek to rule over him (v. 16). The ground was cursed because of the man's abdication of his headship and participation in the woman's disobedience (v. 17). What was formerly a great joy for him, his livelihood, would now become burdensome toil (v. 19). Weeds, dangerous storms, hail, earthquakes, broken relationships, illness, disease, war, depression, death—all are the result of humanity's participation in the devil's plan to overrun and subvert God's creation. The devil's rebellion has brought deception into the world, as well as murder and death (John 8:44).

But God is not unaware of the evils brought about by Satan and his angels. God permitted Satan to attack Job by destroying all of Job's wealth. His herds of oxen, donkeys, sheep, and camels—as well as the servants who took care of them—were either carried off by raiders or killed. His ten children were also killed. The devil afflicted Job with terribly painful boils, which covered his whole body (see Job 1:13–22; 2:7). God allowed the devil to afflict a woman with "a disabling spirit" that would not allow her to walk upright or to straighten up (Luke 13:11–16). The Holy Spirit inspired Paul to describe his thorn in the flesh as "a messenger of Satan" (2 Corinthians 12:7). Paul used the Greek word for messenger, *angel*, for the demon.

When Christ taught that His followers would need to take up the cross to follow Him (Mark 8:34–38), He also included the assaults of the devil and the crosses we Christians bear. But with God's grace sustaining us, we shall gain the victory through our Lord Jesus Christ (Romans 7:24–25; 8:18–39; 1 Corinthians 15:51–58).

Throughout the New Testament we read of the steps the devil took in attempting to thwart our salvation in Christ. He still takes some of these steps today. The devil tempted Jesus to sin by serving Himself apart from His Father's will, by tempting God, and finally by bowing down to the devil and worshiping him. Jesus perfectly resisted the temptations of the devil and overcame him (see Matthew 4:1–11). His death on Calvary's cross destroyed the devil's power. The devil attempted to destroy Christ's work by having Judas betray Jesus into the hands of His enemies (John 13:2). However, the joke was on the devil, for this is exactly what Christ came into the world to do: to suffer and die in payment for the sins of all on Calvary's cross. The devil raises up false prophets and false apostles who twist God's truthful Word. The devil can also appear as an angel of light (2 Corinthians 11:13–15). In this way, the devil and his evil angels turn people from the truth of God to the doctrines of lies, heresies, and false doctrines, which deceive and destroy souls chiefly by leading them away from Christ.

The devil is a liar, a murderer, a deceiver, and a tempter. Zechariah 3:1–2 tells us that the devil is our tempter, deceiver, and accuser. First, the devil leads us into temptation. Then, by his lying deceptions, he leads us into sin. Then, after we fall prey to his temptations and deceptions, he accuses us of doing sin and evil. He whispers in our ears that we are unworthy of God's love, that we are such terrible sinners that God couldn't love us, nor would God want to save us.

> Then comes the devil, pushing and provoking in all directions. But he especially agitates matters that concern the conscience and spiritual affairs. He leads us to despise and disregard both God's Word and works. He tears us away from faith, hope, and love [1 Corinthians 13:13], and he brings us into misbelief, false security, and stubbornness. Or, on the other hand, he leads us to despair, denial of God, blasphemy, and innumerable other shocking things.[4]

Now that Christ has come in the flesh, what is the devil's status as an accuser of believers? Louis A. Brighton writes:

> This war, this casting of Satan out of heaven, took place as a result of Christ's victory and at his ascension and session at the right hand of God (see [Revelation] 5:1–14). . . . It happened when the 'Child was snatched up to God and to his throne,' that is, at the ascension of Christ. Apparently before Christ's victory and ascension, the devil could at will stand before God and bring accusations against God's saints. . . . But at Christ's enthronement at the right of God, Satan was forever banished from God's presence and his place in the heavenly court was taken from him.[5]

In a footnote, Dr. Brighton mentions that though Satan continues to make true accusations against the saints, these accusations no longer stand against the elect because they are justified (declared righteous) by grace through faith in Christ.

Deuteronomy 18:10–14; Jeremiah 27:9–10; Galatians 5:19–21; and Revelation 21:8; 22:15 forbid child sacrifice, divination, fortune-telling, using charms, serving as a medium or wizard, necromancy (consulting the dead or holding séances), false prophecy, dream interpretation, sorcery, idolatry, and sexual immorality, as well as any other occult art or pagan ritual. Christians are also forbidden from participating in non-Christian religious rites (1 Corinthians 10:14), because at their core is demonic activity (vv. 20–22). Scripture is clear that the devil desires to gobble people up (1 Peter 5:8), and that those who participate in such activities have one destination: hell (Revelation 21:8; 22:15). Unbelievers are held in bondage by Satan (Acts 26:18; Colossians 1:13). Their only hope is to repent of their sins and to believe in the Gospel, trusting in Christ's all-sufficient work on the cross, which is personally delivered to them in Holy Baptism (Acts 22:16; Romans 6:3–5; 1 Corinthians 6:9–12).

---

4 LC III 104; *Concordia*, pp. 420–21.

5 Brighton, *Revelation*, 334–36. See also Revelation 12:7–12.

Their Possession of People

Many have discounted demonic possession as an old wives' tale or something from a less enlightened age. But demonic possession was real in Jesus' day, and it is still real today.

In Mark 5:1–20; 9:17–29; John 13:2; and Acts 16:16–17, the biblical accounts demonstrate that those possessed by demons exhibited great physical strength, hysterics, self-harm, seizures, and convulsions (similar to a variety of medical conditions known today); that possessed individuals attempted suicide, betrayed friends, and had the ability to reveal arcane secrets. Generally, the following manifestations of demonic possession are recorded in the Bible:

1. superhuman strength,
2. attempts at the destruction of the human being who is possessed,
3. violent opposition to Christ and His people, and
4. multiple possession or more than one demon possessing an individual.

Of course, as God in human flesh, Jesus Christ is able to overcome such demonic possession, which He does through His Word.

Jesus delivered all those possessed by demons and freed them from the demonic powers that had overtaken them. (See Mark 1:23–28; Luke 4:40–41; Hebrews 2:14–18.) In so doing, Jesus showed His divine power over the demonic powers of evil. Jesus' disciples also were able to cast out demons by God's power in His Word (Matthew 10:8; Mark 6:7, 13; Luke 9:1; 10:17–20; Acts 16:16–18).

Their Torment in Hell

Sinful human beings may be led by God's Spirit through God's Word to genuine repentance and faith in Christ. They will spend an eternity in a new heaven and a new earth. There is no such hope for the sinful angels who rebelled against God. The devil and his cohorts will spend an eternity in hell.

The Scriptures are clear that all who do not trust in Christ for salvation will be cast into hell for eternity, where they will suffer endless torment along with the devil and all his unholy angels (Matthew 13:36–50; Revelation 20:11–15). However, the only cause for their damnation will be their own sin (Romans 6:23; FC SD XI 80–81; *Concordia*, p. 613). God does not want anyone to perish; rather, He desires all to repent of their sins and to trust in His Son for their salvation (2 Peter 3:9). Therefore, until Christ returns, the Church's constant message to the whole world is "Repent and be baptized!" (Acts 2:38–39).

In the end, the devil and his evil angels will be in chains, eternally tormented with fire and in the darkness of hell (the lake of fire and brimstone), which they recognize even now (Matthew 8:29; 25:41; Revelation 20:10). The just judgment they will receive was decreed after they rebelled against God. They were reserved for judgment in hell because of their sin. Unlike humanity, they were given no opportunity to repent and to be saved. Christ did not die to redeem the angels from their sins. Rather, He came to destroy the works of the devil (1 John 3:7; Romans 6:8–11; 1 Corinthians 15:52–57; 2 Timothy 1:10; Revelation 17:14).

Our God-given Victory

The sword of the Spirit is God's Word. The following are powerful Bible passages to help you when you are assaulted by the devil.

> No temptation has overtaken you that is not common to man. God is faithful, and He will not let you be tempted beyond your ability, but with the temptation He will also provide the way of escape, that you may be able to endure it. (1 Corinthians 10:13)

> But thanks be to God, who gives us the victory through our Lord Jesus Christ. (1 Corinthians 15:57)

> The Lord will rescue me from every evil deed and will bring me safely into His heavenly kingdom. To Him be the glory forever and ever. Amen. (2 Timothy 4:18)

> Submit yourselves therefore to God. Resist the devil, and he will flee from you. (James 4:7)

> Be sober-minded; be watchful. Your adversary the devil prowls around like a roaring lion, seeking someone to devour. Resist him, firm in your faith, knowing that the same kinds of suffering are being experienced by your brotherhood throughout the world. (1 Peter 5:8–9)

> Little children, you are from God and have overcome them, for He [Jesus] who is in you is greater than he who is in the world. (1 John 4:4)

Point to Remember

> The reason the Son of God appeared was to destroy the works of the devil. *1 John 3:8*

The Fall and Original Sin

It is impossible to overestimate the effect of Adam and Eve's disobedience. Their decision to disobey God brought sin, decay, and death into God's good creation. In Romans 5:12, Paul points out that "sin came into the world through one man, and death through sin, and so death spread to all men because all sinned." The impact was immediate, affecting human relationships with God and each other and tainting each person in every aspect of life. The disruption even went beyond to affect all of creation in ways that we do not fully understand (see Romans 8:19–22).

Hereditary Sin

Luther defined the affects of Adam and Eve's fall in the following way:

> Here we must confess, as Paul says in Romans 5:12, that sin originated from one man, Adam. By his disobedience, all people were made sinners and became subject to death and the devil. This is called original or the chief sin.
>
> The fruit of this sin are the evil deeds that are forbidden in the Ten Commandments [Galatians 5:19–21]. These include unbelief, false faith, idolatry, being without the fear of God, pride, despair, utter blindness, and, in short, not knowing or regarding God. Also lying, abusing God's name, not praying, not calling on God, not regarding God's Word, being disobedient to parents, murdering, being unchaste, stealing, deceiving, and such. This hereditary sin is such a deep corruption of nature that no reason can understand it. Rather, it must be believed from the revelation of Scripture. (See Psalm 51:5; Romans 6:12–13; Exodus 33:3; Genesis 3:7–19.) (SA III I 1–3; *Concordia*, p. 270)

Because our human nature is inherently corrupt, we cannot even fully understand sin's detrimental effects. Scripture must tell us this, and God's Law constantly makes it known to us, reminding us of how dearly we need the Gospel.

Fear of Death

When Adam and Eve heard God walking in the garden, they tried to hide from Him. This fear and guilt stands in stark contrast to the fellowship in God's grace they once enjoyed. It highlights the personal tragedy of their sin. When God questioned Adam and Eve, they looked for someone, anyone, to blame rather than accept responsibility and ask for forgiveness. After hearing their excuses, God explained the results of their crime.

God first spoke to the serpent:

> "Because you have done this, cursed are you above all livestock and above all beasts of the field; on your belly you shall go, and dust you shall eat all the days of your life. I will put enmity between you and the woman, and between your offspring and her offspring; he shall bruise your head, and you shall bruise his heel." (Genesis 3:14–15)

The humiliation of crawling in the dust punished the serpent's arrogance in disputing and defying God. Enmity replaced the easy conversation in which the serpent and the woman conspired to ignore God's command.

Turning to the woman, God said, "I will surely multiply your pain in childbearing; in pain you shall bring forth children. Your desire shall be for your husband, and he shall rule over you" (Genesis 3:16). Notice that God does not *curse* Eve, as He did the serpent, but describes the consequence of her sin. God's statement to the woman includes a thread of grace in His promise that the human race would continue.

God finally spoke to Adam:

> "Because you have listened to the voice of your wife and have eaten of the tree of which I commanded you, 'You shall not eat of it,' cursed is the ground because of you; in pain you shall eat of it all the days of your life; thorns and thistles it shall bring forth for you; and you shall eat the plants of the field. By the sweat of your face you shall eat bread, till you return to the ground, for out of it you were taken; for you are dust, and to dust you shall return." (Genesis 3:17–19)

These statements also contain elements of curse, judgment, promise, and grace: curse, since the results of sin would hammer all of creation; judgment, because Adam's work changes from joyous service in paradise into a continual struggle to survive; promise, because Adam's work would still bear fruit; and grace, as the human race would continue until God provided the redemption promised through the coming conqueror (Genesis 3:15).

Promise of Life

God forced the man and woman to leave the garden paradise and blocked their return lest they eat of the tree of life and be confirmed in their sinful state. The Scripture does not explain whether Adam grasped the long-term implications of these events. He would certainly learn the hard way as he tilled the soil, witnessed the effects of death and decay, and experienced the damage to his relationships with his wife and with God. However, Genesis 3:20 may give a hint of what Adam *did* understand: only after the fall into sin did Adam name his wife "Eve," which means "Living." Adam seemed to understand that, despite their failure, God promised them life and hope through the birth of a Savior.

What Do Good Angels Do?

To serve and to protect.
—common law enforcement motto

Sometimes the motto "To serve and to protect" is emblazoned on police cars or cruisers. The motto emphasizes that the police are to serve citizens in time of need and to protect them from criminals and evildoers. In the same way, God created His holy angels to serve Him and His people. Now they also protect His people against the evil one and his evil angels.

Most often we are not aware of all the things public servants, such as police officers, firefighters, hospital personnel, armed service members, and so on, do for us. We should be grateful for the faithful exercise of their vocations on our behalf. Likewise, we often are unaware of the service and protection God's holy angels give to us. We do not see them battling evil angels on our behalf, nor do we see them warding off evil or directing our pathways in life. But these things they do for us.

Servants of the Most High

Like our police forces, good angels are God's servants to carry out His will both in heaven and upon earth. And like our police forces, some of the duties of the good angels are pleasant, while others are difficult. This is especially the case when it comes to restraining and punishing evil.

God's goodness and mercy are extended through the ministrations of His holy angels as they protect God's people. God's angels warned and physically rescued Lot and his family from Sodom and Gomorrah, despite Lot's laxity in the matter, before those cities were destroyed (Genesis 19:1–3, 10–12, 15–16). The angels shut the lions' mouths, thus sparing Daniel's life and delivering him from the evil intentions of his enemies (Daniel 6:19–22). After the apostles had faithfully preached and healed many people in Jesus' name, the high priest in league with the Sadducees had them arrested. But the apostles were rescued by an angel, who opened the prison doors so that they could preach in the temple about Jesus (Acts 5:12–21).

God's holy angels also do things that we may find surprising, such as executing God's judgment on wickedness and sin. The ultimate purpose of the activities of the good angels is to protect God's people from evil. On the Last Day, angels will administer God's just judgment. In addition to rescuing Lot and his family, God's angels came to Sodom and Gomorrah to destroy the wicked town by raining down sulfur and fire from heaven. The resulting devastation was so great the town appeared as a giant furnace (Genesis 19:13, 23–28). King Herod was struck dead by an angel because he broke the First Commandment, allowing himself to be exalted as a god rather than giving glory to God (Acts 12:20–23). God's angels exact God's judgment on unbelievers and the devil. This is His alien work, that is, the work that God must do on account of His holiness and His Law, not the work that God wants to do on account of His grace and His Gospel. It is also an alien work for the angels (Revelation 20:1–3). Carrying out God's judgment of wrath on sin does not make God's holy angels evil or bad. God does not want anyone to perish, but He desires that everyone would repent of sin (2 Peter 3:9) and to believe in the atoning sacrifice of His Son (John 3:16; 1 John 4:9–10).

God's created angels ministered on behalf of Jesus before His birth, during His earthly life, and following His ascension into heaven. An angel warned Joseph, Jesus' earthly father, to take the boy and His mother to Egypt into safety (Matthew 1:20–21); angels ministered to Jesus following His temptation by the devil (Mark 1:13); and an angel gave strength to Jesus following His prayer in the Garden of Gethsemane (Luke 22:39–43). Other appearances of angels in the Bible during Jesus' earthly life are listed in a chart on page 174.

Angels also served and protected the apostles as they went forth teaching and baptizing. God's angelic messengers announced Christ's ascension and prophesied about His second coming to judge the living and the dead (Acts 1:10–11). The angel directed Philip to the exact location of the Ethiopian eunuch, a Gentile and the treasurer of the Ethiopian queen. After sharing the Gospel with the eunuch and baptizing him, the Spirit whisked Philip away for another important assignment (Acts 8:26–40). An angel appealed to Cornelius, a centurion, to send for Peter so that he could preach the Gospel to the Gentiles in Caesarea, which is in Philippi (Acts 10:21–33).

As we learned earlier, *angel* means "messenger." God's angels have brought important messages to people. The Word of the Lord, which is Old Testament shorthand for divine revelation, is often accompanied by the presence of an angel. The angel of the Lord, quite possibly the pre-incarnate Christ, proclaimed kind and comforting words to God's prophet. Zechariah was to relay this message about the return of God's people to the land and the restoration of their temple. Zechariah, whose name means "Yahweh remembers," proclaimed numerous prophecies about the coming Messiah, Jesus Christ (Zechariah 1:7–17). The angels announced the resurrection of Jesus Christ to the women at Jesus' tomb (Luke 24:1–6). In the Book of Revelation, God sent an angel to John to mediate the message about Jesus Christ (Revelation 1:1–3).

We have seen how God's holy angels serve Him on earth, but how do they serve God in heaven? The throne of God is in heaven, where angels both praise the Lord and serve Him according to His Word and will (Psalm 103:19–21). Angels worship the Son of God, Jesus Christ, just as they worship the Father and the Holy Spirit (Hebrews 1:1–6), or as the Athanasian Creed says, "The Trinity in Unity and Unity in Trinity is to be worshiped" (*Concordia*, p. 17). The angels praise, glorify, and honor Christ, the Lamb, and the Father, "Him who sits on the throne" (Revelation 5:13).

Companions of God's People

As they serve us, God's angels are our companions here on earth. The elect angels do what they were created to do—God's will. Christians have been given the gift of faith so that we can serve God. Angels help us to do that.

Angels have particular interest in the ministry of the Church, the proclamation of the Gospel of Jesus Christ for the forgiveness of sins. The trials and tribulations suffered by God's apostles are a spectacle observed by both the people of this world and God's angels (1 Corinthians 4:9). In Ephesians 3:8–11, Paul notes that the wisdom of God's plan of salvation by grace through faith in Jesus Christ for both Jew and Gentile is now revealed both in heaven and on earth. Even the angels—"rulers and authorities in the heavenly places" (v. 10)—have this wisdom revealed to them through the Church. Just as the ancient prophets diligently searched the Scriptures concerning the coming of Christ, so, too, do the angels desire to look into the preaching of the Church and its ways of sharing Christ with a lost and sinful world (1 Peter 1:10–12). God's Word tells us that there are times when we entertain angels without being aware of it. If anything, this should teach us to be hospitable at all times (Hebrews 13:2).

Protectors of the Saints

God's holy angels are present as we worship. They pray for us. They observe the struggles of our lives. They help us. God's angels guard and protect us our whole lives.

Before He told the parable of the lost sheep to His disciples, Jesus said, "See that you do not despise one of these little ones. For I tell you that in heaven their angels always see the face of My Father who is in heaven" (Matthew 18:10). While some interpret this verse to mean that each person has a guardian angel, at the very least we may say that God sends angels to watch over children. God's angels take special care of the children in His kingdom. Certainly, if angels have looked out for us while we are living, then they will attend to us when we approach the hour of death (Luke 16:22).

What will angels do for believers on the Last Day? When Christ returns and all the dead are raised by Christ's command (John 5:28), God's countless angels (Hebrews 12:11) will sound the final trumpet and will gather God's elect people from all over the physical world and from heaven to be with Jesus forever. Scripture is clear that the holy angels will accompany Christ at His second coming (Matthew 24:31) and that they will collect the godly and take them up to meet Him in the air (1 Thessalonians 4:17). First Corinthians 6:3 tells us that believers will eventually be the judges of angels at the second coming of Christ. And in Revelation 7:9–17, John describes all the hosts of heaven as the "great multitude that no one could number," which comes from "all tribes and peoples and languages" on the face of this earth (v. 9). The Word of God encourages us to share the Gospel with others so that they, too, would be our spiritual companions and would join us and the holy angels around Christ's throne for all eternity.

Angelic Appearances and Jesus

The following is a list of angelic appearances during our Lord's ministry upon earth, beginning with the announcement of His birth and concluding with the angels' appearance following His ascension into heaven.

The angel Gabriel announces the conception and birth of Jesus to the Virgin Mary.	Luke 1:26–38
An angel encourages Joseph to care for Mary and her unborn, holy Child.	Matthew 1:20–21
The angel and the angelic multitude announce the birth of Jesus to the shepherds.	Luke 2:8–14
An angel warns Joseph to take Mary and the baby Jesus into Egypt.	Matthew 2:13
An angel informs Joseph that it is safe to return with Mary and Jesus to Nazareth.	Matthew 2:19–20
Angels minister to Jesus after His temptation by the devil in the wilderness.	Matthew 4:11; Mark 1:13
An angel ministers to Jesus in the Garden of Gethsemane.	Luke 22:39–43
Two angels converse with Mary Magdalene, Johanna, Mary the mother of James, and Salome about the bodily resurrection of Jesus.	Matthew 28:1–7; Mark 16:1–7; Luke 24:1–7
Two angels appear to Mary Magdalene prior to Jesus' appearance to her.	John 20:11–14
Two angels speak to the disciples following Jesus' ascension into heaven.	Acts 1:10–11

POINT TO REMEMBER

But you have come to Mount Zion and to the city of the living God, the heavenly Jerusalem, and to innumerable angels in festal gathering, and to the assembly of the firstborn who are enrolled in heaven. *Hebrews 12:22–23*

Lutheran Summary of Angels and Demons

Augsburg Confession XVII 1–3

Our churches teach that at the end of the world Christ will appear for judgment and will raise all the dead [1 Thessalonians 4:13–5:2]. He will give the godly and elect eternal life and everlasting joys, but He will condemn ungodly people and the devils to be tormented without end [Matthew 25:31–46]. (*Concordia*, p. 40)

Augsburg Confession XIX

Our churches teach that although God creates and preserves nature, the cause of sin is located in the will of the wicked, that is, the devil and ungodly people. Without God's help, this will turns itself away from God, as Christ says, "When he lies, he speaks out of his own character" (John 8:44). (*Concordia*, p. 41)

Augsburg Confession XX 23, 25–26

People are also warned that the term *faith* does not mean simply a knowledge of a history, such as the ungodly and devil have [James 2:19]. . . . For devils and the ungodly are not able to believe this article: the forgiveness of sins. Hence, they hate God as an enemy [Romans 8:7] and do not call Him [Romans 3:11–12] and expect no good from Him. (*Concordia*, p. 43)

Apology of the Augsburg Confession XXI 8–9

Besides, we also grant that the angels pray for us. For there is a passage in Zechariah 1:12, where an angel prays, "O Lord of hosts, how long will You have no mercy on Jerusalem?" We admit that, just as the saints (when alive) pray for the Church universal in general, so in heaven they pray for the Church in general. However, no passage about the praying of the dead exists in the Scriptures, except the dream taken from the Second Book of Maccabees (15:14). (*Concordia*, p. 202)

Large Catechism III 65

If we would be Christians, therefore, we must surely expect and count on having the devil with all his angels and the world as our enemies [Matthew 25:41; Revelation 12:9]. They will bring every possible misfortune and grief upon us. For where God's Word is preached, accepted, or believed and produces fruit, there the holy cross cannot be missing [Acts 14:22]. (*Concordia*, p. 416)

Large Catechism III 99, 104

And lead us not into temptation. . . . Then comes the devil, pushing and provoking in all directions. But he especially agitates matters that concern the conscience and spiritual affairs. He leads us to despise and disregard both God's Word and works. He tears us away from faith, hope, and love [1 Corinthians 13:13], and he brings us into misbelief, false security, and stubbornness. Or, on the other hand, he leads us to despair, denial of God, blasphemy, and innumerable other shocking things. These are snares and nets [2 Timothy 2:26], indeed, real fiery darts that are shot like poison into the heart, not by flesh and blood, but by the devil [Ephesians 6:12, 16]. (*Concordia*, pp. 420–21)

Large Catechism III 112–13

But deliver us from evil. Amen. In the Greek text this petition reads, "Deliver or preserve us from the evil one," or "the hateful one." It looks like Jesus was speaking about the devil, like He would summarize every petition in one. So the entire substance of all our prayer is directed against our chief enemy. For it is he who hinders among us everything that we pray for: God's name or honor, God's kingdom and will, our daily bread, a cheerful good conscience, and so forth. (*Concordia*, p. 422)

TOPIC SIX

Marriage and Family[1]

Engaging This Topic

"The wedding was beautiful, wasn't it?"
"It certainly was."
"One thing I didn't understand though."
"What's that?"
"In the marriage vows, you Lutherans still say, 'Until death parts us.' Isn't that a little old-fashioned?"

The Bible begins with a marriage (Genesis 1:28; 2:20–24) and ends with a marriage feast (Revelation 19:6–10). Two books of the Bible—Song of Solomon and Ruth—deal extensively with the relationship of husband and wife. In the Old Testament, God is the divine Husband of His Bride, Israel. In the New Testament, Christ is the divine Bridegroom of His Bride, the new Israel, the Church. The Fourth, Sixth, and Tenth Commandments deal with the relationships created and nurtured by marriage and the family.

While the Bible affirms the value of persons whom God has specially called to a single life, it presumes and is permeated with stories about and instructions for man, woman, and child. It describes the joys and heartaches of husband and wife and the pleasures and the pains of bearing and rearing children. The central theme of the Scriptures—a divine Father sends His Son into the world to be born of a virgin mother—is the truth to which every page of Scripture leads.

Yet Christians, at least in the West, seem blind to this biblical emphasis and mute to discussing marriage and the family on the basis of the biblical text. For some, the authority of divine revelation recorded in the Bible and expressed in the created order has been replaced by modern psychology and sociology. Meanwhile, in the public square, the traditional birthright of marriage, family, and community has been traded for a mess of individualist pottage.

1 This chapter adapted from *The Lutheran Difference: Marriage*, written by Gregory Seltz. Copyright © 2006 Concordia Publishing House.

The Bible and the Lutheran Confessions have a great deal to say about marriage and the family. Luther's insight that marriage is not a sacrament but rather a gift of the created order had profound, positive implications for married life in the Christian West. If marriage and family could be viewed—as Luther viewed them—as God's gifts (and not merely personal rights subject to changing public opinion), society might see a renewed appreciation of marriage and the family.

Lutheran Facts

Lutherans believe that God instituted marriage—the lifelong, one-flesh union of husband and wife—in the Garden of Eden when He presented Eve to Adam. Marriage is a First-Article gift (the Creed), having to do with creation. As such, marriage falls under the jurisdiction of the state, not the Church. However, in many countries the Church's ministers can conduct weddings on behalf of the state, and they certainly can bless marriages that have already been solemnized before the State.

Lutherans also believe that the estate of marriage is a divine right established by God and cannot be refused or altered either by the state or the Church. Both the state and the Church are obligated to support and encourage marriage. God issued three commandments to specifically protect marriage and the family: the Sixth ("You shall not commit adultery" [Exodus 20:14]), the Tenth ("You shall not covet your neighbor's wife" [v. 17]), and the Fourth ("Honor your father and your mother" [v. 12]).

When and where God wills, married men and women are given the gift of children. Although God never commands the number of children couples should have, the refusal to have children for selfish reasons violates God's command to "be fruitful and multiply" (Genesis 1:28).

Lutherans teach that all earthly authority, including civil authority, flows from the office of parents. God established the family as the basic building block of society.

Foundation in Creation

In the beginning . . .
—Genesis 1:1

What is marriage? Is marriage merely a civil agreement between two (or possibly more) adults? Is it a relationship based solely on love or sexual attraction? Whatever answers our culture may provide, the Bible says that marriage is part of God's design from the beginning to grow and sustain healthy relationships, families, and communities. There's a lot at stake when people say "I do" and "I will." God instituted marriage in the beginning, and He still guides and blesses it today.

Adam and Eve

Moses writes that the creation of man (Adam and Eve) was different than that of the animals (contrast Genesis 1:20–25 with 1:26–31). Why is this significant? In Genesis 1, animals are said to come from the earth: "Let the earth bring forth living creatures according to their kinds" (Genesis 1:24). Of course, their life also consists in the creative Word of God that calls them forth, but in a different way than man. Man's relationship to his Creator is much more intimate. In Genesis 1:26, God says, "Let Us make man in Our image." God's investment in man as the crown of His creation is seen both in God's more direct participation in this part of His creation and in the unique status that man has reflecting God to creation in original righteousness (Genesis 1:27; Ap II 9, 15–22; *Concordia*, pp. 77, 78). Male and female may be creatures of the earth, but they are creatures unlike any other. This biblical truth is foundational to all discussions about personal human identity, intimacy, and gender issues, as well as personal responsibility and accountability toward other people and God's creation in general.

God placed His stamp of approval on marriage, and indeed all creation, as "very good" (v. 31). The marital relationship was part of God's plan for men and women from the beginning (see Ap XIII 14; *Concordia*, p. 185). It is important to remember that God deemed marriage "very good," namely, that marriage is a normative relationship for human beings in creation. Men and women were meant to be together, reflecting God's goodness, righteousness, and love, not only in their service to each other but also in their mutual service to all creation. While God exempts some from marriage by nature, incapacity, or through the spiritual gift of chastity (see Matthew 19:11–12; 1 Corinthians 7:7–8; Ap XXIII 16–22; *Concordia*, pp. 212–13), marriage remains foundational this side of heaven (see Matthew 22:30; Ap XXIII 7–13; *Concordia*, pp. 211–12).

Jesus Himself reiterates God's intent for marriage by claiming the original, creative plan of marriage as normative.

> He [Jesus] answered, "Have you not read that He who created them from the beginning made them male and female, and said, 'Therefore a man shall leave his father and his mother and hold fast to his wife, and the two shall become one flesh'? So they are no longer two but

> one flesh. What therefore God has joined together, let not man separate." (Matthew 19:4–6)

True, sin challenges God's original plan for marriage; some resist marriage because it binds them to another, while others attempt (and, sadly, succeed) in redefining marriage according to their own terms. They do this against God's Word recorded in the Bible and the creative Word still present and active (and observable!) in creation. But, even now, marriage is to be striven for, sought out as a blessing from God.

"Of the dust from the ground" (Genesis 2:7) and from "the rib that the LORD God had taken from the man" (Genesis 2:22) are important truths for understanding God's sanctified view of physical life. Why? These two phrases root any discussion about the spiritual nature of human relationships where it belongs: in the physical realm of life. In God's plan for humanity, marriage is a spiritual-physical relationship lived to its fullest in the world. In the Christian worldview, there is neither a loathing of the physical nor an unhealthy focus on it alone. Rather, spiritual and physical life for men and women, especially in marriage, is part of God's plan. This applies not only to the hopes and dreams of the couple on their wedding day but also to the fullness of their lives and their children's lives and for the blessing of the communities in which they live.

There are many religious and philosophical traditions that claim the physical or material areas of life are unimportant or even evil. Such was the case among the Gnostics and the Manichaeans in the time of the early Church. That's not the case in Christianity. While the Bible proclaims the depth of the reality of sin and evil, it also proclaims the original goodness of creation and God's redemptive action in the fully divine and fully human Christ not just for the soul but for the whole person: body *and* soul. Creation, Christ's incarnation, crucifixion, and bodily resurrection, the resurrection of all the dead on the Last Day, and the gifts of the Sacraments serve as examples of how God's love is expressed and enjoyed in the flesh. Contemporary views of marriage that focus on the disembodied rights of individuals apart from their created gender differences, or children manufactured in labs apart from real human relationships found in families, eerily reflect those ancient heresies.

How was the marriage of Adam and Eve to bless not only them but also all of God's creation? "God blessed them and said to them, 'Be fruitful and increase in number; fill the earth and subdue it. Rule over the fish of the sea and the birds of the air and over every living creature that moves on the ground'" (Genesis 1:28 NIV). It is important to remember marriage's purposes: the intimate love and mutual support of man and wife, the procreation of children (the building of a family of such love), and the restraining of sexual sins (Genesis 1:27–28; 1 Corinthians 7:2; Ap XXIII

7–17; *Concordia*, pp. 211–12). Genesis 1:28 tells us that God desired that His whole creation would experience that loving leadership in action. Look at God's last instruction there: "Rule over the fish of the sea . . ." *Rule* is a word for service in the Bible. Romans 15:12 tells us that Jesus' rule will be a cause for hope. So also is the family of humanity (male, female, and offspring) to be a blessing to the rest of God's creation as faithful stewards of what God has put under their direction.

God's Design

In Genesis 1 and 2, the Bible teaches God's design for human relationships. Even though sin mars the beautiful gift of marriage, we are to guard and teach marriage as the foundational human relationship. (Keep in mind that there are biblically legitimate reasons for people to live chaste single lives as well.) While God gives His human creatures a variety of relationships in which to exercise our vocations of loving service (mother, uncle, teacher, electrician, student, voter), only marriage encompasses full bodily and spiritual intimacy as designed by the Creator. Also, the Father has endowed no other human relationship with the natural capacity for procreation: extending through children the gift of life.

A healthy marriage extends itself into and influences positively healthy relationships between parents and children. Children who witness parents modeling appropriate behaviors—loving care and service—pattern their behavior and extend it to others. A home filled with love, proper attention and care, and loving discipline when needed is the basis not only for good children but also for good citizens. Stable homes promote stable children, who in turn become stable adults and productive workers, managers, caretakers, nurses, citizens, and so on.

Extended Blessings

Marriage is a relationship rooted in creation, part of God's plan for the human family. The institution of marriage "from the beginning" is intended not only to bless men, women, and children but also to bless all of creation. Fidelity toward marriage's foundational purpose undergirds a healthy sense of human intimacy, sexuality, partnership, family, and through the family, a healthy community.

Whether you are married, have been married, or will never marry, marriage as an institution exists for all. A positive view of marriage calls men and women to direct their love away from themselves and toward each other, their families, and, ultimately, their communities. Practicing such love helps us all become more mature in our care for one another, sensing more clearly what is important in life.

Marriage is also foundational to community life in general, so it is important to resist teachings that reduce marriage's benefits to the happiness of the couple alone. Selfish love is the antithesis to God's love (1 Corinthians 13). Selfish rule is the antithesis to God's servant rule (Psalm 145:15–16; Matthew 20:28). Marriage as an institution is not only to foster healthy, loving relationships but also to curb unhealthy ones (1 Corinthians 7:9–11). Even those who do not seek the triune God's blessing for their marriage realize the value of strong marriages and families to the communities in which they live. Companionship, intimacy, partnership, and family are needs that human beings understand *by nature* to be sustained in and by marriage (Romans 2:14–15; Ap XXIII 8–13; *Concordia*, pp. 211–12).

How, then, are all issues of sexual immorality, including sexual activity outside of the one-flesh union of husband and wife, truly actions that shake peoples' foundations? First and foremost, sexual immorality of any sort challenges the authority of the Genesis account and Christ's reiteration of it in Matthew 19. Male and female were created in God's image for each other, for mutual love and companionship, and for the purposes of family and the building of healthy community. All immoral lifestyles that debase the commitment that undergirds marriage not only shake society, but they also begin to destroy the opportunity for healthy love and intimacy between men and women. Leviticus 18 delineates who can and cannot marry, but the need for such prohibitions also demonstrates how quickly society can unravel into unhealthy, destructive behaviors once the sanctity of marriage and the family has been destroyed (see Romans 1:18–32). As such, this is a warning and an invitation for all to "let the marriage bed be undefiled" (Hebrews 13:4).

For Reflection

> When a man and a woman wed, they enter upon a relationship which in its origin and attendant blessings bears the stamp of divine approval. God, having created His living, breathing masterpiece, the first man, laid down this universal truth for all subsequent ages: "It is not good that the man should be alone" (Genesis 2:18); that is, it is not compatible with his highest happiness, his complete usefulness, to remain unmarried. This declaration of divine wisdom was then translated into divine action; God created for man a helpmate who corresponded to him physically, mentally, and spiritually. And when the first bride in all history was presented to the first groom, "the voice that breathed o'er Eden that earliest wedding-day" pronounced

its primal blessing. This divine benediction, the majestic "And God blessed them," has become the sacred pledge of happiness in Christian marriage.[2]

Point to Remember

We will exult and rejoice in you; we will extol your love more than wine. *Song of Solomon 1:4*

Unique and Distinct

Vive la différence!
—French saying

Are men truly from Mars and women truly from Venus? No, men and women are human beings from the planet earth! While the diversity and gifts of male and female are often misunderstood, it wasn't always so. God's plan for human beings and all His creation was for its beauty and wonder, its harmony in diversity. Men and women have always been unique and distinct, but such distinctions are intended as opportunities for love and service toward each other, not for misunderstanding and domination.

People often think that love is the fullest on a couple's wedding day. But our love for one another ebbs and flows. It often responds positively when emotional and physical needs are met. But such love does not often sustain a marriage. God's love in Christ (1 Corinthians 13) is the kind of love that cares for the unlovable. It seeks to love. It loves not only the friend but also the enemy (see Romans 5:6–8). Such love can begin to recapture the "from the beginning" essence of marriage that was lost in man's rebellion against God.

Male and Female

Genesis 1:27 says that God created male and female in His image, clearly affirming their equality and mutual worth in God's eyes. The Bible's view of male and female is that of intrinsic value. All discussions of the uniqueness of roles, gifts, or abilities must start with this basic biblical principle. Genesis 2:22–23 and Ephesians 5:28 also express the biblical view of the

2 Walter A. Maier, *For Better, Not for Worse* (St. Louis: Concordia, 1939), 17.

mutually high intrinsic value of both male and female as creatures of God. Any discussion about the biblical view of male and female must deal with their uniqueness with respect to each other and their equality before their Creator.

"Bone of my bones and flesh of my flesh" (Genesis 2:23) tells of the intimacy between Adam and Eve. The Bible clearly teaches that men and women were created for each other. Their uniqueness and differentiation is for the sake of the other and not merely for their individuality. Male and female may be unique, but such uniqueness was never meant for isolation. One can't truly appreciate the biblical fullness of what it means to be a man or woman outside the activity of serving another. Marriage is the foundational relationship where this can happen. Adam's declaration of joy concerning Eve is telling. Although Eve was surely different, her intimacy with Adam as well as Adam's with her is proclaimed in Adam's recognition both of Eve's uniqueness ("bone" and "flesh") and of their physical/emotional connection ("of my bones" and "of my flesh"). Each reflected the other. Each was fully human individually and yet was also made to be the spiritual, physical, and emotional partner to the other as part of God's plan. Anti-female or anti-male views of this relationship are based on power and the desire for control. These power plays are not based on the reality of God's call for men and women to be servants to one another as part of God's creation, nor in His purpose for marriage in the redemptive power and example of Jesus.

"It is not good that the man should be alone" (2:18) was God's declaration that His creative process for humanity was not finished with Adam. Genesis 1 and 2 speak about human beings before their fall into sin. Adam was perfect but alone. When God speaks of man's being alone as "not good," it directs humanity toward God's finalized creative purpose in male-female relationships: marriage. God's plan was that men and women would look toward each other in loving service. In fact, it's important to note in Genesis 2:22 that God "brought her to the man." She was God's gift, an opportunity for Adam to learn not only about himself but also about God's love and care for him through Eve. God's resources of life, love, joy, peace, and so on were meant to be shared. Adam without Eve is unfinished business from God's point of view. The original intent for men and women was to find their joy in each other as they not only served the other's needs but also as they reflected God's glory and honor in their stewardship over God's creation.

God defines Eve's relationship to Adam as a helper or partner. Adam sees Eve as part of himself. This helps us to view gender identity as an opportunity to serve the opposite sex. Genesis 2 demonstrates an order in creation. Adam is created out of the dust of the ground and Eve out of

Adam. The relationship between husband and wife is not merely a negotiated contractual agreement but rather a created reality in which men and women learn to serve each other as God intended them to serve. In such service to the other, the Bible shows that a healthy identity of male and female is to be found. Such an understanding of the created unity and diversity of men and women is the key to the biblical intimacy (the one-flesh union) that is built into marriages that honor such teaching.

Self-discovery

People sometimes seek therapy to "find" themselves. But marriage is still one of the best places for men and women to find out who they are, especially from God's viewpoint. Before the fall, Adam cried out that the woman was "bone of my bones and flesh of my flesh" (Genesis 2:23). Adam saw that Eve was unlike any other of God's good creation (2:19–20). This was what Adam learned also about himself as he saw Eve, the one whom God had given him to love. Eve, in her partnership with Adam, demonstrated the fullness of her God-given identity as Adam's helpmate.

Sin corrupted the harmony that existed in the diversity and uniqueness of Adam and Eve. Genesis 3:12–13 shows a radically changed relationship in which both turn on each other and begin to protect themselves. Their uniqueness in status and service to each other now, in the absence of self-sacrificing love, becomes a means for suspicion. Sexuality and intimacy are also now prone to be used as weapons against the other.

Despite the reality of sin, we can envision a healthy relationship in which husband and wife are truly different yet one. The New Testament speaks very matter-of-factly of marriage as a place for mutual love and intimacy (Ephesians 5:19–31), an institution to protect against immorality (1 Corinthians 7:2–5), and as an institution that can be reclaimed in the forgiveness of Jesus Christ (1 Corinthians 6:12–20). In Genesis, Eve was naturally for Adam and Adam for Eve. In the New Testament, our bodies are reclaimed for such service by God's redemptive love in Jesus poured into our lives through Baptism. Our bodies now can be "offered" again in His love to one another (see Romans 6:4–14; 12:1–5). The New Testament calls us to reclaim the original intention of the Creator in our marriages, daily reconciled to God and each other, as we receive and share God's love as His "jars of clay" (2 Corinthians 4:7).

Natural Love

Marriage's relational nature reflects but does not mirror exactly the harmony of God within Himself as three divine persons (one aspect of man being created in God's image). Sin not only destroyed that harmony between persons but also set male and female against each other. Marriages that are blessed by Jesus Christ are not only blessed to be happy but are also blessed to reclaim that love and harmony that was previously so natural.

In John 16:13–15 and 10:29–30, the Bible speaks about the relationship of the trinitarian persons: Father, Son, and Holy Spirit. There is a diversity of person in God even as He is one in nature, or essence. There is a mutual recognition of the uniqueness of the Father, the Son, and the Spirit, yet a oneness in essence, will, love, and purpose. There is a submission of the Spirit to the Son and the Son to Father, even as the Father relates to His creation in redemptive mercy. These realities in God's nature are reflected in the love that men and women have been created to share with each other as they learn to honor and celebrate their unique callings toward each other.

But sin often clouds the positive nature of male and female differences. As Christians, we have an opportunity to reaffirm those differences. Sin turns the unique honor of and specific service that men and women render to each other into competition, man against woman and woman against man. Christians can begin to affirm the unique blessings of men and women according to the Bible, honoring such things because God has called us toward such a view of male and female. Such picturing of men and women according to their scriptural potential (in the reality of real forgiveness and mercy through Christ's death and resurrection) actually enables people to become the men or women God created them to be.

We are taught today that marriages, indeed all relationships, succeed based on compatibility. The Bible's view of marriage is that it is the commitment to learn to love that sustains marriage and not merely a compatibility of interests and talents. In fact, learning to love that which is *not* like you is the core capability and capacity of God's love in Jesus Christ. In the Bible, *porneia* (Romans 7:2) concerns all sexual sins outside of marriage. Each gender was created for the other. Heterosexual immorality uses the opposite sex merely as an object to fulfill its desire. Homosexuality is the ultimate form of self-love: it rejects the biblical proclamation that man and woman were created for each other and that there is a profound oneness and healthy identity in service to the opposite sex. It may be true that on one level men understand men better and women understand women better. However, each are to grow in their understanding of male and female from God's point of view to learn to love that which is different from ourselves and to reflect God's love for us to others.

For Reflection

Christ's endorsement of matrimony is supported throughout the Scriptures. When the prophets of the Old Covenant sought to impress upon their own countrymen the magnificence of Jehovah's grace to Israel and the mystic union that bound Him to His people, they could find no more fitting symbol than marriage, the intimate union that exists between husband and wife. Long into the New Testament the same exaltation of marriage continues. Writing to the Ephesians (5:25) and consciously speaking of a great mystery, St. Paul compares the love which a husband bears for his wife to that self-effacing devotion with which Jesus loved the Church. And as the light of revelation illumines the closing pages of St. John's Apocalypse, the bride, the holy Church, gazes along the horizon of prophecy for the coming of the Bridegroom, Christ.[3]

Point to Remember

As a lily among brambles, so is my love among the young women.
Song of Solomon 2:2

Biblical Intimacy

Love conquers all.
—Virgil

The most precious words that a person can hear are "I love you." The most precious actions a person can see are those that concretely demonstrate "I love you." But love is not merely an emotion. It is a commitment of the will to do for the other person what God says is best. Love is even the willingness to put emotion aside for the sake of another. A love that grows from such a commitment allows space for emotional, physical, and personal intimacy to grow. When a person says, "I will" or "I do," the opportunity for real intimacy begins.

People say that the Bible is prudish about intimacy, especially sexual intimacy. But this caricature is incorrect (see the Song of Solomon; 1 Corinthians 6:18–20; 7:3–5). A few years ago, Dr. Ruth Westheimer became popular by counseling people on intimacy and sex. Dr. Ruth

3 Maier, *For Better, Not for Worse*, 75.

claimed that we needed to quit being so repressed (often blamed on the Church) and be more open with our sexuality and intimacy. However, such a coarse approach, coupled with a mechanical or functional view of sexuality and intimacy, actually limits the intimacy that a person can share with another. The Bible's view of intimacy is something that is built over time with willful commitment. When emotional and sexual intimacy is expressed within a lifelong committed relationship, fear dissipates, apprehension is removed, and intimacy is shared in the context of trust and love.

Leave and Hold Fast

"Therefore a man shall leave his father and his mother and hold fast to his wife, and they shall become one flesh. And the man and his wife were both naked and were not ashamed" (Genesis 2:24–25). Genesis portrays a man setting aside (leaving) familial ties and binding himself (holding fast) to his wife. This oneness is a gift that flows from the action of leaving and holding fast. The image is of something so intimately together that what was once two is now truly one. When Jesus quotes this passage from the Septuagint (the Greek Old Testament), He reiterates both the two-ness and the oneness, the great mystery of love in action within marriage.

"Leave" and "hold fast" speak of the refocusing of the man to the woman and the intimacy that is built when the woman receives such a committed love. "Leave" demonstrates the necessary separation from other concerns, now placing the needs of one's spouse above all other relationships. "Hold fast" speaks of the ongoing connection of that love as the man focuses his energy and his work on loving his wife and, by extension, his family. The wife's reciprocation of that love willingly entrusts her happiness and joy to such a spouse. Intimacy is something that grows in an atmosphere of committed love. Committed love demonstrates itself by leaving, holding fast, and responding. Whenever there seems to be a problem in marriage, one needs to refer to these two actions: leaving and holding fast. If these are violated, the oneness and harmony in marriage that God desires is seriously compromised.

The marriage relationship, the context for a deep emotional, spiritual, and sexual intimacy, begins with commitment. "Leave" and "hold fast" are actions of the will, just like the marriage vows: the "I dos" or "I wills." In essence, both are promises to continually practice such love in the bonds of marriage.

In Matthew 19, Jesus reiterates that male and female were created for each other. "What therefore God has joined together" (v. 6) is an aspect of marriage from the beginning. In Matthew 19, the people challenging Jesus viewed marriage as a disposable partnership. Jesus not only corrects such a misunderstanding ("from the beginning it [divorce] was not so" [v. 8]), but He also teaches the depth of the intimacy lost when marriages are torn apart. His warning, "What therefore God has joined together, let not man separate," compels us to remember that while divorce is sometimes the lesser of two evils (when compared with adultery or abandonment), something very significant is lost. Those who take divorce lightly, almost practicing serial divorce, begin to scar the heart's capacity for intimacy, making that heart more and more callous.

The Bible can't get more down to earth and practical than Paul's instructions to the Corinthians concerning marriage (see 1 Corinthians 7:1–7). God's desire for man and wife is to be so certainly connected to Him by faith and so specifically directed to each other that even their bodies are completely at the disposal of the other. Such a physical availability for each other has to be rooted in more than our best intentions. It is rooted in God's sense of humanity both as the apex of His creation and as full recipients of His gracious mercy. When men's and women's identities are rooted in God's perspective of themselves, such confidence can begin to cause both men and women to submit themselves in loving service to another's needs.

In Genesis, marriage creates the opportunity for physical and spiritual intimacy. In 1 Corinthians 7, marriage helps remedy sinful desire. The Bible again demonstrates itself as both a book of grace and a book of realism. It is true that marriage provides the occasion for intimacy, especially healthy sexual intimacy. But the Bible is very realistic about the depth of sin, its rebelliousness toward God and toward neighbor. It realizes that love is often lost in lust, that desire to have the other often trumps the desire to serve one another. Marriage, then, is an ideal to strive for as well as a relational remedy for men and women's inability to focus on the loving work that needs to be done for intimacy to thrive.

Loving Commitment

The Bible teaches that intimacy flows from commitment; it does not precede it. Cohabitation destroys real intimacy by putting the actions of physical intimacy before lifelong commitment. It makes us physically and emotionally vulnerable to those who have yet to say, "I will love you," "I will learn to love you," and "I do." Nothing more destructive can happen to intimacy than to give oneself over and over again to those who by their actions are saying, "I love you only when you're worth it to me, only when you prove it to me."

Leaving father and mother and holding fast to one's spouse reorders one's relationships in their proper hierarchy. It's not that the extended family is unimportant or that other friendships are to be dispensed with. Rather, marriage requires that all relationships be ordered under the most important human relationship: the relationship to one's spouse. All other relationships are to be judged according to how they help us be the husband or the wife, the father or the mother, that God intends for us to be. Honoring our husband or loving our wife above all other earthly relationships and resisting the temptation to seek an intimacy elsewhere than in our marriage is God's way of keeping the bonds of marriage strong and intimacy intact.

Commitment Comes First

Biblical intimacy is born of a commitment to learn how to love another as he or she needs to be loved. Intimacy is a gift that flows from two actions of one's will: leaving and holding fast.

Such a commitment is to be lifelong. Marriage is that God-ordained relationship of commitment, fidelity, and service that gives a man and a woman the opportunity and the space for such intimacy to grow.

Romance may be the spark that ignites the flame of committed love, but committed love is the fuel that allows romance to be rekindled again and again. Romance is the joy of doing the little things that make our spouses feel loved and cared for. Romance is the up-front desire to love. Mature love is always open to the joys of romance repeatedly rekindled. In fact, all the little romantic things spouses do for each other are like the drops of glue that bond two objects together as one. Leaving/holding-fast love is always willing to start afresh, never taking the blessing of a loving spouse for granted.

The Bible says that sexual sins are especially harmful because they are sins a person commits "against his own body" (1 Corinthians 6:18). This also applies to the embodied oneness of husband and wife. The actions of intimacy in sexual intercourse do not merely solicit pleasure. The spiritual, emotional, and intimate oneness provided only through a pledge of lifelong fidelity should properly precede the physical intimacy of sexual intercourse. Paul's warning against being "joined to a prostitute" is that there is an intimacy there that can't be ignored (1 Corinthians 6:16). Such an intimacy debauched by lack of commitment and selfish desire for sexual pleasure apart from a commitment to one's spouse, or completely closed to the possibility of procreating new life, has ramifications not only for the body and spirit of the individual but also for the oneness of the marriage body. Lack of commitment attacks the oneness of the spirit-flesh unity of husband and wife. Immorality and adultery with another, or even self-centered sexual pleasure for oneself alone, militates against the oneness God desires to give people who seek His blessing of marriage.

For Reflection

> Because marriage comes from God above and not from man or beast below, it involves moral, not merely physical, problems. A sin against the commandment of purity is a sin against God, not simply the outraging of convention, the thoughtlessness of youth, the evidence of bad taste. The Savior tells us that, when God's children are joined in wedlock, they are united by Him, and beneath the evident strength and love that this divine direction promises is an ominous warning. Those who tamper with God's institution have lighted the fuse to the explosive of retributive justice. Marriage is so holy that of all social sins its violation invokes the most appalling consequences. . . . Throughout history red warnings mark the final record of devastated nations that forgot the divine origin of marriage and its holiness.[4]

Point to Remember

My beloved is mine, and I am his. *Song of Solomon 2:16*

Exercising Faith and Love

> What God has joined together, let no one put asunder.
> —from the marriage rite (*LSB*, p. 277)

It has been said that in marriage the husband is the head and the wife is the heart. Paul also uses biological terms when he refers to the husband as the head and the wife as the body. Just as no human being could survive with only a head (absent a body) or only a body (without a head), no marriage can survive without the healthy participation and mutual support of both husband and wife.

Our culture may be beginning to realize that the complementary qualities of men and women are good. The '60s tried to establish the human being as androgynous, as if men and women weren't truly unique. While our society may have begun to remedy inequalities between the sexes, at the same time it appears to have overlooked, diminished, or dismissed the

4 Maier, *For Better, Not for Worse*, 76–77.

unique gifts of male and female. The Bible encourages us to look at the unique and complementary differences created by our heavenly Father as opportunities to serve one another in love within marriage. Love is an exercise.

Mutual Submission, Submission, and Love

> Look carefully then how you walk, not as unwise but as wise, making the best use of the time, because the days are evil. Therefore do not be foolish, but understand what the will of the Lord is. And do not get drunk with wine, for that is debauchery, but be filled with the Spirit, addressing one another in psalms and hymns and spiritual songs, singing and making melody to the Lord with your heart, giving thanks always and for everything to God the Father in the name of our Lord Jesus Christ, submitting to one another out of reverence for Christ. (Ephesians 5:15–21)

It is important to remember that this passage concerns the mutual submission that all believers offer to one another through the work of the Holy Spirit (see Galatians 3:26–29). The Bible emphasizes the mutual submission of believers who, under the inspiration of the Holy Spirit, serve one another in love. Such submissions are acts of the will and commitments to love others as we ourselves were first loved by Christ (1 John 4:7–12, 19). In Christ, we are all "sons of God," "one in Christ," "Abraham's offspring," and "heirs according to promise" (Galatians 3:26–29). Nevertheless, our equality before God in Christ, and the mutual submission we owe to each other, does not destroy ordered social, relational, or sexual distinctions; rather, it transcends them.

This passage also directs us to the biblical focus of loving Christian service to others. Marriage is not only an exercise of love, it is also an exercise of faith. "Out of reverence for Christ" (Ephesians 5:21) is the key to understanding the inter-Christian relationships that have been redeemed and restored for the purposes that God intends. Such reverence sees Christ as the power source, the ultimate reference point in the relationship. In Christ, believers serve one another in love not simply out of respect for one another, but in full view of the gracious relationship they have received through Christ's atoning sacrifice and glorious resurrection. Freed from the power of sin through His blood, the Christian husband and wife exercise both love *and* faith. As we will see later, Christ liberates and enables both husband and wife to enjoy their created and ordered roles and responsibilities in faith-filled, loving service to each other.

Some people see relationships, including marriages, as fifty-fifty propositions in which each person does his or her fair share. Experience proves that such expectations are unrealistic and that relationships based on such expectations will not last. The sustaining power for healthy gender roles and healthy marriages is God our Father, through faith in His Son, by the Spirit's power (see 1 Corinthians 11:11–12). When Christ becomes the reverence point of our loving service, we start asking questions such as "How may I love my neighbor?" At work that becomes "How may I serve my employer?" In marriage it is "How may I serve my wife?" or "How may I serve my husband?"

And as we think about loving service to others, we move to the next, and perhaps more controversial, section of Ephesians:

> Wives, submit to your own husbands, as to the Lord. For the husband is the head of the wife even as Christ is the head of the church, His body, and is Himself its Savior. Now as the church submits to Christ, so also wives should submit in everything to their husbands. Husbands, love your wives, as Christ loved the church and gave Himself up for her, that He might sanctify her, having cleansed her by the washing of water with the word, so that He might present the church to Himself in splendor, without spot or wrinkle or any such thing, that she might be holy and without blemish. In the same way husbands should love their wives as their own bodies. He who loves his wife loves himself. For no one ever hated his own flesh, but nourishes and cherishes it, just as Christ does the church, because we are members of His body. "Therefore a man shall leave his father and mother and hold fast to his wife, and the two shall become one flesh." This mystery is profound, and I am saying that it refers to Christ and the church. However, let each one of you love his wife as himself, and let the wife see that she respects her husband. (Ephesians 5:22–33)

Note how the wife is to "submit" to her husband (vv. 22–24) and how the husband is to "love" his wife in a wholly self-sacrificial way (vv. 25–30). Their actions toward each other are different but complementary. Paul transitions from speaking about the mutual submission believers owe one another in Christ (v. 21) to the submission a wife offers her husband (v. 22; see also Titus 2:4–5; 1 Peter 3:1–6), who is her "head" (v. 23; see also 1 Corinthians 11:3). The equality of man and wife before God in Christ is not lost in this submission, however. For his part, the husband is to model his service toward his wife ("love" [vv. 25, 28, 33]) based on Christ's exemplary service to the Church, which included giving up His own life. The extent of this loving service is even more than the wife is required to do. The wife is the husband's "body" (vv. 28–29; see also 1 Peter 3:7; Colossians 3:19), inferring that his own healthy existence depends upon his full, loving, caring support of her both spiritually and bodily.

What does the Bible mean when it discusses headship (see Matthew 20:25–28; Ephesians 5:25, 28; 1 John 3:16, 18)? Headship is frequently misunderstood as a "who's in charge and who gets to give the orders" proposition. That is not the way of Christian headship. The Greek word *kephale* is used here, and it doesn't mean the "status or position of leader." Rather, *kephale* is a field commander, the one who goes into battle first and who leads by example, even to the point of risking his own life (self-sacrificial love). Such headship entails being ultimately accountable for all whom one leads and serves. The husband and father is accountable to God for how his wife and children are loved, cared for, and served. There are both temporal (Proverbs 29:15; Colossians 3:21) and spiritual (1 Peter 3:7) consequences for husbands and fathers who do not fulfill their duties.

The man is the head and the wife is the body in the marriage relationship (see Genesis 2:18–23; Proverbs 31:10–31). Headship and bodyship have different emphases, different ordered roles to play within the marriage. While the Scriptures indicate the created, redeemed, and sanctified equality of man and woman in God's eyes and according to original righteousness (the "image of God" in Genesis 1:27), the woman was created as "a helper fit for" the man (Genesis 2:18, 20). Without her, it is "not good" for him (2:18), but with her it is "very good" (1:31). In marriage, the wife has a God-created, God-blessed role to play as the recipient of the husband's self-sacrificial love. Proverbs 31:10–31 details the inexpressible value of a wife of noble character, one who fears the Lord (v. 30).

In 1 Peter 3:1–9, the apostle demonstrates how the complementary duties of husband and wife toward each other are supportive and affirming. His phrase "heirs with you of the grace of life" (v. 7) helps define the ultimate purpose of marriage lived out in God's grace. Marriage satisfies body and soul, provides for mutual love and support, and, when and where God wills, results in the gift of children. More than that, in the Christian marriage, husband and wife point to the "mystery" of Christ and the Church (Ephesians 5:31–32). "Heirs with you of the grace of life" shows that in marriage God's grace and forgiveness in Christ are both given and received by husband and wife, who serve each other in love, enabled by God's love in Christ.

Love in Action

The Bible teaches that husbands and wives should serve each other in faith and love because each is unique (and needing forgiveness as well). Marriage is an exciting opportunity to exercise the many facets of love, which flow from faith. It is an adventure of seeing what is and what yet can be in one's marriage. Marriage encompasses the joy of knowing that the fires of romance may ignite at many different times, but they burn most brightly in the actions of committed, loving service to each other, out of reverence for Christ.

Submission is an act of the will to serve another for Christ—a strength rather than a weakness. *Submission* means to commit oneself to serve just as Christ serves us, exercising God's unlimited love in Christ. We readily submit to the advice of our doctors, the direction of our employer, the instruction of our teacher, and to the laws of our government. Submission is simply part of an ordered existence and should not necessarily be construed negatively.

Learning to Love

People say that compatibility is the key to a relationship. While surely helpful, the Bible actually speaks about love as the commitment to serve a person unique and distinct from you. Service toward one's spouse is not merely an act of love but also an exercise of faith in the Christ who fearfully and wonderfully created man as "male and female" for each other (Genesis 1; Matthew 19:5–6). Through faith in our Savior, husband and wife are enabled to practice His forgiving love in marriage.

The mutual submission (Ephesians 5:21) of all believers out of reverence for Christ is a prelude to the self-sacrificial love husbands owe their wives, and the submission wives owe their husbands. Christ has reclaimed the relationship that Adam and Eve shared in the garden prior to their sin. "Submitting to one another" (Ephesians 5:21) not only describes the "what" of our actions, but it also describes the "to whom": our neighbor. The focal point of reverence (Jesus) makes mutual submission happen. The promise of this passage is that God's love is at work in our relationships in such a way that we not only are dependent on Him, but we also are bonded to each other. God, who loves us intimately in Christ, deepens our love for Him and for one another through His Means of Grace. Our confidence, which comes from Christ, means that one's care for one's spouse is given freely (Matthew 10:8). In Christ, a husband's self-sacrificial love and a wife's submission to her husband reclaim the interpersonal relationship enjoyed by Adam and Eve in the Garden of Eden before it was lost through the fall into sin.

A man learns to be a man especially by serving his wife in a self-sacrificial way. A woman learns to be a woman especially by submitting to the service of such a man. Attempts at self-actualization and renewed self-worth fruitlessly search for meaning through endless self-analyzing or narcissistic activities. In contrast, the Bible shows that blessings flow through faith in Christ and are extended through one's service to others. The marriage relationship of husband and wife is the place where such exercising of faith and love is highly blessed to the point of a man more fully realizing his masculinity and a woman, her femininity, within the context of that marriage. Knowing this surely helps us to become the man or the woman that God desires us to be.

For Reflection

> When at Calvary, all history's holy of holies, we pause to survey the extent of Christ's devotion to the Church, we bow before a love that came to give rather than to take, to serve instead of being served, a love that loved until the end, that bitter end when, in the greatest sacrifice of which even divine mercy could conceive, Christ died that His Church might live. By the impulse of this divine love the discussion of the term "obey" becomes more academic than actual in any truly Christian marriage. Glorifying Christ, the husband will be impelled to cherish his wife with an intense affection, to acknowledge her virtues and accomplishments, to minimize her frailties, to perform the many services of love by working for her, providing for her, living for her, and, if necessary, even dying for her, as Christ gave Himself for the Church.[5]

Point to Remember

Eat, friends, drink, and be drunk with love! *Song of Solomon 5:1*

More than Romance

> Love is blind.
>
> —Jessica, in Shakespeare's *The Merchant of Venice*

Marriage isn't merely romance? Impossible! Whoever heard of such a thing! Properly speaking, marriage is about love: the joyful, heartfelt, persevering, committed, "willing to learn" love practiced by folks who can't wait to see what this is all about. Romance may kindle and rekindle that flame, but only love sustains it.

Dietrich Bonhoeffer noted that marriage isn't merely a personal issue; it is an office. Marriage cannot be reduced to the love that one has for another. Rather, the opposite is true. Marriage sustains the love experienced

5 Maier, *For Better, Not for Worse*, 464–65.

and expressed in marriage. Marriage (a gift from God) is meant to create and sustain love. Love is not a feeling; above all it is a commitment, an act of will to serve another rather than oneself. This is the *agape* love that ultimately is God's alone. We can never manufacture such love disconnected from God. However, through faith in Christ, God does indeed share *agape* love with us, and we in turn share *agape* love with others. In the modern mind, where marriage is anything we want it to be and commitment is optional, one wonders if such a love can even be imagined anymore. It is telling that many today believe that long-term marriages are almost extinct, something that existed only in the past. Could past generations have seen such love as possible for all because they viewed marriage as necessary and sacred?

Christ and His Bride

Consider again the passage from Ephesians: "'Therefore a man shall leave his father and mother and hold fast to his wife, and the two shall become one flesh.' This mystery is profound, and I am saying that it refers to Christ and the church" (5:31–32). Paul compares the relationship of husband and wife to Christ and the Church. The marriage relationship is not merely for our individual happiness. It reflects something about God's love to us, just as God's love for the world—especially His Church—teaches us about the purpose of our love for one another. Obviously, the difference between our love and God's love is vast, even incomprehensibly distinct (the mystery of Christ's love for the Church [v. 32]). However, the Christian (one who receives God's love graciously given) does radiate and reflect the love of God to others. In this way, Christ's love for His Bride, the Church, can be an example to men as to how to love their wives, and the Church's submission to its beloved Savior can be an example of how wives should submit to their husbands. The depth of Christ's love for the Church can never be reduced to mere example; it always remains the resource for such love in human relationships.

God's love radiates from Himself in care and service to others. Look at 1 Corinthians 13:1–13; John 15:12–13; and Ecclesiastes 4:7–12. *Agape* is the word used in these passages, and it is by definition "selfless love." (This love is not *philos*—brotherly love; *storge*—family love; or *eros*—sexual love.) In this regard, one could say that not only does God alone love this way, but God also "IS" this love. God desires for His people to receive this love through faith in His Son and to share it with others. Ecclesiastes 4 speaks of the value of true friendship and hints at the blessing of marriage (amid disgust with the world). Throughout the passage, the author speaks about the blessing of another, but at the end he gives the picture of a "threefold cord" that is stronger still. This picture paints not only the value of a husband to his wife or a wife to her husband, but also to God's love in the midst of such a union.

The selfless love of God is vital to marriage. Not only are people unique in how they need to be loved, they are also sinful and self-centered by nature (see again Genesis 3 and its depiction of the unraveling of human relationships). A constant temptation presents itself: to do what is in our own sinful self-interest. God's Word not only exposes that (the work of the Law in our lives, see Romans 3:19–20), but it also provides the Christ-earned declaration of forgiveness and mercy (2 Corinthians 5:17–20) that is needed to overcome these barriers to His love in our relationships with others.

Practically speaking, worship, Bible study, and prayer each have a role in a healthy marriage (see Romans 12:1–2; 1 Corinthians 7:3–5). God's merciful, forgiving love in Christ is not esoteric or otherworldly. It reaches down to the level where we live, the place full of our failures and sins as well as our hopes and dreams. Romans 12 speaks about the priority of mercy in life. All of life is to be redemptively lived "by the mercies of God" (v. 1). Worship, study, and prayerful dialogue with God's Word literally find God bringing His love and mercy in Christ to the place we live. His mercy enables us to "present your bodies" (Romans 12:1) in service to others (to truly live again). Mercy is wonderfully graphic when enfleshed in human nature. It doesn't remove one from the world; it redeems one to live godly lives in this world, with our families, friends, and neighbors. As living sacrifices, we are offered up and poured out, yet we are never extinguished like consumed sacrifices. Service to others in view of God's mercy never exhausts us like service motivated by guilt or greed. First Corinthians 7 wonderfully speaks about the redemption of life in human flesh. It speaks about the physical nature of love amid the issues of prayer and mission. Paul reminds us that Christian teaching does not denigrate the human body. Spiritualistic teachings that overemphasize the human spirit at the expense of the human body or hedonistic teachings that dismiss the human spirit altogether miss the joy of the celebration of the physical level of life and love lived in the sphere of God's acclamation and direction.

In 1 Corinthians 7, Paul is dealing with a very real problem. All of 1 Corinthians 7 speaks about the concerns of family life and the pressing need of sharing the Gospel amid persecution. Families are part of God's plan even amid struggle. Paul speaks about prayer and one's relationship with God as vital to the bond of marriage and a source of joy even for the sexual aspect of love. While one's spiritual relationship with God always takes priority, it never denigrates the love that God wishes for us to express to one another. It elevates both, as this passage clearly teaches.

Colossians 3 is a description of the new life in Christ, which is given through faith in Him. The very gracious love of God certainly received is the source of strength to love and serve others. Notice how Colossians 3:12–17 precedes Paul's exhortation of one's duties to others in one's family. Paul specifically tells us about the "new clothes" that we wear: compassion, kindness, humility, meekness, and patience, forgiving as God in Christ forgave us. It is Christ's action for us that makes our actions for others possible. Paul then invites the Colossian Christians to "let the word of Christ dwell in you richly" (v. 16), which produces a harvest of thanksgiving and thanks-living to those whom we love. Christians believe that the hearing and receiving of God's love and forgiveness in Christ—in Word and Sacraments—is what we need in order to love as He has loved us. It is first and foremost God coming to us to forgive and bless us in Christ. Our songs, offerings, prayers, and lifestyle are responses to what He graciously gives to us through His Son.

The Power of Forgiveness

The Bible understands not only the different needs of men and women as they relate to each other, but also the reality of sin and selfishness in marriage. Why, then, is God's forgiveness in Christ the underlying strength for Christian marriage (see Ephesians 4:31–32)? The struggle in any meaningful relationship is the vulnerability of being transparent in the hands of another sinful person. Our temptation is to keep a record of wrongs, to be moved to anger because of someone's disregard for our thoughts and feelings. We hold on to our anger as a means of self-preservation and protection. In the minds and hearts of sinful people, these thoughts and feelings can burn in us as rage and revenge until they consume us. At this point, sin must be confronted by the justice of a God who never lets sin go unpunished and by the mercy of God in Christ who makes a fresh start truly possible. Paul reminds us that God was just in punishing His Son for our sins (in our stead) and merciful in granting His righteousness to us as a gift when he says, "Forgiving one another, as God in Christ forgave you" (Ephesians 4:32). This reality makes putting away "bitterness and wrath" possible. The Gospel, Baptism, Absolution, and the Lord's Supper are constant reminders of the cost of our forgiveness. These are the very means by which God delivers the forgiveness won by Christ to us. Hebrews 12:1–3 speaks about the joy that Christ had in suffering for His rebellious people because of their coming again to faith and life with God. This is the reality that the Christian returns to daily as he or she seeks to love the other.

Plans for marriage include issues concerning finances, home, children, and, then, the wedding. The most important aspect of a wedding—and a marriage—is the blessing and forgiveness of God and the presence and promise of Christ. Knowing these things will be vital when dealing with the tough challenges that life brings to marriage.

His Love Is Our Strength

Jesus calls us to love as He has loved and continues to love us. That exhortation is never more real than in the marriage relationship. Christ doesn't merely call us to follow His example. Rather, He beckons us to draw on His forgiving grace and love. His forgiving grace received in the Means of Grace enables husbands and wives to put His love into practice.

Romance may ignite people's love for each other, but only God's love can truly sustain a healthy relationship. Only Christ's love can overcome our insecurities. Only Christ's love can give us confidence to serve when our feelings dictate otherwise. Only Christ's love can help one see the impact of one's actions and the opportunities when seeking to love one's spouse as one is loved. Romance burns off of our emotions. For such emotion to rekindle itself over and over again, it must be fueled by the kind of love that cannot be extinguished. Such love is found in the actions of God in Christ, the stories of Christmas and Easter, delivered by His Word and His gifts to us.

God's grace in Christ is the only solid source of power to live life serving one's spouse. This selfless esteem is more powerful than the self-esteem relationships for which our world clamors. "Grace alone" is a clear tenet of Scripture and of the Lutheran faith. One's relationship with God (and with others) can never be certain if it depends on the actions of sinful people. Thank God that He doesn't leave the world's need for His love dependent on our best actions (which amount to nothing before Him and fail time and time again toward the other). Our confidence before God comes from His action in Christ toward us. Our confidence in the resource of His love flows from His promise to bless us, to finish the job with us (Philippians 1:6). That confidence in God's Word, forgiveness, and mercy overflows from us into the lives of others. It is a confidence that doesn't depend on another's reaction to our service (though love in return sure is nice!). It is the confidence, esteem, and strength for service that can only be described as "Christ in you, the hope of glory" (Colossians 1:27; see also 1 Corinthians 6:17–19).

For Reflection

> The avalanche of domestic misunderstanding that starts insignificantly from some small, selfish act and soon assumes devastating

proportions can be averted only by the sincerity of resolution which renews Joshua's promise of old, "As for me and my house, we will serve the Lord" (Joshua 24:15). A home built on this resolution may be shaken by the storms of unemployment, illness, suffering, and death; but it will have a peace which a self-indulgent world knows not, for it will have Christ.[6]

Point to Remember

Set me as a seal upon your heart, as a seal upon your arm, for love is strong as death, jealousy is fierce as the grave. *Song of Solomon 8:6*

Leaving a Legacy

Many children, many cares; no children, no felicity.
—Christian Nestell Bovee

In God's plan, families don't exist for their happiness alone. Families are the place in which father, mother, and children receive and share Christ's forgiveness with one another. In the family, each member learns to live with the other on God's terms. Through the family, generations of children and grandchildren come to know that the Father's love in Jesus Christ, by the power of His Holy Spirit, makes all this possible. Families and family members not only bless each other, but they also are the foundation for a wider community and a civilized society.

What is a family worth today? The value of healthy families to society cannot be overestimated. Each God-given role—father, mother, child—is important. Healthy marriages provide for healthy families; well-cared-for and much-loved children grow to be productive citizens. Healthy families are blessings to the community, which in turn should support the family as an institution.

Doing Your Duty

The family is the primary place in which faith and values are transmitted. Ultimately, the teaching of God's Word is the most essential duty of parents, especially fathers (Deuteronomy 6:7). The goal of such work is the

6 Maier, *For Better, Not for Worse*, 545.

raising up of a family in the faith. As Deuteronomy 6:2 says, this matter is about life itself.

Proverbs 22:6 teaches us that such training will aid our children when they, too, must face life as adults. The purpose of teaching God's Word to children is to prepare our children for life—life lived with God by faith, in worship and study of Him, and in care and support for those we love (work and family). To fail to prepare a child for the opportunity of becoming a godly adult is to fail at what is most basic in God's expectations of parents.

Matthew 23:37 and Hebrews 12:6–10 give us some clues as to the different kinds of love that mothers and fathers bring to parenting. These passages speak about how mother and father might fulfill such duties as God's representatives to their children. Our world senses some value in maternal love, the unconditional love of mothers, but one needs to understand that the disciplinary love of fathers is also vital to a child's maturation. The long-suffering love of a mother may be different than the setting-boundaries love of a disciplining father, but each has its godly purpose. Parental instincts must also be aligned to the Word of God concerning the teaching and moral direction necessary in raising children. Titus 2:1–5 reveals that men and women must constantly be encouraged to strive for what is godly in our love for one another. We are aware of our constant tendency as sinful people to do the opposite. Doing merely what comes naturally is to open oneself up to the dangers of a particular aspect of love—the maternal danger of becoming too attached or the paternal danger of becoming too detached—dominating to the exclusion of the other. Here parents learn to balance each other in the work of godly parenting according to God's lead in the Scripture and for the child's good.

Children are God's blessing to father and mother (Matthew 19:13–14). As in the ancient world, children today sometimes are not valued because they produce nothing society values, yet they cost much. Jesus demonstrates children's value as God's gifts by calling them to Himself amid the rebukes of His own disciples. Children are God's blessing to marriages as both father and mother will have to devote their energies to the love and guiding of another. Child-rearing gives us a very practical glimpse of how God Himself loves us. While children are sinful and selfish from birth, and, indeed, from conception (Psalm 51:5), there is also a simple trust and a joy that children exude, especially when they know they are loved. Such joy is a reflection of our relationship to God as our heavenly Father.

Abortion on demand is the final expression of that idea that children are addenda to our lifestyle on our terms alone. This mentality sees children as having to fit our life expectations and life goals. Conversely, a mind-set that sees children as God's gifts who come into our lives to raise us to maturity (as we do them) in God's love and joy sees that our lives (jobs, time, talents, etc.) are to be used for the sake of our spouse and children. In the Bible's view, nothing is more vital or precious in this world than our spouse and children.

God ordains all earthly authorities for our good. And the home is the place in which children first learn how to respect order and authority. The Fourth Commandment demonstrates clearly the Bible's value of family: father, mother, and child. The state does not tower over the family but is derived from the authority of parents (LC I 141; *Concordia*, p. 375). In this sense, the state is called to serve the goals of the family by maintaining peace and order. In such an environment, the family is able to work and grow. Children develop a healthy respect for all authority as they learn to honor their parents. Honoring one's parents is God's way of building a climate of respectfulness out of which love can grow and be sustained. As the family learns its rightful, joyous place before God the Father, and children learn their place before their parents, a healthy view of civic authority extends. Even with "faulty" parents, one can learn to disagree without disrespect. This lesson learned blesses a community as well.

The wider community is affected by adultery, serial divorce, and abusive or faithless parenting. Adultery destabilizes marriages. Serial divorce creates the mind-set that there is no permanence in love, solidifying the destructive expectation that breakup and loss are the norm in life. Such an expectation not only leaves husbands and wives looking to fend for themselves, but it also leaves children broken and without guidance. Jesus warns in Matthew 19:6, "What therefore God has joined together, let not man separate." Interestingly, Matthew records Jesus' love for the children right after this section about the abuse of divorce. Marriages need an environment of commitment for true intimacy to grow, but families also need that same environment to raise children, to give them time to know and practice the difference between love and lust, between right and wrong, good and bad, selflessness and selfishness. When a community has to do what the family will not, when it is clamoring for government to enforce good behavior, the Church says, "Look first at the families, rebuild there!"

First Peter 2 clearly shows an order of respect: "Be subject for the Lord's sake to every human institution" (v. 13) and "Love the brotherhood. Fear God. Honor the emperor" (v. 17). Governmental authority derives itself from the institutions that God has laid as foundational, namely, the authority of mother and father (see the Fourth Commandment). A modern myth suggests that government can step in and replace many duties of the father and the mother. The Bible warns against such a view. Parental responsibility cannot be replaced by programs or policies. There are times when certain parents abdicate their responsibility and society must step in for the sake of the child. It is in the community's best interest to strengthen our parents for their tasks, challenging them and assisting them to fulfill their responsibilities to their families.

Mother and Father

The teamwork of parenting, learning to work together to raise up children as blessings from God, concretely demonstrates the many facets of God's love to a child. There are many examples of a mother's strength, a father's perseverance, and so on.

Today, some who are born into Christian homes also study, work, and recreate almost exclusively among people of faith, with virtually no contact with non-Christians. Is this God's purpose for the family? Christian families want to be integral parts of their community because God's love always extends outward to others. The temptation today is for many communities to isolate themselves from one another and to love what they like, either out of selfishness or fear. This kind of love stunts the growth of the Christian and the Christian family. Families learn to love by committing themselves to one another, even as they are unique and distinct. Such love is to be extended out from the family to one's neighbors, those like us and those not (for example, see Luke 10, the parable of the Good Samaritan, and Acts 10). God calls us to love that which is unlike us, since that remains the essence of His love for us. The family may be a place of security and growth, the Church may be that as an extended family of faith, but such blessings are always meant to strengthen God's people to reach beyond their zones of comfort to exercise God's love in the power of faith. The post-Communion prayer says it best: "In faith toward You and in fervent love toward one another" (*LSB*, p. 166).

Community Blessing

The family is foremost that place in which the promises of Jesus Christ, the truths of God's Word, are practiced for restoration, redemption, and love. The Church, as God's extended family of faith, exists to gather families to encourage and strengthen them for their work. Such work extends out from godly families to the communities in which they live. Civic authorities exist in God's plan to provide peace and stability for the Church and the family to do their work. The Church and the home are fundamental not only in God's plan of salvation but also in the plan of practicing that salvation for the whole world to see.

God's whole effort to redeem and restore His creation started with a promise (Genesis 3:15), but very soon it was rooted in a family, a bloodline: Abraham's family (Genesis 12:1–3). This family was the place where God firmly established His love in human history so that the whole world might know Him through Abraham's Seed, Jesus Christ.

Children are a common blessing in marriage through which husband and wife must decide together how to love and discipline. Working out such things helps prepare us for work in society as well. Caring for our spouse and our children not only matures us, but it also helps us to rely on God and His Word in very real-world ways. Such wisdom surely extends outward from one's family to one's community. While families not only strive for right actions of husbands, wives, and children, but also for right motivations, learning the value of such things helps one discern the value of civic outward good works as well.

The Bible teaches that the family unit is the foundation of society. It is important to remember that while the government may help in certain family issues, it can never replace the value and work of mothers and fathers for their children. It is too easy to think that the family can be replaced by the functions it provides. Resources, nurture, education, and guidance can come from someplace else, but these serve to support the family, not to replace it. The relationship of father, mother, and child is so intimate that each person sees the other as an extension of self. Rather than seeking to dismiss or replace the family, communities do well to nurture and support the family's ability to care for one another. If mutual responsibility and care does not exist in the family, they cannot exist elsewhere for long.

For Reflection

> With the additional emphasis that the Word of God lays upon the individual in eternity, the names of the elect recorded in the Book of Life, the acknowledgment of each faithful believer by the Savior Himself before His Father in heaven, Dives beholding Abraham and Lazarus in his bosom, no doubt remains in the Christian's mind. He believes that, when the New Testament speaks of "the whole family in heaven" (Ephesians 3:15), it includes in this vast picture of the ten thousand times ten thousand the recognition of those who were united in the Spirit-blessed family here on earth.[7]

Point to Remember

> So Boaz took Ruth, and she became his wife. And he went in to her, and the LORD gave her conception, and she bore a son. . . . They named him Obed. He was the father of Jesse, the father of David. *Ruth 4:13, 17*

7 Maier, *For Better, Not for Worse*, 560.

Homosexuality and Biblical Teaching

The Bible never provides a detailed psychological answer for homosexuality. However, it clearly teaches that homosexual behaviors are sinful, even abominable to God. (See Leviticus 18:22; 1 Corinthians 6:9; 2 Peter 2:4–10.) In Romans 1, the apostle clearly condemns homosexuality as a corruption of God's created order. The male body is not designed to copulate with another male body. The female body is not designed to copulate with another female body. If anyone would argue that the Bible only speaks against extramarital sex but might allow for same-sex "marriage," they have neither understood the biblical doctrine of marriage nor the doctrine of creation. The fact that people crave same-sex relationships proves that something has gone terribly wrong with creation due to the fall into sin (Romans 1:26–28).

Marriage and God's Blessing

Marriage, as God established it in the beginning and as taught by Jesus, is one man married to one woman in lifelong union (Mark 10:4–9). Although the Bible mentions other relations especially in the Old Testament (polygamy, concubinage, fornication), it does not bless them but warns against them (see e.g., Hebrews 13:4). God created sex for the procreation of children and to strengthen the marital bond that supports those children (cf. Genesis 1:28). Within the context of marriage, as God defined it, sex is a wonderful blessing. Outside that relationship, it is idolatry—people rejecting God's order, worshiping what is created rather than the Creator.

Christians should abhor the sin of homosexual behavior as they abhor all sins (Romans 1:28–31; 1 Corinthians 5:9–11; 6:9–10; Galatians 5:19–20; Revelation 21:8). But at the same time, Christians should see homosexuals as people for whom Christ shed His precious blood. God wants us to recognize that "all have sinned and fall short of the glory of God, and are justified by His grace as a gift, through the redemption that is in Christ Jesus" (Romans 3:23–24). A homosexual, like any other sinner, needs to hear God's Law and Gospel applied to his or her life with the goal of repentance and faith.

Lutheran Summary of Marriage and Family

Augsburg Confession XVII 18–21

First, concerning monks who marry, our teachers say that it is lawful for anyone who is not suited for the single life to enter into marriage. Monastic vows cannot destroy what God has commanded and ordained. God's commandment is this, "Because of the temptation to sexual immorality, each man should have his own wife" (1 Corinthians 7:2). It is not just a command given by God. God has created and ordained marriage for those who are not given an exception to natural order by God's special work. This is what is taught according to the text in Genesis 2:18, "It is not good that the man should be alone." Therefore, those who obey this command and ordinance of God do not sin. (*Concordia*, p. 54)

Apology of the Augsburg Confession XIII (VII) 14

Marriage was not first instituted in the New Testament, but in the beginning, immediately after the creation of the human race [Genesis 1:28]. Furthermore, it has God's command. It has also promises, not truly having to do with the New Testament, but rather having to do with bodily life. (*Concordia*, p. 185)

Apology of the Augsburg Confession XXIII (XI) 9–10

Second, because this creation, or divine ordinance, in humanity is a natural right, jurists have said wisely and correctly that the union of male and female belongs to natural right. Natural right is unchangeable. Therefore, the right to contract marriage must always remain. Where nature does not change, that ordinance which God gave nature does not change. It cannot be removed by human laws. Therefore, it is ridiculous for the adversaries to babble that marriage was commanded in the beginning, but is not now. (*Concordia*, p. 212)

Apology of the Augsburg Confession XXIII (XI) 61

The Gospel allows marriage for those to whom it is necessary. Nevertheless, it does not compel marriage for those who can be chaste, provided they are truly chaste. (*Concordia*, p. 217)

Large Catechism I 208

For marriage has the highest importance to God so that people are raised up who may serve the world and promote the knowledge of God, godly living, and all virtues, to fight against wickedness and the devil. (*Concordia*, p. 382)

I Believe in One Lord Jesus Christ

TOPIC SEVEN

God the Son[1]

Engaging This Topic

"My church is a lot more open-minded than yours."
"What do you mean?"
"Well, we teach that Christians, Jewish people, and Muslims all pray to the same God. You talk as if Jesus were *the* Savior, the only path to God."

Muslims believe that Jesus was a great prophet. Jewish people believe that Jesus was a gifted yet unorthodox rabbi. Buddhists regard Jesus as an enlightened person. Scholars acclaim Jesus for His remarkable ethics. Jehovah's Witnesses describe Jesus as an exalted, divine being. Mormons teach that Jesus Christ became a god.

But the early *Christ*ians—the people who first followed Jesus Christ, recorded His teachings, and received Baptism in His name—believed that He *is* God and *became* a man for the salvation of all who receive Him. They knew Him as God the Son, the Second Person of the Holy Trinity.

Christians today hold the same basic beliefs about who Jesus is and about His work of salvation. The earliest centuries of Christian teaching focused on these beliefs and how Christians should describe them from the Scriptures. Because of human weaknesses and misunderstandings, controversies broke out and even divided the fellowship of the early Christians. (The modern notion that earliest Christianity didn't have denominational differences is false.) Through close adherence to the Scriptures, faithful teaching was maintained. The clarification of doctrine that resulted from these controversies is summarized in the three ecumenical creeds: the Apostles' Creed, the Nicene Creed, and the Athanasian Creed (see *Concordia*, pp. 16–18).

1 This chapter adapted from *The Lutheran Difference: God the Son*, written by Alfonso Espinosa, with contributions by Henry Gerike and Edward Engelbrecht. Copyright © 2003 Concordia Publishing House.

Humility and Faith

The controversies that confused and divided the early Christians stemmed from two biblical teachings: (1) Jesus is truly a man and (2) Jesus is truly God. The tension and paradox between these truths caused various teachers to compromise one of the two truths or to find some way to reconcile them through human logic. (See "Comparisons," pp. 223–25.)

Much of the controversy stemmed from the confidence of different teachers who thought they could explain the mystery of the human and divine natures in Christ. Although human reason is one of God's gifts, it is both too weak and too corrupted by sin to explain the eternal mysteries of God. In humility, Christian teachers had to learn that they should simply receive and confess what God teaches about Himself in the Scriptures rather than try to satisfy their reason by figuring it all out.

The most important teaching of all is that, for our salvation, Jesus is both truly God and truly man. He paid the price for our sins on the cross and extends that blessing to us today through His Word and Sacraments.

Lutheran Facts

Lutheran teaching centers on Jesus, through whom a person receives the kingdom of God and learns of the heavenly Father. Saving faith is trusting that Jesus Christ died on the cross for the forgiveness of one's sins and rose again from the dead for one's eternal salvation.

Because Jesus is true and eternal God, Lutherans address prayers to Jesus as well as to the Father and the Holy Spirit.

In honor of Jesus, Lutherans stand during the reading of the Gospel in the Divine Service.

A common table prayer used by Lutherans is "Come, Lord Jesus, be our guest. And let Thy gifts to us be blessed." This prayer reminds Lutherans that the daily blessings of God come through Jesus. It also reminds them of Christ's promise to come again on the Last Day.

Lutherans believe that Jesus gives His true body and blood in the Lord's Supper for the forgiveness of sins. This is the chief blessing in the Lord's Supper and is foundational to Lutheran devotion.

Eternal God and Promised Messiah

> Infidels now are they who say, "Verily God is the Messiah, Son of Mary."
>
> —The Qur'an 5, 19

Jesus Christ was born around 4 BC, the child of Mary, a young Jewish woman from Nazareth in Galilee. But He existed before time began! In other words, the Bible teaches the preexistence of Christ. He is truly "the first and the last" (Revelation 1:17). Jesus is the Savior—the "Messiah" whom the Israelites knew God would send. Today, Christians confess that Jesus Christ is the eternal God and promised Messiah.

The Bible attributes many names and titles to Jesus Christ, such as "Son of God," "Son of Man," "Messiah," and "Christ." "Son of God" does not mean that Jesus is the *Son* of God as opposed to being God Himself. "Son of God" is a divine title. It means that Jesus is of the same *substance* as the Father. (We are God's "sons" in the sense of Galatians 3:26—adopted as a result of Christ's saving work for us. So Christ is the Son, as in having the divine nature, but we are "sons" in the sense of being legal heirs of God by His grace through faith in Jesus Christ.) Jesus often referred to Himself as the "Son of Man." In the Aramaic of Jesus' day, this expression meant simply "a person." However, the prophet Daniel had used a similar expression to describe the Messiah (Daniel 7:13–14). Therefore, Jesus also used this as a divine title, associated with His authority to save and judge all people (Matthew 20:28; 25:31). "Christ" is the Greek equivalent of the Hebrew "Messiah." In Matthew 16:16, Peter identifies Jesus as the Christ—that is, the Anointed One, the long-awaited Messiah who would save His people.

The fact that Jesus is the Messiah was important in the history of the Israelites; the fact that Jesus is God was contrary to the beliefs of most ancient Jews and Gentiles, and it stands in opposition to modern-day beliefs about different paths to "god." Both truths (that Jesus is the Messiah and is God) are vital for knowing Christ. It's possible that some people don't clearly understand the title "Messiah" today, but as Christians, we know it is always appropriate to say, "Jesus is God." The Bible clearly teaches this truth (John 20:28; 1 John 5:20).

For All Eternity

According to Genesis 1:1, God existed "in the beginning." John 1:1 and 14 tell us: "In the beginning was the Word, and the Word was with God, and the Word was God. . . . And the Word became flesh and dwelt among us, and we have seen His glory, glory as of the only Son from the Father, full of grace and truth." Even while the Word was with God, the Word *was* God from all eternity. Yet, in time, God the Word became flesh (Jesus was conceived and born). These verses reveal the preexistence of Christ by clearly identifying Christ as the Word who is God.

In Exodus 3:13–14, God reveals to Moses that His name is "I AM"—or *Yahweh* (represented as LORD in English translations). This name of God teaches that He causes all things to come into existence; He has all power and authority. John 8:58 records that Christ attributed the name "I AM" to Himself. Abraham lived approximately 2,000 years before Jesus was born; nevertheless, as the great "I AM," Jesus existed before Abraham! The Jews who were present when Jesus made this claim "picked up stones to throw at Him" (John 8:59). A "mere man" was claiming to be God, a blasphemous claim in their minds and worthy of the death penalty.

Not everyone responded this way. Andrew announced to his brother, Simon Peter, "We have found the Messiah," that is, the Christ (John 1:41). As a good Israelite, Andrew had been waiting for the coming Anointed One promised in the Old Testament. He recognized Jesus as the Messiah. In John 4:25–26 the Samaritan woman—a descendant of the tribes in the Northern Kingdom of Israel—also knew the prophecies about the Messiah. Jesus told her, "I who speak to you am He" (v. 26). God brought His Old Testament prophecies to fulfillment in the Lord Jesus Christ.

More than 500 years before Jesus' birth, God revealed several messianic prophecies through the prophet Daniel. Daniel saw "one like a son of man" approaching the "Ancient of Days," that is, God (Daniel 7:13). This "son of man" was "given dominion and glory and a kingdom, that all peoples, nations and languages should serve Him" (Daniel 7:14). In Mark 14, Christ was being interrogated before the Jewish Sanhedrin. The high priest asked, "Are You the Christ [Messiah], the Son of the Blessed [and therefore divine]?" (v. 61). "I am," said Jesus (v. 62). Then He cited Daniel 7. Jesus testified that He is the Messiah prophesied by Daniel. The high priest tore his clothes in response, and he accused Christ of blasphemy. He understood *exactly* what Jesus had said and determined to kill Him.

By inspiration of the Holy Spirit, David records a remarkable conversation in Psalm 110:1. The Lord (the heavenly Father) speaks to the Lord (the Son of God), King David's Messiah. God is speaking to God! The proclamation is: "Sit at My right hand, until I make Your enemies Your footstool." Note the reference to "right hand." The Father gives the Son all power and authority. King David lived approximately a thousand years before Jesus was born, yet he already knew Christ as his Lord and King. Hebrews 1:8 also clearly presents the Father as calling the Son "God."

The Appearance of Jesus

You're probably familiar with the saying "Don't judge a book by its cover." In a sense, many people judge Jesus Christ and what He is able to do in terms of His "cover," His appearing as a man.

Jesus can do anything for us because He is almighty God. Nothing is too hard for Him; nothing is impossible for Him. He can and does meet our every need. All resources are at His disposal because all things belong to Him. If we have Christ, we have the answer to all our needs (Luke 10:41–42).

God's people in the Old Testament waited thousands of years for the Messiah (the Christ) to come with His eternal salvation. Since Jesus was faithful to those who waited in Old Testament times for His salvation, what will He do for you as you see clearly that He is the true King of kings? Second Peter 3:9 teaches us that the Lord is not slow in keeping His promises and is patient so that people may come to repentance. He is faithful. The messianic prophecies fulfilled in Christ are proof of that. When we wait for the Lord, we will be blessed (Isaiah 30:18).

Sometimes Jesus is mixed into the bag of world religions and becomes just another name alongside the Buddha, Confucius, Muhammad, the Dalai Lama, and the like. But as Lutherans, we are careful not to do that. All other religious leaders in the history of humankind were mere people created by God. Jesus Christ *is* God.

Comparisons

Jesus Himself recognized that people held different opinions about Him even before His death and resurrection. When the apostle Peter confidently proclaimed who He was (Matthew 16:13–17), Jesus explained that this faith and understanding was a blessing of the heavenly Father. Faith in Christ does not come from a person's ability to "figure Jesus out." It comes as a gift from God through His Word. As you read about Christological controversies below, note how each group respects Jesus, but doesn't understand who He truly is.

Judaism (first century). Some early Jewish-Christian teachers regarded Jesus as truly a man and the Messiah. But they did not believe that He could also be truly God.

Docetism (late first century; named from the Greek word *dokeo*, "to seem or appear"). Influenced by Greek ideas about the corruption of the human body, Docetists taught that Jesus was truly God but only appeared to be human.

Adoptionism (second century). Some taught that Jesus was born an ordinary man but that God adopted Him as His Son at His Baptism.

Arianism (fourth century). Arius, an Alexandrian priest, taught that Jesus was truly a man and was also a god, created by the heavenly Father in the beginning. Arius's teaching greatly threatened early Christianity. After the struggle with Arianism, Christians agreed that Jesus was truly God and truly man. They used Greek terms to speak about God's one divine nature in three persons. Further arguments would arise because the special terms used can be ambiguous and, if misapplied, can allow one to depart from Scripture. Questions arose about how Christ is one person and two natures. Everyone agreed that Jesus was one person. Controversy began to emerge about how the human and divine natures related to each other and that one person.

Nestorianism (fifth century). Nestorius, a patriarch of Constantinople, sparked controversy by rejecting a traditional title for Mary, *Theotokos* "God-bearer." Since Christ has divine and human natures, Mary bore God within her womb. Nestorius insisted on a new term, *Christotokos*, "Christ-bearer," meaning that the human body is the vehicle of the divine, like a garment. Opponents believed that Nestorius was reintroducing Adoptionism by speaking of one person, two "subsistences," and two natures. What he did was change the understanding of "subsistence" taken from the Nicene Creed. He was deposed. Syrian church communities divided according to liturgical rite and doctrine. Many who used the Eastern rite were "Nestorian." Many who used the Western rite were "Monophysite" and "Miaphysite." Some of both Eastern and Western groups remained with orthodox Christianity.

Eutychianism (also called **Monophysitism**, fifth century). Eutyches opposed Nestorius and wanted to emphasize the divinity of Jesus. He taught that Jesus' human nature was like a mere drop of honey absorbed and lost in the ocean of His divine nature. In other words, after the incarnation, Jesus had one person, one subsistence, and one nature. Many rejected Eutyches's views because they were extreme and did not correctly describe the human nature of Jesus. Eutychean churches were at odds with both Orthodox and Miaphysite churches and troubled the Byzantine Empire in Syria and Palestine.

Miaphysitism (also called **Monophysitism**, fifth century). The Council of Chalcedon (451) declared that Jesus had both a human nature and a divine nature inconfusedly, unchangeably, indivisibly, inseparably. In Egypt and Palestine, Eutyches was condemned as a heretic, but many also rejected the Council of Chalcedon. The breakaway churches stated that the *person* of Christ has one subsistence or nature but that it retains divine and human natural qualities. Here they take advantage of ambiguous Greek terms to change the understanding of *nature*. Their formula, held by modern Coptic, Syrian, and Armenian churches, effectively is a Monophysite position, albeit a slippery one.

Point to Remember

No one has ever seen God; the only God, who is at the Father's side, He has made Him known. *John 1:18*

God Became Flesh

Songs of thankfulness and praise,
Jesus, Lord, to Thee we raise,
Manifested by the star
To the sages from afar,
Branch of royal David's stem
In Thy birth at Bethlehem:
Anthems be to Thee addressed,
God in man made manifest.
—Christopher Wordsworth (*LSB* 394:1)

It is one thing to know that Jesus Christ is the God who existed before anything was created and the Messiah of Old Testament prophecies, but it is something else to understand that Jesus was still completely God when He took on human flesh. The fact that God became a man is the miracle and the mystery called the incarnation. (Do not confuse this term with *reincarnation*, a Hindu and Buddhist doctrine—see the Glossary, p. 690.) The Jesus who walked, slept, spoke, ate, cried, thirsted, taught, became tired, suffered, and died was God on earth.

Throughout history the doctrine that Christ is true God has been under attack. In the fourth century AD, a false teacher named Arius asserted that Christ had to be a created being. He thus denied the true divinity of Christ. The ancient Church responded through the Nicene Creed, stating that Jesus Christ is "begotten, not made, being of one substance with the Father" (*Concordia*, p. 16). Distressingly, various forms of Arianism are alive and well today (e.g., Jehovah's Witnesses). The Church must always be prepared to "test the spirits" (1 John 4:1) through the powerful Word of God.

Although the Word of God reveals Christ as fully God and fully man, popular depictions have a tendency to be one-sided, presenting Him either as a human (like a man) or as a divine being (like God). However, many artistic works bring out the biblical revelation that Jesus is both God and man. For example, *Adoration of the Magi* by da Vinci and Fabriano's work of the same title portray the Magi worshiping the Christ Child; both the humanity and divinity of Christ are thus presented.

The doctrine of the incarnation—God taking on human flesh and becoming a man, thereby being both God and man—is vital to our lives. Some people may be tempted to treat this doctrine as nit-picking and not really important, but nothing could be further from the truth. If Christ were *not* what the Scriptures reveal Him to be, He could not be our Savior.

The Birth of Christ

Isaiah 7:14 foretells the Savior's birth: "Therefore the Lord Himself will give you a sign. Behold, the virgin shall conceive and bear a son, and shall call His name Immanuel." This verse describes what comes from the virgin as "child," "son," and "Immanuel." The first two terms point to Christ's human nature. The third points to Christ's divinity. "Mother of God" is a title for Mary from the ancient Christian Church. The virgin gave birth to "Immanuel," God with us.

Now consider Romans 9:5: "To them belong the patriarchs, and from their race, according to the flesh, is the Christ who is God over all, blessed forever. Amen." This verse describes Jesus' human nature in terms of His human ancestry. It is a false claim and myth that Jesus is not actually called "God" in the Bible. He is, here in Romans! (See also FC SD VIII 6; *Concordia*, p. 582.)

Some people ask if the fact that Jesus is both man and God changed during His severe humiliation and suffering. Absolutely not! Here we look to 1 Corinthians 2:8: "None of the rulers of this age understood this, for if they had, they would not have crucified the Lord of glory." This verse clearly states that the one put on the cross is "the Lord of glory." This is yet another title of divinity for Jesus. Christ's true divinity and humanity did not change one iota during His suffering and crucifixion.

"Pay careful attention to yourselves and to all the flock, in which the Holy Spirit has made you overseers, to care for the church of God, which He obtained with His own blood" (Acts 20:28). Here we read about *God's* blood. Some English Bibles note the fact that some Greek manuscripts refer to the "Lord's" blood. Another group of Greek manuscripts have the two words side by side ("Lord and God's"). The blood referred to is from the Lord, who is God. Thus the blood is indeed God's blood. (See FC SD VIII 40, 42, 44; *Concordia*, pp. 588–89). Whoever understands the scriptural revelation that the one person Jesus is truly God and man will understand why "God died" is a biblical and accurate statement.

Besides Christ's work of reconciliation on the cross, the other major work attributed to Jesus Christ is that of creation. Jesus created all things! (See Colossians 1:15–20.)

We know that John tells us "in the beginning was the Word, and the Word was with God, and the Word was God" (1:1). But in his letter to the Colossians, Paul also tells us about the divine and human natures of Christ: "For in Him the whole fullness of deity dwells bodily, and you have been filled in Him, who is the head of all rule and authority" (2:9). Christ's divine nature is described via the words "the whole fullness of deity." Christ's human nature is described by the word "bodily." To be God is to be fully divine. To be human is to have a body. Jesus was fully divine *and* had a body.

Consider what Paul told the Philippians about Christ's nature:

> Your attitude should be the same as that of Christ Jesus: Who, being in very nature God, did not consider equality with God something to be grasped, but made Himself nothing, taking the very nature of a servant, being made in human likeness. And being found in appearance as a man, He humbled Himself and became obedient to death—even death on a cross! Therefore God exalted Him to the highest place and gave Him the name that is above every name, that at the name of Jesus every knee should bow, in heaven and on earth and under the earth, and every tongue confess that Jesus Christ is Lord, to the glory of God the Father. (2:5–11 NIV)

The word *appearance* in verse 8 (NIV) may seem to imply that Jesus was not really a man. But the rest of the passage shows that He was. Verse 6 states that Christ's *being* is by very nature "God" (divine). Verse 7 tells us Jesus "made Himself nothing." This means that He "emptied Himself." Verse 8 says Jesus actually experienced death; thus He was truly a human being. His "appearance as a man" (NIV) means that He came into the world as an actual man even while He was always God at the same time. Verses 9–11 describe the exaltation and worship of Christ. The Bible never attributes this kind of glory and honor to anyone other than *God Himself*!

It is imperative that we understand the meaning of the biblical description "made Himself nothing" (Philippians 2:7). This phrase does not mean that Christ ceased to be God. Consider this insight from Dr. Martin Luther: "He kept it [the majesty of the divine nature] concealed in the state of His humiliation and did not always use it, but only when He wanted to use it" (FC SD VIII 26; *Concordia*, p. 586, citing AE 15:291).

Born for You

The Scriptures clearly teach that God was born in time, coming to us in the plainest and clearest way He could have come—as one of us! One of the saddest and most distressing facets of religion is that some people think they must embark on searches and journeys for God. However, the Bible clearly teaches that God embarked on a "journey" for us. He found us! He came into our flesh and joined us in our life. This has not changed at all for the Christian Church; to this day Christ continues to come to us through His Word and Sacraments. But God does call us to "seek" Him while He may be found (Isaiah 55:6). He is found through Jesus Christ.

The Epistle to the Philippians teaches that Jesus willingly humbled Himself, even to the point of death. What does this say about His love for us? It is easy to forget that all the humiliation, the "emptying," of Christ was totally and completely based on the free and willful choice of Christ Himself. He willed to make Himself nothing; He chose to empty Himself—all for us.

Few Christian doctrines are attacked more than the doctrine of Christ's two natures. Many non-Christian cults claim that it is wrong to say Jesus is God. The following are some verses they use against Christian doctrine. After the verse, a comparison is offered between the false and the proper interpretation of the passage.

Matthew 24:36: "But concerning that day and hour no one knows, not even the angels of heaven, nor the Son, but the Father only." False religions use this Scripture verse to assert that Jesus is not God because Jesus admits to not knowing the day or hour of the end of the world. But Matthew 24:36 contains an example of what Philippians 2:5–7 states: "Christ Jesus, . . . who, though He was in the form of God . . . made Himself nothing." Jesus chose to limit His knowledge in His state of humiliation. However, this does not cancel the fact that He is still God. As God, He knows all things; but this ability He willfully and genuinely laid aside for a time.

Matthew 26:39, 42: "And going a little farther He fell on His face and prayed, saying, 'My Father, if it be possible, let this cup pass from Me; nevertheless, not as I will, but as You will.' . . . Again, for the second time, He went away and prayed, 'My Father, if this cannot pass unless I drink it, Your will be done.'" Cults claim that these verses also prove that Jesus is not God because He is praying *to* God. However, cults exclude the biblical doctrine of Christ's two natures. Because He humbled Himself while on earth, Jesus genuinely needed the heavenly Father. He chose to relate to His Father as a weak and humble man so that He could be the Savior of us all.

Colossians 1:15: "He is the image of the invisible God, the firstborn of all creation." False religions say that this Scripture verse proves that Christ is not God because it describes Jesus as "the firstborn," and Jesus cannot be God because God is not "born." Ironically, the title "firstborn" means the opposite of what false teachers claim. It is a title of position, not substance. For example, Psalm 89:27 indicates that God appointed David as His "firstborn" when He made him king. But David was not "firstborn" in a literal sense (see 1 Samuel 16:10–13). "Firstborn" describes Christ's position of authority as Lord and God. The very next verse (Colossians 1:16) teaches that Christ created all things. According to His human nature He was born, but this in no way contradicts His divine status as "the firstborn of all creation."

Arianism (see "Comparisons," p. 223) is alive and well today. This is especially true in many non-Christian cults, some of which delight in calling themselves "Christian." By knowing the biblical teaching on the two natures of Jesus Christ, you can answer these objections to the Christian faith.

Comparisons

The word *creed* comes from the Latin *credo*, meaning "I believe." Creeds are summary confessions of faith used by the vast majority of Christians. They developed at a time when most people could not read, so they needed a memorable rule of faith. The use of a creed is rooted in the recitation of the *Shema* in ancient Judaism. Part of Jewish daily prayer, the *Shema* (Hebrew for "hear") is drawn from Deuteronomy 6:4–9, 11, 13–21 and Numbers 15:37–41. It served as a summary of biblical teaching and was probably recited by Jesus and the apostles. (See Mark 12:28–31, where Jesus recites a portion of the *Shema* to answer a teacher of the law.)

After Jesus ascended into heaven, the earliest Christians began using summaries of Christian teaching (e.g., see 1 Corinthians 15:3–5). These summaries developed into the creeds listed below.

Apostles' Creed: A summary that began to take shape already at the time of the apostles. This creed developed from a series of questions asked of a person at the time of Baptism. History shows that congregations in Rome were using a form of this creed already in the second century, but the wording did not receive its standard form until much later. Most churches from the Western (Latin) tradition still use the Apostles' Creed for instruction and as a confession of faith in worship.

Nicene Creed: A summary of Christian teaching adopted by congregations of the Roman Empire at the Council of Nicaea in 325. The Council of Constantinople expanded the creed in 381 to help settle other Christological controversies of the fourth century. Today, Eastern Orthodox churches and most churches from the Western (Latin) tradition confess the Nicene Creed in worship, especially during a Communion service. In the Middle Ages the Western churches added the *filioque* statement (see the Glossary, p. 683) and other minor changes, such as changing "we believe" to "I believe."

Athanasian Creed: This longer creed addresses the Christological controversies of the fourth and fifth centuries. Although named for Athanasius (ca. 296–373), the bishop of Alexandria who vigorously opposed Arianism, he did not write this creed, since it emerged much later. Many churches of the Western (Latin) tradition use the Athanasian Creed. Lutheran congregations typically recite it on Trinity Sunday. The creed has been included in Eastern Orthodox services, minus the *filioque* statement (see the Glossary, p. 683).

No creed but the Bible: Congregations of the Restoration movement rejected the use of creeds early in the nineteenth century. They taught that creeds divided Christians from one another and that agreement on the Bible as God's Word was a sufficient basis for unity. Christian Churches, Disciples of Christ, and Churches of Christ descend from this movement.

Liturgical churches (Eastern Orthodox, Lutheran, Reformed, Roman Catholic, and some Wesleyans) regularly recite a creed during their worship services. Many nonliturgical churches accept the teachings of the creeds but do not use them in their worship services.

Point to Remember

And being found in appearance as a man, He humbled Himself and became obedient to death. *Philippians 2:8* (NIV)

Sinless Savior

To what base ends, and by what abject ways,
Are mortals urg'd through sacred lust of praise! . . .
To err is human; to forgive, divine.
—Alexander Pope, *An Essay on Criticism: Part 2*

The Bible teaches us that Jesus did not sin. Some people think that because Jesus did not sin He was not fully human, as in the saying "To err is human." At one time, however, Adam and Eve were both fully human and without sin. Through their desire to be like God, human beings lost their purity. By placing His sinless life under the Law, Jesus sought to restore our purity. Jesus kept the Law, not for Himself but for us. His sinlessness in no way disqualified Him from truly representing us.

The saying "To err is human" is in a sense a serious misconception, because sin is a perversion of God's creation. Not only were Adam and Eve fully human before the fall, but Christians in heaven are also fully human (e.g., they do not "become" angels). What is more, after we rise from the dead, we will still be fully human—even as Christ is still fully human though also fully God. The point is that we often forget sin is an inherited and spiritual disease that does not make us *more* human. We would never say to anyone that he has to have a particular illness or injury to be fully human. Christ took on flesh and became our brother in the sense that He completely joined us in our humanity. Being born under the Law, He was truly our representative and was in the perfect position—as true God and man—to live for us in a vicarious fashion (as our substitute). Being sinless did not disqualify Jesus from living for us. It was the reason His living for us under the Law made Him our Savior. He was able to keep the Law perfectly (without sinning) for us all!

Is there a difference between Jesus being tempted and our being tempted? Absolutely. The fundamental difference is that when we are tempted, we may sin; but Christ never sinned when He was tempted. We cannot fathom what this is like, but from God's Word we know it is true. The life of Christ is often treated as if His only purpose were to teach and to perform the miracles that authenticated His teaching. Many people miss the fact that He was living *for us* under the Law.

One with Us

We know that Christ was "tempted as we are, yet without sin" (Hebrews 4:15). A good example of our Lord being confronted with diverse temptations is the series of episodes in the wilderness (Matthew 4; Mark 1;

Luke 4). But some people believe that since Jesus did not sin, He did not suffer when He was tempted. Hebrews 2:18 tells us otherwise: "For because He Himself has suffered when tempted, He is able to help those who are being tempted." Christ's temptations were completely real and caused Him to suffer. That can be hard for our human brains to reconcile with the fact that after His incarnation, Jesus was holy, which made Him completely separate from sin. But Leviticus 19:1–2 confirms that Jesus was and is and ever will be holy because He *is* God: "And the LORD spoke to Moses, saying, 'Speak to all the congregation of the people of Israel and say to them, You shall be holy, for I the LORD your God am holy.' "

In sinlessness and holiness Jesus came into the world, but another important condition was present at His birth. Galatians 4:4–5 teaches that Jesus was also "born under the law." That is, He subjected Himself to God's Law as given to Moses and to His holy nation, Israel. Even though Jesus as God gave the Law, He put Himself under it and put Himself in the position to keep it. Verse 5 clearly shows that Jesus' purpose for being "born under the law" was "to redeem those who were under the law, so that we might receive adoption as sons." Jesus put Himself under the Law to save us.

This can raise questions about Jesus' Baptism. We need to be baptized because of our sinfulness, but Jesus had no sin. Matthew 3:15 records that Jesus was baptized "to fulfill all righteousness." Through His Baptism, Christ completely identified with us and showed Himself to be our vicarious (substitutionary) representative. He was already perfectly righteous, but He would fulfill all righteousness for all of us, the unrighteous. Jesus was baptized for us, not for Himself!

Jesus did not come "to abolish the Law or the Prophets . . . but to fulfill them" (Matthew 5:17). He fulfilled all the messianic prophecies, thereby giving full meaning to the Law and the Prophets, which pointed forward to Him. He also fulfilled all that the Law and the Prophets required of God's people. Romans 10:4 tells us that "Christ is the end of the law for righteousness to everyone who believes." The word *end* does not mean "termination" but "fulfillment." God's Law is good and holy, and we are to cherish it. But Christ is "the end of the law" because He fulfilled all its righteous requirements for us. Thus as God's people we are no longer "under the law" but are free from its condemnation. God declares us righteous as we believe in His Son, who fulfilled the Law in our stead.

Essential for Salvation

Sometimes people view the sinlessness and holiness of Jesus as a mere expression of piety and respect. But if Christ were not the sinless Son of God, He could never have been in the position to fulfill the Law in our stead. If He had been anything else, we would still be under the Law and its condemnation.

If someone insists that salvation is based on obeying the Law, he or she is saying that the life, death, and resurrection of Jesus were not necessary. Romans 3:20 proves that we cannot make ourselves righteous by observing the Law: "By works of the law no human being will be justified in His sight, since through the law comes knowledge of sin." Apart from Christ, the Law can only show us our sin—it condemns us. We cannot fulfill the Law; we need Christ to do this for us. And He did! God looks at us as if we had perfectly kept the Law, because Christ has kept the Law in our place.

Because of Christ's sinless life under the Law for us, we can relate to the words in Psalm 112:1: "Praise the LORD! Blessed is the man who fears the LORD, who greatly delights in His commandments." God's Law is no longer burdensome, because Christ took away the burden in fulfilling the Law. In Christ, the Law does not condemn us; rather, it shows us the life that Christ lived for us and the life we delight to live.

Comparisons

Through the centuries, different teachers have proposed different ideas or emphases about the meaning of Christ's life and death. These are known as theories of the atonement. Here are some important examples.

Declaratory view. Christ died to show human beings how much God loves them. Some liberal theologians hold this view today.

Dramatic view. Christ tricked the devil by disguising His divine nature with His human nature. The devil attacked Christ and believed that he overcame Him by means of Christ's cross. But Christ arose from death and defeated the devil. This way of describing Christ's work was popular in early Christianity.

Example view. Christ lived and died as an example of goodness for His followers to imitate. The medieval philosopher Peter Abelard (1079–1142) held this view. A group called the Socinians held this view at the time of the Reformation. Some liberal theologians hold this view today.

Martyr view. Christ gave up His life for a principle of truth in opposition to falsehood. A variation holds that Christ died because of misunderstanding, just as others have died because of human sin and hatred. Some liberal theologians hold this view today.

Satisfaction view. Christ died to satisfy God's perfect justice. Anselm (1033–1109) and Thomas Aquinas (1225–74), who were teachers during the Middle Ages, emphasized the satisfaction view. This emphasis has been strong among Roman Catholics.

Substitution view. Christ bore our sins on the cross and received the punishment of death that all people deserved.

Lutherans and other Christian teachers have emphasized *substitutionary satisfaction*, pointing out that the last two views are taught by the Scriptures. Christ both satisfied the Father's justice and substituted His life for ours so that He might reconcile us to God and defeat sin, death, and the devil. Certainly Christ also set a good example for His followers, but following Jesus' example cannot atone for one's own sins.

Point to Remember

We do not have a high priest who is unable to sympathize with our weaknesses, but one who in every respect has been tempted as we are, yet without sin. *Hebrews 4:15*

Sin-Bearer

Jesus atoned for the sins of those who accepted his teaching, by being an infallible example to them.

—Mahatma Gandhi, *All Men Are Brothers*

Although Jesus truly serves as an example, Christians view His work of atonement as something much greater. They teach that Jesus bore the sins of the world as our sacrifice and substitute.

In sports such as baseball, soccer, and football, one player comes in as a substitute for another. By the end of the game, that substitute may have secured either the victory or defeat for the whole team. The greatest substitution in history was no game, but it was something in which we all share. Jesus' death on the cross was, in the eyes of God, *our* death. Jesus' work of redeeming us is finished, and as a result, we are saved.

Romans 6:3 teaches that we "were baptized into His death." In Christ's death, our death died. That is, His death was the result of *our* condemnation for sin. In this sense, Christ's death was our death. For the Christian, temporal death is now much more than a consequence of sin entering the world; it is also a blessing. Paul says, "To me to live is Christ, and to die is gain" (Philippians 1:21). Death is destroyed and no longer threatens the Christian on account of Christ's substitutionary death.

When you see a crucifix, a cross holding a body that depicts Jesus Christ, consider 1 Corinthians 2:2: "I decided to know nothing among you except Jesus Christ and Him crucified." The cross is not a mere *symbol* of God's love or just an *example* of sacrificial living and dying. Paul knew that the cross of Christ is the basis for our salvation—it was where Jesus took away our sins.

Some people find Jesus' crucifixion for our sins to be comforting, while others find it offensive. Paul writes: "The word of the cross is folly to those who are perishing, but to us who are being saved it is the power of God" (1 Corinthians 1:18). There is nothing offensive about the power of God; what is offensive is our sins, which nailed His Son to the cross.

Atonement

Today, people are quick to hold to the truth that God is love. They are not so quick to acknowledge that God has wrath (real and righteous anger that condemns evil). Romans 3:25 tells us that Jesus was presented or displayed as "a propitiation," which can mean "a turning away of wrath." Another translation is "sacrifice of atonement" (NIV). Thus Christ was sacrificed for us to turn God's wrath away from us. In Ap V (III) 261 [382] (*Concordia*, p. 141), we find another way of understanding the effect of propitiation: "our sins have been blotted out by Christ's death." God's wrath has nowhere else to go because it was put fully upon Christ. In effect, therefore, sins paid for are no more. They're gone—"blotted out."

Romans 5:10 clearly teaches that "we were reconciled to God by the death of His Son." Because of our sins, we were enemies of God; but now that Christ has removed our sins, we are God's friends. We have been reunited with Him, brought back together in harmony, and restored to friendship.

Christ came "to serve" and "to give His life" as a ransom for many (Mark 10:45). "Many" does not mean that the benefits of His death are limited to a special few. For example, 1 John 2:2 says: "He is the propitiation [atoning sacrifice] for our sins, and not for ours only but also for the sins of the whole world."

Christ paid the ransom for our sins to the Father. "Ransom" refers to the sum of money used to buy back defeated prisoners or slaves. This process is called "redemption." When the Bible says we are "redeemed," it means that we have been delivered from sin and death. Jesus paid the price through His death on the cross to buy us back from sin. Christ sacrificed or offered Himself once for all (Hebrews 9:26). As a result, Christ was able to "do away with sin" (v. 26 NIV) and "take away the sins of many people" (v. 28 NIV).

We read in 2 Corinthians 5:21 that "for our sake He made Him to be sin who knew no sin, so that in Him we might become the righteousness of God." Jesus was made to be sin because our sin was imputed to Him; we become holy because Christ's righteousness was imputed to us. We are now holy, not by nature but because God declares us holy. On the cross Jesus was declared a sinner, but He was not by nature a sinner.

God "made Him . . . to be sin" does not mean that Jesus became sin *in essence*. He did not *become* sinful in His being. As He hung on the cross, He was considered, treated, and regarded by God as the sacrifice for all sins. He was viewed and counted as bearing our sins. In truth, God has already and finally dealt with all our sins through the cross of Christ!

Galatians 3:13 teaches us that Christ could never be counted as sin in what He did because He was sinless and always kept the Law of God. However, Galatians 3:13 quotes Deuteronomy 21:23, which says that anyone who is hung on a tree is under God's curse. Christ allowed Himself to be hung on a tree so He could be a real and actual substitute for sinners. We are cursed for what we've done; He was cursed for what He allowed to be done to Him. In this way, a cursed one—one who was "made to be sin"—could die for sinners, for cursed people. It would be hard to find a better commentary on Galatians than Luther's 1531 lectures (published in 1535). Luther depicts the Father as sending His Son from heaven to earth to be the worst sinner by taking the sins of all people. The fact that Jesus became a curse for us is the sweetest medicine against a conscience plagued by sin. Our curse is gone. Christ removed it!

Your Defense

Satan is known as "the accuser" (Revelation 12:10). His ongoing practice is to accuse the people of God. He claims that God still holds our sins against us. According to the doctrine of Christ's work, Satan's accusations are an absolute lie because our guilt and shame were put on Christ when He died on the cross. There He cried, "It is finished!" God has indeed dealt with our sin, because Christ was our substitute—"sin for us." As true God and true man, Jesus accepted the punishment, suffering, and death due each of us on account of our sins.

Some people may claim that it's sacrilegious to say that Christ became sin for us. But it is actually sacrilegious to say that He did not. We must say what the Bible clearly teaches. The Gospel cannot be understood apart from the truth that Christ became sin for us.

Of the seven recorded sayings of Christ on the cross, perhaps the most perplexing is His cry: "My God, My God, why have You forsaken Me?"

(Matthew 27:46). Jesus cried out because, by taking our place, He was being treated as we deserved to be treated. On our behalf Christ bore the agony of God's wrath against our sins. As the Father turned away from our sins, He turned away from His Son, who was bearing those sins.

Comparisons

Limited atonement. Reformed churches, which base their teaching on the theology of John Calvin (1509–64), hold that Christ died only for the elect, not for all of humanity.

Universal atonement. Lutherans and most other Christians hold that Jesus died for the sins of all people, not just for those of the elect.

Point to Remember

> There is no distinction: for all have sinned and fall short of the glory of God, and are justified by His grace as a gift, through the redemption that is in Christ Jesus. *Romans 3:22b–24*

Theology of the Cross

Early in Luther's career, while studying St. Paul's first letter to the Corinthians, he noticed some problems in the way theologians of his day thought about God and His work in people's lives. Many theologians believed that by using their reason they could understand God. By studying God's creation and human history, they tried to see and deeply understand God's glorious ways.

But the apostle Paul taught this was not possible. We can't discover God's ways through our reason or by looking for His glory, but through the "word of the cross" (1 Corinthians 1:18). In other words, Paul argued that we know God especially through suffering and weakness (1 Corinthians 1:18–2:16). We learn to trust in Him when we see our own weakness. Here is how Luther described this insight and its significance in the 1518 Heidelberg Disputations (AE 31:40–41; theses 19–24):

> 19. That person does not deserve to be called a theologian who looks upon the invisible things of God as though they were clearly perceptible in those things which have actually happened [Rom. 1:20].
>
> 20. He deserves to be called a theologian, however, who comprehends the visible and manifest things of God seen through suffering and the cross.

In other words, the biblical message of the cross—the Gospel—shows us who God really is. If we try to get to know Him through the glories of creation, the strength of human reason, or through human triumphs in history, we will not see that God works in people's lives through suffering and humility as Jesus did when He redeemed us on the cross. Since medieval theologians lacked this insight of the cross, they became confused. Luther continued:

> 21. A theologian of glory calls evil good and good evil. A theologian of the cross calls the thing what it actually is.
>
> 22. That wisdom which sees the invisible things of God in works as perceived by man is completely puffed up, blinded, and hardened.

The theologians of glory think power is good and weakness is bad. They think triumph is good and suffering is bad. They can't see that God achieved His greatest triumph through Jesus' death for our sins, that Jesus' suffering was the highest good, which sweeps away all our glorious attempts to understand and please God. Also, they cannot see that God still works in our lives through weakness and suffering. Affliction does not automatically make someone a loser. God may allow or send affliction in order to achieve His purposes through our suffering. When we trust in our triumphs and achievements, God is hidden from us rather than revealed. In Luther's day, this happened especially as people believed that obedience to God's Law or man-made rules would bring them closer to God and gain them justification before God. Luther wrote:

> 23. The law brings the wrath of God, kills, reviles, accuses, judges, and condemns everything that is not in Christ [Rom. 4:15].
>
> 24. Yet that wisdom [of the law] is not of itself evil, nor is the law to be evaded; but without the theology of the cross man misuses the best in the worst manner.

The Law is valuable and still has an important place in our lives. But without the cross and the salvation Christ won for us, mankind misuses the Word of God, and people condemn themselves rather than attain to God's glory and salvation as they suppose. For these reasons, Law and Gospel need to be clearly understood, distinguished, and appropriately used.

Theologians of Glory Today

The scholastic theology that Luther combated is less well-known today, but love of glory and triumph are ever with us! Theologians of glory today teach that by obeying certain principles one can lead a triumphant Christian life.

If you are suffering or struggling, they suppose, you have broken the principles or you lack genuine faith.

In the face of such teaching, cling to the cross of Jesus. Certainly follow the wise principles of God's Word but know that God in His wisdom may achieve His good purposes through your struggles and that such times will teach you to look to the Lord. Confess before God and the world that Jesus won your salvation through His suffering on the cross and rose again to be your ever-present Savior. For nothing can separate you from God's love in Christ.

Risen Savior, Living Lord

Seeing is believing.
—popular proverb

In contrast to this popular saying, Jesus said: "Blessed are those who have not seen and yet have believed" (John 20:29). Or as some have put it, "Believing is seeing."

Our faith, however, is not "blind." Our faith rests on the Scriptures, which record numerous eyewitness accounts of the living Jesus after He rose from the dead. Thomas did not touch a ghost; he touched the risen Christ! Since Christ has truly risen from the grave and is alive, our salvation is secure, our faith certain.

Faith is not contrary to reason. Remember the great command to love the Lord our God with all our heart, soul, and mind (Matthew 22:37). We do not practice *fideism*—that is, having faith in faith itself. We do not believe in faith; we believe in Christ. Our faith is therefore intelligent, logical, and rational. God does not call us to blind faith. Jesus Himself led people to believe in Him on the evidence of the miracles He did (John 14:11). Our faith involves real events, people, and places. The historical fact of Jesus' resurrection is the supreme testimony to the truthfulness of the Gospel.

If Christ had not been raised from death, what would that mean for the Christian faith? Paul states: "If Christ has not been raised, then our preaching is in vain and your faith is in vain" (1 Corinthians 15:14). A few verses later, Paul declares: "If Christ has not been raised, your faith is futile and you are still in your sins" (1 Corinthians 15:17). Jesus' resurrection is indispensable. If Christ did not rise, there *is* no Christian faith. Paul concludes: "But in fact Christ has been raised from the dead" (1 Corinthians 15:20).

Some churches hold that the resurrection of Jesus was only spiritual, not physical. But we know that Christ's resurrection was physical. His body was dead; it became alive. Liberal critics hold to the rationalistic assumption that miracles are impossible. Logically speaking, if God exists He can work miracles. History testifies to this fact.

Jesus' Victory

> For Christ also suffered once for sins, the righteous for the unrighteous, that He might bring us to God, being put to death in the flesh but made alive in the spirit, in which He went and proclaimed to the spirits in prison, because they formerly did not obey, when God's patience waited in the days of Noah, while the ark was being prepared, in which a few, that is, eight persons, were brought safely through water. (1 Peter 3:18–20)

While there is some confusion among Christians regarding Christ's descent into hell after His crucifixion, the information Peter provides us seems pretty clear. Christ's descent happened after His death on the cross: He was "put to death in the flesh but made alive in the Spirit" (v. 18b). The textual clue that Jesus went to hell is twofold: (1) "spirits in prison" and (2) "they formerly did not obey." The Bible clearly teaches that after people die, their spirit enters either heaven or hell (Luke 23:43; 16:22–23). "Prison" refers to hell, which is described in terms of agony and suffering. Believers who enter eternal life have had their sins removed by Christ. Their sins are no longer remembered (Isaiah 43:25). The spirits mentioned in 1 Peter 3 disobeyed in Noah's day. They are not in heaven but in hell. Jesus went to "proclaim" there, but nothing indicates that He suffered. The idea that He would suffer after His death contradicts the very words of Christ from the cross: "It is finished" (John 19:30; see also Ephesians 4:7–10). From Peter, John, and Paul, we can be certain that Christ's descent into hell was not for the purpose of suffering; rather, it was a stage of His glorious resurrection from the dead.

As we move our discussion from His crucifixion to His resurrection, we turn to 1 Corinthians 15:3–8. Paul mentions three elements of "first importance":

1. Christ died for our sins.
2. He was buried.
3. He was raised on the third day.

The third element—the resurrection—is elaborated upon by an extensive list of Christ's many appearances, including one to more than 500 followers. Why did the risen Christ make so many appearances? The Lord was providing ample eyewitness testimony! At the time of Paul's recording of the witnesses, he was effectively inviting any skeptics to check out the facts for themselves.

Matthew 28:1–10 tells us that Jesus appeared to the women who had gone early to His tomb (see also Mark 16:1 and Luke 24:10 for the list of women). Verse 9 indicates that the women "took hold of His feet" when they worshiped Jesus. These kinds of details provide further evidence of Christ's physical, bodily resurrection. After He had appeared to the women, to the disciples on the road to Emmaus, and many others, Jesus appeared to His eleven disciples. The first thing He did was rebuke them "for their unbelief and hardness of heart, because they had not believed those who saw Him after He had risen" (Mark 16:14). Jesus made eyewitness testimony a high priority.

While Mark gives a summary of this event, Luke records more details. He tells us that the disciples "were startled and frightened and thought they saw a spirit" (Luke 24:37). Jesus invited them to touch Him and to see His real flesh (v. 39). He then asked for something to eat (vv. 41–43).

In John 20:24–28, we learn about Thomas. (Note that the reference to "the eleven" in Mark 16:14 does not include Thomas, just as the reference to "the Twelve" in John 20:24 does not include Judas Iscariot.) After the other disciples told Thomas about the risen Christ, Thomas reacted as the other disciples had done when they heard the women's testimony of Jesus' resurrection—with doubt and unbelief. Jesus offered the evidence of His physical body and invited Thomas to touch Him. Thomas's response proves that the Bible identifies Jesus as God.

We read about Christ's ascension in Acts 1:9–11. The angels proclaim: "This Jesus, who was taken up from you into heaven, will come in the same way as you saw Him go into heaven" (v. 11). Jesus Christ—true God and true man—is risen, has ascended into heaven, and will come again!

Certainty

None of us were eyewitnesses of the assassination of President Lincoln, yet we have a great deal of certainty that it was an actual historical event because of the accounts of eyewitnesses. Isn't the eyewitness testimony about the resurrection of Jesus as trustworthy and certain? Everyone acknowledges the integrity and usefulness of legitimate eyewitness testimony. None of us doubt the existence of Plato or Aristotle. We are certain of Alexander the Great's conquests. We know that John Adams was the second president of the United States. The quality of the eyewitness testimony concerning the resurrection of Jesus Christ is just as good if not better than that concerning the examples mentioned here.

Many people have recorded evidence concerning Lincoln's assassination. Few, if any, have risked their lives to do so. After Christ rose from the dead and ascended into heaven, the apostles' lives were at stake for preaching the Gospel. This tells us they were certain that Jesus was alive after being crucified. What makes the eyewitness testimony about Christ's resurrection so outstanding is that the disciples were willing to give their very lives as they went about their witnessing. People will sometimes go to great lengths to tell a lie, but they will rarely die for a lie. The apostles were dying for the truth of the resurrection!

After they saw Jesus, the disciples touched the Lord, clasped Him, and ate with Him (see John 21:12–14). These actions are important because they give us proof that Christ truly rose from the dead.

Comparisons

Resurrection of the body. Traditionally, all Christians hold (on the basis of the Scriptures) that Jesus rose from the dead bodily and will reappear bodily at the end of time. He will raise all the dead bodily for the Last Judgment.

Spiritual resurrection. Liberal theologians have been influenced by modern skepticism, which questions the possibility of miracles. As a result, some theologians have proposed "spiritual" views of the resurrection. For example, some believe that Jesus didn't really rise from the dead but that He lives on in the hearts of His followers.

Bodily presence in the Lord's Supper. Eastern Orthodox Christians, Lutherans, Roman Catholics, and some others teach that Jesus gives His true body and blood in the Lord's Supper. For example, the Lutheran Confessions state: "By this communicated ‹divine› power, according to the words of His testament, He can be and is truly present with His body and blood in the Holy Supper. He has pointed this out for us by His Word. This is possible for no other man, because no man is united with the divine nature the way Jesus, the Son of Mary, is. No man is installed in such divine almighty majesty and power through and in the personal union of the two natures in Christ" (FC SD VIII 29; *Concordia*, p. 586).

Bodily presence in heaven only. The Reformed churches and others hold that Christ's human nature must remain in heaven until the Last Day. Therefore, they conclude that Jesus cannot give His true body and blood in the Lord's Supper. For example, the *Westminster Shorter*

Catechism states that people who receive the Lord's Supper are "not after a corporal and carnal manner, but by faith, made partakers of his body and blood" (question 96). In other words, the communing is spiritual and not in the body and blood of Christ.

Point to Remember

For I delivered to you as of first importance what I also received: that Christ died for our sins in accordance with the Scriptures, that He was buried, that He was raised on the third day in accordance with the Scriptures. *1 Corinthians 15:3–4*

Head of the Church and Coming King

We're more popular than Jesus now. I don't know which will go first—rock 'n' roll or Christianity.
—John Lennon

At this moment Jesus Christ is keeping His Church, His body of believers, in the saving faith. By His life, death, and resurrection He secured our salvation; but if not for His sustaining and nourishing service right now, we could never be saved. What is more, by virtue of His holding us now in His Church, we are prepared to meet Christ face-to-face when He comes again in all power and glory.

What evidence do we see that Christ is reigning in heaven right now? Jesus sustains creation and the governments of the world. In His Body, the Church, He sustains us through His Word and Sacraments and keeps us in the forgiveness of sins and the assurance of life eternal. In the kingdom of glory we will experience the fulfillment of all His promises, when we will see our Savior face-to-face.

How people react to the words "Jesus is coming soon" depends much on their knowledge of God's Word and on their spiritual condition. To take comfort in the forgiveness of sins through Christ is also to take comfort in His second coming, because He will welcome into the new heaven and new earth those who trust in Him. On the other hand, if people do not know that their sins are forgiven, the prospect of Christ's coming may be at least disturbing and at worst a terrifying nightmare.

Enthroned in Glory

According to Ephesians 1:20, Christ is seated at the right hand of God in the heavenly realms. The "right hand" of God is not a local or circumscribed place. Jesus is not limited to a geographic point on a heavenly map. The "right hand" is Christ's position of power and authority. Ephesians 1:21–22 describe this position as being "far above all rule and authority and power and dominion, and above every name that is named, not only in this age but also in the one to come," adding that God "put all things under His feet and gave Him as head over all things to the church." The beneficiaries of this rule and authority of Christ are those in the Church.

Romans 8:34 also tells us that Jesus is "at the right hand of God." Christ reigns with all power and authority right now. In this position, Jesus is "interceding for us." We are the beneficiaries of His prayers to the Father on our behalf.

Hebrews 9:28 reminds us that Christ was sacrificed on earth to take away the sins of all people. This passage also teaches that Christ "will appear a second time." In this context, His first appearance refers to His incarnation and birth. The second appearance refers to His glorious second coming. Christ will "save those who are eagerly waiting for Him." This in no way contradicts the fact that we have salvation in Christ today. We do; but throughout the Scriptures our salvation is described as something accomplished, something we are constantly given, and something that is yet to come. These are not contradictory but complementary. The salvation we have now will be confirmed and will lead to a glorious reward in the future.

Matthew 24:30 records that "all the tribes of the earth" will see the second, glorious coming of Christ. The next verse indicates that Christ "will send out His angels with a loud trumpet call" to gather the elect, that is, all Christians. When Christ comes again, He will direct all the events on the Last Day.

First Thessalonians 4:16 lists other signs and events that will accompany Christ's glorious coming. There will be

1. "a cry of command,"
2. "the voice of an archangel," and
3. "the sound of the trumpet of God." Also,
4. "the dead in Christ will rise first."

Verse 17 concludes: "We will always be with the Lord."

According to Matthew 25:31, Christ "will sit on His glorious throne" when He comes again. In verse 32, Jesus teaches us that He will separate people from all nations "as a shepherd separates the sheep from the goats."

This describes the great universal judgment. Verse 34 records that to the sheep Christ will speak words that are sweet: "Come, you who are blessed by My Father, inherit the kingdom prepared for you from the foundation of the world." However, verse 41 records words of terrible judgment spoken to those who rejected Christ: "Depart from Me, you cursed, into the eternal fire prepared for the devil and his angels." Note that Romans 8:1 says: "There is therefore now no condemnation for those who are in Christ Jesus." Galatians 3:13 clearly presents that Christ became a curse for us. But what happens when someone is not "in Christ Jesus"? What happens when anyone rejects Christ's work of becoming a curse for all people? Their curse remains. To be sure, John 3:16; 2 Corinthians 5:15; 1 John 2:2; and other Scripture passages clearly teach that Christ died for the sins *of the world.* But some people never come to saving faith in the glorious work of Christ. When Christians are judged, they are judged in Christ and covered by Him; but when those without Christ are judged, their sins remain without the covering of Christ, whom they rejected.

Revelation 7:16 describes those saved by Christ as never again knowing hunger or thirst; the suffering associated with this temporal realm will be gone. Verse 17 teaches that Jesus is "in the midst of the throne" and that He "will be [our] shepherd." He will lead us to springs of living water, and God will wipe away our every tear. Through our faith in Jesus and by His grace, heaven will be our eternal home!

Coming with the Clouds

Christians comfort fellow believers by saying, "I will pray for you." Even more comforting is the knowledge that God the Son is interceding for us! Perhaps one of the most underestimated assurances we have from the Bible is that our Savior is praying for us. If the prayers of a righteous person are powerful and effective (James 5:16), how much more powerful and effective are Jesus' prayers for us? The answer is self-evident, but we need to celebrate this reality more and more!

A teacher in a vacation Bible school once took his class of first graders outside to have them peer into the sky as he described the second coming of Christ. When the teacher got to the part about Christ's coming on the clouds, a little girl became scared and hid behind a bush. Adults, too, may be confused and unsure about how they can anticipate the glorious coming of Christ.

But we can be filled with joy as we anticipate the Lord's coming because we are saved, promised a gracious reward, comforted, and consoled. The events of the Last Day will all be good for the child of God. All our sins are covered by the blood of Christ and remain that way for eternity. The reason for our confidence is the saving work of Christ for us through His life, crucifixion, and resurrection. Our confidence is created and sustained by virtue of Christ's Word and Sacraments. In other words, we are confident not only because Christ has won our salvation but also because He continually distributes the benefits of this salvation through His Word and Sacraments. Both aspects are indispensable for our confidence and assurance. Having these, we are absolutely prepared for our Lord's second coming.

In our raised and glorified bodies, we will enter the new heaven and earth, we will never again suffer, and we will be filled with unspeakable joy. All these things are true because of Christ's love and mercy toward us; they are true because Jesus lived, died, and rose for us.

While we look forward to entering eternity in our raised and glorified bodies, we have the opportunity to live for Jesus in our earthly bodies right now. We Christians do not live in a foreign dualism that treats the body as inferior to the spirit. We honor our risen and coming Lord as we prepare ourselves in every way, including honoring Him with our bodies—the same ones that will be raised and enter the new heaven and new earth.

Comparisons

Amillennialism. Eastern Orthodox Christians, Lutherans, Roman Catholics, and some Reformed Christians and Wesleyans hold that Christ rules now through His Church. The "thousand years" of Revelation 20 symbolize the present rule of Christ. The Apostles' Creed summarizes the events of the end times from an amillennialist view: Jesus will come to judge the living and the dead, He will resurrect the dead, and the Church will enjoy the life everlasting.

Millennialism. Anabaptists, Baptists, and some Reformed Christians and Wesleyans hold that Christ will establish a literal, thousand-year rule on earth. Postmillennialists believe that Christ will return *after* this thousand-year period; premillennialists believe that Christ will return *before* this thousand-year period.

Liberalism. Liberals seek to establish Christ's kingdom on earth through social justice and peace.

Point to Remember

[Jesus said,] "Then the King will say to those on His right, 'Come, you who are blessed by My Father, inherit the kingdom prepared for you from the foundation of the world.'" *Matthew 25:34*

Lutheran Summary of God the Son

Augsburg Confession III 1–2

Our churches teach that the Word, that is, the Son of God [John 1:14], assumed the human nature in the womb of the Blessed Virgin Mary. So there are two natures—the divine and the human—inseparably joined in one person. There is one Christ, true God and true man, who was born of the Virgin Mary. (*Concordia*, p. 32)

Apology of the Augsburg Confession V (III) 261 [382]

For Christ is an Atoning Sacrifice, as Paul says, "by faith" (Romans 3:25). When fearful consciences are comforted by faith, and are convinced that our sins have been blotted out by Christ's death, and that God has been reconciled to us because of Christ's suffering, then, indeed, Christ's suffering profits us. (*Concordia*, p. 140)

Formula of Concord Epitome IX 4

It is enough if we know that Christ descended into hell, destroyed hell for all believers, and delivered them from the power of death and of the devil, from eternal condemnation and the jaws of hell. (*Concordia*, p. 495)

Formula of Concord Solid Declaration III 15, 58

[The following is an elaboration on the connection between Christ's obedience (keeping and fulfilling the Law) and our being saved.]

For this reason, then, His obedience (not only in His suffering and dying, but also because He was voluntarily made under the Law in our place and fulfilled the Law by this obedience) is credited to us for righteousness. So because of this complete obedience, which He rendered to His heavenly Father for us by doing and suffering and in living and dying, God forgives our sins. He regards us as godly and righteous, and He eternally saves us.

. . . And faith thus values Christ's person because it was made under the Law [Galatians 4:4] for us and bore our sins, and, in His going to the Father, He offered to His heavenly Father for us poor sinners His entire, complete obedience. This extends from His holy birth even unto death. In this way, He has covered all our disobedience, which dwells in our nature, and its thoughts, words, and works. So disobedience is not charged against us for condemnation. It is pardoned and forgiven out of pure grace alone, for Christ's sake. (*Concordia*, pp. 538, 545)

Formula of Concord Solid Declaration VIII 6, 24, 40, 42, 44

We believe, teach, and confess that God's Son from eternity has been a particular, distinct, entire, divine person. Yet He is true, essential, perfect God with the Father and the Holy Spirit. In the fullness of time He received also the human nature into the unity of His person. He did not do this in such a way that there are now two persons or two Christs. Christ Jesus is now in one person at the same time true, eternal God, born of the Father from eternity, and a true man, born of the most blessed Virgin Mary. This is written in Romans 9:5, "from their race, according to the flesh, is the Christ who is God over all, blessed forever." . . .

On account of this personal union and communion of the natures, Mary, the most blessed Virgin, did not bear a mere man. But, as the angel ‹Gabriel› testifies, she bore a man who is truly the Son of the most high God . . . Therefore, she is truly the mother of God . . . .

. . . For if I believe that only the human nature suffered for me, then Christ would be a poor Savior for me, in fact, He Himself would need a Savior. . . . But this person is truly God, and therefore it is correct to say: the Son of God suffers. Although, so to speak, the one part (namely, the divinity) does not suffer, nevertheless the person, who is God, suffers in the other part (namely, in the humanity). For the Son of God truly is crucified for us, i.e., this person who is God. . . . [I]t could be called God's dying, God's martyrdom, God's blood, and God's death. For God in His own nature cannot die; but now that God and man are united in one person, it is called God's death when the man dies who is one substance or one person with God. (*Concordia*, pp. 582, 586, 588–89; the final paragraph cites AE 37:209–11; 41:104)

TOPIC EIGHT

Justification and Sanctification[1]

Engaging This Topic

"Why doesn't your church teach about sanctification?"
"We *do* teach about sanctification."
"Then what steps are you taking to become a better Christian?"

The words *justification* and *sanctification* weigh in at five syllables each, which make them technical terms. Yet they are not just jargon; rather, they are central for understanding the Christian life. Sin and its guilt are removed. Faith is given. Faith is maintained. Believers die, are raised, and live forever with God. This is the best happy ending that God has to offer, and it is a true story.

Different approaches to the biblical witness about these topics define relationships and differences among Protestants, between Protestants and Roman Catholics, and between Western and Eastern Christianity. The concepts themselves come from the Bible in such representative passages as Romans 3:22–25; 4:25; James 2:24; and elsewhere. Controversy about these terms arose when Augustine, bishop of Hippo in North Africa, contended with Pelagius, a popular lay theologian from Rome. Augustine gave us these big words to describe how God removes sin and guilt from a person and how that person grows in right faith and behavior.

One often hears talk about justification and sanctification in Western Christianity, whereas Eastern Orthodox Christians speak of *theosis*, of becoming like God in Christ. There the emphasis remains on the incarnation and entire life and work of Christ, from which flow the stages of purification, illumination, and sainthood in the lives of believers. It is for this reason that Orthodox Christians commune infants after Baptism. The cross does not play a central role here.

Western Christianity has a more specific focus on sin and guilt, thereby seeing a primary place for the cross and Christ's atonement for sinners.

1 This chapter adapted from *The Lutheran Difference: Justification and Sanctification*, written by Korey Maas. Copyright © 2005 Concordia Publishing House

Roman Catholics speak of initial and final justification, between which is a life in which one is gradually made more holy in a cleansing manner through the sacraments. Since the Reformation, Lutheran and Reformed Protestants have generally agreed that the doctrine of justification as God's total declaration of righteousness is the foundation and cornerstone of the Christian Church and its faith, though differences about how one is given faith and maintained in faith affect their respective understanding of the doctrine of justification. Arminians and Methodists, on the other hand, have placed greater emphasis on sanctification and the human will.

Since the time of Augustine, few have agreed upon the definition and content of justification. Especially among Western Christians, debates arise about whether God justifies by *declaring* sinners holy or by actually *making* them holy. Does God alone effect justification, or must we in some way cooperate with or assent to God's action? Furthermore, how does God maintain believers in faith?

Remaining in faith is a concern that shifts the focus from justification to sanctification, again depending on one's definitions. This area of concern is perhaps even more hotly debated. What is the definition of *sanctification*, the means by which it takes place, and the reasons for retaining or losing it? Such questions are especially worth exploring from a Lutheran perspective because, while they are widely recognized to have a strong doctrine of justification, Lutherans are often accused of downplaying—or even ignoring—the doctrine of sanctification.

This chapter aims to clarify the contributions of Lutheran theology to the discussions about how one's sins are forgiven, how one remains in faith, and how one finally goes to heaven. These discussions are important because Christians do more than believe teachings for the sake of just believing. Christian faith ultimately is caught up in the great saving work of God, the passing away of the old creation, and the creation of the new, eternal heaven and earth.

Some of this chapter speaks to debates internal to the Lutheran Church. To some Lutherans who may be tempted to downplay sanctification, they will see the rich biblical and confessional testimonies to the importance of sanctification. Likewise, the biblical doctrine of justification emphasizes to those possibly influenced by Methodism the truth that justification is indeed "the article on which the church stands or falls." In fact, we will see just how intimately related justification and sanctification are.

Lutheran Facts

The Lutheran Church, following Scripture, considers the doctrine of justification the central teaching of the Christian faith. By inheritance from

Adam and Eve and by thought, word, and deed, people are transgressors of God's Law, subject to His wrath, and condemned to eternal death. However, God is moved to justify us unworthy sinners by grace. He did this through Christ, who fulfilled God's Law and through His sufferings and death satisfied divine justice. In Christ, God reconciled the world to Himself.

Through the Gospel and the Sacraments, God gives us Christ's righteousness and offers, gives, and seals to us His forgiveness for Christ's sake. These are apprehended by faith, which itself is a divine gift given through the Means of Grace. All human merit is excluded.

Sanctification is the spiritual growth that follows justification. By God's grace, a Christian cooperates in this work. Through the Holy Spirit's work in the Means of Grace, faith is increased, love strengthened, and the image of God renewed. Lutherans believe that sanctification will be complete only in heaven.

The Curse and the Cure

> Houston, we've had a problem.
> —Apollo 13 astronaut James Lovell

The near-fatal Apollo 13 mission of 1970 has become part of America's national memory. It gripped people's attention at the time. Its events were later turned into a successful film, and Lovell's statement has become a proverb. The Apollo 13 mission had a happy ending. Since that narrowly averted disaster, however, the world has witnessed tragedies on an enormous scale: genocide, terrorism, and natural disasters, to name just a few. Anyone who looks at the television, browses the Internet, or opens a newspaper will almost surely conclude that, indeed, we have a problem. As Christians, we know that the fundamental problem with the world is bondage to sin.

Diagnosing the Disease

After describing the creation of the world and the plant and animal life to populate it, Scripture records God's crowning act of creation: man and woman. But Moses not only records this fact, he also highlights the great distinction between God's creation of man and all that came before. Unlike all other creatures, "God created man in His own image, in the image of

God He created him" (Genesis 1:27). A precise definition of God's image is difficult to summarize, since God in Himself remains beyond the grasp of fallen man's reason. On the basis of what He has revealed in Scripture, however, the reformers were able to conclude that "man was made in the image and likeness of God. What else was this image and likeness other than that man was created with wisdom and righteousness so that he could apprehend God and reflect God?" (Ap II [I] 18; *Concordia*, p. 78). In this light, it is hardly surprising that God would look upon His human creation and declare it "very good" (Genesis 1:31).

Genesis 3 records man's first act of disobedience. In response to man's disregard for the one command he had received, God pronounced a new judgment upon His creation. Speaking first to the serpent, which had deceived the woman, God said, "Cursed are you" (Genesis 3:14). Speaking to the man, God also said, "Cursed is the ground because of you" (Genesis 3:17). The created world, which God had previously called "very good," fell under a curse, the consequences of which God's human creation cannot avoid. The woman will experience pain in childbirth, the man will toil and sweat to support his family and life, and finally, in accordance with the warning pronounced in Genesis 2:17, both will die. Not only does this curse involve physical death, but, apart from redemption in Christ, it also involves spiritual and eternal death, as Luther summarized: "For when we had been created by God the Father and had received from Him all kinds of good, the devil came and led us into disobedience, sin, death, and all evil [Genesis 3]. So we fell under God's wrath and displeasure and were doomed to eternal damnation" (LC II 28; *Concordia*, pp. 401–2).

Although God's curse was first announced to the serpent and those whom he had tempted, Scripture also makes clear that the curse and its effects are not limited to these individuals. Adam and Eve were cursed because they refused to obey God's command. The same is true of their descendents. Something similar to God's dialogue with Adam and Eve occurs when He speaks to the people of Israel: "I am setting before you today a blessing and a curse: the blessing, if you obey the commandments of the Lord your God . . . and the curse, if you do not obey" (Deuteronomy 11:26–28). In the New Testament, Paul makes clear that this remains no less true. "Cursed," he says, "be everyone who does not abide by all things written in the Book of the Law, and do them" (Galatians 3:10). That word *all* is worth emphasizing, as James also states: "Whoever keeps the whole law but fails in *one point* has become accountable for all of it" (James 2:10, emphasis added). For this reason, the Lutheran Confessions rightly conclude: "By their own strength, people cannot fulfill God's Law. They are all under sin, subject to eternal wrath and death. Because of this, we cannot be freed by the Law from sin and be justified" (Ap IV [II] 40; *Concordia*, p. 87).

It is understandable that, just as Adam sinned and was punished, so should all who willfully break God's Law be punished. This, however, does not tell the whole story of sin and its effects. We all commit *actual* sins. But we are also infected with *original* sin, a sinful nature. By this we mean that "even if a person would not think, speak, or do anything evil (which, however, is impossible in this life, since the fall of our first parents), his nature and person are nevertheless sinful. Before God they are thoroughly and utterly infected and corrupted by original sin, as by a spiritual leprosy. . . . So we are by nature the children of wrath, death, and damnation, unless we are delivered from them by Christ's merit" (FC SD I 6; *Concordia*, p. 512). This is precisely what Paul teaches when he writes that sin and its consequences reign "even over those whose sinning was not like the transgression of Adam" (Romans 5:14), which was a willful breaking of God's command. This is why, for example, the psalmist confesses that he was conceived in sin (Psalm 51:5). That even those who *commit* no sin should be judged guilty of sin may be difficult to accept, even to understand. But this is why Luther stressed that "this hereditary sin is such a deep corruption of nature that no reason can understand it. Rather, it must be believed from the revelation of Scripture" (SA III I 3; *Concordia*, p. 270).

As is evident from the creation account, in which man was created and declared "very good," God did not desire His people to be sinful. The fall into sin, and our continual sinfulness, is in direct contradiction of God's will. In fact, He explicitly states as much when He commands His people to "be holy, for I am holy" (Leviticus 11:44). This command is repeated in the New Testament by Peter, who encourages the Christian to "be holy in all your conduct, since it is written, 'You shall be holy, for I am holy' " (1 Peter 1:15–16).

It is depressingly obvious that left to our own devices we are hopelessly lost. Our first parents introduced a curse upon creation. We inherit original sin. We commit actual sins. We are not holy as God demands. Therefore, we are all subject to the just penalties for sin: death and condemnation. In light of all this, what hope is there for human beings living under the curse of sin and death? Despite the severity of this message, all is not hopeless. We have not been left to our own devices. We have not been left under a curse, but we have been redeemed from it. As Paul announces in Galatians 3:13: "Christ redeemed us from the curse of the law by becoming a curse for us—for it is written, 'Cursed is everyone who is hanged on a tree'—so that in Christ Jesus the blessing of Abraham might come to the Gentiles, so that we might receive the promised Spirit through faith." In His suffering and death, Christ experienced the full effects of God's curse upon sin. Because He underwent this suffering on our behalf, we need no longer fear the eternal consequences of our sin. As the Confessions summarize: "The

Law condemns all people. But Christ—without sin—has borne the punishment of sin. He has been made a victim for us and has removed that right of the Law to accuse and condemn those who believe in Him. He Himself is the Atonement for them. For His sake they are now counted righteous" (Ap V [III] 58 [179]; *Concordia*, p. 109).

Rejoicing in the Cure

Scripture is explicit in its diagnosis of human sinfulness: it is not only inherited from our first parents, but it also comes forth in our own thoughts, words, and deeds. Scripture is clear in its presentation of the deadly consequences of sin. Thankfully, however, Scripture is equally explicit in proclaiming that our problem has been solved in the person and work of Jesus Christ, the Savior who removed the curse of sin with His atoning death and resurrection.

Recognizing our inherent sinfulness, how will we daily approach our Lord in prayer? Let's compare the two approaches in Luke 18:9–14. This parable epitomizes two ways in which sinners might approach God. The Pharisee shows the approach that is unacceptable in the Lord's sight. Rather than freely admitting his sinfulness, the Pharisee attempts to excuse himself; literally, he declares himself just or righteous by pointing out the good he does and the evil he avoids. But even if his claims are true, he is mistaken in believing that such obedience can compensate for other faults or for that original sin that even he has inherited. By way of contrast, we read that the tax collector "went down to his house justified" (Luke 18:14). Yet all he did was approach God to pray, "Be merciful to me, a sinner!" (v. 13). Recognizing his sinfulness, the tax collector also recognized that God alone is capable of justifying him, of declaring him righteous.

In his Epistle, John states even more explicitly what is illustrated by the parable in Luke 18. He warns, "If we say we have no sin, we deceive ourselves." But he also offers this comforting promise: "If we confess our sins, He is faithful and just to forgive us our sins and to cleanse us from all unrighteousness" (1 John 1:8–9). That is why we do not enter worship as if we have a right to stand before God. Instead, we come into His presence confessing our sins and asking that He "cleanse us from all unrighteousness." In His great mercy, this He does, proclaiming our forgiveness in the words of Absolution, words that are spoken "in the stead and by the command" of Christ Himself.

The Last Word?

The doctrine of original sin is impossible to grasp without the aid of divine revelation. However, for many people, it is also extremely offensive. But the proclamation of the Gospel—the forgiveness of sin—only makes sense if one is first made aware of one's own need for forgiveness. That is why the Law—which accuses individuals of sin—must also be proclaimed. The Law is never to be the last word; nevertheless, only after the curse has been diagnosed can the cure be appreciated in all its sweetness.

Knowing that, how do we respond to a friend who tells us, "We all make mistakes sometimes, but at heart people are basically good"? The doctrine of original sin, as Luther explained, "must be believed from the revelation of Scripture" (SA III I 3; *Concordia*, p. 270). We can point out to such friends, as C. S. Lewis does in *Mere Christianity*, that we are incapable of perfectly obeying even our self-imposed moral codes. How much less will we then believe we can fulfill the commands of a holy God? Ultimately, we must stress that actual sins are but symptoms of the deeper problem of a sinful nature, which prevents us from being "basically good." Then we must follow the proclamation of human sinfulness with a proclamation of Christ's saving work.

Comparisons

Eastern Orthodox: "What is necessary in order to please God and to save one's own soul? In the first place, a knowledge of the true God, and a right faith in Him; in the second place, a life according to faith, and good works" (*The Longer Catechism of the Eastern Church*, Question 3).

Lutheran: "Our churches teach that people cannot be justified before God by their own strength, merits, or works. People are freely justified for Christ's sake, through faith, when they believe that they are received into favor and that their sins are forgiven for Christ's sake" (AC IV 1–2; *Concordia*, p. 33).

Reformed/Presbyterian: "Those whom God effectually calleth He also freely justifieth; not by infusing righteousness into them, but by pardoning their sins ... for Christ's sake alone" (*The Westminster Confession of Faith*, chapter 21.1).

Roman Catholic: "Whereas all men had lost their innocence in the prevarication of Adam ... free will ... was by no means extinguished in them" (*Canons and Decrees of the Council of Trent*, Session 6, Decree on Justification; cf. CCC2 paras. 1730–48).

Baptist: "We believe that the great gospel blessing which Christ secures to such as believe in him is Justification; that Justification includes the pardon of sin, and the promise of eternal life on principles of righteousness; that it is bestowed . . . solely through faith in the Redeemer's blood" (*New Hampshire Baptist Confession*, article 5).

Wesleyan/Methodist: "We are accounted righteous before God only for the merit of our Lord and Saviour Jesus Christ by faith, and not for our own works or deservings" (*Methodist Articles of Religion*, article 9).

Liberal: "The traditional soteriology presupposed the historicity of Adam's fall and started from the assumption that mankind needs to be saved primarily from the taint inherited from Adam. But modern anthropology has discredited this way of determining the nature of man and of sin" (Gerald Birney Smith, ed., *Guide to the Study of the Christian Religion* [Chicago: University of Chicago Press, 1916], p. 519).

Point to Remember

Christ redeemed us from the curse of the law by becoming a curse for us—for it is written, "Cursed is everyone who is hanged on a tree." *Galatians 3:13*

Stumbling Stone and Cornerstone

Justify my love.
—1980s pop star Madonna

Despite their occasional protestations to the contrary, pop stars are not typically those we would consider to be "just like us." But, frequently, musicians and entertainers achieve popularity precisely because they so accurately reflect the thoughts and feelings of a great many people. Madonna's quotation might be taken as a case in point. How often are we given to believe that love must somehow be justified? That is, love must be earned, merited, or deserved by the one who receives it. Of course, this partially reflects that our society rarely thinks of love except in terms of romance. But think for a moment about other—and, arguably, higher—forms of love.

Are there people in your life for whom you simply cannot justify your love yet whom you love nonetheless? If you are a parent of young children, you likely recognize that infants are a good example of those who are loved without having done anything to deserve such love. Although they might say so in jest, parents of teenagers might feel the same way! Of course, we also often hear of those who are in a coma or are in some way debilitated and unable to respond to those who care for them; yet those who do care for them often do so precisely because they love them.

The Unlovely Beloved

The universal human condition is succinctly diagnosed with Paul's opening statement in Romans 3:10: "None is righteous, no, not one." But Paul does not stop there. Verses 10–18 quote the Old Testament at length, proclaiming that no one understands, seeks, or fears God. No one does good. Rather, people deceive, curse, and shed blood. These are the results of original sin. As the Confessions summarize: "Original sin contains these diseases: ignorance of God, contempt for God, not having fear and trust in God, [and] the inability to love God" (Ap II [I] 14; *Concordia*, p. 78). Since these are the results of inherited sinfulness, it follows that there is nothing we have done or can do to merit God's love. In fact, contrary to some opinions, Paul explains that this diagnosis of the human condition is not meant to spur us to do better or to try harder to justify God's love. Instead, Paul writes that it is proclaimed "so that every mouth may be stopped" (Romans 3:19), so that we might cease our attempts to justify ourselves. That is the primary purpose of the Law: to reveal our sinfulness and subsequent need for a Savior.

The depth and nature of God's love is revealed when Paul contrasts it with the self-interested love of sinful men. Unlike those who are unlikely to give up their lives even for a deserving individual, Paul confirms that "Christ died for the ungodly" while we were "still weak" (Romans 5:6) and "still sinners" (Romans 5:8), while we were "dead in our trespasses" (Ephesians 2:5). That is, Christ's love was showered upon us precisely when we did not deserve it, when we were still in rebellion against Him, and when, being "dead," we could do nothing to change this predicament. This is the very reason a Savior is necessary. As the Confessions pointedly ask: "Why do we need Christ's grace if we can be justified as a result of our own righteousness?" (Ap II [I] 10; *Concordia*, p. 77).

As we discussed earlier, sin results in death. Death is a consequence of the sinful nature all have inherited from Adam; therefore, all can expect to die. However, it would be a mistake to believe that Christ's death was the inevitable result of His being human. He certainly is, as we confess in the Athanasian Creed, "perfect God and perfect man" (*Concordia*, p. 17). But in one crucial respect Jesus differs from all other men. He is, as the Epistle to the Hebrews records, "without sin" (4:15) and "without blemish" (9:14).

Therefore, the confessors could state that He did not have to die "for His own sake." But He did so for our sake. "For this reason, then, His obedience (not only in His suffering and dying, but also because He was voluntarily made under the Law in our place and fulfilled the Law by this obedience) is credited to us for righteousness. So, because of this complete obedience, which He rendered to His heavenly Father for us by doing and suffering and in living and dying, God forgives our sins" (FC SD III 15; *Concordia*, p. 538).

Some have ridiculed Christ's sinless death for us as a "legal fiction." Such critics say that it would be neither logical nor just for an innocent man to pay the penalty for others, or for that man's righteousness to be conferred to others. The Lord Himself responds to this: "My thoughts are not your thoughts, neither are your ways My ways" (Isaiah 55:8). Scripture also provides another answer. Although sinless in and of Himself, Christ did bear sins deserving God's wrath. These were not His own sins, but ours and those of the entire world. This was prophesied already in the Old Testament, where it is proclaimed that "the LORD has laid on Him the iniquity of us all" (Isaiah 53:6) and that "He bore the sin of many" (Isaiah 53:12). Looking back on Christ's death, Peter emphasized the same fact: "He Himself bore our sins in His body" (1 Peter 2:24). What this means is that God did not pour out His wrath on Jesus *instead of* sending punishment for our sins; God dealt with our sin in Christ's suffering and death.

Christ and His crucifixion on our behalf is indeed a stumbling block to many. Specifically, Peter says that Christ is a stumbling stone to "those who do not believe" (1 Peter 2:7). Paul expresses the same thing, calling Christ's death a stumbling block to the Jews and Greeks who preferred to see something more in keeping with their conception of God's character (see 1 Corinthians 1:23–24). The imagery of a stone, upon which some will trip and fall, vividly illustrates the incomprehensibility of Christ and His salvation to those without faith. Interestingly, the imagery of a stone is also employed in a more positive light. For those who have been granted faith, Christ crucified becomes the cornerstone, the very foundation of our salvation. It is hardly surprising, then, that the confessors often call our justification on account of Christ's atoning death "the chief article in all Christian doctrine" (FC SD III 6; *Concordia*, p. 536). The image of a cornerstone is also reflected in the familiar Lutheran phrase that describes justification as "the article on which the church stands or falls."

The clear connection between Christ's death and our salvation is expressed by Paul, who declares that we are "justified by [God's] grace as a gift, through the redemption that is in Christ Jesus" (Romans 3:24). Specifically, Paul says that this redemption occurs in Christ because Christ alone was "a propitiation by His blood" (Romans 3:25). That is, Christ's blood shed on the cross is an atonement for our sins. The author of Hebrews says precisely the same thing: "by means of His own blood" Jesus secured for us "an eternal redemption" (9:12). It is nothing other than this proclamation of pure Gospel that we learned in the Small Catechism, professing our belief that Christ "purchased and won me from all sins, from death, and from the power of the devil. He did this not with gold or silver, but with His holy, precious blood and with His innocent suffering and death" (SC II; *Concordia*, p. 329).

The Centrality of the Cross

Despite the world's frequent preoccupation with romantic love, Scripture plainly declares:

> Greater love has no one than this, that someone lay down his life for his friends. (John 15:13)

> By this we know love, that He laid down His life for us. (1 John 3:16)

The purest and most perfect love is to be found in that apparently most unlovely event, the suffering and death of Christ. With this selfless act, our Lord Himself redeemed those who had done, and could do, nothing to justify His love.

Despite the fact that some consider Christ and His death foolishness, we know that this—and nothing else—is our sure salvation. Not only does Scripture declare that we are, in and of ourselves, sinful and deserving of condemnation, but it also constantly reminds us that there are no thoughts, words, or deeds by which we can justify ourselves. Instead, God became man, took our sins upon Himself, and in His death He justifies us. Therefore, like Paul, we cannot boast in our own works, but only "in the cross of our Lord Jesus Christ" (Galatians 6:14).

What is true for us as individuals is also true for all people. Salvation has been won once, for all, on the cross. This is why, when speaking of our salvation, we will only boast in the cross. But the cross will be central not only in thinking about and rejoicing in our own justification but also in proclaiming salvation to others. We will, of course, say to friends and family, "God loves you," and other similar truths. But we will also remember that God's love is not generic and that His saving love comes at a price. This is not a price that we must pay but one that Christ has paid on the cross. Therefore, there can be no proclamation of God's love and salvation without the proclamation of the cross. This clearly informed Paul's evangelism efforts, for he says, "I decided to know nothing among you except Jesus Christ and Him crucified" (1 Corinthians 2:2).

All Too Easy?

The apostle Paul often commented that Christ's death was an offense and a stumbling block to many. This is no less true today than it was in Paul's day. Not only is the idea of God Himself suffering in human flesh offensive, but so, too, is the proclamation that His death *alone* is the means of salvation. "That's too easy," some would say. "Surely we must contribute *something* to our salvation." But Scripture declares otherwise. Justification is the free gift of God, won and bestowed solely on account of Christ.

We can use this biblical evidence to respond to the popular opinion that God will reward all those who "do their best to live a good life." We are sinful by nature. It is also true that we are legalists by nature. That is, we want to justify ourselves by means of the Law—by *doing* something. Any honest assessment of our lives will reveal that we have not lived perfectly, so we are sometimes tempted to believe that God doesn't demand perfection but only that we do our best. But such a view denies the clear testimony of God Himself. Thus when confronted with someone who holds to the "live a good life" philosophy, we want to draw attention to the words of Scripture and emphasize that, though God demands perfect righteousness, this very righteousness becomes ours on account of Christ's sinless death on our behalf.

Comparisons

How many religions are there in the world? There are not a thousand, not four (pagan, Jewish, Muslim, Christian), but only two essentially different religions: *the religion of the Law*, that is, the endeavor to reconcile ourselves to God through our works, and *the religion of the Gospel*, that is, faith in the Lord Jesus Christ, belief worked in us through the Gospel by the Holy Spirit, belief that we have a gracious God through the reconciliation already effected by Christ, and not because of our own works.[2]

Point to Remember

> For if while we were enemies we were reconciled to God by the death of His Son, much more, now that we are reconciled, shall we be saved by His life. *Romans 5:10*

2 Adapted from Francis Pieper, *Christian Dogmatics* (St. Louis: Concordia, 1950), 1:9–10.

Just Words

A man is but a man, and words are but words.
—Elizabethan playwright Anthony Munday

Although we use words every day and, indeed, could not get by without them, it is not uncommon to hear "mere words" being denigrated. For example, each of us has probably thought or said that "actions speak louder than words." Children still regularly repeat the schoolyard chant that, unlike sticks and stones, "words can never hurt me." In a political age characterized by what the pundits call *spin*, it has become increasingly easy to dismiss even the announcement of good news as just words. But do these clichés actually reflect the truth?

How important are words? How powerful are they? Most people will probably agree that words are very important. Most people will also agree that words can have both positive and negative power. But if even human words have such power and importance, how much more significant are the very words of God?

Word Perfect

Paul begins two of his Epistles with helpful definitions. To the Romans, he writes that the Gospel is "the power of God for salvation" (1:16). In his first letter to the Corinthians he writes: "The word of the cross . . . is the power of God" (1:18). Each definition is extremely significant; each refers the power of God to words. It is "the word of the cross"—the proclamation of Christ's death—in which God powerfully acts. It is the Gospel—the word of Good News—by which salvation comes. True, our *objective* justification occurred with Christ's death. But as Luther writes in the Large Catechism: "Neither you nor I could ever know anything about Christ, or believe on Him, and have Him for our Lord, unless it were offered to us and granted to our hearts by the Holy Spirit through the preaching of the Gospel" (LC II 38; *Concordia*, p. 403). Christ's death secured our salvation, but the *subjective* appropriation of this salvation only comes to us with its verbal proclamation.

Scripture clearly indicates that Jesus taught about the saving power of words. Speaking to His disciples, He said, "The words that I have spoken to you are spirit and life" (John 6:63). Speaking of the command to preach the Gospel received from His heavenly Father, He said, "His commandment is eternal life" (John 12:50). According to Jesus, divine words do not merely convey information; they actually convey life. Indeed, they are life. Speaking of this power of divine words, the Confessions therefore state that we "are given not only bodily, but also eternal things: eternal righteousness, the Holy Spirit, and eternal life. These things cannot reach us except by the ministry of the Word" (AC XXVIII 8–9; *Concordia*, p. 58).

In one of many biblical metaphors, Paul describes the Word of God as "the sword of the Spirit" (Ephesians 6:17). This is not the only time such imagery is used. The Epistle to the Hebrews likewise explains that "the word of God is living and active, sharper than any two-edged sword" (4:12). The Word of God is not a "dead letter." It is living, active, and effective; it actually does something. In fact, it does that which nothing else is given the power to do: bestow forgiveness. Because this promise of forgiveness is attached to nothing but God's own Word, the Confessions insist that "in issues relating to the spoken, outward Word, we must firmly hold that God grants His Spirit or grace to no one except through or with the preceding outward Word" (SA III VIII 3; *Concordia*, p. 280).

Although God's Word is indeed living and active, we should not regard it as magical. Humans can and, sadly, sometimes do reject God's Word and the salvation it bestows. Thus Scripture exhorts us not to reject God's Word but to receive it in faith. In Acts 13:38–39, Paul speaks of the "forgiveness of sins [which] is proclaimed to you," and then continues by saying that "everyone who believes is freed from everything from which you could not be freed by the law" (sin, death, hell). This emphasis on the necessity of belief is expressed in the classic Lutheran expression that we are "justified by faith." This is not to detract from the fact that, objectively, Christ alone justifies. But, as the Confessions explain: "Christ is Mediator . . . . For how will Christ be Mediator if we do not use Him as Mediator in justification, if we do not hold that we are counted righteous for His sake? To believe is to trust in Christ's merits, that for His sake God certainly wishes to be reconciled with us" (Ap IV [II] 69; *Concordia*, p. 91). Nor should it be understood that our believing is a good work, attributable to our own strength. On the contrary, "faith is God's gift" (FC SD III 11; *Concordia*, p. 538). Indeed, faith is not something we contribute to God's Word, but "faith is conceived from the Word" (Ap IV [II] 73; *Concordia*, p. 91). Finally, this is why God has so graciously provided for the regular proclamation of His Word: "So that we may obtain this faith, the ministry of teaching the Gospel and administering the Sacraments was instituted" (AC V 1; *Concordia*, p. 33).

In describing the manner in which Christ has justified His Church, Paul says that He "cleansed her by the washing of water with the word" (Ephesians 5:26). The reference to Baptism—water with the Word—is unmistakable. In fact, Luther would describe this Sacrament by saying that "Baptism is nothing other than God's Word in the water" (SA III V 1; *Concordia*, p. 278). But is it appropriate to say Baptism actually justifies, or saves? According to Peter, it certainly is. He explicitly says that

Baptism "now saves you" (1 Peter 3:21). But not by water alone. As the Small Catechism reminds us, "without the Word of God the water is simple water and no Baptism. But with the Word of God it is a Baptism, that is, a gracious water of life and a washing of regeneration in the Holy Spirit" (*Concordia*, p. 340).

Matthew 26:26–28 records the words Jesus used to institute the Lord's Supper; they are repeated at each celebration of this Sacrament. These words also reveal the reason for which the Sacrament was instituted. Christ here offers His body and blood, He says, "for the forgiveness of sins." But as with Baptism, it is not simply the elements themselves that bestow forgiveness, "but the words, which are given here, 'Given . . . and shed for you, for the forgiveness of sins.' These words are, beside the bodily eating and drinking, the chief thing in the Sacrament. The person who believes these words has what they say and express, namely, the forgiveness of sins" (SC VI; *Concordia*, p. 343). The intimate connection between the justification secured at Calvary and the justification bestowed in Word and Sacrament is further highlighted by Luther: "It is useless talk when they say that Christ's body and blood are not given and shed for us in the Lord's Supper, so we could not have forgiveness of sins in the Sacrament. Although the work is done and the forgiveness of sins is secured on the cross [John 19:30], it cannot come to us in any other way than through the Word" (LC V 31; *Concordia*, p. 435).

Same Word, Many Accents

It may be easy to grow cynical about words spoken by sinful and self-interested human beings. But Scripture clearly and consistently posits a radical distinction between the Word of God and the word of man. The Gospel is never mere words. But it most certainly is "just words"—that is, words which convey and bestow forgiveness, declaring us just and righteous in the sight of God. Our Lord is so gracious that He presents His Gospel to us in several Means of Grace.

Consider Jesus' promise to His apostles in John 20:21–23. "Jesus said to them again, 'Peace be with you. As the Father has sent Me, even so I am sending you.' And when He had said this, He breathed on them and said to them, 'Receive the Holy Spirit. If you forgive the sins of any, they are forgiven them; if you withhold forgiveness from any, it is withheld.'" This promise helps us to understand the practice of Confession and Absolution. Visitors to Lutheran churches sometimes take offense at the Absolution pronounced during the Divine Service, asking, "What right does the pastor have to forgive sin?" The answer is given by Jesus, who tells His apostles, "If you forgive the sins of any, they are forgiven them." Called and ordained pastors, those who inhabit and exercise the pastoral office by virtue of the congregation's call, truly do forgive "in the stead and by the command" of Jesus. With this Absolution, justification is pronounced and received. In fact, Lutherans confess that "the word *justify* means . . . 'to absolve, that is, to declare free from sins'" (FC Ep III 7; *Concordia*, pp. 480–81). This is true because the Absolution pronounced is nothing other than the Word of God. "Because God truly brings a person to life through the Word, the Keys truly forgive sins before God" (Ap XIIa [V] 40; *Concordia*, p. 162). This is why Luther encouraged pastors to ask of the penitent, "Do you believe that my forgiveness is God's forgiveness?" (SC V; *Concordia*, p. 342). Believing that the justification pronounced in Absolution is indeed God's justification, we are eager to receive this word of the Lord as often as it is made available, whether corporately in worship or individually in private Confession and Absolution.

There is more than one way to say, "I love you." Married couples usually know this. The Bride of Christ, the Church, also knows it, because Christ reveals and bestows His saving love for her in numerous ways. His justifying love comes in the Means of Grace, those expressions of "the Gospel, which does not give us counsel and aid against sin in only one way. God is superabundantly generous in His grace: First, through the spoken Word, by which the forgiveness of sins is preached . . . . Second, through Baptism. Third, through the holy Sacrament of the Altar. Fourth, through the Power of the Keys. Also through the mutual conversation and consolation of brethren" (SA III IV; *Concordia*, p. 278). Such superabundant love not only makes us aware of God's great desire that we be justified but also prompts us joyously to make use of the various Means of Grace He provides.

Let's Hear It Again

Despite our many clichés about "mere words," it is clear that even human words are powerful and effective. Few people would envy a marriage where the words "I love you" are never spoken. Indeed, even one who knows he or she is loved will want and need to hear those words repeated often. How much more, then, can the Bride of Christ, the Church, rejoice in the fact that her Bridegroom so often and so variously proclaims His word of love.

In response, we proclaim our love for the Bridegroom through regular worship. Some friends may not understand this and ask why we spend so much time attending church. Many reasons can be given for regular church attendance: habit, coercion, a sense of duty. None of these answers is likely to encourage a positive view of Christian worship. But one who recognizes that God is present in the Divine Service to justify us by means of His Word and Sacrament will eagerly anticipate the opportunity to receive these gifts. We rejoice to come into the Lord's house because we know that there He promises to meet us, to speak to us, and to grant us the salvation won by the death and resurrection of Christ.

Comparisons

Verbal inspiration: The Holy Spirit led the prophets, evangelists, and apostles to write the books of the Bible. He guided their writing, inspiring their very words while working through their particular styles of expression. Therefore, the Bible's words are God's Word. Conservative Christian churches hold this view. Many also maintain that the original writings of the Bible were without error (the doctrine of inerrancy) but that some mistakes entered the text as the scribes copied, edited, or translated the Scriptures over the centuries.

Partial inspiration: Christians affected by theological liberalism hold different views of the inspiration of the Bible. For example, some would assert that the Bible is God's Word but that the authors erred in some factual details. Others would say that the Bible *contains* God's Word and that the Spirit leads people today to determine which parts of the Bible God wants them to follow. Still others would say that the Bible is one testimony to God's Word, along with writings used in other religions.

Inspired translations: Some churches hold that God inspired certain translations of the Bible. For example, the Eastern Orthodox Church holds that God inspired the Greek Septuagint translation of the Old Testament. Some English-speaking Protestants hold that God inspired the King James translation of the Bible.

Point to Remember

The word of the cross is folly to those who are perishing, but to us who are being saved it is the power of God. *1 Corinthians 1:18*

Creeds, Deeds, and Needs

Necessity knows no law.
—Latin proverb

The misguided but still popular slogan "deeds, not creeds" is sometimes heard within the Church. The point made by this phrase is that Christians should focus *less* on what they believe and confess and *more* on the manner in which they lead their lives. But since that which Christians believe first and foremost is the Good News of justification and since the manner in which Christians live pertains to sanctification, the slogan quoted above seems to imply that sanctification rather than justification is the essence of Christianity. Some might even be led to believe that the Law rather than the Gospel is the essence of Christianity.

Christians are sometimes accused of hypocrisy for saying they believe certain truths while living as if they do not believe them. So, while some who use this phrase may indeed believe that deeds rather than creeds are the essence of Christianity, it is also quite possible that it is repeated more innocently as a call for Christians to live in accordance with their profession of faith. However, deeds and creeds are not to be played one against the other; our works flow naturally and inevitably from our faith.

One Thing Needful?

In typically blunt language, Paul states: "This is the will of God, your sanctification" (1 Thessalonians 4:3). These words of God's inspired apostle leave no doubt that the Lord intends His people to be sanctified, that is, to be made pure and holy. In fact, Paul continues: "Whoever disregards this, disregards not man but God, who gives His Holy Spirit to you" (v. 8) for the purpose of sanctification. We are to act "in holiness" because God, through His Spirit, has called us "in holiness." The Lutheran Confessions are in full agreement with this, even saying: "For this very reason we are justified: being righteous, we may begin to do good works and to obey God's Law. We are regenerated and receive the Holy Spirit for the very reason that the new life may produce new works, new dispositions, the fear and love of God, hatred of lustful desires (concupiscence), and so on" (Ap V [III] 227–28 [348–49]; *Concordia*, pp. 135–36). Sanctification is not merely an option. It is God's will and one of the very purposes for which He justifies us.

In Luke 10:38–42, sisters Mary and Martha were obviously thrilled that Jesus had chosen to visit them personally. But their joy was expressed in two very different ways. Mary simply sat at the feet of Jesus and "listened to His teaching" (v. 38). Martha, on the other hand, "was distracted with much serving" (v. 40). She certainly wanted to please her Lord, but instead she became "anxious and troubled" (v. 41)—not only with her own work but also because Mary, in her eyes, was doing no work! Yet Jesus does not rebuke Mary. He says, "One thing is necessary. Mary has chosen the good portion" (v. 42). Paul is quick to tell the same to all those whom Christ has visited in His Word and Sacraments. One thing is necessary for salvation: grace. "By grace you have been saved," he says; "this is not your own doing"; it is "not a result of works" (Ephesians 2:8–9). As with Mary and the Ephesians, so with us. When we speak of justification and salvation, we must be clear that only one thing is needed, and this has been given us by God Himself.

The teaching of justification by grace through faith without works is sometimes obscured by a misunderstanding of important biblical texts. In 1 Corinthians 13:2, for example, Paul says, "If I have all faith . . . but have not love, I am nothing." Likewise, James asks, "What good is it, my brothers, if someone says he has faith but does not have works?" He concludes, "Faith by itself, if it does not have works, is dead" (James 2:14–17). Paul teaches that love is required. Do Lutherans deny this? No, say the Confessions: "We also require this." The confessors note that "renewal and beginning to fulfill the Law must exist in us" (Ap V [III] 98 [219]; *Concordia*, p. 115). But they also clarify that here Paul does not "talk about the way of justification. Instead, he writes to those who, after they had been justified, should be urged to bring forth good fruit" (Ap V [III] 99 [220]; *Concordia*, p. 115). The same is true concerning James. "It is clear," the Confessions state, "that James does not contradict us." But when we speak of faith we do not mean "passive knowledge" but faith, which "is a new life"; therefore, "it necessarily produces new movements and works" (Ap V [III] 127–29 [248–50]; *Concordia*, p. 119).

Paul also writes to young pastor Titus and encourages him to preach good works to his congregation. But he is quick to clarify that God saved us "not because of works done by us," but by the mercy shown us in our Baptism (Titus 3:5). After having received this justifying grace, Christians will then live out a sanctified life as they "devote themselves to good works" (Titus 3:8). This ordering of justification and sanctification is also maintained in the Confessions, where it is taught that "love and works must also follow faith. Therefore, they are not excluded so that they do not follow faith, but *confidence in the merit of love or of works is excluded in justification*" (Ap IV [II] 74, *emphasis added*; *Concordia*, pp. 91–92).

The words of Jesus in Matthew 7:17–18 illustrate the relationship between faith and works, justification and sanctification. Jesus does this when He describes the relationship between a tree and its fruit. Every healthy tree by its very nature bears good fruit. The Augsburg Confession therefore states that the Lutheran churches "teach that this faith is bound to bring forth good fruit [Galatians 5:22–23]. It is necessary to do good works commanded by God [Ephesians 2:10]" (AC VI 1; *Concordia*, p. 33). This illustration and explanation also reveal a subtle but important distinction between the ways in which the term *necessary* can be used. On the one hand, we must do good works because God commands them. But good works are also necessary in another sense. They necessarily (i.e., naturally and inevitably) flow from justifying faith, just as good fruit is naturally and inevitably produced by a good tree. In other words, sanctification is the inevitable fruit of justification.

Using an illustration similar to that in Matthew 7:17–18, Jesus says in John 15 that He alone is the source of our justification, our sanctification, and our salvation. In John's Gospel, this is partially revealed in yet another agricultural illustration. "Already you are clean," Jesus says, "because of the word that I have spoken" (John 15:3). Already you are justified and united with Christ. But Jesus goes on to explain that it is only by remaining in Him that sanctification takes place: "As the branch cannot bear fruit by itself, unless it abides in the vine, neither can you, unless you abide in Me" (v. 4). Thus the Confessions also explain: "First, in conversion faith is kindled in us by the Holy Spirit from the hearing of the Gospel. Faith lays hold of God's grace in Christ, by which the person is justified. Then, when the person is justified, he is also renewed and sanctified by the Holy Spirit. From this renewal and sanctification the fruit of good works then follow"(FC SD III 41; *Concordia*, pp. 542–43).

Law or Gospel?

The phrase "deeds, not creeds" can be understood (and can be intended) to mean "Law, not Gospel," and God's Law does declare that sanctification and good works are necessary. But *necessity* can also be a Gospel word. There is a considerable difference between saying "The Christian *must* be sanctified" and saying "The Christian *will* be sanctified." So while it might truthfully be said that "sanctification is necessary," it might also be said that "necessity knows no law." That is, Christian sanctification, though necessary, is not motivated by the coercion of the Law; it is a fruit of the Gospel.

In Galatians 2:20, Paul vividly describes the manner in which his faith and life are related. Paul, the great preacher of justification, is also the great defender of sanctification. He preaches faith but also teaches concerning the Christian life that flows from faith. Speaking of his own life, he can say, "It is no longer I who live, but Christ who lives in me. And the life I now live in the flesh I live by faith in the Son of God." Christ lives in him and thus works through him. The same is true of all Christians. So we can also say, "It is a living, busy, active, mighty thing, this faith. It is impossible for it not to be doing good works incessantly. It does not ask whether good works are to be done, but before the question is asked, it has already done them, and is constantly doing them" (FC SD IV 10–11; *Concordia*, p. 548, citing AE 35:370).

Lutherans are sometimes accused of neglecting the doctrine of sanctification. This, however, is certainly not true of the Lutherans who wrote and compiled the Confessions. Indeed, Luther himself has much to say on the topic in the most widely read of all Lutheran works: the Small Catechism. Not only does this booklet include the Ten Commandments, which reflect God's will for our lives, but it also includes a Table of Duties, which describes how all Christians should live and act in relation to others. But even when commenting upon the Second Article of the Creed—an article explicitly concerned with justification—Luther confesses that Christ justifies so "that I may be His own, live under Him in His kingdom, and serve Him in everlasting righteousness, innocence, and blessedness" (*Concordia*, p. 329). It is the Lutheran teaching that God justified us so that we might serve Him here on earth, where our sanctification remains imperfect, as well as in heaven, where we will serve Him in "everlasting righteousness."

Why and for What?

The informed Christian will never seek to pit Law against Gospel, sanctification against justification, or deeds against creeds. Each is intimately related to the other. The Law reveals our need for the Gospel. Being justified by the Gospel, our sanctification begins to find its expression in the cheerful and spontaneous fulfillment of the Law. Our creed—that Christ died and rose again for our salvation—motivates our deeds of love and thanksgiving. Each is necessary. The real question is, "Why and for what?"

And that begs the question, Are good works necessary? Lutherans should never deny that sanctification and good works are necessary. Their necessity is precisely what the Formula of Concord confesses. "Good works are necessary," it says; "we necessarily are to do, and must do, the kind of good works God has commanded. In the Holy Scriptures themselves the words *necessity*, *needful*, and *necessary*, as well as *ought* and *must*, are used to describe what we are bound to do because of God's ordinance, command, and will" (FC SD IV 14; *Concordia*, p. 548). But, as the Formula also states, we must always be careful of the context in which this confession is made. Good works pertain to sanctification only, not justification. "We must be on our guard well to make sure that works are not brought in and mixed into the article of justification and salvation," the formulators write, expressly condemning the statement that "*good works are necessary for believers to be saved*" (FC SD IV 22, *emphasis added*; *Concordia*, p. 549).

Comparisons

Eastern Orthodox: "How have we salvation by Christ's doctrine? When we receive it with all our heart, and walk according to it" (*The Longer Catechism of the Eastern Church*, question 197).

Lutheran: "Our churches teach that this faith is bound to bring forth good fruit [Galatians 5:22–23]. It is necessary to do good works commanded by God [Ephesians 2:10], because of God's will. We should not rely on those works to merit justification before God. The forgiveness of sins and justification is received through faith' " (AC VI 1–2; *Concordia*, p. 33).

Reformed/Presbyterian: "They who are effectually called and regenerated . . . are further sanctified . . . by His Word and Spirit dwelling in them" (*The Westminster Confession of Faith*, chapter 13.1).

Roman Catholic: "Having, therefore, been thus justified . . . through the observance of the commandments of God and of the Church, faith cooperating with good works, [they] increase in that justice . . . and are still further justified" (*Canons and Decrees of the Council of Trent* X; cf. CCC2 para. 2001).

Baptist: "We believe that Sanctification is the process by which, according to the will of God, we are made partakers of His holiness" (*New Hampshire Baptist Confession*, article 10).

Wesleyan/Methodist: "Good works . . . are . . . pleasing and acceptable to God in Christ, and spring out of a true and lively faith" (*Methodist Articles of Religion*, article 10).

Liberal: "We cannot define Christian ethics in terms of a church-controlled society. Neither can we regard Christian duty as identical with biblical precepts . . ." (Gerald Birney Smith, ed., *Guide to the Study of the Christian Religion* [Chicago: University of Chicago Press, 1916], p. 570).

Point to Remember

I have been crucified with Christ. It is no longer I who live, but Christ who lives in me. *Galatians 2:20*

Dying to Live

No life that breathes with human breath
Has ever truly longed for death.
—Tennyson, "The Two Voices"

At first glance, Tennyson's observation might seem self-evident. The dying day is something people attempt to postpone for as long as possible; it is not an event to be longed for. Yet even a passing familiarity with current affairs reveals that some apparently do long for death, whether they are suicide bombers or terminally ill advocates of euthanasia.

It is the Christian confession, however, that death is not simply the natural and inevitable end of life. Death is the final consequence—and final condemnation—of sin. But many others, it seems, welcome or even embrace death as good.

Take, for example, cases of euthanasia. In the face of terrible suffering, even some Christians may propose that a quick, assisted death is preferable to prolonged pain. They may even assume that, since God is merciful, such "mercy killings" reflect God's will. However, death is in fact not God's will, but the undesired result of our rejection of God's will with the first sin of Adam.

Wanted Dead *or* Alive?

James understood that death is something we do not desire: "For as the body apart from the spirit is dead, so also faith apart from works is dead" (James 2:26). But just as we seek to avoid physical death, so should we seek to avoid a dead faith. This he describes as "faith apart from works." James's words offer a salutary warning that sanctification and good works are never to be shunned or rejected. So, too, do the words of Luther, who not only confessed that "faith, renewal, and forgiveness of sins are followed by good works" but also insisted that "if good works do not follow, the faith is false and not true" (SA III XIII 2, 4; *Concordia*, p. 283). Just as we desire bodily life, so we desire a living faith, a faith that expresses itself in deeds.

In Ephesians 2:5, Paul notes that when we were "dead in our trespasses," God "made us alive" with Christ. In verses 8–9, Paul summarizes the doctrine of justification when he writes that "by grace you have been saved through faith. And this is not your own doing; it is the gift of God, not a result of works." But Paul is also clear that we were not justified so that we might continue to sin. Quite to the contrary, we were "created in Christ Jesus for good works" (v. 10). Finally, he explains that these works are not of our own invention or choosing; rather, "God prepared beforehand, that we should walk in them" (v. 10). That is, God not only effected our justification, but He also plays the central role in our sanctification, having prepared for us the very works in which our sanctification is carried out.

Let's look at several verses that show us the ultimate source of the good works that God has prepared for us.

Ezekiel 36:27: "And I will put My Spirit within you, and cause you to walk in My statutes and be careful to obey My rules."

John 15:5: "I am the vine; you are the branches. Whoever abides in Me and I in him, he it is that bears much fruit, for apart from Me you can do nothing."

Philippians 2:12–13: "Therefore, my beloved, as you have always obeyed, so now, not only as in my presence but much more in my absence, work out your own salvation with fear and trembling, for it is God who works in you, both to will and to work for His good pleasure."

These passages reveal the great extent to which God desires our sanctification. The prophets, apostles, and even Jesus Himself declare that God not only prepares the good works in which our sanctification is expressed but also is personally active in us to produce these works. Paul says that it is "God who works in you"; Jesus says, "Whoever abides in Me and I in him, he it is that bears much fruit"; and through Ezekiel, the Lord says, "I will put My Spirit within you, and cause you to walk in My statutes." The trinitarian God who justified us is also the God who sanctifies us. It is true that, unlike justification—which God alone effects—we are able to cooperate in our sanctification. But Jesus makes clear that we do not work alone. "Apart from Me," He says, "you can do nothing." The Confessions say the same when they state: "Even in this life the regenerate advance to the point that they want to do what is good and love it, and even do good and grow in it. Still, this (as stated above) is not of our will and ability, but of the Holy Spirit. . . . The Spirit works such *willing and doing*" (FC SD II 39; *Concordia*, p. 528).

Because it is the Holy Spirit who lives and works in us to effect our sanctification, Paul can refer to the good works of the sanctified life as the "fruit of the Spirit" (see Galatians 5:22–23). Thus the Confessions explain that the Christian "lives according to God's unchangeable will revealed in the Law. Since he is born anew, he does everything from a free, cheerful spirit. These works are not properly called 'works of the Law,' but works and 'fruit of the Spirit'" (FC SD VI 17; *Concordia*, p. 560). Because we are grafted into the living vine, Jesus Christ, we, too, live and are nourished by Christ and His Holy Spirit. But while we live, something must die: our sinful flesh "with its passions and desires" (Galatians 5:24). Like unwanted weeds, our sinful desires, if unchecked, can grow up to choke out the healthy fruits of sanctification. Therefore Paul refers to such desires as "crucified," put to death. This is a death the Christian truly does long for—the death of the sinful passions that are contrary to God's will.

Our desire that sinful passions be crucified and that good works might flourish is not merely a pious hope. It is precisely this for which Jesus prays when He asks of His Father: "Sanctify them in the truth." Moreover, Jesus indicated the very means by which this sanctification is effected: "Your Word is truth" (John 17:17). Paul echoes this when he notes that the Word does crucify our sinful desires because it is profitable "for reproof" and "for correction." Likewise, it encourages in us the living fruits of the Spirit, since it is also profitable "for teaching" and "for training in righteousness, that the man of God may be competent, equipped for every good work" (2 Timothy 3:16–17). Something of this is expressed in the Small Catechism's explanation of the Third Petition of the Lord's Prayer. God's will is done, Luther observes, "when God breaks and hinders every evil counsel and will that would not let us hallow the name of God nor let His kingdom come, such as the will of the devil, the world, and our flesh. Instead, He strengthens and keeps us steadfast in His Word" (*Concordia*, p. 334).

The Christian is no longer dead in sin. Having been made alive in justification, we, even now, "like living stones are being built up as a spiritual house" (1 Peter 2:5). God's work in us, through us, and for us did not end with our justification. It is He who continues to build us up and to sanctify us so that we might "offer spiritual sacrifices acceptable to God" (1 Peter 2:5). This dual emphasis on God's work and our work is very significant. As the Confessions note: "As soon as the Holy Spirit has begun His work of regeneration and renewal in us through the Word and holy Sacraments, we can and should cooperate" (FC SD II 65; *Concordia*, p. 532). Lest we become tempted to overestimate our own abilities, however, the Confessions continue by saying that the Christian "does good to such an extent and as long as God by His Holy Spirit rules, guides, and leads him. As soon as God would withdraw His gracious hand from that person, he could not for a moment keep obeying God" (FC SD II 66; *Concordia*, p. 532).

Wanted Dead *and* Alive

As much of the above makes clear, Christians do not hold the positive view of death that some have. "Dead" faith is condemned. While we were "dead" in sin, Christ "made us alive" in justification. We are now "living stones" with which Christ builds His Church. But death is not always bad. It is for our good that our sinful nature is "crucified." Indeed, the sanctified life is described as one of both dying and rising. In fact, we *die* in order to *live*.

Romans 6 shows that Paul, the great preacher of Christ's death, also preaches our death—not our physical death, but our death to sin. This, he states, took place in our Baptism into Christ. We were "baptized into His death" (v. 3) and "buried therefore with Him by baptism into death" (v. 4). But our death with Christ and death to sin is not the whole of the Good News Paul proclaims. As was the case with Christ, our death is followed by our resurrection. We were raised especially that "we too might walk in newness of life" (v. 4). The font of our justification is also the font of our sanctification. This is precisely what Luther wrote concerning Baptism in his Small Catechism. Our Baptism was not a rite only significant for a day; rather, "it signifies that the old Adam in us should, by daily contrition and repentance, be drowned and die with all sins and evil lusts. And it also shows that a new man should daily come forth and arise" (*Concordia*, p. 340).

Paul knew full well that the sanctified life was not always a pleasant life. Even he was afflicted, perplexed, persecuted, and struck down. Indeed, Paul describes these sufferings as only to be expected by the Christian in this world. They are, he says, "always being given over to death for Jesus' sake" (2 Corinthians 4:11). But he is also clear that this fact does not lead to despair. In a very real sense, Paul shares in the suffering of Christ. Having been baptized into Christ's death, he was "always carrying in the body the death of Jesus." But at the same time, this takes place "so that the life of Jesus also may be manifested in our bodies" (2 Corinthians 4:10). The sanctified life—whether expressed in worship, in our daily vocations, in good works, or even in suffering—is a life lived in and with Christ, a life that reveals Christ and the fruits of His Spirit.

In Life, in Death, in Christ

We may not look forward to death. But given the frustrations and difficulties that beset us in this world, even life may sometimes look less than appealing. We can therefore rejoice in the fact that, whether we live or die, we do so with Christ as our Savior.

It is sometimes assumed that since Christ alone was responsible for our justification, sanctification must be defined as our response. This is not untrue. But we want to beware of the temptation to assume it is our response alone. The Christian does indeed cooperate with the action of God in sanctification, but he or she never acts without God's concurrent action. In fact, as much of the above has revealed, it is God Himself who initiates and sustains our sanctification. Thus, in his commentary on the

Third Article of the Creed in his Large Catechism, Luther could say quite simply: "I believe that the Holy Spirit makes me holy, as His name implies" (LC II 40; *Concordia*, p. 403).

Comparisons

Monergism: The biblical doctrine that God's grace is the only efficient cause in beginning and effecting conversion. Scripture teaches that people are by nature spiritually dead and antagonistic to spiritual things. People are saved by God's grace, not by works. Whatever synergism there is, in the proper sense of the term, follows conversion and is a result of God's monergism in a person's conversion.

Synergism: Concept that people cooperate with their own conversion. Developed out of an attempt to reconcile apparent contradictions in Scripture concerning humankind's native corruption, God's all-inclusive redemption, and people being saved by faith. Generally speaking, the synergistic view holds that people are by nature not altogether spiritually dead and that some resist God's call to faith less violently than others.

Point to Remember

> We were buried therefore with Him by baptism into death, in order that, just as Christ was raised from the dead by the glory of the Father, we too might walk in newness of life. *Romans 6:4*

Holy, Wholly, Holy

> I want a perfect body
> I want a perfect soul
> —"Creep" by Thom Yorke of British band Radiohead

In our often narcissistic and image-conscious society, it is not uncommon to hear people expressing a desire for the perfect body. An abundance of industries—from tanning salons to fitness centers to plastic surgery clinics—have sprouted up to fulfill that desire. Less obvious, but no less true, is that a host of individuals and organizations now also promise assistance in the perfection of the soul. From popular self-help seminars to the cult teachings of Scientology, we are increasingly being told that we can acquire a pure soul and reach a state of perfect spirituality.

Is our desire for perfection, whether physical or spiritual, healthy or unhealthy? In this life, neither physical nor moral perfection is attainable. Both body and soul are corrupted by sin, and though this sin is forgiven, its effects and consequences remain with us as long as we live.

Now and Not Yet

There can be no misunderstanding of the fact that God desires our holiness (Leviticus 11:45; 1 Peter 1:15–16). As the Confessions remind us, humankind "was originally created by God pure and holy" (FC Ep I 2; *Concordia*, p. 474). There was no need for God to tell our first parents to "be holy"; that is the state in which they were created by Him. But since the fall into sin, we must confess with St. Paul that "none is righteous," no one is holy in and of themselves (Romans 3:10). Yet God continues to exhort His people to "be holy." In fact, so much does God desire our holiness that He not only commands it but also effects it Himself. As Luther confessed with the Second Article of the Creed in his Large Catechism: "This is the Holy Spirit's office and work. He begins and daily increases holiness upon earth" (LC II 59; *Concordia*, p. 405). The Christian is always in the process of becoming what God says he or she already is. That is the dialectic and paradox of justification and sanctification.

The Holy Spirit is not the only person of the Trinity whose work effects our holiness. Referring to Christ, who "offered for all time a single sacrifice for sins" on the cross, the author of Hebrews wrote that by this "single offering He has perfected for all time those who are being sanctified" (10:12, 14). On account of Christ's atoning death, we are now called perfect—"perfected for all time." The past tense indicates that this has already taken place; even now we are *judged* holy in God's sight. In our Baptism, we have been clothed with the perfect holiness of Christ, yet this perfection belongs to those "who are being sanctified." The verb tense here is equally significant. We are still being sanctified, still being *made* holy. That is, we are even now holy in the eyes of God, but we are not yet holy in and of ourselves.

In Romans 7, Paul certainly makes no claim to being perfect. Quite the opposite, he admits that he knows what the holy Law of God commands, but he is still unable to keep the Law. In fact, "I do the very thing I hate" (v. 15) that is, sin. Paul explains that this is because there is "in my members another law waging war against the law of my mind" (v. 23). He calls this "the law of sin" (v. 23). What Paul describes is the paradoxical nature of the Christian: both saint and sinner at the same time—sinners in ourselves, saints in Christ. Thus the Confessions explain: "We teach that through the Holy Spirit's work we are born anew and justified. But the sense is not that after regeneration no unrighteousness clings anymore to the justified and regenerate in their being and life. It means that Christ covers all their sins (which in this life still dwell in nature) with His complete obedience" (FC SD III 22; *Concordia*, p. 539).

Christian sanctification is not perfected in this life, not even in one such as the apostle Paul. But this lack of earthly, visible perfection, Paul also says, is no cause for despair: "We do not lose heart," he says and explains that "though our outer self is wasting away, our inner self is being renewed day by day" (2 Corinthians 4:16–17). That is, though we quite obviously still stumble in sin, and though we also still experience the very visible consequences of sin in this world, God continues His work of sanctification in us. He is daily renewing, reviving, and restoring us, and "preparing for us an eternal weight of glory" (2 Corinthians 4:17). We see here another very important distinction between the work of Christ in justification and the work of the Spirit in sanctification. As Luther summarizes in his explanation of the Third Article of the Creed in his Large Catechism, our redemption in Christ is finished, "but the Holy Spirit carries on His work without ceasing to the Last Day" (LC II 61; *Concordia*, p. 406). Neither justification nor sanctification is necessarily obvious to our senses and emotions. But just as God assures us in His Word that we *have been* justified, so, too, He assures us that we *are being* sanctified.

The continual process of our sanctification will come to an end. There will come a day—though not in this life—when we are no longer "saint and sinner," but wholly and only saints. Paul looks forward to this day when he assures his readers that "just as we have borne the image of the man of dust, we shall also bear the image of the man of heaven" (1 Corinthians 15:49). Just as we now bear the image of our sinful forefather Adam, we will in heaven bear the image of our perfectly sinless Savior, Jesus Christ. This doctrine of Paul is also the doctrine of the Lutheran Church, which teaches: "While sanctification has begun and is growing daily [2 Thessalonians 1:3], we expect that our flesh will be destroyed and buried with all its uncleanness [Romans 6:4–11]. Then we will come forth gloriously and arise in a new, eternal life of entire and perfect holiness" (LC II 57; *Concordia*, p. 405).

When Paul wrote his second letter to Timothy and his letter to the Philippians, it was conceivable that his own death would soon arrive. It is obvious, though, that Paul does not look upon death with fear or terror. Instead, he says, "to die is gain," and "that is far better" (Philippians 1:21, 23). It is far better, he explains to Timothy, because "there is laid up for me the crown of righteousness" (2 Timothy 4:8). That is, Paul will be crowned with the purity and holiness of the resurrected and perfectly sanctified saints. Paul's cheerful acceptance of possible death is the result of his firm belief in this promise of God. Therefore, commenting on this passage, the confessors write: "The justified are due the crown because of the promise. Saints should know this promise" (Ap V [III] 242–43 [363–64]; *Concordia*, p. 137). Because Paul's faith is also our faith, we, too, can approach death with the sure hope that "to die is gain"—it is to gain that perfect holiness denied us here on earth.

Here and There

Many Christians are unlikely to be seduced by the naïve promises of radical plastic surgeons or the bizarre claims of modern cults. Sadly, however, some have succumbed to the erroneous idea that people are, in this life, capable of perfection. So-called "faith healers," for instance, imply that illness and disease will be cured if one simply believes hard enough. John Wesley, the father of Methodism, preached a doctrine of Christian perfectionism that suggested sanctified believers could live without sin.

God has not guaranteed us perfection in this life. But read 2 Corinthians 5:1–5. In contrast to any who would preach perfection in this life, Paul insists that here "we groan" and remain "burdened" by the weight of our sinfulness (v. 4). For this reason, though, we long for that day when "what is mortal may be swallowed up by life." This is no idle hope. Paul informs us that "He who has prepared us for this very thing is God" (v. 5). Because God Himself will effect our perfect sanctification, there can be no reason to doubt it. Indeed, Paul continues, God has given us a guarantee of His promise in the person of His Holy Spirit. This Spirit, through His activity in the Word of God, "bestows, increases, and strengthens faith. So when He has done it all, and we abide in this and die to the world and to all evil, He may finally make us perfectly and forever holy. Even now we expect this in faith through the Word" (LC II 62; *Concordia*, p. 406).

While fitness instructors and radical plastic surgeons would have us focus on our physical appearance, Paul counsels otherwise: "We look not to the things that are seen but to the things that are unseen" (2 Corinthians 4:18). What we see in ourselves, sin and its consequences, these Paul calls "transient." They will pass away. But that unseen righteousness and holiness that have already been accounted to us for the sake of Christ will remain ours in heaven. Indeed, even in this earthly life, it is only this that God sees in His children. As the Smalcald Articles state: "Although sin in the flesh has not yet been completely removed or become dead [Romans 7:18], yet He will not punish or remember it" (SA III XIII 1; *Concordia*, p. 283).

Looking to Jesus

In contrast to our culture, which constantly encourages us to look to ourselves, compete with others, and compare ourselves with others, the call of the Gospel encourages us to look to Jesus (Hebrews 12:2). He alone is the perfect example of holiness. By means of our Baptism into His death and resurrection, His perfection has been made our perfection.

The biblical command to be holy is explained with reference to God's own holiness. God is the only true standard of holiness and perfection, and as Scripture reminds us, "all have sinned and fall short of the glory of God" (Romans 3:23). There can be little good, therefore, in comparing ourselves with fellow sinners. Indeed, this may even tempt us to believe that, since we appear less sinful than some, we are less deserving of the Law's condemnation or less needful of the Gospel's forgiveness. This is hardly the case, however. Reflection on our own sanctification, therefore, should never lead us to measure ourselves against others. Instead, we should honestly measure ourselves against the unfailing standard of God's Word, freely confess our failures, and rejoice in the fact that God has not only forgiven all our sins but also continues to work in us through His Holy Spirit to crucify our sinful passions and desires.

Comparisons

Perfect love: Medieval Christian thinkers such as Francis of Assisi (ca. 1182–1226) and Thomas Aquinas (ca. 1224–74) proposed different theories of perfection. By grace, Christians could attain higher degrees of love and ultimately fulfill the law of love. They could overcome all temptation. The views of Francis and Thomas still influence many Roman Catholics.

Perfect holiness: Many Wesleyans (followers of John Wesley, such as Methodists, as well as Holiness and Pentecostal churches that follow his teachings) teach that there is a second work of grace after salvation. This work of grace totally sanctifies or perfects a person so that he or she no longer sins.

Sanctification: Lutherans, like many other Christians, teach that believers continue to struggle with temptation throughout life and do not attain sinless perfection until they are brought to heaven.

Point to Remember

Just as we have borne the image of the man of dust, we shall also bear the image of the man of heaven. *1 Corinthians 15:49*

Lutheran Summary of Justification and Sanctification

Augsburg Confession IV

Our churches teach that people cannot be justified before God by their own strength, merits, or works. People are freely justified for Christ's sake, through faith, when they believe that they are received into favor and that their sins are forgiven for Christ's sake. By His death, Christ made satisfaction for our sins. God counts this faith for righteousness in His sight (Romans 3 and 4 [3:21–26; 4:5]). (*Concordia*, p. 33)

Augsburg Confession VI

Our churches teach that this faith is bound to bring forth good fruit [Galatians 5:22–23]. It is necessary to do good works commanded by God [Ephesians 2:10], because of God's will. We should not rely on those works to merit justification before God. The forgiveness of sins and justification is received through faith. The voice of Christ testifies, "So you also, when you have done all that you were commanded, say, 'We are unworthy servants; we have only done what was our duty'" (Luke 17:10). The Fathers teach the same thing. Ambrose says, "It is ordained of God that he who believes in Christ is saved, freely receiving forgiveness of sins, without works, through faith alone." (*Concordia*, pp. 33–34)

Smalcald Articles III XIII

I do not know how to change in the least what I have previously and constantly taught about justification. Namely, that through faith, as St. Peter says, we have a new and clean heart [Acts 15:9–11], and God will and does account us entirely righteous and holy for the sake of Christ, our Mediator [1 Timothy 2:5]. Although sin in the flesh has not yet been completely removed or become dead [Romans 7:18], yet He will not punish or remember it.

Such faith, renewal, and forgiveness of sins are followed by good works [Ephesians 2:8–9]. What is still sinful or imperfect in them will not be counted as sin or defect, for Christ's sake [Psalm 32:1–2; Romans 4:7–8]. The entire individual, both his person and his works, is declared to be righteous and holy from pure grace and mercy, shed upon us and spread over us in Christ. Therefore, we cannot boast of many merits and works, if they are viewed apart from grace and mercy. As it is written, "Let the one who boasts, boast in the Lord" (1 Corinthians 1:31); namely, that he has a gracious God. For with that, all is well. We say, besides, that if good works do not follow, the faith is false and not true. (*Concordia*, p. 283)

TOPIC NINE

Predestination[1]

Engaging This Topic

"Don't you believe that God has a plan for your life? A destiny?"
"Yes. But I also believe that God gives me freedom to make choices."
"How can both of these things be true? Your faith seems so inconsistent."

> This doctrine provides glorious consolation under the cross and amid temptations. In other words, God in His counsel, before the time of the world, determined and decreed that He would assist us in all distresses. He determined to grant patience, give consolation, nourish and encourage hope, and produce an outcome for us that would contribute to our salvation.
>
> —Formula of Concord Solid Declaration XI 48 (*Concordia*, p. 609)

This is the claim concerning the biblical doctrine of predestination set forth by the founders of the Lutheran Church more than 425 years ago. Other Christians, and at times some dissenting Lutherans, have not approached the subject of predestination with the same sense of consolation. In fact, many Christians would rather avoid the subject completely.

Traditional Lutherans like to say that the doctrine of predestination is a final examination for a theologian, testing his general commitment to Christian doctrine. The questions in this final exam would read something like the following:

1. Isn't it arrogant or presumptuous to claim that God has chosen you?

2. Can anyone ever really be sure?

1 This chapter adapted from *Lutheran Difference: Predestination*, written by Thomas Manteufel, with contributions by Edward Engelbrecht. Copyright © 2003 Concordia Publishing House.

3. Should a person accept everything taught by Scripture about this subject simply because it is taught there?
4. Can this Lutheran doctrine be proved from Scripture?
5. Isn't predestination a form of fatalism?
6. Do Lutherans agree with the teaching that God has predestined some to eternal life and therefore must have predestined the rest to damnation?
7. Does predestination ignore human responsibility for repenting and believing in Christ?
8. Did God choose people to salvation because of what He foresaw they would do?
9. Did God choose people on the basis of the faith He foreknew they would have?

This chapter will give attention to these points and help you learn what the Bible teaches and what it does not teach. As you read, pray for God's wisdom and remember Paul's words in Romans, "Oh, the depth of the riches and wisdom and knowledge of God! How unsearchable are His judgments and how inscrutable His ways! 'For who has known the mind of the Lord, or who has been His counselor?' 'Or who has given a gift to Him that He might be repaid?' For from Him and through Him and to Him are all things. To Him be glory forever. Amen" (11:33–36).

Lutheran Facts

One of Luther's most important writings was *The Bondage of the Will*, which overturned many misconceptions about predestination.

A common closing found in letters by Lutheran pastors has been "D. V." (*Deo volente*), which means "God willing." This note reminds both the writer and the recipient that the future is in God's hands.

Lutherans believe people can be sure they will go to heaven because of the sure promise of salvation God gives through Jesus Christ.

Lutherans hold that in the New Testament the Church is the "chosen people." They do not support the idea that the Jewish people today or the modern nation of Israel have a special relationship with God as Israel did during the Old Testament.

Three popular Lutheran hymns that mention God's election or choice are "Baptized into Your Name Most Holy" (*LSB* 590); "A Mighty Fortress Is Our God" (*LSB* 656); and "Alleluia! Let Praises Ring" (*LSB* 822).

Chosen from Eternity

From eternity, O God,
In Thy Son Thou didst elect me;
Therefore, Father, on life's road
Graciously to heav'n direct me;
Send to me Thy Holy Spirit
That His gifts I may inherit.
—*The Lutheran Hymnal* 411:1

This hymn stanza expresses a belief important to Lutherans. But the idea often is not well understood, even by Lutherans. It has at times led to confusion and disputes. Some people feel that this teaching speaks of people as though they were puppets controlled by a supernatural puppet-master, that it denies the dignity of human beings as decision-makers, or that it means some people are predestined to hell. This important doctrine is sometimes called *election*, and sometimes it is called *predestination*. Do these words mean the same thing, or do they point to different aspects of God's action? *Election* refers to choosing; *predestination* means determining something beforehand.

Chosen

The Bible refers to various acts of election (or choosing) by God. God's election of Israel as the chosen nation shows His love and amazing grace and generosity, not basing His choice on population or on righteousness (Deuteronomy 7:6–8; 9:4–6). God's election of Paul (Acts 9:15) and the Twelve (Luke 6:13) to apostleship shows His wise, serious intention to appoint some persons to special experiences and purposes. From eternity, God chose His only-begotten Son to be Jesus the Messiah (Luke 23:35; 1 Peter 1:19–20; 2:4). The Christian Church as a whole is a chosen people (1 Peter 2:9), a New Testament Israel dear to God. The election of individuals to be saved believers (see Colossians 3:12; James 2:5; 1 Corinthians 1:28–29) expresses the same love and appointing purpose.

Ephesians 1:3–14 speaks of God's election of those who are saved. According to verses 4–5, God had two intended purposes in mind in this election. First, He chose believers to be "holy and blameless" in His sight. They are holy and blameless because He has forgiven their sins and justified them, that is, declared them righteous. This purpose involves the creation of justifying faith (Romans 3:28). Believers also are holy by the life-sanctifying work of the Holy Spirit, who is given to all who have justifying faith, so that the fruit of good works is included in predestination

(Galatians 3:11–14; Ephesians 2:8–10). Second, God chose to adopt them as His sons, graciously accepted by Him as their Father.

Since election leads to adoption for sonship, some people think it involves only persons of the male sex. But women are not excluded from the family of God (Galatians 3:26–28). The blessing is called *sonship* to emphasize the assurance of rights of inheritance, as Galatians 3:29 and 4:7 show. In ancient Israel, daughters did not always have the inheritance rights that sons had. (For example, see Numbers 27:1–8.) But Paul calls believing women "sons" to indicate that they can be sure of a son's right when it comes to receiving the heavenly inheritance. According to Ephesians 1:4, this divine election took place before creation, before the adoptees existed.

What moved God to choose the elect persons? It was an act of His love (Ephesians 1:5), His freely given grace (v. 6). Furthermore, He chose the elect "in Him" (v. 4)—that is, in Christ—because of His redemptive work and merits.

The Second and Third Persons of the Holy Trinity showed their oneness with the Father by cooperating in carrying out His election decision. The Son's work of atonement is applied for the redemption of the elect (Ephesians 1:5–8), and He acts as their head as they find their hope in Him (vv. 10–13). The Holy Spirit brings about that hope and faith and gives them a guarantee of the heavenly inheritance by beginning the new life in them (vv. 13–14; 1 Corinthians 12:3; Acts 13:48).

"Blessed be the God and Father of our Lord Jesus Christ, who has blessed us in Christ with every spiritual blessing in the heavenly places, even as He chose us in Him before the foundation of the world, that we should be holy and blameless before Him" (Ephesians 1:3–4). The word translated as "blessed be" in verse 3 is a form of the same Greek word translated "blessed" in the same verse. Blessings are invocations of well-being and good things, pronouncements of well-wishing. In the first place, God blesses the elect by declaring and bringing about their redemption, and in turn Paul calls upon the elect to join him in blessing and praising God in grateful response for His glorious grace.

Chosen to What?

If Christians take Ephesians 1:3–14 seriously, what results of predestination may they expect and look for in their lives? Recall the benefits for which we have been chosen: forgiveness, holiness, the work of the Spirit, faith, and adoption. We will want to appreciate and use these realities.

If human beings are expected to use free will to decide to believe in the Gospel in order to have salvation, why did Paul tell the Ephesian believers that they were predestined to be saved? But Paul goes on to say in Ephesians

2:1 that we "were dead in the trespasses and sins." Here Paul teaches that the unconverted are dead in sin. Since the dead cannot raise themselves, human beings *cannot* use their will to turn to God or believe the Gospel. The origin of turning and believing is in God, who predestines it.

An acquaintance says to you, "I don't think salvation is just a matter of being predestined. If you tell people that, they will get lazy in their spiritual life, and they will believe there is no need to live good lives and think and act like true Christians. Isn't it better to say, 'God has made it possible for you to be saved, but in the end it's up to you to go on the right path'?" God has predestined more than the mere possibility of salvation. In love, He chooses people. No doubt people will abuse God's grace. But that doesn't mean we should hide or obscure His message of love. In fact, what message is more likely to inspire faithfulness and good works?

The teaching of a predestined salvation does not contradict the truth that sinners are saved by the merits of Jesus Christ, through faith in Him as the Redeemer. The predestination of salvation of people also includes the foreordaining of how it is to come to pass.

Fatalism involves the belief that every event is governed by an impersonal fate, or perhaps spirits that have no sympathy with people and their problems. Some think that the doctrine of predestination is a form of this belief. On the contrary, the act of divine election shows how concerned God is about the elect one.

Since predestination and election are so hard to understand and so easily applied in a wrong way, would it not be better to ignore the matter and devote time and thought to more important questions of the Christian life? This proposal is always attractive to some. But Paul treats the teaching as an important, valuable truth for which we praise God. It belongs to "the whole counsel of God," which ought to be proclaimed for the building up of Christians (Acts 20:27, 32). What could be more important than the Lord's provision for eternal life with Him?

Blessed!

Look at the apostle Paul's emotional response, which breaks forth with praise: "Blessed be the God and Father of our Lord Jesus Christ, who has blessed us in Christ with every spiritual blessing in the heavenly places . . . to the praise of His glorious grace, with which He has blessed us in the Beloved. . . . [He] is the guarantee of our inheritance until we acquire possession of it, to the praise of His glory" (Ephesians 1:3, 6, 14). Let's follow the apostle's example by praising God and reveling in the positive, encouraging attitude Paul expresses toward fellow believers.

Comparisons

All major religions and philosophies wrestle with issues of God's will, human freedom, and the future. Based on the Scriptures, predestination (or election) is taught by most Christian churches. Differences in these teachings will be clarified in later comparisons.

Eastern Orthodox: "With what design did God create man? With this, that he should know God, love, and glorify him, and so be happy forever. Has not that will of God, by which man is designed for eternal happiness, its own proper name in theology? It is called *predestination* of God" (*The Longer Catechism of the Eastern Church*, questions 120–21).

Lutheran: "God's Word leads us to Christ, who is the Book of Life, in whom all are written and elected who are to be saved in eternity. For it is written Ephesians 1:4, "Even as He chose us in Him [Christ] before the foundation of the world" (FC Ep XI 7; *Concordia*, p. 498).

Reformed and Particular Baptist: "By the decrees of God, for the manifestation of his glory, some men and angels are predestined unto everlasting life, and others foreordained to everlasting death" (*The Westminster Confession of Faith*, chapter 3.3).

Anabaptist: "Concerning the restoration of the first man and his posterity we confess and believe, that God, notwithstanding their fall, transgression, and sin, and their utter inability, was nevertheless not willing to cast them off entirely, or to let them be forever lost; but that He called them again to Him, comforted them, and showed them that with Him there was yet a means for their reconciliation, namely, the immaculate Lamb, the Son of God, who had been foreordained thereto before the foundation of the world, and was promised them while they were yet in Paradise, for consolation, redemption, and salvation, for themselves as well as for their posterity" (*The Dordrecht Confession*, article 3).

Roman Catholic: According to the *Catechism of the Catholic Church*, the perfectly purified elect can go directly to heaven when they die (para. 1023). The imperfect elect must spend time in purgatory (para. 1031).

Free-Will Baptist and Wesleyan: "Salvation is rendered equally possible to all; and if any fail of eternal life, the fault is wholly their own" (*Confession of the Free-Will Baptists*, chapter 8).

Liberal: "In the place of the older kind of 'assurance,' which declared that God's absolute word had been proclaimed to us in final form, we must develop a type of assurance which looks confidently toward the establishment of truer dynamic relationships with God through the practical experience of using the best conceptions we have, while striving always for better ones if these are to be found" (Gerald Birney Smith, ed., *Guide to the Study of the Christian Religion* [Chicago: University of Chicago Press, 1916], p. 550; in other words, Christians cannot know with certainty about the doctrine of predestination and other doctrines because they cannot be sure that Scripture is reliable).

Point to Remember

He chose us in Him [Christ] before the foundation of the world, that we should be holy and blameless before Him. *Ephesians 1:4*

For Jesus' Sake

You shall and you shan't—
You will and you won't—
And you will be damned if you do—
And you will be damned if you don't.
—Lorenzo Dow, *On the Doctrine of Particular Election* (1836)

This rhyme is often quoted as a criticism of the teaching of particular election (the idea that only a certain number of people are predestined to be saved). The complaint is that this teaching leads to the following thought: all are told to believe the Gospel, but if you are not one of the elect, you will be damned if you do believe and also if you don't. Although this rhyme is written in fun, it expresses serious frustration.

Christ the Savior

In predestination God has appointed the elect persons for obedience to Him, that is, a healing of hostile, disobedient sinners so they can trust and serve Him. They are also appointed for an application of Jesus' atoning blood for justification and its results. These blessings come about through the sanctifying work of the Holy Spirit.

First Peter 1:2–7 and 11 point to Jesus Christ as Lord, to His atoning sacrifice. He is the Lamb, sacrificed for the unrighteous, to reconcile them to God (1 Peter 1:19–20; 3:18). He died for the whole world (2 Corinthians 5:15, 19), for God wants all to be saved (1 Timothy 2:4; 2 Peter 3:9). Election was a special act of God's grace by which He determined to apply the atoning blood of Jesus to the elect. According to 1 Peter 1:10–12 and 23–25, it is the work of the Spirit of Christ to reveal the saving message of Christ's atonement through predictions of the atonement by Old Testament prophets and apostolic preaching about the atonement after it took place. This revelation is the Word of the Gospel, which regenerates sinners with the new life of hope, in which 1 Peter 3:9 exalts.

God has determined to bring about the healing and restoration of the elect by applying to them the atonement Jesus was appointed to make for all mankind and bringing them to faith in Him as their Redeemer (1 Peter 1:2–9, 19). He will shield and guard them in faith until the culmination of their salvation (vv. 4–5). Thus the Good Shepherd promises that no one can snatch them out of His hand (John 10:27–29). These predestined actions will come to pass in the lives of Christians. And 1 Peter 1:3, 6, 8 tells us that the believers react with unending joy, praise, and love for Christ.

Christ the Focus of Faith

The Lutheran Confessions call Christ "the Book of Life" in which all who shall be eternally saved are inscribed and in which Christians are to look for knowledge of their election. Those who trust in Christ look to Him for knowledge of their election. In their faith in Him they see their election being carried out. The more they gaze at Him and His redemption, the more surely they recognize their election. He is the Word of God (John 1:1), in whom the Father expresses love for His creatures and which His people can hear and read with endless pleasure.

In His universal grace God has predestined no one to damnation. Christ died for all, and when the elect are brought to faith, they realize that an atonement for all includes atonement for them and rejoice in that fact. Why, then, has the loving God not elected all people to be justified by faith? Many have puzzled over this question. But it is never answered in God's Word and so during this life must remain among the unsearchable judgments of God (Romans 11:33).

How is Lorenzo Dow's rhyme at the beginning of this section a distortion of the scriptural doctrine of election? In itself the teaching of particular election is correct. All who are predestined to salvation will be glorified (Romans 8:30), yet some people will receive everlasting punishment (Matthew 25:46). The predicament described in Lorenzo Dow's rhyme will not actually arise: no one will come to an abiding faith in Christ as Savior and yet be denied eternal life because of not being one of the elect. Those who come to such a faith do so because they are elected to do so (Romans 8:30; Acts 13:48) and because of the work of the Holy Spirit through God's Word.

Fatalism discourages people from living by faith because in fatalism the things we do make no difference in the end. Some people connect this thought with predestination by arguing, "Why should I make use of Baptism or Absolution, or even believe and repent at all, if I am guaranteed to be saved no matter what happens in my life?" To answer this, we consult 1 Peter 1:8–9; 3:21; and Acts 2:38 to see whether Peter urged his hearers to have a fatalistic attitude. The election to salvation is a predestination to the means of conferring grace (Word, Absolution, and Sacraments) and the means of receiving repentant faith. One's salvation comes about in the course of time. Peter taught nothing else but this.

Election in Christ and faith in Christ are not merely isolated, independent experiences of individuals. For example, Peter and his readers could rejoice together in their common experience of Christ's benefits, God's electing love, and their union in the elect community of the Christian Church (1 Peter 1:1–3, 10–12; 2:9). The Old Testament prophets and the New Testament believers were united in their Christ-centered focus. In Ephesians 1, Paul also refers to this shared focus on Christ as Redeemer, Lord, and Head and the love for the saints, who are aware of the eternal riches they all share (see vv. 1–10, 15–18, 22–23). The doctrine of predestination helps them to regard each other as "brothers beloved by the Lord" (2 Thessalonians 2:13). Nevertheless, it would be a mistake to attempt to base membership lists on determination of who is elect or who has faith. A Christian can know his or her own faith and election and relation to Christ. A Christian may express confidence or encouragement about another person's confession of the Gospel (e.g., 1 Thessalonians 1:4). But Christians cannot know the hearts of others with certainty. Only the Lord has infallible knowledge of His seal on those who are His, for "the Lord sees not as man sees: man looks on the outward appearance, but the Lord looks on the heart" (1 Samuel 16:7; see also 2 Timothy 2:19). In the Church we recognize each one's confession of Christ and in love regard it as genuine unless the hypocrisy of a "brother's" confession becomes clear (as in 1 Corinthians 5).

God's election involves His foreknowledge (1 Peter 1:2). This fact was comforting to Peter's readers, who were suffering persecution and tribulation. Their troubles have never been unknown to God or beyond His power or concern. He knew they would play a role in the demonstration, exercise, and maintaining of their saving faith (1 Peter 1:5–9). Believers can be sure that God's purposes for them are far older than their present troubles, extending back before creation.

Comparisons

Christians state different reasons why God predestines, or elects, someone to salvation. This issue sparked controversy in the fifth century when a monk named Pelagius argued that people had the power to overcome sin and save themselves. St. Augustine, in response, emphasized that people had no power to save themselves and were utterly dependent on God for salvation. He argued that God chose who would be saved and who would be damned. In response, other monks began teaching that the human will had power to choose salvation but that God also added His grace to help in conversion (semi-Pelagianism).

In 529 a church council gathered at Orange, France. It rejected the teachings of Pelagius and the semi-Pelagians and largely restated Augustine's views as compatible with Scripture. However, unlike Augustine, the council concluded that God did not predestine anyone to hell. The different views summarized below still reflect the issues of this early debate.

Double predestination: This view was emphasized by John Calvin and follows the teaching of Augustine in emphasizing election solely on the basis of grace. Traditional Reformed churches and Particular Baptists hold this teaching. "By the decrees of God, for the manifestation of his glory, some men and angels are predestined unto everlasting life, and others foreordained to everlasting death" (*The Westminster Confession of Faith*, chapter 3.3).

In view of faith or obedience: Wesleyans, Free-Will Baptists, and others emphasize the freedom and power of the human will. They teach that God chose to save certain people because He foresaw that they would believe the Gospel or obey His Word.

Unresolved cause of election: Roman Catholics do not explain why God chose the elect, whether by grace, faith, or obedience. They teach that God predestined no one for hell (*Catechism of the Catholic Church*, para. 1037).

Universalism: This view was expressed by the early Christian teacher Origen and has grown popular among Christians influenced by liberalism. It teaches that all people will eventually be saved. Some hold that there may be a time of punishment for the wicked, but no eternal punishment.

The mystery of God's love in Christ: Lutherans assert that God's Word teaches the election of all true believers by His grace in Christ. They also assert that, though the Bible teaches that some people will go to hell, it does not state that God predestined these people to hell.

Lutherans do not attempt to solve this paradox since Scripture itself does not resolve it. They emphasize that election is a mystery, which human reason cannot solve.

Point to Remember

He predestined us for adoption as sons through Jesus Christ. *Ephesians 1:5*

Not a Dark Cloud

> I don't know if we each have a destiny, or if we're all just floating around accidental-like on a breeze, but I, I think maybe it's both. Maybe both is happening at the same time.
>
> —from the film *Forrest Gump*.

At the heart of the film *Forrest Gump* are questions of God's will and the future, which troubled the main characters. For many people, the issue of predestination hangs over their hearts like a dark cloud.

When the congregation pastored by Dr. C. F. W. Walther, the first president of the LCMS, raised questions about predestination, Walther addressed their concerns by showing the connection between predestination and the joy of Christmas. He explained that predestination does not hang over believing Christians as a dark, threatening storm cloud, so that they must always anxiously ask, "Am I also a chosen one?" No, far from being a dark cloud, the doctrine of predestination is much more a brightly shining sun of grace, comfort, and joy, which rises over every person as soon as he has been called by the Gospel and thereby has become a believer (see Walther, "Sermon on Predestination," 1881).

The fact that only some people are predestined to eternal life is an age-old concern in the Church. Because the names of these elect are not spelled out in Scripture, therefore an individual may well wonder: "Am I one of them?"[2]

2 Editor's Note: When I was in college, my friend Jim went through a great personal struggle over the doctrine of election. He carefully read various opinions on the topic but was not able to "figure it out." At one point, he locked himself in his dorm room and wouldn't talk with any of us for three days. Eventually, he received God's peace concerning this topic. Always remember that this teaching is more than an intellectual problem. It remains a mystery of God's grace. Have patience with those who struggle to understand.

Thank God!

The Word of God takes for granted that one *can* know of one's election. As a recurring theme in their correspondence, the apostles direct the Colossians, the Thessalonians, the Ephesians, and the Christians of Asia Minor (Pontus, Galatia, Cappadocia, Asia, Bithynia) to think of their election. For example, Paul writes: "But we ought always to give thanks to God for you, brothers beloved by the Lord, because God chose you as the firstfruits to be saved, through sanctification by the Spirit and belief in the truth" (2 Thessalonians 2:13). God has chosen to bring about the salvation of the elect by means of the Spirit's sanctifying work and by means of faith in the truth. There need be no dark cloud of doubt for a child of God about whether he is elect. If one is a believer in Christ, he or she may confidently trace faith, justification, and renewal back to God's election.

After speaking of thankful recognition of election, Paul says that it follows that they should stand firm in all the apostolic teaching and with God's help be encouraged and strengthened in good words and works (2 Thessalonians 2:15–17). They will know that they are living in the life to which God has ordained them and are glad of it.

The apostolic teachings emphasized in 2 Thessalonians 2:15 give vital instruction to God's people about election, the Savior, the faith indispensably connected with election, and the life into which it brings believers. In order to carry out the purposes of election, God has entrusted apostles such as Paul with proclaiming His wholesome and illuminating Word, so that by it the hearers may be brought to faith and reconciliation with Him and be fully guided in living in it throughout their lives. Paul speaks of this task to Titus: "Paul, a servant of God and an apostle of Jesus Christ, for the sake of the faith of God's elect and their knowledge of the truth, which accords with godliness, in hope of eternal life, which God, who never lies, promised before the ages began and at the proper time manifested in His word through the preaching with which I have been entrusted by the command of God our Savior" (1:1–3). In his second letter to Timothy, Paul says that he faithfully endures much to serve the elect (2:10).

Through the Gospel

Since lost and condemned sinners are in a predicament from which no human resources can help them escape, are they in fact without hope? No, there is help coming from outside of them—from God, who elects and calls to salvation and glory through a Gospel call. His grace gives good hope (2 Thessalonians 2:16).

The elect are predestined to be saved through faith in the truth, and this saving truth is stated in the Gospel, by which they are called (or summoned) to receive the eternal glory Christ has gained for them (2 Thessalonians 2:13–14). In 1 Thessalonians 1:4–10, Paul told the Thessalonian Christians that their election was knowable from their welcome of the Gospel message he brought to them and its effect in their lives. The dark cloud of predestination is dispelled and turned to sunshine when they read Christ as the Book of Life and rejoice in the Savior, in whom God has brought them to trust.

The doctrine of election was not set forth to the pagans on Mars Hill (Acts 17), but rather to Christian believers (Romans 8–11; Ephesians 1). Human beings first come to faith, and in that faith they find certainty that they have been elected by God to receive His blessings. Pagans, as people who do not yet have faith, are not in a position to make use of the doctrine of election.[3]

Stand Firm

How can firmness and certainty about the Christian teaching of election be maintained in the life of the Christian? To answer this, we look to the benefit mentioned by Peter and to the use of prayers to implore the Lord that it come to pass in our life as well as in the lives of our fellow believers. As part of the fulfillment of predestination, God will guard and keep the believer in the state of grace until the entrance into the heavenly inheritance (1 Peter 1:3–5). Even if an elect person temporarily falls from grace, God will restore that person before death. This happened to some of the Galatians (see Galatians 5:4). God's fulfillment of His predestination of individuals will include bringing about prayers in their lives like those in 1 Thessalonians 3 and 2 Thessalonians 2 for preservation in grace and continuance in it. He will answer these prayers by leading His children finally into life eternal.

Comparisons

The strict Calvinism of New England Puritans and other Reformed churches made the subject of predestination a matter of grave fear and uncertainty during the First Great Awakening in North America (1726–60). As a result, more and more preachers focused on a personal experience of salvation and a life of obedience as ways to tell whether one was truly chosen by God. In time these proofs of experience and obedience became the reasons people believed that God chose some for salvation but not others. These

3 As you discuss matters of faith in your own personal conversations, remember that the doctrine of election is typically a doctrine to discuss with those who are mature in faith.

proofs were features of the Second Great Awakening (1800–1830) and have remained key features of revivalism.

Religious awakenings and revivalism affected Lutherans in North America, sparking much debate about church practice. Although Lutherans were divided by the topic of election during the Predestination Controversy of the 1880s, they did not dramatically change their teaching, as did the Reformed. Today, Lutherans continue to emphasize that election is a mystery of God. They focus on God's promises in Christ and the Means of Grace.

Point to Remember

> We ought always to give thanks to God for you, brothers beloved by the Lord, because God chose you as the firstfruits to be saved. *2 Thessalonians 2:13*

By Grace Alone

> "But Halvor, tell me, what is really your opinion about this election or predestination business, or whatever you call it?"
>
> "Oh, to tell you the truth, I haven't been lying awake nights thinking about it. It's a very difficult and involved affair, perhaps a mystery best left alone by mortals. But in my own simple way I am inclined to believe what a certain wise man has said, namely, that one can't expect to be elected unless he agrees to be a candidate."
>
> —from *Halvor*, by Peer Strømme

Many people, like Halvor Helgeson, the Norwegian pastor in this story, have considered how they could become elected as possessors of eternal life. The same idea appears in another story, *Hellbent for Election*, in which a man condemned to hell finally is elected to become a resident of heaven, after he turns toward the Lord in repentance. Of course, we don't choose to be candidates of election. God calls us by grace through faith in Christ.

Not Because of Works

God's purpose of good pleasure toward the elect was centered in Christ, and He chose us in Him (Ephesians 1:4, 9, 11). The elect have been called in accordance with this purpose and have also been justified and glorified

(Romans 8:28–29). A key and eternal purpose is to cause us to lead a holy life (2 Timothy 1:9).

God's saving purpose is not founded upon our works at all but was prior to the beginning of time and all the works done in time. Election was the application to us of grace, God's favor, in Christ the Redeemer. A holy life of works is certainly God's purpose for us and is the way in which it is realized in us. But the purpose is before the works, and not vice versa. Even the saving faith active in works was not the cause of election or appointment to salvation, but was the result of it, as Acts 13:48 tells us: "And when the Gentiles heard this, they began rejoicing and glorifying the word of the Lord, and as many as were appointed to eternal life believed."

God chose the elect by His good pleasure and grace, the same principle by which He forgives sinners for Jesus' sake (Ephesians 1:5–9). In Ephesians, Paul goes on to stress that God's grace is His kindness, which is not based on our works (2:7–9). Romans 11:5–6 says that in Israel, while some are hardened and lost, there is still a remnant chosen by grace, and if it is by grace, it cannot be by works. According to 2 Timothy 1:9, the intent of God to elect people to eternal grace was before any good works and led to the doing of the works.

Second Timothy 1:7 calls for a spirit of power, of love, and of self-discipline. If you know that God has elected you to be Christ's follower, you are aware that He wills to give you this spirit and will help you express it and grow in the use of it. The attitude of being willing to suffer and endure opposition and losses for the sake of the Gospel (vv. 8 and 12) stems from the conviction that the Lord has power to guard and keep those whom He has chosen through all difficulties until the Last Day and in fact uses that power to enable us to suffer all for Him.

Paul writes: "Therefore do not be ashamed of the testimony about our Lord, nor of me His prisoner, but share in suffering for the gospel by the power of God" (2 Timothy 1:8). Timothy might be ashamed of being the spokesman of a message unpopular in his society, or of being associated with a religious "jailbird" (Paul, who is in prison). He seems to have fear (1 Corinthians 16:10–11) and belittling criticism directed at him (1 Timothy 4:12). But no one who is called by a gracious, elective purpose of an all-powerful God needs to be ashamed of the Gospel. Paul commends to Timothy the good example of Onesiphorus, who had a clear vision of God's purpose: "He often refreshed me and was not ashamed of my chains, but when he arrived in Rome he searched for me earnestly and found me—may the Lord grant him to find mercy from the Lord on that Day!—and you well know all the service he rendered at Ephesus" (2 Timothy 1:16–18).

In 2 Timothy 1:3–5, 9–11 Paul mentions how God brought about His purpose of predestination. God has saved us by the work of Christ, the death-conquering Savior. He appointed Paul and others to be heralds of this work, called us through their Gospel message, heard and answered the prayers of Christians for each other, and provided for the passing of faith from one heart to another—through instruction in His Word. The teaching work of Paul and the other apostles is part of the carrying out of God's gracious purpose and is to be steadfastly maintained as the pattern of sound teaching in the Church. The apostolic teaching should be handled with faith and love in Christ, used not just to win arguments but with sincere concern to promote sound teaching in every way.

The crucified and risen Savior has removed the curse of death by His atonement for sin, and the Gospel promises eternal life and glorious immortality to all who put their trust in Christ (2 Timothy 1:10). The application of this life-giving grace through the Gospel of Christ was predestined for the elect before the beginning of time.

Paul's themes in 2 Timothy 1 have implications for the whole people of God. The scope of thankfulness and mutual love extends to all in whom God's gracious elective purpose is carried out. This is the whole people of God, including Paul's believing, God-serving forefathers; Timothy; Paul; Timothy's pious mother and grandmother; and all who are blessed with the pattern of sound teaching.

Gospel Grace

When an elderly pious woman heard of some arguments going on about predestination, she said, "Ah, I have long settled that point in my own mind. For if God had not chosen me long before I was born, I am sure He would have seen nothing in me that would lead Him to choose me afterward." Her thinking is right on target, in accord with the fact that the election of grace is not based on our works. Although she was pious like Lois and Eunice in 2 Timothy 1, she also recognized her unworthiness before God. Election by grace happens neither because God sees that any good works have been done nor because He foresees that they will be done in time to come.

Someone (improperly) explained the doctrine of election in this way: "The Lord is always voting for a man, and the devil is always voting against him. Then the man himself votes, and that breaks the tie!" Yet the unconverted man cannot vote for his conversion and for the Gospel. He is dead in sin (Ephesians 2:1) and does not accept the things that come from the Spirit (1 Corinthians 2:14). This dreadful condition has been called the "bondage of the will." Martin Luther famously wrote about this.

Someone may state: "We surely do need God's grace and couldn't be saved without it. But I know that we have to do our part too." However, those who are in the darkness of unbelief cannot "do their part" to come to faith. God must turn on the light in us (2 Corinthians 4:6). Conversion is purely a gift of God.

Second Thessalonians 2:14 and 2 Timothy 1:9 speak of how the Lord called the elect through the Gospel. The call to believe in Christ is based on His death for *all* human beings and is to be spoken to *all* the world (Matthew 28:19). Many hearers will not respond with faith. But God uses this Gospel call to bring the elect to faith.

He Is Able

Second Timothy 1:12 teaches that God is able to guard and keep us in our relationship with Him until the Last Day. Romans 14:4; 16:25; and other passages give the same assurance. Some think that this promise to preserve people in the faith is the meaning and comfort of election—namely, that God has determined to preserve the faith *of all those who turn to Him* and is able to keep them unto the end. But we can't turn to Him by our own reason and strength. The proposal presented here is another version of the idea that the unconverted can come to faith by their own decision, or cooperate in doing it, and election is God's promise to guard the faith of all who do so. But the same objections must be raised. God is indeed able to preserve faith. But He is also able to originate faith, as He has predetermined to do in election.

Comparisons

The following illustrates how different groups might respond to the question "How do you know you are going to heaven?"

Typical response: I am a good person.

Liberal: Heaven is a state of mind.

Eastern Orthodox: I pray, have faith, and do good works. I belong to the true Church.

Roman Catholic: I can't be sure I'm going to heaven because that would be prideful. But I belong to the true Church.

Calvinist/Reformed: God chose me by grace to believe His Word and live according to it (proofs of faith).

Revivalist: I have accepted Jesus Christ as my personal Savior (personal commitment).

Lutheran: The Holy Spirit has called me by the Gospel of Jesus Christ through Baptism and God's Word (Means of Grace).

Point to Remember

> [God] saved us and called us to a holy calling, not because of our works but because of His own purpose and grace. *2 Timothy 1:9*

Predestination by Lamplight

> Moreover, who knows whether I am elected to salvation?
>
> Answer: Look at the words, I beseech you, to determine how and of whom He is speaking. "God so loved the world," and "that whosoever believeth in Him." Now, the "world" does not mean Saints Peter and Paul alone but the entire human race, all together. And no one is here excluded. God's Son was given for all. All should believe, and all who do believe should not perish, etc. Take hold of your own nose, I beseech you, to determine whether you are not a human being (that is, part of the world) and, like any other man, belong to the number of those comprised by the word "all."
>
> —Martin Luther[4]

Luther's remark shows how the Word of God can be used to guide our teaching and understanding of election and salvation. This is lamplight shining on our path (and, in this case, on our nose).

Luther does not mean that everyone is elect or that the Bible teaches universalism (Luther never believed that). But he is saying to the questioner that there can be no doubt, in the Gospel statements, that Jesus Christ is the Savior who made atonement for all people and that all are invited to believe in Him. Faith, rightly understood, is the personal appropriation of Christ, which says, "If He came for all, He came also for me." Everyone who does come to faith can then contemplate the truth that "God has elected me to be His child and has called me by this Gospel call." This contemplation is done in the lamplight of the Gospel statements.

We Know

"For I am sure that neither death nor life, nor angels nor rulers, nor things present nor things to come, nor powers, nor height nor depth, nor anything else in all creation, will be able to separate us from the love of God in Christ Jesus our Lord" (Romans 8:38–39). Paul is convinced that nothing

4 Ewald Plass, comp., *What Luther Says* (St. Louis: Concordia, 1959), § 1859.

can separate God's people from His love in Christ Jesus, that is, turn it into hostility and damnation and delete its benefits. This conviction is inextricably connected to Paul's assertion in verse 28 that "we know" that God will work in all things for the ultimate good of His people. He goes on in the passage to explain that all this flows from God's predestination of them for a glorious purpose.

What the elect know, or should know, is the truth of God's Word, which is a lamp and a light-giver (Psalm 119:105, 130), filled with God's great "Yes" in Christ (2 Corinthians 1:20) and wonderful promises that serve the faith of the elect (Titus 1:1–3). God's Word is convincing to them (Acts 28:23), leads them to know the truth (John 8:31–32), is the power for salvation, and brings about faith (Romans 1:16; 10:17).

The lamplight of Romans 8:29 reveals how the Father bestows predestined sonship (Ephesians 1:5): He conforms the elect to be like His own Son, making them His dear brothers (and, of course, dear brothers of one another). Here, "brother" refers to the technical, legal status of being an heir (Galatians 4:7), and it also includes female Christians.

Like 1 Peter 1:2, Romans 8:29 teaches that predestination involves *foreknowledge*. Paul also sheds light on the relationship of predestination, foreknowledge, and saving faith in 2 Thessalonians 2:13: "But we ought always to give thanks to God for you, brothers beloved by the Lord, because God chose you as the firstfruits to be saved, through sanctification by the Spirit and belief in the truth." Many have understood this verse to mean that God elected certain persons to salvation on the basis of His foreknowledge of their faith and/or work. But it has already been shown in this chapter that faith is a result, not a cause, of election. Therefore, Bible teachers have often pointed out that the foreknowledge mentioned in Romans 8:29 is not simply God's awareness of all that ever happens, but rather the knowledge of a loving relationship between persons. Scripture sometimes speaks of this kind of knowledge, as in Galatians 4:9: "But now that you have come to know God, or rather to be known by God, how can you turn back again to the weak and worthless elementary principles of the world, whose slaves you want to be once more?"

Justification is part of the fulfillment of the intention of election (Romans 8:30). So is God's unfailing manifestation of love toward His elect as He prepares them for eternal glory (vv. 31–36). He treats those who are justified and reconciled to Him as His children and brings good out of evil for them, even out of suffering. They *do* suffer, but they conquer their troubles in various ways, and their eternal destiny is sure.

Note Paul's wording in Romans 8: Christ is the pattern of predestined destiny (v. 29); the basis of redemption (v. 32); the dying, raised, and exalted One, our intercessor (v. 34); and the loving Lord (vv. 35, 37–39).

Light for Faith

The Word of God shows the connection between election and other Christian teachings. These are some examples of the integration of doctrines in the light of Scripture.

Damnation. There is no predestination to eternal death (1 Timothy 2:4). But the Son of God was predestined to be damned for sinners (1 Peter 1:19–20), and because of this the elect shall escape damnation.

Saving faith. We are predestined *to* it, not predestined *because* of it (2 Thessalonians 2:13).

Grace. Predestination is an election of grace, showing God's loving concern for the salvation of sinners. But it is based on grace alone, not works (2 Timothy 1:9; Romans 11:5–6).

Means of Grace. We are elected to be saved through the Means of Grace (2 Thessalonians 2:13–14).

Warning. The scriptural doctrine of election will disturb people who rely for salvation on works or on something other than the merits of Christ.

Comfort. It assures the elect of their salvation (Romans 8:28–39; John 10:28).

The Church. The members of the Church are united as beneficiaries of election (1 Peter 1:1–2; Romans 8:29). Election guarantees the survival of the Christian Church (Matthew 24:24; 16:18). The Lord will bring about justice for His elect who pray to Him (Luke 18:7), watch over them in the last days (Matthew 24:22, 24), and gather together the elect on earth and those in heaven at the second coming (Matthew 24:31; Mark 13:27).

Another key question in discussions of election and predestination is this: How is God's control of all outcomes related to the decisions people make? God does control all outcomes in the world (Proverbs 20:24). Predestination to salvation is one facet of this (Ephesians 1:11). Human beings can make decisions and plans about many things, and have a free will to do so, but whether these work out or come to pass is subject to God's control (James 4:13–15; 1 Corinthians 16:7; Proverbs 16:9). But unconverted people cannot even decide to believe in Christ, to come to Him, to be converted. In spiritual matters they have bondage of the will. Divine predestination pertains to these matters.

Light for Living

Mark Twain's *Huckleberry Finn* describes a sermon preached to feuding families who keep their guns handy. "Everybody said it was a good sermon," Huck notes, "and they all talked it over going home, and had such a powerful lot to say about faith and good works and free grace and preforeordestination, and I don't know what all, that it did seem to me to be one of the roughest Sundays I had run across yet." Twain's suggestion that the topic of predestination has no usefulness at all for the way people live is intended as an amusing comment. This reaction is an exact match for the attitudes of many people.

Does the teaching of predestination promote Christian sanctification or not? Those who have a grateful knowledge of their election will want to live in the holy life to which they have been predestined. Note what Paul says the elect are to put on because they *are* elect: "compassionate hearts, kindness, humility, meekness, and patience," as well as forgiveness and, above all, "love, which binds everything together in perfect harmony" (Colossians 3:12, 14).

Why, then, does God let Christians suffer for their faith? This is all part of the working out of the purpose of election. If we are elected to conformity with the Son of God, we shall share in His sufferings in order that we may also share in His glory (Romans 8:14–18, 29). The refinement and purification that take place in such suffering are part of the holiness to which we are elected (1 Peter 1:2–7).

How do you "make your . . . election sure" (2 Peter 1:10)? Peter says that our election is made sure by diligence in good works, productive knowledge of the Lord Jesus, and remembrance of our forgiveness (2 Peter 1:5–9). This statement might seem to mean that good works and a Christian life are the basis of our election and make us qualified for it, or perhaps that election is provisional until we become worthy of it. But these thoughts contradict the fact that election is by grace alone. We should note here that forms of the same Greek word for "making sure" in the original text are applied to "election" (v. 10) and the Word of the prophets about Christ (v. 19). Both of these are certain and true in themselves. But the word refers to a demonstration that something is true and reliable. The prophecy about Christ is demonstrated to be true by the transfiguration (vv. 16–18). And our election to faith, to a Christian life, and to eternal glory is demonstrated by living in that life to which we are predestined and expressing the fruit of faith. Thereby, we may grow in the awareness that God is carrying out His purpose of election in us.

Point to Remember

Those whom He predestined He also called, and those whom He called He also justified, and those whom He justified He also glorified. *Romans 8:30*

Lutheran Summary of Predestination

Apology of the Augsburg Confession XVII 66

[He] will give eternal life and eternal joys to the godly . . . . (*Concordia*, p. 197)

Formula of Concord Epitome XI 6–7, 16–20

5. It [the predestination of God] is not to be investigated in God's secret counsel. It is to be sought in God's Word, where it is revealed.

6. God's Word leads us to Christ, who is the Book of Life, in whom all are written and elected who are to be saved in eternity. For it is written in Ephesians 1:4, "Even as He chose us in Him [Christ] before the foundation of the world."

. . . When anyone teaches the doctrine about God's gracious election to eternal life in such a way that troubled Christians cannot comfort themselves with this teaching, but are led to despondency or despair, or when the unrepentant are strengthened in their wild living, then‹, wickedly and erroneously,› the doctrine of election is not treated according to God's Word and will. Instead, this doctrine is being taught according to reason and by the encouragement of cursed Satan. It is as the apostle testifies in Romans 15:4: "Whatever was written in former days was written for our instruction, that through endurance and through the encouragement of the Scriptures we might have hope." Therefore, we reject the following errors:

1. God is unwilling that all people repent and believe the Gospel.

2. When God calls us to Himself, He is not eager that all people should come to Him.

3. God is unwilling that everyone should be saved. But some—without regard to their sins, from God's mere counsel, purpose, and will—are chosen for condemnation so that they cannot be saved.

4. Something in us causes God's election—not just God's mercy and Christ's most holy merit—because of which God has elected us to everlasting life. (cf. *Concordia*, pp. 498, 499–500).

Formula of Concord Solid Declaration II 57

If a person will not listen to preaching or read God's Word, but despises God's Word and community, and so dies and perishes in his sins, he cannot comfort himself with God's eternal election or receive His mercy. For Christ, in whom we are chosen, offers to all people His grace in the Word and holy Sacraments. (*Concordia*, pp. 530–31)

Formula of Concord Solid Declaration XI 8, 87–90

God's eternal election does not just foresee and foreknow the salvation of the elect. From God's gracious will and pleasure in Christ Jesus, election is a cause that gains, works, helps, and promotes our salvation and what belongs to it. Our salvation is so founded on it that "the gates of hell shall not prevail against it" (Matthew 16:18) . . . .

This doctrine and explanation of the eternal and saving choice of God's elect children entirely gives God all the glory. In Christ He saves us out of pure mercy, without any merits or good works of ours. He does this according to the purpose of His will, as it is written, "He predestined us for adoption through Jesus Christ, according to the purpose of His will, to the praise of His glorious grace, with which He has blessed us in the Beloved" (Ephesians 1:5–6). Therefore, it is false and wrong when it is taught that not only God's mercy and Christ's most holy merit, but also something in us is a cause of God's election, on account of which God has chosen us to eternal life. Before we had done anything good, also before we were born, yes, even before the foundations of the world were laid, He elected us in Christ. . . .

Furthermore, this teaching gives no one a cause either for despair or for a shameless, loose life. By this teaching, people are taught that they must seek eternal election in Christ and His Holy Gospel, as in the Book of Life. This excludes no penitent sinner, but beckons and calls all poor, heavy-laden, and troubled sinners to repentance and the knowledge of their sins. It calls them to faith in Christ and promises the Holy Spirit for purification and renewal. It gives the most enduring consolation to all troubled, afflicted people, so that they know that their salvation is not placed in their own hands. Otherwise they would lose their salvation much more easily than was the case with Adam and Eve in Paradise, yes, every hour and moment. But salvation is in God's gracious election, which He has revealed to us in Christ, out of whose hand no person shall snatch us (John 10:28; 2 Timothy 2:19). (*Concordia*, pp. 603–4, 614–15)

I Believe in the Holy Spirit

TOPIC TEN

The Holy Spirit[1]

Engaging This Topic

"Are you filled with the Holy Spirit?"
"Sure . . . well, aren't all Christians filled with the Holy Spirit?"

Even in our increasingly irreligious society, people continue to talk about God, often in terms of His Fatherhood. The general public recognizes the name, person, and work of Jesus Christ. But what do those outside the Church know of the Third Person of the Trinity? What do those *inside* the Church know about the Holy Spirit?

The Lutheran Church is perhaps especially open to the charge of "neglecting" the Holy Spirit. While one will not hear a Lutheran pastor preach even the shortest sermon without proclaiming Christ, Lutheran preaching often does not explicitly mention the Holy Spirit. Although this may be noted and criticized at times, Lutherans can say truthfully—if perhaps somewhat surprisingly—that it is neither an oversight nor an accident. Rather, it is entirely in keeping with Scripture's depiction of the office and work of the Spirit Himself.

As Jesus proclaimed to His disciples before His departure, the Spirit's task will be to "bring to your remembrance all that I have said to you" (John 14:26) and to "glorify Me" (John 16:14). The Third Person of the Trinity has no desire to draw attention to Himself; He has instead been sent for the purpose of directing our attention to God's saving work in Christ. In this regard Dr. Martin Luther explained: "That, then, is the Holy Spirit's office and work, that He through the Gospel reveal what great and glorious things God has done for us through Christ, namely, ransomed us from sin, death, and the power of the devil, received us into His grace and care, and given us Himself wholly and sufficiently" (WA 28:82).

Where Christ is preached, Lutherans rejoice to believe, teach, and confess that the Spirit is always present and active. Far from neglecting the

1 This chapter adapted from *Lutheran Difference: Holy Spirit*, written by Korey Maas. Copyright © 2002 Concordia Publishing House.

Spirit, Lutherans praise, honor, and glorify Him as God. This occurs not only when they speak *about* Him, but especially when in humble silence they allow Him to speak *to* them, to reveal the Savior and proclaim His salvation.

Lutheran Facts

Lutherans focus most specifically on the work of the Holy Spirit on particular holidays: The Feast of the Baptism of Our Lord, the Second Sunday of Easter (Quasimodogeniti), and Pentecost.

During the service of confirmation, Lutherans publicly confirm the work of the Spirit in a person's life. The service commemorates the work of the Spirit through Baptism and the Word, leading a person to publicly confess faith in Jesus.

During the service of confirmation, the pastor lays his hand on the confirmand's head and prays for the sevenfold gift of the Spirit as described in Isaiah 11:2.

During the ordination and installation of pastors, Lutherans call especially on the work and guidance of the Holy Spirit, who appoints men to the pastoral office (John 20:21–23; Acts 20:28).

During the 1970s, Lutheran churches, like most churches, were affected by the charismatic movement. A small percentage of Lutherans claim special gifts of the Spirit. Most Lutherans, however, continue to emphasize the work of the Holy Spirit through the Word of God rather than through specially anointed individuals.

Lutherans worship and pray to the Holy Spirit as the Third Person of the Holy Trinity.

The Spirit Speaks

> Sticks and stones may break my bones,
> but words can never hurt me.
> —a nursery rhyme

Words. Are they really so powerless? Mere scribbles and sound bites can stop a dispute or end a friendship. Words can begin a marriage or begin a war. Stronger even than human speech are the words that proceed from the mouth of God. Thankfully, unlike so many of our words, God's strong Word was written—and is still preached—for our benefit.

Human beings have almost limitless reasons, both positive and negative, for speaking with one another. We also have numerous methods for communication—from writing to sign language to verbal speech. For what reason might God feel it necessary or desirable to verbally speak with those He has created? And why did He choose to communicate by the particular means of the external, written Word of Scripture?

Discerning Spirit

Let's begin by looking at several passages from Scripture that have something to say about words that come from God's mouth.

Psalm 33:6: "By the word of the Lord the heavens were made, and by the breath of His mouth all their host."

2 Peter 3:5: "For they deliberately overlook this fact, that the heavens existed long ago, and the earth was formed out of water and through water by the word of God."

Hebrews 4:12: "For the word of God is living and active, sharper than any two-edged sword, piercing to the division of soul and of spirit, of joints and of marrow, and discerning the thoughts and intentions of the heart."

Ephesians 6:17: "And take the helmet of salvation, and the sword of the Spirit, which is the word of God."

The authors of the Old and New Testaments are in complete agreement: the heavens and the earth were created by God. They are also in agreement regarding the manner in which He created. Out of nothing, God *spoke* the universe into being (Genesis 1). The spoken word of God is a tremendously powerful thing; it is, as the author of Hebrews calls it, "living and active." How can mere words do such things? Of course, they are not "mere" words; they are God's own words. They are living and active because the Spirit lives in them and acts through them. They are, in the language of Paul, the Spirit's "sword"—the powerful tool or instrument by which the Spirit carries out His divine work. God's Word moves more than molecules of air and stirs more than breath. His Word can move and stir the heart.

The Spirit continued to speak through the words of the New Testament apostles. Acts 1:2 tells of the commands Jesus gave the apostles "through the Holy Spirit." First Corinthians 2:12–13 says we have received "the Spirit who is from God" and that the apostles shared "words not taught by human wisdom but taught by the Spirit." And 2 Peter 3:15–16 ascribes to the words of the apostle Paul authority equal to that of the prophets. The apostles gathered in Jerusalem do not act apart from the Spirit, but according to His revealed will (Acts 15:23–29). Unlike many medieval and modern councils of the Roman Church, the apostolic council agrees wholly with Scripture when it proclaims the will of the Spirit according to the Word and the office of prophet in the New Testament (Acts 15:30–35). The Spirit inspired the authors of both the Old and New Testaments to reveal Him who stands at the center of all Scripture—Christ, whose life and death won our salvation.

God spoke His creation into being, but divine speech did not end there. Peter declares that though the prophets spoke and wrote to God's people, they did not do so of their own accord. They spoke "from God," being "carried along by the Holy Spirit" (2 Peter 1:21). Paul echoes this thought as he writes to the young pastor Timothy, saying, "All Scripture is breathed out by God" (2 Timothy 3:16). Such passages proclaim the doctrine of Scripture's inspiration. Although Scripture does not explain the precise manner in which it was inspired, it teaches that its words come from God Himself through the Spirit.

While rejoicing that God would speak to His creation in human language, Christians also realize that some readers have difficulty understanding the Bible. Our understanding of the written Word of Scripture could not take place without the Spirit's activity. This is Paul's point when he writes: "The natural person does not accept the things of the Spirit . . . and he is not able to understand them" (1 Corinthians 2:14). Writing again to the Corinthians, he further explains by way of illustration. There are some, he says, who read Scripture as though a veil were draped between them and its true meaning. But with the Spirit "the veil is removed" (2 Corinthians 3:15).

To understand Scripture—or any literature—requires an awareness of its major themes. Believing that the Holy Spirit inspired Scripture and works through it, the Old and New Testament authors speak also of the Spirit's work in terms of Law and Gospel. Nehemiah, for example, records a prayer of the Levites in which the Spirit is said to have admonished Israel (9:30). Likewise, Jesus announces in John 16 that the Spirit will "convict the world concerning sin" (vv. 7–8). Although He must convict and condemn, the Spirit's "proper" work is to proclaim Christ. St. Paul assures us that the Gospel is very much the concern of the Spirit. "He saved us," Paul writes to Titus, "by the washing of regeneration and renewal of the Holy Spirit" (3:5). This rebirth and renewal through the forgiveness of sins is, as seen in John 20, the specific purpose for which the Holy Spirit was bestowed upon the apostles (vv. 22–23).

So intimately and essentially related are the Spirit and the preaching of Christ that Luther was led to declare in the Large Catechism that "where Christ is not preached, there is no Holy Spirit" (LC II 45; *Concordia*, p. 404).

Jesus declared that the Scriptures testify about Him (John 5:39). Likewise, Jesus ascribes this work to the Holy Spirit. The Spirit will remind the disciples of all that Jesus has said (John 14:26) and will bring glory to Him (John 16:14).

Although the Holy Spirit speaks and acts through God's external Word, there are spirits who do not do so. The knowledge that God's Spirit is constantly working through God's Word offers great assurance to the Christian. But, as John notes in his first letter, there also exist false spirits, those who are not God's. Therefore, be on guard, always testing the spirits and those who speak by them (1 John 4:1). But how? The intimate relationship between the Holy Spirit and Holy Scripture provides the basis on which to test the spirits. That is, if a spirit seems to call, gather, or enlighten and yet does so without the Word of God, it is not the Spirit of God.

Word and Spirit

The Holy Spirit not only inspired the ancient and original authors of the Bible, but He also works even today through the external Word, continuing to fulfill God's holy will.

Knowing the Holy Spirit's purpose in revealing God's Word helps us to properly read and understand it. As Jesus declared, the Scriptures testify to Him (John 5:39; 20:31). Understanding this, we read Scripture knowing that in all its parts it speaks of our salvation in Christ—and our need for salvation.

The Scriptures have been written for our salvation. However, this is far from all that Scripture has to offer. It not only speaks about our salvation; it also *effects* our personal salvation. The external Word of Scripture, in which the Holy Spirit is living and active, is the means by which God forgives our sin and declares us to be His children. God promises that His Word "shall accomplish that which I purpose, and shall succeed in the thing for which I sent it" (Isaiah 55:11).

Sure Word

Where God's Word is, there also is His Spirit. Not only is He present, but He is also active, and powerfully too. Acting through the Word of Scripture, He continually—and convincingly—convicts us of sin. But thanks be to God, He also pardons us for the sake of Christ.

That God's Spirit has called, gathered, enlightened, and sanctified us by means of His Word prompts us, when speaking to Him in worship and prayer, to offer heartfelt praise and thanksgiving. Also, knowing that His Word offers a clear and truthful expression of His holy will, we are often stimulated to worship and pray using His own words, saying back to Him what He has already said to us.

How might you respond to a friend who believes that God has spoken—or wonders if God has spoken—to him or her through means other than the revealed Word of Scripture? Statements such as "I really think God is telling me to . . ." or "I feel that the Holy Spirit has laid it on my heart to . . ." are common expressions in some Christian churches. The problem, of course, is that if one only "thinks" or "feels," then there can be no certainty that it is God Himself who is speaking. Such certainty comes only when we look for God to speak where He has promised to do so—in His revealed, written Word. One manner in which we might respond to these statements is by simply asking questions: "What is it that makes you feel God is speaking?" "How might you test these thoughts and feelings?" "Is what you've heard consistent with what has been revealed in Scripture?" Such questions could be followed by briefly studying together some of the pertinent passages above.

Comparisons

Verbal inspiration: The Holy Spirit led the prophets, evangelists, and apostles to write the books of the Bible. He guided their writing, inspiring their very words while working through their particular styles of expression. Therefore, the Bible's words are God's Word. Conservative Christian churches hold this view. Many also maintain that the original writings of the Bible were without error (the doctrine of inerrancy) but that some mistakes entered the text as the scribes copied, edited, or translated the Scriptures over the centuries.

Partial inspiration: Christians affected by theological liberalism hold different views of the inspiration of the Bible. For example, some would assert that the Bible is God's Word but that the authors erred in some factual details. Others would say that the Bible *contains* God's Word and that the Spirit leads people today to determine which parts of the Bible God wants them to follow. Still others would say that the Bible is one testimony to God's Word, along with writings used in other religions.

Inspired translations: Some churches hold that God inspired certain translations of the Bible. For example, the Eastern Orthodox Church holds that God inspired the Greek Septuagint translation of the Old Testament. Some English-speaking Protestants hold that God inspired the King James translation of the Bible.

The Spirit of God

Your life and the world you live in will never be the same.
—the character "Trinity," from the film *The Matrix*

Trinity. Christians hear this word so often they may sometimes fail to appreciate its true meaning. *Coequal, coeternal*—Christians use these words so little that they may not even know what they mean! The Holy Trinity is, to be sure, a great mystery. What's more, the Third Person of the Trinity, the Holy Spirit, may be the most mysterious.

What comes to mind when you hear the terms *holy* and *spirit*? Such words are used frequently even by non-Christians. When combined in the Christian Church, however, they take on a very specific—though perhaps not always clearly understood—meaning.

A Personal Being

We learn about the nature of the Holy Spirit in Psalm 139:7–10 and 1 Corinthians 2:10–11. The psalmist confesses that there is no place—on the earth, below it, or above it—in which he can escape the Spirit of God. In fact, following the format of ancient Hebrew poetry, David "parallels" God's Spirit with His presence, using these terms to describe each other. Where God is—everywhere!—there also is the Spirit. Not only is the Holy Spirit omnipresent, being in all places, He is also omniscient, that is, He knows all things. Paul notes this in 1 Corinthians 2:10 when he acknowledges that the Spirit searches "everything, even the depths of God." Omniscience and omnipresence are attributes of God alone. To ascribe them to the Holy Spirit is to claim for Him a divine status.

Jesus professes in John 4:24 that "God is Spirit," while Paul declares even more clearly in 2 Corinthians 3:17 that "the Lord is the Spirit." Based on such evidence, the Church confesses in the Athanasian Creed her belief that "the Father is God, the Son is God, the Holy Spirit is God" (*Concordia*, p. 17).

Many people, when hearing the word *spirit*, think of an impersonal energy or "life force." New Age and Eastern religions are not alone in speaking of a vague, impersonal spirit inhabiting the world. In contrast, the Lord's Old and New Testament people have always confessed that the Spirit of God is a person. As a person, He speaks (Acts 13:2), He makes choices (1 Corinthians 12:11), and He teaches (1 Corinthians 2:13). Also, like a person—and very much unlike an impersonal energy or "life force"—He loves (Romans 15:30) and experiences grief (Isaiah 63:10).

Another false impression worth touching on is the translation of the Latin word *spiritus* into English as *ghost*. The word *ghost* originally referred to the driving force, the self-aware human soul that animates the body, as well as to fury and anger. With the coming of Christianity to the Germanic tribes, the Church added to this concept any spiritual being that is active and self-aware, including angels, demons, and the Holy Spirit. The use of *ghost* as the soul of a dead human dates from the fourteenth century when the Black Death ravaged Europe. When the King James Bible was published in 1611, *ghost* did not have the immediate ties with Halloween that it does today. The popular notion of a comically frightening "spook" only became common in the United States—and later in Europe—during the nineteenth and twentieth centuries.

But what exactly does it mean to use the term *person* in reference to the Holy Spirit? The authors of the Athanasian Creed confessed that "the Father is one person, the Son is another, and the Holy Spirit is another" (*Concordia*, p. 17). Commenting on this and other testimonies of the early Christian Church, the Lutheran reformers insisted that "the term *person* [should be used] as the Fathers have used it. We use it to signify, not a part or quality in another, but that which subsists of itself " (AC I 4; *Concordia*, p. 31). That is, the Spirit is not merely a part of God or God's energy, He is God Himself.

Peter, Paul, and even Jesus Himself confess the Christian belief that the Holy Spirit is truly God, yet a person distinct from both the Father and the Son. In Acts 5, Peter rebukes Ananias for having lied to the Holy Spirit. Since one could hardly lie to an inanimate or impersonal object, Peter's words reveal the apostolic belief in the Spirit's personhood. But Peter does not stop there. His condemnation goes on to reveal the true nature of this Holy Spirit to whom Ananias has lied: "You have not lied to men but to God" (Acts 5:4). Paul invokes the three persons of the Trinity in the benediction given to the Christians at Corinth (2 Corinthians 13:14). Even Christ Himself, in the familiar words of the Great Commission, charges His disciples to baptize "in the name of the Father and of the Son and of the Holy Spirit" (Matthew 28:19). The words are familiar; what may sometimes go unnoticed, however, is Jesus' use of the singular "name." Father, Son, and Holy Spirit are three persons, yet they share one and the same name, that of the almighty God Himself.

Given the mystery of the Trinity, it is not surprising that there was much argument in the early Church about the exact nature of the relationship between Father, Son, and Holy Spirit. Much of the debate focused on terms such as *begotten* and *proceeds*, words we know today from the creeds formulated during those early controversies.

Although it is impossible for human reason to understand how three persons are one God and one God is three persons, Scripture is not silent about this mystery. With regard to the Spirit's eternal relation to the Father, Jesus describes Him in John 15 as going out, or proceeding, from the Father (v. 26). The Nicene Creed, however, refers to the Spirit "who proceeds from the Father *and* the Son" (*Concordia*, p. 16, *emphasis added*). A comparison of Matthew 10:20 and Galatians 4:6 helps to explain this. In these passages the Holy Spirit is referred to as both "the Spirit of Your Father" and "the Spirit of His Son." Being "of" both the Father and the Son, He also proceeds from both. Such is the confession of the Athanasian Creed: "The Holy Spirit is of the Father and of the Son, neither made nor created nor begotten but proceeding."

The Bible not only describes the relationship of the Spirit to the Father and Son with regard to their essence and being, but it also describes this relationship as it applies to their work in the world and for the world. It is common, and certainly not incorrect, to classify the work of the Father as creation, that of the Son as redemption, and that of the Holy Spirit as sanctification (see, for example, Luther's introduction to the Apostles' Creed in his Large Catechism; *Concordia*, pp. 398–99). It would be an error, however, to *limit* the three persons of the Trinity to these works, possibly giving the impression that the work of each is unrelated to the work of the others.

In John 16:14, Jesus describes the work of the Holy Spirit, saying that He will reveal Christ to His people as He "[takes] what is Mine and [declares] it to you." In a comparable manner, Jesus' own work is described in John 1:18 as that of making "Him known" or revealing the Father. All the Father's work has a common goal: making His love and salvation known to us through Christ, by the power of the Holy Spirit.

Jesus explains to the Samaritan woman that God must be worshiped according to His nature. Because "God is spirit," Jesus explains, He must be worshiped "in spirit" (John 4:24). Likewise, because God and His Word—both the written and incarnate Word (cf. John 14:6 and 17:17)—are truth, God is to be worshiped "in . . . truth" (John 4:24).

To worship God according to His nature is to worship Him as He is. He is not only the Father or the Son or the Spirit alone, but the triune God, Father, Son, and Holy Spirit together. Therefore the Church confesses in the Nicene Creed: "I believe in the Holy Spirit . . . who with the Father and the Son together is worshiped and glorified" (*Concordia*, p. 16). Likewise, the Church confesses in the Athanasian Creed: "the Trinity in Unity and Unity in Trinity is to be worshiped" (*Concordia*, p. 17).

A Personal Faith

Christians do not merely believe in "spirit" but in *the* Spirit, the Holy Spirit, the Third Person of the Trinity, God Himself. This biblical faith offers the believer great comfort.

The Christian Church does not believe in fate. Rather, the Church confesses that a holy, loving, and *personal* God oversees, guides, and even intervenes in the world, the Church, and the lives of its members. When Christians pray, they pray "in the Spirit" to a God who hears and answers them. Even in those times that we forget to pray or do not know what to pray, the person of the Holy Spirit is interceding and offering petitions on our behalf (Romans 8:26–27).

When tempted by the spirits of the world, we are reassured to know that the Spirit of God never ceases His work of creating and strengthening faith, bringing forgiveness in Word and Sacraments, and directing our lives in accordance with the will of God.

Although many people would deny the existence of spirits, demons, and angels, Scripture clearly states that they are present and active in the world. They are constantly attempting to lead us into temptation, doubt, and despair. They not only tempt us to deny God's holiness, but they may also lead us to doubt that He has in fact declared us holy and continues to make us so.

Mystery and Revelation

The mystery of the Holy Trinity is incomprehensible to human reason. Nevertheless, it is true, as God's true Word declares. Although we are unable to comprehend the "how," we joyfully confess the "who" of the Trinity: Father, Son, and Holy Spirit.

How do we answer a friend who questions the nature of the Holy Spirit and His relation to God the Father and God the Son? The Holy Spirit Himself reveals and instructs in God's truth. We prayerfully request that He work in the hearts and minds of those who do not believe. Furthermore, since the Spirit has inspired Scripture and continues to speak and act through this means, we can encourage questioning friends to seek answers in the Bible. Many of the passages found in this chapter may be helpful starting points for discussing the nature and work of the Spirit.

Although Christians frequently begin prayer in the name of the Father and end in the name of Jesus, they often pray without specific mention of the Holy Spirit. There is certainly nothing wrong with this, as Christians always pray "in the Spirit." One simple way to specifically mention the Spirit, however, would be to close prayers to our heavenly Father with the trinitarian phrase "through Jesus Christ, who lives and reigns with You and the Holy Spirit."

Comparisons

Proceeds from the Father and the Son: Christians of the Western tradition teach that the Holy Spirit proceeds from the Father *and the Son* (*filioque* in Latin). They tend to emphasize the coequal divinity of the Father, Son, and Holy Spirit.

Proceeds from the Father: Eastern Orthodox churches have never accepted the *filioque* statement added by Western churches to the Nicene Creed. They contend that the Spirit proceeds from the Father *through* the Son, emphasizing more of a hierarchy among the persons of the Trinity.

Pseudo-Christian beliefs: A variety of groups reject the divinity of the Holy Spirit and the doctrine of the Trinity. For example, the Jehovah's Witnesses regard the Holy Spirit as an impersonal force. The United Pentecostal Church teaches that the Father, Son, and Holy Spirit are all manifestations of the same person ("Jesus only"). Mormons hold that the Holy Spirit is a spiritual god alongside the Father and the Son, who are gods with physical bodies.

Life-giving Spirit

In Your radiance
Life from heaven
Now is given
Overflowing,
Gift of gifts beyond all knowing.
—Michael Schirmer (*Lutheran Worship* 160:1)

Every day we make choices. Sometimes we clamor for more options from which to choose; sometimes we wish there were not so many options. Whether or not we enjoy them—or even notice them—each and every day our lives are filled with countless choices. How strange, then, that no one made the first and most important decision: to begin lie.

Breath of God

Although it is sometimes assumed that the Holy Spirit was not introduced until Pentecost, the opening verses of Scripture remind us that He was present even at the time of creation. What is more, He was *active* in creation (Genesis 1:2). Although we read in Genesis 2:7 that God breathed into man "the breath of life," the translators of both the Hebrew language of the Old Testament and the Greek language of the New Testament often use *breath* and *spirit* interchangeably. Since the same word is used for both, Job is able to synonymously parallel the terms in his confident confession that the "Spirit of God has made me, and the breath of the Almighty gives me life" (33:4). In the same manner, when reciting the Nicene Creed, the Church confidently confesses its faith in "the Holy Spirit, the Lord and Giver of Life" (*Concordia*, p. 16).

Although God breathed the Spirit into man at his creation, man did not long maintain his holy and "spiritual" status. In the Garden of Eden man fell, and all since have been born in a "natural" or "fleshly," that is, sinful, state. In contrast to the life given at creation, Paul described death in transgressions. Paul was not alone in proclaiming the dire consequences of man's sinful separation from the Holy Spirit. Before Paul's conversion—during a persecution of Christians to which he gave his assent!—Stephen preached the Law. Not only is natural man not endowed with the Spirit, Stephen says, but "you always resist the Holy Spirit" (Acts 7:51).

Being dead in trespasses (Ephesians 2:1), the sinner must be reborn or re-created if he or she is to have life. In David's well-known psalm of repentance, he asks that the Lord might "create in me a clean heart" (51:10). It is no coincidence that David appeals to God's creative power. Creation—that which God alone can do—is precisely what must take place. Psalm 104 notes the one through whom this creative act takes place: "When You send forth Your Spirit, they are created" (v. 30). Men who are dead in sin must be brought to life, created anew. We, however, have no power to do this ourselves. Jesus Himself explains this to His visitor Nicodemus. Just as man cannot live without first having been born, so, too, must he be born again, "born of water and the Spirit," if he is to enter God's kingdom (John 3:5). With the psalmist and with Christ, Paul declares that this takes place "through His Spirit" (Romans 8:11). Only the Holy Spirit who first gave life can bestow the new and eternal life that comes with forgiveness. New life is given only on account of the life sacrificed by Christ. In this life given for us, the Holy Spirit played a prominent role.

The Gospels make plain that Jesus was no ordinary man. Luke's Gospel, in particular, provides the details surrounding His birth, His early life, and the beginning of His earthly ministry. As these details make clear, the Holy Spirit was, from Jesus' very conception, intimately involved with

His earthly life and ministry. The Holy Spirit came upon Mary that her child might truly be called the Son of God. Together with the Father, the Spirit was present at Jesus' Baptism, a sign and a testimony that Jesus' ministry was divinely ordained. The Spirit's role as a witness to Jesus' divine nature and work is later echoed in Jesus' own words. Just before His arrest, Jesus promised His disciples the Counselor, the Spirit of truth, whose work it would be to "bear witness about Me" (John 15:26). This testimony, He goes on to explain, "will glorify Me, for He will take what is Mine and declare it to you" (John 16:14).

The life of Jesus, the life given into death for our sins, is the one and only basis for our salvation. That we might know of His glorious work on our behalf, the Spirit has been given as His witness. For this we must truly give thanks.

Not only does the Spirit play a role in the life of Jesus, but He is also involved in our own lives: "But you were washed, you were sanctified, you were justified in the name of the Lord Jesus Christ and by the Spirit of our God" (1 Corinthians 6:11). Lest we conclude that the Spirit's work stops with bearing witness to Christ, Paul explains that the Holy Spirit makes the benefits of Christ's work our own.

"Justification by faith" is a phrase familiar to Lutherans. Both Scripture and the Lutheran Confessions proclaim the doctrine of "grace alone," that our justification is a free gift of God, given by His Spirit working through the Word (1 Corinthians 12:3). The Confessions also teach the doctrine of "faith alone," that this gift of salvation is received only by faith. Paul teaches that, like grace itself, faith is a free gift of the Spirit.

Lively Spirit

The Holy Spirit acts without our asking, without our effort, and at times without our knowledge. But knowing how and for what purpose the Spirit is active can be a source of great comfort and encouragement for the Christian.

Christians are not immune to feelings of insignificance, meaninglessness, or loneliness. The modern world teaches a "closed universe." God—if He exists at all—does not intervene in our lives. This teaching leaves people alone to question their life's meaning and purpose. It certainly does nothing to alleviate negative thoughts.

The assurance that we were given life by a personal and loving God, a God who breathed His own Spirit into our first parent, offers significance and meaning beyond compare. In the same manner, the promise that His Spirit is constantly at work in our lives, comforting and counseling (as His very names declare), offers us the assurance that we are certainly not alone.

Knowing that the Holy Spirit's work is to testify to Christ, we can be encouraged in our own evangelism efforts. Many find personal evangelism a difficult and, at times, frustrating task. On those occasions when we might become hesitant, nervous, or frustrated, it is comforting to know that the conversion of unbelievers does not ultimately rest upon our own words or works. Rather, the Spirit Himself is at work. It is He who testifies to Christ through our sharing of Scripture.

Live in the Spirit

Acting through Word and Sacraments, the Spirit testifies to the person and work of Jesus Christ. What is more, through these means the Holy Spirit not only points to our salvation in Christ, but He also effects our salvation! Without our cooperation, He raises us from death in sin to new life in Christ.

We are not burdened with the misconception of worship as a good work that must be done to please God. Instead, we gather together to hear the reassuring promise of eternal life granted in Jesus' name. We come to *receive* life in His Word and Sacraments. And we come to offer our praise and thanksgiving for this wonderful, free, certain gift of God.

The biblical parallels between creation and re-creation, birth and rebirth, speak against the notion that we must in some way cooperate with the Holy Spirit's work of justification. We can respond to a friend who believes that one must "make a decision" or otherwise work with the Spirit in salvation that, just as Adam did not choose to be created and we do not cooperate in our birth, neither do we have the option of taking part in our own rebirth.

Comparison

As you read the following comparisons, look for how the different churches talk about the work of the Holy Spirit, whether through the Means of Grace or within a person.

Eastern Orthodox: "Is the Holy Ghost communicated to men even now likewise? He is communicated to all true Christians. . . . How may we be made partakers of the Holy Ghost? Through fervent prayer, and through the Sacraments" (*The Longer Catechism of the Eastern Church*, questions 249–50).

Lutheran: "I believe that I cannot by my own reason or strength believe in Jesus Christ, my Lord, or come to Him. But the Holy Spirit has called me by the Gospel, enlightened me with His gifts, sanctified and kept me in the true faith" (SC II; *Concordia*, p. 330; Lutherans emphasize that the Holy Spirit works through the Means of Grace: the Word and Sacraments).

Reformed: "But when God accomplishes His good pleasure in the elect, or works in them true conversion, He not only causes the gospel to be externally preached to them, and powerfully illuminates their minds by His Holy Spirit . . . but by the efficacy of the same regenerating Spirit He pervades the inmost recesses of the man" (*Canons of the Synod of Dort*, article 11).

Roman Catholic: The Holy Spirit awakens faith in unbelievers and communicates new life to them through the ministry of the Church. Cf. CCC2 paras. 1098, 1432–33.

Anabaptist: This movement emphasizes the mystical work of the Spirit in the heart rather than through Word and Sacraments. Only holy people have received the Holy Spirit and are members of the Church.

Baptist: "We believe that Repentance and Faith are sacred duties, and also inseparable graces, wrought in our souls by the regenerating Spirit of God" (*New Hampshire Baptist Confession*).

Wesleyan: "But as soon as he is born of God . . . he is now capable of hearing the inward voice of God, saying, 'Be of good cheer; thy sins are forgiven thee'; 'Go and sin no more.' . . . He 'feels in his heart,' to use the language of our Church, 'the mighty working of the Spirit of God'" (*Standard Sermons of John Wesley*, 39.4).

The Spirit of Holiness

The gods help those who help themselves.
—*Aesop's Fables*

Whether it be through "twelve steps" or "seven habits," it seems that everyone—both in and out of the Church—is engaging in some sort of self-help or self-improvement. We want to look better, feel better, and act better. Our constant desire to better ourselves is driven by unhappiness, which is an inevitable consequence of sin. We—both Christians and non-Christians—are often unhappy with who we are because we are not who we were meant to be: God's holy people, created without sin to live in communion with Him. But even our so-called self-help is rarely done by ourselves. We enlist the aid of books, support groups, and personal trainers. If we need the help of others to become sober, thin, or better able to communicate with our spouse, how much more is divine assistance needed if we are to become holy?

The Helpless Self

Working through the Scripture, the Holy Spirit fulfills the purpose of Scripture: bringing sinners to salvation. As Paul writes to Timothy and to the church at Rome, Scripture has many purposes (Romans 15:4). Through it the Holy Spirit teaches, rebukes, corrects, and trains in righteousness. The Spirit does this so that the Christian might be "equipped for every good work" (2 Timothy 3:16–17).

Since even those forgiven by Christ continue to struggle with the effects of original sin, we are not yet the perfectly pure and holy people our gracious God first created us to be. Thus Martin Luther wrote in his Large Catechism that

> for now we are only half pure and holy. So the Holy Spirit always has some reason to continue His work in us through the Word. He must daily administer forgiveness until we reach the life to come. At that time there will be no more forgiveness, but only perfectly pure and holy people [1 Corinthians 13:10]. We will be full of godliness and righteousness, removed and free from sin, death, and all evil, in a new, immortal, and glorified body. (LC II 58; *Concordia*, p. 405)

Paul describes the Spirit's work of sanctification as a "debt" to "put to death the deeds of the body" (Romans 8:13). This, however, is an obligation we remain unable to fulfill by our own power. Therefore, Paul emphasizes that this putting to death is done "by the Spirit." As the misdeeds of the body are daily put to death, Paul also explains that we are "being transformed into the same image from one degree of glory to another." This, too, comes not from our own power, but it "comes from the Lord who is the Spirit" (2 Corinthians 3:18).

As we discussed in the last chapter, *sanctification* is daily putting to death sin and being transformed into the likeness of our holy God. Paul declares to the Corinthians who had formerly been immoral, idolaters, thieves, and drunkards: "you were washed, you were sanctified, you were justified" (1 Corinthians 6:11). Paul's use of passive vocabulary cannot be overemphasized. These things were not done by the Corinthians themselves; they were done *for* them. These themes are repeated in the closing of Paul's first letter to the Thessalonian church. He prays, "May the God of peace Himself sanctify you" (5:23). This reference to the One who both calls and sanctifies is reflected in the language of the Small Catechism, in which we confess that "the Holy Spirit has called me by the Gospel, enlightened me with His gifts, sanctified and kept me in the true faith" (SC II; *Concordia*, p. 330).

We are sanctified by the truth, which is God's own Word, the means through which the Spirit is always at work. It is by the power of God's Word that the Church is called into existence, sins are forgiven, and eternal life is granted. Hence the words of the Large Catechism: "'I believe that the Holy Spirit makes me holy, as His name implies.' 'But how does He accomplish this, or what are His method and means to this end?' Answer, 'By the Christian Church, the forgiveness of sins, the resurrection of the body, and the life everlasting" (LC II 40–42; *Concordia*, p. 403).

In his first letter to the Corinthians, Paul explains that all who have been baptized "in one Spirit" and "made to drink of one Spirit" are together members of this one body (12:13). In Ephesians Paul uses a different metaphor, describing the Church as "the household of God," a "holy temple," and a "dwelling place for God" (2:19–22). Through different illustrations, Paul makes the same points. The one Holy Christian Church is called and gathered by the Spirit, it consists of those who have received the Holy Spirit in Baptism, and in it God continues to dwell "by the Spirit."

The Spirit's presence and activity are in fact the only basis on which the Church can rightly be called "holy." The Church is not always in its outward and visible life more holy than other organizations. Without the Holy Spirit, there is no Holy Christian Church.

Prayer is associated with the sanctified Christian life. The Church that has been called, gathered, enlightened, and sanctified by God Himself also desires to speak with Him who has done such great things. God, in fact, desires that we speak with Him. Therefore, His apostle exhorts Christians to pray "at all times," to pray "in the Holy Spirit" (Ephesians 6:18), and to "pray without ceasing" (1 Thessalonians 5:17). We are told not only what to do but also how to do it. As Paul and Jude (20) proclaim, Christians pray "in the Holy Spirit." This, however, is not the Spirit's only work regarding prayer. Even being strengthened by the Spirit who dwells within us, we sometimes do not know how to pray or what to pray for. Paul's words to the Romans are infinitely encouraging. He assures his audience that "the Spirit intercedes for the saints" (8:27). Even prayer, part of the life of the sanctified Christian, is something God in His wisdom and mercy has not left to our strength alone.

The Christian's sanctification is not limited to deeds that seem outwardly holy. Often when we hear the word *sanctification*, we may call to mind stereotypes of good works, such as regular church attendance or even the Boy Scout helping an elderly lady across the street. Few of us, perhaps, immediately call to mind factory workers building tractors, technicians programming computers, or teachers at the front of a public school classroom—things not explicitly mentioned in the Law of God. Yet we read in Exodus that the gift of God's Spirit is associated with the so-called mundane tasks of masonry, carpentry, and design (see Exodus 31:1–6; 35:30–33).

The examples from Exodus may seem strange until we realize that, in the same way that God gave these men the skills that were used for the tabernacle, He also gives skills to people for more "mundane" purposes of life. "Good works" are merely works done by "good people," that is, those who have been declared holy and good by God Himself. The Christian is doing the will of God, living out the life of sanctification, when he or she faithfully carries out the tasks of his or her vocations. The many callings we have received—pastor or parishioner, parent or child, employer or employee—are, when carried out faithfully, means by which our neighbor is loved and served. For this reason, Martin Luther appended to his Small Catechism a Table of Duties (*Concordia*, pp. 346–48), concluding them with reference to Romans 13:8: "The one who loves another has fulfilled the law."

Ever-present Help

In Leviticus 19:2 the Lord's people are told: "Be holy, for I the Lord your God am holy." That's a tall order! Although we are assured that God, for the sake of Christ's all-sufficient death and resurrection, no longer accounts to us our sin, the Christian still daily struggles with what Scripture calls the "flesh" or the "sinful nature" that still dwells in all descendants of Adam. This daily conflict reminds us that we are not yet the entirely holy people we should be and one day will be. When this struggle becomes discouraging and disheartening—as even Paul recognized it to be (Romans 7:14–24)—we can take comfort in knowing that we do not struggle alone.

Most Christians would agree that they ought to spend more time in prayer. Many of us fall into the trap of only remembering to whisper a hasty prayer before meals or before drifting off to sleep. Even when special effort is made to spend time with God in prayer, we sometimes simply can't find the words to pray as we would like. Because we recognize our own weakness, Paul's words in Romans 8:26–27 are a comforting reminder that our prayers are not the only ones being heard by God. The Holy Spirit Himself intercedes for us.

Aside from participating in worship, many Christians do not find time to be actively involved in the affairs of the Church. Works done in and for the congregation are not the sole means by which we live the sanctified Christian life. Being a faithful and loving spouse is a good work. Being an honest and able employee pleases God. Being an obedient child fulfills

God's Law. Even in the most common acts of daily life, Christians can be confident that the Holy Spirit is at work in them and sanctifying them.

Beyond Self-Help

The Christian's sanctification, we can joyously confess, is no mere matter of self-help. God assures us that He has not only declared us holy, but that His Holy Spirit also is constantly at work in us, with us, and through us to make us holy.

How might we respond to a friend who attempts to simplify the Christian experience by claiming that God works our justification, but we must work our own sanctification? Clarifying and explaining the Holy Spirit's necessary role in sanctification might begin most profitably with those passages that explicitly mention God as the subject of our sanctification (e.g., John 17:17; 1 Corinthians 6:11). Also, Paul's words in Romans 7:14–24 illustrate how powerless even the great apostle was to work out his own sanctification: "For I know that nothing good dwells in me, that is, in my flesh. For I have the desire to do what is right, but not the ability to carry it out. For I do not do the good I want, but the evil I do not want is what I keep on doing" (vv. 18–19).

God has placed each of us in specific situations in life: mother, father, son, daughter, employee, employer, volunteer, mentor, etc. Another word for these situations is "vocation." Luther's Small Catechism includes a section called the "Table of Duties" (*Concordia*, pp. 346–48). As you review the "Table of Duties," consider how the Holy Spirit is at work through these vocations to work out your sanctification. The passages listed can be used to guide your prayers as you include petitions for the strength to faithfully carry out your vocations.

Comparisons

Since the Reformation, the confessional writings of Christians have generally agreed that sanctification or holiness is a result of God's justifying grace in Christ. However, different traditions emphasize different teachings about holiness based on their views of sin and the abilities of the human will.

Perfect holiness only in heaven: Lutherans, the Reformed, and Baptists of the Calvinist tradition teach that Christians do not attain perfection in this life because of the taint of original sin. The Holy Spirit sanctifies believers in lives of greater service to God and others.

Degrees of holiness: Roman Catholics and the Eastern Orthodox Church teach that the saints attain a greater degree of holiness than most Christians. They attain this through fervent prayer, good works, and self-deprivation. Roman Catholics also teach that Mary was born without the taint of original sin.

Perfectionism: Churches of the Wesleyan and Anabaptist traditions, as well as others of the Arminian tradition, teach that it is possible to reach a state of perfection. Perfection is a second work of grace following justification and is usually accompanied by a mystical, personal experience.

Ethics: Liberalism, as an heir to the individualistic form of religion known as Pietism that was popular after the Thirty Years' War (1618–48), emphasizes personal or corporate standards of conduct, which the human will can attain through love and discipline.

Baptized with the Spirit

The Word by seers or sibyls told,
In groves of oak, or fanes of gold,
Still floats upon the morning wind,
Still whispers to the willing mind.
One accent of the Holy Ghost
The heedless world hath never lost.
—Ralph Waldo Emerson, *The Problem*

Emerson's poetry signaled an important shift in American religious thought away from the words of Scripture toward "natural" spirituality.

Human beings reveal strange inner contrasts. We waver between the emotional and the empirical. At times we just want to feel things, and at times we want definitely to know things. Sometimes we want an internal experience, and sometimes we want external proof. However, these otherwise wonderful impulses—as with all human inclinations—can confuse or mislead.

Can you think of times when you may have ignored what seemed obviously to be true just because it didn't "feel right"? Are there some instances when it may be inappropriate to demand hard evidence for something? There are stark contrasts between emotionalism and rationalism, confidence in things felt and trust in things seen. And most of us have experienced times when an overreliance on internal feelings or on external evidence resulted in less-than-desirable consequences.

The Promised Spirit

Although the Spirit was certainly present and at work in the era of the Old Testament, the Lord promised a future event when "on the male and female servants in those days I will pour out My Spirit" (Joel 2:29). Even centuries later, however, John informs his readers that "the Spirit had not been given, because Jesus was not yet glorified" (7:39). It was not until the days before His ascension that Jesus told His disciples that they should "wait for the promise of the Father," that "you will be baptized with the Holy Spirit not many days from now" (Acts 1:4–5). That this promised gift was the outpouring of the Spirit is made clear a few days later—on Pentecost. Following the Spirit's dramatic entrance, the apostle Peter refers his audience to the prophet Joel to explain the morning's events (Acts 2:16–21). Nearing the end of his impromptu sermon, Peter again makes reference to the promise of the Holy Spirit, saying this promise is for "everyone whom the Lord our God calls to Himself" (2:39).

John the Baptist prophesied that the one whose coming he announced would baptize "with the Holy Spirit" (Mark 1:8). This reference to Baptism with the Holy Spirit (or *in* or *by*; the English renderings are sometimes inconsistent—each is a translation of the Greek preposition *en*) recurs in all the Gospels, the Book of Acts, and Paul's first letter to the Corinthians. While John does not specify who will be so baptized, Paul announces that "in one Spirit we were all baptized" (1 Corinthians 12:13).

While some may not even realize they have been baptized with the Spirit (1 Corinthians 3:16), and while some may show little evidence of the Spirit—as was the case in the carnal Corinthian church—Paul writes quite emphatically that "anyone who does not have the Spirit of Christ does not belong to Him" (Romans 8:9). That is, if one has not received the Spirit, one is not a Christian.

Although God has promised to pour out the Spirit on all of His redeemed, He has not promised to do so without means. As Peter preached to them, the Holy Spirit was received by those in the house of Cornelius. Note what Peter was preaching when this happened: "Everyone who believes in Him receives forgiveness of sins through His name" (Acts 10:43). Peter proclaimed the Gospel! Through God's spoken, written, and sacramental Word of grace comes God's Spirit. He has not promised to do so otherwise.

Just as the Holy Spirit comes with faith, so, too, is He inseparable from the object of our faith: Jesus Christ. Alternating his emphasis on the

Second and Third Persons of the Trinity, Paul argues in Romans that "the Spirit of God dwells in you" (8:9), that "Christ is in you" (v. 10), and twice again that the Spirit "dwells in you" (v. 11). This, Paul proclaims, is true of all Christians without exception.

The office and work of the Holy Spirit are that of proclaiming, revealing, and making present Christ and His salvation. This He does in and through the Word; this He does also in and through His work of Baptism. Paul declares this to be true when he explains that, being baptized into Christ, the Christian is baptized into His saving death and resurrection (Romans 6:3–4). The apostle Peter states even more clearly that "baptism . . . now saves you" (1 Peter 3:21).

Paul urges the Ephesians to "maintain the unity of the Spirit," recognizing that there is only "one body and one Spirit," only "one Lord, one faith, one baptism" (4:3–6). This unity becomes endangered when it is stated or implied that there may be two sorts of Christians—those who have been baptized with water and those who have received an additional and immediate "baptism with the Spirit."

While Paul makes clear that the Church recognizes only one Baptism, the value of this Baptism sometimes comes into question if the Spirit's presence and activity are not always or explicitly felt and seen. What is often sought is an obvious manifestation of the Spirit, such as prophesying, speaking in tongues, or healing. Against placing too much confidence in one's senses, however, both Jesus and Paul warn that signs are not to be demanded.

Comforting Spirit

Even before the birth of His Son, God promised that His Spirit would be poured out on all people. The promise of Joel, as with all Old Testament prophecies, has been fulfilled in Christ. It was He who sent the Spirit from His Father on Pentecost, and it is He whose name we are baptized into even today.

The Church rejoices to know that God's Word does not fail, that all His promises come true, and that in Christ we are fulfilled for our benefit and for God's own glory.

We can take consolation in knowing that all Christians—even those as sin-steeped as the Corinthians—have been baptized in the Spirit. While Christians will want at all times to avoid ranking, measuring, or comparing holiness, it comes as a great comfort to be reassured that the Holy Spirit received in Baptism is a free gift given to all of God's redeemed people, even those in whom His presence and fruits are not always obvious. The Spirit is not dependent on our holiness, our works, or even our prayer, but

He is poured out with water and the Word for the sake of our Lord, Jesus Christ.

We can also take comfort in knowing that we have not been baptized in the Spirit alone, but into the name of the Trinity itself: Father, Son, *and* Holy Spirit. In the last chapter of Matthew, our Lord instituted the Sacrament of Christian Baptism. We can do no better—indeed, no other!—than to receive this gift according to His mandate, His institution, and His words: "in the name of the Father and of the Son and of the Holy Spirit" (Matthew 28:19). Members in the one Holy Church receive their one Holy Baptism in the name of the God who also is one and holy. In the formula for Baptism, the unity in Trinity and Trinity in unity is confessed, and all of His great gifts and benefits are received.

Life in the Spirit

Quite frequently Christians do not feel holy inwardly. Just as often, we appear outwardly unholy. We rejoice, therefore, to be assured that our holiness is not a matter of internal feelings or external evidence. Our personal holiness rests upon God's Word and Spirit having, in our Baptism, declared and made it true.

What loving response can we give to those who might downplay our Baptism with water and the Word by asking, "Yes, but have you been baptized *with the Holy Spirit*?" We can confess, "Jesus is Lord," and remind them that we could not make this confession without the Holy Spirit!

The morning and evening prayers found in Martin Luther's Small Catechism are preceded with encouragement to "bless yourself with the holy cross and say: In the name of God the Father, Son, and Holy Spirit" (*Concordia*, p. 344). This sign and these words serve as a daily reminder of the Baptism with which we were received into God's household and through which we received His promised Holy Spirit, together with all His gifts and blessings.

Comparisons

Eastern Orthodox: "Baptism is a Sacrament, in which a man who believes . . . dies to the carnal life of sin, and is born again of the Holy Ghost to a life spiritual and holy" (*The Longer Catechism of the Eastern Church*, question 288).

Lutheran: "For without the Word of God the water is simple water and no Baptism. But with the Word of God it is a Baptism, that is, a gracious water of life and a washing of regeneration in the Holy Spirit" (SC IV; *Concordia*, p. 340).

Reformed: "By the right use of this ordinance [Baptism] the grace promised is not only offered, but really exhibited and conferred by the Holy Ghost, to such (whether of age or infants) as that grace belongeth unto, according to the counsel of God's own will, in his appointed time" (*The Westminster Confession of Faith*, chapter 28.6).

Anabaptist: "Concerning baptism we confess that penitent believers, who, through faith, regeneration, and the renewing of the Holy Ghost, are made one with God, and are written in heaven, must, upon such Scriptural confession of faith, and renewing of life, be baptized with water" (*The Dordrecht Confession*, article 7).

Roman Catholic: Baptism both signifies and causes the new birth of water and the Spirit. Cf. CCC2 paras. 1425–29.

Baptist: "Sinners must be regenerated or born again; that regeneration consists in giving a holy disposition to the mind; that it is effected in a manner above our comprehension by the power of the Holy Spirit, in connection with divine truth, so as to secure our voluntary obedience to the gospel" (*New Hampshire Baptist Confession*, article 7).

Wesleyan: "Baptism is not only a sign of profession and mark of difference whereby Christians are distinguished from others that are not baptized; but it is also a sign of regeneration, or the new birth" (*Methodist Articles of Religion*, article 17; Holiness churches and Pentecostals teach a second work of grace, after regeneration, by which God "perfects" a person or baptizes them in the Holy Spirit.

The Fruit and Gifts of the Spirit

> LORD, shall we not bring these gifts to Your service?
> Shall we not bring to Your service all our powers?
> For life, for dignity, grace and order,
> And intellectual pleasures of the senses?
> —T. S. Eliot, choruses from "The Rock"

Have you ever heard someone say, "She's at the top of her class, she sings in the choir, and she's captain of the swim team. She's really quite gifted."

We often hear teachers, counselors, and researchers speak of gifted children. And we certainly rejoice if they're talking about our children!

But what about children who are not given the "gifted" label? Do they lack gifts?

Why is the term *gifted* so often used in place of *able* or *talented*? Even in its common, secular usage, the term is passive. That is, there is an implication that things such as intellect and athleticism are received from someone else rather than developed independently.

God's Gifts

In describing the sanctified life that Christians live by the Spirit, Paul describes some of the fruit produced in believers. "Against such things," he writes, "there is no law" (Galatians 5:22). In fact, such things, when performed by those regenerated by the Spirit, are a fulfillment of God's holy Law. The Christian, however, having been raised to new life by the Spirit, no longer lives under the Law (Galatians 5:18). In his letter to the Romans, Paul reminds us that our sanctification is never complete in this life. Although we exhibit in our lives the fruit of the Spirit who sanctifies us, these are only "firstfruits." Until we are finally made entirely pure and holy upon our arrival in God's heavenly presence, we continue to "groan inwardly" and "wait eagerly" for our final redemption (Romans 8:22–23).

On several occasions Paul discusses what are called "spiritual gifts." He lists these gifts as follows.

ROMANS 12:6–8	1 CORINTHIANS 12:4–10	1 CORINTHIANS 12:28
Prophecy	Speaking wisdom	Apostleship
Serving	Speaking knowledge	Prophecy
Teaching	Faith	Teaching
Encouraging	Gifts of healing	Miracles
Contributing	Working miracles	Healing
Leading	Prophecy	Helping others
Doing acts of mercy	Distinguishing spirits	Administration
	Tongues	Tongues
	Interpreting tongues	

In our own day there is frequent and often confusing discussion of spiritual gifts. The same was true even in the days of the apostles. Paul therefore begins his discussion in 1 Corinthians 12 by saying, "Now concerning spiritual gifts, brothers, I do not want you to be uninformed."

Of what, then, does Paul inform us? First, as noted in Romans, Christians do not necessarily have the same gifts. They do, however, regardless of their gift or gifts, have the same Spirit (1 Corinthians 12:4). Second, it should be noted that even while the above lists were given by the same author—and the Corinthian lists even to the same audience—Paul never enumerates precisely the same gifts. Nor does he even clarify what he means by particular gifts.

It seems that Paul's purpose is *not* to give a definitive or exhaustive list of spiritual gifts. Instead, his purpose is to confirm that Christians do indeed have gifts given by God Himself and that the use of these gifts should not cause division in the Church.

The gifts that come with sanctification are very different from the Gift given for our justification. Christ gave His life, as we confess in the Nicene Creed, "for us men and for our salvation" (*Concordia*, p. 16). Spiritual gifts, however, are not given for our own personal benefit, but for the good of others. Paul, who has the most to say about spiritual gifts, insists that they are to be used "for the common good" of the Church (1 Corinthians 12:7). Likewise, Peter exhorts Christians to use their gifts "to serve one another" (1 Peter 4:10).

The Corinthian church was, when Paul wrote, a complete mess. It was divided by factions. It was tolerant of sexual immorality unheard of even among pagans. Members were suing one another, and there were disputes concerning marriage, worship, and the Lord's Supper. And yet Paul begins his first letter by claiming that the Christians at Corinth "are not lacking in any spiritual gift" (1:7). He could say such a thing, as he later explains by way of repetition, because the gifts of the spirit are given "to each" in the Christian Church. All those who have been baptized have received the Holy Spirit together with His gifts (1 Corinthians 12:7, 11).

To be sure, we can use God's gifts selfishly or unwisely, as was the case in Corinth. We may also at times be unaware of the Holy Spirit's gifts—in ourselves and in others. This is because these manifestations are given by the Spirit as He determines and "as He wills" (1 Corinthians 12:11; cf. John 3:8). They may not always be obvious, especially when our sinfulness is!

It may at first strike us as strange that Paul would consider the ability to teach, encourage, lead, administer, help, or serve as a "spiritual" gift. As we well know, there are many "unspiritual" people in the world who are quite competent teachers and administrators. There are plenty of non-Christians who still go out of their way to encourage, help, and serve others. These do not seem to be in any way supernatural gifts; they seem to be talents exercised even by some who have not received the Holy Spirit. Remember that all we have—our goods, our health, our talents and abilities—we have as a gift from God. Rather than assuming that the adjective *spiritual* refers to the nature of the gifts that Paul describes, we might more readily conclude that it refers to the source of these gifts, that is, the God who "is spirit" (John 4:24).

Just as "the wind blows where it wishes" (John 3:8), Jesus explains that the activity of the Holy Spirit is in some ways incomprehensible. Paul reiterates Jesus' thought when he declares that the Spirit gives His gifts "as He wills" (1 Corinthians 12:11). Recognizing this, the Church is also reminded that the gifts of the Spirit are precisely that: gifts. We can only receive them as they are given. We dare not demand that God give, or even assume that He gives, Christians today all of the gifts that He once gave to the apostolic Church.

Christ instituted the Means of Grace as the unchanging instruments by which He provides for our *spiritual* needs, working both our justification and our sanctification. As means by which to serve the *material* needs of the Church and her members, however, different gifts of the Spirit may be given as different circumstances require.

Gifts of Service

The Holy Spirit in whom Christians have been baptized has not only provided us with the free gift of salvation and eternal life in heaven, but He also bestows on us many and various gifts to be used in service to the Church on earth.

Many of us may fall into that category of people who were not considered "gifted" children. We were not born with certain outstanding abilities that the world admires. But we have been born anew, we have been made God's children, and He certainly considers us gifted. There is great comfort in knowing that our heavenly Father knows our true worth and that He makes use of our gifts for His own glory.

When we are at times tempted to envy the gifts of others, Paul's words in 1 Corinthians 12 are a great encouragement. He reminds us that "the body does not consist of one member but of many" (v. 14) and that "God arranged the members in the body, each one of them, as He chose" (v. 18). No matter what our gifts or how seemingly unspectacular, we can be assured that they are precisely those that God meant us to have.

Gifted Children

As God's sure Word declares, *all* of His children are gifted. Having received, we then also give. We give of our time and talent to serve others.

How can we respond to someone who questions those who do not exhibit some of the more spectacular gifts of the Spirit, such as speaking in tongues or miraculous healing? The Spirit gives His good gifts, as St. Paul declares, "as He wills" (1 Corinthians 12:11). We are not at leisure to dictate what gifts are given, when, and to whom. Instead, we can only rejoice to be assured that God's wisdom is greater than our own, that He distributes His gifts for His glory and for the benefit of the Church. We should also remember that, being gifts, these are given freely and with no merit on our part. That is, they are not rewards. Nor are they a means by which to determine if some are "more holy" than others. In Baptism, all Christians receive the Holy Spirit together with the full and sufficient forgiveness of sins. On this basis alone—not on account of any other gifts, talents, or abilities—we are reckoned holy.

Spiritual gifts are given to use in service to others. In your daily devotions, take time to thank God for the talents and abilities He has given you and other members in the Church. How might your talents best be put into service in your own congregation?

Comparisons

Natural gifts: God gives talents to all people (whether Christian or not) as part of the created order. Christians should use these gifts in service to the Creator and the Church.

Spiritual gifts: Pentecostals and Charismatics teach that special, miraculous gifts are normally part of every believer's life. They place special emphasis on "speaking in tongues" as a sign of receiving a "baptism with the Holy Spirit." Lutherans and other Christians have taught that the Holy Spirit bestows spiritual gifts through Baptism. The Eastern Orthodox Church and Roman Catholics teach that the Holy Spirit bestows or strengthens spiritual gifts through confirmation.

Church, Unity, and Fellowship

When the apostle Paul bade farewell to a gathering of church leaders at Ephesus, he told them, "The Holy Spirit has made you overseers, to care for the church of God" (Acts 20:28). In other words, the life of the Church depends on the Holy Spirit. In view of this, it is fitting that the Apostles' Creed places its comments about the Church right after those about the Holy Spirit, "I believe in the Holy Spirit, the holy Christian Church, the communion of saints" (Third Article). The following paragraphs will comment briefly on what the Church is, the unity of the Church, and the fellowship of the Church.

Defining Church

Surprisingly, the word "church" appears only three times in the Gospels—each time in the Gospel according to Matthew. In the first occurrence, Jesus tells the disciples, "I will build My church, and the gates of hell shall not prevail against it" (Matthew 16:18). What a marvelous promise! We know from the start and from our Lord that the Church will endure until He returns. The second and third instances of "church" occur together as Jesus teaches about forgiveness (Matthew 18:15–20), that essential doctrine and practice for life in the Church, since without forgiveness there is no Church.

One may wonder why doesn't Jesus mention the Church more often if the Church and her life are so important. In fact, He does, but not with the word "Church." When Jesus began to teach, He proclaimed, "Repent, for the kingdom of heaven is at hand" (Matthew 4:17). In the Old Testament and in the Gospels, God's people commonly talk about the kingdom of God—His reign among believers. However, the Book of Acts and the letters of the apostles refer less to the kingdom and more to the Church. The early Christians slowly transitioned from talking about inheriting "the kingdom prepared for you from the foundation of the world" (Matthew 25:34) to speak instead about the hell-conquering Church. They likely did not want to confuse their hearers into thinking that God's kingdom was like a political, earthly kingdom. It was something more, "For the kingdom of God is not a matter of eating and drinking but of righteousness and peace and joy in the Holy Spirit" (Romans 14:17), a fitting description of what God desires for us in congregational life. The Church is spiritual, the institution of the Spirit. Its members live, eat, and drink not focused on this life but on the life to come (Mark 14:25; Acts 14:22).

Unity of the Church

Since the resurrected Savior reigns over all creation and God's Spirit is everywhere present, there is only one true Church (Ephesians 1:20–23; Colossians 1:17–18). In the Nicene Creed, the early Christians referred to the "one holy catholic and apostolic Church" (the *una sancta*; Third Article). All who trust in Jesus Christ for the forgiveness of sins and who worship the triune God are members of this one Church (cf. Romans 12:4–5). However, most often, the Bible speaks practically about local or regional churches—local gatherings of believers. Ninety percent of the time when you come across the word "church" in your Bible, it means a local group, as we experience life together as God's people today.

Church Fellowship

A unique blessing in our churches is fellowship (Gr. *koinonia*). The word *church* literally means "ones called out," a gathering or assembly of those called together (Gr. *ekklesia*). Paul writes to the Corinthian congregation, "You were called into the fellowship of His Son, Jesus Christ our Lord" (1 Corinthians 1:9). To the Philippians, he writes, "that I may know [Jesus] and the power of His resurrection, and may share [Gr. *koinonia*] His sufferings, becoming like Him in His death, that by any means possible I may attain the resurrection of the dead" (Philippians 3:10–11). As the Holy Spirit brings us into fellowship with our Lord, He naturally also draws us to one another. We run together, seeking to share in the benefits of Jesus' passion and resurrection for our salvation; we also seek opportunities to extend that partnership (Gr. *koinonia* in Philippians 1:5) to others through the call of the Gospel (cf. Acts 2:40–42).

Sadly, as Christians come together, they also tend to come apart. As saints set apart by the Holy Spirit, they have fellowship with God and with one another; as sinners, they offend and hurt one another. They fail to share the forgiveness God intends for them. This problem of divisions among believers is nothing new. Already in the Old Testament kingdom of God, people departed from God's ways (1 Corinthians 10:6). To the Corinthian congregation, the apostle Paul writes, "I appeal to you, brothers, by the name of our Lord Jesus Christ, that all of you agree and that there be no divisions among you, but that you be united in the same mind and the same judgment" (1 Corinthians 1:10; cf. Psalm 133:1; Ephesians 4:3).

The apostle John writes that in his day some departed from the faith, dividing the fellowship (1 John 2:19; cf. 1 Timothy 1:19; 4:1; 6:3–5). The apostle Paul likewise warns, "I appeal to you, brothers, to watch out for those who cause divisions and create obstacles contrary to the doctrine that you have been taught; avoid them" (Romans 16:17; cf. Titus 3:9–11; 2 John 10–11). Because man-made divisions affect the Church, there are naturally different denominations of Christians, something the Lord Jesus did not intend but did foresee would happen, which drove Him to pray for our unity (John 17:20–21).

Working Together

The fact that there are divisions—whether doctrinal, practical, cultural, or geographical—should not deter sincere believers from organizing their lives and service together for the sake of fellowship and mission work. The Lord's Church shall advance against the gates of hell and overcome them. Leaders in Lutheran churches enter into dialogue with leaders of other churches, seeking unity based on the Holy Scriptures and sound practice, which are essential for genuine unity. For example, the International Lutheran Council is a worldwide fellowship of regional churches. Where opportunities for cooperative work become available without compromising sound doctrine and practice, Lutheran churches may work respectfully with other Christian churches and organizations (e.g., the cooperative efforts of Lutheran World Relief to relieve suffering and improve lives around the world).

Lutheran Summary of the Holy spirit

Apology of the Augsburg Confession VII & VIII (IV) 13–16

We should understand what chiefly makes us members—living members—of the Church. If we will define the Church only as an outward political order of the good and wicked, people will not understand that Christ's kingdom is righteousness of heart and the gift of the Holy Spirit [Romans 14:17]. People will conclude that the Church is only the outward observance of certain forms of worship and rites. Likewise, what difference will there be between the people of the Law and the Church if the Church is only an outward political order? But Paul distinguishes the Church from the people of the Law [Israel] in this way: The Church is a spiritual people. It has not been distinguished from the pagans by civil rites ‹its polity and civil affairs›. Instead, it is God's true people, reborn by the Holy Spirit. Among the people of the Law [Israel], apart from Christ's promise, even the earthly seed had promises about bodily things such as government. Even though the wicked among them were called God's people (because God had separated this earthly seed from other nations by certain outward ordinances and promises), the wicked did not please God [Deuteronomy 7:6–11]. But the Gospel brings not merely the shadow of eternal things, but the eternal things themselves: the Holy Spirit and righteousness. By the Gospel we are righteous before God.

Only those people who receive this promise of the Spirit receive it according to the Gospel Besides, the Church is Christ's kingdom, distinguished from the devil's kingdom. It is certain, however, that the wicked are in the devil's power, and members of his kingdom. Paul teaches this when he says that the devil "is now at work in the sons of disobedience" (Ephesians 2:2). Christ says to the Pharisees, who certainly had outward fellowship with the Church, that is, with the saints among the people of the

Law (as officeholders, sacrificers, and teachers), "You are of your father the devil" (John 8:44). Therefore, the Church, which is truly Christ's kingdom, is properly the congregation of saints. For the wicked are ruled by the devil. They are not ruled by the Spirit of Christ. (*Concordia*, p. 145)

SMALCALD ARTICLES III III 1–8, 40

The New Testament keeps and urges this office ‹of the Law›, as St. Paul does when he says, "The wrath of God is revealed from heaven against all ungodliness and unrighteousness of men" (Romans 1:18). Also, "the whole world may be accountable to God. . . . No human being will be justified in His sight" (Romans 3:19–20). And Christ says, the Holy Spirit will convict the world of sin (John 16:8).

This is God's thunderbolt. By the Law He strikes down both obvious sinners and false saints. He declares no one to be in the right, but drives them all together to terror and despair. This is the hammer. As Jeremiah says, "Is not My Word like . . . a hammer that breaks the rock in pieces?" (23:29). This is not active contrition or manufactured repentance. It is passive contrition, true sorrow of heart, suffering, and the sensation of death.

This is what true repentance means. Here a person needs to hear something like this, "You are all of no account, whether you are obvious sinners or saints ‹in your own opinions›. You have to become different from what you are now. You have to act differently than you are now acting, however great, wise, powerful, and holy you try to be. Here no one is godly."

But to this office of the Law, the New Testament immediately adds the consoling promise of grace through the Gospel. This must be believed. As Christ declares, "Repent and believe in the gospel" (Mark 1:15). That is, become different, act differently, and believe My promise. John the Baptist (preceding Christ) is called a preacher of repentance, but this is for the forgiveness of sins. That is, John was to accuse all and convict them of being sinners. This is so they can know what they are before God and acknowledge that they are lost. So they can be prepared for the Lord [Mark 1:3] to receive grace and to expect and accept from Him the forgiveness of sins. This is what Christ Himself says, "Repentance and forgiveness of sins should be proclaimed in [My] name to all nations" (Luke 24:47).

Whenever the Law alone exercises its office, without the Gospel being added, there is nothing but death and hell, and one must despair, as Saul and Judas did [1 Samuel 31; Matthew 27:5]. St. Paul says, through sin the Law kills. [See Romans 7:10.] On the other hand, the Gospel brings consolation and forgiveness. It does so not just in one way, but through the Word and the Sacraments and the like, as we will discuss later. As Psalm 130:7 says against the dreadful captivity of sin, "with the LORD is . . . plentiful redemption." . . .

In Christians, this repentance continues until death. For through one's entire life, repentance contends with the sin remaining in the flesh. Paul testifies that he wars with the law in his members (Romans 7:14–25) not by his own powers, but by the gift of the Holy Spirit that follows the forgiveness of sins [Romans 8:1–17]. This gift daily cleanses and sweeps out the remaining sins and works to make a person truly pure and holy. (*Concordia*, pp. 272–73, 276)

Formula of Concord Epitome II 2–6

1. This is our teaching, faith, and confession on this subject: in spiritual matters the understanding and reason of mankind are ‹completely› blind and by their own powers understand nothing, as it is written in 1 Corinthians 2:14, "The natural person does not accept the things of the Spirit of God, for they are folly to him, and he is not able to understand them because they are spiritually discerned."

2. Likewise, we believe, teach, and confess that the unregenerate will of mankind is not only turned away from God, but also has become God's enemy. So it only has an inclination and desire for that which is evil and contrary to God, as it is written in Genesis 8:21, "the intention of man's heart is evil from his youth." Romans 8:7 says, "The mind that is set on the flesh is hostile to God, for it does not submit to God's law; indeed, it cannot." Just as a dead body cannot raise itself to bodily, earthly life, so a person who by sin is spiritually dead cannot raise himself to spiritual life. For it is written in Ephesians 2:5, "even when we were dead in our trespasses, [He] made us alive together with Christ." And 2 Corinthians 3:5 says, "Not that we are sufficient in ourselves to claim anything as coming from us, but our sufficiency is from God."

3. God the Holy Spirit, however, does not bring about conversion without means. For this purpose He uses the preaching and hearing of God's Word, as it is written in Romans 1:16, the Gospel "is the power of God for salvation to everyone who believes." Also Romans 10:17 says, "Faith comes from hearing, and hearing through the word of Christ." It is God's will that His Word should be heard and that a person's ears should not be closed (Psalm 95:8). With this Word the Holy Spirit is present and opens hearts, so that people (like Lydia in Acts 16:14) pay attention to it and are converted only through the Holy Spirit's grace and power, who alone does the work of converting a person. For without His grace, and if He does not grant the increase, our willing and running, our planting, sowing, and watering (1 Corinthians 3:5–7)—are all nothing. As Christ says ‹in John 15:5›, "apart from Me you can do nothing." With these brief words the Spirit denies free will its powers and ascribes everything to God's grace, in order that no one may boast before God (1 Corinthians 1:29; [2 Corinthians 12:5; Jeremiah 9:23]). (*Concordia*, pp. 477–78).

Formula of Concord Solid Declaration II 56, 58–60

For we should not and cannot always judge from feeling about the presence, work, and gifts of the Holy Spirit, as to how and when they are experienced in the heart. They are often covered and happen in great weakness. Therefore, we should be certain about and agree with the promise that God's Word preached and heard is ‹truly› an office and work of the Holy Spirit. He is certainly effective and works in our hearts by them (2 Corinthians 2:14–17; 3:5–6). . . .

When such a person despises the instrument of the Holy Spirit and will not listen, no injustice is done to him if the Holy Spirit does not enlighten him but allows him to remain in the darkness of his unbelief and to perish. For it is written about this matter, "How often would I have gathered your children together as a hen gathers her brood under her wings, and you would not!" (Matthew 23:37).

In this respect it may well be said that a person is not a stone or block. For a stone or block does not resist the person who moves it. It does not understand and doesn't care what is being done with it. But a person with his will resists God the Lord until he is converted. It is true that a person before his conversion is still a rational creature, having an understanding and will. However, he does not understand divine things. He does not have the will to desire something good and helpful. He can do nothing at all about his conversion (as has also been said above ‹frequently›), and is in this way much worse than a stone and block. For he resists God's Word and will, until God awakens him from the death of sin, enlightens, and renews him.

God does not force a person to become godly. (Those who always resist the Holy Spirit and persistently oppose the known truth are not converted, as Stephen says about the hardened Jewish people [Acts 7:51].) Yet God the Lord draws the person whom He wants to convert [John 6:44]. He draws him in such a way that his darkened understanding is turned into an enlightened one and his perverse will into an obedient one. This is what the Scriptures call creating a clean heart [Psalm 51:10]. (*Concordia*, pp. 530–31)

TOPIC ELEVEN

Daily Prayer[1]

Engaging This Topic

"Thanks for inviting me to church. I really learned a lot from the service. But I have a question. Why does your pastor pray the same prayers over and over again?"
"What do you mean?"
"He uses written prayers, doesn't he? And you repeat the Lord's Prayer too."
"That's right. . . . But your church doesn't pray that way?"
"I think God doesn't want us to use written prayers or repeat the Lord's Prayer. He wants us to pray from our heart."

Exalted and hallowed be His great name in the world which He created according to His will.
May He rule His kingdom.
—the Kaddish, a Jewish prayer

When Jesus' disciples asked, "Lord, teach us to pray" (Luke 11:1), Jesus didn't say, "Just pray from your heart, whatever you feel." Jesus gave the disciples specific requests, specific words, which we know today as the Lord's Prayer or the "Our Father."

The disciples' question about prayer came from a curiosity that existed in Judaism. Many rabbis taught their followers how to pray. For example, the ancient Jewish Kaddish (also Qaddish), part of which is quoted above, shows marked similarity to the first two petitions of the Lord's Prayer. Although historians have not discovered a direct link between the Lord's Prayer and the Kaddish, it is entirely likely that Jesus gave His disciples a form of prayer they knew, His personal version of the Kaddish.

Early Christians received the Lord's Prayer not just as an example of how one could pray but also as a model of how one should pray. The *Didache*, the earliest Christian book about worship outside the New

1 This chapter adapted from *The Lutheran Difference: Daily Prayer*, written by Patra Pfotenhauer. Copyright © 2002 Concordia Publishing House.

Testament, records the Lord's Prayer and encourages people to recite it three times a day. This builds on the Jewish tradition of daily prayer and its Old Testament roots.

Today the vast majority of Christians continue to recite the Lord's Prayer. Ask Christians from a variety of denominations how they pray and you'll soon discover that they share a common use of the Lord's Prayer. Lutherans recite the Lord's Prayer in personal devotions and in public worship. However, Lutherans also use the Lord's Prayer as a confession of faith, to teach the faith to new believers.

This section on the Lord's Prayer builds on that tradition epitomized in Luther's Small Catechism. Following ancient custom, Martin Luther divided the Lord's Prayer in the following way according to the German wording that follows the Greek and Latin texts:

Introduction
Our Father, Thou who art in heaven.

Seven Petitions
Hallowed be Thy name.
Thy kingdom come.
Thy will be done, as it is in heaven, so on earth [on earth as it is in heaven].
Give us this day our daily bread.
And forgive us our debts as we forgive our debtors [our trespasses, as we forgive those who trespass against us].
And lead us not into temptation.
But deliver us from evil.

Conclusion
Amen.

The text comes from Matthew 6:9–13. Luke 11:2–4 records Jesus' prayer with slightly different wording. English-speaking Lutherans often use the wording in brackets, which comes from liturgical tradition and the use of Matthew 6:14–15. Lutherans usually end the Lord's Prayer with the ancient doxology "For Thine is the kingdom and the power and the glory forever and ever." This word of praise is based on 1 Chronicles 29:11 and has many witnesses in documents of the early Church, including the *Didache* that was written about AD 100. It was included by later Greek scribes in Matthew 6:13, likely based on early Christian tradition and common Jewish prayers of the time. Historic Lutheran orders of service use the tradition of chanting the doxology as a response to the Lord's Prayer.

For Lutherans, the Lord's Prayer highlights all the basic elements of prayer:

Praise: the introduction
Requests: the "Thy" petitions (1–3)
Thanksgiving: the first "us" petition (4)
Intercession: all of the "us" petitions (4–7)

Take special note of how much space Jesus gives to "spiritual" requests from God. Only the Fourth Petition focuses on earthly goods (and only for the current day, implying daily use of the prayer). So often our prayers falter into requests for "things." But consider anew the spiritual blessings God wants you to have through the death and resurrection of His Son, Jesus, and confidently make your requests in His name.

Lutheran Facts

Although Martin Luther did not give fixed rules about prayer, he encouraged Christians to pray in the morning, the evening, and before and after meals.

Lutheran prayer and worship services tend to be less formal than Roman Catholic and Eastern Orthodox services but more formal than other Protestant services.

Most Lutherans pray quietly and listen as a pastor or layperson leads them in prayer. A prayer often ends with a recognizable conclusion so that everyone may say "Amen" together. Lutherans usually recite the Lord's Prayer together.

At home, the head of a Lutheran family is expected to lead the rest of the family in prayer.

Lutherans pray directly to God and not through the intercession of saints. They believe that God hears and answers prayer today, according to His good and gracious will. Lutherans are encouraged by Scripture to "pray without ceasing" (1 Thessalonians 5:17).

Our Father Is Holy

> But what is worship? thought I. Do you suppose now, Ishmael, that the magnanimous God of heaven and earth—pagans and all included—can possibly be jealous of an insignificant bit of black wood?
>
> —Herman Melville, *Moby Dick*

Melville asks this question about God and prayer at the beginning of his famous novel to describe the tense friendship between Ishmael (a Christian) and Queequeg (an idol worshiper). He wonders whether God hears the prayers of all people or only the prayers of Christians.

Many Christians today ask similar difficult questions about prayer. Why pray if God knows everything anyway? Does prayer really make a difference? Does prayer change God's mind?

The purpose of prayer is not to receive every item on our wish list from our heavenly Father. Rather, Jesus commanded us to pray as a response to God for all He has done for us. Prayer is an opportunity to express our thanks and praise, as well as our deepest needs. As we present our requests to God, we act in faith, believing that God will answer our prayers according to His will.

Lord, Teach Us

Jesus wanted His disciples to know the importance of prayer. In Matthew 6:4–13 Jesus introduces the Lord's Prayer. He specifically tells His disciples to avoid drawing attention to themselves when they pray. Rather, He wants to reinforce the practice of praying simply with a contrite heart. This section of Scripture is included in the Sermon on the Mount, where Jesus is contrasting Jewish legalistic traditions with His own teachings. Therefore, the concept of a simple and sincere prayer as outlined in the Lord's Prayer was another way Jesus illustrated that childlike faith is desired more than outward and showy prayers.

According to Matthew 6:5–8, Jesus is telling His disciples to avoid praying as a show for others. Rather, they were instructed to pray to their Father in secret. Seven hundred years earlier, God spoke through Isaiah to tell His people that though they were going through the motions of worship, they were not believing with their hearts (29:13).

In the introduction to the Lord's Prayer, Jesus teaches us to begin by addressing our "Father." Although some passages of the Old Testament describe God as Father, Jesus makes God's fatherhood a central teaching of the New Testament. Through Christ's death and resurrection, we can now have an intimate relationship with God. We don't have to address Him as Lord, God, or Judge. In Romans 8:15–17, Paul states that we can call Him Father because God's Spirit is alive in us and we are no longer dead. Through His Spirit, we are empowered to believe that God is our Father who sent Jesus to rescue us from sin, Satan, and evil.

A good earthly father does not ignore the requests of his children. How much more does our heavenly Father hear our requests and answer them? He loves His children and desires to give them what is best for them (Luke 11:9–13).

The First Petition of the Lord's Prayer states that God's name is to be hallowed, literally, "set apart." In the Second Commandment, God commands us to keep His name holy by not profaning or misusing it (Exodus 20:7). He says He is "jealous" when people worship other gods, and He responds with punishment (Exodus 20:4–6). As we are empowered by the Spirit, we honor God's name through word and deed.

Following the terrorist attacks on the United States on September 11, 2001, some Christians, Jews, Muslims, and others held interfaith prayer services to express their national unity. Before condoning or condemning such services, we should consider the following passages from the New Testament.

Luke 24:52–53: "And they worshiped Him and returned to Jerusalem with great joy, and were continually in the temple blessing God."

Acts 5:12: "Now many signs and wonders were regularly done among the people by the hands of the apostles. And they were all together in Solomon's Portico."

These verses show us that as Jewish Christians, early believers gathered for worship at the temple in Jerusalem, alongside other Jewish people. Let's look at several more passages from Acts.

Acts 9:11: "And the Lord said to him [Ananias], 'Rise and go to the street called Straight, and at the house of Judas look for a man of Tarsus named Saul, for behold, he is praying.' "

Acts 10:1–20: "At Caesarea there was a man named Cornelius, a centurion of what was known as the Italian Cohort, a devout man who feared God with all his household, gave alms generously to the people, and prayed continually to God. About the ninth hour of the day he saw clearly in a vision an angel of God come in and say to him, 'Cornelius.' And he stared at him in terror and said, 'What is it, Lord?' And he said to him, 'Your prayers and your alms have ascended as a memorial before God. And now send men to Joppa and bring one Simon who is called Peter. He is lodging with one Simon, a tanner, whose house is by the sea.' When the angel who spoke to him had departed, he called two of his servants and a devout soldier from among those who attended him, and having related everything to them, he sent them to Joppa. The next day, as they were on their journey and approaching the city, Peter went up on the housetop about the sixth hour to pray. And he became hungry and wanted something to eat, but while they were preparing it, he fell into a trance and saw the heavens opened and something like a great sheet descending, being let down by its four corners upon the earth. In it were all kinds of animals and reptiles and birds of the air. And there came a voice to him: 'Rise, Peter; kill and eat.' But Peter said, 'By no means, Lord; for I have never eaten anything that is common or unclean.' And the voice came to him again a second time, 'What God has made clean, do not call common.' This happened three times, and the thing was taken up at once to heaven. Now while Peter was inwardly perplexed as to what the vision that he had seen might mean, behold, the men who were sent by Cornelius, having made inquiry for Simon's house, stood at the gate and called out to ask whether Simon who was called Peter was lodging there. And while Peter was pondering the vision, the Spirit said to him, "Behold, three men are looking for you. Rise and go down and accompany them without hesitation, for I have sent them."

Acts 17:22–23: "So Paul, standing in the midst of the Areopagus, said: 'Men of Athens, I perceive that in every way you are very religious. For as I passed along and observed the objects of your worship, I found also an altar with this inscription, "To the unknown god." What therefore you worship as unknown, this I proclaim to you.' "

Acts 17:26–30: "And He made from one man every nation of mankind to live on all the face of the earth, having determined allotted periods and the boundaries of their dwelling place, that they should seek God, in the hope that they might feel their way toward Him and find Him. Yet He is actually not far from each one of us, for 'In Him we live and move and have our being'; as even some of your own poets have said, 'For we are indeed His offspring.' Being then God's offspring, we ought not to think that the divine being is like gold or silver or stone, an image formed by the art and imagination of man. The times of ignorance God overlooked, but now He commands all people everywhere to repent."

These verses describe God's reaction to the prayers of religious people who do not yet know Christ as the Savior. God patiently bears with the ignorance of people who have not yet received the Gospel (Saul, a persecutor of believers; Cornelius, a disciple of Judaism; Athenian idolaters). In the examples from Acts, He responds mercifully by sending someone to proclaim Christ (SA III VIII 8; *Concordia*, p. 281). When people reject the Gospel, Christians should seek out other people who will listen.

Christians must not allow the Gospel to be compromised or perverted by false religious beliefs. If a body of people wishes to hear the Gospel, certainly Christians should willingly share it with them. However, if that body of people wishes to change or suppress the preaching of the Gospel, Christians ought not to comply with their requests in order to please them.

Dear Father

Human fathers may be good or bad. For children from broken or abusive homes, the term "father" may cause more anxiety than encouragement or comfort. In contrast, several New Testament passages reveal that the first Christians prayed to God with the Aramaic word *Abba* (i.e., "daddy").

Prayer was given as a gift for us to communicate intimately with our God. The death and resurrection of Jesus made a way for us to address God as Father or *Abba*. If you have not had a positive experience with your earthly father, the title of God as your "Father" may be difficult. Those hurts from the past are real and painful. But through the power of the Gospel, you can forgive and begin the healing process. Earthly fathers make mistakes and are sinful. You have a perfect heavenly Father who loves you unconditionally.

When you address God with the intimate title of "Father," you are speaking to God, whose name is to be hallowed. In the Church over the last thirty years, the practice of approaching God with awe and respect has waned. Through Christ's death and resurrection, we can now approach the throne of God with confidence. However, we should not forget that it is the throne of our almighty God that we are approaching. God is holy and most deserving of our honor and respect and awe.

Our modern culture has made an impact on values. Whether you think the impact has been positive or negative, we as Christians have an opportunity to honor God's name through our words and actions as an example for others. We have the opportunity to honor God in our daily lives. It is a response to God's love for us, and through His Spirit we are empowered to live lives that honor God's name.

Comparisons

Use of the Lord's Prayer as a model: Anabaptists, Baptists, and some Wesleyans emphasize that Jesus gave the Lord's Prayer as a model and not as a form of prayer for repetition. They encourage spontaneous prayers from the heart rather than repeated prayers.

Formal use of the Lord's Prayer: Most other Christians pray the Lord's Prayer daily or frequently in public worship. The official catechisms of the Eastern Orthodox, Lutheran, Reformed, and Roman Catholic churches contain commentaries on the Lord's Prayer. Repetition is only a problem if people repeat the words without considering what they say. Jesus Himself repeated prayers (see Matthew 26:44).

Prayer with non-Christians: Today, some Christians hold public prayer services with people of other religions. Interreligious services are most popular among Christians who have questioned traditional beliefs about the triune nature of God and do not consider joint services with non-Christians a threat to the Gospel. (In 1964 the papal decree *Lumen Gentium* taught that Christians, Jews, and Muslims all pray to the same Creator.)

Point to Remember

For you did not receive the spirit of slavery to fall back into fear, but you received the Spirit of adoption as sons, by whom we cry, "Abba! Father!" The Spirit Himself bears witness with our spirit that we are children of God. *Romans 8:15–16*

God's Reign

Here we may reign secure; and, in my choice
To reign is worth ambition, though in Hell:
Better to reign in Hell than serve in Heaven.
—John Milton, *Paradise Lost*

These rebellious words, attributed to Satan, are a helpful reminder as we study prayer. Although our Father reigns by His grace, Satan also has a kingdom or reign. Since all people on earth live in the crossfire of these two warring kingdoms, we have an urgent need to pray!

Despite Jesus' careful teaching, His disciples struggled to understand the coming of God's kingdom. For example, James and John longed to rule with Jesus on earth, even though God's kingdom is contrary to any earthly kingdom. In Jesus' kingdom, if you want to be first, you will become last and be a servant to many. In this kingdom His Spirit leads you so that you are not conformed to the pattern of this world, but rather transformed by the renewing of your mind.

See the Kingdom

Nicodemus was a Pharisee and a member of the Jewish ruling council. He was considered an enemy of Jesus. Nicodemus approached Jesus at night so he could not be seen; though he tried to hide himself, he had great courage to ask the questions he did. But Nicodemus was confused by Jesus' answers to his questions. According to John 3:1–18, Nicodemus thought that Jesus was referring to a physical rebirth. Jesus explained that God's kingdom is a spiritual kingdom that begins at Baptism through water and the Spirit. In John 3:3, 5, 12, and 16, we are reassured that we dwell in God's kingdom through Baptism and faith that Christ died for us.

Romans 14:17 reinforces the fact that God's kingdom is a spiritual kingdom that does not consist of man-made ceremonial practices. God makes us members of His kingdom through the death and resurrection of Jesus, and empowers us through His Spirit to live lives filled with peace and joy.

Luke 12:32 states that God is pleased to give us His kingdom. Earlier in that chapter, Jesus addresses His disciples and admonishes them to seek God's kingdom above all earthly desires (vv. 22–31). We often get distracted by earthly desires and don't trust God or accept that His kingdom is at work among us.

But God desires that all people will be saved and come to the knowledge of Him (1 Timothy 2:3–6). Jesus is the Mediator who makes it possible for us to approach God's throne. The Holy Spirit dwells in us and empowers us to share God's kingdom with others. We pray that God's kingdom would come to all people when we pray "Thy kingdom come."

A Gracious Will

Both 1 John 2:15–17 and Romans 12:1–2 describe the battle between the desires of the world and the kingdom of God. First, John clearly states that anyone who loves the world cannot have the love of the Father within. Paul reinforces this thought as he admonishes the Christians in Rome to remember that the kingdom of God is at work in their minds. In the same way, as we are led by the Spirit, God will carry out His will in our lives.

In Galatians 5:16–21, Paul describes the battle between the sinful nature and the Spirit of God that occurs in all believers. This battle makes it difficult to follow the will of God. It is important to remember here that all believers are both saints and sinners. But we have victory over our sinful nature through Christ's death and resurrection (Romans 7:7–25; Galatians 5:22–26).

What a comfort! The kingdom of God belongs to us! Yet we still sometimes doubt that we belong to God's kingdom. At those times, it is important to remember that the coming of God's kingdom is not based on our actions. When we pray "Thy kingdom come," we are acknowledging that God's kingdom *has* come to us and *will* come to us in eternity. Through Baptism, we entered God's kingdom; however, we get distracted by our sinful nature, rather than being led by the Spirit. At times we get caught up in the details of our lives and miss the bigger picture of God's will and the opportunity to share the Good News of God's kingdom with others.

Comparisons

Eastern Orthodox: God's kingdom of grace is "righteousness and peace and joy in the Holy Spirit" (Romans 14:17). This has not come to every person in its full sense, since many people continue to sin. God's kingdom comes secretly and inwardly. The kingdom of glory is the perfect bliss of the faithful.

Lutheran: God's kingdom comes when the heavenly Father gives us His Holy Spirit through the Word, so that we believe the Gospel and lead godly lives now and in eternity. The Church (true believers) is Christ's kingdom (see SC III and Ap VII 16; *Concordia*, pp. 333, 145).

Reformed and Baptist: Christ acts as our King "in subduing us to Himself, in ruling and defending us, and in restraining and conquering all His and our enemies" (*Westminster Shorter Catechism*, question 26).

Anabaptist: According to Menno Simons, founder of the Mennonites, the Church is Christ's spiritual kingdom. Members of this kingdom cannot bear arms or fight. The quarrelsome, slanderous, and wrathful cannot enter the kingdom and the Church of Christ even if they have the outward appearance of being Christians.

Roman Catholic: God's kingdom came in the death and resurrection of Christ. It continues to come through the Eucharist. The Lord's Prayer asks primarily for the final appearance of God's reign through Christ's return. We must distinguish social progress and God's reign, which energizes us to serve justice and peace until Christ returns. The Church is a sign of God's kingdom. Cf. CCC2 para. 2818.

Wesleyan: God's kingdom is true religion: repentance, faith, and holiness. Christians pray for the fullness of God's kingdom, when Jesus returns.

Liberal: Following the teaching of the Baptist minister Walter Rauschenbusch (1861–1918), liberal Christians identify the coming of God's kingdom with social progress. "Liberation theology," a subsequent movement popular in developing countries, encourages political and even military action as ways of bringing God's rule (social equality, peace, and justice).

Today, many interfaith movements offer their own teaching about God's kingdom. For example, the Manila Manifesto, drafted by the Lausanne Committee for World Evangelization, states that the Church is a sign of God's kingdom and that proclamation of God's rule "demands the prophetic denunciation of all that is incompatible with it."

Point to Remember

Fear not, little flock, for it is your Father's good pleasure to give you the kingdom. *Luke 12:32*

Our Daily Bread

[Ichabod] pictured to himself every roasting-pig running about with a pudding in his belly, and an apple in his mouth; the pigeons were snugly put to bed in a comfortable pie, and tucked in with a coverlet of crust.

—Washington Irving, *The Legend of Sleepy Hollow*

"Super-size it!" shouts our appetite. Whether in Sleepy Hollow or at a modern drive-through, we love to consume. Like Ichabod we dream about getting more. We crave not only roasting-pigs or more fries but also larger homes with a television and a telephone in every room. We imagine boats, sports cars, motorcycles, snowmobiles, and jet skis parked in our driveways.

In contrast, Jesus teaches us to pray for *daily* bread and encourages contentment.

Bread of Mercy

Matthew 5:45 says that God provides rain and sunshine for the wicked as well as the righteous. Psalm 145:15–16 tells us that all creation looks to

God to supply its needs, and He satisfies the desires of every living thing. However, unbelievers do not realize that God is the supplier of all their needs. Believers, on the other hand, join with the psalmist in praising God and acknowledging that all good gifts come from His hand. God is just and He cares for all of His creation. Don't worry about what others have, rather rejoice in the gifts God has given to you. Even when the trials of life consume you, through God's Spirit you can say with Paul that you have learned the secret of contentment: Jesus Christ (Philippians 4:12).

In Romans 13:9, Paul lists some of the commandments, including "You shall not covet"; then he goes on to say that all the commandments can be summed up in one rule: "Love your neighbor as yourself." This is a guiding principle as we apply the Fourth Petition of the Lord's Prayer to daily life. When we love others as much as we love ourselves, we are challenged to rejoice with them and thank God for the gifts He gives to them.

In 1 Timothy, Paul directs Timothy and other church leaders to live godly lives and be examples for the believers. Apparently some of the leaders in the church at Ephesus were using their positions of leadership for financial gain. Therefore, Paul is addressing that particular issue in chapter six. Paul clearly illustrates that we do not need to be concerned about our physical needs, because God will provide for us. He goes on to warn Timothy that the *love* of money can be destructive to one's faith. Examples include those people who obsessively pursue gambling and the stock market.

In Matthew 19:16–26, Jesus clarifies that outward acts do not bring about salvation; rather, salvation is the result of God's mercy. According to verse 26, salvation—as well as following the commandments—is only possible through God's power. In verse 24, Jesus compares a rich man's efforts to enter God's kingdom to a camel going through the eye of a needle. Jesus was comparing a very large thing (a camel) with a very small thing (a needle's eye) to show the impossibility of gaining eternal life by one's own merit.

In Matthew 6:19–24, the section that follows the Lord's Prayer, Jesus teaches about priorities. He reinforces the fact that material items do not have eternal value. However, material possessions dictate many people's priorities and decisions. Jesus' point is summed up in the First Commandment. Satan wants us to be distracted by the things of this world, whereas God wants us to focus on and celebrate His kingdom.

The main point Jesus makes in Matthew 6:25–34 is that God is the great Provider and none of His children need to worry about material things. Jesus compares God's provision for His people to the way He provides for birds and flowers. He emphasizes that people are much more valuable to Him and He will take care of them. He instructs His people to focus on God and His kingdom rather than earthly goods, because He will provide for them.

In Philippians 4:6, Paul writes to the church of Philippi and encourages them to present their requests to God with thankful hearts, rather than experience anxiety. In the explanation of the Third Article of the Apostles' Creed, Luther also exhorts believers to know and acknowledge that all good gifts come from God. We are to receive our blessings with an attitude of thanksgiving.

Thanksgiving with Contentment

Do you realize how much God loves you? Consider all the different blessings we depend on right now: food, shelter, light, and the very air we breathe. Only by God's power are we able to live with balanced priorities. God displays His unconditional love for us by providing for all of our needs. His ultimate gift is Jesus, whose death and resurrection offer hope for living each day, as well as the assurance of eternal life in the future. God's love motivates us to share our gifts with others.

Stewards

If we were to list all the blessings we daily receive from God, we would be overwhelmed. Even without asking for it, God daily provides everything we need. God owns everything we have and has given us the privilege to be stewards (or caretakers) of His gifts.

Comparison

Daily bread: All Christians believe that it is appropriate to pray for the necessities of bodily life and to offer thanks to God for earthly goods.

Daily bread refers to the Means of Grace: For the Eastern Orthodox and Roman Catholics, *daily bread* refers not simply to the needs of the body but also to the bread of the Eucharist and the Word of God as the bread of the soul.

Friedrich Heiler studied various religions and denominations for his classic book *Prayer*. He described several different types of prayer as practiced by various groups:

Primitive: God is viewed as a great power, but not almighty. Prayers express fears and the desire for safety from God or other powers.

Ritual: The form of the prayer, not the content, causes God to answer.

Greek: God is favorable toward mankind and not almighty. Moral living (and prayer as a moral deed) attains God's favor.

Philosophical: Prayer becomes thankfulness, reflection on life and its meaning rather than specific requests.

Mystical: Prayer seeks to unite the person with God's essence so that one becomes a part of God's being. God communicates with the person praying through inner illumination.

Prophetic: Prayer is based on love and heartfelt supplication. The person praying may beg or even complain to God in a relationship of trust.

Lutheran attitudes about prayer are best described by Heiler's "prophetic" category.

In recent years, many people have shown "primitive" attitudes toward prayer. Radio and television preachers who emphasize prayers for wealth or prosperity have especially caused great confusion.

Point to Remember

But seek first the kingdom of God and His righteousness, and all these things will be added to you. *Matthew 6:33*

Forgiveness

I pardon you.

—from the film *Schindler's List*

As commander of a Nazi concentration camp, Amon Goeth stands before his bathroom mirror. He stares at himself. He ponders a conversation from the previous evening, when Oskar Schindler suggested that the power of granting pardon—the power to forgive—is greater than the power to kill. After this hesitation, Goeth casually steps to his balcony, aims his rifle into the compound of prisoners, and calmly takes another life.

The idea of forgiveness is easy to ponder. The practice of forgiveness is another matter. Two brothers haven't spoken for years because they have unresolved issues about the family business. A son weeps at his dying father's bedside after years of silence brought about by bitterness and anger from the past. Broken relationships are commonplace and they result in further pain and anguish.

In the Fifth Petition of the Lord's Prayer, Jesus is trying to spare His people such pain by teaching His disciples the importance of forgiveness. God empowers us to forgive one another so we can avoid pain and hardship. Without God's forgiveness through Jesus Christ's death and resurrection, we would be lost.

Broken by Sin

Many scholars believe that King Solomon wrote Ecclesiastes later in his life. One theme throughout the book is that no one can possess enough wisdom to comprehend God and His ways. In Ecclesiastes 7:20, Solomon explains the reason for this human weakness is that no one on earth does right and never sins. This confirms what King David wrote in Psalm 51:5: "Behold, I was brought forth in iniquity, and in sin did my mother conceive me." (See also Psalm 14:3.) However, the Good News is that through Christ's death and resurrection, we receive the free gift of eternal life. Take a moment to really think about what you deserve from God as a result of your sin. Although this is uncomfortable to consider, it is important to remember that all of us deserve to die, and without Christ we are destined for eternal separation from God.

Luke 15:11–32 tells the familiar and powerful parable of the lost son. It is a beautiful picture of what God does for us. Even though we have intentionally rebelled and disobeyed Him, God runs with open arms to meet us and offer us forgiveness. He longs to give us His best. However, we are only ready to receive His gifts after God's Spirit has softened our hearts and helped us realize that we are in dire need of a Savior. Often, like the younger son, we have to hit rock bottom and find ourselves eating the food of the swine before we realize how much we need Jesus and the new life He freely offers.

Many people relate to the older son in the parable, the one who thinks that he deserves a special favor because of all the good things he has done in his life. He believes that he has worked hard to earn a place of importance in his father's household. Therefore, he is jealous when his younger sibling receives such grace from his father. Similarly, as Christians, we may see ourselves as better than others who haven't been "lifelong" Christians. At times like these, we remember that we can do nothing to be saved, but simply receive what the Father has to offer. As the father in the parable said to his older son, "All that is mine is yours" (Luke 15:31).

Psalm 103 is a hymn of praise written by King David, thanking God for all of His blessings. Verse 12 paints a picture of what God does with our sin: "As far as the east is from the west, so far does He remove our transgressions from us." David's point is that God removes our sins completely from us. However, we still have to live with the consequences of our sin, but we can do so with a clean conscience, not burdened by the weight of guilt.

Out of God's love for us, we are empowered to love and forgive others. In Colossians 3:12–13, Paul describes how the Holy Spirit clothes His chosen people. Through His power and the fruit of His Spirit, we forgive others as Christ forgives us. Forgiveness is not a feeling. The feelings will follow the act of forgiveness. Sometimes, it may take years for the feelings of peace and love to occur, but the act of forgiveness is the first step. There are some situations that seem impossible to forgive by human standards, such as marital unfaithfulness or cases of abuse. But Matthew 19:26 tells us that "with God all things are possible." That includes not only our salvation, which is the direct meaning of Christ's words in Matthew 19, but also our ability as Christians to forgive as we have been forgiven.

In Matthew 5:23–26, Jesus is describing the urgency of reconciliation. He does not want His children to be separated through sin, as was the unforgiving servant (Matthew 18:23–35). Our separation from each other has the potential to separate us from God if, like the servant, we act deliberately and especially publicly to hurt those who have caused us injury. Christ offers His eternal strength and empowers us with His perfect love to forgive others.

The Greatest Gift

Forgiveness is the greatest gift offered through Christ, the very heart of the Christian faith. Yet we often take God's forgiveness for granted or are too stubborn to accept an apology from a close friend. It is easy to justify our behavior and allow ourselves to be guided by our sinful nature rather than by God's Spirit. Ask God to empower you to follow His Spirit's leading in your life.

Comparisons

For Lutherans, prayer is not a Means of Grace, that is, a way by which God grants us forgiveness, life, and salvation. This is a key difference between a Lutheran view of prayer and the views expressed by other denominations and religions. Luther did not view grace as a "thing" that a person could use to gain strength and please God. Grace is God's undeserved favor and loving-kindness toward sinners. Occasionally Luther mentioned "imploring" God's grace, by which he meant studying and repeating the promises of Scripture, such as the Fifth Petition of the Lord's Prayer. While many

Christian teachers have encouraged troubled hearts to "pray for grace" until they feel better, Luther pointed troubled hearts to the promises of God's Word and to the Sacraments for comfort. Prayer was to follow as a thankful response to God's grace.

Eastern Orthodox: "What are the means for attaining to a saving hope? The means to this are, first, prayer; secondly, the true doctrine of blessedness, and its practical application" (*The Longer Catechism of the Eastern Church*, question 388).

Lutheran: God's Word and Sacraments are the Means of Grace because God promises forgiveness through them. Prayer is not a Means of Grace. In prayer we respond to God's grace and request His help for spiritual and physical needs.

Reformed: "Why is prayer necessary for Christians? Because it is the chief part of the thankfulness which God requires of us, and because God will give His grace and Holy Spirit only to such as earnestly and without ceasing beg them from Him and render thanks unto Him for them" (*The Heidelberg Catechism*, question 116).

Anabaptist: "Everything which you have unwittingly done and confessed as evil doing is forgiven you through the believing prayer which is offered by us in our meeting for all our shortcomings and guilt" (*The Schleitheim Confession*, closing remarks).

Roman Catholic: "Is there any other means of obtaining God's grace than the Sacraments? There is another means of obtaining God's grace, and it is prayer" (*The Baltimore Catechism*, question 303; cf. CCC2 2000–2003, 2010).

Baptist: "How is the Word to be read and heard that it may become effectual to salvation? That the Word may become effectual to salvation we must attend thereunto with diligence, preparation and prayer, receive it in faith and love, lay it up in our hearts and practice it in our lives" (*Keach's Catechism*, question 97).

Wesleyan: "The chief of these means [of grace] are prayer . . . searching the Scriptures . . . and receiving the Lord's Supper . . ." (*Wesley's Standard Sermons* 12.2.1).

Liberal: "Christianity means the growing experience of a social relationship with God. But the very means by which this social relationship is established is prayer" (Errett Gates, in *Guide to the Study of the Christian Religion*, edited by Gerald Birney Smith [Chicago: University of Chicago Press, 1916]). Liberals believe prayer has psychological benefits akin to meditation in Eastern religions. It is a never-ceasing quest for communion with the divine. This is apart from the philosophical question of whether the divine exists.

Point to Remember

As far as the east is from the west, so far does He remove our transgressions from us. *Psalm 103:12*

God's Protection

> I swear by God . . . neither America nor the people who live in it will dream of security . . .
>
> —Osama bin Laden

Pain, disease, loss, and disaster surround us. Many of us have experienced firsthand the grief that comes from the loss of a dream, a job, or even a loved one. The evening news constantly reminds us that we live in a broken world. David wrote in Psalm 51:5: "I was brought forth in iniquity, and in sin did my mother conceive me." Daily we are tempted by the devil, the world, and our sinful nature.

The devil wants to drive us away from God and His kingdom. In the Sixth Petition of the Lord's Prayer, we pray for God's protection from temptation; in the Seventh Petition, we acknowledge that God does protect and deliver us from evil.

A Way Out

In Matthew 4:1–11 Jesus comes face-to-face with temptation and evil. Jesus was tempted in three different ways. Satan tempted Jesus with physical desires (represented by hunger), to show His Godly power before the right time, and to gain earthly power and wealth. With every temptation, Jesus uses God's Word to refute Satan. "Let no one say when he is tempted, 'I am being tempted by God,' for God cannot be tempted with evil, and He Himself tempts no one. But each person is tempted when he is lured and enticed by his own desire" (James 1:13–14). James was encouraging the early Christian Church that was scattered as far as Phoenicia, Cyprus, and Syrian Antioch. They were experiencing trials in their faith, and his main purpose was to encourage them. In this particular section he is clarifying that God does not tempt believers. In fact, God Himself cannot be tempted because by His very nature He is holy. James is clearly making the point that each one of us is tempted when our own sinful nature "is lured and enticed." James outlines the process of temptation that leads to sin.

In 1 Corinthians 10:6–13, Paul is writing to the church at Corinth, which is primarily Jewish. Therefore, he uses the Jewish forefathers as examples to help the Corinthians understand how easy it is to fall into temptation. In verses 6–12, the Law is clearly illustrated, convicting the hearts of the people in Corinth to know that they are also susceptible to temptation. Then, in verse 13, the Gospel message is shared, informing the people that there is no temptation that they cannot overcome through God's power.

What hope does this give us as we face temptations in our life? It tells us that God is on our side. We can always look to God to give us strength when we are faced with temptations.

Resist

On December 29, 1890, the U.S. cavalry confronted and attempted to disarm a band of more than 300 Sioux Indians at Wounded Knee (in South Dakota). The Indians believed that their ritual clothing, "Ghost Shirts," would protect them from the soldiers' bullets. When the shooting stopped, 25 cavalrymen had died, but more than 150 Sioux men, women, and children had also died. Still others were wounded. Their "Ghost Shirts" had not protected them. What was missing in the faith of the people who were shot at Wounded Knee? Simple truth. Because their beliefs were rooted in falsehood, they suffered horribly. Human "faith" leads to destruction, but faith in God is a blessing.

In Daniel 3:16–18, we read about Shadrach, Meshach, and Abednego. The faith expressed by these young men connects with God's promises and the reality that His people suffer. They understood that they were in God's hands, not left alone to suffer the whims of people. They believed that God would care for them, but they also were ready to suffer for the truth. Through Christ's death and resurrection, we have unlimited power in our lives to overcome temptation. At the name of Jesus, demons flee.

Comparisons

Perfect love: Medieval Christian thinkers such as Francis of Assisi (ca. 1182–1226) and Thomas Aquinas (ca. 1224–74) proposed different theories of perfection. By grace, Christians could attain higher degrees of love and ultimately fulfill the law of love. They could overcome all temptation. The views of Francis and Thomas still influence many Roman Catholics.

Perfect holiness: Many Wesleyans (followers of John Wesley, such as Methodists, as well as Holiness and Pentecostal churches that follow his teachings) teach that there is a second work of grace after salvation. This work of grace totally sanctifies or perfects a person so that he or she no longer sins.

Sanctification: Lutherans, like many other Christians, teach that believers continue to struggle with temptation throughout life and do not attain sinless perfection until they are brought to heaven.

Point to Remember

> No temptation has overtaken you that is not common to man. God is faithful, and He will not let you be tempted beyond your ability, but with the temptation He will also provide a way of escape, that you may be able to endure it. *1 Corinthians 10:13*

Amen

> We ought to consider the end of everything, in what way it will end; for the god having shown a glimpse of happiness to many, has afterward utterly overthrown them.
>
> —Herodotus, *The History*

Like the ancient Greeks, many people today cannot trust heaven. They pray but they do not believe God will give them what they ask. They fear that if He does give them happiness or contentment, He will likely pluck it away at any moment.

In the conclusion of the Lord's Prayer, we have the opportunity to respond to God with boldness and confidence as we place all of our petitions into His care. It is a final time in the prayer to acknowledge that God is supreme and beyond our comprehension. As we pray the conclusion, we are trusting that God is in control of all things. By faith we place our lives and all things into the caring hands of our Father.

You of Little Faith

Matthew 14:22–36 illustrates the fact that faith is truly a gift from God. The disciples were clueless about the power Jesus possessed. They had just witnessed Jesus' miraculous feeding of 5,000 people and then saw Him walking on water. They were afraid because they thought He was a ghost. Jesus was frustrated with their lack of faith and understanding. They still did not get it—He is the Son of God!

Peter wanted to illustrate his faith in Jesus, so he stepped out of the boat and walked on water. This is a well-known passage, but we don't often think of its powerful application to the conclusion of the Lord's Prayer. We are called, like Peter, to step out of our comfort zones and trust God with the difficult areas in our lives. This is impossible without the Holy Spirit's power. We can't do it on our own. But God will give us the strength to take the step and trust Him. This story clearly illustrates what it means to surrender and trust in God.

Obviously, Peter realized that walking on water was out of the natural realm of human possibilities, and then he sank. His fear controlled his faith; he didn't allow the Spirit to calm his fear. This has some definite applications for daily living. Is our natural response one of fear or one of faith? Jesus responded by rescuing Peter and then challenging him in his faith. Jesus made the ultimate rescue when He suffered on Calvary on our behalf.

In Ephesians 3:14–21, Paul shares a beautiful prayer for spiritual strength. He paints a picture of the love God has for each one of His children. It is beyond understanding.

> For this reason I bow my knees before the Father, from whom every family in heaven and on earth is named, that according to the riches of His glory He may grant you to be strengthened with power through His Spirit in your inner being, so that Christ may dwell in your hearts through faith—that you, being rooted and grounded in love, may have strength to comprehend with all the saints what is the breadth and length and height and depth, and to know the love of Christ that surpasses knowledge, that you may be filled with all the fullness of God. Now to Him who is able to do far more abundantly than all that we ask or think, according to the power at work within us, to Him be glory in the church and in Christ Jesus throughout all generations, forever and ever. Amen.

Walk by Faith

Can you relate to Peter? Is God asking you to "walk on water" and trust Jesus in areas of your life? What fears cause you to sink?

On September 11, 2001, Todd Beamer dialed for an operator on an air phone and reached Lisa Jefferson, an operator in Chicago. Todd explained that his plane, United Airlines Flight 93, had been hijacked. He calmly described the plans of the passengers to retake the plane as a means to prevent the hijackers from crashing it into a populated area. As Todd waited for his fellow passengers to organize, he told Lisa about his family. They recited the Lord's Prayer and Psalm 23 together.

Suddenly, Lisa realized that Todd had set the phone down. She heard him say, "God help me. Jesus help me." Then she heard him ask: "Are you guys ready? Let's roll."

Although the plane crashed near Pittsburgh, God had heard Todd's plea for help. He helped Todd and the other passengers do the right thing in a moment of paralyzing fear. God enabled Todd to walk by faith. In our Baptism, we received God's Spirit, who daily empowers us to trust God and surrender to His will and way. In Romans 8:28–39, Paul reminds us that there is nothing that can separate us from God's love in Christ Jesus! This section of Scripture reinforces the fact that there is no temptation or sin so great that it can separate a person from God's love. So step out of the boat. In the conclusion of the Lord's Prayer, we are professing that through God's Spirit, we will walk by faith with confidence in God our Father.

Comparisons

Faith as God's gift: Lutherans, Reformed, Particular Baptists, Roman Catholics, and some Wesleyans teach that faith is a gift of God. Lutherans emphasize that the Holy Spirit creates faith through the Means of Grace (Word and Sacraments).

Faith as a human power: Eastern Orthodox, Anabaptists, General Baptists, and some Wesleyans teach that each person has faith and must offer it to God of his or her own free will.

Point to Remember

For by grace you have been saved through faith. And this is not your own doing; it is the gift of God, not a result of works, so that no one may boast. *Ephesians 2:8–9*

Lutheran Summary of Daily Prayer

Apology of the augsburg Confession V (III) 210–12 [331–33]

So Daniel teaches us in praying to seize mercy, that is, to trust in God's mercy and not to trust in our own merits before God. We also wonder what our adversaries do in prayer, if the ungodly people ever ask anything of God. If they declare that they are worthy because they have love and good works and ask for grace as a debt, they pray precisely like the Pharisee who says, "I am not like other men" (Luke 18:11). He who prays for grace in this way does not rely upon God's mercy and treats Christ with disrespect. After all, He is our High Priest, who intercedes for us. So prayer relies upon God's mercy, when we believe that we are heard for Christ's sake. He is our High Priest, as He Himself says, "Whatever you ask in My name, this I will do, that the Father may be glorified in the Son. If you ask Me anything in My name, I will do it" (John 14:13–14). Without this High Priest we cannot approach the Father. (*Concordia*, p. 133)

Large Catechism III 4–6, 17–23, 28–32

But before we explain the Lord's Prayer part by part, it is most necessary first to encourage and stir people to prayer, as Christ and the apostles also have done [Matthew 6:5–15]. And the first thing to know is that it is our duty to pray because of God's commandment. For that's what we heard in the Second Commandment, "You shall not take the name of the Lord your God in vain" [Exodus 20:7]. We are required to praise that holy name and call upon it in every need, or to pray. To call upon God's name is nothing other than to pray [e.g., 1 Kings 18:24]. Prayer is just as strictly and seriously commanded as all other commandments: to have no other God, not to kill, not to steal, and so on. Let no one think that it makes no difference whether he prays or not. Common people think this, who grope in such delusion and ask, "Why should I pray? Who knows whether God heeds or will hear my prayer? If I do not pray, some one else will." And so they fall into the habit of never praying. They build a false argument, as though we taught that there is no duty or need for prayer, because we reject false and hypocritical prayers [Matthew 6:5]. . . .

Let this be the first and most important point, that all our prayers must be based and rest upon obedience to God, regardless of who we are, whether we are sinners or saints, worthy or unworthy. We must know that God will not have our prayer treated as a joke. But He will be angry and punish all who do not pray, just as surely as He punishes all other disobedience. Furthermore, He will not allow our prayers to be in vain or lost. For if

He did not intend to answer your prayer, He would not ask you to pray and add such a severe commandment to it.

In the second place, we should be more encouraged and moved to pray because God has also added a promise and declared that it shall surely be done for us as we pray. He says in Psalm 50:15, "Call upon Me in the day of trouble; I will deliver you." And Christ says in the Gospel of St. Matthew, "Ask, and it will be given to you; . . . for everyone who asks receives" (7:7–8). Such promises certainly ought to encourage and kindle our hearts to pray with pleasure and delight. For He testifies with His own Word that our prayer is heartily pleasing to Him. Furthermore, it shall certainly be heard and granted, in order that we may not despise it or think lightly of it and pray based on chance.

You can raise this point with Him and say, "Here I come, dear Father, and pray, not because of my own purpose or because of my own worthiness. But I pray because of Your commandment and promise, which cannot fail or deceive me." Whoever, therefore, does not believe this promise must note again that he outrages God like a person who thoroughly dishonors Him and accuses Him of falsehood.

Besides this, we should be moved and drawn to prayer. For in addition to this commandment and promise, God expects us and He Himself arranges the words and form of prayer for us. He places them on our lips for how and what we should pray [Psalm 51:15], so that we may see how heartily He pities us in our distress [Psalm 4:1], and we may never doubt that such prayer is pleasing to Him and shall certainly be answered. This ‹the Lord's Prayer› is a great advantage indeed over all other prayers that we might compose ourselves. For in our own prayers the conscience would ever be in doubt and say, "I have prayed, but who knows if it pleases Him or whether I have hit upon the right proportions and form?" Therefore, there is no nobler prayer to be found upon earth than the Lord's Prayer. We pray it daily [Matthew 6:11], because it has this excellent testimony, that God loves to hear it. We ought not to surrender this for all the riches of the world. . . .

Every one of us should form the daily habit from his youth of praying for all his needs. He should pray whenever he notices anything affecting his interests or that of other people among whom he may live. He should pray for preachers, the government, neighbors, household servants, and always (as we have said) to hold up to God His commandment and promise, knowing that He will not have them disregarded. This I say because I would like to see these things brought home again to the people so that they might learn to pray truly and not go about coldly and indifferently. They become daily more unfit for prayer because of indifference. That is just what the devil desires, and for which he works with all his powers. He is well aware what damage and harm it does him when prayer is done properly.

We need to know this: all our shelter and protection rest in prayer alone. For we are far too weak to deal with the devil and all his power and followers who set themselves against us. They might easily crush us under their feet. Therefore, we must consider and take up those weapons with which Christians must be armed in order to stand against the devil [2 Corinthians 10:4; Ephesians 6:11]. For what do you imagine has done such great things up till now? What has stopped or quelled the counsels, purposes, murder, and riot of our enemies, by which the devil thought he would crush us, together with the Gospel? It was the prayer of a few godly people standing in the middle like an iron wall for our side. Otherwise they would have witnessed a far different tragedy. They would have seen how the devil would have destroyed all Germany in its own blood. But now our enemies may confidently ridicule prayer and make a mockery of it. However, we shall still be a match both for them and the devil by prayer alone, if we only persevere diligently and do not become slack. For whenever a godly Christian prays, "Dear Father, let Your will be done" [see Matthew 6:10], God speaks from on high and says, "Yes, dear child, it shall be so, in spite of the devil and all the world." (*Concordia*, pp. 408–9, 410–12)

Large Catechism III 92–98

For where the heart is not in a right relationship with God, or cannot take such confidence, it will not dare to pray anymore. Such a confident and joyful heart can spring from nothing else than the certain knowledge of the forgiveness of sin [Psalm 32:1–2; Romans 4:7–8].

There is here attached a necessary, yet comforting addition: "As we forgive." He has promised that we shall be sure that everything is forgiven and pardoned, in the way that we also forgive our neighbor. Just as we daily sin much against God, and yet He forgives everything through grace, so we, too, must ever forgive our neighbor who does us injury, violence, and wrong, shows malice toward us, and so on. If, therefore, you do not forgive, then do not think that God forgives you [Matthew 18:23–25]. But if you forgive, you have this comfort and assurance, that you are forgiven in heaven. This is not because of your forgiving. For God forgives freely and without condition, out of pure grace, because He has so promised, as the Gospel teaches. But God says this in order that He may establish forgiveness as our confirmation and assurance, as a sign alongside of the promise, which agrees with this prayer in Luke 6:37, "Forgive, and you will be forgiven." Therefore, Christ also repeats it soon after the Lord's Prayer, and says in Matthew 6:14, "For if you forgive others their trespasses, your heavenly Father will also forgive you," and so on.

This sign is therefore attached to this petition. When we pray, we remember the promise and think, "Dear Father, for this reason I come and pray for You to forgive me, not so that I can make satisfaction or can merit anything by my works. I pray because You have promised and attached the seal to this prayer that I should be as sure about it as though I had Absolution pronounced by You Yourself." For Baptism and the Lord's Supper—appointed as outward signs—work as seals [Ephesians 1:13]. In the same way also, this sign can serve to confirm our consciences and cause them to rejoice. It is especially given for this purpose, so that we may use and practice forgiveness every hour, as a thing that we have with us at all times. (*Concordia*, pp. 419–20)

TOPIC TWELVE

BAPTISM[1]

ENGAGING THIS TOPIC

"I'm so excited! My brother asked me to be a godparent for my niece. She's getting baptized on Sunday."
"You mean the one who was just born? That isn't right. She's too young to be baptized."
"What do you mean?"
"She's too young to make a decision for Christ or even remember her Baptism. What good will it do her?"

- In the mid-1980s feminist theologians in the United Church of Canada raised questions about the words traditionally spoken at Baptism (Matthew 28:19). They proposed that, instead of using the masculine words "Father" and "Son," Baptism should be done "in the name of the Creator and of the Redeemer and of the Sanctifier."

- Boulevard Baptist Church of Anderson, South Carolina, was dismissed from its local Southern Baptist Association because the congregation accepted as members Christians who had been baptized by pouring or sprinkling.

- When the Reformed Church of France, a mixture of Protestant groups, decided that it should offer the Lord's Supper to the "nonbaptized," Bishop Michel Viot resigned his office. He announced that he would convert to Roman Catholicism because the Reformed Church's decision undermined the Sacraments given by Christ.

Around the world the doctrine and practice of Baptism continues to complicate relationships among Christians. While some churches wish to de-emphasize Baptism in order to foster greater unity, other churches respond with revulsion to such proposals. They regard Baptism as so

1 This chapter adapted from *The Lutheran Difference: Baptism*, written by Robert Rossow, with contributions by Edward Engelbrecht. Copyright © 2003 Concordia Publishing House.

central to their identity that they reject such compromises for the sake of unity.

The reformer Dr. Martin Luther regarded Baptism as *the* identifying mark of a Christian. In fact, for Luther, Baptism *made* a Christian. Luther thought Baptism so central to the Christian faith that he encouraged fellow Christians to repeat the words of their Baptism each day.

The Headwaters of Baptism

Jesus was not the first person to encourage Baptism. Nor was John the Baptist. The beginnings of Baptism spring from the Old Testament washings God commanded through Moses. To minister at the tabernacle, the priests needed to wash. Likewise, when the people visited the tabernacle for worship, they needed cleansing. Many ancient religions included ritual washing as part of their practice. But God made cleansing, purity, and holiness the focus of Old Testament life (Leviticus 11:44–45; 19:1–2; 20:7–8). You could not approach the Holy One of Israel if you were unclean.

After the Lord scattered the children of Israel among the nations because they broke His covenant, He promised that He would provide them with a new washing that surpassed the rituals of the old covenant. This washing would not simply purify the body; it would cleanse the heart, transform it, and bestow the Holy Spirit (Ezekiel 36:24–27).

As the people of Judah returned from exile in Babylon, they intermarried with the Gentiles who had settled in the land of Israel (Nehemiah 13:25–30). The rabbis were faced with the problem of purifying these foreigners. For boys and men, the old covenant provided a means to cleanse them and receive them into the covenant: circumcision (Genesis 17). But the old covenant did not provide such a means for cleansing girls and women. It appears that the rabbis solved this problem by drawing on the Old Testament cleansing rituals.[2]

Thus ritual washing was part of conversion in Judaism in the first century before Christ, as demonstrated by the services of covenant renewal described in the Dead Sea Scrolls (*The Community Rule*, 1 QS III). For devout Jewish groups such as the Essenes, ritual washing became a frequent or even daily religious practice (see Mark 7:1–4, where *washing* is the Greek word for Baptism; note the plural in Hebrews 6:2). In fact, archaeologists have found ritual washing pools (*mikvehs*) near the Temple Mount and at Qumran.

2 See Joachim Jeremias, *Infant Baptism in the First Four Centuries* (London: SCM, 1960), 24–40.

A New Covenant

When John the Baptist began calling the people of Judah to repentance, he was following the practice of devout people in his day. However, John's preaching showed that his Baptism was different from the washings of other Jewish groups (Matthew 3:5–12). John's preaching and Baptism were preparing the way for the coming of Jesus, for the new washing prophesied by Ezekiel and Jeremiah:

> I will sprinkle clean water on you, and you shall be clean from all your uncleannesses, and from all your idols I will cleanse you. And I will give you a new heart, and a new spirit I will put within you. And I will remove the heart of stone from your flesh and give you a heart of flesh. And I will put My Spirit within you, and cause you to walk in My statutes and be careful to obey My rules. (Ezekiel 36:25–27)

> But this is the covenant that I will make with the house of Israel after those days, declares the LORD: I will put My law within them, and I will write it on their hearts. And I will be their God, and they shall be My people. (Jeremiah 31:33)

These Old Testament prophesies were fulfilled in the New Testament:

> How much more will the blood of Christ, who through the eternal Spirit offered Himself without blemish to God, purify our conscience from dead works to serve the living God. Therefore He is the mediator of a new covenant, so that those who are called may receive the promised eternal inheritance, since a death has occurred that redeems them from the transgressions committed under the first covenant. (Hebrews 9:14–15)

The Baptism provided by Jesus would make all other ritual washings obsolete.

As we dive into the New Testament's teaching about Baptism, bear in mind this Old Testament background and Ezekiel's prophecy. They will help you understand the full blessings of Baptism "in the name of the Father and of the Son and of the Holy Spirit" (Matthew 28:19).

Lutheran Facts

Lutherans may baptize by pouring, sprinkling, or immersing someone with water "in the name of the Father and of the Son and of the Holy Spirit." The mode of Baptism is usually decided by the setting and local custom, not by specific rules about how to apply the water.

When a person is baptized at a Lutheran church, that person is regarded as a member of the congregation and a member of the Church universal.

Lutherans baptize people of all ages and all mental abilities, including infants and the mentally handicapped.

Although pastors usually administer Baptism, any layperson can baptize when special need arises (such as the imminence of death).

Following ancient church practice, Lutherans usually choose baptismal sponsors or "godparents" for the person being baptized. The role of a sponsor is to support and encourage the newly baptized person in the Christian faith (mentoring).

Today Lutherans usually baptize during the regular Sunday morning service.

When a person is baptized by another Christian church "in the name of the Father and of the Son and of the Holy Spirit," Lutherans regard this as a valid Baptism. They do not re-baptize.

What Is Baptism?

> They said our Christian gods were demons and that they would burn down our houses . . . [but] I am staying a Christian.
>
> —Mr. Umra Mohan Pawar, Dangs, India, 1999

Many religions and cultures have special ritual washings. When a group of Hindu radicals poured water on Mr. Pawar and other Christians in India, they sought to undo their Christian Baptism. They gave Mr. Pawar a locket of the Hindu monkey god and told him that he was now a Hindu. But in the face of such bold persecution, Mr. Pawar quietly clung to his Baptism into Christ.

This Hindu ritual could not undo the blessings Mr. Pawar and other Christians receive in Baptism. God in His grace has chosen to come to us in simple means—water and the Word of Christ. His presence bears much power and bestows many blessings. A culture that seems obsessed with the extraordinary might not recognize God's extraordinary presence and promise in ordinary means—including Holy Baptism. Our Lord promised to come to us in His Word and Sacraments. God can also reach others through us and our everyday encounters in how we live and speak.

God's Affinity for the Finite

A central teaching of the Bible is that the almighty, eternal God loved all people so much that He determined to reach us with His salvation. God became human in Christ (incarnation) to reach us and to remedy our sinful condition: "And the Word became flesh and dwelt among us, and we have seen His glory, glory as of the only Son from the Father, full of grace and truth. . . . No one has ever seen God; the only God, who is at the Father's side, He has made Him known" (John 1:14, 18). Although we can learn things about God through the beauty, power, and order of creation, we can only know God through Christ.

Further examples of God's love through His presence in a finite, tangible way are included in Scripture. God reaches down to us; we cannot get to Him. Sometimes God "shows up" with a blaze of glory, as in Exodus 3:1–6 where God appears in a burning bush. At other times, He appears in very "ordinary" ways. For example, God "shows up" in 1 Kings 19:11–13 not in the wind nor the earthquake nor even the fire; rather, He comes in the low whisper. In Matthew 13:34, God the Son "shows" the kingdom of God through words (parables). In Matthew 21:1–11, God the Son "shows" Himself to the people, riding on a donkey. And in Mark 1:9–11, God the Holy Spirit appears like a dove and the Father's voice is heard. He certainly used ordinary things—a bush, a whisper, human language, human form, and a dove—but He is anything but ordinary.

The Means of Grace

The Means of Grace are ways or vehicles through which God gives us His gifts—forgiveness of sins and eternal life. The Means of Grace include God's Word and God's Sacraments of Holy Baptism and the Lord's Supper. Scripture teaches that the Sacraments

- are instituted and commanded by God (Matthew 28:19).
- include a visible element connected with God's Word (Ephesians 5:26).
- convey God's grace, the promise of forgiveness of sins, and eternal life through faith in Christ Jesus (Galatians 3:26; Acts 2:38–39).

Through the Means of Grace, God creates saving faith in Christ Jesus and strengthens and preserves the faith of believers. *Baptism* means a washing with water (Matthew 28:19–20). Yet 1 Peter 3:21 makes clear that it is also the washing away of our sins.

Holy Baptism

Matthew 28:19–20 tells us that God Himself commanded Baptism. This command wasn't given to just a select few. All nations are included in the command to baptize. This means all kinds of people without respect to nationality, age, or ability, because God gave Baptism as a blessing for everyone. Paul writes:

> But when the goodness and loving kindness of God our Savior appeared, He saved us, not because of works done by us in righteousness, but according to His own mercy, by the washing of regeneration and renewal of the Holy Spirit, whom He poured out on us richly through Jesus Christ our Savior, so that being justified by His grace we might become heirs according to the hope of eternal life. (Titus 3:4–7)

God's attitude toward us is one of kindness and love. Our salvation is not based on our worth or merit but only in God's mercy for the sake of Christ. In verse 5, the "washing of regeneration" refers to the Sacrament of Holy Baptism.

Lost and Found

When the children of Israel left their homeland and settled in Egypt (ca. 1875 BC), they forgot about God's promises to their forefathers. They were lost until the Lord spoke to Moses and called him to preach to the people and lead them out of Egypt. Instead of appearing to the leaders of Israel, God chose to reach Israel through an eighty-year-old sheepherder, Moses.

God has told us that He communicates His presence and power through rather simple means. We are to look for God where He promised to be—in His Word and Sacraments. Regular devotion time and worship provide us with the opportunity to encounter God and His promises, as do receiving the Lord's Supper and remembering our Baptism.

God found us and claimed us through the Gospel—the visible Gospel in Holy Baptism or from the spoken Gospel heard and then received in faith. Through simple means God provides the creation of saving faith in Christ Jesus and the strengthening of that faith, which clings to the gifts of forgiveness of sins and eternal life.

How, then, can we respond to someone who claims that Baptism is only a church tradition with simple symbolic qualities? We can tell him or her that God instituted and commanded Holy Baptism; through it He provides forgiveness of sins and eternal life.

Comparisons

Most Christian churches regard Baptism as a sacrament. They teach that God bestows grace through Baptism. Eastern Orthodox, Lutheran, Roman Catholic, Episcopal, Reformed, and some Wesleyan churches hold to a sacramental view.

Eastern Orthodox: "What virtue is there in each of these Sacraments? In Baptism man is mysteriously born to a spiritual life" (*The Longer Catechism of the Eastern Church*, question 286).

Lutheran: "[The Sacrament of Holy] Baptism . . . [is] a gracious water of life and a washing of regeneration in the Holy Spirit" (SC IV; *Concordia*, p. 340).

Roman Catholic: "If any one saith that in the Roman church, which is the mother and mistress of all churches, there is not the true doctrine concerning the sacrament of baptism; let him be anathema" (*Canons and Decrees of the Council of Trent*, Session 7, On Baptism, Canon 3; cf. CCC2 para. 1214).

Reformed: "Baptism is a sacrament of the New Testament, ordained by Jesus Christ, not only for the solemn admission of the party baptized into the visible Church; but also, to be unto him a sign and seal of the covenant of grace" (*The Westminster Confession of Faith*, chapter 28.1).

Methodist: "Sacraments ordained of Christ are . . . certain signs of grace, and God's good will toward us, by which he doth work invisibly in us, and doth not only quicken, but also strengthen and confirm, our faith in him. There are two Sacraments ordained of Christ our Lord in the Gospel; that is to say, Baptism and the Supper of our Lord" (*Methodist Articles of Religion*, article 16).

Some Christian churches hold that Baptism is an ordinance. They view Baptism as a public declaration of faith and commitment, which only the mature should receive. Anabaptists, Baptists, and some Wesleyans hold to an ordinance view.

Baptist: Baptism is an ordinance of the New Testament, ordained by Jesus Christ, to be unto the party baptized as a sign of his fellowship with him, in his death and resurrection (1689 *London Baptist Confession of Faith*, chapter 29: Of Baptism, 1).

Anabaptist: "[Leaders of the church should] be an example, light, and pattern in all godliness and good works, worthily administering the Lord's ordinances—baptism and supper" (*The Dordrecht Confession*, article 9).

Point to Remember

> He saved us . . . by the washing of regeneration and renewal of the Holy Spirit, whom He poured out on us richly through Jesus Christ our Savior, so that being justified by His grace we might become heirs according to the hope of eternal life. *Titus 3:5–7*

What Baptism Bestows

> Even as a boy I had heard of eternal life promised to us through the humility of the Lord our God condescending to our pride . . . I solicited from the piety of my mother, and of Thy Church, the mother of us all, the baptism of Thy Christ, my Lord and my God.
>
> —St. Augustine, *Confessions* 21.17

To appreciate the special quality of Baptism, we must first understand the depth of human need. Paul wrote: "For the wages of sin is death, but the free gift of God is eternal life in Christ Jesus our Lord" (Romans 6:23). When it comes to our relationship with God, all we "bring to the table" is sin and death. But God brings the gift of eternal life in Christ.

King David tells us that we are sinful from conception, that sin is an inherited disease that corrupts our human nature (Psalm 51:1–12). This original sin is the result of the fall and means that human beings are condemned to hell without God's regeneration. "Since the fall of Adam, all who are naturally born are born with sin . . . . Concupiscence is a disease and original vice that is truly sin. It damns and brings eternal death on those who are not born anew through Baptism and the Holy Spirit" (AC II 1–2; *Concordia*, pp. 31–32). As Paul explains, the sinful nature is hostile to God and cannot please Him (Romans 8:5–8). Self-help religions deny the harsh facts of original sin and pretend that we can do what only God can do through the Holy Spirit (see Luther's explanation of the Third Article of the Apostles' Creed in the Small Catechism; *Concordia*, p. 330).

Our thoughts, words, or deeds can make us feel guilty. But we find assurance in God's unconditional love for us. We have a habit of rationalizing our sinful condition as well as our sinful actions. When all such rationalizations are stripped away, we find assurance of God's love and mercy in His Word. God's love and mercy is communicated to us in Baptism. Thus remembering our Baptism edifies and assures us.

The Greatest Gifts

In his Pentecost sermon, Peter told the crowd: "Repent and be baptized every one of you in the name of Jesus Christ for the forgiveness of your sins, and you will receive the gift of the Holy Spirit. For the promise is for you and for your children and for all who are far off, everyone whom the Lord our God calls to Himself" (Acts 2:38–39). Two gifts are mentioned here in connection with Baptism: forgiveness of sins and the gift of the Holy Spirit. The punctuation in some translations of these verses can be misleading. Verses 38–39 are one sentence in Greek, emphasizing that both forgiveness *and* the Holy Spirit are bestowed in Baptism "for you and for your children." Note the apostle's words. The promise of these gifts is for all—young and old. Age is not the important factor. The calling of God in Christ is what Peter emphasizes.

How did the gift of salvation start? Paul tells us in Romans 5:8: "God shows His love for us in that while we were still sinners, Christ died for us." God's gift of forgiveness flows from His love for us in Christ rather than from our love for Him. Likewise, righteousness comes to us from outside of ourselves—only through Christ Jesus (1 Corinthians 1:30). In order for us to be declared righteous, Jesus had to be declared guilty in our place. God declares us righteous only for the sake of Christ (2 Corinthians 5:21).

Paul explains in Romans 8 that, through the power of the Holy Spirit, we are no longer enemies of God, but rather, through Christ, we are "sons of God" (Romans 8:14), "children of God" (v. 16), and His "heirs" (v. 17). As heirs, we inherit Christ's merits and benefits. Because of Christ's perfect righteousness, our "Spirit is life" (v. 10) and "He who raised Christ Jesus from the dead will also give life to your mortal bodies" (v. 11). In the parable of the prodigal son (Luke 15:11–32), we see how we walked away from God in our sin. Through the Law, God calls us to repentance. But this cannot save us. Our God is like the prodigal son's father who saw him far off and "felt compassion" (v. 20). Our heavenly Father welcomes back His lost sons and daughters and gives them the full rights of heirs.

How, then, do we receive Christ's righteousness? God accomplished and conveyed our salvation (forgiveness and eternal life) entirely by His grace. Nothing we are or do merits His gifts. We receive forgiveness of sins and eternal life through faith in the merits of Christ Jesus won for us on the cross. (See Ephesians 2:8 and Titus 3:3–7.)

In Romans 6:3–11, Paul tells us that our old self and its slavery to sin died with Christ in our Baptism. And a new life rose with Christ in our Baptism. This new life occurs even now as we receive Christ's righteousness—and will be finally and fully received on Judgment Day.

By Christ's death on the cross, God prepared our rescue from the devil's kingdom. Colossians 1:13–14 speaks of the "domain of darkness"—the power of the devil and all of his evil. But even that "domain of darkness" need not concern us. Baptism delivers us from the power of the devil and shields us from all the evil accusations of the old evil foe. Christ took these accusations with Him to the cross.

How does God connect us to the salvation won for us by Christ? We are saved "by the washing of regeneration and renewal of the Holy Spirit . . . poured out on us richly through Jesus Christ our Savior" (Titus 3:5–6). God calls Christians to faith through certain "proper channels," the Means of Grace (Word and Sacrament). One of these is Baptism. As Paul explains, in Baptism our sinful nature is put to death and we are given a new life in Christ. In Baptism, the Holy Spirit connects us to Christ: we are baptized into Christ's death and resurrection.

In the Great Commission, Jesus commands Baptism for people of "all nations" (Matthew 28:19). He makes no qualifications about age, and it is clear that Baptism is completely passive. The power of Baptism has nothing to do with how educated a person is or how "ready" he or she feels. This, and the fact that Baptism reconnects the lost to Christ, shows the importance of infant Baptism. In Baptism, the physical element (water) has no magical power, but the water is connected to the Word (the invocation of the name of our triune God), through which the Holy Spirit works to regenerate the lost.

Genesis 1:28 tells us: "And God blessed them. And God said to them, 'Be fruitful and multiply and fill the earth and subdue it and have dominion over the fish of the sea and over the birds of the heavens and over every living thing that moves on the earth.'" We are born of human parents and there is an important similarity between our physical existence and our new life in Christ. Our God is a God of means, who institutes a proper way in which His calls us. Although God could create us directly, He calls us into human existence through the means of our human parents. Since we now inherit a corrupted human nature, our merciful God has instituted other means to restore us and to incorporate us into His family. Baptism is the means of new birth God institutes to create the new life in Christ that our human existence cannot claim for itself.

Comfort in Christ

Scripture clearly connects the forgiveness of sins with Baptism. So how do we respond to someone who claims that Baptism is only a symbol or confession of faith by the person baptized? Through Holy Baptism, God comes with His love in Christ through His Word. Any confession of faith accompanying this act of God is purely a response to God's grace.

A person plays no active role in receiving the forgiveness of sins. God acts to redeem us through Jesus Christ. God declares His mercy upon us for the sake of Christ. In other words, God creates and sustains our faith.

We were buried with Christ through Baptism into death. And just as Christ was raised, so we, too, are raised to a new life (Romans 6:3–4). This biblical truth brings us comfort when our sins weigh heavily upon us. Our sin was buried with Christ. Now we need to let those old, dead, buried sins rot and not bring them back to life. Christ and His righteousness are alive in us. Setting our hearts and minds on Christ brings much comfort.

Comparisons

Eastern Orthodox, Lutheran, Roman Catholic, and some other churches teach that God bestows salvation or new birth through Baptism. (*Regeneration* is from a Latin term meaning "born again.")

Eastern Orthodox: "Baptism is a Sacrament, in which a man . . . is born again of the Holy Ghost to a life spiritual and holy" (*The Longer Catechism of the Eastern Church*, question 288).

Lutheran: "Baptism . . . [is] a gracious water of life and a washing of regeneration in the Holy Spirit" (SC IV; *Concordia*, p. 340).

Roman Catholic: Through Baptism we are born again and made members of the Church. It is the gateway to the whole Christian life. Cf. CCC2 para. 1213.

Reformed churches teach that Baptism places a person in a covenant relationship with God.

Reformed: "Baptism . . . doth signify and seal our ingrafting into Christ, and partaking of the benefits of the covenant of grace, and our engagement to be the Lord's" (*Westminster Shorter Catechism*, question 94).

Anabaptist, Baptists, and some Wesleyans regard Baptism as a symbol of a person's personal commitment to Christ and a new way of life.

Baptist: "We believe that Christian Baptism is the immersion in water of a believer, into the name of the Father, and Son, and Holy Ghost; to show forth in a solemn and beautiful emblem, our faith in the crucified, buried, and risen Savior" (*New Hampshire [Baptist] Confession of Faith*, declaration 14).

Anabaptist: "Concerning baptism we confess that penitent believers who, through faith, regeneration, and the renewing of the Holy Ghost, are made one with God, and are written in heaven, must, upon such Scriptural confession of faith, and renewing of life, be baptized with water" (*The Dordrecht Confession*, article 7).

Point to Remember

We were buried therefore with Him by Baptism into death, in order that, just as Christ was raised from the dead by the glory of the Father, we too might walk in newness of life. *Romans 6:4*

What Baptism Does

We are CHRISTians.
—Missionary Harley L. Kopitske

Mankind's identity is by nature connected with the old Adam and is defined by sin and death. To be redefined by righteousness and life, we need a new identity—one that is connected with the new Adam, Christ Jesus. Baptism provides this new connection and new life.

Since medieval times, Christians have used another name for Baptism: *christening*. This special term reminds Christians of what Baptism does. It gives them a new identity, uniting them with Christ.

There's an old saying: "Show me your friends and I'll show you your future." We all have times in our lives when the company we keep tarnishes or polishes our identity. At other times, we experience the profound realization that we are children of God. This can change the way we feel and act. In Baptism, *God* acts, not us. We passively receive His active grace. There is no merit or worthiness in ourselves; instead we focus on the merits and worthiness Christ earned for us on the cross.

The Garment of Salvation

Paul tells Titus quite clearly that God saved us in Christ. Titus 3:8 is an admonition from Paul: "The saying is trustworthy, and I want you to insist on these things, so that those who have believed in God may be careful to devote themselves to good works. These things are excellent and profitable for people." This is important information Paul is sharing with Titus, and he takes extra steps to make sure Titus understands that our salvation is based not upon who we are or what we do; rather, God's love moved Him to save us for the sake of His Son, Jesus Christ. God saved us "by the washing of regeneration and renewal of the Holy Spirit"—Holy Baptism (Titus 3:5). This washing produces in us a faith that clings to the merits of Christ.

In every culture, clothing and jewelry provide important means for identifying who people are and what they do. In American culture, for example, a businessperson wears a suit, a judge wears black robes, an athlete wears sneakers, a Christian wears a cross, and a farmer wears overalls. These examples are pretty simplistic. But in Galatians 3:26–27, Paul tells us that we are clothed with Christ. Christ's righteousness now covers our sinful nature. God the Father now sees that righteousness, which not only covers us but has also been credited to us. Our sinful nature with its "passions and desires" (Galatians 5:24) will plague us until we go to heaven, but it no longer defines our identity. We now belong to Jesus. This new ownership provides for us a secure identity.

So how do the people around us see our "new clothes"? How do people identify our faith by our outward actions? We can positively express our faith to others through word and deed. As the old song says, "They'll know we are Christians by our love." As we share the love of Christ with those around us, they will see the "new clothes" of Christ that are ours in Baptism.

Paul instructs the church at Ephesus to "put off your old self, which . . . is corrupt . . . and to put on the new self" (4:22–24). The "old self" includes things such as self-centeredness, immorality, and despair. These are gone now. Instead, we have a "new self," a new attitude and new actions. Love, joy, peace, patience, kindness, goodness, faithfulness, gentleness, and self-control flow from those who have been clothed by Christ through Holy Baptism (Galatians 5:22–26).

The New You

Many people search for identity or go on a quest to "find themselves." We can direct a fellow Christian struggling with his or her identity to God's unconditional love. Christ's righteousness covers us. We can direct friends who are searching back to their Baptism, where they were adopted into the family of God.

In today's fashion-obsessed world, "you are what you wear." This misguided perception can actually help us understand our true spiritual identity. Those who have put on Christ in Baptism are truly children of God. They not only wear Christ, but their identity also comes from Christ.

The white cloth presented to a child at Baptism signifies that this child has now put on Christ and is clothed with Christ's righteousness. The baptized child or adult now makes a "fashion statement" for Christ.

Comparisons

Revivalism: In some Protestant church bodies, people are baptized numerous times, each time they experience a religious conversion and wish to declare the new direction for their lives.

One Baptism: Most churches teach that Baptism makes a person a member of the kingdom of God—His Church—despite denominational affiliation. These churches do not re-baptize people who have been properly baptized by a different church (e.g., a Lutheran would not re-baptize a person baptized in the Roman Catholic Church).

Anabaptism: During the sixteenth century, churches that believed only in adult Baptisms insisted that people baptized as infants be re-baptized as a testimony to their faith. Anabaptists, Baptists, and some Wesleyans practice re-baptism.

Point to Remember

For as many of you as were baptized into Christ have put on Christ. *Galatians 3:27*

Why Baptize Infants?

Today you will be baptized a Christian.
—Dietrich Bonhoeffer, *Letters and Papers from Prison*

From a Nazi prison in 1944, Pastor Bonhoeffer wrote his newborn nephew, Dietrich Wilhelm, a letter for the day of his Baptism. It would be years before Dietrich Wilhelm could understand or read this letter for himself. For cynical minds, Pastor Bonhoeffer's letter may seem like a waste of effort, a waste of words.

But words are not so powerless. Pastor Bonhoeffer realized that he was passing on to his nephew a heritage and inheritance through the counsel and encouragement of words. With this letter, he left something of enduring value for his nephew.

A newborn baby cannot understand the words of his parents' lullaby or the legal implications of his parents' will. Does that mean parents should not sing lullabies or prepare wills with their children as beneficiaries? Absolutely not. Although infants cannot understand such words, they are still able to receive the blessings and benefits of their parents' love and care. Most objections to infant Baptism are based upon human conditions. Yet God's grace is unconditional. The direction of giving in Holy Baptism is from God to us, not from us to God.

Those who object to the practice of infant Baptism often do so because they believe infants

- don't need it (condition of innocence).
- can't understand what they are doing or receiving (condition of noncognition).
- are incapable of deciding or willing Baptism (condition of nonvolition).

Those who object to infant Baptism fail to recognize the dire need of all people because of sin. They likewise fail to appreciate the power of God's Word. Scripture clearly states that all people, including infants, are diseased with the condition of sin (Romans 3:10–18, 23). Because of sin, the human reason and the will are *always* hostile to God. They do not preclude God's ability to convey His grace.

We did not decide to be born. Nor does an infant who is adopted play any part in determining who adopts her or what rights and privileges of the family she receives. Instead, an infant receives all the blessings and privileges from being adopted into the family simply because the family chose to adopt her. The same is true for our adoption by God. He chose us to be His sons and daughters. He clothes us in Christ. We are recipients of His grace in our Baptism.

Dead in Sin

In Psalm 51:5, the psalmist tells us that sin begins at conception. And in Romans 5:18–19, Paul tells us that we inherit our sin from our parents. Ultimately, sin is inherited from Adam. So we are dead in our sins (Ephesians 2:1) and cannot become righteous on our own. Christ's active obedience (keeping God's Law perfectly) and His passive obedience (paying the penalty for our disobedience on the cross) have been credited to us through faith. His obedience becomes our righteousness by God's grace through faith.

Our Inheritance

Children inherit physiological and psychological traits from their parents. Friends may say, "He has his father's eyes" or "She has her mother's smile." We don't speak as frequently about the spiritual trait we inherit from our parents: sin.

Are we to remain with that inheritance? No. Matthew tells us: "Then the children were brought to Him that He might lay His hands on them and pray. The disciples rebuked the people, but Jesus said, 'Let the little children come to Me and do not hinder them, for to such belongs the kingdom of heaven.' And He laid His hands on them and went away" (19:13–15). Jesus invites and welcomes children. They are included in the kingdom of heaven. But how do people receive the kingdom of heaven? According to John, we must be "born again . . . born of water and the Spirit" (3:3–5); Luke says it's our "Father's good pleasure" to give us His kingdom (12:32); and Paul says we inherit the kingdom "by grace . . . through faith . . . [as a] gift of God" (Ephesians 2:8). The kingdom of heaven is received by grace alone through faith alone in Christ Jesus; it is a gift to us from God, given at our Baptism. If the kingdom of heaven belongs to little children, and the kingdom of heaven is received by faith, then we may conclude that little children have the capacity for faith created by the Holy Spirit!

"But to all who did receive Him, who believed in His name, He gave the right to become children of God, who were born, not of blood nor of the will of the flesh nor of the will of man, but of God" (John 1:12–13). Parents make the decision for a child's natural birth, but God alone decides and effects spiritual birth. Christian parents can bring their children to Baptism, through which God bestows forgiveness of sins and eternal life.

This brings us to the sometimes uncomfortable question of whether the Bible says it's appropriate to baptize infants. Scripture reveals who should and should not receive the Sacrament of the Lord's Supper (1 Corinthians 11:28–32). We do not find similar guidelines concerning Baptism. We do, however, have the statement of Peter in Acts 2:38–39: "Repent and be baptized every one of you in the name of Jesus Christ for the forgiveness of your sins, and you will receive the gift of the Holy Spirit. For the promise is for you and for your children and for all who are far off, everyone whom the Lord our God calls to Himself." Peter supports the practice of infant Baptism by giving those who can believe the promise of salvation in Baptism along with their children. Throughout Acts we see entire households baptized; no one is excluded (Acts 10:44–48; 11:14; 16:15; 18:8; 1 Corinthians 1:16). No specific prohibitions against baptizing infants exist in the biblical accounts of Peter and Paul as they baptize and teach according to Christ's mandate in Matthew 28. Why not baptize infants? They certainly need the same forgiveness of sins as adults. And they certainly are included in our

Lord's Great Commission to make disciples of all people by baptizing and teaching. Since human reason and will are by nature enemies of God, they could never be conditions for receiving God's grace.

Faith cannot be reduced to a cognitive understanding or an articulate confession of the Christian faith, though ordinarily it includes both. Faith, in its simplest form, is trust that clings to God's promises. The Holy Spirit, working through Baptism, elicits such a trust in infants.

What can we say to a friend or relative who is planning to wait to have his or her child baptized until the child is old enough to decide? The Holy Spirit can and does create faith wherever and in whomever He pleases (John 3:5–8). Luther wrote in his explanation to the Third Article of the Apostles' Creed: "I believe that I cannot by my own reason or strength believe in Jesus Christ, my Lord, or come to Him. But the Holy Spirit has called me by the Gospel, enlightened me with His gifts, sanctified and kept me in the true faith" (*Concordia*, p. 330). The Holy Spirit is present and at work in Baptism. Therefore, He can and does create faith in infants through this Means of Grace.

Comparisons

Eastern Orthodox, Lutheran, Roman Catholic, Reformed, and some Wesleyan churches baptize infants as well as adults (including the mentally handicapped). These churches note that Jesus does not put an age limit on Baptism (Matthew 28:19). They view the Bible references to "household" Baptisms as including people of all ages (Acts 11:14; 16:15, 33; 18:8; the Greek term for "household" included every resident of a house, including servants and their families).

Eastern Orthodox: "How can you show from holy Scripture that we ought to baptize infants? In the time of the Old Testament, infants were circumcised when eight days old; but Baptism in the New Testament takes the place of circumcision; consequently infants should be baptized" (*The Longer Catechism of the Eastern Church*, question 293).

Lutheran: "The Baptism of infants is pleasing to Christ, as is proved well enough from His own work. For God sanctifies many of those who have been baptized as infants and has given them the Holy Spirit" (LC IV 49; *Concordia*, p. 428).

Roman Catholic: "If any one saith that little children, for that they have not actual faith, are not, after having received baptism, to be reckoned amongst the faithful; and that, for this cause, they are to be rebaptized when they have attained to years of discretion ... let him be anathema" (*Canons and Decrees of the Council of Trent*, Session 7, On Baptism, Canon 13; cf. CCC2 paras. 1250–52).

Reformed: "Are infants also to be baptized? Yes: for since they, as well as the adult, are included in the covenant and church of God; and since redemption from sin by the blood of Christ, and the Holy Ghost, the author of faith, is promised to them no less than to the adult; they must therefore by baptism, as a sign of the covenant, be also admitted into the Christian Church" (*The Heidelberg Catechism*, question 74).

Methodist: "The baptism of young children is to be retained in the church" (*Methodist Articles of Religion*, article 17).

Anabaptists, Baptists, and some Wesleyans baptize only those who are mature enough to state their faith and express a desire for Baptism (teen years or late childhood at the earliest). They point out that particular examples of Baptism describe adult participants and do not explicitly mention children.

Some teach a particular "age of accountability." They teach that before this age, God does not hold people accountable for things they do wrong.

Baptist: "Those who do actually profess repentance towards God, faith in, and obedience to, our Lord Jesus Christ, are the only proper subjects of this ordinance" (1689 *London Baptist Confession of Faith*, chapter 29: On Baptism, 2).

Anabaptist: "Concerning baptism we confess that penitent believers, who, through faith, regeneration, and the renewing of the Holy Ghost, are made one with God, and are written in heaven, must, upon such Scriptural confessions of faith, and renewing of life, be baptized with water" (*The Dordrecht Confession*, article 7).

Point to Remember

And Peter said to them, "Repent and be baptized every one of you in the name of Jesus Christ for the forgiveness of your sins, and you will receive the gift of the Holy Spirit. For the promise is for you and for your children and for all who are far off, everyone whom the Lord our God calls to Himself." *Acts 2:38–39*

Living the New Life

I am baptized.

—Martin Luther (LC IV 44; *Concordia*, p. 427)

Martin Luther would tell people, "I *am* baptized" (present passive verb), rather than "I *was* baptized." By this he meant that Baptism affects our ongoing identity. It is not simply an isolated and ineffectual act of the past. Baptism defines both who we are and what we do now.

An identity crisis often results in sporadic and even pathological behavior. Security in one's identity, on the other hand, provides for more consistent and appropriate behavior. Baptism provides us with a very secure identity.

New Creation

At the dawn of creation the Lord said, "Let there be light" (Genesis 1:3). Since that moment, light has shone forth, making life possible and perpetually sustaining life. God made His light shine in our hearts. He creates our new life in Christ (2 Corinthians 3:18; 4:6.) The lighted candle often presented at Baptism symbolizes that God's light now shines in the heart of the one baptized. It also reminds us to live in that light daily.

A Change for the Better

Baptism changes our hearts. In Baptism God comes to us in love. This love then changes our hearts, enabling and motivating us to love God. Baptism also changes our minds. Christ's righteousness is credited to us in Holy Baptism. We now can turn our attention to that righteousness and all else that is above in Christ (Colossians 2:12–13a; 3:1–2). Further, Baptism changes our behavior. In Baptism we become connected to the vine, that is Jesus Christ. As branches, we now live out that connection in acts of love and service (Colossians 3:5–17). At our Baptism we received the promise of forgiveness of sins, eternal life, and the gift of the Holy Spirit (Acts 2:38–39). In Hebrews 10:22–25, the author instructs:

> Let us draw near with a true heart in full assurance of faith, with our hearts sprinkled clean from an evil conscience and our bodies washed with pure water. Let us hold fast the confession of our hope without wavering, for He who promised is faithful. And let us consider how to stir up one another to love and good works, not neglecting to meet together, as is the habit of some, but encouraging one another, and all the more as you see the Day drawing near.

By meeting on a regular basis with fellow Christians in prayer, Bible study, and worship, we are enabled by God to remember with joy the promises we received in our Baptism.

One in Christ

"But you were washed, you were sanctified, you were justified in the name of the Lord Jesus Christ and by the Spirit of our God" (1 Corinthians 6:11). The Holy Spirit washed and sanctified us at our Baptism. The Holy Spirit created our new life in Christ and also sustains it. The Holy Spirit has promised to come to us regularly through God's Word and Sacrament. Therefore, regular contact with such Word and Sacrament provides us with the Holy Spirit's continued guidance.

A change of identity translates into a change in living. This does not always mean that we do new things. Sometimes it simply means that we do the same things better. For example, we may improve our relationships with our spouses or children, have a better attitude at work or school, and have a more intentional and sincere worship life.

Regular church attendance facilitates remembering our Baptism. Several parts of the Divine Service can help us personally remember our Baptism. The Invocation reminds us of God's presence in our lives. The Confession and Absolution remind us of the promise of forgiveness we received in Baptism. The reading of God's Word reminds us that the Word gives Baptism its power and promise. The Lord's Supper strengthens our faith given in the Sacrament of Baptism. The Benediction reminds us to live in the peace and joy of our baptismal promise.

Comparisons

Confirmation. Churches that baptize infants also practice confirmation (Eastern Orthodox, Lutheran, Roman Catholic, Reformed, and some Wesleyan churches). Confirmation instruction is a way of following the mandate of Jesus to both baptize and teach. The teaching has the goal of readying confirmands to confess the faith not by proxy—as with infant Baptism—but for themselves. Based on Matthew 10:32–33; 28:19–20, Lutheran children are expected to receive diligent instruction in the teachings of the Christian faith, leading to a public confession of Jesus Christ.

Point to Remember

Let us draw near with a true heart in full assurance of faith, with our hearts sprinkled clean from an evil conscience and our bodies washed with pure water. *Hebrews 10:22*

Lutheran Summary of Baptism

Augsburg Confession IX 1–2

Concerning Baptism, our churches teach that Baptism is necessary for salvation [Mark 16:16] and that God's grace is offered through Baptism [Titus 3:4–7]. They teach that children are to be baptized [Acts 2:38–39]. Being offered to God through Baptism, they are received into God's grace. (*Concordia*, p. 35)

Smalcald Articles III V

Baptism is nothing other than God's Word in the water, commanded by His institution. As Paul says, it is a "washing . . . with the word" [Ephesians 5:26]. As Augustine says, "When the Word is joined to the element or natural substance, it becomes a Sacrament." This is why we do not agree with Thomas Aquinas and the monastic preachers who forget the Word (God's institution). They say that God has imparted to the water a spiritual power, which through the water washes away sin. Nor do we agree with Scotus and the Barefooted Monks, who teach that Baptism washes away sins by the assistance of the divine will. They believe this washing occurs only through God's will, and not at all through the Word or water.

Of the Baptism of children, we hold that children should be baptized, for they belong to the promised redemption made through Christ [Acts 2:39]. Therefore, the Church should administer Baptism to them. (*Concordia*, p. 278)

Large Catechism IV 47–49, 52–53, 64–65

Here a question arises by which the devil, through his sects, confuses the world: Infant Baptism. Do children also believe? Are they rightly baptized? Briefly we say about this, let the simple dismiss this question from their minds. Refer it to the learned. But if you wish to answer, answer as follows:

The Baptism of infants is pleasing to Christ, as is proved well enough from His own work. For God sanctifies many of those who have been baptized as infants and has given them the Holy Spirit. There are still many people even today in whom we perceive that they have the Holy Spirit both because of their doctrine and life. It is also given to us by God's grace that we can explain the Scriptures and come to the knowledge of Christ, which is impossible without the Holy Spirit [1 Corinthians 12:3]. . . .

Further, we say that we are not very concerned to know whether the person baptized believes or not. For Baptism does not become invalid on that account. But everything depends on God's Word and command. Now this point is perhaps somewhat difficult. But it rests entirely on what I have said, that Baptism is nothing other than water and God's Word in and with each other [Ephesians 5:26]. That is, when the Word is added to the water, Baptism is valid, even though faith is lacking. For my faith does not make Baptism, but receives it. . . .

Lastly, we must also know what Baptism signifies and why God has ordained just this outward sign and ceremony for the Sacrament by which we are first received into the Christian Church. The act or ceremony is this: we are sunk under the water, which passes over us, and afterward are drawn out again. These two parts, (a) to be sunk under the water and (b) drawn out again, signify Baptism's power and work. It is nothing other than putting to death the old Adam and effecting the new man's resurrection after that [Romans 6:4–6]. Both of these things must take place in us all our lives. So a truly Christian life is nothing other than a daily Baptism, once begun and ever to be continued. For this must be done without ceasing, that we always keep purging away whatever belongs to the old Adam. Then what belongs to the new man may come forth. (cf. *Concordia*, pp. 428, 429–30)

TOPIC THIRTEEN

CONFESSION[1]

ENGAGING THIS TOPIC

"You Lutherans are just like the Roman Catholics."
"What? Why do you say that?"
"Your pastors wear robes, baptize babies, and even think they can forgive sins."
"Well, that's true. . . ."
"But when your pastors say in the worship service, 'I forgive you all your sins,' that's blasphemy! Only God can forgive sins."

"When I urge you to go to confession, I am simply urging you to be a Christian." This quote from Martin Luther's "Brief Exhortation to Confession" (*Concordia*, p. 653) is not merely a phrase exhorting pious practice. Nor is it an exaggeration. Confession and Christianity are indeed so intimately entwined that they could be used almost synonymously. For Lutherans, the practice of Confession and Absolution as revealed in Scripture stands at the heart of Christian faith and life. Christian confession is not simply a historic practice of the Church or a pious ritual; it is a profound summary of the whole Christian faith.

In Confession and Absolution, the two great emphases of Christianity—man as sinner and God, in Christ, as man's Savior—are brought sharply and unmistakably into focus. In Confession we humbly and sorrowfully admit all that we are: sinners in need of divine mercy. In Absolution, we receive that which God so earnestly desires to give: forgiveness, consolation, and the firm assurance that the death and resurrection of His only Son have overcome our sin.

Given the central place of Confession and Absolution in Christianity, it is not surprising that these practices also stood at the heart of the Reformation. As a young monk plagued by the knowledge of his own

1 This chapter adapted from *The Lutheran Difference: Confession*, written by Korey Maas. Copyright © 2001 Concordia Publishing House.

sinfulness, Martin Luther went to private confession. But Luther found that confession, as practiced by the church of his day, proved as burdensome to the conscience as did the sin for which he sought forgiveness! As a result, Luther turned to God's Word for help. And in God's Word he found the glorious and consoling truth: that forgiveness is a free, unconditional gift, won by Jesus Christ on the cross and freely bestowed in His name.

Luther and his fellow reformers unceasingly proclaimed this good news of forgiveness from the pulpit, in private confession, and even in the home. This good news of Absolution—forgiveness for the sake of and in the name of Christ—remains central to the faith and life of the Lutheran Church because when a person is urged to confess his sin and to be absolved, he is simply urged to be a Christian.

Lutheran Facts

The Lutheran emphasis on judging according to Scripture alone (*sola scriptura*) arose from opposition to the pope's granting of *indulgences*, certificates that offered forgiveness of sins in exchange for money. This practice originally allowed people to offer financial support to the Crusades. Later, indulgences helped to fund the building of cathedrals and monasteries, as well as to defray the costs of corrupt church officials.

Martin Luther saw this practice as unethical. He saw no basis in Scripture for the doctrine of purgatory and the granting of indulgences. In Scripture, Luther read how Jesus offers forgiveness freely. Luther's Ninety-five Theses spoke to this issue and sparked the Reformation.

Even as he rejected indulgences and purgatory, neither Luther nor the other reformers did away with private confession of sins and Absolution. In fact, the Augsburg Confession and its Apology both mention how Lutherans maintain this practice.

Repent!

> With a convulsive motion, he tore away the ministerial band from before his breast. It was revealed!
>
> —Nathaniel Hawthorne, *The Scarlet Letter*

Hawthorne's desperate character Rev. Dimmesdale spends his life hiding his sin of adultery. He abandons his love, Hester, to a life of shame while he pretends he has done nothing wrong. As a result, Dimmesdale dies young, revealing his sin only moments before his death.

"I'm sorry. I was wrong." We rarely enjoy speaking these words. Nobody likes to admit being wrong or doing wrong. Even when we know it's true, admitting blame and saying "I'm sorry" can humble us and make us feel uncomfortable. In fact, for some, confession means weakness. Saying "I'm sorry" means playing the sap.

We sometimes give excuses for not admitting a wrong or to get out of saying we are sorry. The admission of guilt or wrongdoing is difficult and so we avoid it because of pride, fear, or shame. Such feelings not only discourage us from admitting our faults to others, they can at times prevent us from honestly confessing our sin before God.

This is hardly new: "And the man and his wife were both naked and were not ashamed" (Genesis 2:25) leads to "But the Lord God called to the man and said to him, 'Where are you?' And he said, 'I heard the sound of You in the garden, and I was afraid, because I was naked, and I hid myself'" (Genesis 3:9–10). What made Adam go from not knowing or caring that he was naked to feeling shame in his nakedness? The answer is simple: sin. Our feelings of pride, fear, and shame not only prevent us from confessing our sins, they are themselves a result of sin and the sinfulness we have inherited from our first parents.

Living Repentance

John the Baptist prepared the way for Jesus' ministry of forgiveness (Matthew 3:1–12). John's central message can be summarized with the imperative "Repent!" As he prepared the way for the Lord, John preached repentance (v. 3), baptized for repentance (v. 11), and exhorted his audience to produce fruit in keeping with repentance (v. 8). Anticipating Jesus' declaration that the Son of Man did "not come to call the righteous but sinners" (Luke 5:32), John's ministry impressed upon people that they were indeed sinners and in need of repentance. Those who did not reject John's message willingly, repented and confessed their sins (v. 6).

What does Jesus Himself have to say about repentance? "From that time Jesus began to preach, saying, 'Repent, for the kingdom of heaven is at hand'" (Matthew 4:17). And from Luke 13: "Unless you repent, you will all likewise perish" (v. 5). Jesus begins His ministry with the theme previously proclaimed by John. Without mincing words, Jesus declares that repentance is a matter of life or death, a matter of heaven or hell! Or, put another way, repentance is a matter of Law and Gospel. Those who ignore the Law's call to repent will suffer the full penalty of the Law's condemnation. Those hearing the call to repent, however, find refuge from its accusation and condemnation in the Gospel's promise of forgiveness.

Both John the Baptist and Jesus speak with a sense of urgency. The opening chapters of Paul's letter to the church at Rome build one of Scripture's most damning arguments. Paul's discussion of man's sinfulness culminates in chapter three, where he concludes on the basis of many Old Testament passages that, without exception, all people are sinful. "None is righteous" (Romans 3:10), "all have turned aside" (v. 12), "no one does good" (v. 12). He further explains that we are in no position to change our sinful status. Attempts to "do good" or to follow the law are of no avail. On the contrary, Paul explains that "through the law comes knowledge of sin" (v. 20). Why is repentance such a pressing need? When we see that we have broken God's Law and we cannot make amends, repentance and God's mercy are our only refuge.

Although Scripture often emphasizes human sinfulness and demands repentance, it also assures us that those who confess their sin find mercy. In Proverbs we read: "Whoever conceals his transgressions will not prosper, but he who confesses and forsakes them will obtain mercy" (28:13). The words of the apostle John, which find familiar expression in the church's liturgy, are especially comforting: "If we confess our sin, He is faithful and just and will forgive us our sins and purify us from all unrighteousness" (1 John 1:8–9).

The Psalms make clear that people not only commit actual sins, but they are also burdened with the guilt of original sin. David confesses in Psalm 51 that, being sinful from conception, his sin is always before him. He also acknowledges in Psalm 19 that man's sinfulness is so great that many faults must remain hidden and indiscernible. That is, they remain hidden to those whose faults they are; God is, of course, aware of all our transgressions.

Just as Scripture notes different forms and forums for the confession of sin, Luther's Small Catechism (*Concordia*, p. 341) distinguishes between confession made before God and before one's pastor. In Psalm 32 David sings: "I will confess my transgressions to the LORD" (v. 5). The apostle James exhorts: "Confess your sins to one another" (5:16). And Luke records that many in the city of Ephesus confessed their sin openly and publicly before the church (Acts 19:18). God has not limited our opportunities for confession to particular times, places, or people.

Welcome Relief

Although confessing one's sins can be an uncomfortable experience, God does not intend it to be a burdensome task. Quite the opposite! Some people feel that confession provides relief because it allows us to "get things off our chest." While this reason is understandable, we must also recognize that unless someone else bears our sin, we are not rid of it. The Gospel proclaims that our sin has in fact been placed on someone else: Christ, who conquered sin on the cross. Knowing that Christ has borne our sins emboldens us to confess our faults. Confession provides welcome relief because with it comes Absolution—complete forgiveness.[2]

The Divine Service provides the opportunity for corporate and public confession of sin. This is beneficial, especially in the context of worship. As we come to worship, we enter the house of the almighty God. As we call on His name, we also realize that we are, on the basis of our own merits, entirely unworthy to stand in His presence. In fact the only thing we bring to God in worship is our sin. With such a realization comes the desire to confess our sin and to hear God's reassuring word of Absolution. We desire to hear that He Himself wants us as His forgiven children to worship in His presence. If the Divine Service includes the celebration of the Lord's Supper, we also take seriously Paul's admonition to examine ourselves before communing (1 Corinthians 11:28). Part of this examination includes recognizing and repenting of our sin.

Facing the Mirror

Just as a morning look in the mirror reveals our outward flaws, a look into God's Word reveals our flaws in thought, word, and deed. We may hate to say, "I was wrong," but God's Law shows just how wrong, how sinful, we are. The good news, however, is that God responds to our confession of "I was wrong" by declaring clearly and surely: "You are forgiven."

In his famous Ninety-five Theses, Martin Luther wrote, "When our Lord and Master Jesus Christ said, 'Repent' [Matt. 4:17], He willed the entire life of believers to be one of repentance" (AE 31:25).

Confession or repentance is to be part of daily Christian life. In the Lord's Prayer, we say, "Give us this day our daily bread, and forgive us our debts, as we also have forgiven our debtors" (Matthew 6:11–12). Although few will go to church or seek their pastor daily for Confession and Absolution, we can cultivate the habit of confession before God as part of our private devotion and prayer. One simple way of doing this includes reflecting on the Ten Commandments and their catechetical explanations. Likewise, recitation of the Lord's Prayer includes asking that God "forgive us our sins, as we forgive those who sin against us."

We can also daily express our thanks to God for hearing our confession and forgiving our sin. Our thanksgiving for forgiveness takes place

2 See "Brief Exhortation to Confession": *Concordia*, pp. 649–53.

as we remember the forgiveness Jesus won for us on the cross. In our Baptism, God washed away all guilt and punishment due for our transgressions. As forgiveness in the name of the triune God covers all sin, we also daily remember our Baptism and daily live our lives in the righteousness and purity God has granted. For this reason Luther's Small Catechism encourages Christians to make the sign of the holy cross and say, "In the name of God the Father, Son, and Holy Spirit" at morning and evening prayer (*Concordia*, p. 344). These words and sign remind us of our Baptism and the forgiveness and new life God gave us there. For this we offer our humble thanks and praise to God.

Comparisons

Penance: A sacrament for the Eastern Orthodox and Roman Catholics. When someone repents, he must feel sorrow for sin, confess, and perform certain works to amend his life ("make satisfaction" for Roman Catholics). The penitential system developed from the early Christian practice of counseling people after Confession and Absolution. For example, if a man stole a sheep, the pastor would counsel him to return the sheep.

Daily repentance: Lutherans teach that repentance is not an occasional action but should be part of daily Christian life and prayer. Worship usually begins with Confession and Absolution. Lutherans expect people to repent before receiving the Lord's Supper.

Crisis repentance: For many Protestants, repentance is something done once or only occasionally, when one experiences a spiritual crisis. During the religious revivals of the 1800s, many introduced the practice of an "altar call" by which people are encouraged to commit or recommit their lives to Christ.

Point to Remember

Give us this day our daily bread, and forgive us our debts, as we also have forgiven our debtors. *Matthew 6:11–12*

Absolution

Alone, alone, all, all alone,
Alone on a wide wide sea!
And never a saint took pity on
My soul in agony.
—Samuel Taylor Coleridge, *The Rime of the Ancient Mariner*

Coleridge's poem illustrates the incredible burden of loneliness caused by sin. The Mariner anguishes over his foolish error and has no one to comfort him. Instead, the eyes of his fallen companions hang open—and stare!

The "wages of sin" is not only death (Romans 6:23), but it also includes the death of relationships. Because of sin, marriage, parenthood, and friendship seem to face insurmountable obstacles. Personalities conflict, rebellion flares, motives become selfish, and feelings are frequently hurt. As witnesses to many of these struggles, marriage and family counselors note that healthy and lasting relationships develop best as people learn to practice forgiveness.

Forgiveness is essential even to *healthy* relationships. Since all people are sinners, we cannot have a healthy relationship without forgiveness. God frequently describes His relationship with His people in family terms. The Church is called the Bride of Christ. God's Word compares His love to the selfless love parents have for their children. Likewise, Scripture describes our response to God's love as that of unfaithful spouses or selfish and rebellious children. When we, by sinning, damage or reject the relationship God desires to have with us, there is only one remedy: the forgiveness won by His Son on the cross.

Sweet Forgiveness

In Mark 2:1–12, we read the story of Jesus healing the paralytic man. The teachers of the law were quite right to ask, "Who can forgive sins but God alone?" (v. 7). As teachers of the law, they knew what the Old Testament had to say regarding sin and forgiveness. They knew well the words David addressed to God: "Against You, You only, have I sinned" (Psalm 51:4). Sin is never merely a mistake. Nor is it ever simply a wrong done against one's neighbor. Sin is, in its essence, rebellion against the almighty God; it is the breaking of His holy and perfect Law. Therefore, forgiveness must come from the one who has been offended—God Himself. The teachers' mistake was not in believing that God alone can forgive sin, but in failing to recognize who it was that stood before them, saying, "Son, your sins are forgiven." They failed to realize what Jesus was in fact revealing to them: that

He is God Himself, God incarnate. And as God, He exercises His divine authority: "The Son of Man has authority on earth to forgive sins" (Mark 2:10).

The events of 2 Samuel 11–12 form the background against which David wrote Psalm 51. Chapter 11 describes David's sins of adultery and murder. In chapter 12, Nathan, a prophet sent by the Lord, confronts David with his crimes. Upon realizing the enormity of his sins and hearing the judgment pronounced upon him, David can only respond with the words, "I have sinned against the LORD" (2 Samuel 12:13). He offers no excuses. He does not attempt to shift the blame. Nor does he qualify his repentance in any way. He simply confesses. And Nathan, in response, pronounces God's forgiveness. He does not further chastise David for his sin. He does not pry into the motivation behind David's actions. Nor does he question David's sincerity. As the Lord's mouthpiece, Nathan announces the judgment of the Lord: "The LORD also has put away your sin" (v. 13).

In his memorable psalm of repentance, David pleads: "Have mercy on me, O God, according to Your steadfast love; according to Your abundant mercy" (51:1). David approaches God as a sinner. He makes no claims on God; he does not attempt to persuade the Lord of his worthiness. On the contrary, David appeals to the merciful, loving, and compassionate character of God Himself. He asks only that God act according to His nature—and forgive. Likewise, Daniel makes his appeal on the basis of God's merciful nature: "We do not present our pleas before You because of our righteousness, but because of Your great mercy" (Daniel 9:18). The psalmist and the prophet approach God knowing that God desires to forgive, not on the basis of one's merit but on the basis of His mercy. Daniel emphasizes this conviction by repeating the refrain: "For Your own sake, O Lord" (v. 17), "For Your own sake, O my God" (v. 19).

God's love and mercy are not abstract attributes. God is love in action. God's love manifests itself in real life and in real death. Paul dramatically stresses this point in his letter to the Romans: "God shows His love for us in that while we were still sinners, Christ died for us" (5:8). Paul highlights the magnitude of this divine love as he explains that very few would give their life even for a righteous or good man. And yet—mercy of mercies—God allowed His only Son to die for the ungodly, for those who remained mired in sin. Just as God demonstrates His love for our lives, so, too, does His sacrificial love transform the lives of His people. God did not demonstrate His love for sinners so that people might merely see or understand this love. The love made visible on the cross actually affects the relationship between God and His people. Through His act of mercy God justified us. God declares us innocent for Jesus' sake. The Lord no longer remembers the sin that separated us from Him. Paul goes on to state that with this declaration of innocence, God has reconciled us to Himself. Although our sinful rebellion once made us God's enemies, the blood of Christ has spared us God's wrath and brought us again into a loving relationship with Him.

So how do individuals receive Christ's forgiveness won on the cross? In recalling the story of Abraham, the apostle Paul directs his readers' attention to the all-important words "it was counted to him" (Romans 4:23). God credited righteousness to Abraham. Although Abraham honestly faced the fact that his body was "as good as dead," and that his wife Sarah's womb was also "dead," he believed that God would fulfill His promise to grant them children. "In hope he believed against hope" (v. 18). That is, Abraham had faith; he trusted the word of the Lord. And on the basis of this trust, God credited to him righteousness. But Paul's concern is not only with Abraham. He goes on to proclaim: "The words 'it was counted to him' were not written for his sake alone, but for ours also" (vv. 23–24). On account of our sin we honestly recognize that before God we are "as good as dead." We deserve death. But just as God credited righteousness to Abraham on account of his faith in the promise, so also God credits righteousness to those who believe the promise given with Christ: He "was delivered up for our trespasses and raised for our justification" (v. 25). This is God's gracious promise, that the death and resurrection of Christ took place for our justification, for our forgiveness. Although this death and resurrection occurred long ago, the benefits of that sacrifice are received through faith even today.

Abraham has sometimes been called the "father of faith." Many biblical authors use Abraham's great trust in the Lord as an example. The author of Hebrews repeats what Paul says about Abraham (Hebrews 6:13–20). But he also further explains the implications of God's promise to Abraham. He realizes that, even when God Himself makes a promise, believing that promise is not always easy. The Lord has therefore taken an oath by His promise, and "an oath is final for confirmation" (Hebrews 6:16). Since, as the author reminds us, it is impossible for God to lie, His promises cease all arguments and all doubts—"We have this [hope] as a sure and steadfast anchor of the soul" (v. 19).

The Heart of Christianity

A survey of high school and college students showed that the most recognizable example of Christianity was Nedward Flanders, a character in *The Simpsons* cartoon by Matt Groening. Whereas previous generations identified Christianity with missionary preachers such as Billy Graham, this generation has identified Christianity with a stereotype that is really a satire of Christian teaching and practice. This satire involves a basic misunderstanding of the Gospel and a superficial caricature of the "religious right." For example, as the story goes, Flanders was a wild, rebellious hippie whose parents were beatniks. After undergoing radical therapy he became incapable of expressing anger, went to Oral Roberts University, had a series of successful careers, and became a pillar of the community through selfless charity work. His Christianity embraces goodness and salvation, yet is focused on the perceived suppression of one's "true" nature under a veneer of morality, works-righteousness and its perceived good to society. This portrayal of Christianity includes a literalistic pickiness regarding doctrine and the Bible, and what secular culture would view as selective intolerance to homosexuality and non-Christian religions.

So how can we explain to someone what it means to be a Christian? Many in our society would describe Christians as people whose morality is defined by their actions: attending church, performing works of charity, or following Christ by trying to emulate His works (consider the "What Would Jesus Do" idea). The Christian certainly will take advantage of every opportunity to worship and to do good works in service to his neighbor. Likewise, the Christian most definitely wants to follow Christ. Yet these acts focus on what a human being does.

We cannot limit Christianity to good works because forgiveness and the means by which it was won—Jesus' sacrificial death on the cross—stand at the heart of Christianity. To our great relief, the Christian faith is first and foremost not about what we do, but about what God has done for us in the person and work of Christ. In contrast to popular, works-centered explanations of what it means to be a Christian, we point to Jesus when asked who we are. As Christians, we are those whom God bought by the blood of His only Son, Jesus Christ. We are those upon whom, in Baptism, Christ has put His name. We are those whom God has forgiven through faith in the sacrifice of Jesus on the cross.

Particular sins may often weigh heavily on our conscience. In such instances, the account of David's Confession and Absolution in 2 Samuel 12:1–15 proves especially comforting. David had committed adultery and murder. While we may never be convicted of such sins, neither should we take refuge in our little sins! In the eyes of God, sin is sin. Whether large or small, sin is an act of rebellion against His divine Law. And, acting as a mirror to reflect our sinfulness, this Law never ceases to accuse us. The circumstances of David's Confession and Absolution, however, may provide great comfort and consolation when our conscience condemns us. No matter how great our sin, God offers full and complete forgiveness. Like David, we hear from His called servant, "The Lord has put away your sin."

Times change. Styles change. People change. And not always for the better! But in the midst of an ever-changing world, Scripture assures us that God does not change. He remains ever merciful, ever compassionate, and ever willing to forgive us. His promises are sure; they do not expire and He does not revoke them. He invites us to come confidently before Him, seeking Absolution and requesting forgiveness "for Your own sake, O Lord."

Seriously and Sincerely

God takes our sin very seriously. We rejoice to be assured, however, that He takes our forgiveness just as seriously by sending His only Son to suffer sin's consequences and to win our forgiveness. This forgiveness forms the foundation for our intimate relationship with God.

Relationships built on love are strengthened as that love is continually expressed. Our relationship with God is founded on the forgiving love He so dramatically demonstrated on the cross of Calvary. Likewise, this relationship grows, matures, and is strengthened as we continue to hear God speak to us the good news of His forgiveness. We have regular opportunities to hear the Gospel through His Word spoken in Scripture, through His Word placed in the mouth of pastors and confessors, and in His Word attached to the physical elements of the Lord's Supper.

We are children who have been forgiven; the power of forgiveness can also affect our relationships with others. In the Lord's Prayer we pray that God would forgive our sins. We also ask that He might daily strengthen us to forgive those who sin against us. In this fallen world, we will lack opportunities to forgive those who have wronged or offended us. Strengthened by the Holy Spirit, we can love our neighbor as God has loved us. We can strengthen, repair, and renew strained or broken relationships by willingly forgiving and demonstrating our love for those who have hurt us.

Comparisons

Eastern Orthodox: To receive Absolution, one must be contrite, intend to amend one's life, and have faith in Christ's mercy. "Is there not besides these [fasting and prayer] a certain special mean used by holy Church for cleansing and giving peace to the conscience of the penitent? Such a mean is the *epitimia*, or penance. What is *epitimia*? The word means punishment." (*The Longer Catechism of the Eastern Church*, questions 355–56.)

Lutheran: God's Law causes a person to repent. Absolution, which is simply a declaration of forgiveness through Christ, takes away sin and consoles the repentant heart. As a result of God's forgiveness, Christians naturally amend their lives. Most worship services include public Absolution. Private Absolution is encouraged for those especially troubled by their sins.

Roman Catholic: To receive Absolution, one must be contrite, confess, and agree to make satisfaction. ". . . [W]e are able, through Christ Jesus, to make satisfaction to God the Father, not only by punishments voluntarily assumed by us for the punishment of sin, or imposed at the discretion of the priest in proportion to the transgression, but even (which is a great evidence of love) by temporal scourgings inflicted by God and patiently borne by us" (*Canons and Decrees of the Council of Trent*, Session 8, chapter IX; see also *Catechism of the Catholic Church* §§ 1459–60).

Reformed, Baptist, Anabaptist, and Wesleyan: Declaration of forgiveness through Absolution is not practiced. Confession is usually made to God directly but may include a public commitment as evidence of faith in God's forgiveness. (For example: "being deeply convinced of our guilt, danger, and helplessness, and of the way of salvation by Christ, we turn to God with unfeigned contrition, confession, and supplication for mercy . . ." [*New Hampshire Baptist Confession*, article 8].) Some churches emphasize discipline, under which a person expresses repentance before church leaders in order to be restored to communion.

Point to Remember

But God shows His love for us in that while we were still sinners, Christ died for us. *Romans 5:8*

Keys of the Kingdom

Go in; and tell my lady I am gone,
Having displeas'd my father, to Lawrence' cell
To make confession, and to be absolv'd.
—Shakespeare, *Romeo and Juliet*

The romance of Romeo and Juliet revolves around the "cell" of Father Lawrence, who hears their confessions and forgives their sins. The couple comes to a tragic end only after they are cut off from Father Lawrence's help and cannot heed his counsel. Rather than "love moderately," as Lawrence encourages, they love "like fire and powder, which as they kiss consume."

The Keys of the kingdom of heaven, which Father Lawrence applied in his cell, set God's people free from sin. But they also bind us to one another. We are baptized by another's hand, we receive the Lord's Supper in the communion of saints, we hear Absolution from our pastor's lips. The Office of the Keys, or the authority to forgive and retain sins, serves as *the* key to Christian life.

God's Gift

Amid all the confusion about who Jesus is and what He had come to do, Peter confesses his belief that Jesus is the Christ, the Son of God (Matthew 16:16). That is, Jesus is the fulfillment of God's promise of a Savior. Upon hearing this confession, Jesus responds, "I will give you the keys of the kingdom of heaven" (v. 19). Jesus explains that the Keys are for binding and loosing (v. 19; see also Matthew 18:18). In the more familiar language of John 20:21–23, Jesus explains that loosing and binding mean forgiving or not forgiving sins. The clear implication is that entrance into the kingdom of heaven is a matter of one's sins being loosed, that is, forgiven or absolved.

In Matthew 16, Jesus promised that He would give the Keys of the kingdom to Peter. Parallel passages make clear, however, that Jesus gave the Keys to others as well. The promise of Matthew 16 ("I will give . . .") is fulfilled in the post-resurrection story of John 20. Here Jesus speaks not only to Peter but also to the other disciples. Bestowing on them the Holy Spirit, He declares, "If you [plural] forgive the sins of any, they are forgiven them" (John 20:23). With this gift of the Spirit, the disciples are empowered to announce the forgiveness of sins won by Christ's death and resurrection. A more literal translation of verse 23 ("Those whose sins you forgive have already been forgiven.") emphasizes that this forgiveness has already been effected by Christ's atoning work. It is an objective fact, which the disciples are to announce, preach, and proclaim. The context of Matthew 18 also makes clear that the Keys are given not to Peter alone, but as a gift to the Church. Jesus here explains to His disciples how sin is to be confronted in the Church and by the Church. He repeats that which He had earlier stated: "Truly, I say to you [plural], whatever you [plural] bind on earth shall be bound in heaven, and whatever you [plural] loose on earth shall be loosed in heaven." It is also noteworthy that, in the four Gospels, only Matthew uses the word *church*. More significantly, he does so in only two locations, both involving the discussion of the power of the Keys to bind and loose sin (16:18; 18:17). The Keys are for the Church!

First Corinthians helps us understand the special role of pastors. Members of the Corinthian congregation were divided by issues relating to those who served as their pastors (1:11–12; 3:3–5). Some claimed to follow the apostle Paul, who had founded the church at Corinth (Acts 18:1–11). Others claimed to follow Apollos, Paul's successor there (Acts 18:24–19:1). Paul condemns such divisions, emphasizing that in their pastoral roles both he and Apollos are to be regarded as "servants of Christ and stewards of the mysteries of God" (1 Corinthians 4:1) or, in the King James translation, "ministers of Christ, and stewards of the mysteries of God."

Although the Keys have been given to the whole Christian Church, their public use has been entrusted to specific individuals. The term *steward*, as used elsewhere in Scripture, means one who acts as a manager or trustee (cf. Luke 12:42; Galatians 4:2). That with which he is entrusted is not his own but belongs to someone else. Likewise, that with which he is entrusted is not for his use alone, but it is to be administered for the sake of others. The reference to ministers as stewards highlights Paul's claim that the "mysteries" belong to God; the minister of Christ does not act on his own authority or for his own sake, but he acts on behalf of Christ and for the sake of the Church.

In Ephesians 3:2–12, Paul speaks a great deal about "the mystery." As a steward of God's mysteries, Paul also refers to his task as that of an administrator. For the sake of the Church he was to carry out "the plan of the mystery" (v. 9), "the stewardship of God's grace" (v. 2). Paul also explains the content of this gracious mystery: "This mystery is that the Gentiles are fellow heirs, members of the same body, and partakers of the promise in Christ Jesus through the gospel" (v. 6). The mystery that was entrusted to Paul is the Gospel itself (Ephesians 6:19). It is the Good News of Christ's promise, His grace, and His unsearchable riches, which are for all people.

In Colossians 2:2–3 and 1 Timothy 3:16, Paul again talks about the great "mystery." Not only does Paul explain that the mystery of God is the Good News of Jesus Christ, but he goes on to state that this mystery is Christ Himself. His incarnation, death, and resurrection are the foundation upon which the mystery of forgiveness rests. Jesus is not merely the subject of the Good News—He *is* the Good News! When forgiveness is proclaimed, Christ Himself is proclaimed, and vice versa. Paul expresses this very thought when he famously declares: "We preach Christ crucified" (1 Corinthians 1:23). Such is a fitting motto for those entrusted with the mysteries of God and the administration of the Keys of the kingdom of heaven.

Upon appointing and sending out preachers to proclaim the kingdom of God, Jesus assures them that they speak with His authority: "The one who hears you hears Me" (Luke 10:16). In matters pertaining to the kingdom of heaven, the Lord removes all doubt and uncertainty. Those whom He has called and sent to speak His Word can do so with confidence. Likewise, those who hear the Word of God spoken by those called and sent can do so with certainty. To prevent all doubt of the promise and power of the Keys, the Lutheran Confessions frequently emphasize the truth found in Luke 10: "Our people are taught that they should highly prize the Absolution as being God's voice and pronounced by God's command" (AC XXV 3; *Concordia*, p. 50).

Speak for God

The complaint is often heard that Christians presume to "speak for God." It would certainly be unwise (and untrue!) to state that Christians always and everywhere speak for God. There are many topics on which God has chosen to remain silent. Where God has not clearly revealed His will in Scripture, the Christian will not presume to guess His mind or to speak in His stead. But the Lord has clearly and unmistakably revealed His desire for people's forgiveness. In the same manner He has revealed His desire that we proclaim to others the forgiveness won by Christ on the cross. When we do so, we need have no doubt that we are speaking for the God who assures us that "the one who hears you hears Me" (Luke 10:16).

Christ has given His Keys to the Church as a gift. Whether it be a child's first bicycle or a wife's diamond earrings, good gifts evoke thanksgiving. And those who give such gifts delight to see them used and enjoyed. So it is with the Keys of the kingdom of God. God delights to provide His forgiveness and we are eager to receive it. Our thanksgiving for such a gracious gift expresses itself in prayer, praise, and—perhaps most important—in our frequent return to receive the benefits provided through the Office of the Keys.

With the Office of the Keys, as with all of God's promises, we can be confident that He does not lie; His promise will be kept. This is particularly comforting when the promise is that of Absolution. When we hear the words "In the stead and by the command of my Lord Jesus Christ I forgive you all your sins," we can take comfort, knowing that this forgiveness is indeed spoken in Christ's stead and by His command. The pastor does not merely announce that he absolves us, He proclaims that God in heaven has forgiven our sin. Our Lord's own promise assures us that this proclamation is true.

The Office of the Keys

Forgiveness is a gift that we always need. So that we might never be confused or in doubt about where to find this gift, Christ assures us that He has located it in a specific place. We can be certain that Christ's own Absolution is found in the Church, in the Office of the Keys exercised by called pastors.

Knowing that Christ has located the Keys in His Church, what practical advice can we give to a person (even ourselves!) who sometimes questions whether he or she is truly forgiven? Almost without fail, biographies of Martin Luther explain that his "road to Reformation" began with the pressing question of how he might find a gracious God. The confessional practice in Luther's day demanded lengthy and explicit enumeration of sins. How could he be sure he had not forgotten some? How could he be sure that he was truly sorry for those he had remembered? Luther's study of Scripture eventually led him to the comforting realization that God's forgiveness does not depend on the accuracy of one's memory or a measurable amount of sorrow. It does not depend on anything within us. It is found outside of us; it rests solely on God's Word and God's promise. The fulfillment of that promise is announced in the words of Absolution. If and when we are tempted to question our forgiveness, we need not wonder where to go for assurance. We can look for comfort to those in the Church who have been charged with the exercise of the Keys, those called and placed in office for the very purpose of proclaiming Christ's forgiveness.

The "stewards of the mysteries of God" perform a needful but often thankless task. Preaching, Absolution, the distribution of the Sacraments—these applications of the Gospel stand at the heart of the Christian Church. Together with them God has also instituted an office for their administration in the Church. But the men called into this office remain men. They are subject to the same temptations, frustrations, and shortcomings we all face. We who benefit from the mysteries of which they are stewards can do much to encourage them in their work with simple words of thanks and appreciation. Words of encouragement, prayers for health and faithfulness, along with prayers of thanksgiving, will certainly be appreciated.

Comparisons

Eastern Orthodox: Christ gave the Keys to the apostles. This authority is now exercised by bishops.

Lutheran: Christ gave the Keys to the Church. Pastors exercise the Office of the Keys publicly. Christ also calls Christians to forgive one another personally and privately.

Reformed: Episcopalians and some Reformed teach that Christ gave the Keys to the apostles. This authority is now exercised by bishops/clergy. Other Reformed hold that Christ gave the Keys to the Church.

Roman Catholic: Christ gave the Keys to Peter, the first pope; therefore, the papacy holds the authority to forgive sins on Christ's behalf. Priests exercise this authority locally. Cf. CCC2 paras. 551–53.

Anabaptist: Christ gave the Keys to ministers and all those anointed with the Spirit.

Baptist: Christ gave the Keys to the Church. The Church calls pastors and preachers to exercise that authority by proclaiming the Gospel.

Wesleyan: John Wesley believed that Christ gave the Keys to the apostles. The Wesleyan tradition is divided over who holds the Keys today: bishops, clergy, or all Christians.

Point to Remember

> If your brother sins against you, go and tell him his fault, between you and him alone. If he listens to you, you have gained your brother. *Matthew 18:15*

Not Guilty

> Always acknowledge a fault frankly. This will throw those in authority off their guard and give you an opportunity to commit more.
> —Mark Twain

Despite Mark Twain's advice, every year thousands of defendants plead "Not guilty." Their claim of innocence creates high drama. Crucial evidence is weighed, emotional testimony is heard, passionate arguments are presented. The tension builds to a climactic conclusion: a verdict is announced by those vested with the authority do so. Only then does the tension finally dissolve in audible sighs, cheers, or tears of joy.

As TV ratings attest, audiences find courtroom dramas very appealing. And in real life, the judge's vocation is given high honor and respect. Why does the courtroom hold such fascination for audiences? Is it simply the appeal of well-scripted Hollywood fiction, or is there a certain drama inherent in all decisions of guilt and innocence? Perhaps much of the appealing tension—on the big screen and in real life—is the result of our inability to know, until announced, what the judge's final verdict will be. The Bible makes frequent use of courtroom metaphors as it outlines the divine drama of salvation. Think of the familiar scriptural terms such as *law*, *witness*, *testimony*, *righteousness*, and *justification*. In this biblical drama, God Himself is the judge; His verdict is final. But in the daily drama of our own lives, in our continual struggles with guilt, we need never be anxious about what God's final verdict will be. On the cross, His Son suffered so that we might be declared "not guilty." And this heavenly judge has authorized and exhorted Christians to announce to one another the good news of this verdict.

Private Confession

Although we are assured that God Himself hears our confession and forgives us, Scripture also exhorts Christians to practice confession of another sort. In Matthew 18:15, Jesus tells those listening to His parable: "If your brother sins against you, go and tell him his fault, between you and him alone. If he listens to you, you have gained your brother." And James tells his readers: "Therefore, confess your sins to one another and pray for one another, that you may be healed. The prayer of a righteous person has great power as it is working" (5:16). In the Matthew passage, Jesus gives His disciples instructions regarding the proper manner in which the Church is to deal with those who have committed known sins. Before anything else is done, one is to be shown his fault "between you and him alone." Likewise, James encourages those burdened with their own transgressions to "confess your sins to one another." Such passages make clear that Confession and Absolution is not only a private matter between an individual and God, or a public matter as in corporate worship, but that all Christians are exhorted to confess to one another and to be willing to forgive one another. On the basis of Matthew 18, Luther's Large Catechism emphasizes the same.[3]

Scripture also provides examples of this type of Confession and Absolution. Think back to our earlier discussion of David's confession of adultery and murder to Nathan in 2 Samuel 12:1–14. Nathan's confrontation of David fittingly illustrates the principle expounded by Jesus in Matthew 18. David, privately confronted with his crimes, confesses to and is absolved by the prophet Nathan. Likewise, the well-known parable of Luke 15 depicts the prodigal son confessing his fault to his father. Although the father does not explicitly announce forgiveness, he calls the prodigal his son and announces that he is alive again.

3 See "Brief Exhortation to Confession" 13–14; *Concordia*, p. 651.

An excellent example of sinful nature—and our need for Confession and Absolution—is found in Romans 7:15–25. Paul's complaint here is that of every Christian: "I do not understand my own actions. . . . For I know that nothing good dwells in me, that is, in my flesh. For I have the desire to do what is right, but not the ability to carry it out" (vv. 15, 18). Even this great evangelist of the apostolic church and author of nearly half of the New Testament laments that he remains tormented by sin and his inability to control it. He knows God's Law and delights in it. He desires to do what is good. But he cannot; rather, he does precisely that which he hates to do. He confesses that he is, in effect, a prisoner of his own sinful nature and trapped in a body of death. In such dire straits he can only confess his great need of rescue.

Certainty of forgiveness is received only from God's Word. Psalm 119 can be read as a devotion concerning God's Word. As a pious and well-educated Israelite, the apostle Paul certainly knew the Word of God as revealed in the Old Testament. While lamenting his sinful nature he may also have taken comfort in reading or remembering Psalm 119. Here the psalmist, too, confesses that his soul "clings to the dust" (v. 25) and "melts away for sorrow" (v. 28), asking God to "give me life according to Your word" (v. 25) and to "strengthen me according to Your word" (v. 28). The psalmist's confidence that the Lord will indeed do so is evident as he declares: "This is my comfort in my affliction, that Your promise gives me life" (v. 50). With God's Word comes life, salvation, strength, and hope. In this promising Word the psalmist puts his trust (v. 42). The author of Psalm 119 had good reason to put his trust in the Word of the Lord. It is, as noted elsewhere in Scripture, "living and active" (Hebrews 4:12). God's Word, similar to that of a judge in his courtroom, has an active power; it does what it says and accomplishes its purpose. This the Lord Himself declares in Isaiah: "[My word] shall not return to Me empty, but it shall accomplish that which I purpose, and shall succeed in the thing for which I sent it" (55:11). What the Lord most ardently desires is the faith and salvation of His people. For this reason He also promises that "everyone who calls on the name of the LORD shall be saved" (Joel 2:32).

Faith in God's forgiveness is faith in His word and promise. But from where does this faith come? By what means is it received? In the New Testament Paul repeats this promise (Romans 10:13–17), but at the same time notes that one cannot call on someone in whom he has not believed. And there can be no believing without first hearing. Nor can there be hearing without preaching, or preaching without those who have been sent to do so. Paul urgently commends the preaching of the Word of Christ because from this Word alone comes saving faith. For the same reason, the Lutheran Confessions uphold the necessity of proclaiming and hearing this external word: "We must constantly maintain this point: God does not want to deal with us in any other way than though the spoken Word and the Sacraments" (SA III VIII 10; *Concordia*, p. 281).

Those who have been called and sent to proclaim God's word of forgiveness are given various titles and responsibilities. In the Book of Acts, Paul charges the overseers of the church in Ephesus to keep watch over their flock, acting as shepherds of the church of God (20:28). Writing later to the Ephesian church, he also refers to apostles, prophets, evangelists, and those who are pastors and teachers. These, he also notes, have been given this ministry by Christ Himself (4:11–13). While the devil and our own sinful nature attempt to distract, tear down, and divide the church of God, pastors and overseers are charged with the task of preparing, building up, and uniting the church in faith and knowledge of the Son of God. Such are the effects of the Gospel, the word of Absolution they have been called and sent to proclaim.

In what are known as the "Pastoral Epistles," Paul writes to Timothy and Titus, young pastors who have been sent to proclaim the Word of God in their respective churches. In addition to encouraging them to remain faithful ministers of the Gospel, he also describes the qualifications for those in their positions. Overseers must be, among other things, blameless and above reproach, self-controlled, disciplined, and gentle. Such qualifications are particularly important for those entrusted with God's Word and work. In the context of hearing confession, it is especially important that a pastor be self-controlled and disciplined so that he might not presume to speak anything other than that which God, in His Word, has given him to speak. Likewise, gentleness will be appreciated by those seeking comfort and consolation (1 Timothy 3:1–7; Titus 1:7–9).

Counsel and Consolation

Paul's complaint in Romans 7 says a great deal about our need for frequent Confession and Absolution. Paul's great distress serves to confirm the fact that all are sinful and—to use his own word—wretched beings. On the one hand, it is perhaps comforting to know that our experiences are not ours alone, that even such devout Christians as the apostle Paul continually struggled with sin. On the other hand, we may be led to ask, "If even Paul was such a great sinner, how much more so must I be?" More important than the sin shared by Paul and all Christians, however, are Christ and His Word, the means by which all sin is forgiven. As Christ and His Word of forgiveness are most clearly and concisely proclaimed in Confession and Absolution, Luther was led to write in his "Brief Exhortation to Confession" that "he who feels his misery and need will no doubt develop such a longing for [confession] that he will run toward it with joy." Recognizing the depths of human misery and need, Luther also went on to warn: "But those who pay no attention to it and do not come of their own accord, we let go their way. Let them be sure of this, however, that we do not regard them as Christians" (*Concordia*, p. 652).

James 5:16 is worth repeating here: "Therefore, confess your sins to one another and pray for one another, that you may be healed. The prayer of a righteous person has great power as it is working." Although Scripture nowhere commands private confession to a pastor, we can receive benefits by confessing to, and being absolved by, one called and placed into the office of the pastoral ministry. We've all experienced the frustration of being transferred from one telephone extension to another—and another and another—each time being told that the person who could help us just stepped away from his or her desk. In an age of increasingly narrow job descriptions, it is often difficult to locate the specific person charged with the particular task we need fulfilled. When that which we need fulfilled so desperately is the promise of God's own forgiveness, it would indeed be taxing if we did not know to whom we could go. We have been assured, however, that Christ Himself has called and sent people for this particular purpose. Coming for confession to the pastors placed in our midst, we need have no doubt about their divinely instituted authority to proclaim Absolution. This assurance is also highlighted in the Lutheran Confessions (see AC XXV; *Concordia*, p. 50).

In light of the biblical qualifications for those placed into the pastoral office, we can trust that a pastor will be self-controlled and disciplined, neither intentionally nor accidentally revealing to others what has been privately confessed. To be blameless and above reproach certainly implies keeping in confidence that which has been confessed.

Good News Indeed

To someone on trial, few words are sweeter than "Not guilty." With those two words, spoken audibly by a judge or jury, all accusations are swept away. In their place are given joy, relief, and the freedom to begin life anew. Good news indeed!

How are we to respond to someone who asks to be forgiven for a sin he or she has committed against us? How do we respond to someone asking forgiveness for some sin not committed against us personally? Having been forgiven, we will not hesitate to forgive others. To be sure, this is often difficult, especially if a person's sin has directly affected or offended us. In such instances it may be helpful to remember that we do not speak our own words, but we announce what God has already declared to be true.

It may occur that we are even sought out to console those who have not sinned against us personally. In these cases it will be our strong desire to assure them with clear passages of Scripture that God remembers their sin no more.

Both the Small Catechism (*Concordia*, p. 342) and *Lutheran Service Book* (pp. 292–93) contain short orders for individual Confession and Absolution. But few Lutheran congregations today encourage the regular practice of private Confession and Absolution. In most cases this practice has been replaced by counseling. Although pastoral counseling is a worthy practice, the Lutheran Confessions also state that private Absolution "should not be despised, but greatly and highly esteemed, along with all other offices of the Christian Church" (SA III VIII 2; *Concordia* p. 280; see also AC XI; *Concordia*, pp. 35–36). With that in mind, we might begin again to take advantage of the services for Confession and Absolution found in the church's catechetical and worship material. When in need of consolation, we may ask our pastor to use the order of Individual Confession and Absolution found in *Lutheran Service Book*. The brief order found in Luther's Small Catechism may also find appropriate use in the home, where offenses and the need for reconciliation are certainly not absent.

Comparisons

Private confession and counseling: Eastern Orthodox, Lutherans, and Roman Catholics practice private Confession and Absolution. They also offer pastoral counseling. All conversations are kept strictly confidential. By law, clergy cannot be forced to say what they have heard in private confession. Roman Catholics require private confession at least once a year, usually starting when someone prepares for first Communion. Lutherans do not set rules about how often someone should come to private confession nor do they expect enumeration of all sins. People should confess the sins that trouble them most.

Counseling: Reformed, Anabaptists, Baptists, and Wesleyans offer pastoral counseling but do not pronounce Absolution.

Point to Remember

> Therefore, confess your sins to one another and pray for one another, that you may be healed. The prayer of a righteous person has great power as it is working. *James 5:16*

The Kindest Way to Handle Accusations

As noted on p. 381, Christians are still sinners in need of daily repentance. In any community or gathering of Christians, things are bound to go wrong at some point. As a result, one Christian might make accusations against another Christian; one Christian might hear an accusation made against another Christian. When you hear an accusation, what should you do?

Maintain perspective. Perhaps the first thing to recall is that an accusation is not evidence that someone is guilty. For example, our Lord Jesus was frequently accused in a variety of ways. He was called a glutton and a drunkard (Matthew 11:19); a friend of tax collectors and sinners (Matthew 11:19); a man acting without authority (Matthew 21:23); one plotting to destroy the temple (Matthew 26:61); a blasphemer (Matthew 26:65); a breaker of the Sabbath (Luke 13:14); a false prophet (Luke 22:64); one interfering with paying taxes, who claimed to be a king (Luke 23:2); an insurrectionist (Luke 23:5); a false Christ (Luke 23:35, 39); an illegitimate son (John 8:41); a demoniac (John 8:48); and disrespectful (John 18:22). Despite all these accusations, Jesus' enemies found it difficult to charge Him at His trial (Matthew 26:59–60; Mark 14:55–59). Scripture likewise clearly testifies that Jesus had done nothing wrong (Luke 23:39–41); He was without sin (2 Corinthians 5:21; Hebrews 4:15; 1 Peter 2:22; 1 John 3:5). If the sinless Lord Jesus did not escape accusation, we should not be surprised to find our fellow Christians accused on occasion, and we should not rush to condemn them.

Consider the motive of the accuser. Perhaps ask yourself, "Does the accuser have something to gain by speaking ill of someone else?" (cf. Proverbs 6:16–19; 12:6; 24:28–29). "Why is the accuser telling this to me? Am I in a position of authority that allows or requires me to do something about this concern?" If you don't have such authority, be doubly wary about supposing the accusation is true since you probably should not have heard it in the first place.

Consider the circumstances. Since a person's reputation is precious and difficult to restore if damaged (Proverbs 22:1), consider whether there is a kinder way to explain what has happened. Don't assume the worst. Jesus teaches us not to rush to condemn (Matthew 7:1), which may result in others condemning us (Matthew 7:2–5). Often an accusation is based on misunderstanding or lack of empathy (Joshua 22:10–34).

Avoid spreading rumors, gossip, or slander. If you hear an accusation against someone, you may feel tempted to discuss it with others, saying something such as, "I heard this. Have you heard anything?" Spreading an accusation is sin, which is persistently rebuked in Scripture along with other vices (Leviticus 19:16; Psalm 101:5; 140:11; Proverbs 10:18; 11:13; 20:19; 30:10; Jeremiah 6:28; 9:4; Matthew 15:19; Mark 7:22; Romans 1:29–30; 2 Corinthians 12:20; Ephesians 4:31; Colossians 3:8; 2 Thessalonians 3:11–12 ["busybodies"]; 1 Timothy 3:11; 5:13; 6:4; 2 Timothy 3:3; 1 Peter 2:1). In biblical practice, a false witness receives the punishment that the person he accuses would receive if judged guilty (Deuteronomy 19:18–20)! This illustrates seriousness of false accusations. You may want to remind the accuser of this biblical standard to discern whether he is exercising appropriate caution in what he is saying about someone else.

Establish the facts. If you are in a position of authority that requires you to consider the accusation, the truthfulness of an accusation must be established on solid evidence. A common biblical standard of evidence is that two or three witnesses must agree independently on what happened (Deuteronomy 17:6–7; 19:15–21; 1 Timothy 5:19–20; cf. Matthew 18:19–20). One witness, or conflicting witnesses, do not offer enough evidence for concluding that someone has sinned. Note also that witnesses are not always able to discern a person's motives (Joshua 22:10–34), which is why it is so important to speak directly and clearly with the person accused, as Jesus taught (Matthew 5:23–24; 18:15).

Seek to restore your brother or sister. In Matthew 18:15–20, Jesus carefully outlined a process for restoring those who have sinned (cf. Luke 17:3–4; 2 Thessalonians 3:14–15), which is rooted in the Old Testament standards of evidence found in Deuteronomy 19. It involves speaking to a person privately first (v. 15); speaking to him before witnesses, if necessary (v. 16); and confronting him publicly before the church only as a last resort (v. 17). In cases where a sin has taken place publicly, an authority may rebuke the person publicly without first doing so privately (e.g., Galatians 2:11–14). Nevertheless, to proceed privately first is the best way.

Cover your brother's sin. When a brother repents, do not punish him by making his mistakes known to others. "Love covers a multitude of sins" (1 Peter 4:8; cf. Proverbs 10:12; 1 Corinthians 13:7). This does not mean a cover-up, allowing the person to remain sinning, but an effort to maintain and restore his reputation.

In Luther's explanation of the Eighth Commandment, he provided some general advice on this issue, which has become proverbial among Lutherans. He wrote, "Defend [your neighbor], speak well of him, and explain everything in the kindest way." In other words, don't immediately assume that your neighbor is guilty of an accusation. Recognize that there is often a better explanation for what has happened or that some circumstances require patience and care.

Lutheran Summary of Confession

Augsburg Confession XI 1–2

Our churches teach that private Absolution should be retained in the churches, although listing all sins is not necessary for Confession. For according to the Psalm, it is impossible. "Who can discern his errors?" (Psalm 19:12). (*Concordia*, pp. 35, 37)

Augsburg Confession XII 1–10

Our churches teach that there is forgiveness of sins for those who have fallen after Baptism whenever they are converted. The Church ought to impart Absolution to those who return to repentance [Jeremiah 3:12]. Now, strictly speaking, repentance consists of two parts. One part is contrition, that is, terrors striking the conscience through the knowledge of sin. The other part is faith, which is born of the Gospel [Romans 10:17] or the Absolution and believes that for Christ's sake, sins are forgiven. It comforts the conscience and delivers it from terror. Then good works are bound to follow, which are the fruit of repentance [Galatians 5:22–23].

Our churches condemn the Anabaptists, who deny that those who have once been justified can lose the Holy Spirit. They also condemn those who argue that some may reach such a state of perfection in this life that they cannot sin.

The Novatians also are condemned, who would not absolve those who had fallen after Baptism, though they returned to repentance.

Our churches also reject those who do not teach that forgiveness of sins comes through faith, but command us to merit grace through satisfactions of our own. (*Concordia*, p. 38)

Smalcald Articles III VII 1–3

The Keys are an office and power given by Christ to the Church for binding and loosing sin [Matthew 16:19]. This applies not only to gross and well-known sins, but also the subtle, hidden sins that are known only to God. As it is written, "Who can discern his errors?" (Psalm 19:12). And St. Paul himself complains that "with the flesh I serve the law of sin" (Romans 7:25). It is not in our power to judge which, how great, and how many the sins are. This belongs to God alone. As it is written, "Enter not into judgment with Your servant, for no one living is righteous before You" (Psalm 143:2). Paul says, "I am not aware of anything against myself, but I am not thereby acquitted" (1 Corinthians 4:4). (*Concordia*, p. 279)

Smalcald Articles III VIII 1–2

Absolution, or the Power of the Keys, is an aid against sin and a consolation for a bad conscience; it is ordained by Christ in the Gospel [Matthew 16:19]. Therefore, Confession and Absolution should by no means be abolished in the Church. This is especially for the sake of timid consciences and untrained young people, so they may be examined and instructed in Christian doctrine.

But the listing of sins should be free to everyone, as to what a person wishes to list or not to list. For as long as we are in the flesh, we will not lie when we say, "I am a poor man, full of sin"; "I see in my members another law"; and such (Romans 7:23). Since private Absolution originates in the Office of the Keys, it should not be despised, but greatly and highly esteemed, along with all other offices of the Christian Church. (*Concordia*, p. 280)

TOPIC FOURTEEN

The Lord's Supper[1]

Engaging This Topic

"You believe *what* about the Lord's Supper?"
"I know. It's hard to explain. But that's what Jesus says."
"Oh, come on! That's just *your* interpretation."

Lutherans, like all Christians, believe in celebrating the Lord's Supper. Jesus' words—which consecrate the Lord's Supper—stir the deepest devotion in Lutheran hearts. This is because His words promise forgiveness, which Lutherans regard as the central blessing of the Christian faith.

To understand Lutheran attitudes about the Lord's Supper more thoroughly, we have to understand what Lutherans have experienced because of their beliefs.

Excommunicated by the Pope (1521)

On January 3, 1521, Pope Leo X issued a letter stating that Dr. Martin Luther could not receive the Lord's Supper, damning him to hell, and calling on public officials to capture him so that he could be burned at the stake. These condemnations also applied to those who agreed with Luther's teachings (namely, Lutherans).

Persecution greatly influenced the attitudes of early Lutherans. For example, from the beginning of the Reformation to 1600, the Spanish Inquisition punished 1,995 people for Lutheranism. Many were burned at the stake. Also, in the early 1600s, Holy Roman Emperor Ferdinand II began a vicious persecution of Protestants, which led to the Thirty Years' War. During the conflict, one-third of the German population died.

1 This chapter adapted from *The Lutheran Difference: The Lord's Supper*, written by Gregory Seltz. Copyright © 2002 Concordia Publishing House.

Covert Calvinists (1573)

After Luther's death in 1546, his close friend and colleague Philip Melanchthon wavered in his beliefs. Melanchthon wanted to create better relations with the Roman Catholics and the Swiss Reformed. He often left many people confused about Lutheran teaching, especially about the Lord's Supper.

Calvinists (Reformed) secretly worked their way into teaching positions in Saxony. All the while affirming that they were Lutherans, they convinced August, the elector, to depose genuine Lutherans and appoint Calvinists instead. More than one hundred Lutheran pastors and teachers were deposed or banished. The Calvinists felt so confident in their deception that they published an anonymous tract attacking Luther's teaching about the Lord's Supper.

Then the Calvinists made a mistake. A Wittenberg professor, Caspar Peucer, wrote to a Calvinist friend who was a court preacher in Dresden. He addressed the letter to the court preacher's wife so that no one would suspect him of organizing the Calvinists. By mistake, the letter was delivered to the wife of a different court preacher! When she opened the letter and saw that it was in Latin, she gave it to her husband. He immediately recognized its importance and gave it to Elector August.

In the letter, Peucer asked the court preacher to deliver a Calvinist prayer book into the hands of Anna, the elector's wife. He wrote: "If first we have Mother Anna on our side, there will be no difficulty in winning his Lordship [Elector August] too." Outraged, Elector August imprisoned Peucer for his deception and halted the Calvinist plot to take over his territory. He funded the publication of the Lutheran *Formula of Concord* and insisted that all Lutheran pastors and teachers publicly subscribe to its teaching. Not surprisingly, the deceptive efforts of the Reformed created lasting mistrust.

The *Agende* Controversy (1830s)

Relations with the Reformed grew still worse when the king of Prussia decided to unite the Protestant churches in his realm. Frederick William III had led the German states in the fight against Napoleon. After the war, he wanted to create the strongest nation possible by uniting all the churches. However, some of the churches in his territory were Reformed while others were Lutheran.

To support his union effort, Frederick created his own "agende," or book of worship services. To satisfy the Reformed churches, he changed the wording for the distribution of the Lord's Supper. This outraged many Lutherans. They refused to use the king's *agende*.

Frederick tried to force the Lutherans to conform. He insisted that Lutherans and Reformed take Communion together. Government officials broke into Lutheran churches and took away their old service books to replace them with the king's *agende*. Resisting pastors were forbidden to baptize or to administer the Lord's Supper. Parents were punished if they refused to send their children to schools supervised by state church pastors. Persecution grew very intense. For example, by the end of 1835, all the resisting pastors in the state of Silesia were in prison. Prussian troops even attacked a congregation in Hönigern as they kept vigil outside their church on Christmas Eve (see pp. 446–50). As a result of this persecution, many Lutherans fled to North America and settled in the Midwest.

In North America, Lutherans enjoyed a very different experience. For example, when German Lutheran immigrants from the kingdom of Saxony reached St. Louis, Missouri, in 1839, Christ Episcopal Church allowed them to gather for services in the church basement. These immigrants would later have C. F. W. Walther as their leading pastor and form a core group within the Missouri Synod. During their first harsh winter, Lutheran settlers in Perry County, Missouri, received merciful treatment from their neighbors. In particular, members of the Brazeau Presbyterian Church offered life-saving assistance.

The Ecumenical Movement (1910)

When Protestant missionaries from around the world gathered at Edinburgh, Scotland, to coordinate their mission efforts, they began a movement to unite all churches. Key aspects of this effort emphasized how churches agreed and minimized how they disagreed, especially regarding the Lord's Supper. The ecumenical movement encouraged the practice known today as "open Communion."

The Prussian Union used force to unite churches; in contrast, the ecumenical movement used persuasion. They argued that differences between churches weren't important enough to keep them apart. They contended that "if you really love me, you'll commune me." Many liberal or progressive churches have adopted these arguments, leading to declarations of intercommunion.

However, many churches continue to hold that, in view of their differences, they should respect one another, pray for one another, yet worship and seek to fulfill God's calling separately. The vast majority of Christian congregations worldwide continue to practice "close Communion" (e.g., Eastern Orthodox, Roman Catholic, and numerous Protestant churches).

Lutheran Facts

Reception of the Lord's Supper is not based on age but rather on preparation. Most Lutherans begin receiving the Lord's Supper between the ages of 10 and 13, after receiving instruction in Luther's Small Catechism. Communing is not a right to be assumed or demanded but a privilege based on preparation.

Lutherans receive the Lord's Supper often.

Lutheran congregations usually ask people to "announce" their intention to receive the Lord's Supper. For example, some have communicants gather at the altar for a special service of preparation. Others ask people to personally register with the pastor before the service. In the United States and Canada, members often register by signing a card and presenting it to the usher or elder.

Following Jesus' practice at the Last Supper, Lutherans use unleavened bread and wine to celebrate the Lord's Supper.

To receive the Lord's Supper, Lutherans usually go forward to the altar in groups ("tables") that either stand or kneel together before or around the altar, depending on the architecture. This commemorates the gathering of Jesus with His disciples around the table of the Last Supper. In some congregations communicants follow a more recent practice of receiving the sacrament at "stations" where they stop only briefly. While Scripture does not forbid this form of communing that is specialized for large groups, neither does Scripture portray such a practice.

After partaking of the Lord's Supper, Lutherans offer a personal prayer of thanks to Jesus. Many kneel to offer this prayer.

An Ancient Meal

> Wherefore is this night distinguished from all other nights?
> —the Haggadah for Passover

Jesus introduced the Lord's Supper during Passover on the night He was betrayed. Around the table were His twelve disciples, confident that they would never let Jesus down. All that would change quickly.

Have you ever felt the swing from confidence in Christ to despair with yourself? That's what hit the disciples on Passover night. What would Jesus do with such fickle followers? What would He do with people whose strength would soon give way? He instituted a Supper that would feed them

His body and blood. Because their grip would soon give way, He would firmly take hold of them. That's grace in action! We have the certainty of God's grace in Jesus in contrast to the uncertainty and even unbelief of the disciples.

In light of Jesus' actions that night, what do the words "Take, eat, this is My body. Take, drink; this is My blood shed for you for the forgiveness of your sin" mean for us? Jesus' offer to "take, eat; take, drink" is truly an incredible offer of grace to those who would shortly abandon Him—including us.

A Special Night

We often forget the historical setting of the first Lord's Supper. But, if we look closely, it tells us so much about human failings and God's grace to save. Jesus' gracious grip on the disciples doesn't slip, even as all "hell" breaks loose. The gracious character of Jesus' ministry is clearly evident on that night when He was betrayed—He willingly provided spiritual protection and forgiveness for those who did not deserve these gifts.

The first Lord's Supper took place on the night before Christ's betrayal, in the midst of the Passover celebration (Mark 14:12). This roots God's acts of grace in history, at a certain time and in a specific place. The night of His betrayal also demonstrates clearly the contrast of the certainty and power of Christ's gracious gift to the disciples and their sinful bravado and weakness.

The Lord's Supper is like the Passover meal—but it is so much more. Jesus instituted the Lord's Supper in the context of a Passover meal. Passover was the Jewish festival commemorating the time when the angel of the Lord passed over the homes of the Hebrews rather than kill their firstborn sons as He did in the Egyptian homes. The lambs (or kids) used in the feast were killed on the fourteenth day of Nisan (March–April), and the meal was eaten the same evening between sundown and midnight. Since the Jewish day began at sundown, the Passover feast took place on the fifteenth day of Nisan.[2] In the Lord's Supper, God protects us as well. As God's provision of grace, the Lord's Supper forgives our sins and strengthens our faith, protecting us from the bondage to sin, death, and the power of Satan that would otherwise ensnare us. The difference between the two meals is Christ. Whereas the Passover lamb was the food that bound the Israelites together, Christ, the Lamb of God, becomes the food that feeds our bodies and souls. The angel of death passed over the houses of the Israelites because the blood of the lamb was on the doorposts. The blood

2 Adapted from *Concordia Self-Study Bible*, p. 1530, note on Mark 14:1; see also *The Lutheran Study Bible*, p. 1819, note on John 18:28.

of Jesus Christ shed on the cross shields us from God's righteous judgment against our sins. (See also Ephesians 2:13; 1 John 1:7; Revelation 1:5b.)

As we look at Mark's account of Jesus' institution of the Lord's Supper that Passover evening (14:17–31), we learn a great deal about the disciples' strength of commitment to Jesus. And we are given an opportunity to examine how we would respond in the same situation. Sadly, the text exposes the deceptive self-confidence of each and every disciple. Even Peter, the "rock" (Matthew 16:18), soon denied Christ and cursed His name. When we examine the response of the disciples, we must admit that we would have done the same or worse.

But we also have the opportunity here to see Jesus' commitment to the disciples. Jesus knew the disciples would deny Him. He even spoke face-to-face with Judas, who would betray Him. Yet, in view of all this, He instituted the Supper, where miraculously His body and blood were given to strengthen the disciples' faith in their weakest hour. Incredibly, Jesus offers this same grace to us every time His Supper is available to us in His Church. Again, grace in action.

Let's take a closer look at Jesus' institution of the Lord's Supper in Mark 14:22–26. Jesus took the bread and the wine and said, "Take; this is My body. . . . This is My blood of the covenant, which is poured out for many." His body and blood are unique gifts to His disciples in this gracious Supper. Miraculously, Christ became the sustenance of body and soul for the disciples. The Lord's Supper was called "the medicine for immortality" in the early Church. You can see that supernatural power clearly at work that first night. There was surely no power and strength in the disciples themselves.

Jesus responded to the needs of His disciples. Their faith was failing. Their strength waned and His arrest loomed. Jesus knew this was a time to put grace into action. Through the Lord's Supper, God offered His protection and care just in time!

A Personal Meal

Mark shows us that Jesus not only instituted the Supper but also gave Himself in the Supper for the forgiveness of sins. The very purpose of Christ's ministry was to forgive sins. In the institution of the first Lord's Supper, Jesus applied His forgiveness personally to His disciples. Jesus earned our salvation on the cross and also promised to be with us in His saving presence, even to the end of the age (Matthew 18:20; 28:20). He fulfills that promise personally to us every time we receive His Supper.

Many today call Holy Communion the "Christian's supper." But Scripture teaches us that this description is less than what the Supper truly is. Holy Communion is the *Lord's* Supper for Christians, not the Christian's supper for the Lord. While both descriptions sound "spiritual," one rests on the power of Christ and His word while the other rests on the power of our commitment and resolve to love Jesus. We must call it the *Lord's* Supper because forgiveness, life, and salvation are at stake. These benefits need to be "sure things" in the life of sinful people. Any movement away from the certainty of Christ's presence for us and the fact that, above all, this is *His* Supper, His provision, is a movement toward spiritual disaster.

Sinners are always welcome at the Lord's Supper because Christ instituted the meal to forgive sins. Each of Jesus' disciples was a poor, miserable sinner who experienced the joy of His forgiveness offered freely by God's grace. Sinners who desire no forgiveness or who believe they do not need forgiveness should be excluded from the meal out of concern for their spiritual well-being. While sin doesn't disqualify one from the Table, a lack of repentance does.

The Certain Savior

The Lord's Supper is a "grace event" created by a grace-giving Savior to forgive the sins of people who, even at their best, don't deserve forgiveness. In this event one sees the certainty of Jesus contrasted with the uncertainty of the disciples. One sees the forgiving, loving Savior contrasted with the treachery of the betrayer. One also sees the determination of a Messiah heading to the cross yet willing to strengthen His people before the storm of their disobedience.

Knowing this about Jesus, we can make sure we receive the Lord's Supper often. This gift is so wonderful that no effort on our part is too great to find out when the Supper is offered. If something is valuable to us, we need to find out how we can access it as much as possible.

Jesus treats us with undeserved grace. He makes Himself available in ways that we can receive. He earned our forgiveness through His death and resurrection, with no strings attached. The question in any relationship or difficult situation must be "How has Jesus treated me despite my sin?" The answer becomes our motivation to love others.

Comparisons

During the Middle Ages, most congregations of Western Christendom celebrated the Lord's Supper four times a year. Influenced by the modern liturgical movement, most Christians celebrate the Lord's Supper much more frequently today.

Eastern Orthodox and Roman Catholic: The Lord's Supper is celebrated each Sunday and on special feast days. Roman Catholics are encouraged to commune frequently, but expected to commune at least once a year.

Lutheran and Reformed: Practice varies from congregation to congregation, but most celebrate the Lord's Supper several times a month and on special feast days. In recent years, more congregations have celebrated the Lord's Supper weekly. Some Reformed congregations use grape juice instead of wine.

Anabaptist: Practice varies among Anabaptists. For example, most Mennonites celebrate the Lord's Supper only twice a year. Other Anabaptists celebrate more frequently. Many congregations use grape juice instead of wine. Foot washing is an important part of their Lord's Supper service.

Baptist: The Lord's Supper is celebrated monthly in many congregations. However, congregations of the Restoration movement celebrate the Lord's Supper weekly (Disciples of Christ, Christian Churches, and Churches of Christ). Many Baptist congregations use grape juice instead of wine.

Wesleyan: Practice varies from congregation to congregation. Most celebrate the Lord's Supper quarterly or monthly. Many congregations use grape juice instead of wine.

Point to Remember

On the first day of Unleavened Bread, when they sacrificed the Passover lamb, His disciples said to Him, "Where will you have us go and prepare for You to eat the Passover?" *Mark 14:12*

Miracle of Miracles

King of kings yet born of Mary,
As of old on earth He stood,
Lord of lords in human vesture,
In the body and the blood,
He will give to all the faithful
His own self for heav'nly food.
—Liturgy of St. James, *LSB* 621

Some people have a difficult time with the Lord's Supper. They ask, "How could Jesus' body and blood be present in bread and wine?" But that's the wrong question. Instead, people need to ask, "Why?" The Bible says He came looking for all people from the Garden of Eden (Genesis 3), to the manger (Matthew 1:22–23), and in, with, and under the bread and wine of the Lord's Supper. When Jesus comes looking, people are found and forgiven. Whether it's in the Garden of Eden, the Tent of Meeting, the Tabernacle, Baptism, or the Lord's Supper, grace "in the flesh" coming among us to save us has always been God's way.

Comfort

> An angel of the Lord appeared to him in a dream, saying, "Joseph, son of David, do not fear to take Mary as your wife, for that which is conceived in her is from the Holy Spirit. She will bear a son, and you shall call His name Jesus, for He will save His people from their sins." All this took place to fulfill what the Lord had spoken by the prophet: "Behold, the virgin shall conceive and bear a son, and they shall call His name Immanuel" (which means, God with us). (Matthew 1:20–23)

Christians take great comfort and joy in Christmas because God came in the flesh to save us. Christmas is the celebration of the miraculous birth of Christ, who came to save His people from their sins.

But the story of Christmas is very hard for some people to believe. Whenever we start to ask, "How did God do that?" we get into trouble. How did God become man? How did Jesus suffer our damnation on the cross? How will God raise the dead on the Last Day? The Bible tells us simply that He did or will do these things. He became man when the Holy Spirit "overshadowed" Mary. He was able to take our place because He was fully man, and He earned our salvation because He was fully God. He will raise the dead "in a moment, in the twinkling of an eye" (1 Corinthians 15:52). All these things are clearly taught in the Bible, but to probe the complete depths of these truths remains beyond our grasp. The miraculous is always in God's arena, even as we witness it with our own eyes.

Christians never explain how Christmas happens; instead, we proclaim, "It did happen!" This Christian confession of faith concerning the virgin birth is related to our confession about Christ's body and blood present in, with, and under the bread and wine in the Lord's Supper. As Christians, we take our stand on the sure and completely reliable Word of God. We stand on the person and work of Jesus Christ. If He tells us something, we can be certain His Word is truth. His words are spirit and life (John 6:63). "If it were not so, would I have told you?" Jesus says to His disciples (John 14:2). We trust in the miraculous character of the Lord's Supper. No one claims to fully understand how the Lord makes it work. But His Word does what it says: "Let there be light," and it is so. "This is My body. . . . This is My blood," and it is so. Whenever Jesus says, "Here for you, for your forgiveness," we say "Thank You" and receive what He offers.

The Bible makes another connection between Christmas and the Lord's Supper in Hebrews 2:14–15: "Since therefore the children share in flesh and blood, He Himself likewise partook of the same things, that through death He might destroy the one who has the power of death, that is, the devil, and deliver all those who through fear of death were subject to lifelong slavery." This passage refers to the Christmas event using the same biblical word often used to describe the Lord's Supper. The word is *koinonia*, which means "communion" ("shared" in some translations). God's real communion with humanity helps us to understand His real presence in the Lord's Supper. Hebrews 2:14 says that Jesus "shared," or participated, communed, in our humanity. That's the word Paul uses in 1 Corinthians 10:16 when he asks: "The cup of blessing that we bless, is it not a participation [sharing, communing] in the blood of Christ? The bread that we break, is it not a participation [sharing, communing] in the body of Christ?" His answer is yes! There is no figurative emphasis in the words. This is not just participation with the Church in an act that it calls "the Lord's Supper." It is Jesus giving Himself—the complete, literal gift of His own body and blood—to His Church. Miraculously, Jesus shared in our humanity, our flesh and blood. We also really receive His body and blood for the forgiveness of our sins, as Scripture teaches. Following the verse above, the Lord's body and blood are distributed with the bread and the wine according to the practice of Jesus and the apostles. Withholding the cup runs contrary to the Lord's institution.

John 6:29–35, 53–60 also helps us understand the Lord's Supper. Here Jesus calls Himself the bread of life. In this portion of Scripture, Jesus draws attention to the fact that only He can create and sustain faith. He is the source, the resource, the very "food for faith." His words are spirit and life (John 6:63). Lutherans would say that they are *sacramental*, full of the presence and power of Jesus Christ.

Many people say that John 6 isn't about the Lord's Supper because the Supper wasn't instituted yet. And though it is true that John 6 does not teach specifically about the Lord's Supper, it does help us make connections to and prepare for the Sacrament. It could be that in these words, Jesus was preparing His disciples to receive Him in whatever way He chose to come (through His Word and Sacraments). After all, He talked about His death, preparing them for its occurrence long before it happened.

A Familiar Feast

Just as an anchor secures a ship during a storm, the proclamation of Christmas and the action of the Lord's Supper can anchor our life in Christ. The Christmas event and the teachings of the Lord's Supper both tell about God's work for the salvation of all people. God's work is sure. God's promises are sure. God's invitations are sure. God's Word anchors our faith in the certainty of Jesus' forgiveness and His accomplished work on the cross amid a world full of broken promises and temporary commitments.

There are times when we don't feel deserving or don't even feel the presence of Jesus in our lives. But Christ's words "This is My body; this is My blood" challenge us to look to His promises in the midst of difficult times. We have the promise of Christ, namely, that He is present for us. Our faith tells us to hold on to His promise over and against our feelings. Feelings can be wrong; the promise of Christ cannot.

At His birth, He was named *Jesus*, for He would save His people from their sins. The main blessing Jesus provides in the Lord's Supper is forgiveness of sins. If Jesus' main work was to earn forgiveness for His people, it stands to reason that He provides a special gift to deliver His forgiveness to those He saved. In 1 Corinthians 11:23 Paul talks about himself being a "delivery person" of the Lord's Supper—a very special delivery package indeed.

On Our Lord

The truth about Jesus is often hard to believe. His miraculous birth has caused many to scratch their heads in wonder. But for those who trust the sure Word of God, He provides power and comfort in the Christmas Christ. In the Lord's Supper we receive the same Christ, who comes all the way to our level (the flesh level) so that we might truly be certain of His forgiving presence in our lives.

This security helps us in our relationships with others as well. Secure relationships help us to become better friends, neighbors, husbands, wives, and so on. In fact, a strong family that demonstrates committed love gives children the security they need to enter into healthy relationships when they grow up. Our relationship with the Lord is the most necessary one of all. The Lord's Supper demonstrates over and over again Christ's willingness to call us His forgiven brothers, His forgiven sisters. Through the certainty of Christ, we can risk loving one another the way He first loved us. The Lord's Supper is Christ's clear voice of forgiveness and community amid the chaos we face daily.

Comparisons

Eastern Orthodox: "[A believer] under the forms of bread and wine, partakes of the very Body and Blood of Christ, to everlasting salvation" (*The Longer Catechism of the Eastern Church*, question 315).

Lutheran: "It is the true body and blood of our Lord Jesus Christ, under the bread and wine, for us Christians to eat and drink, instituted by Christ Himself" (SC VI; *Concordia*, p. 343).

Reformed: "The Lord's Supper is a sacrament, wherein . . . his death is showed forth, and the worthy receivers are, not after a corporal and carnal manner, but by faith, made partakers of his body and blood" (*Westminster Shorter Catechism*, question 96).

Anabaptist: "We also confess and observe the breaking of bread, or Supper, as the Lord Christ Jesus before His suffering instituted it with bread and wine, and observed and ate with His apostles, commanding them to observe it in remembrance of Him" (*The Dordrecht Confession*, article 10).

Roman Catholic: "Through consecration of the bread and wine there comes about a conversion of the whole substance of the bread into the substance of the body of Christ our Lord, and of the whole substance of the wine into the substance of his blood" (*Canons and Decrees of the Council of Trent*, On Transubstantiation; cf. CCC2 paras. 1373–77).

Baptist: "We believe [in] . . . the Lord's Supper, in which the members of the Church, by the sacred use of bread and wine, are to commemorate together the dying love of Christ" (*New Hampshire Baptist Confession*, article 14).

Wesleyan: "The body of Christ is given, taken, and eaten in the Supper only after a heavenly and spiritual manner" (*Methodist Articles of Religion*, article 18).

Liberal: Liberal Christians, strongly influenced by rationalism, usually don't believe in miracles. Therefore, they don't believe Christ gives His body and blood for the forgiveness of sins in the Lord's Supper.

Point to Remember

Since therefore the children share in flesh and blood, He Himself likewise partook of the same things, that through death He might destroy the one who has the power of death, that is, the devil. *Hebrews 2:14*

Given for You

The cup, the cup itself from which our Lord drank . . . if a man could touch or see it, he was heal'd at once, by faith, of all his ills.
—Alfred, Lord Tennyson, "The Holy Grail"

The many medieval tales about the Holy Grail tried to explain the mystery and wonder of the Lord's Supper. They became popular in a twelfth-century poem, a part of which describes a serving dish with a communion wafer that has miraculous healing powers. Stories about miracles caused by the Lord's Supper were common in medieval times, yet the setting for such tales was often a location apart from the divine service, the place intended by Christ for the Lord's Supper. The grail stories later spoke of the sacred cup used at the Last Supper that contains Christ's royal blood. This change happened because the Old French words *san graal*, holy dish, sound like *sang real*, royal blood.

What helped to create these stories? People's lives were short, harsh, and full of sorrow. They found comfort in heavenly things that last forever, are never unpleasant, and are full of joy. As a result, they craved miracles that they could see and touch. The medieval Church and local economies profited from pilgrimages and alms based on miracles, allowing some to take biblical truth out of context. In the proper context of the Divine Service, however, God brings the real, miraculous, completely free, yet precious gift of the Lord's Supper to His people.

Some gifts seem to be so incredible, so beyond everyday experience, that we struggle to accept that they are really ours until we actually receive them! We don't believe the gift is true until the letter is in our hands, the money is in the bank, the ring is on our finger, or the baby is in the cradle.

The Lord's Supper is such an amazing and undeserved gift because Christ earned it for us by His death on the cross. It is a gift for each of us personally: Jesus said, "Given for you" (Luke 22:19).

Benefits

We tend to think of the benefit of forgiveness of sins as nothing special today. People say they're sorry as if that would atone for their sin. Much more is needed to overcome real guilt before God. What makes forgiveness so incredible for us is the high price Christ paid—His death on the cross—for us.

As it presents the institution of the Lord's Supper, Matthew 26:26–30 emphasizes the "forgiveness of sins." While that is self-evident in the very presence of Jesus, Matthew wishes his hearers to make no mistake about the essence of this gift. As Jesus teaches, He has the authority to forgive sins (Matthew 9:1–8). Wherever and whenever Jesus is present, He desires to forgive sins. Jesus' real presence in the Lord's Supper is cause enough for us to know that His forgiveness is present.

Whenever Christ Jesus is truly present, life and salvation are also present. This is good news for all who receive the Lord's Supper in faith. Luther wrote: "Where there is forgiveness of sins, there is also life and salvation" (SC VI; *Concordia*, p. 343). When we receive Jesus by listening to His Word, receiving His name in Baptism, or receiving His body and blood in the Lord's Supper, the destructiveness of guilt and the pain caused by our sinfulness and weakness give way to real life. Now that's an incredible gift!

In 1 Corinthians 11:23–26, we read about the purpose of public ministry among God's people. Paul says that what he received, he now passes along to others. He emphasizes that what he gives is something that was "given to give." A pastor's job is really to say "yes" when Christ says "yes," and "no" when Christ says "no." Pastors deliver to people the gifts that Christ has certified them to carry. Paul confesses that this Supper isn't his; it is Christ's. People place their confidence in Jesus, not in the messenger.

In 1 Corinthians 11:24, the same benefit of forgiveness is proclaimed with two little words: "for you." Nothing sweeter can be said than the words *for you*. It is one thing to think about Jesus' forgiveness for the whole world; it's another thing entirely to realize His forgiveness is for each of us, personally. As people gather at the altar to receive the Lord's Supper, watch their faces. People are in awe of the fact that Jesus forgives them personally.

In 1 Corinthians 11:25, Jesus takes the cup and says, "This cup is the new covenant in My blood. Do this, as often as you drink it, in remembrance of Me." The word *covenant* (or *testament* in some translations) brings to mind the last will and testament that someone might make prior to his or her death. Jesus' death on the cross enabled His "estate" of forgiveness of sins, life, and salvation to be delivered to His "heirs" in faith. That's why it is so important to take the words "This is My body. . . . This is My blood" just as they are. Receiving His body and blood delivers His benefits to us with certainty.

For You

Some have said that the only certainty in life is that each person struggles with a sense of inadequacy, personal guilt, or remorse. Today many people seek answers to questions about self-fulfillment. We as Christians can run to the Lord's Table, where Jesus tells us who we are in His name. The benefit of the Lord's Supper goes right to the heart of our soul problem. It builds a solid ground for self-worth and self-fulfillment. Redeemed, forgiven, and empowered by the presence and promises of Jesus Christ, we undergo real change.

"For you" is a beautiful phrase spoken by someone who loves you and gives you a gift. Think of the awesome truth of the gift of forgiveness offered to us by Christ Himself. Paul reminds the Corinthians about what is central to their life as a church—gathering around the Table of the Lord as mutually repentant and forgiven people. It is a gift that keeps on giving. Trying to celebrate the personal value of such a gesture of love is the beginning of a "Lord's Supper lifestyle."

Love and *forgiveness* are action words. Jesus doesn't just talk about love and forgiveness; He gives them (1 Corinthians 11:26). Paul demonstrates the effort of love and forgiveness by bringing the Lord's Supper to the congregation in Corinth, which causes him all sorts of trouble and pain. When the Lord brings salvation, there is always a price to be paid, and He paid it on the cross. His words are backed by His actions. This Supper doesn't just talk about forgiveness and community; it creates and sustains them.

Special Delivery

"Take, eat" and "take, drink . . . for the forgiveness of sins" are action words of grace, delivered to God's people. Jesus doesn't just say, "I love you." He shows it by His death on the cross and delivers it through the gift of His

Supper. Going to Holy Communion is in many ways like opening the greatest gift in life, knowing for sure that it is meant for you.

This main benefit of Holy Communion—forgiveness—shows us what is really important in our lives: our relationship to Jesus. Since our relationship to Jesus is the most important thing in life, and forgiveness is the way He created and continues to sustain this relationship, then knowing and growing in His forgiveness must be our first priority. The power of forgiveness is not only to receive, but also to share with others.

Jesus demonstrated the price that had to be paid to bring forgiveness and life to our lives. Paul demonstrated the same in his ministry. Motivated by God's love for us, we become God's forgiving agents in this world.

Comparisons

Eastern Orthodox: "What benefit does he receive who communicates in the Body and Blood of Christ? He is in closest manner united to Jesus Christ himself, and, in him, is made partaker of everlasting life" (*The Longer Catechism of the Eastern Church*, question 342).

Lutheran: "These words, 'Given for you' and 'shed for you for the forgiveness of sins.' This means that in the Sacrament forgiveness of sins, life, and salvation are given us through these words. For where there is forgiveness of sins, there is also life and salvation" (SC VI; *Concordia*, p. 343).

Reformed: "Our Lord Jesus . . . instituted the sacrament . . . for the perpetual remembrance of the sacrifice of himself in his death, the sealing all benefits thereof unto true believers, their spiritual nourishment and growth in him, their further engagement in, and to all duties which they owe unto him; and to be a bond and pledge of their communion with him, and with each other, as members of his mystical body" (*The Westminster Confession of Faith*, article 29).

Anabaptist: "[In the Holy Supper] we are admonished to the utmost, to love and forgive one another and our neighbor, as He has done unto us, and to be mindful to maintain and live up to the unity and fellowship which we have with God and one another, which is signified to us by this breaking of bread" (*The Dordrecht Confession*, article 10).

Roman Catholic: "And He would also that this sacrament should be received as the spiritual food of souls . . . and as an antidote, whereby we may be freed from daily faults, and be preserved from mortal sins. He would furthermore, have it as a pledge of our glory to come"

(*Canons and Decrees of the Council of Trent*, Session 13.2; cf. CCC2 paras. 1391–1401).

Baptist: "The Lord's Supper is a holy ordinance, wherein, by giving and receiving bread and wine, according to Christ's appointment, His death is showed forth, and the worthy receivers are, not after a corporeal and carnal manner, but by faith, made partakers of His body and blood, with all His benefits, to their spiritual nourishment, and growth in grace" (*Keach's Catechism*, question 107).

Wesleyan: "The Supper of the Lord is not only a sign of the love that Christians ought to have among themselves one to another, but rather is a sacrament of our redemption by Christ's death" (*Methodist Articles of Religion*, article 18).

Point to Remember

For as often as you eat this bread and drink the cup, you proclaim the Lord's death until He comes. *1 Corinthians 11:26*

Fellowship Divine

Lord Jesus Christ, we humbly pray
That we may feast on You today;
Beneath these forms of bread and wine
Enrich us with Your grace divine.
—H. E. Jacobs (*LSB* 623:1)

Through faith in Christ Jesus we belong to something bigger than ourselves. God re-created people through Holy Baptism to be in a loving relationship with Him and with one another. That's community! The Lord's Supper is not just a meal shared between you and God. In the Lord's Supper we confess an extended faith family, a forgiven community—His Church.

The Lord's presence in the Church makes it a different kind of community. No other place in the world has the promise of Christ's presence, power, and protection. But the Lord's Supper deepens that promise. When we receive His body and blood, we all receive Christ in common; He unites us. We serve Christ as we serve one another. His gift binds us together in a way that even our earthly family relationships cannot match.

Things shared in common bind families together. The joys, the pains, the experiences, and the common traditions make us family. The mutual receiving of the real, present, forgiving, empowering, protecting body and blood of Christ makes us an eternal family.

Is Means *Is*

People search for something big enough to believe in. People search for community that lasts. The Lord's Supper calls us to that community and empowers us to begin to live that eternal reality now. The unity we share in the Lord's Supper overcomes ethnic, racial, and economic divisions. In the Lord's Supper, true community exists in Christ and is available to all.

For explanation, we go back to Paul's letter to the church at Corinth. "Therefore, my beloved, flee from idolatry. I speak as to sensible people; judge for yourselves what I say. The cup of blessing that we bless, is it not a participation in the blood of Christ? The bread that we break, is it not a participation in the body of Christ? Because there is one bread, we who are many are one body, for we all partake of the one bread" (1 Corinthians 10:14–17). What does Paul mean by "participation in the blood of Christ" and "participation in the body of Christ"? Is receiving the bread and wine a "participation in the body and blood of Christ"? Paul's answer is a resounding, "Yes!" The phrase means participating in a common, real thing that binds us together. The real thing is Christ's body and blood. It is so real that when we receive it, He binds us together. "We who are many are one body, for we all partake of the one bread" (1 Corinthians 10:17).

This emphasizes the truth that "*is* means *is*" when it comes to the Lord's Supper. People have challenged the word "is" when their ideas about the world start to collide with objective truth. Created truth exists apart from human opinion because the Creator exists apart from human opinion. When opinion collides with fact, conflict occurs. When people come into conflict with God, they depend on Christ to mediate it. If they warp Christ's own words, however, they run the risk of damaging the situation to the point where they may lose salvation (Revelation 22:18–19).

Americans may recall President Bill Clinton's reinterpretation of the word "is" in order to sidestep personal scandal. That attempt failed, and he became the second U.S. president to be impeached, an indelible mark on his term in office. Yet he was not the first person to tangle with this two-letter word. Swiss theologian Ulrich Zwingli had some specific ideas about how God ought to work; in 1529 he famously interpreted the word "is" to make the words of Christ work according to his ideas. Zwingli rejected the idea that God works through any physical means. He concluded that the Lord's Supper is only a symbol for the "real" activity of God in the heart and mind. However much "spin" Zwingli applied, Dr. Luther's "no spin" approach won out: "*is* means *is*." That little word carries a big impact, as big as the "I Am" Himself. It is Christ, not we, who creates the reality of the Lord's Supper. After all, it belongs to Him. Paul underscores what this meal offers: forgiveness of sins and eternal life received by believers through faith. We take the Lord at His word. In this meal Christ gives us real power to serve our brothers and sisters in the faith.

Paul also tells us that the Supper creates the "body of believers." The body and blood of Christ create and sustain the Church. Communion in the body and blood of Christ makes us a real community. The real presence also means the real power of Christ. We seek community with one another, but often we seem so helpless to make it happen. The Lord's Supper calls us to community, empowers us in community, and enables us to maintain community. Real community flows from Christ's selfless love and sacrificing presence.

In 1 Corinthians 12:12–27, we read Paul's famous description of the Church as one body with many members. These verses reveal incredible diversity within the Church. Paul tells us that the only way to keep such a diverse group together in unity is that "in one Spirit we were all baptized into one body" (v. 13). He goes on to explain the different parts of the body; each member has special gifts and talents. What an array! What a blessing! What a community! No human could hold it all together. Only the presence of Christ and the power of the Holy Spirit can sustain this reality. Only the confession of our sin and our reliance on Christ's grace, especially received in the Supper, can keep us focused on the things that matter.

Paul explains our corporate responsibility to one another. He illustrates the truth that Holy Communion is personal, but never private. We don't have the right to disregard the work of Jesus in the lives of others or to value our status with the Lord as any greater than another's. We are tempted to see a hierarchy of spiritual maturity and gifts as something special because we believe that we are something special. Such pride always demeans someone, somewhere. We share with others the personal forgiveness of sins won by Jesus on the cross. Even our best efforts are uncertain and powerless. The Church is always God's creation, not man's decision. Nothing but the presence and forgiveness of Christ will see us through.

Family of Faith

It's easy to forget what is lasting in life. Family and church concerns often rank low on our list. The Lord's Supper challenges us to see the family of faith as God's answer to our need—part of something eternal, bigger than ourselves.

In 1 Corinthians 12:12–13, Paul shows us that we are part of a faith family. In worship we not only celebrate what Christ has done for us, we also celebrate what He has done for others. God called us into community through faith so that we might love as He first loved us. Through faith all who worship are celebrated members of the Body of Christ.

In 1 Corinthians 10:15–17, Paul tells us that Christ binds us together. That bond extends outward to family, friends, and even to the stranger at the Communion rail. To receive Christ in the Supper assures us we are His and enables us to live as He lived—in a loving way, looking out for others. It is amazing what needs, hurts, and even celebrations we miss when discontent dominates our thinking.

Body of Christ

The Lord's Supper gives us a different vision of community—created and sustained by the present Christ who binds us together in love and unity. His body and blood create the Body of Christ, His Church. His gifts create and sustain the extended family of faith. We are brothers and sisters in Christ.

The next time you go to Communion, look at the people communing with you. Does the Lord's Supper make you more accepting of those who are not like you? Again, His love motivates us to ask, "If Christ values this person, how can I get to know him or her?" We can even say, "If that person values Christ at the Supper, I need to get to know him or her."

Comparisons

Physical "body": Churches which teach that Christ gives His actual body and blood in the Lord's Supper (Eastern Orthodox, Roman Catholic, Lutheran) view Paul's reference to the "body" in 1 Corinthians 11:29 as a reference to Jesus' physical body given in the Sacrament. These churches emphasize the forgiveness provided by the Sacrament. They believe that Jesus' divine and human natures are united in such a way that Jesus' physical body is not restricted to one location like our physical bodies. He can be physically present in the Lord's Supper. (See John 20:19–20 for an example of how Jesus' body behaves differently from our bodies because of its union with the divine nature.)

"Body" of believers: Other churches view Paul's reference to the "body" in 1 Corinthians 11:29 as a reference to the body of believers. These churches emphasize the community nature of the Lord's Supper. They believe that Jesus' physical body—His human nature—remains in heaven and therefore cannot be present in the Lord's Supper.

Point to Remember

Because there is one bread, we who are many are one body, for we all partake of the one bread. *1 Corinthians 10:17*

Communion Means Union

May God bestow on us His grace and favor
That we follow Christ our Savior
And live together here in love and union
Nor despise this blest communion.
—Martin Luther (*LSB* 617:3)

There is a big difference between an obligation and a loving commitment. An obligation is often met grudgingly, sometimes even resentfully. It's something we *have* to do. On the other hand, people will sacrifice for one another when those efforts grow out of commitments. When people share *loving* commitment, the burden of serving others seems light.

The Lord's Supper motivates us to a loving commitment to serve others. We can no longer treat each other just as Bill, Mary, Tom, Greg, Yvette, Devin—fill in the name. No, Christ has made His home among us. He has declared our bodies to be part of His holy ground. Each Christian's loving obligation is to serve as Christ serves, if for no other reason than to proclaim the power of the Lord's Supper in our lives. Sharing real love is not really a burden. We can never exhaust what Christ wants to give us, even if we try to give it all away.

Divisions

Although Christians are called to unity and service, the actual state of some Christian congregations may be something closer to the opposite. For example, the Corinthian church in Paul's day was a mess. Many people felt that they were God's special people because they were spirit-filled, an impression that filled them with vain pride. Others interpreted freedom in the Gospel to mean living according to the loose morality of the time. Such pride and self-gratification caused divisions and abuse, including a denigration of Paul's ministry. It was no surprise that even the Lord's Supper was being abused within the church. Real change needed to happen. Paul explained that to rebuild the community of believers, they had to return to a faithful celebration of the Lord's Supper, the community meal.

At that time there were two meals in the church. The *agape* (love feast) we might call the "potluck." The other meal was Holy Communion, the Lord's Supper. The Corinthians celebrated the Lord's Supper as if it were any other meal. One can see the social hierarchy at work in 1 Corinthians 11:17–22. The poor were made to eat at other tables. The rich indulged themselves. But worst of all, the Lord's Supper was viewed as merely a social convention. Probably as a result of conditions similar to these, the love feast disappeared from the regular practice of the Church. Today's potluck meals are not confused with church services and have a recognizably different context.

While this scene in the Corinthian church probably represents the infighting of certain social groups, one must never forget that all sin against our neighbor is ultimately sin against God. God calls us into human relationships and instructs us how to live with and for one another. To dismiss or demean our neighbor is to disobey God. We see the same kind of attitude in some churches today. Many churches "major in minors." They allow their prideful sin to overshadow God's love in Christ. Jesus won the forgiveness for all sins, including our sinful pride.

But Paul had an antidote for the Corinthians' squabbling. He called them back to the basics: putting the Lord's Supper and the obligation to community back in their proper places. With Christ as the center of the church, there would be hope for change. (See 1 Corinthians 11:23–27, 33–34.) In his first letter, Paul told the Corinthians to "wait for one another" (11:33). He was asking them to treat others differently than the world expected. The poor had no expectation of the loving concern of the rich. The outcasts had no reason to believe that the upstanding people would pay them any mind. The Lord's Supper turns such conventions upside down. Let those who lead serve! Let the first become last!

Paul discusses the problem of the Corinthian congregation in the context of human freedom and our obligation to serve others (1 Corinthians 10:23–24, 31–33). Paul's description of God's desire for the lives of His children is a paradox. We are freely bound to one another. We are free to serve! It's not an obligation to love; it's an opportunity. And the purpose is to be part of God's redemption of every person by sharing the Gospel.

Invitation

Because of sin, people's natural inclination is to love things and use people. In contrast, receiving Jesus' forgiveness means living sacrificially for others.

Ponder for a moment the biblical fact that each person at the Lord's Table receives the body and blood of Christ. Christ comes to us sacrificially, as a servant, and dwells in us. To serve Jesus is our greatest honor. Through His Supper, the Holy Spirit strengthens our faith, empowering us to serve our brothers and sisters in the faith—starting with those next to us at the Communion rail.

The Lord's continued willingness to serve, demonstrated among people like those at Corinth, makes our burdens in service to one another light by comparison. The whole Bible declares the stubborn commitment of our God to love us despite ourselves. Romans 5:8 says, "While we were still sinners, Christ died for us." What Jesus endured for us—Gethsemane, the trial, the whip, the cross, and the separation from the Father—makes our burden for sharing love with others small in comparison.

Risk Love

Real relationships take a certain amount of risk. To love and to serve someone means we might get hurt. The Lord's Supper teaches us to find our strength only in Christ. In our certain relationship with Jesus, He frees and empowers us to risk when serving others.

Knowing that our relationship with Jesus is secure, we can be more Christlike in our service to others. Again, the Lord's Supper builds certainty of faith in our relationship with God. That allows us to commit ourselves to learn to love one another. Too many people fail to realize that relationships are faith exercises whereby we draw all our strength from God and His gifts so that we might be able to love others free of charge, the way Christ loves us.

Comparisons

Close(d) Communion: The vast majority of Christian congregations in the world hold to the ancient practice of close(d) Communion. For example, the Eastern Orthodox Church, Roman Catholics, The Lutheran Church—Missouri Synod, the Wisconsin Evangelical Lutheran Synod, the Evangelical Lutheran Synod, the Association of Reformed Presbyterian Churches, and some conservative Anabaptist churches practice close(d) Communion. That is, they only commune members of congregations with which they have official fellowship. Exceptions may be made in cases of pastoral care.

Open Communion: A minority of congregations, influenced especially by the ecumenical movement of the nineteenth century, practice open Communion. That is, they commune people without regard to belief or denominational membership (most expect that a person will be baptized before he or she receives the Lord's Supper).

Point to Remember

[I am] not seeking my own advantage, but that of many, that they may be saved. *1 Corinthians 10:33b*

Prepare the Way

During the second week in Lent it was Raskolnikov's turn to fast and go to Communion, together with the rest of his [prison] barrack.
—Fyodor Dostoevsky, *Crime and Punishment*

The novel *Crime and Punishment* ends with the emotional repentance of Raskolnikov, a brutal murderer despised by his fellow inmates. The prisoners protest his opportunity to go to the Lord's Supper and would discourage him, believing that he's not worthy or prepared.

Lutherans believe that no one is worthy to receive the Lord's Supper *unless* the Lord prepares them.

The Lord's Supper is a grace event where Jesus calls us in repentance to receive what He alone can provide—forgiveness of sins and eternal life. And even more, His Supper empowers us to serve one another.

So what can we do to get ready to receive the Lord's Supper? How does this readiness prepare us to receive Christ when He comes again in glory to judge the living and the dead? Preparation should focus on (a) our need (especially from God's viewpoint), (b) God's provision, and (c) our desire to be part of the serving community that God has created and continues to sustain. After all, this is what a foretaste of heaven will be like.

Worthy

Preparation for the Lord's Supper has become a lost art. Many Christians neglect preparation before receiving the Sacrament. To those who understand its value and its power, godly preparation is a must. Let's focus our attention on the preparation necessary to receive over and over again Jesus' body and His blood shed to empower and sustain us as His people until He comes again in glory.

Paul says that eating in an unworthy manner is sinning against the body and the blood of the Lord (1 Corinthians 11:27). To receive the Supper with no repentance or to receive it while sinning against a brother or sister is ultimately sinning against the gift Jesus offers at the Table, His body and blood shed for the forgiveness of sins. In so doing, we sin against our Lord. The statement "Christ is present at His Supper whether you believe it or not" is true. The question is whether we are receiving Him to our benefit or to our judgment.

To "examine yourself" prior to communing means to test yourself, critique yourself, demonstrate the truth about yourself. We are not to play games with ourselves or with God. Instead, we are to use the Ten Commandments as a godly diagnostic tool, asking ourselves, "Have I kept them with all my heart, all my soul, all my mind?" When we are honest before God, we must answer, "No." He already knows us just as we are and stands ready to forgive us.

Paul says that unworthy participation in the Lord's Supper has personal ramifications. We also know today that unforgiven guilt can have physical side effects. It seems that the Corinthians compounded their guilt as they trifled with God's presence in His Supper. Their disobedience to the Lord and His Supper was also at the heart of their community problems. Once the true teaching and celebration of Jesus in the Lord's Supper are lost, we are left to our own sinful devices. That was quite evident in the Corinthian congregation.

A large part of their problem was spiritual pride. According to 2 Corinthians 13:5–10, the Corinthian Christians disrespected Paul and the foundation of the Church, Jesus Christ. How could they be so foolish? They thought they were strong in some spiritually unique way without Christ. We also need to recognize the power of God's grace in our weakness! The simple things of God are our strength.

Paul talks about weakness and strength, saying it is better to be weak and reliant on the Lord rather than strong and unfaithful. Paul was attacked as spiritually weak because he didn't seem to demonstrate a bold enough spirit. The Corinthians challenged his authority. In 2 Corinthians 12:7–10, he teaches the church, as well as us, that our power is found in Christ alone. Our weakness always looks to Christ's strength. Our own strength tends to make us look away from Christ, thereby making us weak.

In the Small Catechism, Martin Luther writes: "A person is truly worthy and well prepared who has faith in these words, 'Given . . . and shed for you for the forgiveness of your sins'" (SC IV; *Concordia*, p. 343). There is comfort in knowing that our worthiness to receive the Lord's Supper comes not from our own doing, but instead through faith—faith given to us by God. Faith is the essence of worthy preparation. Faith is not something we do for God. Faith is empowered because of its object—Jesus Christ. Worthy preparation comes from God alone through saving faith in Jesus. Many people quote this passage from Luther without considering the context. Luther assumes that people will have studied the other parts of the catechism before coming to the Lord's Supper. That way they will be ready to examine themselves.

Guarded Hearts

It is awesome to be in the presence of Jesus Christ. We draw near because He invites us. Faith trusts that invitation. At the Table we meet Christ, truly present. As we receive Him through faith, He empowers us to live boldly in service to Him and others.

As we examine ourselves, we must guard against the temptation to think that we've earned the right to be at the Lord's Table (2 Corinthians 13:5). Satan wants us to believe that God needs us more than we need Him. Satan wants us to turn God's gifts into something we do for Him. But Christ is in us in Baptism, Confession and Absolution, Holy Communion, and His Word. Preparation makes us aware of our desperate need and His amazing grace.

We also must guard against the feeling that our sins make us unworthy. Remember Peter's denial of Christ? The danger here is to become so aware of our sin that we let it drive us away from Jesus. Satan loves to make people believe that their sin makes them unworthy. In some ways this is pride in reverse. It's almost like telling God, "I need something other than Your Supper for forgiveness, because that provision is not big enough for a sinner like me." God's gracious forgiveness offered in His Supper is great enough to forgive even the chief of sinners.

Self-examination

"Worthiness" is crucial to receiving the body and blood of Christ for our benefit. But what makes us worthy is not something we do; rather, it is something God has done for us—He has given us faith. We are worthy through faith in Christ Jesus to receive the gifts He offers in Holy Communion. Examination means to (a) repent of our sin, (b) trust in the real presence of Jesus Christ and His offer to forgive our sins, and (c) desire to amend our sinful life by the power of the Holy Spirit.

Many Christians spend Saturday in preparation for Holy Communion on Sunday. We can examine our lives using the Ten Commandments and focusing on the promises of God in Scripture. Preparation enables us to take an honest inventory of our lives and makes us even more anxious to meet our loving, forgiving Savior at His Table.

There are other ways we can prepare ourselves to receive our Lord's Supper. We can fast, pray, or meditate on certain portions of Scripture. But above all, knowing our need for forgiveness and trusting Christ's offer of grace makes us worthy and well-prepared. Come! Take and eat. Take and drink. The Meal for eternal life is now ready, and God has reserved a place for us at His Table.

Comparisons

Eastern Orthodox: They expect Baptism, catechesis, self-examination, confession of sins, and faith as preparation. "What is required individually of every one who desires to approach the Sacrament of the Communion? To examine his conscience before God, and to cleanse it from sin by penitence; for doing which he has helps in fasting and prayer" (*The Longer Catechism of the Eastern Church*, question 341).

Lutheran: They expect Baptism, catechesis, self-examination, confession of sins, and faith as preparation. "But a person is truly worthy and well prepared who has faith in these words, 'Given . . . and shed for you for the forgiveness of sins'" (SC VI; *Concordia*, p. 343).

Reformed: They expect Baptism, catechesis, self-examination, and faith as preparation. "What is required of them that would worthily partake of the Lord's Supper, that they examine themselves of their knowledge to discern the Lord's body, of their faith to feed upon him, of their repentance, love, and new obedience" (*Westminster Shorter Catechism*, question 97).

Anabaptist: They expect Baptism, catechesis, self-examination, and faith as preparation. "Concerning baptism we confess that penitent believers, who, through faith, regeneration, and the renewing of the Holy Ghost, are made one with God, and are written in heaven, must, upon such Scriptural confession of faith, and renewing of life, be baptized with water . . . and thus be incorporated into the communion of the saints" (*The Dordrecht Confession*, article 7).

Roman Catholic: The "Latin Church" requires Baptism and "reserves admission to Holy Communion to those who have attained the age of reason." They require some catechesis regarding self-examination, that one know how to discern "grave sins" and receive "the sacrament of reconciliation," that is, confession, absolution, and penance. The "faithful should observe the fast required in their Church." The

Church requires the faithful "to take part in the Divine Liturgy on Sundays and feast-days" (*Catechism of the Catholic Church*, §§ 1244, 1385–89).

Baptist: They expect Baptism, catechesis, self-examination, and faith as preparation. "We believe that Christian Baptism . . . is prerequisite to the privileges of a Church relation; and to the Lord's Supper, in which the members of the Church . . . are to communicate together the dying love of Christ; preceded always by solemn self-examination" (*New Hampshire Baptist Confession*, article 15).

Wesleyan: They expect Baptism, catechesis, self-examination, and faith as preparation. "To such as rightly, worthily, and with faith receive the same, the bread which we break is a partaking of the body of Christ; and likewise the cup of blessing is a partaking of the blood of Christ" (*Methodist Articles of Religion*, article 18).

Liberal: Liberalism has undermined traditional preparation for the Sacrament. For example, some people today question the need for Baptism and thorough catechesis. Individualism emphasizes the "self" in self-examination, taking this to mean that each person should do or believe what he or she feels is best, without regard to congregational beliefs or practices.

Point to Remember

Let a person examine himself, then, and so eat of the bread and drink of the cup. *1 Corinthians 11:28*

Close Communion

The following are excerpts from a CPH Bible study produced with the aid of former LCMS president Dr. A. L. Barry. The text is written by the Secretary of the Synod, Raymond L. Hartwig.

Major issues are being discussed in today's church, including worship style, the office of the public ministry, and the service of women in the church. But one of the most pronounced and debated issues is associated with the Sacrament of the Altar.

Thankfully not everything having to do with Holy Communion is at issue among Lutherans. Basic teachings regarding the Sacrament of the Altar, although questioned and contested in other Christian circles, remain for all Lutherans securely anchored in the Holy Scriptures and the Lutheran Confessions. Together, Lutheran churches confess with Martin Luther in his Small Catechism: "What is the Sacrament of the Altar? It is the true body and blood of our Lord Jesus Christ under the bread and wine, instituted by Christ Himself for us Christians to eat and to drink."

Much must be rightly understood, of course, regarding that brief description of the Sacrament. But this common conviction among us of the real presence of Christ's body and blood is a great blessing that continues to unite in conviction Lutheran Christians all over the world. So also is the conviction that this Lord's Supper has both vertical and horizontal dimensions. On the one hand, it is a vertical impartation from God to man of all the marvelous blessings included in the words "Given and shed for you for the remission of sins." On the other hand, the Sacrament is also a horizontal celebration of Christian fellowship. Both dimensions are clearly recognized in our Lutheran Confessions: "After the Last Supper, as he was about to begin his bitter passion and death for our sin, in this sad, last hour of his life, this truthful and almighty Lord, our Creator and Redeemer Jesus Christ, selected his words with great deliberation and care in ordaining and instituting this most venerable sacrament, which was to be observed with great reverence and obedience until the end of the world, and which was to be an abiding memorial of his bitter passion and death and of all his blessings, a seal of the new covenant, a comfort for all sorrowing hearts, and a true bond and union of Christians with Christ their head *and with one another*" (*Formula of Concord, Solid Declaration*, Article VII, 44, *emphasis added*).

All Lutherans continue to hold such a vertical-horizontal understanding of the Lord's Supper, which results in pastoral care regarding practice, care that was certainly also evident in the early Christian church. The well-known church historian Werner Elert (1885–1954), in his first book, *Eucharist and Church Fellowship in the First Four Centuries*, presents a comprehensive description of the Communion practice of the early church. Elert discusses at length the reasoning behind their very restrictive practice. As he points out, the church universally recognized that inadmissible altar fellowship injures the integrity of the church. It would have been unthinkable for them to admit a person of a differing confession to the Sacrament—or even that people could participate without significant proof of being in full church fellowship.

Even more important than historical practice, of course, is the testimony of Holy Scripture, which contains God's inspired instruction regarding the proper use of His Sacrament. Clearly the vertical and horizontal dimensions of the Sacrament can be harmed by careless participation. Certainly those who are ungodly and unrepentant, including those who take part in non-Christian religions, must be prevented from participation: "You must not associate with anyone who calls himself a brother but is sexually immoral or greedy, an idolater or a slanderer, a drunkard, or a swindler. With such a man do not even eat. . . . Expel the wicked man from among you" (1 Corinthians 5:11, 13). "The sacrifices of pagans are offered to demons, not to God, and I do not want you to be participants with demons. You cannot drink the cup of the Lord and the cup of demons too; you cannot have a part in both the Lord's Table and the table of demons" (1 Corinthians 10:20–21).

Also to be excluded are those who are unforgiving and refuse to be reconciled, showing by their behavior that they do not really believe and appreciate the forgiveness that God offers to them in the Sacrament. Jesus clearly teaches, "If you do not forgive men their sins, your Father will not forgive your sins" (Matthew 6:15).

Most Lutheran Christians also agree that those who are unable to examine themselves, such as infants, the unconscious, and the people who have not received proper instruction, should not be admitted to the Sacrament for their own safety's sake, following the instruction of St. Paul: "A man ought to examine himself before he eats of the bread and drinks of the cup. For anyone who eats and drinks without recognizing the body of the Lord eats and drinks judgment on himself. That is why many among you are weak and sick, and a number of you have fallen asleep. But if we judged ourselves, we would not come under judgment" (1 Corinthians 11:28–31).

Finally, the Scriptures speak also of the exclusion from the Sacrament of those of a different confession of faith, since the Lord's Supper contains the heart of the Gospel and is a testimony of the unity of faith. Again it is St. Paul who provides important instruction: "Whenever you eat this bread and drink this cup, you proclaim the Lord's death until He comes" (1 Corinthians 11:26). "Watch out for those who cause divisions and put obstacles in your way that are contrary to the teaching you have learned. Keep away from them" (Romans 16:17).

The Lutheran Church—Missouri Synod has continued the practice of the early church that we know today as close or close(d) Communion. Its first president, Dr. C. F. W. Walther, argued in his "Theses on Communion Fellowship with the Heterodox" of 1870 that "participation in the Sacrament is church fellowship and cannot exist when there are different confessions involved." This early conviction was later repeated by theologian John Fritz in his book *Pastoral Theology*, maintaining that one who "communes at the altar of any church, he thereby, by a public act, confesses the faith of that church." More recently, campus pastor Donald Deffner, in a tract entitled "Why Close Communion?" concludes, "And so in welcoming such a person who holds to false doctrines, even though he be a practicing Christian, we would become partakers of that person's sins and teaching."

In response to growing discussion in the church, the Missouri Synod already in 1967 resolved by convention resolution to continue to formally support and advocate the practice of close Communion. It noted that "the celebration and reception of Holy Communion not only implies but is a confession of the unity of faith." It further resolved "that pastors and congregations of The Lutheran Church—Missouri Synod, except in situations of emergency and in special cases of pastoral care, commune individuals of only those Lutheran synods which are now in fellowship with us" (Resolution 2–19). This resolution has been repeated and underscored in several subsequent conventions as well.

The Commission on Theology and Church Relations of The Lutheran Church—Missouri Synod, in its report *Theology and Practice of the Lord's Supper* (May 1983), has added this further explanation: "A heavy responsibility rests on pastors in making decisions as they evaluate those exceptional cases of pastoral care where persons who are members of denominations not in fellowship with the LCMS desire to receive the Lord's Supper. However, part of the pastor's responsibility in such situations involves informing individuals desiring Communion also of *their* responsibility regarding an action which identifies them with the confessional position of the church body to which the host congregation belongs and their willingness to place themselves under the spiritual care of the pastor in that place."

It should be noted that the majority of Christians today still maintain a practice of close Communion and that most Lutheran groups in the United States, including those with a differing practice today, did at one time concur in the practice of close(d) Communion. The predecessor bodies of the largest Lutheran body in the United States today, the Evangelical Lutheran Church of America (ELCA), consistently subscribed to the Akron/Galesburg Rule of 1870: "I. The rule is: Lutheran pulpits are for Lutheran ministers only; Lutheran altars are for Lutheran communicants only. II. The exceptions to the rule belong to the sphere of privilege, not right. III. The determination of the exceptions is to be made in consonance with these principles, by the conscientious judgment of pastors, as the case arises."

This responsibility can be a difficult one for pastors, resulting in some of the most difficult moments in ministry. Herman von Bezzel captured the feeling of many a pastor in carrying out this important stewardship,

"If things were to be according to my heart, I would let everyone come to the altar." And yet Bezzel also rightly concluded, "However, I do not have my heart to ask in these matters, but rather my obedience." How important for pastors to become as knowledgeable as possible regarding this important stewardship, and how important for the people of the congregation also rightly to understand this Communion practice and to support their pastor as he carries out this significant responsibility. This is the purpose of this Bible study.[3]

The Fight for the Church Keys

The following story describes one congregation (Hönigern, now in western Poland) that rebelled against the Prussian Union. Their suffering and persistence will help you understand what Lutherans experienced because of their beliefs about the Lord's Supper. The story picks up after Pastor Kellner refused to use the king's new worship service (*Agende*). The royal consistory commission summoned Kellner, threatened him with punishment, and fined him. The church deputies locked the church and refused to turn over the keys to the commission.

Now afterward alarmed expectation drove the congregation to very eager use of Word and Sacrament, both of which appeared endangered. In eight weeks about 2,000 communion-ready people sought communion of the holy sacrament 2,930 times. Many from out of town who often traveled ten miles (often more than one hundred people in surrounding villages found hospitable admission) worked powerfully by their speech and example in order to strengthen the Hönigern congregation members. In the congregation many came to acknowledge their sins and the salvation of Christ, so that in those eight weeks at Hönigern more lives had been roused than otherwise in eight years.

At last, on September 11, appeared the commission sent by the consistory.

Yet before 8 o'clock one saw the children of the congregation on the different sidewalks run toward the dear house of God, most in Sunday dress, all with hymnals under their arms. Among their number were also three little children, born on the day or night before, whom their parents would still see baptized according to the Lutheran order in the Lutheran

3 *Close Communion: Sharing God's Meal* (St. Louis: Concordia, 1995), 7–11.

church. About two thousand congregation members had assembled themselves at the open place under the trees of the church graveyard. Under them [also] about 9 o'clock walked their pastor, [who] exhorted them to rest and to devotion in God's will. The entire assembly answered with the singing of songs: "Abide, O Dearest Jesus" and "Dear Christians, One and All, Rejoice."

During the singing the pastor went with the deputies into the parsonage and turned over to them church keys, the church seal, and the cashbox (with about 28 Thaler); the church books remained in the locked sacristy. The pastor asked the deputies, that they might advise one another, whether they would bring the church books. With these words he went out and sang further with the congregation the songs "We All Believe in One True God," "O Holy Spirit, Enter In," "O You Giver of True Joy," and "From Eternity, O God."

After 10 o'clock two military police appeared, who, unperturbed by the singing crowd, went on. Then appeared the commission. . . . The District President walked to the singing pastor and let the local tribunal, church, and school principles form a circle into which the commission and Pastor Kellner entered. Finally once more Kellner was asked whether he would receive the new *Agende* with the August 16 authorized modifications. He answered [that] he would receive it if someone had disproved the reasons he raised for opposition. To this came the reply that here is not the time or place to refute reasons; he should simply answer with a yes or no. If he answered no, the superintendent would immediately declare his suspension. The pastor answered that he could not acknowledge this suspension, since the union consistory had no authority to ordain it. Since the District President demanded the church keys, the forty deputies declared the same way that they would not give them up. "This is the fruit of your eight-year operation," said the superintendent to the pastor. "You should be ashamed of yourself." The pastor answered, "It's a trifle to me that I am judged by you, Mr. Superintendent, or by a human day; Jesus Christ is a true judging judge." "Yes," said the superintendent, "who *will* judge." "Yes," dismissed the congregation members standing about, "who will judge you, Mr. Superintendent!"

Now, while the District President with the remaining men of the commission negotiated about the local spiritual caregiver and the church principals were in the schoolhouse, the entire congregation drew together and sang on the spot before the schoolhouse "Commit Whatever Grieves You." . . .

The further discussions, in which the deputies pled that they must not take their good pastor away from them, had no success. The District President made known that the negotiations broke off and at 2 o'clock would be continued. In the meantime he sent out a riding military policeman in order to acquire someone who might break open the church doors. Both horseshoers and community smiths of Hönigern and of Eckendorf had refused this service, and finally a smith came from out of town, who under the rebukes of the congregation members set out to perform his handiwork. . . .

Now the commission broke out toward the church, the District President, the military police, and the smith going before. At some distance followed the Superintendent and Pastor Bauch. Kellner, however, got down on his knees in his study and wrestled with the Lord in prayer, that He might still rule the congregation according to His counsel and will. The women, however, had positioned themselves before the church doors and remained singing. The commission withdrew.

With consent of the District President, Pastor Kellner assembled the forty deputies yet once more at the church graveyard—first of all he called upon the Lord concerning His Holy Spirit, and then [he] called the deputies—still once more to consider whether they would hand over the church that day. They might weigh the difficult quartering cost, which stood before them. They replied again: "Our conscience would rebuke us if we willingly turn our Lutheran church into a union church from fear of bare threats; also we owe our children witness that we have let them take only by force the doors we mutually inherited from our fathers." And when their votes were counted, thirty-eight set themselves against the transfer and two for the transfer.

While the commission drew back to the protocol recording in the schoolroom, Pastor Kellner walked to the threshold of the church doors, prayed the Our Father, and spoke the Blessing over the people who had gathered. All together, 2,000 participants fell on their knees. . . .

On September 12 the church patron Herzog of Würtemburg arrived about 5 o'clock in Hönigern. Since more than a thousand of the congregation members were gathered, he asked the deputies for the church keys and set before them the possible result of their insubordination. They continued, however, in their refusal. Since not all deputies were opposed, Herzog decided that about 10 o'clock a written decision should be sent to him. Many ladies dropped to his feet and begged him about support for the pastor and the old *Agende*. In the written answer the deputies declared that they could not and would not receive the new *Agende* willingly; against force they would raise no resistance other than standing unarmed before the door singing, and quiet songs would certainly not mention force. . . .

On September 14 the deputies delivered the church keys to Pastor Kellner with the request that he preach to them and administer the Sacrament. He did so and was committing hereby—up to that point he had declared with words that he would not acknowledge the suspension—the first acts of disobedience against the royal commission. Five hundred communicants received the Holy Sacrament. After conducting the service, the deputies locked the church again and subsequently kept the keys in their care.

Tuesday next appeared government board member Storch in the company of the District President in the parsonage and set the choice before the pastor, whether to acknowledge the suspension and produce the church keys or to follow him as a captive. The pastor asked whether he came in the name of the District government or in the name of the royal consistory. Since the District President answered in the name of the District government, Kellner complied without refusal of the police arrest.

The separation of the pastor from his sick wife, who had recently given birth, and from his child and congregation was deeply bitter and penetrating to the depths of his heart. The assembled crowd sobbed and stretched their arms toward their pastor, seized his suitcase and at first would not let go of it until his express word that whoever resisted his arrest by the police sinned against God's commandment. They allowed it. . . .

On December 22 a commission arrived again. . . . Consistory President Hahn attempted to instruct the congregation with kindness. The schoolteacher Leib presented to him the question: "Mr. Consistory President, you entrusted yourself in the past before God's tribunal to maintain that after introduction of the new *Agende* our church would remain a pure Lutheran church?" He answered resoundingly, "You indeed retain the Lutheran Lord's Supper; also the Lutheran symbolic books apply!" The District President, however, threatened the schoolteacher with dismissal if he did not go into the church.

Thereby enacted the commission a publication, the contents of which stated that the congregation be summoned for handing over the church keys at the next church inventory, that in the meantime the Lutheran faith would not be abandoned by the revised *Agende*, but that further insubordination would be broken up by armed force. This publication was posted everywhere; however, they were torn down in some places. . . .

On Monday was read after that a royal cabinet order dated December 12, in which the king found fault with the previous order, then in cover of the *Agende* gave reassurance that the Lutheran faith would not be renounced by it. "The symbolic books of the Lutheran church remain, as I already many times publicly have said, in their full authority, and each preacher whom you present shall, after my appointment, as soon as the congregation wishes, expressly be pledged on the Augsburg Confession." Because of constant reluctance, however, the necessary coercive measures were already set in motion. . . .

On Tuesday, on the day before Christmas Eve, the Crown Prince was traveling with Baron von Kottwitz and was saying to him: "Today's a difficult day for me; they allow soldiers to march against Hönigern." On the same day at 12 o'clock moved on to the location four hundred infantry, thirty dragoons, and fifty Hussars, which up to that time had remained a mile from Hönigern. On Holy Christmas Eve, at 5:30 a.m., the military surrounded the church on all sides, so that also two hundred congregation members, who had kept watch, saw themselves surrounded. They were asked to remove themselves. Five minutes to consider—they sang. The summons repeated, the same time to consider—they sang. For the third time the crowd was summoned, and at the same time the soldiers loaded. At this point went off some soldier's rifle, which one of the congregation members would snatch away from him in order to see whether it was really loaded. The bullet punched through the window into the church. The church railing was broken. The soldiers moved forward and struck the people with rifle butts and the flat side of swords, smashed a door, and entered. The congregation members fled and scattered in every direction, still with blows pursued, whereby some, both women and youths, were wounded. Unaided out of the shelters were individuals fetched by the hair; others were ridden down. The pursuit continued two hours. In the empty parsonage the pantry and wash cupboard were broken open and other outrages committed. Eight persons were led away to Namslau captured, and the soldiers assigned quartering in homes. The eager Lutheran homes received most of them, some as many as twenty men.[4]

Later that day a new pastor was installed who would lead the congregation with the new *Agende*. This and other incidents caused many Lutherans to emigrate to North America and Australia.

4 Hermann Theodor Wangemann, *Prussian Church History*, vol. 2 (W. Schultze, 1859–60), 66–88; translated by Edward Engelbrecht.

TOPIC FIFTEEN

Priesthood and Ministry[1]

Engaging This Topic

"So, what's the deal?"
"What do you mean?"
"Well, you Lutherans say that every Christian is a priest to God, but you have ministers dressed up in fancy robes who speak on behalf of God."
"That's true. Our pastors speak in the stead and by the command of Jesus Christ."
"But doesn't every Christian do that? I just don't get it."

Priesthood and ministry—it seems so simple in theory. Every Christian is a member of Christ's holy priesthood by virtue of his or her Baptism. Some members of the holy priesthood are called and ordained to be pastors in the Office of the Holy Ministry. As our Lutheran Confessions so clearly state: "Our churches teach that no one should publicly teach in the Church, or administer the Sacraments, without a rightly ordered call" (AC XIV; *Concordia*, p. 39). That appears simple enough to understand. While every baptized believer is a priest in the royal priesthood of Jesus Christ, not every Christian holds the Office of the Holy Ministry. Martin Luther put it very succinctly, when he wrote to the Senate of Prague in 1523: "A Priest is not identical with Presbyter or Minister—for one is born to be priest, one becomes a minister."[2]

The proper distinction of priesthood and ministry lies at the heart of the Lutheran Reformation. In Luther's day, priests (i.e., ministers or pastors) were seen as a more holy group of Christians, closer to God and separated from the people. They had special power by virtue of their ordination to change the bread and wine into the body and blood of Christ in the Lord's Supper. They also offered the body and blood of Christ to the

1 This chapter adapted from *The Lutheran Difference: Priesthood and Ministry*, written by William M. Cwirla. Copyright © 2007 Concordia Publishing House.

2 AE 40:18.

Father as an unbloody sacrifice to atone for the sins of the people. Priests were seen as analogous to the Old Testament priesthood of the tabernacle and the temple, a holy order set apart to make sacrifices for the people.

Luther and the reformers realized that the New Testament does not have a priesthood like that of the Old Testament. Jesus Christ is the one and only High Priest of a new covenant, established by the sacrifice that He made on the cross. This once-for-all sacrifice of Christ as the Lamb of God who takes away the sin of the world put an end to all bloody sacrifices for sin. And it ended the Old Testament priesthood of the sons of Aaron. Christ, our High Priest, has an eternal priesthood like that of Melchizedek. And now, every Christian is anointed a priest in Baptism, not to offer bloody sacrifices for sin but to offer his or her body as a living sacrifice in thanksgiving to God.

Luther and the reformers also recognized that the Church as a priesthood has an ordered ministry, an office that is charged with publicly preaching the Word and administering the gifts of Christ's sacrifice. Priesthood and ministry—both are gifts of God to His holy people and through His people to the world.

Lutheran Facts

Nearly every Christian group has some form of the Office of the Holy Ministry. Even the most independent congregations have pastors, some of whom hold considerable authority.

Still there are considerable differences and questions among Christians regarding the priesthood of Christians and the Office of the Holy Ministry. Is every Christian a minister in the same sense that every Christian is a priest? What are the distinctive duties and authorities of the Holy Ministry? How is the concept of priesthood different from ministry? How does God call a person to the Holy Ministry, and who is eligible to serve?

As with many other issues at the time of the Reformation, Luther and his fellow reformers steered a careful path between the Roman Church, on the one hand, and the radical reformers, on the other. Affirming both priesthood and ministry, the Lutheran Reformation retained both the dignity of every Christian before God as a priest and the special office in the Church that is charged with preaching the Word and administering the Sacraments. Unlike Rome, the Lutherans held that every Christian is a member of the priestly caste. Unlike the radical Anabaptists and others, Lutherans held that not everyone is called to be a minister or pastor in the church. In this way, Lutherans preserved both scriptural teachings without compromising one for the sake of the other.

Baptism and Priesthood

For a priest, especially in the New Testament, was not made but born. He was created, not ordained. He was born not indeed of flesh, but through a birth of the Spirit, by water and Spirit in the washing of regeneration.

—Martin Luther, "Concerning the Ministry" (AE 40:19)

When you think of a priest, what images come to your mind? A holy man, perhaps, set apart from the rest? Someone who wears long robes and black shirts with a white-tabbed collar? A religious person who is close to God? But do you think of a little child, or a mother caring for her baby, or a car mechanic servicing a transmission, or a farmer tending his crops? Those activities somehow don't seem very priestly, yet they are! One of the great insights of the Reformation was that every baptized believer in Jesus Christ is a priest to God in the priesthood of Christ.

Baptismal Beginnings

First Peter is an exercise in reading between the lines. If we pay attention to what Peter is saying to his audience, we can find evidence that he is writing this letter to newly baptized Christians. In the first chapter, he talks about new birth (v. 3) and calls his readers "born again" (v. 23). Peter continues in chapter 2 by saying that like newborn infants, they "long for the pure spiritual milk" (v. 2). Peter includes a reference to Exodus when he calls his readers "a chosen race, a royal priesthood, a holy nation, a people for [God's] own possession" (1 Peter 2:9). Finally, in chapter 3, Peter tells his readers that "Baptism . . . now saves you" (v. 21).

In chapter 2, Peter talks about his readers' relationship to God. He says they are "chosen" by God and "precious" to Him. Peter speaks of them as a "spiritual house" (i.e., temple) and a "holy priesthood." Both of these are images from the Old Testament, referring to the Levitical priesthood and the tabernacle or temple (see Exodus 37–39). The purpose of the New Testament priesthood is to offer "spiritual sacrifices" that are acceptable to God through Jesus Christ. This stands in contrast to the sacrifices of the Old Testament, which were sacrifices of blood for the atonement of sin.

The baptized are also called a chosen people, royal priesthood, holy nation, God's possession, and kings and priests in Revelation 1:4–6. *Chosen* implies election in grace; *royal priesthood* suggests kingly, sacrificial service; *holy nation* says that the Church is the New Testament Israel of God (Galatians 6:16). Each is granted in Christ through Holy Baptism.

If we compare Exodus 19:3–6 with 1 Peter 2:9–10, we see that the Church is similar to Old Testament Israel. Both come through water (the Red Sea and Baptism) and into the Promised Land as God's holy nation and priesthood. Israel's "baptism" was in the Red Sea under Moses' guidance, since he was the covenant leader (1 Corinthians 10:2).

Once we were not God's people and not recipients of His mercy, as we read in Hosea: "[Gomer] conceived again and bore a daughter. And the LORD said to [Hosea], 'Call her name No Mercy, for I will no more have mercy on the house of Israel, to forgive them all.' . . . When [Gomer] had weaned No Mercy, she conceived and bore a son. And the LORD said, 'Call his name Not My People, for you are not my people, and I am not your God'" (Hosea 1:6, 8–9). The Hebrew names for Hosea's children of Gomer's adultery were, respectively, Lo-ruhama and Lo-ammi. Our sin and the sin of Adam have alienated us from God and placed us under His wrath. But we can be certain that we are part of the people of God and recipients of His mercy, as we read in Hosea 2:1, 22–23:

> Say to your brothers, "You are my people," and to your sisters, "You have received mercy." . . . "And in that day I will answer, declares the LORD, I will answer the heavens, and they shall answer the earth, and the earth shall answer the grain, the wine, and the oil, and they shall answer Jezreel, and I will sow her for myself in the land. And I will have mercy on No Mercy, and I will say to Not My People, 'You are My people'; and he shall say, 'You are my God.'"

In Baptism, God restores us in Christ, the beloved Son, so that we are beloved and belong to God as His priestly people.

Baptism joins us to Christ in His death (Romans 6:1–7), washes us with the Word (Ephesians 5:26), clothes us with Christ (Galatians 3:27), works rebirth and renewal by the Holy Spirit (Titus 3:5), and saves us through the death and resurrection of Jesus (1 Peter 3:21). This means we are born again and clothed for a life of priestly service to God, to live under Christ in His kingdom, and to serve Him, as it says in the explanation of the Second Article of the Apostles' Creed in the Small Catechism, in "everlasting righteousness, innocence, and blessedness" (*Concordia*, p. 329). Our priestly vestments are the righteousness of Christ, which we wear as a robe covering our sin.

Holy Priests in a Priesthood

In the Old Testament, priests were considered holy, that is, set apart by God for service to Him and to His people. The high priest wore special clothing showing that he represented Israel before God and God before Israel (Exodus 28). He had a headpiece, a turban with the phrase "Holy to the LORD" written on it (Exodus 28:36), a visible reminder of his being set apart for priestly service. The high priest and his priesthood were specially consecrated for their office by washing, anointing with oil, and sacrifice (Exodus 29).

In Exodus 28, we read that the high priest wore a breastplate, ephod, robe, tunic, sash, and turban. The breastplate and ephod carried the names of the tribes of Israel. The high priest literally represented the people before God; the turban with its insignia also indicated that he literally represented God before the people. In Galatians, Paul states that in Baptism we are clothed with Christ, that is, we wear the vestments of Jesus Christ, our High Priest, as priests in His royal priesthood (3:27).

In Exodus 29, we see that Baptism is an anointing into the priesthood of Christ. A priest was washed with water and anointed with oil. Sacrifices were made at priests' ordinations, and blood was sprinkled on them. In Baptism, we are cleansed by the blood of Christ and anointed by Him as priests to serve Him. As 1 Peter 2:9 indicates, Baptism is a consecration into the royal priesthood, wherein Christ anoints us for priestly service.

A Greater Priest

The Book of Hebrews makes the argument that Christ is a superior priest in a greater priesthood than the Old Testament priesthood of Aaron. Christ is a sinless High Priest in a greater order (that of Melchizedek, not Aaron), who offers His blood in a greater and superior sacrifice in a greater covenant at a greater, eternal tabernacle.

Given that Christ's priesthood is eternal, we would expect the New Testament priesthood to reflect the once-for-all character of Jesus' priestly sacrifice. No longer is the shedding of blood called for in the New Testament, because the atoning blood of Christ has been shed one time for all time. The priesthood of the New Testament does not deal with the atonement for sin but with offerings of thanksgiving in view of Christ's all-atoning sacrifice. The Apology of the Augsburg Confession states clearly:

> These are the sacrifices of the New Testament, as Peter teaches, "a holy priesthood, to offer spiritual sacrifices" (1 Peter 2:5). Spiritual sacrifices, however, are contrasted not only with those of cattle, but even with human works offered by the outward act, because *spiritual* refers to the movements of the Holy Spirit in us. (Ap XXIV 26; *Concordia*, p. 224)

Comparisons

Eastern Orthodox: "What ecclesiastical institution is there through which the succession of the Apostolical ministry is preserved? The ecclesiastical *Hierarchy*" (*The Longer Catechism of the Eastern Church*, question 276).

Lutheran: "Here belong the statements of Christ that testify that the Keys have been given to the Church, and not merely to certain persons, 'Where two or three are gathered in My name . . .' [Matthew 18:20]. Finally, Peter's statement also confirms this, 'You are . . . a royal priesthood' [1 Peter 2:9]" (Tr 68–69; *Concordia*, p. 304).

Reformed/Presbyterian: "All saints that are united to Jesus Christ their head, by his Spirit and by faith, have fellowship with him in his graces, sufferings, death, resurrection, and glory; and being united to one another in love, they have communion in each other's gifts and graces, and are obliged to the performance of such duties, public and private, as do conduce to their mutual good, both in the inward and outward man" (*The Westminster Confession of Faith*, chapter 26.1).

Roman Catholic: "If any one saith, that there is not in the New Testament a visible and external priesthood; or, that there is not any power of consecrating and offering the true body and blood of the Lord, and of forgiving and retaining sins, but only an office and bare ministry of preaching the Gospel; or, that those who do not preach are not priests at all: let him be anathema" (*Canons and Decrees of the Council of Trent*, Session 4, 1; cf. CCC2 paras. 1581–89).

Baptist: "The members of these churches are saints by calling, visibly manifesting and evidencing (in and by their profession and walking) their obedience unto that call of Christ" (*The Baptist Confession of 1688*, 6).

Point to Remember

But you are a chosen race, a royal priesthood, a holy nation, a people for His own possession, that you may proclaim the excellencies of Him who called you out of darkness into His marvelous light. *1 Peter 2:9*

The Priesthood at Worship

> Life is worship. The real issue in worship is set between idolatry, which is death, and faith, which is participation in the life of God.
>
> —Kenneth F. Korby, "The Church at Worship," in *The Lively Function of the Gospel*

Priests worship, and a priesthood is a worshiping community. Strictly speaking, worship is a two-way street. The Lord serves His people through His Word, and His people serve Him through their prayers and praise. These two ways we commonly call Sacrament and sacrifice. Sacraments run from God to us; sacrifices run from us to God. In the Old Testament, these were sacrifices of blood, grain, wine, or money. In the New Testament, the sacrifices are unbloody, offered not for sin but in thanksgiving for what God has done. Like smoke rising up from the altar, the sacrifices of God's priestly people rise up to Him.

Think of all that goes on in the worship of God. The focus is on worship and the various activities in the liturgy. The sacrificial actions include prayer, confession, praise, and the singing of hymns. Sacramental actions include hearing the Word, receiving the Sacrament, and so on. The priestly direction of worship goes from us to God, while the sacramental direction of worship runs from God to us. This is in important distinction in a Lutheran understanding of worship (see Ap XXIV 26; *Concordia*, pp. 224–25).

Spiritual Sacrifices

Paul tells the Romans: "I appeal to you therefore, brothers, by the mercies of God, to present your bodies as a living sacrifice, holy and acceptable to God, which is your spiritual worship. Do not be conformed to this world, but be transformed by the renewal of your mind, that by testing you may discern what is the will of God, what is good and acceptable and perfect" (12:1–2). Priests in the New Testament offer their bodies as living sacrifices, which are their spiritual worship. Notice that *spiritual* does not mean non-material or having nothing to do with the body. Rather, the word *spiritual* means, as the Confessions state, that which is worked by the Holy Spirit (Ap XXIV 26; *Concordia*, pp. 224–25). The sacrifices are living, since the one sacrifice into death that atones for all sin has been accomplished in the cross of Jesus. It is this sacrifice, once for all, that makes the spiritual sacrifices of God's priestly people acceptable to Him. They are offered in view of God's mercy in Jesus Christ.

Paul goes on to talk about God's gifts of grace (Romans 12:3–8). Here we learn that everyone has different gifts and responsibilities, and this diversity is a good thing for the priesthood (see 1 Corinthians 12:12–30).[3] An individual priest is to the priesthood as a member is to the whole body. This is a very important concept. No person is a priest unto himself or herself but a priest *within a priesthood.* Just as a body has a diversity of parts with differing functions, so the priesthood of Christ has several priests with a diversity of duties and gifts. In Romans, Paul specifically lists prophesying (in the sense of proclaiming the Word), serving, teaching, encouraging, contributing, leading, and showing mercy. In 1 Corinthians, he lists apostles, prophets, and teachers, followed by workers of miracles, healers, administrators, those speaking in various tongues, and the like. This is clearly not intended as some comprehensive inventory of gifts, but these are examples of how the Spirit arranges a diversity of gifts in a given congregation for the common good. Every baptized believer has a place and purpose in the priesthood of Christ, and no task or gift is insignificant or unimportant. This diversity of gifts and persons strengthens the priesthood by placing a variety of resources at the disposal of the Holy Spirit who unites all believers in the one Body of Christ.

In Colossians, Paul describes the baptismal clothing of God's chosen people: "compassion, kindness, humility, meekness, and patience" (3:12). The priestly vestments of Christ's people are not vestments made of cloth but are the robe of Christ's righteousness and His perfect obedience under the Law. These vestments describe Christ and the baptized believer in Christ. In addition, Paul commends the virtues of forgiveness and love, which preserve the unity of the priesthood. Without forgiveness and love, the priests of God would not be united as a priesthood. The priesthood as a united whole, forgiving one another and uniting in love, is called to peace, to thanksgiving, to teaching, and to admonishing one another with the Word of Christ through psalms, hymns, and spiritual songs (Colossians 3:16).

The liturgy guides and shapes this priestly praise in the congregation, and the daily offices of prayer and the Word do the same in the Christian household. Here, the disciplines of daily prayer, as taught in the Small Catechism, are of special importance as the priests of God pray together as a family, where the father presides and the mother assists in the instruction and prayers of the children. As Peter reminds us, we are to "proclaim the excellencies of Him who called you out of darkness into His marvelous light" (1 Peter 2:9). "Proclaiming the excellencies" includes singing hymns, witnessing to others, proclaiming the Gospel to one another, and showing the mercy of Christ to those in need in our various callings.

3 In the topic on Christian vocation, we will explore this diversity of gifts more deeply.

In Hebrews 12:18–29, the author compares Mount Sinai of the old covenant to Mount Zion of the new. Hebrews lists seven things that pertain to the greater worship of the New Testament:

1. Mount Zion, the heavenly Jerusalem, the city of God;
2. countless angels;
3. the assembly of the firstborn;
4. the Judge of all;
5. the spirits of the justified;
6. Jesus, the Mediator of a new covenant; and
7. His sprinkled blood.

These are all given as a present tense reality, not something that will happen in the future. This is the present tense reality of Christian worship, which has much more to it than meets the eye. In view of these gifts, Hebrews 12:29 states that we are to worship God with reverence (fear) and awe, "for our God is a consuming fire." Priestly worship is never comfortable, but it is comforting. To enter into the presence of God is an awe-full experience because He can destroy you and He can save you.

"Worthy Is the Lamb"

Revelation 4–5 gives a marvelous depiction of worship from a heavenly perspective. These chapters provide a foretaste of what is to come and a revelation of the mystery of worship that already is. At the center of worship is the Lamb, enthroned in the very center, who appears slain and alive at the same time. Surrounding the Lamb (Christ) are twenty-four enthroned elders, representing the Church as God's Israel, both Old and New Testament. At the four corners are the four living ones, the seraphim that Isaiah saw when he was called (Isaiah 6), but now their faces are uncovered. Their faces reflect their constituencies—an eagle, the foremost creature of the air; an ox, the chief domestic beast; a lion, the chief of the wild beasts; and a man, the head of the creation. Together, they represent the whole creation that worships the Father and the Son and the Holy Spirit. Around them are myriads of angels who chant an endless hymn to Christ: "Worthy is the Lamb who was slain" (Revelation 5:12). God is praised as Creator, "for You created all things, and by Your will they existed and were created" (Revelation 4:11). God is praised for the work of redemption through His Son: "By Your blood You ransomed people for God from every tribe and language and people and nation." Creation and redemption are the twin pillars on which all of worship rests. It is centered in Christ, the Lamb of God, who takes away the sin of the world. So today Christian worship always has Jesus Christ at the center. Christ is the Word through whom all things were made (John 1:1–2), and He is the Lamb whose blood redeems men for God. Without Christ at the center, no hymn or sermon or worship can properly be called Christian.

Everything in Order

Worship is an ordered event. That shouldn't be surprising. Most human activities are. When we go to a ball game, we sit in assigned seats, and the players play their assigned positions. The ordered activity of worship is no different. But according to 1 Corinthians 14:26–39, the Corinthian congregation had some problems with disorderly conduct in worship, and Paul had to lay down some rules for them. The Corinthian congregation was deeply divided. Apparently, some were disrupting the services by babbling in strange tongues, and others were insisting on speaking, even to the point of interrupting others. Women, ordinarily quiet, were asking questions and commenting, to the embarrassment of their husbands. In view of the "everything goes" approach to worship, the apostle gave the Corinthians some simple rules. Only two or three may speak, each in turn. There is no speaking in tongues unless it can be made intelligible, and the women are to remain silent. Since God is a God of order and peace, everything conducted in His name should be done in an appropriate and orderly manner.

The liturgy provides an orderly framework in which the Word of God may be heard and taught, and the priestly people of God have scope and room for their prayers and praises as one body. Since the liturgy is primarily drawn from the Scriptures, it ensures that the Word of God dwells richly among the priesthood.

As priests in Christ's royal priesthood, we each have a place and purpose in corporate worship. Too often, we are concerned only with our "being fed" or what we "get out of" worship. Every priest has a purpose in the worship of the priesthood, whether to sing, to pray, or to encourage. Those priests who are called and ordained as pastors are given to preach, teach, and administer the Sacraments. One often neglected priestly act is the word *Amen*, which is often intercepted by overeager presiders. *Amen* is the priestly word of the royal priesthood. It is saying "yes" to the prayers and blessings spoken. If nothing else, every priest belongs in church to say his or her "Amen."

Comparisons

Eastern Orthodox: "Whence originates the Hierarchy of the Orthodox Christian Church? From Jesus Christ himself, and from the descent of the Holy Ghost on the Apostles; from which time it is continued, in unbroken succession, through the laying on of hands, in the Sacrament of Orders" (*The Longer Catechism of the Eastern Church*, question 277).

Lutheran: "So that we may obtain this faith, the ministry of teaching the Gospel and administering the Sacraments was instituted. Through the Word and Sacraments, as through instruments, the Holy Spirit is given [John 20:22]" (AC V 1–2; *Concordia*, p. 33). "Our churches teach that no one should publicly teach in the Church, or administer the Sacraments, without a rightly ordered call" (AC XIV; *Concordia*, p. 39).

Reformed/Presbyterian: "Saints, by profession, are bound to maintain an holy fellowship and communion in the worship of God, and in performing such other spiritual services as tend to their mutual edification; as also in relieving each other in outward things, according to their several abilities and necessities" (*The Westminster Confession of Faith*, chapter 26.2).

Roman Catholic: "If anyone saith, that order, or sacred ordination, is not truly and properly a sacrament instituted by Christ the Lord; or, that it is a kind of human figment devised by men unskilled in ecclesiastical matters; or, that it is only a kind of rite for choosing ministers of the Word of God and of the sacraments: let him be anathema" (*The Canons and Decrees of the Council of Trent*, Session 4, 3; cf. CCC2 para. 1581).

Baptist: "To each of these churches thus gathered, according to his mind declared in his Word, he hath given all that power and authority which is any way needful for the carrying on that order in worship and discipline which he hath instituted for them to observe, with commands and rules for the due and right exerting and executing of that power" (*The Baptist Confession of 1688*, 7).

Point to Remember

I appeal to you therefore, brothers, by the mercies of God, to present your bodies as a living sacrifice, holy and acceptable to God, which is your spiritual worship. *Romans 12:1*

The Priesthood in the World

> We conclude therefore that a Christian man does not live in himself, but in Christ and in his neighbor, or else is no Christian: in Christ by faith; in his neighbor by love.
>
> —Martin Luther, "The Freedom of the Christian" (AE 31:371)

One of the great contributions of the Lutheran Reformation is the concept, derived from God's Word, of vocation or calling. Every Christian has a calling from God, defined by where God has located us in relation to those He has placed around us. There each Christian as a priest to God serves his or her neighbor, and in so doing serves God Himself.[4]

Different denominations have different understandings of the Church and vocation. Roman Catholic and Eastern Orthodox traditions usually see the Church as the ordained priesthood. Some consider holy orders of monks, friars, nuns, and so on, to be "more" a part of the Church than laypeople. Some define the Church as a means of government, with elective offices, boards, and so on. Some see the Church only at the local level, while others see a national or global body as primarily Church. Scripture, however, cuts through any number of human definitions to tell us what God says about His Church.

Priestly work goes on not only in church but also in the home, the workplace, and the community in which the priest lives. A helpful guide for the work of the priesthood in vocation is the "Table of Duties" in the Small Catechism (see *Concordia*, pp. 346–48). There, the life of the priest is organized in three areas: church, civil society, and home (and, by extension, the workplace). But does Scripture talk like this? Consider this quote from Scripture found in the Augsburg Confession: "True Christian perfection is to fear God from the heart, to have great faith, and to trust that for Christ's sake we have a God who has been reconciled [2 Corinthians 5:18–19]. It means to ask for and expect from God His help in all things with confident assurance that we are to live according to our calling in life, being diligent in outward good works, serving in our calling" (AC XXVII 49; *Concordia*, p. 57).

Sometimes people have a romantic view of the Christian life as being religious or always involved in church work. The Lutheran understanding of priesthood as a calling or vocation emphasizes that Christ can be and is served in our various callings, no matter how mundane or worldly they might appear. Christian perfection is not found in some religious life removed from the world but is found in true fear of God under the Law,

4 This section will touch in brief the material that is more fully covered in the chapter on vocation.

and true faith in Christ according to the Gospel, that for His sake our sins are forgiven and that He clothes us with His perfect righteousness. In that liberty, we serve God and the neighbor in our various callings. This was the genius of the Lutheran Reformation that restored the dignity of priesthood to the various callings of people in the world.

Where has God located you with respect to home, congregation, and community? Whom has God placed around you as your neighbor in terms of family, friends, congregation, and neighborhood? What are the various hats that you currently wear? Perhaps your answer includes some of the following: father, mother, son, daughter, employer, employee, citizen, and congregation member. In identifying our various "hats," we are also indicating the places where and the people whom we serve.

Priests in Church

God orders the Church as those who preach and those who hear. The priesthood supports their pastor with a fair wage and support for his family as laborers worthy of their hire (1 Corinthians 9:14; Galatians 6:6–7; 1 Timothy 5:17–18). Pastors should also be given the honor and obedience that befits their office as those who speak "in the stead and by the command" of Jesus Christ (see 1 Thessalonians 5:12–13). Each member of the priesthood is responsible for the support of his or her pastor.

God orders pastors to serve the Church in special ways that give blessing and benefit to His people. In 1 Samuel 13:1–13, Saul becomes impatient when Samuel is delayed in arriving, so he offers the sacrifice himself. God did not give Saul the office to make acceptable sacrifices, and Saul's rejection of the Lord's plan, however "expedient," did not please the Lord and resulted in judgment against Saul. In a similar way, God has provided an office for the preaching of His Word, the administration of His Sacraments, and for the pronouncement of His Absolution.

Although the Lord's Supper is given to the whole Church, it is not given to all to administer it. In the case of an emergency, a layperson may administer Baptism where death appears to be imminent and no pastor is available. No one should be left to die apart from the Gospel of Jesus Christ. Such a case is similar to a citizen's arrest in which a citizen, though not authorized to enforce the law, does so to protect his neighbor and then only until the authorities arrive. At any other time, other than an emergency, the citizen would be arrested for impersonating a police officer. In the case of Samuel, Saul was impersonating a sacrificial minister.

What does this mean in relation to Christ as our High Priest and our own priesthood and vocations? The Epistle to the Hebrews makes the strong argument that Jesus did not make Himself to be the High Priest of the world, but He was called and anointed by God the Father, as the psalms tell us. If this is true of Christ, the eternal Son of God, it is true of His priests. We do not baptize ourselves, but we are baptized into the priesthood by God through His minister. Likewise, God is the one who places us into our various callings and offices, which we receive as a gift from Him. For this reason, we do not speak of our rights as a priesthood but of the gift of our priesthood, since this comes from God and not from ourselves.

Priests at Home

God has an order for the Christian home and family. God orders the home as husbands over wives, and parents over children. The husband is the head of the family as Christ is the Head of the Church (see Ephesians 5:22–33; 1 Peter 3:1–7). The wife is subordinate to her husband, that is, ordered under him as the Church is ordered under Christ. Note that the word for *subordinate* is a word used in the military to indicate every person in his or her rank. The common translation of *submission* does not quite capture the nuance. The wife is not submissive to her husband but subordinate to him. He is the bishop of the household, and she is the deaconess who is there to assist him. Similarly, children are ordered under their parents and are to be obedient to them in the Lord, that is, so long as what parents command is according to God's will. Since a parent's word is God's Word for a child, parents are not to frustrate their children with too many rules, but nurture them in the instruction and discipline of the Lord (Ephesians 6:1–4). Christian parents fulfill their priesthood by bringing their children to Holy Baptism, teaching them the catechism and the Scriptures, and preparing them for Holy Communion and full adult participation in the Church.

Priests in Public

Paul instructed the church at Ephesus about the priesthood of the Christian worker toward his or her boss or subordinates. Paul says the priesthood of the worker is to serve his or her boss as though serving the Lord Himself (6:5–9). Paul reminds us that Christians ought to be the best workers they can be, since they are serving Christ in their work. The priesthood of a boss is to be kind and fair to his or her workers, knowing that we all have one master who is Jesus Christ, who came to be the servant of all.

Scripture also tells us about the Christian's priestly service toward the government. The priesthood of a citizen is to render obedience, honor, respect, revenue, and taxes to the governing authority as God's minister (see Romans 13:1–7; Titus 3:1; 1 Peter 2:13–14). In Lutheran theology, temporal government is sometimes called the kingdom of the left as compared to the kingdom of the right, a kingdom of grace that is manifested in the Church. The Lutheran distinction of the two kingdoms orients the Christian favorably toward the government. Lutherans do not believe in a Christian nation but in a nation in which Christians actively participate in government as their priestly vocation.

In fact, Christians are to pray for those in government regardless of political party: "First of all, then, I urge that supplications, prayers, intercessions, and thanksgivings be made for all people, for kings and all who are in high positions, that we may lead a peaceful and quiet life, godly and dignified in every way. This is good, and it is pleasing in the sight of God our Savior, who desires all people to be saved and to come to the knowledge of the truth" (1 Timothy 2:1–4). The Christian's priesthood calls him or her to pray for those in authority, since intercession for others is uniquely priestly work. If the Christian does not intercede on behalf of the state, who will?

Christians are bound to obey the government as God's representative of law. However, when the government forces someone to go against the Word of God or conscience, which is the Law of God written in men's hearts (Romans 2:14–15), then, as Peter told the high priest, "We must obey God rather than men" (Acts 5:29).

The following comparisons help to illustrate different approaches to Christian vocation and how those differences affect the settings of church, home, employment, and government.

Comparisons

Eastern Orthodox: "What are *Orders*? Orders are a Sacrament, in which the Holy Ghost, by the laying on of the Bishop's hands, ordains them that be rightly chosen to minister sacraments, and to feed the flock of Christ" (*The Longer Catechism of the Eastern Church*, question 357).

Lutheran: "Therefore, when the regular bishops become enemies of the Church or are unwilling to administer ordination, the churches retain their own right ‹to ordain their own ministers›. Wherever the Church is, there is the authority to administer the Gospel" (Tr 66–67; *Concordia*, p. 303).

Reformed/Presbyterian: "The Lord Jesus, as king and head of his Church, hath therein appointed a government in the hand of Church officers, distinct from the civil magistrate" (*The Westminster Confession of Faith*, chapter 30.1).

Roman Catholic: "If anyone saith, that, by sacred ordination, the Holy Ghost is not given; and that vainly therefore do the bishops say, *Receive ye the Holy Ghost*; or, that a character is not imprinted by that ordination; or, that he who has once been a priest can again become a layman: let him be anathema" (*Canons and Decrees of the Council of Trent*, Session 4, 4; cf. CCC2 para. 1581).

Baptist: "A particular church gathered and completely organized, according to the mind of Christ, consists of officers and members; and the officers appointed by Christ to be chosen and set apart by the Church (so-called and gathered) for the peculiar administration of ordinances, and execution of power and duty, which he intrusts them with or calls them to, to be continued to the end of the world, are bishops or elders and deacons" (*The Baptist Confession of 1688*, 8).

Point to Remember

[Submit] to one another out of reverence for Christ. *Ephesians 5:21*

The Office of the Holy Ministry

The ministry of the Word, or the preaching office, is not a human institution but an office that God Himself has established.
—C. F. W. Walther, "Thesis II on the Office" (*Church and Ministry*)

When we hear the word *authority*, we usually think of the law, judges in black robes, and police officers with guns. In the Bible, the word *authority* is actually derived from the word *permission*. Authority, as it is used in the Scriptures, is permission granted to someone to do something. This is where we get the notion of the office. Authority doesn't float in the air like gas but is located in an office, enabling a person to do a given task.

We are under the authority of government in civil society and under the authority of parents in the home. Without parents and government, ordered society quickly degenerates into anarchy. Likewise, the Church without the Office of the Holy Ministry is no longer an ordered priesthood but a random collection of individual priests.

Think about some of the authority structures under which we live. What would happen if there were no notion of office, where literally anyone could be mayor of the city or president of the nation any time he or she felt like it? We live under many authority structures according to the Fourth Commandment: parents, employers, government, the Church. If there were no notion of authority, there would be chaos and anarchy. When the authority structures break down or are disabled, civilized society is impossible. We recognize the need for authority, especially in the civil realm. Although we say that anyone can be president, in fact, only one person is the president. If everyone is in charge, then in fact no one is truly in charge. Knowing where the authority is and who holds it is essential for life together. It is liberating to be under authority, because then we are free to perform our vocation without looking over our shoulder at what's happening around us.

Disciples and Apostles

To understand *authority* in Scripture, consider Mark 3:13–19:

> And He went up on the mountain and called to Him those whom He desired, and they came to Him. And He appointed twelve (whom He also named apostles) so that they might be with Him and He might send them out to preach and have authority to cast out demons. He appointed the twelve: Simon (to whom He gave the name Peter); James the son of Zebedee and John the brother of James (to whom He gave the name Boanerges, that is, Sons of Thunder); Andrew, and Philip, and Bartholomew, and Matthew, and Thomas, and James the son of Alphaeus, and Thaddeus, and Simon the Cananaean, and Judas Iscariot, who betrayed Him.

Notice that Mark makes a distinction that these twelve disciples were apostles. The word *disciple* means "one who follows or learns from another," while the word *apostle* means "one who is sent with authority." Although all apostles were disciples, not all disciples were apostles. Jesus had a large circle of disciples who were loosely associated with Him. Included in that wider circle were the women who followed Him and attended to Him. In Jesus' day, it was unheard of for a rabbi to have female disciples. Out of that greater crowd of disciples, Jesus called twelve apostles. A *disciple* is one who follows and learns from His teacher. All Christians are made disciples through Baptism and teaching (Matthew 28:16–20). An *apostle* is one who is sent with the authority of another. Jesus here specifically authorizes them to preach the kingdom and to drive out demons. They would do precisely what Jesus was doing, "in His stead and by His command." This was a limited authorization, a kind of internship for the apostles, in which they would learn what it means to be authorized by the Son of God Himself.

After Jesus' death and resurrection, He met with His Eleven (the Twelve minus Judas) to authorize them. Jesus has all authority in heaven and on earth, which He received from the Father. On the basis of His authority, Jesus authorized the disciples to make disciples or to disciple the nations (Matthew 28:16–20). The means for accomplishing this task was through Baptism in the triune name and through teaching. Jesus' mandate extended to all nations until the end of the age. Clearly, this was more than eleven men could accomplish in a lifetime. When men are called and ordained into the Office of the Holy Ministry today, their work is an extension of this original apostolic work, discipling the nations through Baptism and teaching (see also Acts 14:23; Titus 1:5). For this reason, the pastoral office is seen as an apostolic office, which is in continuity with the apostles Jesus sent.

When Jesus sent out His apostles—and when He sends us—He promises that the words of His apostles are His words and are to be heard as though He Himself were speaking. The forgiveness of the apostle is the forgiveness of Christ, crucified and risen with the wounds to prove it (Luke 10:16). In the Small Catechism instruction on Confession and Absolution, Luther has the pastor ask the penitent, "Do you believe that my forgiveness is God's forgiveness?" (*Concordia*, p. 342). The answer to that question hinges on our understanding of what it means to speak with the authority of another. When a called and ordained servant of Christ speaks out of Christ's office, we can be as certain of this as if a voice from heaven called out to us and spoke into our own ears. Of course, this authority to speak for Christ pertains to forgiveness of sins, not the color of the walls or the kind of carpet laid on the church floor.

In Romans 10:14–15, there is a progression of rhetorical questions that move from faith to hearing to preaching to having been sent to preach. Faith seeks an object. It clings to the objective Word of Christ, which was preached and heard. The preaching of the Word is objective as well. It is not the result of a person's subjective feeling that God has called him to preach but an objective reality that God has specifically sent him to a particular place and people to proclaim the Word.

So what about Judas? He was called and sent just like the other eleven. Acts 1:12–26 helps us understand what happens to faithless or wicked pastors. This episode in Acts is vitally important in our ability to understand the nature of the office. Judas was unfaithful and betrayed the Lord. He killed himself and left his office vacant. But the apostolic office remains even when the apostle goes bad. This is the beauty of the gift of office, because the office does not derive its authority from the person but the person from the office. Therefore, as our Lutheran Confessions remind us, "both the Sacraments and Word are effective because of Christ's institution and command, even if they are administered by evil men" (AC VIII 2; *Concordia*, p. 34). The office provides an objective certainty that a person cannot. So, if even Judas forgave sins, they were forgiven by virtue of his office.

Some people think God gives all Christians to the Church as pastors. But Ephesians 4:7–13 (NIV) tells us otherwise:

> But to each one of us grace has been given as Christ apportioned it. This is why it says: "When He ascended on high, He led captives in His train and gave gifts to men." (What does "He ascended" mean except that He also descended to the lower, earthly regions? He who descended is the very one who ascended higher than all the heavens, in order to fill the whole universe.) It was He who gave some to be apostles, some to be prophets, some to be evangelists, and some to be pastors and teachers, to prepare God's people for works of service, so that the body of Christ may be built up until we all reach unity in the faith and in the knowledge of the Son of God and become mature, attaining to the whole measure of the fullness of Christ.

The key word in this passage is *some*. Some are given to be prophets, apostles, evangelists, pastors, and teachers. We aren't sure what all these titles refer to in this passage or even if these offices were in effect at the time of Paul. He might be referring to the various offices of the Word throughout the course of history. Nonetheless, it is the crucified, risen, and ascended Christ who gives these gifts to His Church so that the whole priesthood of God, that is, the whole Church, attains the unity of the faith and grows in knowledge to full maturity in Christ. As the Church is built up by Word and Sacrament, it grows together into Christ, the Head of the Church, and builds itself up in love as each priest of the royal priesthood does his or her work.

First Corinthians 3:5–9 sheds some light on how pastors functioned in the early Church. It appears from this passage that Paul preached the Word and Apollos baptized. The issue in Corinth was that people were playing favorites. Some preferred Paul, some Cephas, and some Apollos. Some said, "I belong to Christ," perhaps rejecting all pastoral leadership. Over and against this, Paul (an *apostle*, one who was sent out with Christ's authority) points out that he preached and Apollos watered (perhaps meaning that Apollos baptized), but it was God who gave the growth. This is one reason that pastors typically wear vestments that covered their own persons and personality. Pastors are interchangeable instruments who speak the Word of Jesus Christ, who wishes to be heard through them. As the Apology of the Augsburg Confession notes: "Christ requires that they [pastors and bishops] teach in such a way that He Himself is heard because He says, 'The one . . . hears Me.' Therefore, He wishes His own voice, His own Word, to be heard, not human traditions" (Ap XXVIII 19; *Concordia*, p. 250).

A Stewardship

A steward is a household office in which someone is responsible to see to it that every servant gets his or her fair share of the household goods (Luke 12:42). The pastoral office is an office of stewardship charged with caring for the household of God and distributing the gifts of Christ to His priesthood.

The apostle Paul calls his apostolic office a stewardship of the mysteries of God (1 Corinthians 4:1). A mystery is a hidden thing that is revealed by the Word of God. The Office of the Holy Ministry reveals these hidden things of Christ by the preaching of the Word of Christ. Among the mysteries in the New Testament are the resurrection and change of our bodies on the Last Day (1 Corinthians 15:51), the uniting of all things under Christ (Ephesians 1:9–10), Christ Himself (Colossians 2:2), and the incarnation and reign of Christ (1 Timothy 3:16). One might also include the Sacraments as *mysteries*, which was the earliest term for the Sacraments in Greek. (*Sacrament* is a borrowed term in Latin.) Our rebirth in Baptism is a mystery, something hidden from sight that must be revealed by the Word, as are the body and blood of Christ in the Lord's Supper. The Office of the Holy Ministry is Christ's authorized steward of these mysteries, dispensing the gifts of Christ to His royal priesthood as a household steward sees to it that all the servants receive their fair share (Luke 12:42).

The Lord's Supper, Holy Baptism, and Holy Absolution were all entrusted to the inner core of apostles who were the first pastors of the Church. This does not mean that the Sacraments belong to the clergy as a private possession. Rather, the Word and Sacraments are entrusted to the whole Church in the Office of the Holy Ministry, which also belongs to the whole Church, so that these things might go on in the stead and by the command of Christ. The Office of the Holy Ministry is authorized to preach the Gospel and administer the Sacraments for the blessing and benefit of the whole Church.

Accountability

With authority comes accountability to the one granting the authority. Those who govern are accountable to the people. God holds parents accountable for their care of their children. Likewise, pastors are accountable for their stewardship of the Word of God.

In 1 Corinthians 3:10–15, Paul uses the image of a builder to describe the work of the Holy Ministry. One lays the foundation, and another builds on it. Pastoral work is always building on what came before. Paul indicates that a pastor's work will be judged most severely by the Lord, since it is the Lord's office. If the builder builds with cheap materials, the structure will not withstand the fire of testing. If he builds with good materials, the structure will endure. This is a call for pastors to preach the Word as Law and Gospel and not their own pious opinions. Notice that though the work of the builder is judged, the builder is not judged by his work. He will be saved, though the one who builds shoddily will suffer loss. This is why a pastor's concerns may not be the same as his congregation's or church body's leadership. His concern is faithfulness to the Gospel of Jesus Christ, over and against any institutional concerns, for he is accountable to God for the kind of material he uses to build.

Is the pastor accountable to anyone else? Acts 20:28 tells us: "Pay careful attention to yourselves and to all the flock, in which the Holy Spirit has made you overseers, to care for the church of God, which He obtained with His own blood." The Greek word for *overseer* is the word *episkopos*, commonly translated "bishop." This passage is important from a number of aspects. The elders of Ephesus are also called overseers (bishops) and shepherds (pastors). At this time, these three terms were interchangeable. We don't know how the elders of Ephesus were called or placed into office. We do know that the Holy Spirit was the one who made them overseers, and it is to God Himself that they and Paul were finally accountable. The Church is God's flock, purchased with the holy, precious blood and innocent suffering and death of Jesus Christ. The Office of the Holy Ministry is called to care for God's treasured possession—His royal and holy priesthood.

James and the author of the Epistle to the Hebrews both underscore the accountability of the Office of the Holy Ministry. Pastors must give an account of their stewardship (Hebrews 13:17; James 3:1). For this reason, the priesthood desires to support and obey its pastors, unless, of course, they teach contrary to the Word of God. Again, as with all other authority structures, "we must obey God rather than men" (Acts 5:29). So what are we to do when a pastor goes against God's Word? Respect and honor for the office must be maintained at all times, even when those who hold it are less than honorable. Usually, church bodies are able to supply other pastors and counselors who can help address a situation in which a pastor is teaching false doctrine. Every Christian is called, by virtue of his or her priesthood, to be a discerning hearer of God's Word and to respectfully hold pastors accountable for their teaching and practice.

Comparisons

Eastern Orthodox: "What is it to feed the Church? To instruct the people in faith, piety, and good works" (*The Longer Catechism of the Eastern Church*, question 358).

Lutheran: "[The Holy Spirit] works faith, when and where it pleases God [John 3:8], in those who hear the good news that God justifies those who believe that they are received into grace for Christ's sake. This happens not through our own merits, but for Christ's sake" (AC V 2–3; *Concordia*, p. 33).

Reformed/Presbyterian: "To these [Church] officers the keys of the kingdom of heaven are committed, by virtue whereof they have power respectively to retain and remit sins, to shut that kingdom against the impenitent, both by the Word and censures; and to open it unto penitent sinners, by the ministry of the gospel, and by absolution from censures, as occasion shall require" (*The Westminster Confession of Faith*, chapter 30.2).

Roman Catholic: "If anyone saith, that, in the Catholic Church there is not a hierarchy by divine ordination instituted, consisting of bishops, priests, and ministers: let him be anathema" (*The Canons and Decrees of the Council of Trent*, Session 4, 6; cf. CCC2 paras. 871–945).

Baptist: "The way appointed by Christ for the calling of any person, fitted and gifted by the Holy Spirit, unto the office of bishop or elder in the church is that he be chosen thereunto by the common suffrage of the church itself, and solemnly set apart by fasting and prayer, with imposition of hands of the eldership of the church, if there be any before constituted therein; and of a deacon, that he be chosen by the like suffrage, and set apart by prayer, and the like imposition of hands" (*The Baptist Confession of 1688*, 9).

Point to Remember

The one who hears you hears Me, and the one who rejects you rejects Me, and the one who rejects Me rejects Him who sent Me.
Luke 10:16

Qualities and Tasks

> Show me the man who keeps his house in hand; he's fit for public authority.
>
> —Sophocles, *Antigone*

An office is never simply bare authority; there are always responsibilities and accountability. There are standards for virtually every office and task in our lives. Not everyone is qualified to be president of the United States. Nor is everyone capable of being a firefighter or a police officer. Some offices require specific gifts, others specific training and experience. Certain situations, such as a criminal conviction, may even disqualify a person from holding a particular office.

The Office of the Holy Ministry also requires certain qualities and abilities of those who are chosen for it, and it lays on them certain duties and responsibilities along with accountability for the execution of that office. The Holy Ministry is not a special kind of priesthood but a particular calling within the royal priesthood of Christians.

Everyone has expectations, even of their pastors. Opinions vary on what qualities are important for a pastor or even essential for the Office of the Holy Ministry. Let's look at what Scripture says is necessary for those called to this office.

A Noble Task

The apostle Paul lists a variety of qualities and characteristics of the man who desires the office of overseer in the Christian congregation. Among them, he must be the husband of only one wife, be a good father, manage his household, be temperate, disciplined, respectable, hospitable, able to teach and refute false teaching, be gentle, sober, and neither quarrelsome nor greedy (1 Timothy 3:1–13; Titus 1:6–9). The overall picture is of a man with a sound reputation both inside and outside the Church. This is essential, since scandals in the pastoral office can cause people to doubt the Word or drift away from the Church. The apostle Paul recognized that pastoral work puts a man on the front lines against the devil's schemes, where the slightest weakness of character can give opportunity for the evil one to work his wiles.

Women are excluded from holding pastoral authority according to 1 Timothy 2:12: "I do not permit a woman to teach or to exercise authority over a man; rather, she is to remain quiet." This is not to suggest that women are inferior to men, only that it is not God's will that they serve in this capacity. The apostle Paul cites the deception of Eve as her unique part in the fall, but he counterbalances it with a reference to woman's unique place in the incarnation (the bearing of the child). In 1 Corinthians 14, Paul addresses a similar issue in Corinth, where the women of the congregation were speaking in the presence of the assembly. Paul enjoins them to be silent, citing four reasons:

1. It is the common practice in all the churches.
2. It is written in the Torah that they are subordinate.
3. It is a shame for them to speak in the presence of the assembly, thereby dishonoring them.
4. It is the Lord's command.

While people vigorously debate the applicability of these verses in the Church today, an important underlying fact needs to be acknowledged. Male and female are each unique and not interchangeable with each other. The unique gifts of being male and female has implications for the way each fulfills his or her priesthood in a way that honors God. The key question to be asked is not "What are my rights?" but "What honors Christ and His Word?" To this end, the Church historically has not ordained women to the Office of the Holy Ministry but has created many avenues of priestly service for women such as deaconess, teacher, and the like.

The Holy Scriptures are foundational for the work of the Holy Ministry. The Office of the Holy Ministry is apostolic in three senses:

1. It is sent by God.
2. It is a continuation of the ministry of the apostles.
3. It teaches the doctrine of the apostles as recorded in the Scriptures.

Paul charges young pastor Timothy to attend to the public reading of the Scriptures (reading also included preaching) and reminded him that the Scriptures, as the very breath of God, are useful for doctrine, rebuke, correction, and training in righteousness so he might be fully equipped for his work (see 1 Timothy 4:11–14; 2 Timothy 3:14–17). For this reason, it is essential for the pastor to be the chief student of the Scriptures and to have ample time for the deep study of God's Word above and beyond the usual tasks of sermon preparation and Bible study.

To characterize the preaching of the pastoral office, Paul uses the image of a craftsman, a workman who is not ashamed of his work because it meets a high level of craftsmanship (2 Timothy 2:15; 4:1–2). To correctly handle the Word of truth means to interpret it accurately and to apply it in a way that properly distinguishes the Law and the Gospel. The Law must be preached lawfully, especially to those who are unaware or unrepentant of their sins. The Gospel must be preached evangelically without compromise or conditions. The preacher of the Word must be willing to preach in season and out of season, when the Word is producing much fruit and also when there is little or no fruit on the congregational vine. One of the greatest challenges for a preacher, especially one who is young and inexperienced, is not to let the frustrations of parish life creep into the pulpit. Regardless of what happened at the last council meeting, the preacher is called to correct, rebuke, and encourage with patience and careful instruction, using nothing other than the Word of God.

In 1 Timothy 5:17–20, Paul discusses the activities of the pastoral office and even discusses salary rationale. (Note: The term *elder* in this passage is synonymous with *overseer* or *pastor*. See Acts 20:17ff.) The apostle states that elders (presbyters or pastors) who govern the affairs of the congregation are worthy of double pay for their efforts, especially considering that they are also involved in preaching and teaching. The additional time and energy needed to administer the temporal affairs of a congregation would preclude any other income source. Paul himself worked at times in order not to be a financial burden on the young congregations he was gathering. Paul is also very careful to say that proper procedure should be followed if a charge is made against a pastor. It must be substantiated by two or three witnesses, which was the legal standard in Judaism (see Matthew 18:18). Those who are found guilty are to be rebuked publicly, since a public office requires a public rebuke. Like any public office, pastors are visible examples for those under them.

Paul also discusses the dangers of false doctrine in the Church (1 Timothy 6:3–10). False doctrine is a cancer that eats away at the life of the Church. It stirs up controversies and divisions along with endless quarrels over words that wind up in envy, strife, harsh words, evil suspicions, and continual animosity and friction. Paul knew of such things in his own day and warned Timothy that things would not get better as the time of the end drew near.

Another cancer that eats away at the Church is greed and financial corruption. Paul warns that some see godliness as an opportunity to profit, and he knew nothing of the television and the lucrative publishing industry we have today. His warning applies to pastor and priesthood alike: the love of money is the root of all sorts of evil. Money itself is not evil; it is a gift from God. But the love of money turns the good gift into an idol that consumes.

The Lord Is My Pastor

In our North American Lutheran tradition, the most common title for those who hold the Office of the Holy Ministry is *pastor*. This word comes from the Latin *pastores*, which means "shepherd." In Acts 20:28, to be an overseer is to be a shepherd.

Some consider Psalm 23 to be the job description of a good pastor. Of course, Psalm 23 is about the Lord. David, the shepherd-king, writes a sheep's-eye view of what it is like to have the Lord as His shepherd. But a pastor is a shepherd of a flock. His flock lacks nothing. He makes them rest in the green pastures of God's Word; he leads them to the quiet, restful waters of their Baptism, and he restores their soul, picking them up when they fall. He guides his congregation in the well-worn ruts of righteousness that are the way of Jesus' dying and rising. He walks with them through the dark valley as they face their own death. He brings them the comfort of the Word—the rod of the Law, the staff of the Gospel. He prepares a rich table, the body and blood of the Good Shepherd, in the presence of the enemy—sin, death, the devil. He anoints the head of each of his flock with the healing balm of forgiveness. Their cup overflows, so that goodness and mercy follow them all the days of their lives in the confidence that they will dwell with God forever.

Peter also describes pastors as shepherds (1 Peter 5:1–4). He addresses the elders (pastors) and exhorts them to be shepherds to the flocks entrusted to their care, watching over the priesthood willingly and eagerly. They are not to use their position to lord it over their people but to lead them by example. That's the curious thing about sheep. They only respond to being led. They can't be driven like cattle. Pastors are not ranchers, driving their people, nor are they executives, managing their people. They are humble shepherds serving under the chief shepherd and bishop, Jesus Christ. His promise is a crown of life that won't fade away, a crown that awaits all who trust in Christ. The goal of pastoral work is not success but faith and faithfulness.

Preaching and Prayer

The authority of the pastoral office is not a blanket authority to do anything and everything in the Church but to oversee the life of the congregation, to preach, teach, administer the Sacraments, warn, rebuke, and restore. Other tasks can often intrude, diluting the effectiveness of the office.

We read in Acts 6:1–7 about a situation in the Jerusalem congregation that caused difficulties for the apostles. The Greek widows were being neglected in the distribution of food. This could have turned into a divisive thing for the first congregation of Christians, since animosity between Hebraic and Greek people was strong. The twelve apostles wisely gathered the whole company of disciples together. (Note the distinction of *apostle* and *disciple* in this passage.) The apostles advised the disciples to choose seven godly men from among them. Having done so, the congregation presented these seven men to the apostles who ordained them into their office with prayer and the laying on of hands. Although the passage does not refer to these seven as *deacons*, it refers to their works as to "serve [*diakonia*] tables." The apostles wisely focused on the essence of their office, namely "prayer and the ministry of the word." The Augsburg Confession states that the essential authority of the Office of the Holy Ministry is "to preach the Gospel, to forgive and retain sins, and to administer Sacraments" (AC XXVIII 5; *Concordia*, p. 58)

Recognizing the essence of the Office of the Holy Ministry as preaching the Word and administering the Sacraments, the congregation as a priesthood has the opportunity to free its pastor to do his proper work and to open up new possibilities through outreach and works of service in the community. The potential distractions to the ministry of Word and Sacrament are many and varied, from congregational issues to personal crises to synodical and church body politics. While these may be important, they are not essential. The pastor and the baptized priesthood can work together to ensure that the Office of the Holy Ministry is able to run unencumbered so that the Word may be preached, the Sacraments administered and distributed, and the priesthood may have ample opportunity for prayer.

Comparisons

Eastern Orthodox: "How many necessary *degrees* are there of Orders? Three: those of *Bishop*, *Priest*, and *Deacon*" (*The Longer Catechism of the Eastern Church*, question 359).

Lutheran: "Since the grades of bishop and pastor are not different by divine authority, it is clear that ordination administered by a pastor in his own church is valid by divine law" (Tr 65; *Concordia*, p. 303).

Reformed/Presbyterian: "Church censures are necessary for the reclaiming and gaining of offending brethren; for deterring of others from the like offenses; for purging out of that leaven which might infect the whole lump; for vindicating the honor of Christ, and the holy profession of the gospel; and for preventing the wrath of God, which might justly fall upon the Church, if they should suffer his covenant, and the seals thereof, to be profaned by notorious and obstinate offenders" (*The Westminster Confession of Faith*, chapter 30.3).

Roman Catholic: "If any one saith, that bishops are not superior to priests; or, that they have not the power of confirming and ordaining; or, that the power which they possess is common to them and to priests; or, that orders, conferred by them, without the consent or vocation of the people, or of the secular power, are invalid; or, that those who have neither been rightly ordained, nor sent, by ecclesiastical and canonical power, but come from elsewhere, are lawful ministers of the Word and of the sacraments: let him be anathema" (*The Canon and Decrees of the Council of Trent*, Session 4, 7; cf. CCC2 paras. 880–87).

Baptist: "The work of pastors being constantly to attend the service of Christ in his churches, in the ministry of the Word and prayer, with watching for their souls, as they that must give an account to him" (*The Baptist Confession of 1688*, 10).

Point to Remember

Do your best to present yourself to God as one approved, a worker who has no need to be ashamed, rightly handling the word of truth. *2 Timothy 2:15*

Call and Ordination

Our churches teach that no one should publicly teach in the Church, or administer the Sacraments, without a rightly ordered call.
—Augsburg Confession XIV (*Concordia*, p. 39)

How do you come into an office? Never on your own! You cannot place yourself into an office; it must be given to you. In the United States, we choose our public officials by election or by appointment depending on the office, and then they are formally and publicly placed into office by those authorized to do so. For example, the president of the United States is elected on the first Tuesday of November and placed into office with a solemn oath administered by the chief justice on January 20 the next year. Only then is that person rightfully in the office.

The Church, likewise, deals with the Office of the Holy Ministry as a public office. Men are chosen by election or appointment and then are solemnly placed into office with a vow, prayer, and the Word of God. These traditional procedures, handed down from the early Church, reflect the divine character of the Office of the Holy Ministry. It is the Lord's office, and it is His Church. He calls and ordains certain priests to be pastors in His Church.

We have a variety of mechanisms for choosing people for public office. In the United States, this is most often done by democratic election. Sometimes, officials are appointed and their appointment is ratified. We also have mechanisms for placing people into public office. These ceremonies may be simple or quite elaborate, as in the inauguration of a president. There is a specified rite for inaugurating a president that includes a solemn vow, made with a hand on the Bible, to defend the Constitution of the United States. We can be certain that people belong in office as they have been lawfully chosen and installed. In fact, the chief purpose of an inauguration is to make public the fact that this person is now assuming the office to which he or she has been elected. The Office of the Holy Ministry is a public office in the Church and is treated in a similar fashion. Men are chosen to serve by call and are ordained to office.

Chosen to Serve

When faced with the vacancy left by Judas, the apostles chose two men who had been with them the entire time from John's Baptism to Jesus' resurrection and who were eyewitnesses to Jesus' resurrection. They then commended the matter to God in prayer and drew lots (Acts 1:12–26). While this episode is descriptive of what was done and not prescriptive of what must be done, it is nevertheless enlightening and instructive. The apostles used the best reasoned judgment to arrive at a short list of candidates and then left the final decision to the Lord. However, the Church chooses and places its candidates for the Office of the Holy Ministry, and the procedure should reflect the fact that it is God who calls through the various mechanisms of the congregation, not the congregation by itself.

In our earlier example from Acts 6:1–7, the congregation of disciples picked the seven men who were to serve, and the apostles prayed over them with the laying on of hands. In the Books of Acts, 1 Timothy, and Titus, it appears that elders (pastors) were appointed. Paul and Barnabas appointed elders in all the cities where congregations had been gathered. Paul instructs Timothy and Titus to select suitable men to be elders and overseers and gives the criteria for their selection.

The Lutheran Confessions state that the right to have a pastor may never be denied a congregation, and because the Church alone possesses the priesthood, it has the right to elect and ordain ministers (Tr 67–69; *Concordia*, pp. 303–4). Historically, this right to elect and ordain has been exercised in various ways. Sometimes, pastors are appointed by bishops or consistories (committees that oversee regions); other times they are elected directly by congregations. While the right and authority to call and ordain lies with every gathering of the priesthood, it does not follow that each congregation may or should act autonomously. When the Treatise on the Power and Primacy of the Pope was written, bishops were refusing to ordain pastors to Evangelical (Lutheran) congregations. Faced with the prospect of no pastors, the Lutheran reformers reasoned that the Church as the royal priesthood may never be denied pastors. So, when the existing structures refuse to provide pastors, for the sake of the Gospel the priesthood steps in to fulfill the responsibility that was abdicated. However a man is selected, whether by a congregational vote or by a committee or by appointment, the method and means should reflect God's activity. A congregation acting alone may call someone who will confirm them in their error and scratch their itching ears, as Paul said. A bishop appointing a pastor may have his own interests in mind and not those of a congregation. When both cooperate, that may yield the best results. Lutherans have a historic tendency not to force a pastor on a congregation but to seek the consent of a congregation when issuing a call.

It is important for us to recognize that God is the one who calls through whatever instruments are used. In Acts 20:28, we see that the Holy Spirit made the elders of Ephesus overseers of God's flock. The tendency on our part is to concern ourselves with how something is done more than over what is being done. While the process of calling a pastor may seem tinged by special interests and politics or some people may not be happy with the particular choice, it is helpful to remember that it is God who calls the man in, with, and under the machinery of the call.

Congregations should guard against the notion that they are hiring a pastor instead of God calling a pastor through them. Certainly, employing the Word of God and prayer in all facets of the call process helps to underscore God's hidden hand in this matter. Further, the involvement of neighboring pastors helps to emphasize the catholicity of the pastoral office, that this is not simply an isolated congregation, but one in fellowship with other congregations who also recognize the Office of the Holy Ministry in that place.

With the Laying on of Hands

The liturgical gesture of laying on of hands is an ancient practice going back to the Old Testament. When Moses laid his hands on Joshua as his successor, Joshua received the "spirit of wisdom" that Moses had (Deuteronomy 34:9). This is not to suggest that power is transmitted mechanically through a succession of hands laid on heads. The laying on of hands was a sign of specificity, indicating that a particular person was involved whether for prayer, healing, or placing into office. Hands were laid on the Old Testament sacrifices prior to slaughter. Jesus laid hands on the sick and demonized for healing and on the little children for blessing. The practice of installing into office with the laying on of hands likely came from the synagogue and the ordination of a rabbi.

Paul and the company of elders laid hands on Timothy at his ordination. Paul refers to a gift that was given through a prophetic utterance (1 Timothy 4:14) and a gift of God that was given through the laying on of hands. While it is not clear what exactly those gifts were, it is clear that Timothy was gifted for the office into which he was placed. The gifts pertaining to the Office of the Holy Ministry do not inhere to the pastor but to the pastoral office. Since the Office of the Holy Ministry is an office of the Word as the pastor is a servant of the Word, it stands to reason that this office would come with the requisite gifts to fulfill the duties of the office. The laying on of hands indicates that Timothy specifically had been chosen by God to occupy the office, and this was being publicly ratified and confirmed by the Word of God and prayer.

Ordained

Ordination is a liturgical rite by which a person who has been previously called is publicly placed into office. It is the churchly equivalent of inauguration in the political realm.

In 2 Timothy 1:6–7, we see that Timothy's ordination brought comfort and confidence to this young pastor in the midst of great trial and testing. Timothy did not take his position on his own initiative or by his own scheming; it was given to him as a gift. This provided him confidence in his work. Timothy was quite young in a culture that valued the wisdom of age and looked down upon the young as ignorant and inexperienced. He would be challenged by older men as well as the lusts of youth. New and complex heresies were on the horizon that would test his doctrinal acumen. The fact that his office came with the promises of God's blessing and the gifts of the Spirit would certainly bring comfort to Timothy, and to any pastor, in times of doubt and despair.

Ordination is traditionally done by neighboring pastors outside the congregation. This practice underscores the fact that a pastor is a gift of the ascended Christ to His congregation (see Ephesians 4:11). From ancient times in the Church, ordination was assigned to the bishops or overseers. Our Lutheran Confessions acknowledge this but point out that this is by human, not divine, arrangement (Tr 63–67; *Concordia*, pp. 303–4). Although the congregation may have a direct role in calling its pastor, it nevertheless receives its pastor as a gift through the ordination of fellow pastors. This outside-of-ourselves character of ordination serves to underscore that these are gifts of Christ, who sits enthroned at the right hand of

God as the Head of the Church. In summary, the holy priesthood of the baptized and the Office of the Holy Ministry are not two competing entities or two classes of Christian. To serve in the Office of the Holy Ministry is a priestly calling like every other vocation. Priesthood is our baptismal dignity before God whereby our lives are made living sacrifices through the one atoning sacrifice of Jesus Christ. The Office of the Holy Ministry is the office that serves the priesthood with the gifts of Word and Sacrament, enabling and enlivening them to live in the fear of God, faith in Christ, and service of love to the neighbor.

Comparisons

Eastern Orthodox: "What difference is there between them [bishop, priest, and deacon]? The Deacon serves at the Sacraments; the Priest hallows Sacraments in dependence on the Bishop; the bishop not only hallows the Sacraments himself, but has power also to impart to others, by the laying on of his hands, the gift and grace to hallow them" (*The Longer Catechism of the Eastern Church*, question 360).

Lutheran: "Wherever the Church is, there is the authority to administer the Gospel. Therefore, it is necessary for the Church to retain the authority to call, elect, and ordain ministers. This authority is a gift that in reality is given to the Church. No human power can take this gift away from the Church" (Tr 67; *Concordia*, p. 303).

Reformed/Presbyterian: "For the better attaining of these ends, the officers of the Church are to proceed by admonition, suspension from the Sacrament of the Lord's Supper for a season, and by excommunication from the Church, according to the nature of the crime and demerit of the person" (*The Westminster Confession of Faith*, chapter 30.4).

Roman Catholic: "If any one saith, that the bishops, who are assumed by authority of the Roman Pontiff, are not legitimate and true bishops, but are a human figment: let him be anathema" (*Canons and Decrees of the Council of Trent*, Session 4, 8; cf. CCC2 paras. 880–87).

Baptist: "Although it be incumbent on the bishops or pastors of the churches to be instant in preaching the Word by way of office, yet the work of preaching the Word is not so peculiarly confined to them that others also, gifted and fitted by the Holy Spirit for it, and approved and called by the Church, may and ought to perform it" (*The Baptist Confession of 1688*, 11).

Point to Remember

For this reason I remind you to fan into flame the gift of God, which is in you through the laying on of my hands, for God gave us a spirit not of fear but of power and love and self-control. *2 Timothy 1:6–7*

Lutheran Summary of Priesthood and Ministry

Augsburg Confession V

So that we may obtain this faith, the ministry of teaching the Gospel and administering the Sacraments was instituted. Through the Word and Sacraments, as through instruments, the Holy Spirit is given [John 20:22]. He works faith, when and where it pleases God [John 3:8], in those who hear the good news that God justifies those who believe that they are received into grace for Christ's sake. This happens not through our own merits, but for Christ's sake.

Our churches condemn the Anabaptists and others who think that through their own preparations and works the Holy Spirit comes to them without the external Word. (*Concordia*, p. 33)

Augsburg Confession XIV

Our churches teach that no one should publicly teach in the Church, or administer the Sacraments, without a rightly ordered call. (*Concordia*, p. 39)

Augsburg Confession XXVII 5–12

Many entered monastic life through ignorance. They were not able to judge their own strength, though they were old enough. They were trapped and compelled to remain, even though some could have been freed by the kind provision of canon law. This was more the case in convents of women than of monks, although more consideration should have been shown the weaker sex [1 Peter 3:7]. This rigor displeased many good people before this time, who saw that young men and women were thrown into convents for a living. They saw what unfortunate results came of this procedure, how it created scandals, and what snares were cast upon consciences! They were sad that the authority of canon law in so great a matter was utterly set aside and despised. In addition to all these evil things, a view of vows was added that displeased even the more considerate monks. They taught that monastic vows were equal to Baptism. They taught that a monastic life merited forgiveness of sins and justification before God. Yes, they even added that the monastic life not only merited righteousness before God, but even greater merit, since it was said that the monastic life not only kept God's basic law, but also the so-called "evangelical counsels." (*Concordia*, p. 54)

Apology of the Augsburg Confession XIII 7–13

The adversaries understand priesthood not about the ministry of the Word, and giving out the Sacraments to others, but as referring to sacrifice. This is as though there should be a priesthood like the Levitical one [Leviticus 8–9] to sacrifice for the people and merit the forgiveness of sins for others in the New Testament. We teach that the sacrifice of Christ dying on the cross has been enough for the sins of the whole world. There is no need for other sacrifices, as though Christ's sacrifice were not enough for our sins. So people are justified not because of any other sacrifices, but because of this one sacrifice of Christ, if they believe that they have been redeemed by this sacrifice. So they are called priests, not in order to make any sacrifices for the people as in the Law, that by these they may merit forgiveness of sins for the people. Rather, they are called to teach the Gospel and administer the Sacraments to the people. Nor do we have another priesthood like the Levitical, as the Epistle to the Hebrews teaches well enough [Hebrews 8]. But if ordination is understood as carrying out the ministry of the Word, we are willing to call ordination a Sacrament. For the ministry of the Word has God's command and has glorious promises, "The gospel . . . is the power of God for salvation to everyone who believes" (Romans 1:16). Likewise, "So shall My word be that goes out from My mouth; it shall not return to Me empty, but it shall accomplish that which I purpose" (Isaiah 55:11). If ordination is understood in this way, neither will we refuse to call the laying on of hands a Sacrament. For the Church has the command to appoint ministers, which should be most pleasing to us, because we know that God approves this ministry and is present in the ministry ‹that God will preach and work through men and those who have been chosen by men›. It is helpful, so far as can be done, to honor the ministry of the Word with every kind of praise against fanatical people. These fanatics imagine that the Holy Spirit is given not through the Word, but through certain preparations of their own. For example, they imagine He is given if they sit unoccupied and silent in far-off places, waiting for illumination, as the Enthusiasts formerly taught and the Anabaptists now teach. (*Concordia*, p. 185)

Treatise on the Power and Primacy of the Pope 65–70

Since the grades of bishop and pastor are not different by divine authority, it is clear that ordination administered by a pastor in his own church is valid by divine law.

Therefore, when the regular bishops become enemies of the Church or are unwilling to administer ordination, the churches retain their own right ‹to ordain their own ministers›.

Wherever the Church is, there is the authority to administer the Gospel. Therefore, it is necessary for the Church to retain the authority to call, elect, and ordain ministers. This authority is a gift that in reality is given to the Church. No human power can take this gift away from the Church. As Paul testifies to the Ephesians, when "He ascended . . . He gave gifts to men" (Ephesians [4:8]). He lists among the gifts specifically belonging to the Church "pastors and teachers" [4:11], and adds that they are given for the ministry, "for building up the body of Christ" [4:12]. So wherever there is a True Church, the right to elect and ordain ministers necessarily exists. In the same way, in a case of necessity even a layman absolves and becomes the minister and pastor of another. Augustine tells the story of two Christians in a ship, one of whom baptized the catechumen, who after Baptism then absolved the baptizer.

Here belong the statements of Christ that testify that the Keys have been given to the Church, and not merely to certain persons, "Where two or three are gathered in My name . . ." [Matthew 18:20].

Finally, Peter's statement also confirms this, "You are . . . a royal priesthood" [1 Peter 2:9]. These words apply to the True Church, which certainly has the right to elect and ordain ministers, since it alone has the priesthood.

A most common custom of the Church also testifies to this. Formerly, the people elected pastors and bishops [Acts 14:23]. Then came a bishop, either of that church or a neighboring one, who confirmed the one elected by the laying on of hands [1 Timothy 4:14]. Ordination was nothing else than such a ratification. (*Concordia*, pp. 303–4)

TOPIC SIXTEEN

VOCATION[1]

ENGAGING THIS TOPIC

"It's just a job. I can leave any time that I want."
"Well, it's more than a job."
"What do you mean?"
"It's your *vocation*. God has given you gifts to serve others."

Today, Christians are pressed from every side to limit the role of faith in their life. A politician can have Christian convictions so long as they are not related to his or her public office. Christians can express their faith in worship, but often see little connection between faith and their work life. Not only secularists but also some Christians believe that faith should be truncated in this way. We often hear the mantra: "My faith is one thing, my profession another." Indeed, some Christians integrate faith and work in quite inappropriate ways. A Christian auto mechanic who leaves evangelistic tracts in each car but fails to repair them well is not a good Christian witness.

What is missing from the discussion is an understanding of *vocation*, or calling. Lutherans are aware that clergy and other church workers are not simply hired but are *called* by God through the congregation. Catechized Lutherans are also aware of a wider sense in which all Christians are servants: the priesthood of all believers. This is often taken to mean only that each Christian is called to spread the Gospel and to lead an ethical life. But there is much more to it than that. God provides each Christian with gifts and circumstances that define a *station* in life. The purpose of this station is to serve our neighbors, to play a part in God's providential care of humanity. This means that even work with low worldly status is something God calls us to do.

In our age, intense spiritual experience is exalted as the sign of God's favor. Ordinary work is often seen as a spiritually dead, practical necessity.

1 This chapter adapted from *The Lutheran Difference: Vocation*, written by Angus Menuge. Copyright © 2006 Concordia Publishing House.

However, God did not save humankind with spectacular displays of power but through the crucifixion of Jesus. God does not call us to revel in private spiritual gifts, but to take up our crosses and to do His work. It is here that we find what Gene Edward Veith calls the "spirituality of ordinary life." The life-changing implications of this perspective are the focus of this chapter.

Lutheran Facts

Late medieval Roman Catholic theology emphasized the holiness of religious vocations (clergy, members of various religious orders, and so on). In contrast, Luther emphasized the holiness of everyday life. Christian mothers caring for their children, Christian fathers working to support their families, Christian soldiers following orders and doing their duty—each of these are God-given vocations of service toward one's neighbor.

Lutheran Christians understand that vocation is exercised in relationships. Before God, Christians are alone in their relationship with God, a relationship in which *He* serves *them*. But with their neighbor they are in a relationship in which *God* serves their neighbor *through them*. Father, mother, son, and daughter are, according to one Lutheran theologian, "biological orders" in which God serves members of the family. Other spheres of service include our daily work as employees or employers, citizens, teachers, electricians, or volunteers. God even uses people without faith to serve others here on earth. However, only the work of Christians done in faith is truly a good work in God's eyes.

Although God's work of love through our vocations serves our neighbor, our service does not obtain the forgiveness of sins. Our full forgiveness was won by Christ through His spotless life, bitter sufferings and death, and glorious resurrection. The fulfilling of our vocations is merely the fruit of lives transformed by God's redeeming grace.

Called to Be Christ's

I fled Him, down the nights and down the days;
I fled Him, down the arches of the years;
. . . But with unhurrying chase,
And unperturbèd pace,
. . . Came on the following Feet,
And a Voice above their beat—
. . . 'Whom wilt thou find to love ignoble thee
Save Me, save only Me?
. . . Rise, clasp My hand, and come!'
—Francis Thompson, *The Hound of Heaven*

Since the fall into sin, all humans are by nature enemies of God. There is a huge chasm between a holy God and sinful humanity. Humans have no power to change the situation: we are not only lost but also incapable of reorienting ourselves. However, our God is a gracious God, a good shepherd who seeks out His lost sheep. He sent His only Son to lead the perfect life and to atone for our inability to do so by suffering and dying on a cross. God shows that Jesus' sacrifice is complete by raising Him bodily from the dead. But there is more. Our sinful nature must also be put to death so that we find new life in Christ. God does this by uniting us in Holy Baptism with Christ's death and resurrection, calling us out of the darkness of sin to the light of Christ.

Have you ever found yourself in a difficult situation in which there was *nothing* you could do to repair the situation, but someone else was able to help? There is a difference between problems we can fix and chronic conditions that only someone else can help with. Think about medical, financial, employment, or relationship issues that are beyond our control but that, with the help of a professional in that area, can be taken care of or even fixed. Similarly, we humans cannot save ourselves from sin; this is a "schoolmaster unto salvation," by showing our need for a savior. Two important roles are played by Jesus' death and resurrection: There is a distinction between the fact of justification (Christ's atonement for the sins of all people) and its effect on us (the believer's justification in Baptism).

A Royal Family

Sin is not a problem like a leaky sink or a car that does not start. Such problems can be fixed by human reason and ingenuity. Sin is an illness beyond our capacity to fix. But Christ Himself is our great physician, atoning for our sin and then offering healing and regeneration in the waters of Holy Baptism.

Being put right with God does not earn the world's favor. However, Christians are the adopted children of God Himself; we belong to the most royal family. "You are a chosen race, a royal priesthood, a holy nation, a people for His own possession, that you may proclaim the excellencies of Him who called you out of darkness into His marvelous light. Once you were not a people, but now you are God's people; once you had not received mercy, but now you have received mercy" (1 Peter 2:9–10).

The family and household of God are special indeed. God has elected us, as Paul tells the Romans:

> And we know that for those who love God all things work together for good, for those who are called according to His purpose. For those whom He foreknew He also predestined to be conformed to the image of His Son, in order that He might be the firstborn among many brothers. And those whom He predestined He also called, and those whom He called He also justified, and those whom He justified He also glorified. (Romans 8:28–30)

This election shows God's special care for every one of us. Many people suffer from feelings of insignificance because they lack wealth, fame, or an exciting job. It is vital that all Christians see that God has given them the highest approval and status possible. By adopting us as His own sons and daughters, God has incorporated us into the royal family of the King of the universe! Paul explains that this was all according to His plan, since God has always known each individual that He would save. As Christians, we can never say that God has forgotten about us or has faulty records. Think about the analogy in C. S. Lewis's *The Lion, the Witch and the Wardrobe*, in which four ordinary, secular children, Edmund, Peter, Lucy, and Susan are called to be kings and queens of Narnia.

So does election mean that non-Christians we know are without hope and are not loved by God? From Ephesians 1:13, we learn that it is God alone who saves. We must not assume that someone who claims to reject Christ by words or deeds cannot be saved. Consider the example of Paul. He was "chief of sinners," yet God called Him to repent and change his ways. As he told Timothy, "This is good, and it is pleasing in the sight of God our Savior, who desires all people to be saved and to come to the knowledge of the truth" (1 Timothy 2:3–4). We know that God wants all people to be saved and that He can work through even our halting efforts to witness. In Ephesians 1:13, we see that those who had been outside of Christ's salvation were included when they "heard the word of truth, the gospel of . . . salvation." God can and does work through our proclamation of that word to bring people to faith, so all Christians are called to witness.

Gifted and Talented

God does not *save* us to *shelve* us. God has work for us to do, and He knows that workers need the right tools for the job. We have natural gifts, but we also need spiritual ones to see and do His will, so He gladly provides them.

God does not only save us by grace, but He also *gifts* us by grace to do His work. We are God's "workmanship, created in Christ Jesus for good works, which God prepared beforehand, that we should walk in them" (Ephesians 2:10). As we are incorporated into Christ's royal family, we are given the gifts we need to do His work. Think back to *The Lion, the Witch and the Wardrobe*, where Aslan provides Peter, Susan, and Lucy each with distinctive gifts that define their distinctive callings. Lewis's analogy is to the gifts the Father gives to each of us. The spiritual gifts of all Christians include many pieces of "armor": "the belt of truth," the "breastplate of righteousness," the "shield of faith," the "helmet of salvation" and the "sword of the spirit" (Ephesians 6:14–17). Each of these gifts aids us in our daily life. For example, being grounded in God's truth gives Christians a solid place to stand, independent of the shifting sands of politics and philosophy. Having Christ's righteousness as a gift means that we do not need to depend on our own inadequate righteousness, which is like "a polluted garment" (Isaiah 64:6) before God.

There is also a practical connection between spiritual gifts and God's will. Spiritual gifts are not merely powers to do things. They are given along with the Spirit immediately in and through Baptism. With the power of the Holy Spirit, the eyes of faith are opened to a realm of spiritual reality. We can see the truth of God's love amid a world of suffering and evil. We are taught words of divine wisdom from above that human reason can never reach up to or comprehend. We find the divine truth that God saves and renews us through grace, even though the truths of the Gospel remain "folly" to the non-Christian, who cannot "understand them because they are spiritually discerned" (1 Corinthians 2:14). And we also discern God's will for our life. This includes the ability to recognize our vocation. No longer are we bound to conform to the patterns of this world: our mind is renewed so that we can believe and live differently from those who find their home in this world (see Romans 12:2). We have a citizenship from heaven and live here as resident aliens. Think about the specific ways Christians see the purpose of their lives differently than non-Christians: putting less store in accumulating possessions, doing work as a service to others and not merely for reward, and seeing that work as an opportunity to witness to co-workers and clients.

Comparisons

Eastern Orthodox: "What is necessary in order to please God and to save one's own soul? In the first place, a knowledge of the true God, and a right faith in Him; in the second place, a life according to faith, and good works" (*The Longer Catechism of the Eastern Church*, question 3).

Lutheran: "Our churches teach that people cannot be justified before God by their own strength, merits, or works. People are freely justified for Christ's sake, through faith, when they believe that they are received into favor and that their sins are forgiven for Christ's sake" (AC IV 1–2; *Concordia*, p. 33).

Reformed/Presbyterian: "Those whom God effectually calleth, He also freely justifieth; not by infusing righteousness into them, but by pardoning their sins . . . for Christ's sake alone" (*The Westminster Confession of Faith*, chapter 21.1).

Roman Catholic: "Whereas all men had lost their innocence in the prevarication of Adam . . . free will . . . was by no means extinguished in them" (*Canons and Decrees of the Council of Trent*, Session 6, Decree on Justification; cf. CCC2 paras. 154–55).

Baptist: "We believe that the great gospel blessing which Christ secures to such as believe in him is Justification; that Justification includes the pardon of sin, and the promise of eternal life on principles of righteousness; that it is bestowed . . . solely through faith in the Redeemer's blood" (*New Hampshire Baptist Confession*, article 5).

Wesleyan/Methodist: "We are accounted righteous before God only for the merit of our Lord and Saviour Jesus Christ, by faith, and not for our own works or deservings" (*Methodist Articles of Religion*, article 9).

Liberal: "The traditional soteriology presupposed the historicity of Adam's fall and started from the assumption that mankind needs to be saved primarily from the taint inherited from Adam. But modern anthropology has discredited this way of determining the nature of man and of sin" (Gerald Birney Smith, ed., *Guide to the Study of the Christian Religion* [Chicago: University of Chicago Press, 1916], p. 519).

Point to Remember

Now if we have died with Christ, we believe that we will also live with Him. *Romans 6:8*

Redeemed into Service

> Yet take thy way; for sure thy way is best:
> Stretch or contract me, thy poore debter:
> This is but tuning of my breast,
> To make the musick better.
> —George Herbert, *The Temper*

Modern consumer society panders to our preferences. This tempts us to suppose that service to God is simply a matter of choice. But when it comes to our relationship with God, He always chooses us. He creates us, elects us, redeems us, and brings us to saving faith. We were redeemed at a price—the ransom Jesus paid for us on the cross. But we are redeemed for a purpose. The natural and spiritual gifts that God provides us are to be used to serve our neighbor, attending to his or her physical and spiritual needs.

The calling to serve others is not a mystery of faith, but a concrete reality defined by our specific gifts and circumstances. Someone with the gift of teaching among those who need to learn has already been given a vocation. We may reject our calling, or embrace it but perform it badly, but the calling remains as an objective reality all the same. Calls change people; they are crosses that crucify our sinful egoism. Through Christ's suffering and death upon the cross, we are brought new life and become servants who follow Christ by putting the needs of others before our own.

Think of a time when you were required to go somewhere you really did not want to go, but then found meaning and even joy in the opportunity to serve. God is not just being nice when He provides us with natural and spiritual gifts; He's enabling us to do the work He wants us to do. There is a difference between the paths we choose and the paths that God chooses for us. We are used to seeing everything as our choice, and the idea of someone else choosing us and our path in life is alien and even threatening to our autonomy. But when we humble ourselves to God's will for our lives, even when we don't want to, we can find meaning in our lives and experience growth. Human nature resists God's will, but God changes us through vocation so that, to our surprise, we find fulfillment in serving others.

God's Eyes and Hands

Paul tells the church at Corinth: "Only let each person lead the life that the Lord has assigned to him, and to which God has called him. This is my rule in all the churches" (1 Corinthians 7:17). God does not call us out of our circumstances into a special kind of holy Christian living. Unless our activities are inherently sinful (as were Paul's before his conversion), God expects us to remain at our station. It is here, and with the gifts that God has provided, that we are called to serve our neighbor. If we can avoid degrading or difficult work, we may do so, but even the worst work is an opportunity to serve and to witness. The suffering slave may change the slave owner's heart.

So who, exactly, is our neighbor? In practice, our neighbor is always the person we encounter where we are, whether we like the person or not. The Good Samaritan found the robbery victim and had the gifts to help him. His calling was perfectly clear, defined by his circumstances and abilities, not some mystery requiring deep contemplation.

In Luke 19:11–27, we read the parable of the ten minas. A nobleman was going on a business trip. He gave ten of his servants a mina each (one mina was about three months' wages for a laborer) and told them, "Engage in business until I come" (v. 13). When he returned, he called his servants to see what they had done with the money. The first told him he'd earned ten more minas; the second earned five more minas; the third had just the original mina, which he had hidden away. The nobleman richly rewarded the first two and chastised the third, taking the mina from him and giving it to the first servant. When the other servants cried *Unfair!* the nobleman said, "I tell you that to everyone who has, more will be given, but from the one who has not, even what he has will be taken away" (v. 26).

What did Jesus want us to learn from this parable? What results does God expect from the talents He gives us? God's talents are an investment. An investor expects some return on his investment. When God "plants" us with gifts, He expects growth and fruit. When we discern our gifts, we simultaneously discern a call to use them. The more we are given, the more that is expected of us. Neglecting our talents is a sinful rejection of God's will and purpose for our life. But our God is a gracious God, and when we neglect or abuse our talents He calls us to repentance and a renewed life of service, graciously forgiving us our sins.

Paul expended a lot of effort explaining God's "gift giving" to the church at Rome.

> For by the grace given to me I say to everyone among you not to think of himself more highly than he ought to think, but to think with sober judgment, each according to the measure of faith that God has assigned. For as in one body we have many members, and the members do not all have the same function, so we, though many, are one body in Christ, and individually members one of another. Having gifts that differ according to the grace given to us, let us use them: if prophecy, in proportion to our faith; if service, in our serving; the one who teaches, in his teaching; the one who exhorts, in

> his exhortation; the one who contributes, in generosity; the one who leads, with zeal; the one who does acts of mercy, with cheerfulness. (Romans 12:3–8)

Some of us may, with the servants in Luke's parable, cry *Unfair!* thinking God is being arbitrary when He gives different gifts to different Christians. Some gifts are certainly more high-profile than others, and some receive greater acclaim. So it can certainly seem unfair that God gives different gifts to different people. But we must remember two things. First, we are entitled to none of these gifts and should therefore be thankful for those we do have. Second, God's purpose is for us to live in a community, in the Body of Christ. A community cannot work if everyone does the same kind of work (e.g., everyone is a lawyer or doctor) or if some kinds of work are neglected (no one collects the garbage or keeps hospitals clean). Likewise, an effective body cannot be made by many parts with the same function (e.g., many eyes). God wants us to discern our contribution to the proper functioning of civil society and the Church.

Paul used a similar analogy in his first letter to the Corinthians when discussing the Church as the Body of Christ. He told them that each part of the Body of Christ needs the other parts: "The eye cannot say to the hand 'I have no need of you'" (1 Corinthians 12:21). Paul did not, however, intend this instruction to stop at the church door. Part of his calling as an apostle brought him to Aquila and Priscilla at Corinth, where he stayed and worked with them as tentmakers so that he could support his preaching and other missionary activities (Acts 18:3). He used what some might call menial labor together with a direct call from Jesus Christ to preach to the nations. God used this tent-making as part of His glorious plan. God made Paul's work holy through Paul's calling. The world often makes all sorts of distinctions between different types of work in terms of pay and status, and some conclude that some people's work is unimportant. But the fact is that just as each part of the body is indispensable to the proper functioning of the body, so each vocation is indispensable to the Body of Christ and to society. No vocations are more important than others. All are God-pleasing means of serving our neighbor. God *sanctifies* the work that Christians do through their calling in Baptism.

But we are still sinful human beings and are prone to jealousy and discord over the differences in our gifts. When we think too closely about how our role compares with others, we sometimes lose sight of how all of these roles combine to fulfill God's intentions for community. We must remember that in the Body of Christ our responsibility is to live a life "worthy of the calling to which [we] have been called" (Ephesians 4:1), that we are required to have "humility" and "patience, bearing with one another in love" (v. 2). We are also called to unity in the Spirit. Jealousy and discord are enemies of this unity, and we should remind ourselves that, though we have different gifts, "there is one body and one Spirit," and we are called to one hope, founded in "one Lord, one faith, one baptism" (vv. 4–5).

Loving Our Neighbor

When God commands us to love our neighbor, He is not calling for a warm fuzzy feeling, but a life of self-sacrificial service. God calls us to love our neighbor through the vocations He sends to us.

Although a pleasant disposition can be a good witness, this call from God does not simply mean being a nice, polite person on the job. True love is the fulfillment of God's Law, and requires us to love our neighbor as ourselves (Romans 13:9–10). This love is "patient and kind" and avoids "envy" (1 Corinthians 13:4). "It does not insist on its own way" (v. 5) but puts our neighbor's needs above our own. Our vocations are means of showing love by giving our neighbor what he really needs. This is accomplished by honest, trustworthy work of high quality, not by shoddy work adorned with superficial piety. As Luther reputedly said, the Christian cobbler should make good shoes, not poor shoes covered in crosses.

We get a pretty good picture of what love is in 1 Corinthians 13, but we are told what to do with that love and how to use it in 1 John 3:

> For this is the message that you have heard from the beginning, that we should love one another. . . . Whoever does not love abides in death. . . . By this we know love, that He laid down His life for us, and we ought to lay down our lives for the brothers. But if anyone has the world's good and sees his brother in need, yet closes his heart against him, how does God's love abide in him? Little children, let us not love in word or talk but in deed and in truth. (vv. 1, 14, 16–18)

The pattern of true love is found in the cross of Christ. It is self-sacrificial love, love shown to others that seeks nothing in return. If need be, Christians are called to lay down their very life for others as Christ did for us. In our vocations, there is a sense in which we already do this, because we lay down the selfish cravings of our ego in order to serve others. In that sense, vocation, like Baptism, involves a kind of crucifixion and resurrection. We are not merely called to say the right words, to pay lip service to God's love, but to show our love "in deed and in truth" (1 John 3:18). Think of the New York firefighters, police officers, and other rescue workers who ran into the World Trade Center on September 11, 2001, to save those trapped inside. They are a dramatic example of showing love in service to their fellow man. But Jesus didn't say we are to show our love only dramatically or in dangerous situations. We are to show it daily, no matter our vocation. Consider some more ordinary vocations such as plumbers, carpenters, teachers, or businessmen. They daily have the opportunity to kill their own desires and instead serve others. God sanctifies their work through their calling in Baptism.

No Longer Aliens

Every vocation involves a relationship. Sin breaks relationships, making us aliens to God, our neighbor, and even to ourselves. But the new life in Christ received through faith restores these relationships, making us friends and loyal subjects.

God's love in Christ overcomes the conflicts that undermine our relationships. Conflict arises from self-love, which makes us resent the accomplishments of others when we should be rejoicing in them. Self-sacrificial love makes us "love one another with brotherly affection" and honors others above ourselves (Romans 12:10). United with Christ in Baptism, we find in Him a source of joyful hope, patience, and faithful prayer (v. 12) that binds us together as a community and keeps us focused outward on those in need (v. 13). Unconditional love can love the persecutor (v. 14) and "associate with the lowly" (v. 16). The power of this love is found in its lack of self-conscious pride, which causes us to take revenge and become angry at others because they harm us or thwart our preferences (vv. 17–20). True love can "overcome evil with good" (v. 21). There are countless stories of people whose lives were turned around because someone took the time to show them love. That's what God calls us to do every day: show His love.

Relationships are destroyed when we choose to live for ourselves, neglecting our obligations to others. Christ restores relationships because He died for us all, so that we no longer live for ourselves but for Him (2 Corinthians 5:14–15). As a result, we should not look at other Christians "according to the flesh" (v. 16), but as a "new creation" (v. 17). Our God is not a "Do as I say, not as I do" kind of God. When God calls Christians to harmonious relationships, the foundation is God's own action of reconciliation. God "through Christ reconciled us to Himself and gave us the ministry of reconciliation" (v. 18). As God has reconciled us to Himself through Christ, we are called to be "ambassadors for Christ" (v. 20), creating new relationships by sharing this message of reconciliation with others. At some point, we will all experience relationship problems and need reconciliation. It may be something big like a married couple who disagrees about having children or spouses who find jobs in cities thousands of miles apart. As Christians, we are called to handle these difficult decisions in ways that reflect God's reconciling, selfless love.

Comparisons

Eastern Orthodox: "How have we salvation by Christ's doctrine? When we receive it with all our heart, and walk according to it" (*The Longer Catechism of the Eastern Church*, question 197).

Lutheran: "Our churches teach that this faith is bound to bring forth good fruit [Galatians 5:22–23]. It is necessary to do good works commanded by God [Ephesians 2:10], because of God's will. We should not rely on those works to merit justification before God. The forgiveness of sins and justification is received through faith" (AC VI 1–2; *Concordia*, p. 33).

Reformed/Presbyterian: "They who are once effectually called, and regenerated . . . are further sanctified . . . by His Word and Spirit dwelling in them" (*The Westminster Confession of Faith*, chapter 13.1).

Roman Catholic: "Having, therefore, been thus justified . . . through the observance of the commandments of God and of the Church, faith co-operating with good works, [they] increase in that justice . . . and are still further justified" (*Canons and Decrees of the Council of Trent*, Session 6, 10; cf. CCC2 paras. 1700, 1993, 2008–10).

Baptist: "We believe that Sanctification is the process by which, according to the will of God, we are made partakers of His holiness" (*New Hampshire Baptist Confession*, article 10).

Wesleyan/Methodist: "Good works . . . are . . . pleasing and acceptable to God in Christ, and spring out of a true and lively faith" (*Methodist Articles of Religion*, article 10).

Liberal: "We cannot define Christian ethics in terms of a church-controlled society. Neither can we regard Christian duty as identical with biblical precepts . . ." (Gerald Birney Smith, ed., *Guide to the Study of the Christian Religion* [Chicago: University of Chicago Press, 1916], p. 570).

Point to Remember

Beloved, if God so loved us, we also ought to love one another.
1 John 4:11

Ruler of the Realms

> Now is the time for all good men to come to the aid of their country.
> —manual typewriting exercise

Our God governs us through two kingdoms or realms. In the kingdom of the left (civil government), God governs us through human authorities, such as parents, the legal system, and our political leaders. In the kingdom of the right (the Church), God governs believers through the Gospel in Word and Sacrament. Although saved by grace, Christians belong to both realms. In this life, we are simultaneously saints and sinners.

Most of the time, our obligation to earthly authorities is clear. However, these authorities are under God's Law, and when an officeholder requires us to do something against God's Law, the Christian must serve God rather than men. A human judgment that contradicts God's Law is not valid, for though there are two kingdoms, there is only one King, God.

Consider someone who claims to be Christian but rejects the state's authority because the only boss he recognizes is the "Jewish carpenter." Is his rejection of human authority justified? Is he missing something important? When a Christian nurse is required to participate in a legal abortion procedure, she discovers a conflict between human law and God's Word. Whose authority should prevail? In this case, God's Law prevails, even if it costs the nurse her job. Christians should obey man-made laws, such as those controlling speed limits, voter registration, and taxes. If most people dissent from human laws, chaos arises and we cannot protect our own families or freely proclaim the Gospel. However, human laws cannot save us and they remain subject to God's Law. If human laws obstruct the Gospel or contradict God's direct commands to a Christian, then those laws violate God's purpose and the Christian should be obedient to Christ's command.

Under His Authority

Humble obedience to authority is a crucial element of the Christian life. Christians are called to obey earthly authorities, starting with their parents, but also to reflect Christ's rule in their hearts by living lives of self-sacrificial love. The Christian is subject to both authorities in his vocation, where he must obey the law and do what his employer requires, yet also serve his neighbor in gratitude for what Christ has done for him.

Jesus' own life reveals His acceptance of God the Father's authority. Jesus models acceptance of authority by humbling Himself to be baptized even though He was without sin. We learn from the Father's response

(Matthew 3:17) that those who humble themselves to authority are exalted. Jesus' calling is to bear and atone for the sins of the world. Even with what lies before Him, Jesus humbly accepts His Father's will (Matthew 26:39). In our earthly vocations, we also are called to humbly accept God's will, seeing our neighbor as an opportunity for love, not an obstacle to self-fulfillment. When we follow this path, we discover a higher fulfillment in service well done than we could ever find in self-gratification. We must lose our lives to find them.

The apostle Paul explains the connection between Christ's humility and our own. We see that the pattern of Christ's vocation is humiliation and exaltation (Philippians 2:6–11). This same pattern is laid out for our earthly vocations. We are called to be imitators of Christ's humility (vv. 1–5), which means accepting God's authority. Since this authority is manifest in two kingdoms or realms, we must live as humble citizens of both realms, obedient to earthly authority and to the fact that we are saved by God's grace through faith in Christ to serve others.

So Christians are to respect man-made rules as long as they don't violate God's Law, but does an earthly ruler derive authority from the power of his military or the number of votes she received? Tolstoy believed that all human laws violated the supremacy of Christ's rule in our heart, but he neglected the fact that Christ Himself said we should pay the taxes due to Caesar (Matthew 22:21). Paul explains that human authorities are established by God Himself (Romans 13:1) as means of maintaining order. Remember the first, or civil, use of the Law, which serves as a curb against the worst consequences of outward sin. Robert Bolt makes the point dramatically in his play *A Man for All Seasons*, in which Thomas More says that he would give the devil himself the benefit of law for his own safety's sake. Paul clarifies that rebellion against human authority instituted by God is also rebellion against God (Romans 13:2). Anyone who holds a position of authority is "God's servant," called to do God's will. The function of such an office is not to oppress the people, but to do them "good." Yet to maintain order, the officeholder is granted special powers to punish wrongdoers and is authorized to levy a tax (vv. 4–7).

The offices of human authority are instituted by God. But human *officeholders* may violate their office by acts of oppression that are contrary to God's intentions for maintaining an orderly society. Some societies make evangelism illegal; yet, in the Great Commission, Christ calls the Church to spread the Gospel. As in the early Church, so in China, Saudi Arabia, the Sudan, and Indonesia Christians are called to obey God rather than men (see Acts 5:27–32). The cost can be high, as anyone can discover by reading the magazine *The Voice of the Martyrs*. Although we Christians must increasingly endure the scorn of secularists in the media, we can be thankful that in the United States we are not imprisoned, tortured, or killed for our faith.

But some people still have oppressive vocations, such as slavery or working for unfair pay, for unreasonable hours, or in unsafe conditions. How should Christians in these circumstances behave? They can show a Christlike submission to authority and love for others even in unfair and oppressive vocations, such as slavery. Paul explains that the slave is certainly entitled to try to gain his freedom by legal means (1 Corinthians 7:21) and discourages anyone from allowing themselves to be a slave (v. 23; see also Philemon 15–16). But the Christian is not justified in using violence to escape and, if there is no legal recourse, should see slavery as a means of Christlike service and witness (Ephesians 6:6).

Family Matters

In the Large Catechism, Luther tells us that parents are the preeminent representatives of God's authority on earth. Children who reject their parents' authority typically reject every other authority as well and become dysfunctional citizens and poor employees. Rejection of God's representatives is rejection of God's authority, and such rejection flows from unbelief.

By contrast, children who humbly accept the authority of their parents learn to accept God's representatives in society and the Church. They become valued citizens and workers and are more likely to remain faithful members of a church.

Paul notes that the Fourth Commandment—"Honor your father and your mother"—is the first one connected with a promise (Ephesians 6:1–4). The honoring of parents is connected to a good life here on earth, which is clearly impossible without an orderly society. Paul is saying that reverence for parental authority is necessary for a peaceful civil society. In his commentary on the Fourth Commandment in the Large Catechism, Luther explains that "honor" goes beyond the love we are enjoined to show to our neighbor. We are called to revere our parents as God's primary human representatives on earth. The Christian family is a small society, with parents as its rulers. It is a small church in which the earthly father models Christ, and his wife, the Church (Ephesians 5:24–25). In this way, the family is the primary building block for both civil society and the Church. It plays a foundational role in building both the earthly and heavenly kingdoms. This shows that defending and supporting family is not merely a fashionable political agenda; it is crucial to God's governance of humanity and calls for the commitment of all Christians.

Families frequently act as a unit. Just as a family is bound together by biological similarities, God calls whole families to be bound to Christ, the

Head of the Body of Christ. Consider the story of the Philippian jailer in Acts 16:25–34. Paul and Silas are in jail, in chains, when an earthquake shakes the foundations of the prison, breaks open the doors, and breaks all the chains holding the prisoners. The jailer wakes up and is about to kill himself, assuming that all the prisoners have escaped. But Paul stops him and tells him all the prisoners are still there. The jailer's response is to ask Paul and Silas, "Sirs, what must I do to be saved?" (v. 30). They replied, "Believe in the Lord Jesus, and you will be saved, you and your household" (v. 31). Then they preached the Word of God to him and his household. When the jailer was converted, he knew his Christian duty to baptize his whole family, thereby putting their old selves to death and calling forth new life in Christ. This practice of family conversion is still common in Africa today, but modern individualism sometimes undermines it in the West.

Church and State

Church and state have different vocations. The state does not save, nor is the Church called to maintain law and order. Yet Christians should support the state unless it violates God's Law or impedes the Gospel.

Jesus explains that the kingdom of grace is not of this world. Our salvation does not depend on who has the most power here on earth, and the Church cannot win souls by the use of force (John 18:36). Force belongs to the earthly kingdom, and it is our government that has been authorized to bear the sword (Romans 13:4). But the sword can never change a person's heart or make him believe in Christ. Only the Holy Spirit can do this through the Gospel and the Sacraments. On the other hand, arrogant leaders are wrong in supposing that their authority is self-made. The power they do have to maintain order is always from above (John 19:11). But this power cannot save. We should obey our earthly leaders, but never entrust our souls to them (Psalm 146:3). Totalitarian regimes frequently require exclusive allegiance to the state, as if it were our Savior. But our salvation is found only in Christ, whose Means of Grace are offered by the Church and not the state.

Jesus does not call us out of the world into a separate, holy life. Nor does He call us to be worldly and conform our thoughts to worldly patterns of thinking (Romans 12:2). Instead, Jesus calls us to be in the world, but not of it (John 17:15–16). This is made possible by the "renewal of [our] mind" (Romans 12:2), a mind enabled to see God's will. Our vocation is where all of this happens. We are not asked to do amazing signs or to attain an elevated state of enlightenment, but to show Christ's love by forgetting ourselves and serving our neighbor right where we are. There are temptations both to hide from the world and to become too worldly. When we are tempted, we can remember how Christ came into this world, pursuing His vocations yet not resorting to worldly means of power and self-promotion. We can truthfully say that Christ fulfilled His vocations for us.

Comparisons

Lutheran: "Our teachers' position is this: the authority of the Keys [Matthew 16:19], or the authority of bishops—according to the Gospel—is a power or commandment of God, to preach the Gospel, to forgive and retain sins, and to administer the Sacraments. . . . For civil government deals with other things than the Gospel does. Civil rulers do not defend minds, but bodies and bodily things against obvious injuries. They restrain people with the sword and physical punishment in order to preserve civil justice and peace [Romans 13:1–7]. Therefore, the Church's authority and the State's authority must not be confused" (AC XXVIII 5, 11–12; *Concordia*, p. 58).

Reformed: "The civil magistrate may not assume to himself the administration of the Word and Sacraments, or the power of the keys of the kingdom of heaven: yet he hath authority, and it is his duty to take order that unity and peace be preserved in the Church, that the truth of God be kept pure and entire, that all blasphemies and heresies be suppressed, all corruptions and abuses in worship and discipline prevented or reformed, and all the ordinances of God duly settled, administered, and observed. For the better effecting whereof he hath power to call synods, to be present at them, and to provide that whatsoever is transacted in them be according to the mind of God" (*The Westminster Confession of Faith*, chapter 23.3, 1647; the U.S. revision to this confession was adapted to the separation of church and state).

Roman Catholic: [The following points are rejected; the opposite points are considered true.] "54. Kings and princes are not only exempt from the jurisdiction of the Church, but are superior to the Church, in litigated questions of jurisdiction. . . . 55. The Church ought to be separated from the State, and the State from the Church" (*The Papal Syllabus of Errors*, section 7, decreed by Pope Pius IX, December 8, 1864; individual condemnations are considered infallible by some Roman Catholic theologians).

Point to Remember

> Obey your leaders and submit to them, for they are keeping watch over your souls, as those who will have to give an account.
> *Hebrews 13:17*

Ordered by Design

> Turning and turning in the widening gyre
> The falcon cannot hear the falconer;
> Things fall apart; the centre cannot hold;
> Mere anarchy is loosed upon the world.
> —W. B. Yeats, *The Second Coming*

Modern secular society emphasizes equality and democracy. In many ways this is good. Everyone is equally valuable to God, and everyone should have a voice in how government is run. But that does not mean that vocations are interchangeable. And the right to voice an opinion does not make all opinions equally authoritative.

God created order out of chaos. This order is reflected in distinctions in vocation. Not every living thing has the same purpose. Only humans are called to be stewards over creation. Men and women are not interchangeable units in an androgynous society. *Husband* is a different vocation from *wife. Father* is a different vocation from *mother.* The fact that vocations have equal importance does not imply that no one has to submit to anyone else. Children are as important as parents but must submit to their parents' authority. Wives are as important as husbands, but must submit to their husbands' authority. Parents, however, must not embitter but serve their children. Husbands are called to love their wives in self-sacrifice as Christ loves the Church.

Sometimes, however, people resist order in groups. Have you ever encountered a group in which a bossy person usurped someone else's job? He likely caused the group damage. Secularists often reject the special status God gives to humanity by claiming that we are no different than other animals. Some feminists reject the distinctive offices of wife and mother, appearing to resent the fact that God made men and women different. Statists would prefer that the state was our parent and that the "traditional family" would wither away, as it is beginning to do in Scandinavia. But order is part of God's providential design for His creation and is necessary for harmonious living. Selfish, self-important people hurt others because they are not willing to entrust them with anything "important." We have all suffered the kitchen with too many cooks. All of God's work is important and needs to be done. We are called to follow God's design for our lives and use the gifts we have rather than trying to be something we are not able to do so, or to do something we are not called to do.

Made to Order

God made human beings different from other creatures because He had special work for them to do. Likewise, He made women different from men and assigns distinctive roles to husband and wife, father and mother. Distinctions in God's design reflect God's desire for harmonious order, where each element in creation minds its own business and contributes to the functioning of the whole.

Genesis 1:26–28 shows us the special task given to human beings alone in all of creation. "Be fruitful and multiply and fill the earth and subdue it and have dominion over the fish of the sea and over the birds of the heavens and over every living thing that moves on the earth" (v. 28). God is the Supreme Creator, who created all things out of nothing, and He created male and female in His image. He calls humans to be subcreators, and He gives them the responsibility of governing natural resources. We are called to do this through procreation and exercising the vocation of steward. Although God is the landlord who owns everything (Psalm 24:1), we are His stewards (Psalm 8:6), entrusted with the management of the natural world.

Genesis 2:15–24 shows that male/female distinctions are part of God's *original* design and not simply the consequence of the fall, as some have argued. The first man was made *good* as was all of creation. Although he was good after his own kind, the man was made incomplete. Human beings are relational, social beings, and though Adam had a perfect relation with God, he did not have a social relation with another human being. For this reason, God says, "It is not good that the man should be alone; I will make him a helper fit for him" (Genesis 2:18). We see that woman is created to help man and to complete him in a one-flesh union (v. 24). Woman is not created in the same way as man (vv. 22–23), and she is not assigned a completely independent role, just as the man is not completely independent of the woman. It is clear that Adam can only be completed by someone like him (human) yet different from him (designed and made differently). Adam would not have been completed by another man. The difference between man and woman therefore traces to an original difference in design and is not merely a consequence of the conflict brought into the world by the fall.

But Genesis 3:14–19 tells us that curses were laid upon the vocations of men and women as a consequence of the fall. Through Eve, the curse brings pains in childbearing, and just as humans were tempted to be like gods, the woman will desire to be like the man and to usurp his role as head of the woman (Genesis 3:16). This verse is sometimes misread by feminists as claiming that male headship is only a consequence of the fall and that our renewal in Christ removes this distinction. As we saw, however, the distinction between man and woman is part of the original design of God. Through Adam, the curse brings pain and effort in our vocations, and it brings sickness, weakness, and death. But in verse 15 we see the first promise of a Messiah, who will save us from the consequences of sin by suffering and dying for our sins.

As Adam brought condemnation and death into the world, Christ brought justification and eternal life (see Romans 5:12–21). Christ justifies by the great exchange. He took all of our sin upon Himself on the cross and atoned for it. In exchange, He then makes us righteous by giving us His own perfect righteousness. This righteousness is offered freely; it is not something we have earned. We are declared righteous because God accepted Christ's payment on our behalf, not because we have erased our debt. As a result, though we were "dead in our trespasses," God "made us alive together with Christ" (Ephesians 2:5). With this new life, we are thoroughly restored and re-equipped, "created in Christ Jesus for good works" (v. 10) out of gratitude for His salvation.

Also in response to this new life, we are called to "[give] thanks always and for everything to God the Father in the name of our Lord Jesus Christ, submitting to one another out of reverence for Christ" (Ephesians 5:20–21). Right after this verse in his letter to the Ephesians, Paul lays out quite clearly God's design for husbands and wives. Marriage is patterned on and expresses (in the case of believers) the relationship of Christ and His Church. All believers are called to submit "to one another out of reverence for Christ" (v. 21). Man and woman form a completed whole, a one-flesh marriage under the lordship of Christ. In marriage, submitting to each other means that both man and woman accept the role appointed to them by God's design. But, as we said earlier, God did not design man and woman in the same way. Wives are called to submit to their husbands in the same way that the Church submits to Christ (vv. 22–24) and to respect their husbands (v. 33). Since the man represents Christ, he must love his wife in the same way Christ loves the Church. The man is called to self-sacrificial love, to be a servant leader who puts his wife's interests ahead of his own. The husband who loves his wife like his own body will look after and care for his wife (vv. 28–29), in sickness and in health, until death.

Order in Society

In *King Lear*, Shakespeare shows how family breakdown leads to the decline of civilization. Our vocations call us to maintain God's order in family and society by respecting God's design for humanity.

What happens to society when people reject authority? Here are some prime examples from Scripture: "In those days there was no king in Israel. Everyone did what was right in his own eyes" (Judges 21:25). It's hard to follow authority when there is none; it's even harder to have order when it's every man for himself. When people reject external authority, they become their own authority. Each person becomes his own king. But people have different desires and interests, and so the many self-appointed kings, each of whom rejects the authority of all the others, make conflict inevitable. There will be constant battles for power, wealth, and prestige. In his second letter to Timothy, Paul tells us that, in the last days, there will be an increase of narcissism, greed for money, rudeness and disobedience, ingratitude, an inability to forgive, slander, brutality, false piety, Machiavellian scheming, and suppression of the truth (3:1–5). We see these things today in disrespect for teachers, the police, political leaders, and the clergy, to name a few. Paul's instruction to Timothy at the end of verse 5 is solid advice for us as well: "Avoid such people."

But avoiding such people doesn't mean burying our heads in the sand. Just as in Paul's time, Christians today are called to give up the selfish desires that cause disorder and disrespect for God's design for family and society. We must eschew uncontrolled sensuality (1 Peter 4:2–4), but remain "self-controlled and sober-minded" (v. 7) so that we can pray and show love and hospitality to others (vv. 8–9). The gifts we have are entrusted to us so that we may use them to faithfully serve others (v. 10). When we do this, we contribute to maintaining an orderly community. Christians can be seen as the "doctors" for our society, diagnosing its ills and offering remedies.

Order in the Church

Today we suffer from vocational confusion in the Church. Laity sometimes usurp pastoral work. Pastors take on work better handled by qualified laity. Many want more "exciting" worship. Some women "feel" called to be a pastor. All of this distracts from the life of humble, selfless service to which Christ calls us.

Since our God is a God of order, it is important that we observe order in the Church. In worship, each contribution should help build up the Church (1 Corinthians 14:26). Liturgy has been devised so that we understand the proper relation between God and man. We invoke God's name to show our submission to His authority. We confess our sins and hear the words of Absolution from a pastor who stands in the place of Christ Himself. We respond with songs of praise. Worship is not focused on us and our words, but on God's Word for our life. The Word of God did not originate with us. Cutesy self-help sermons and people-centered hymns teach the false doctrine that we save ourselves by getting ourselves right with God or by improving our lives.

We also show respect for God's design by understanding that He has distinctive work for women in the Church. As men are called to represent Christ in the context of marriage, they are also called to represent Christ in the Church. Women are every bit as valuable and important to God as men, but women are not called to be pastors. We must remember that God exalts the humble and humiliates the proud. Mary is granted a gift, given to no man, of being the very mother of God. It is women, not men, who first bring the news of the risen Christ. Mary's *Magnificat* (Luke 1:46–55) provides a wonderful model for women's vocations in the Church.

For Reflection

> Christ's endorsement of matrimony is supported throughout the Scriptures. When the prophets of the Old Covenant sought to impress upon their own countrymen the magnificence of [God's] grace to Israel and the mystic union that bound Him to His people, they could find no more fitting symbol than marriage, the intimate union that exists between husband and wife. Long into the New Testament the same exaltation of marriage continues. Writing to the Ephesians (5:25) and consciously speaking of a great mystery, St. Paul compares the love which a husband bears for his wife to that self-effacing devotion with which Jesus loved the Church. And as the light of revelation illumines the closing pages of St. John's Apocalypse, the bride, the holy Church, gazes along the horizon of prophecy for the coming of the Bridegroom, Christ.[2]

Point to Remember

> He is before all things, and in Him all things hold together. *Colossians 1:17*

---

2 Walter A. Maier, *For Better, Not for Worse* (St. Louis: Concordia, 1939), 75.

The Great Dance

O chestnut-tree, great-rooted blossomer
Are you the leaf, the blossom or the bole?
O body swayed to music, O brightening glance,
How can we know the dancer from the dance?
—W. B. Yeats, *Among School Children*

Our triune God shows diversity, order, and relationship within His own being. Although the Son is coequal with the Father, the Son chooses the way of obedience, humbling Himself to become man and dying on a cross for our sins. Then the dance changes, and the Son is exalted to the right hand of the Father. The Holy Spirit is also an active participant with a special role. He proceeds from the Father and the Son, convicting the world of sin, calling people to faith and making them holy.

There is another dance, the great dance of marriage, where man and woman become one flesh, living in reverence for Christ. The dance widens to family and then community. Each person has many roles in the dance. Men and women are born into the vocation of son and daughter, and may later find themselves husband and wife, father and mother, worker, volunteer, and member of a congregation.

Have you ever been at a meeting or in a group situation where one person seemed to dominate and wanted to do all the work? Most of us know someone with the "If I don't do it myself, it won't get done correctly" attitude. Proud people do not trust other people to do a good job, so they take on all the work by themselves. The contributions of others are ignored, causing hard feelings. The results are often poor. The soccer player who will not pass when he should is usually tackled, so the whole team loses an opportunity to score. When each player thinks of his work as a contribution to the team's objective, the team functions effectively. In the same way, vocations are not isolated walks of life, but contributions to a collaborative project.

A Play with Many Parts

Vocations exist in interdependence. One actor says his line to set up the next actor for her line. Otherwise we have one character taking everyone's part and doing a monologue. This ignores the gifts that other actors have been given and rejects the author's intention for the play. Recognizing vocation is recognizing our particular contribution to a community project that also involves the vocations of others. It rejects an "I can do it all" or "I did it my way" approach. Frank Sinatra's song fails to capture the fact that human beings flourish in community, not by self-assertion but by a combination of humble service and dependence on the gifts of others.

When John the Baptist called the crowds to repentance, he wasn't asking them to give up their worldly vocations and abandon their communities. "Tax collectors also came to be baptized and said to [John], 'Teacher, what shall we do?' And he said to them, 'Collect no more than you are authorized to do.' Soldiers also asked him, 'And we, what shall we do?' And he said to them, 'Do not extort money from anyone by threats or by false accusation, and be content with your wages'" (Luke 3:12–14). He told them to do their jobs well and to be fair in their dealings with others.

Repenting of our sin is not repenting of our existence in the world. God created the world and called it *good*. Even after the fall, He expects Christians to remain in their various stations where they can best show His love to their neighbor. John tells tax collectors and soldiers to conduct their work ethically, but he does not tell them to resign. This reflects the fact that both taxation and the military are part of the human government that God institutes to maintain order on earth. It also shows that every vocation is under God's Law. Tax collectors and soldiers who extort money or make false accusations are acting outside of their vocation.

Let's review what we learned earlier from Romans 12:4–8 and 1 Corinthians 12:14–26. There are many different vocations because God has assigned different functions and distributed different gifts to different people. Just as the various parts of the body have different functions but each contributes to the life of the body, so there are different callings that together support the life of a community.

In God's eyes no vocation is unimportant. Different vocations connect to serve the society as a whole. It is easy to suppose that eyes are more important than hands because we need eyes to see where we are going. Likewise, political leaders may be tempted to think they are more important than workers. But what use is it to see the steering wheel if one has no hands to control it? And what government could survive in a world without farmers and factory workers? Yet those workers also need political leaders so that society is well run and taxes are collected for education, services, and the military. Otherwise the workers are not trained, have no infrastructure to get to work, and are vulnerable to attack. The fact is that each vocation is dependent on the others. Each vocation is crucial to the healthy functioning of the civil community and of the Body of Christ.

Paul gives the Thessalonians some great advice on contributing to the great dance of community. In order for the great dance to work, each Christian must be self-controlled (1 Thessalonians 4:4–5), should avoid wronging or taking advantage of his brother or sister (v. 6), and should love others (vv. 9–10). This love is shown in part through obedience to vocation, accepting the assigned role that God has given us. In verse 11, Christians are called to "live quietly" (avoiding conflict and discord), to mind their "own affairs" (focusing on serving their neighbor through their own vocation and not trespassing on the vocations of others), and to work with their "hands" (actually do the work themselves and not make others do it for them). All of this is done to create a harmonious working community so that the daily lives of Christians "may walk properly before outsiders" (v. 12) by serving as a collective witness to Christ through a life of cooperative self-sacrifice.

Paul also has some choice words for those who would prefer to sit out the dance.

> Now we command you, brothers, in the name of our Lord Jesus Christ, that you keep away from any brother who is walking in idleness and not in accord with the tradition that you received from us. For you yourselves know how you ought to imitate us, because we were not idle when we were with you, nor did we eat anyone's bread without paying for it, but with toil and labor we worked night and day, that we might not be a burden to any of you. It was not because we do not have that right, but to give you in ourselves an example to imitate. For even when we were with you, we would give you this command: If anyone is not willing to work, let him not eat. (2 Thessalonians 3:6–10)

Vocations are not our choices, but God's choices for us. When we abdicate vocation, it is like an organ of our body shutting down. The whole body suffers because a function critical to the whole is not being performed. Those who neglect their talents let down not only themselves but also the whole community, which is justified in imposing punishment on the idler. Paul argues that the person who refuses to use his gifts to support the whole cannot expect support from others until he repents and makes his contribution.

Paul goes on in that same chapter to distinguish between being busy and being a busybody. He says that hard workers are busy pursuing their assigned vocation. A busybody ignores his own vocation and interferes with everyone else's because he is so sure he can do it better. A good way to annoy people is to appoint yourself as supervisor, constantly critiquing everyone else's work while doing absolutely none of your own. Paul says that such people are called to return to their own vocation and to "earn their own living" (2 Thessalonians 3:12) like everyone else. Vocation opposes self-importance and self-appointed, self-made people, and it exalts those who allow God to make of them servants for the whole.

Wearing Many Hats

The same person can have many callings at the same time. A Christian businessman is simultaneously called to be a Christian, a church member, a husband and father, and a salesman. The callings affect one another in important ways. For example, a Christian businessman should not allow his work to undermine his familial roles and should see his work as a means of supporting his family and of witness. Additionally, he should conduct his business in a fair and honest manner, his actions reflecting his beliefs positively to unbelievers.

In 1 Timothy, Paul tells us about holding many vocations simultaneously. Anyone who serves as an overseer (or bishop or pastor) will at the same time be a monogamous husband, a teacher (1 Timothy 3:2), a parent (v. 4), and a longtime Christian (v. 6). He makes it clear that overseers and deacons must pursue their other vocations in ways compatible with their vocation as a minister. It is important to see that a Christian businessman and parent is called to conduct business *and* to raise his children in ways that reflect his primary call to be a Christian. A crooked businessman, wife-beater, or child abuser who worships regularly is not a good witness or a faithful servant, despite his outward but false piety.

In Acts 26, Paul uses his multiplicity of vocations to be a more effective witness for Christ. From Paul, we can learn that every vocation is an opportunity for witness. Paul uses his vocation as teacher of the Jewish Law to defend the Gospel "against all the accusations of the Jews" (Acts 26:2) by arguing that Jesus fulfills the promises given to the twelve tribes of Israel (v. 7). Using his expertise in Greek philosophy, Paul also witnesses to the Gentiles (v. 20) and as a lawyer provides public evidence to support his case for Christ (v. 26). Finally, he uses his vocation as Roman citizen so that he can appeal to Caesar (v. 32) and witness in Rome. The lesson for us is that we have opportunities to witness as spouse, parent, worker, citizen, and member of a congregation. Each vocation is a distinctive avenue for witness. By pursuing that vocation in a Christlike manner, we embody the Gospel for those with whom the vocation connects us.

A Road Less Traveled

Some of the best things that happen to us are not our idea. Changes in circumstance or relationships can be painful, yet they also provide new opportunities for service.

Joseph's story (Genesis 50:15–21) is an excellent example of how God can even work through human evil to provide an important calling. Joseph's brothers sold Joseph into slavery, wresting him away from his vocations at home. But God drew Joseph to a new calling: he was put in charge of "all the land of Egypt" (Genesis 41:41), where he exercised wise stewardship by storing grain from the abundant years so that famine could be endured. Although Joseph's brothers had meant to harm him, God used their evil actions to work good for Israel. Joseph's new vocation enables him to do God's providential work by saving Israel from starvation. Even if we suffer hardships such as job loss, illness, or divorce, which tear us away from our current vocations, God will provide new work for us to do. A painful experience may lead to a new opportunity to serve.

The examples of Moses and Paul also illustrate how God calls us out of our "comfort zone." We can be mistaken in supposing something is not our calling when it is. Moses thought he had no gift to lead Israel because he was not a confident speaker. But God made Moses the leader, saying what God commanded and working through the medium of Aaron (Exodus 7:1–2). Paul thought his goal in life was to round up Christian "blasphemers" for extradition, but he was chosen by God to carry His name "before the Gentiles and kings and the children of Israel" (Acts 9:15). Today, teachers are often required to teach in areas outside their original training. In the business world, retraining and reassignment is common. Pastors are called to different congregations, to mission work, or to become members of a theology faculty.

Point to Remember

> If one member suffers, all suffer together; if one member is honored, all rejoice together. *1 Corinthians 12:26*

God at Work

> In co-operation in vocation, man becomes God's mask on earth . . . God reveals himself to others through man's actions.
> —Gustaf Wingren, *Luther on Vocation*

Everything we have is God's. We are saved by grace and not by works. So God does not *need* any of our vocations. But our neighbor does. God calls us into vocations to serve our neighbor, not to save or serve ourselves. But vocations are not merely human works. God works through us.

As Luther explains, we are God's masks (*larvae Dei*): His eyes, hands, and feet. Although God could provide everything directly, He chooses to work through human beings. Just as the Gospel is communicated through the Means of Grace (Word and Sacrament), so God's providential care for humanity is channeled through the means of vocations. To use Gene Edward Veith's example in *God at Work*, God could provide bread directly, as He did to Israel in the desert. But normally God provides through the vocations of farmer, truck driver, baker, and store clerk. Vocations are the channels of God's ongoing love for creation.

Occasionally we find ourselves doing something that helps someone else even though we had not planned on doing it. Everyone runs into unexpected demands. Someone else needs heavy lifting, dishes to pass, or repairs on the house. Sometimes we can help, sometimes we cannot, and sometimes we are the ones who need help. God works through people where they are and with the gifts that He has given them. Ability and opportunity suffice to make the call to serve. This is often unexpected, and sometimes we are unwilling to help. God prefers a willing helper who forgets herself, but He will still work through an unwilling helper, changing her as He does so. I am sometimes reluctant to put up the Christmas tree, but I am always glad when I have done it.

Our Servant God

God serves us in order to call forth our service to others. But God does not merely tell us to serve. Through faith, the Gospel changes us, so that we find a new desire to serve. God does this by working through us, by uniting us with Christ and giving us the love of Christ.

God also provides what we need to serve. He is concerned for our temporal needs of food, drink, and clothing (Matthew 6:27–34). He provides the raw materials for all of this in our natural environment and calls human beings to create the products. But He wants us to remember that salvation is not found here. God's providence for this life must always be held secondary to the gift of eternal life. Our vocations are important to serve our neighbor, but God ultimately calls us home to live with Him.

Jesus gives us an excellent example of leading a life of service. He humbled Himself to wash His disciples' feet (John 13:14) so that we would see our calling to forget our pride and serve others in humility. A Christian should not be like the butler who "doesn't do floors." Even a Christian CEO may be called to help a disabled person rake leaves or shovel snow. Those who humble themselves to meet the real needs of others are exalted by God as heroes of the faith, even if the world takes no notice. What matters is the love and the witness given to the person who is helped.

God works through us by filling us "with the knowledge of His will in all spiritual wisdom and understanding" (Colossians 1:9). This spiritual discernment enables us to see our vocation. We are also provided with power to bear "fruit in every good work" (v. 10) and receive gifts of endurance, patience, and joyful gratitude for being made heirs of Christ's inheritance (vv. 11–13). Paul tells us that the fruit of the Spirit includes "love, joy, peace, patience, kindness, goodness, faithfulness, gentleness, [and] self-control" (Galatians 5:22–23).

From Paul we also learn to focus our hearts and minds on our heavenly Father, not on our neighbor.

> For when one says, "I follow Paul," and another, "I follow Apollos," are you not being merely human? What then is Apollos? What is Paul? Servants through whom you believed, as the Lord assigned to each. I planted, Apollos watered, but God gave the growth. So neither he who plants nor he who waters is anything, but only God who gives the growth. He who plants and he who waters are one, and each will receive his wages according to his labor. For we are God's fellow workers. You are God's field, God's building. (1 Corinthians 3:4–9)

Paul addresses factions in the church of Corinth that arose from disagreements about who was the best human leader. These disagreements show a failure to understand that human beings are servants and conduits of God's saving grace (1 Corinthians 3:5). None of us has any power to save in ourselves: "neither he who plants nor he who waters is anything, but only God who gives the growth" (v. 7). Thus we are "God's fellow workers" (v. 9) in the same sense that tenant farmers are fellow workers with the landowner. The landowner works through the tenants to produce crops, but the land and the crops are his. Although all vocations are opportunities for evangelism, we never save anyone. God saves by the power of the Holy Spirit working through the Gospel. Likewise, though all vocations are opportunities to show love to our neighbor, it is God's love that is being shown through us.

God works even through our weaker efforts here on earth. God can work through insincere people (Philippians 1:18). Even if the Gospel is preached insincerely, the Holy Spirit can still work through the Word. More generally, God is at work in humans even when they do not cooperate. Although Paul tells the Philippians that he would like to be with the Lord in heaven, he recognizes that God has work for him to do here on earth (vv. 24–25). Like the captain of a ship, we are not authorized to abandon our station when we feel like it.

God builds the Christian community by working through us. As John 15:1–8 tells us, we are to Christ as the branches are to the vine. We have no spiritual life of our own, no natural ability to bear fruit (John 15:4), but, if we are connected to Christ, we will bear abundant fruit (v. 5). Paul explores several similar analogies. He says we are no longer aliens but "fellow citizens," no longer outcasts but "members of the household of God" (Ephesians 2:19). And we are stones of a building raised "on the foundation of the apostles and prophets" (God's Word) with "Christ Jesus Himself being the cornerstone" (v. 20). The common bond of each stone in the building is its incorporation in Christ and submission to God's Word. The Holy Spirit also is a tie that binds us together into God's dwelling place (v. 22).

Mutual Dependence

In his book *Civility*, Stephen Carter argues that we often fall prey to *individualism*, the idea that we are independent and completely in charge of our lives. But a great piano player needs a music teacher, the composers and printers of the music, the parent who took him to lessons, the automobile workers who built the car, the road workers who build and maintain the roads, and many others.

God's plan for us rejects individualism. God made us social beings. We are designed for relationship, to work together. Our gifts are not provided to exalt ourselves in isolation from others but are means of playing our part in a wider community. Everyone needs the support of others with different gifts. Many people cannot fix their own plumbing or electrical systems and do not know how to put on a new roof or fix their cars. God does not want "division in the body" (1 Corinthians 12:25) where some people view themselves as self-sufficient or superior, so He distributes His gifts in such a way that everyone depends on others. That helps us to see that we are in this together, that the suffering and honor of some impacts everyone (v. 26). God creates this mutual dependence "for building up the body of Christ, until we all attain to the unity of the faith and of the knowledge of the Son of God" (Ephesians 4:12–13). As each part does its work, Christians abandon deception by "speaking the truth in love," and the Body of Christ grows up into the Head, Christ (vv. 15–16).

God calls us to carry our own load yet also to bear one another's burdens. Each of us has assigned vocations, a burden we are called to carry. But our vocations are not unrelated to other people's. As we bear our own load (Galatians 6:5) by following our vocation, we must also "bear one another's burdens" (v. 2) by supporting other people's vocations. For example, a builder is called to build, but his work will fail if the architect's blueprint is faulty or if the contractors do not deliver the materials on time. Likewise, the architect is called to design the house to be structurally sound, but his plans are not realized if the builder deviates from the plan or if the contractors deliver defective materials. We always have a twofold responsibility to complete the work assigned to us, and to make sure that it serves those other workers who depend on it.

Consider the Source

All pride and boasting comes from the tendency to take credit for the works of our own hands. But we are stewards, not landlords, of everything we have. Our very lives, bodies, and minds are gifts. So are our callings to serve others. God is love and transmits it like the light of the sun. At best we are like the moon. We are marred by the "craters" of sin and produce no light of our own. But by God's grace in Christ, we can reflect the light of God's love to others.

John explains that all true, unconditional (*agape*) love comes from God. Anyone capable of showing this divine love "has been born of God" (has been regenerated) and "knows God" (1 John 4:7). In Christ, God came into the world so that we see His love and share in that love by living through Christ (v. 9). By ourselves, we cannot love God, but God's love empowers us to love others (vv. 11–12). It is not possible to live in God's love without loving our neighbor (vv. 20–21). Because of this love, we become "good Samaritans," sacrificing our own interests to serve our neighbors. We cannot claim to show the love of God if we are unloving to the poor, other races, the divorced, homosexuals, or drug addicts. Christ is the ultimate "good Samaritan" because He sacrificed Himself to save helpless humanity.

James reminds us "that every good gift and every perfect gift is from above" (James 1:17). God gave us a new birth through the Gospel (v. 18). This creates a free heartfelt desire to help. We can trust that "He who supplies seed to the sower and bread for food will" also supply our hearts with spiritual seeds that produce a "harvest of . . . righteousness" (2 Corinthians 9:10). Our generous Father enriches us so that we may be generous to others (v. 11). God values generosity because it reflects gratitude to Him (v. 12) and because it causes men to "glorify God because of your submission flowing from your confession of the gospel of Christ" (v. 13). Churches witness most effectively when they combine evangelism with a concern for the temporal needs of others. Food pantries, parish nurse programs, and church schools are a few among many examples.

Comparisons

The word *vocation* ("calling") is used in a variety of ways. The different uses of the word stem from different traditions in Western Christendom.

Medieval: The word *vocation* was used mainly to describe God's calling of servants in the Church. A *clerical vocation* meant a parish pastor. A *religious vocation* meant a person who lived as a monk or nun in isolation from broader society. (*Vocation* could also describe the fixed states in which people labored in medieval society: serfs, lords, and so on.) A sharp contrast was made between those called to serve God in the Church and all other workers. This view of vocation was important for later Roman Catholicism.

Lutheran: Martin Luther applied the word *vocation* not only to clergy but also to all workers. He emphasized that God commanded, blessed, and worked through all types of legitimate labor. The heavenly Father called people to different types of work so that they might bless one another.

Calvinist: John Calvin largely accepted Luther's view of vocation but added that labor should lead to profit as a mark of God's blessing. Later, some Calvinists came to view profit as a mark of election to salvation.

Anabaptist: Menno Simons and Jacob Hutter were influenced by Luther's view on vocation, but they taught that Christians could not legitimately serve in government. They also emphasized communal sharing of profit.

Modern: Since the Enlightenment, the tendency has been to separate vocation from God's call to work. Christianity taught people to live in service to God and His goals. In contrast, modern movements have taught people to live their lives for personal goals, state goals, or collective social goals. Vocation has come to mean one's career with no reference to God's calling.

Point to Remember

And God is able to make all grace abound to you, so that having all sufficiency in all things at all times, you may abound in every good work. *2 Corinthians 9:8*

Lutheran Summary of Vocation

Vocation intersects with every major theological doctrine. God calls human beings into vocations by creating them for special work. He brings hardship to these vocations by the curse of the fall. But vocations continue as channels of God's providential love of His creation. Non-Christians are compelled to serve so that social order is maintained. But Christians are reborn in Christ to a new willingness to serve their neighbor and spread the Gospel. Finally, Christ calls believers out of this world into life eternal with Him.

Augsburg Confession II 1–2

Our churches teach that since the fall of Adam [Romans 5:12], all who are naturally born are born with sin [Psalm 51:5], that is, without the fear of God, without trust in God, and with the inclination to sin, called concupiscence. Concupiscence is a disease and original vice that is truly sin. It damns and brings eternal death on those who are not born anew through Baptism and the Holy Spirit [John 3:5]. (*Concordia*, pp. 31–32)

Augsburg Confession VI 1–2

Our churches teach that this faith is bound to bring forth good fruit [Galatians 5:22–23]. It is necessary to do good works commanded by God [Ephesians 2:10], because of God's will. We should not rely on those works to merit justification before God. The forgiveness of sins and justification is received through faith. (*Concordia*, p. 33)

Augsburg Confession XIV

Our churches teach that no one should publicly teach in the Church, or administer the Sacraments, without a rightly ordered call. (*Concordia*, pp. 39)

Augsburg Confession XVI 1–2

Our churches teach that lawful civil regulations are good works of God. They teach that it is right for Christians to hold political office, to serve as judges, to judge matters by imperial laws and other existing laws, to impose just punishments, to engage in just wars, to serve as soldiers, to make legal contracts, to hold property, to take oaths when required by magistrates, for a man to marry a wife, or a woman to be given in marriage [Romans 13; 1 Corinthians 7:2]. (*Concordia*, pp. 39–40)

Augsburg Confession XX 9–10, 27–28

First, [our teachers] teach that our works cannot reconcile God to us or merit forgiveness of sins, grace, and justification. We obtain reconciliation only by faith when we believe that we are received into favor for Christ's sake. He alone has been set forth as the Mediator and Atoning Sacrifice (1 Timothy 2:5), in order that the Father may be reconciled through Him. Therefore, whoever believes that he merits grace by works despises the merit and grace of Christ [Galatians 5:4]. . . . We teach that it is necessary to do good works. This does not mean that we merit grace by doing good works, but because it is God's will [Ephesians 2:10]. It is only by faith, and nothing else, that forgiveness of sins is apprehended. The Holy Spirit is received through faith, hearts are renewed and given new affections, and then they are able to bring forth good works. (*Concordia*, pp. 42, 43)

Small Catechism: Apostles' Creed

I believe in God, the Father Almighty, maker of heaven and earth. *What does this mean?* Answer: I believe that God has made me and all creatures. He has given me my body and soul, eyes, ears, and all my limbs, my reason, and all my senses, and still preserves them. In addition, He has given me clothing and shoes, meat and drink, house and home, wife and children, fields, cattle, and all my goods. He provides me richly and daily with all that I need to support this body and life. He protects me from all danger and guards me and preserves me from all evil. He does all this out of pure, fatherly, divine goodness and mercy, without any merit or worthiness in me. For all this I ought to thank Him, praise Him, serve Him, and obey Him. This is most certainly true.

And in Jesus Christ, His only Son, our Lord, who was conceived by the Holy Spirit, born of the Virgin Mary, suffered under Pontius Pilate, was crucified, died and was buried. He descended into hell. The third day He rose again from the dead. He ascended into heaven and sits at the right hand of God the Father Almighty. From thence He will come to judge the living and the dead. *What does this mean?* Answer: I believe that Jesus Christ, true God, begotten of the Father from eternity, and also true man, born of the Virgin Mary, is my Lord. He has redeemed me, a lost and condemned creature, purchased and won me from all sins, from death, and from the power of the devil. He did this not with gold or silver, but with His holy, precious blood and with His innocent suffering and death, so that I may be His own, live under Him in His kingdom, and serve Him in everlasting righteousness, innocence, and blessedness, just as He is risen from the dead, lives and reigns to all eternity. This is most certainly true.

I believe in the Holy Spirit, the holy Christian Church, the communion of saints, the forgiveness of sins, the resurrection of the body, and the life everlasting. Amen. *What does this mean?* Answer: I believe that I cannot by my own reason or strength believe in Jesus Christ, my Lord, or come to Him. But the Holy Spirit has called me by the Gospel, enlightened me with His gifts, sanctified and kept me in the true faith. In the same way

He calls, gathers, enlightens, and sanctifies the whole Christian Church on earth and keeps it with Jesus Christ in the one true faith. In this Christian Church He daily and richly forgives all my sins and the sins of all believers. On the Last Day He will raise up me and all the dead and will give eternal life to me and to all believers in Christ. This is most certainly true. (*Concordia*, pp. 328–30)

TOPIC SEVENTEEN

Worship[1]

Engaging This Topic

"I'm having trouble understanding you Lutherans."
"Why's that?"
"Well, you preach and pray like Baptists but your worship services are just like the Roman Catholics."
"I've always thought our worship tradition was unique."
"Well, why should tradition matter at all? Shouldn't we just follow the Bible?"

Lutheran Facts

Lutherans are led in worship by a pastor.

The service follows an *order*, an outline of worship that addresses spiritual needs such as forgiveness, learning from God's Word, and spiritual care through the proper administration of the Sacraments.

Lutheran orders of service are from the Western (Latin) liturgical tradition. This, in turn, stems from the synagogue and temple worship practiced by the earliest Christians, who were Jewish.

The Lutheran Reformation helped to encourage the practice of congregational singing, which had largely disappeared during the Middle Ages. The Lutheran Church has been called "the singing church."

Lutheran *chorales* spread to every nation touched by the Reformation. The chorales stem from the simple congregational songs of the early Middle Ages (Gregorian chant or plainsong).

Lutheran hymns have typically focused on the gracious work of the Holy Trinity for our salvation.

1 This chapter adapted from *The Lutheran Difference: Worship*, written by Steven P. Mueller, with contributions by Edward Engelbrecht. Copyright © 2004 Concordia Publishing House.

THE GOD WE WORSHIP

> Surely my heart cannot truly rest, nor be entirely contented, unless it rest in Thee.
>
> —Thomas à Kempis

What first comes to mind when you think of worship? Possibly your thoughts are of a church service, a prayer, a sermon, or a song. Perhaps you think of a certain building. Maybe a discussion that you've had with another Christian over worship forms or styles comes to mind. Chances are that your first reaction is to focus on something that we do or are involved in when we worship.

Our first reactions may fall short of what they should be. It is easy to get caught up in discussing the details of worship, or the controversies that often surround it, while forgetting the true focus of our worship. Worship needs to be focused on God and His Word.

WHY WORSHIP?

God is worthy of worship. His glory, splendor, holiness, and greatness are so wonderful that all creatures should be moved to worship Him (Psalm 29). Every good thing, all that we are and have, comes from Him. He deserves our worship because He is God (Psalm 145:3; Revelation 5:12).

Exodus 20:8 reveals the Third Commandment to us. God commands His people to worship Him. Hebrews 10:25 reminds us that worship does not end with the coming of Christ. Christians are also called to continue to worship together—in part to give each other encouragement in the last days.

In the Small Catechism, Martin Luther wrote that the Third Commandment means that "we should fear and love God so that we may not despise preaching and His Word, but hold it sacred, and gladly hear and learn it" (*Concordia*, p. 319). This explanation helps to focus our understanding of the commandment. Luther reminds us that the purpose of the Sabbath was not simply to have a day off from work, but to provide opportunity to worship. He directed people's attention to the Word of God. We hear God's voice, and receive His direction through His Word. True worship must involve the proclamation and belief of God's Holy Word. God knows that we will be blessed as we hear His Word.

Worship isn't simply a set of activities to do or words to speak. Worship needs an object. We are to worship God. In the explanation of the First Commandment in the Large Catechism, Luther writes: "A god means that from which we are to expect all good and in which we are to take refuge in all distress. So, to have [the One] God is nothing other than trusting and believing Him with the heart" (I 2; *Concordia*, p. 359). According to this definition, a god is whatever we trust and believe in. Whatever being or thing that we trust above all other things is, in fact, our god. To be sure, there is only one true, living God. Only the true God can save us. Only He has the power that we need. Only He is truly worthy of worship. Yet many people continue to worship false gods. Understood in this way, every person has a god.

If we are to worship the true God, we must know who He is. Deuteronomy 6:4 reminds us that there is only one God. Matthew 28:19 reveals that this one God consists of three persons: Father, Son, and Holy Spirit. The biblical doctrine of the Trinity is beyond our human comprehension. Our limited brains are incapable of fully understanding the nature of God. We can, however, trust and believe His Word. The only true God is the Holy Trinity. The three persons, Father, Son, and Holy Spirit, are each fully God, and yet are only one God. This is how God has revealed Himself to us.

There are many people in our world who deny the doctrine of the Trinity, and yet they still claim to worship God. Jesus, who is the way, the truth, and the life, says that it is impossible to access the Father apart from the Son (John 14:6). Without the Son, we do not really know the Father. First Corinthians 12:3 teaches us that we cannot believe in Jesus without the Holy Spirit. We are not free to ignore the Trinity or any of the three persons. We come to the Father through Jesus. We believe in Jesus through the Spirit. The Trinity is the only true God. This is the God we worship.

The triune God is worthy of our worship. Nothing or no one else deserves or rightly receives our worship. In Isaiah 42:8, God forbids worshiping false gods or any created thing. In Revelation 22:8–9, John was about to worship an angel who had shown him wondrous things. The angel rebuked him. Angels are not worthy of worship—they are servants of God along with human beings. (This shows us also that mere human beings are not worthy of worship either.) Only God is worthy of worship.

True Worship

God commands our worship, and invites us to worship Him by offering us His blessings of forgiveness, life, and salvation. True worship must be focused on the true God. God has revealed Himself as the Holy Trinity. We have certainly engaged in false worship. We have let other things take the place of God. (Indeed, every sin we commit is also a sin against the First Commandment. When we sin, we show that we prefer sin to God.) Since we have done these things, we should do as God says: confess our sins and receive His forgiveness for Jesus' sake.

In the Athanasian Creed we confess "the catholic [i.e. universal] faith is this, that we worship one God in Trinity and Trinity in unity" (*Concordia*, p. 17). Notice that the Creed doesn't just say we *believe* in the Trinity, but that we *worship* the Trinity. Worship and faith are directly related. Worship reflects our faith, and the content of our faith is affected by the way we worship. God's revelation of Himself moves us to worship Him as He is. Our faith and doctrine were never meant to be merely thoughts or words. Our faith impacts every aspect of our lives—including worship. We worship God because of who He is, in thanksgiving for the salvation that is ours in Jesus Christ, in praise of His goodness to us, and because He gives us His gifts in worship.

One Triune God

Exodus 20:1–8 is commonly known as the *First Table of the Law.* Each of these commands is about worship. They appear at the beginning of the Ten Commandments because our relationship with God has the highest priority. In Matthew 22:37, Jesus summarizes these commands with one word: *love.*

Our liturgy and music affirm that the Holy Trinity is the true God. Common expressions in our liturgy such as "Glory be to the Father and to the Son and to the Holy Spirit" focus our worship on the Holy Trinity.

Comparisons

The word *creed* comes from the Latin *credo*, meaning "I believe." Creeds are summary confessions of faith used by the vast majority of Christians. They developed at a time when most people could not read, so they needed a memorable rule of faith. The use of a creed is rooted in the recitation of the *Shema* in ancient Judaism. Part of Jewish daily prayer, the *Shema* (Hebrew for "hear") is drawn from Deuteronomy 6:4–9, 11, 13–21 and Numbers 15:37–41. It served as a summary of biblical teaching and was probably recited by Jesus and the apostles. (See Mark 12:28–31, where Jesus recites a portion of the *Shema* to answer a teacher of the law.)

After Jesus ascended into heaven, the earliest Christians began using summaries of Christian teaching (e.g., see 1 Corinthians 15:3–5). These summaries developed into the creeds listed below.

Apostles' Creed: A summary that began to take shape already at the time of the apostles. This creed developed from a series of questions asked of a person at the time of Baptism. History shows that congregations in

Rome were using a form of this creed already in the second century, but the wording did not receive its standard form until much later. Most churches from the Western (Latin) tradition still use the Apostles' Creed for instruction and as a confession of faith in worship.

Nicene Creed: A summary of Christian teaching adopted by congregations of the Roman Empire at the Council of Nicaea in 325. The Council of Constantinople expanded the creed in 381 to help settle other Christological controversies of the fourth century. Today, Eastern Orthodox churches and most churches from the Western (Latin) tradition confess the Nicene Creed in worship, especially during a Communion service. In the Middle Ages the Western churches added the *filioque* statement (see the Glossary, p. 683) and other minor changes, such as changing "we believe" to "I believe."

Athanasian Creed: This longer creed addresses the Christological controversies of the fourth and fifth centuries. Although named for Athanasius (ca. 296–373), the bishop of Alexandria who vigorously opposed Arianism, he did not write this creed, since it emerged much later. Many churches of the Western (Latin) tradition use the Athanasian Creed. Lutheran congregations typically recite it on Trinity Sunday. The creed has been included in Eastern Orthodox services, minus the *filioque* statement (see the Glossary, p. 683).

No creed but the Bible: Congregations of the Restoration movement rejected the use of creeds early in the nineteenth century. They taught that creeds divided Christians from one another and that agreement on the Bible as God's Word was a sufficient basis for unity. Christian Churches, Disciples of Christ, and Churches of Christ descend from this movement.

Liturgical churches (Eastern Orthodox, Lutheran, Reformed, Roman Catholic, and some Wesleyans) regularly recite a creed during their worship services. Many nonliturgical churches accept the teachings of the creeds but do not use them in their worship services.

Point to Remember

You shall have no other gods before Me. . . . You shall not take the name of the Lord your God in vain . . . . Remember the Sabbath day, to keep it holy. *Exodus 20:3, 7–8*

The People Who Worship

> God wants us to believe Him and to receive from Him blessings. He declares this to be true divine service.
>
> —Philip Melanchthon, Ap V (III) 107 [228] (*Concordia*, p. 116)

Driving home from worship one Sunday morning, Susan pondered Pastor Gomez's sermon. He drew a connection between the Gospel reading and their community in a way she had not considered before. Intrigued, she asked her family what they thought of the message. Her question was met with an awkward silence. When she pressed further, it seemed that no one else had listened to the sermon. "Come on, Mom," her son complained, "isn't it enough that we went to church?"

How would you respond to the son? His words seem to indicate he's uncomfortable with his mother's question. Perhaps he is masking his guilt at being unable to answer her. Maybe he did not want to attend worship. We may be tempted to lash out at words like these, but chances are we can relate to them at times. It is not enough to simply "go to church." If we are not hearing the Word of God and thereby receiving His blessings, we are not really worshiping Him.

Are you ever tempted to think of worship as something to attend and watch, but not really something in which to participate? There may be times that we treat worship more as a "spectator sport" than something that we are called to participate in gladly and freely. We may do this because it is easier just to attend a service than to take part in it. We may participate less if we are not familiar with the worship forms or with what is expected of us. There may be times when we seem less able to take part in a service. We need to be careful that we do not use times like these as an excuse. Worship is not a magical formula or ritual that we simply witness. It calls for the involvement of each Christian.

In Spirit and Truth

In John 4:19–26, Jesus talks with a Samaritan woman who had led a sad and sinful life. When His questions get too personal, she tries to sidetrack Jesus by bringing up a point of controversy between the Jews and the Samaritans—the proper place for worship. She wants to know where people have to worship. Does it have to be in Jerusalem as the Jews teach, or is she free to worship in other places? Jesus does not mandate any city as the one place of worship. Instead, He teaches that true worshipers worship "in spirit and truth" (John 4:24). It is true that God once taught that worship should take place in the temple in Jerusalem. Now that God has become incarnate in Jesus Christ, worship was not limited to this one place. It is not the place of worship that matters, but the God who is worshiped. The woman wanted to know where to worship. Jesus was teaching her how to worship. She needed to worship not by simply going to a place of worship, but by worshiping in spirit. The inclination of her heart was vital. To worship in spirit means to believe, to worship with your heart as well as your mind and body.

Let's look back at the quote at the beginning of this section: "God wants us to believe Him and to receive from Him blessings. He declares this to be true divine service" (Ap V [III] 107 [228]; *Concordia*, p. 116). The Apology of the Augsburg Confession echoes Jesus' words by stressing the necessity of belief. Faith and worship are completely connected. Worship is not only something we do because we believe—our faith itself is worship. Trusting and believing God is worship. When we receive His gifts (and we only receive His spiritual gifts by faith), we are worshiping. This is part of God's plan for us. He is pleased when we believe Him and receive His gifts.

Many of our worship services begin with Confession and Absolution. First John 1:8–9 and Psalm 32:5 (which are often used in worship) remind us that we are sinners in need of God's forgiveness. This is true even if we try to ignore this fact. We can be thankful that God is gracious and merciful. He forgives our sins for Christ's sake. When we confess our sins, we are acknowledging what we bring to worship—our sinfulness. We are utterly reliant on God's grace if we are to come into His presence and receive His blessing. Faith knows that we owe everything to Christ, and it boldly reaches out to receive His blessings. Even when the service does not begin with Confession and Absolution, we come before God with repentant hearts each day of our lives, knowing that, because faith in the Gospel means to receive God's gift of forgiveness in Jesus Christ. (See Ap V [III] 188–89 [309–10]; *Concordia*, p. 130.)

In John 4:23–24, Jesus told the Samaritan woman that true worshipers worship in spirit and in truth. In John 17:17, He says, "Sanctify them in the truth; Your word is truth." It is not sufficient to do or say anything we want. God tells us to worship in truth. Our worship must be true—it is normed and guided by the Word of God, which is truth. This does not mean that everything we say must be a word-for-word quote from the Bible, but we judge our words and our worship by the standard of God's Holy Word. It is our only infallible guide. As our guide, the Holy Scriptures direct us to proclaim the Truth made flesh, Jesus Christ. The apostle John uses the word *truth* in his Gospel to describe Jesus (John 1:14, 17; 14:6), Jesus' teachings (John 8:31–32, 45–46), and the Spirit's testimony about Jesus (14:7; 15:26; 16:13). Worshiping "in spirit and truth" will not center on emotional experiences, seeking miracles, or so-called "spiritual" phenomena, but on the clear proclamation of the Gospel of Jesus Christ in Word and Sacrament. The Scriptures assure us that the Holy Spirit works powerfully through these Means of Grace: we have been born again through God's Word (1 Peter 1:23); we are washed and renewed by the Holy Spirit (Titus 3:5); through the Holy Spirit, we have the Office of the Keys (John 20:22–23); we receive forgiveness of sins through the Lord's Supper (Matthew 26:27–28).

Sometimes, Christians speak as if this emphasis on "spirit and truth" is unique to the New Testament. But Hosea 6:6 (which Jesus quotes in Matthew 9:13; 12:7) makes it clear that God was never asking simply for outward obedience: "For I desire steadfast love and not sacrifice, the knowledge of God rather than burnt offerings." He has always sought the whole person. Repeatedly in the Old Testament, God calls Israel to offer sacrifices. When the sacrifices were offered without faith, God called His people to acknowledge Him and show mercy. Without these responses of faith, the sacrifices meant nothing. In the same way, Christians who have been freed from offering animal sacrifices are still called to trust and believe our God. Without faith in Christ, we are not worshiping.

Hosea calls us to a living faith. Romans 12:1 calls us to offer ourselves, our bodies, as living sacrifices to God. We do this in response to God's goodness to us. He has freely shown us His mercy. We respond by gratefully offering ourselves to Him. This is not a sacrifice of blood and death. Christ has already offered the final sacrifice of His body on the cross. Instead, God calls us to offer ourselves as a living sacrifice. When our lives reflect our faith, we are doing this. Yet even the opportunity and ability to do this are blessings from God. We would be unable to serve God unless He had first served us.

By Faith Alone

Focusing on this biblical teaching on worship, we know it is never proper for us to consider worship simply as "going through the motions" or mindlessly repeating words or actions. Whatever forms or words we use to worship, we may be tempted to believe that the acts themselves are worship. We need to confess this attitude and receive God's forgiveness. He calls us to worship in spirit and truth.

Every religion in the world has some form of worship. Most of the members of these religions seem sincere and many seem to live good lives. But without faith in Christ, they are not engaged in true worship. Don't question the sincerity of people in other religions. People can be sincere but also wrong! No act of worship is of any use if it is not directed, in faith, to the true and living God, the Holy Trinity. Non-Christians are not engaged in true worship or belief (see LC II 66; *Concordia*, p. 406).

God reveals Himself to us and calls us to worship Him. God wants all people to believe in Him and to receive His gift of salvation (1 Peter 3:15). Those who have received this gift respond in worship and thanksgiving. When we encounter people who do not worship the true God, we need to remember that Jesus Christ also died and rose for them. We should share the Gospel with them so that they may receive God's salvation and join us in worshiping Him.

Taking Stock

We have seen how our worship is rightly preceded by Confession and Absolution. Matthew 6:11–12 tells us that we are to pray daily, asking for God's provision. We also need God's forgiveness not only before services but also daily. We are to take the time to confess our sins and hear His forgiveness each day.

Comparisons

Christians have typically defined their doctrine of worship under the doctrine of the church and ministry.

Eastern Orthodox: "What is to be noted of the *place* where the Liturgy is celebrated? It must always be consecrated in a *temple*, the *table* in which, or at least, if there be no such table, the *antimense* [altar cloth] on which the Sacrament is consecrated, must have been consecrated by a Bishop. Why is the *temple* called a *church*? Because the faithful, who compose the Church, meet in it for prayer and Sacraments" (*The Longer Catechism of the Eastern Church*, questions 320–21).

Lutheran: "So that we may obtain this faith, the ministry of teaching the Gospel and administering the Sacraments was instituted. . . . The Church is the congregation of saints [Psalm 149:1] in which the Gospel is purely taught and the Sacraments are correctly administered" (AC V 1, VII 1; *Concordia*, p. 33, 34).

Reformed: "This catholic Church hath been sometimes more, sometimes less visible. And particular churches, which are members thereof, are more or less pure, according as the doctrine of the gospel is taught and embraced, ordinances administered, and public worship performed more or less purely in them" (*The Westminster Confession of Faith*, chapter 25.4).

Anabaptist: "We believe in, and confess a visible church of God, namely, those who, as has been said before, truly repent and believe, and are rightly baptized; . . . this church, we say, may be known by their Scriptural faith, doctrine, love, and godly conversation, as, also, by the fruitful observance, practice, and maintenance of the true ordinances of Christ, which He so highly enjoined upon His disciples" (*The Dordrecht Confession*, article 8).

Roman Catholic: "The sacred and holy, ecumenical and general Synod of Trent—lawfully assembled in the Holy Ghost, the same Legates of the Apostolic See presiding therein—to the end that the ancient, complete, and in every part perfect faith and doctrine touching the great mystery of the Eucharist may be retained in the holy Catholic Church. . . . The Catholic Church instituted, many years ago, the sacred Canon, so pure from every error. . . . For it is composed, out of the very words of the Lord, the traditions of the apostles, and the pious institutions also of holy pontiffs" (*Canons and Decrees of the Council of Trent*, Session 22, Doctrine of the Sacrifice of the Mass; cf. CCC2 paras. 1324, 1345–55).

Baptist: "We believe that a visible Church of Christ is a congregation of baptized believers, associated by covenant in the faith and fellowship of the gospel; observing the ordinances of Christ; governed by his laws, and exercising the gifts, rights, and privileges invested in them by his Word; that its only scriptural officers are Bishops, or Pastors, and Deacons, whose qualifications, claims, and duties are defined in the Epistles of Timothy and Titus" (*New Hampshire Baptist Confession*, article 13).

Wesleyan: "The visible Church of Christ is a congregation of faithful men, in which the pure Word of God is preached, and the sacraments duly administered, according to Christ's ordinance, in all those things that of necessity are requisite to the same" (*Methodist Articles of Religion*, article 13).

Liberal: "We can no longer think of the [worship] service as something demanded by God to which the worshiper is therefore compelled to submit. We must think of it as an exercise designed entirely to help the worshiper in securing the right religious attitude toward God, life, and duty. We must consider, then, the presuppositions with which our worshiper enters the church. The psychology of apperception is important here. We must estimate his attitude toward each element of worship. We must consider what may check the rising tide of emotion and what may carry it on to the full" (Gerald Birney Smith, ed., *Guide to the Study of the Christian Religion* [Chicago: University of Chicago Press, 1916], p. 617).

Point to Remember

God is spirit, and those who worship Him must worship in spirit and truth. *John 4:24*

The Way of the Church

Is it then the walls that make Christians?
—Victorinus, in *The Confessions of St. Augustine*

As an elder in his church, Nathan stopped to visit one of his fellow members who hadn't come to worship in several months. "We've missed you, Harold. Is anything wrong? Can we help you with anything?"

"No, Nathan, nothing's really wrong. I've just been busy. A lot of important business demanded my attention, and I haven't had much time for church. But it's made me wonder, Nathan, do we really need to go to church? I believe that God is everywhere. Can't God bless me here just as easily as He can at church?"

Nathan sighed to himself. He'd heard these questions before. Saying a silent prayer, he began to share his faith with Harold.

Is Harold right? Can God bless us anywhere—even if we're not within the walls of the church? Harold has a point. God truly is omnipresent. He is not limited by our human restrictions. He can bless us anywhere. In fact, He does bless us. All good things that we receive in this life are from God. He blesses us even when we fail to recognize Him as the source of our blessings.

If God is with us everywhere, and will bless us, why does He want us to worship together? God can bless us anywhere, but He promises His blessings of forgiveness, life, and salvation in His Word and Sacraments. He promises that He is present where two or more Christians are gathered in Jesus' name. We worship together because this is God's plan for us. He has told us to do this and has promised us great blessings when we worship together.

Connected by Christ

When Christians gather together for worship, we experience a number of relationships. We are connected to the people we join for worship. We are brought into the presence of God "with angels and archangels and with all the company of heaven" (from the Communion liturgy, based on Hebrews 12:22–24 and elsewhere). In this section, we explore the nature of these relationships in worship.

Different Christian churches use various terms to refer to worship services. For Lutherans, a common term is *Divine Service*. When you think about it, this term can seem vague. Who is serving whom in worship? Is worship the act of humans serving God, or is it God serving humans? Does God need our worship? These very important questions help to illustrate some of the differences in how various denominations conceive of worship. Many Christians think worship is primarily something that we do for God. We praise Him. We give Him offerings. We serve Him. Yet as we consider various elements of worship, we will see that many of them are occasions where He serves us. Christian worship may contain both aspects. God graciously gives to us, and we respond to Him in faith and thanksgiving. It is important that we recognize that God does not need our worship. There is nothing that God needs. He is God no matter how His creation responds to Him.

Look at this list of elements that are often present in Christian worship. Some show God serving or giving to humans; in others, humans respond to God by serving or giving back to Him.

Time to worship. Time is part of God's gift to us. It is His creation. In Exodus 20:8–11, we hear the Third Commandment's call for us to worship, yet in that command is also the blessing of time. God gave His people a day of rest so they would have the opportunity to worship Him. While Christians are not obligated to keep the Sabbath (Matthew 12:8; Colossians 2:16–17), Acts 20:7 shows us that they commonly met together on Sunday, "the Lord's Day." They met for worship on the day Christ rose from the dead, as well as at other times. It is true that we use some of "our" time for worship, but we should remember that the time itself was first a gift from God.

Confession of sins. God provides us with the opportunity and invitation to confess our sins. We are sinners who need God's forgiveness. At His invitation, we acknowledge our sinful nature, and admit where we have disobeyed God's commands in thought, word, and deed.

Absolution (forgiveness) of sins. Absolution (and the forgiveness of sins we hear in other parts of the service) is a gracious gift of God. Nothing we do earns or merits this treatment. God has given to us what we did not deserve—forgiveness and life in Jesus Christ (1 John 1:9).

Praise. Psalm 9:1–2; 100:4; and Revelation 5:12 are just a few examples of the many passages that call for God's people to praise Him. We praise

God as we respond to His gifts, acknowledge His identity and goodness to us, as we proclaim His greatness, and as we sing and rejoice in Him. Revelation 5:12 reminds us that we praise Him because He is worthy of all praise and glory.

The Word of God. While it is people who read the Word, the Word itself comes from God. All Scripture is inspired by God (2 Timothy 3:14–17). He has given us His Word so that we may know His will and come to faith in His Son. We do not need to guess what God desires or what He might say. He freely communicates to us in the Bible. The Word is one of His gifts to us.

Offerings. Our offerings are clearly examples of us giving to God. We give financial offerings, but we also offer ourselves and our time. We support the mission and ministry of His Church in our offerings. However, even here we are not taking the initiative. God has first given us all things. We only give back a portion of what He has given to us (Psalm 116:12–14, 17–19).

Baptism. In Baptism, God gives His blessings to His people. He gives forgiveness of sins and salvation through this blessed washing (Acts 2:38). We do nothing to deserve these blessings, but He still gives them to us (1 Peter 3:21). While we only undergo Baptism once, we continue to live in its blessings each day. In fact, the words that begin most worship services are meant to remind us of Baptism: "In the name of the Father and of the Son and of the Holy Spirit." Each service begins with a reminder that we worship as the baptized and forgiven children of God.

The Lord's Supper. In the Lord's Supper, Christ our risen Lord is the host who invites us to eat His true body and drink His true blood, once offered in sacrifice on the cross (1 Corinthians 11:23–26). He gives us life and forgiveness again. He gives Himself to us.

Prayer. As we pray, we bring our concerns, requests, and supplications before God. We do this, however, at His invitation and with His help. He tells us to ask Him for His help, because He wants to help, even as a father wants to help his children (Matthew 7:7–8). Luther's Small Catechism summarizes this well in its explanation of the introduction of the Lord's Prayer: "God would tenderly encourage us to believe that He is our true Father and that we are His true children, so that we may ask Him confidently with all assurance, as dear children ask their dear father" (*Concordia*, p. 331).

Benediction. A benediction is a blessing (literally, a "good word"). God blesses us and sends us forth in His peace (Numbers 6:24). This is also His work.

Analyzing all of these elements of worship, who really is the servant in worship? While we are indeed responding to God's gifts, He gives far more than we could ever give. All that we do is return a tiny portion of what He has first given to us. God graciously serves us in worship.

Our relationship to God is part of worship. As we worship, however, He has also brought us together with other people. First Corinthians 12:12–14 (and the verses that follow) compare the Church to a body. God has brought us together to be one Body in Christ. Christ is the Head of the Body, and each of us is a part of this collective Body. The word *member* refers to a part of a body (such as a limb). The idea of church membership is rooted in this understanding and should not be compared with participation in a club. We worship together because God has placed us together in one body. He has given us different gifts and abilities so that together, living under Him, we can accomplish more things than we could do separately. The Church and corporate worship are His idea. We need one another.

Hebrews 10:25 reminds us that as we worship together we are able to encourage one another. We cannot do this if we are not with other Christians.

In the Smalcald Articles, Martin Luther writes that God gives His Gospel to us in many ways, including the Word, Baptism, the Sacrament of the Altar, through the Office of the Keys (Absolution), and "also through the mutual conversation and consolation of brethren" (III IV; *Concordia*, p. 278). This is a powerful argument for worshiping together. Luther supports these words with Matthew 18:20: "For where two or three are gathered in My name, there am I among them." God blesses us as Christians fellowship together, share God's Word and counsel with one another, and support one another in the Christian faith. These are functions of the Church that we simply cannot do alone. We need one another. I can be a Christian by myself, but I cannot be the Church by myself.

Challenges and Blessings

In worship God gives His gifts to us, but we often describe worship as our work. It does feel like we are the ones acting at times, but still we know that God gives us the means and the ability to do these things. It may be that we want to be in control. We want to feel useful and needed. In much of our spiritual life, we may struggle with wanting a greater role for ourselves than we really have. Yet God still loves us and blesses us for Jesus' sake. Even when we make too much of ourselves, He blesses us.

Psalm 116:12 asks: "What shall I render to the LORD for all His benefits to me?" Can we really give God anything to thank Him for His mercy? The psalmist answers this question. In a very real sense, there is nothing we can do to repay God. We might give Him offerings, but these are only a return of things He has given us first. He graciously receives our gifts and our worship not because of the intrinsic value of these things, but because He loves us. A parent, who receives an otherwise ugly and useless gift, loves the gift if it was given to him in love by his child. So our Father graciously receives our worship because He loves us. He loves us because of who we are in Jesus. So the psalmist answers that we can repay God by receiving His salvation and responding in worship.

God calls us together to be His Church. Since the Church is made up of redeemed sinners, there will be both challenges and blessings when we come together to worship. There are challenges when sinners worship together. Not all members will likely see things the same way. There will be different preferences for style, music, time, and many other aspects of worship. Some of these have a scriptural basis, others may not. Whatever the challenges may be, God has called us to be a Church. The blessings of our relationship far outweigh the challenges. God intends to bless us as we live together in the Body of Christ. He knows how much we need one another.

Comparisons

As you read the following comparisons, look for how the different churches talk about the work of the Holy Spirit, whether through the Means of Grace or within a person.

Eastern Orthodox: "Is the Holy Ghost communicated to men even now likewise? He is communicated to all true Christians. . . . How may we be made partakers of the Holy Ghost? Through fervent prayer, and through the Sacraments" (*The Longer Catechism of the Eastern Church*, questions 249–50).

Lutheran: "I believe that I cannot by my own reason or strength believe in Jesus Christ, my Lord, or come to Him. But the Holy Spirit has called me by the Gospel, enlightened me with His gifts, sanctified and kept me in the true faith" (SC II; *Concordia*, p. 330; Lutherans emphasize that the Holy Spirit works through the Means of Grace: the Word and Sacraments).

Reformed: "But when God accomplishes His good pleasure in the elect, or works in them true conversion, He not only causes the gospel to be externally preached to them, and powerfully illuminates their minds by His Holy Spirit . . . but by the efficacy of the same regenerating Spirit He pervades the inmost recesses of the man" (*Canons of the Synod of Dort*, article 11).

Roman Catholic: The Holy Spirit awakens faith in unbelievers and communicates new life to them through the ministry of the Church. Cf. CCC2 paras. 1098, 1432–33.

Anabaptist: This movement emphasizes the mystical work of the Spirit in the heart rather than through Word and Sacraments. Only holy people have received the Holy Spirit and are members of the Church.

Baptist: "We believe that Repentance and Faith are sacred duties, and also inseparable graces, wrought in our souls by the regenerating Spirit of God" (*New Hampshire Baptist Confession*).

Wesleyan: "But as soon as he is born of God . . . he is now capable of hearing the inward voice of God, saying, 'Be of good cheer; thy sins are forgiven thee'; 'Go and sin no more.' . . . He 'feels in his heart,' to use the language of our Church, 'the mighty working of the Spirit of God'" (*Standard Sermons of John Wesley*, 39.4).

Point to Remember

The body is one and has many members, and all the members of the body, though many, are one body, so it is with Christ. For in one Spirit we were all baptized into one body—Jews or Greeks, slaves or free—and all were made to drink of one Spirit. *1 Corinthians 12:12–13*

Elements of Christian Worship

The standard of prayer is the standard of faith.
—attributed to Prosper of Aquitaine

Janet has been your friend since you were in high school. She has little background in Christianity but always was curious about your faith. Recently, she has become a Christian and is looking for a church to join. "I'm confused," she says. "All of these churches say they are Christian, but they seem so different. They all have a worship service, but they all do different things. How can one religion have so many different expressions?"

Janet is correct in noticing differences in the way that different Christians worship. Some of the major differences include the type of music that is used, the role of the pastor and other leaders, the presence of vestments or other special clothing, the "formality" or "informality" of the service, the degree of involvement by the congregation, and the use (or non-use) of the Sacraments.

Many differences in worship reflect different theological understandings. For example, the use of the Lord's Supper will reflect what a church believes about this Sacrament. Some differences may be the result of cultural background. Some differences reflect different views of the purpose of worship, and some may be questions of style or preference. These are only a few of the sources of the differences.

The Bible and Worship

When we look in the Bible, we might be surprised by what we find about worship. The Old Testament gives very specific directions on how to worship. In Exodus 25, God tells His people how to construct the ark of the covenant, the table for the bread of the presence, and the lampstand. In Exodus 26–27, God gives the design for the tabernacle—the place where His glory would dwell—and for the altar where the priests were to offer burnt offerings. Chapter 28 gives specific directions for the type of clothing that the priests would wear in worship. In chapter 29, the priests are consecrated and set apart for service in the tabernacle. Exodus 30–31 involves the production of various furnishings for the temple, and give instructions for their use. Chapter 31 also tells about the Sabbath. This is an amazing amount of detail. God tells Israel exactly what they are to do in worship. We must note that these things are part of the old covenant and are no longer practiced by Christians. John 1:14 tells us that Christ, the Word, became flesh and *tabernacled* among us. In Christ, God is no longer limiting Himself to the tabernacle of the old covenant. The Book of Hebrews teaches us that Christ is the fulfillment of the priesthood and of sacrifice. We do not worship in the manner prescribed in the Old Testament now that Christ has come and has offered Himself as the final sacrifice.

In contrast, the New Testament provides no detailed list of instructions on how Christians must worship. Yet it does provide descriptions of some early Christian worship and some guiding principles for our worship. One of the first descriptions of worship after Pentecost is found in Acts 2:42. This verse contains four elements of Christian worship. The first is that the early Christians devoted themselves to the apostles' teaching. The content of the apostles' teaching is the Word of God, as 1 Thessalonians 2:13 reminds us. (Remember that Acts 2 records events at the very beginning of the Christian Church. The New Testament has not yet been written by the apostles. As eyewitnesses to Jesus, they themselves were the source of information about Jesus.) As the early Church listened to the apostles' teaching in worship, so we do also. The presence of God's Word is a vital element of Christian worship. Without the reading of Holy Scripture, we are not hearing the Word of God, but the word of men. Most Lutheran congregations, like many other Christian churches, choose to read the Scriptures from a schedule of readings called a *lectionary*. This schedule is designed to read a wide variety of Scripture in worship, and it keeps us from reading only our favorite passages. It helps us to hear the whole counsel of God. The Word is also present as it is proclaimed and applied to our current situation by the sermon.

The second element of worship is fellowship (in Greek, *koinonia*). Fellowship is a very close relationship, a group of people who share things in common. Christians gather in fellowship when we have a common faith, share the same beliefs, and hold a set of common, biblical values. Fellowship reminds us that we are called not only to be individual Christians but also to be part of the Church. This is still true today. While we will engage in a devotional life and private or individual worship of God, we are also called to fellowship with the people of God. We worship together, just as the early Christians did. So much did they value this fellowship that they continued to worship together even when the Church was facing persecution and Christians were being killed for their faith.

The third element of worship reflected in Acts 2:42 is "the breaking of bread." While "breaking bread" can refer to any meal shared together (as in Acts 2:46), here, in the context of worship, it refers to Holy Communion. The early Christians were not only hearing the Word when they came to worship in fellowship, but they were also communing together (Luke 22:19; 1 Corinthians 10:16). We see this reflected in worship whenever the Lord's Supper is celebrated according to Christ's institution.

The Lutheran Confessions assume that the Lord's Supper will be celebrated regularly in Lutheran congregations. In fact, the Confessions repeatedly claim that Lutheran congregations celebrate the Eucharist every Sunday (AC XXIV 34; *Concordia*, p. 49). Lutherans have a frequent celebration of the Lord's Supper because of Christ's gracious invitation to do this, and because of its benefits. We believe that Christ is truly present in this Sacrament, in His body and blood, for our forgiveness. Seeing these wonderful gifts, and hearing God's invitation to commune, why wouldn't we want to celebrate the Supper often? In contrast, some churches that do not believe Christ is really present, or that think that the bread and wine are mere symbols, tend to have Communion less frequently.

The fourth element of worship referenced in Acts 2:42 is prayer. God has invited His children to come to Him in prayer at any time. Prayer should certainly be a part of our corporate worship, but it should also be part of our personal devotions and daily lives. We are exhorted to pray at all times and for all of our concerns and needs. First Timothy 2:1–2 shows us some of the things for which we ought to pray. We should offer requests, prayers, intercessions, and thanksgiving. We ask God for what we need and desire, we pray for others, and we thank God for His goodness. We pray for all people, especially for those who do not yet know the Savior. We pray for our government and for peace. Our Father invites us to bring all of our needs and concerns to Him in prayer.

James 5:16 reminds us of the importance of Confession and Absolution. As we enter into the presence of our God, we do so dressed only in Christ's righteousness. We confess our sins and hear His forgiveness. While Confession and Absolution are not present in every worship service, they are a part of our daily Christian lives. Even when there is not a specific order of Confession and Absolution, no Christian worship service is complete without a call to repentance and the proclamation of the forgiveness of sins.

Hebrews 13:15 enjoins us to offer God a sacrifice of praise. It specifies that we do this when we confess His name. Philippians 2 points to the great day when every knee will bow before Christ and every tongue will confess that He is Lord. When we worship, we are confessing our faith. We acknowledge to one another and to the world that we believe in the true God. We proclaim to anyone who will listen that we know that Jesus Christ is the Savior of the world. We see this as we confess our faith together in the Creeds—summaries of our belief.

Every element of worship we have examined can be enacted with spoken words alone. This is appropriate, but Scripture also indicates that another dimension may be used to amplify the Word. Ephesians 5:19–20 reminds us of the helpfulness of music. We make music in our heart to the Lord, but we also speak to one another in hymns, songs, and spiritual songs. Music can be a beautiful and enriching aspect of worship.

Christian Freedom

Scripture doesn't give us these elements as a law. It never says, "Do these things or you are not a Christian." The early Christians did these things because they found that they were important elements of worship. They joined together, heard God's Word, celebrated the Lord's Supper, and prayed. They sang songs, confessed their sins and their faith, and heard God's blessing. These were not a burden to them but a blessing. They knew that God was working in their lives through these things. So we also receive these elements of worship, not as a burden but as a wonderful invitation. God allows and invites us to do these things.

People often characterize worship by the label of the denomination. There are some differences in how denominations understand particular elements (e.g., What is the Lord's Supper? Is the Bible really the Word of God?) Nonetheless, these elements are used, to some degree, in all Christian denominations. Even the historic liturgy is not specifically Lutheran. We share liturgical texts and structures, hymns and songs with other Christians. Our use of these elements will reflect our biblical doctrine, yet to the degree they are shared with other Christians, they testify to the true unity of the "one, holy, Christian and apostolic Church."

Simply having Bible readings or prayers or any other element does not automatically make the worship appropriate or good. One can read the Scriptures without reference to Christ and His salvation. That would not be Christian worship. Some people pray to other gods or for things that are rejected by the Bible. This is not Christian worship. We need to evaluate our worship (and everything we do) in the light of God's Word.

Comparisons

The form and content of Jewish worship in the first century greatly influenced the form and content of early Christian services (see p. 539 on the use of the psalms in Old Testament worship). Below are some elements of worship that Jewish people are known to have used at the synagogue and at home during the first century. Note how they compare with some elements of the traditional Lutheran Divine Service.

SYNAGOGUE SERVICE	SERVICE OF THE WORD
Readings from the Torah and the Prophets	Reading from the Bible
Sermon	Sermon
Shema Yisrael confession	Apostles' or Nicene Creed
Eighteen Benedictions	Congregational prayers

SEDER SERVICE	SERVICE OF THE SACRAMENT
The *Kaddish* prayer	The Lord's Prayer
Cups of wine	Cup of the Lord's Supper
Matzah bread	Bread of the Lord's Supper
Narration of the Exodus	Narration of the Words of Institution
Singing of the Hallel (Psalms 113–18)	Post-Communion canticle and hymns

A popular Aramaic prayer used in ancient Judaism is known as the *Kaddish* or *Qaddish* ("consecration"). Portions of this prayer are almost word for word the same as the Lord's Prayer, taught by Jesus. Note how the prayers are similar (italic text) and how they differ (regular text).

THE *KADDISH*	THE LORD'S PRAYER
Extolled and *hallowed be the name of God* throughout the world which He has created, and which He governs according to His righteous will. Just is He in all His ways and wise are all His decrees. *May His kingdom come*, and *His will be done in all the earth.* Praised be the Lord of life, the righteous Judge forever more. Whatsoever praise we would render unto God, howsoever we would adore the Most High, we would yet fail to give Him the glory due to His great name.	Our Father who art in heaven, *hallowed be thy name,* *thy kingdom come,* *thy will be done on earth* as it is in heaven. Give us this day our daily bread; and forgive us our trespasses as we forgive those who trespass against us; and lead us not into temptation but deliver us from evil.

Point to Remember

I will dwell among the people of Israel and will be their God. And they shall know that I am the Lord their God, who brought them out of the land of Egypt that I might dwell among them. I am the Lord their God. *Exodus 29:45–46*

When Scripture Is Silent

> For to those who believe in Christ whatever things are either enjoined or forbidden in the way of external ceremonies and bodily righteousnesses are all pure, adiaphora, and are permissible, except insofar as the believers are willing to subject themselves to these things of their own accord or for the sake of love.
>
> —Martin Luther, *Commentary on Galatians* (AE 27:161)

Holy Cross Lutheran Church was at a turning point. They had outgrown their building and had to do something. Should they seek a way to expand their sanctuary, or should they build a new one? The congregation was divided. They decided that they would search the Scriptures to see what God wanted them to do. Both sides tried to quote Bible verses to support their position, but observers were quick to note that the verses really didn't fit this situation. They finally came to the conclusion that no Bible verse would give them a direct answer. These situations are known as *adiaphora* (see Glossary, p. 676.)

Many things that we face every day are not directly addressed by Scripture. The example above is one: should a church remodel or rebuild? Where should a church be built? What should it look like? What times should services be held? Which of our faithful and qualified Christians will teach a Sunday school class? The Bible may give us some principles to consider, but we cannot look in our concordances to see what color the church should be painted.

Christians do try at times to make Scripture answer questions that it doesn't address. But this is a dangerous, slippery slope. If Scripture really does speak to an issue, we must listen. But we must not take Scripture out of context or twist it to say things that are not really there. When we make it appear that Scripture says something that it really doesn't, we are taking the place of God. We are making our word more important than His Word. We also risk the faith of other people. If they reject our misuse of Scripture, they may also reject the proper use of Scripture. It is vitally important to read Scripture in context. We are blessed when we hear the Word of God and keep it (Luke 11:28).

God's Will

Christians determine God's will by consulting His Word. It is the only infallible guide we have. We carefully search the Scriptures to see if they address the topic we are considering. If the Bible does speak to an issue, we are to listen to the Word. We are not free to ignore God's Word. He has the final say. When we ignore the Bible, we may end up in the situation Jesus warns about in Matthew 15:8–9: proclaiming human teachings instead of God's Word. When we do this, we worship Him in vain, having already rejected Him and His will.

All Scripture is inspired by God and is His Word. However, Christ Jesus has fulfilled the Law and freed us from its demands. We no longer offer animal sacrifices, for example, because Christ has offered the final sacrifice of Himself on the cross. We are not required to eat kosher foods or outwardly observe the Sabbath Day because Jesus has fulfilled these things for us. We no longer live under the Law, but by the Gospel. This does not mean, however, that we should go on sinning. Romans 6:15 makes it clear that we are not to use God's grace as an excuse for sinning. We are no longer slaves to sin, but we are servants of God.

Issues on which Scripture is truly silent are known as *adiaphora*. When you think about it, many things that we deal with every day are adiaphora. In cases where the Bible doesn't tell us to do something, and doesn't tell us not to do it, the Christian is free to act according to his own conscience and preference. Romans 14:13–23 uses the example of foods. Are Christians to follow Jewish dietary restrictions? Scripture does not require us to do this, nor does it forbid us to follow kosher guidelines. A Christian is free to eat kosher or non-kosher food. Paul gives two guiding principles. One is that whatever we do must come from faith. If we doubt whether something is right, we shouldn't do it. But if we are confident that God does not forbid it, we are free to act as we see fit.

When addressing issues on which Scripture is silent, we are bound to encounter differences of opinion. We need to be careful that we do not use our God-given freedom in a manner that causes a weaker Christian to stumble in the faith. We are not to become stumbling blocks or obstacles to other Christians (1 Corinthians 8:9). This word is sometimes translated as *offense*. An "offense" in this case does not mean something that another person doesn't like. It means something that can cause our neighbor to stumble or fall from the faith. We are indeed free to do many things, but we do not want to use our freedom in such a careless manner that we cause another person to fall from faith. This calls stronger Christians to be watchful for those who are weak. We may need to be careful in our use of freedom so that we do not harm the faith of a weaker brother or sister. The Lutheran Confessions emphasize the responsible use of freedom, saying that we should not give offense to the weak and cause them to grow hostile toward the Gospel. We also should not use our freedom frivolously and so cause others to take offense (see FC Ep X 5; *Concordia*, pp. 496–97).

There is another danger in adiaphora. Those who are not truly weak in faith may try to bind other Christians to their own practice, and thus rob them of the freedom of the Gospel. Paul encountered this situation regarding the issue of circumcision. The Judaizers, a sect claiming to be part of the early Christian Church, were insisting that all Christian men be circumcised even though the Bible does not require this. This is not true, and is an offense to the Gospel. It places our human regulations above God's Word. Our observance of human rites does not make us Christians. In the face of such persecution, Paul did not allow Titus to undergo circumcision, and Paul advised the Galatian church to likewise reject the demand for circumcision (Galatians 2:3–5; 5:1). It was not the outward act that was the problem, but the motive. The Judaizers would not be allowed to steal the freedom of the Gospel from others. It is interesting to note that in Acts 16:3, Paul was taking Timothy to evangelize practicing Jews. These Jews would genuinely have stumbled if they learned that Timothy was not circumcised. In this situation, Paul circumcised Timothy. For the sake of the weak, they were happy to concede. In Galatia, the Judaizers were not weak in faith. They were trying to control the lives of others, to make everyone like they were.

Another application of adiaphora may be seen in cases in which no one seems to be in a position of taking offense. First Corinthians 14:40 reminds us that when we worship together, we need to be concerned about how our actions affect others. Even if we have freedom to do certain things, we don't want worship to be chaotic or disorderly. We don't want to use our freedom in a way that is disruptive to the worship of others. Instead, everything done in worship should be done "in a fitting and orderly way."

Another danger of adiaphora is that we begin to think that our human rites or customs are good works that earn us something before God. First Timothy 4:1–5 calls the restriction of Christian freedom a demonic doctrine. If we are restricting people from doing what God has freed them to do, we are not serving Him, but serving the devil. Ephesians 2:8 emphatically tells us that we are saved by God's grace, not by our own works. We dare not offer our own works and ideas as a substitute for the work of Christ. We are saved by His life, death, and resurrection alone. The Lutheran Confessions deal extensively with the question of adiaphora. (See AC XXIV; Ap XXIV; FC Ep X; *Concordia*, pp. 47–49, 220–37, 496–97.)

The Bible and Tradition

Issues of adiaphora, and therefore tensions, often arise as we are considering the traditions of a church. At times like this, we might be prone to point out that another person's viewpoint is just tradition, so we can get rid of it. Many useful or cherished things that we do are part of the traditions of our church. It is far too easy to criticize the traditions of others without looking at our own. While many traditions are obvious, others are easily overlooked. Things such as the date of Christmas, the time and day when worship services are held, wedding customs, and countless other aspects of our church life are not directly addressed in Scripture. These traditions help give us a group identity. They make it possible for us to worship together. They provide order and structure to the things that we do together. If we are not careful, however, our traditions can eclipse the Gospel. Our traditions can cause us to exclude others. We can begin to assume that everything we do is found in Scripture. We should boldly and freely use the best of our human traditions, but acknowledge them for what they are. Many of the traditions of the Christian Church were developed for good reasons. Perhaps the best way to view a tradition is to ask why it was started in the first place, evaluate if this is a good reason, and consider if those reasons still apply today.

The topic of adiaphora may make us uncomfortable. Two extreme reactions to these issues lead to problems. Legalism seeks to find a rule for everything. If Scripture doesn't speak, legalism fills in the blanks with regulations. The other extreme is antinomianism—a rejection of God's Law, and an irresponsible, chaotic use of freedom. Both of these fall short of God's plan and compromise God's Word. Legalism strips away the freedom that Christ has won for us and binds us to the Law again. It ultimately relies on works and our own efforts. As it binds consciences to human standards, it eclipses the Gospel and leads to despair. Antinomianism, on the other hand, seeks freedom at any cost. It cares little for the effect it has on other people. It is self-serving and creates stumbling blocks for other people. Both are abuses that fall short of God's plan. Sadly, we are inclined to both errors. We want freedom for ourselves while seeking to bind other people to our own preferences and understanding. We want to be legalistic for them and antinomian for ourselves.

Freedom in adiaphora means that we do not all have to do things the same way. An individual congregation may choose to do a variety of things (on which Scripture is silent) that are different from other congregations. There may be significant advantages to be found, however, when churches choose to work together. When we work together, we may find it much easier to worship with other Christian congregations. Uniformity in our practice helps children learn and remember and is a source of comfort for the elderly. (Think how hard it would be if we all used different versions of the Lord's Prayer!) Christians do not have to worship on Sunday, but the availability and prevalence of worship on Sunday mornings is a strong witness to our world. A considerate use of our freedom may even promote peace in the Church.

Comparisons

Eastern Orthodox: "What is meant by the name *holy tradition*? By the name holy tradition is meant the doctrine of the faith, the law of God, the sacraments, and the ritual as handed down by the true believers and worshipers of God by word and example from one to another, and from generation to generation. . . . Why is tradition necessary even now? As a guide to the right understanding of holy Scripture, for the right ministration of the sacraments, and the preservation of sacred rites and ceremonies in purity of their original institution" (*The Longer Catechism of the Eastern Church*, questions 320–21).

Lutheran: "We believe, teach, and confess that the community of God ‹the churches of God› (in every place ‹in every land› and at every time according to its circumstances) has the power to change such worship ceremonies in a way that may be most useful and edifying to the community of God ‹the churches of God›. Nevertheless, all frivolity and offense should be avoided in this manner. Special care should be taken to exercise patience toward the weak in faith" (FC Ep X 4–5; *Concordia*, pp. 496–97).

Reformed: "The greater the heap of ceremonies in the Church, so much the more is taken, not only from Christian liberty, but also from Christ, and from faith in Him; while the people seek those things in ceremonies which they should seek in the only Son of God, Jesus Christ, through faith. Wherefore a few moderate and simple rites, that are not contrary to the Word of God, do suffice the godly" (*Second Helvetic Confession*, chapter 27).

Anabaptist: The Anabaptists rejected all earlier liturgies. They emphasized weekly gatherings where people would seek the will of God and encourage one another to greater discipleship. They also taught that if Scripture did not command a practice, it probably should not be done by a Christian. As a result many Anabaptist groups have refused to use or own modern technology (cars, electricity, etc.) since Scripture does not mention these things.

Roman Catholic: An extensive tradition of canon law regulates the duties and practices of Roman Catholicism. At the heart of their worship is the canon of the Mass.

Baptist: "In cases of difficulties or differences, either in point of doctrine or administration . . . it is according to the mind of Christ that many churches, holding communion together, do by their messengers meet to consider and give their advice in or about that matter in difference, to be reported to all the churches concerned; howbeit these messengers assembled are not intrusted with any church power properly so called, or with any jurisdiction over the churches themselves, to exercise any censures either over any churches or persons, to impose their determination of the churches or officers" (*Baptist Confession of 1688*, para. 15).

Wesleyan: "It is not necessary that rites and ceremonies should in all places be the same, or exactly alike; for they have been always different, and may be changed according to the diversity of countries, times, and men's manners, so that nothing be ordained against God's Word. Whosoever, through private judgment, willingly and purposely doth openly break the rites and ceremonies of the Church to which he belongs, which are not repugnant to the Word of God, and are ordained and approved by common authority, ought to be rebuked openly" (*Methodist Articles of Religion*, article 22).

Point to Remember

Let us pursue what makes for peace and for mutual upbuilding.
Romans 14:19

The Bible in Worship

Lord, open now my heart to hear,
And through Your Word
to me draw near;
Preserve that Word in purity
That I Your child and heir may be.
—Johannes Olearius

"Do I have to?" pleaded Andy.

Theresa did not give in to her son. "Your grandparents sent you a wonderful present for your birthday. It is polite to thank them for their gift, and since you like it so much, to tell them."

"I know," he replied, "but I don't know what to say."

"I'll help you with the words," she said. "Let's work on it together." So Andy sat down to write a thank-you note.

Have you ever struggled to find the right words for a letter or a thank-you note? This is a common experience. The more we care about the letter or about the people receiving it, the more we want the words to be just right. We don't want to say the wrong thing, and we want to be sure we communicate accurately.

It can be hard to learn new and challenging things, but this is part of our maturation. Often we teach and learn by example. We may suggest words or ways in which something might be done. Children follow our example, and use our words or ideas until they accomplish their task. In time, they need less help. It can be very satisfying for a child to learn and develop competency in something that once was challenging.

Do we need to *learn* how to worship? All God's people respond to Him in worship. When we believe in Him and trust Him, we are worshiping. Worship seems so familiar to us, yet it can intimidate us. Just watch what happens when someone is asked to volunteer to say a prayer in front of a group of people. Few may want to do it because they are afraid of saying the wrong thing or looking foolish. We don't need to be afraid as we worship our God. By His grace we will grow in confidence as He guides us in worship. This guidance can deepen our understanding and our relationship with our God. It can open new understanding to us as well.

Growing through Worship

How do Christians learn to worship? For many, our education occurs simply through the Divine Services we have attended. We learn about worship by worshiping with God's people. While there are different ways Christians worship, many Christians have found it helpful to use scriptural verses and passages as the backbone of the Divine Service. God gives us His Word, and we respond to Him with His Word. We are not obligated to worship in this way, but we may find a great blessing through such richly biblical forms.

Matthew 28:18–20 is the Great Commission of Jesus to His Church. In verse 18 we find the Invocation—the words used at the beginning of our worship service. When we hear these words, we are reminded of our own Baptism and of Jesus' promise to be with us always. We gather as the baptized and forgiven children of God. Because these words remind us of our Baptism, many Christians make the sign of the cross on themselves as they hear these words. This is a way of reminding ourselves that we, too, are baptized into Christ.

Matthew 15:22 records the words of a Canaanite woman and Mark 10:47 those of Bartimaeus, a blind man. Both people seek Jesus' blessing and healing, and so they cry out, "Lord . . . have mercy!" They knew that only Jesus could give them the healing they needed. Our worship uses these words in the part of the service known as the Kyrie (the Greek word for "Lord.") We, too, call out to God for His mercy. In one version of the Kyrie, we simply pray, "Lord, have mercy. Christ, have mercy. Lord, have mercy." In other versions, brief prayers are said before the congregation responds, "Lord, have mercy."

The Hymn of Praise is another portion of the Divine Service. We sing many songs of praise at different times, but several texts find particular use in our worship. Luke 2:14 records the song of the angels at Jesus' birth: "Glory to God in the highest, and on earth peace among those with whom He is pleased." These words are ordinarily referred to as the Gloria in Excelsis (Latin for "Glory in the highest"). When we sing them, we are joining the song of the angels in praising our Lord. Revelation 5:8–14 is repeated in the song "Worthy Is Christ" (sometimes called "This Is the Feast"). In this passage we hear the song of heaven. Christ is praised because He is the Redeemer of the world. John tells us that these words are sung by the heavenly angels and echoed by every creature God has made. In other words, we sing them too!

We sing John 6:68 as part of the Alleluia verse (*LSB*, p. 173). This sung verse precedes the reading of the Gospel for the day. Peter's words remind us that only Jesus has the words of eternal life. We hear that Word in the Gospel. This is not a mere recitation of an historical event. In the Gospel, God again offers us His grace and eternal life.

There are several texts that are used as offertory songs. In Psalm 51:10–12, we join David in praying that God would create a new heart within us. We are sinful people who need God to forgive our sin. We pray that He will be merciful to us, grant us forgiveness, and restore us to be His people. He does these things through Christ Jesus. By singing these words, we are reminded that our offerings, though they are a response to God's blessings, are nothing compared to what God has given us. His giving far exceeds the small gifts that we bring. Another passage of Scripture used as an offertory (usually during Lent) is "What Shall I Render to the Lord." This is based on Psalm 116:12–14, 17–19.

While these are common texts in worship, not all are in use in all congregations. One of the most universally used passages of Scripture is Matthew 6:9–13, the words of the Lord's Prayer (which is also found in Luke 11:1–4). We are not obligated to use these words. They are not the only acceptable words for prayer. However, they are an excellent model for prayer. This prayer covers a multitude of human needs. When we pray this prayer, we are again following the pattern of God's words in worship.

As we prepare for Holy Communion, we know that we are about to enter the presence of almighty God. Without His mercy we would not survive this encounter, but God does deal graciously with us. Isaiah 6:3–6 and Matthew 21:9 are behind the song known as the Sanctus (the Latin word for "holy"). Like Isaiah, we are coming into God's presence. As sinners we would be consumed by His glory. Isaiah was spared when an angel took a coal from the heavenly altar, touched his lips with it, and said that he was forgiven. In Holy Communion, the body and blood of Christ are taken from the altar and placed on our lips. We are forgiven and able to enter God's presence. In singing the Sanctus, we add the words of Matthew 21:9: "Blessed is He who comes in the name of the Lord! Hosanna in the highest!" These words remind us that Christ, whose body and blood we are about to receive, is the holy and almighty God.

After the Words of Institution have been said, we sing a song asking Christ, the Lamb of God, for His mercy and peace. Jesus is the Lamb of God (in Latin, *Agnus Dei*) who takes away the sin of the world. He does this by sacrificing Himself on the cross for us. As Colossians 1:20 tells us, He has made "peace by the blood of His cross." His sacrifice was sufficient to pay for the sins of the entire world.

Several different songs of thanksgiving are sung after we have received the blessed Sacrament. One of the oldest is found in Luke 2:29–32, the Nunc Dimittis or Song of Simeon. God had promised Simeon that he would not die without seeing the Messiah with his own eyes. When Simeon was an old man, the baby Jesus was brought to the temple. Simeon responded by glorifying God. The promised Messiah had come, and Simeon was ready to die and go to heaven. We may sing the same words after we commune. Just as God promised, we have seen and tasted the Lord. We have been blessed with His forgiveness and love. When God wills, we are prepared to enter His kingdom forever!

From the Heart

We have looked at some of the biblical texts reflected in our worship. There are many more in the Divine Service and in other orders of worship. There are also many biblical quotations, references, and allusions in our hymns and songs. Knowledge of God's Word is a blessing to His people. The more familiar we are with the Bible, the more use it will be in our lives. We ought to regularly hear and read God's Word for this very reason. It may surprise us, however, to see how much Scripture we have memorized through worship without even realizing it. There are other ways this can happen as well, but here is a strong example of how the Word might "dwell in [us] richly" (Colossians 3:16).

The liturgical texts that we have looked at are all part of "the ordinary." These are words that are repeated week after week in the Divine Service.

The repetition of texts does not mean that worship is always the same. We have looked at the repeating parts of worship—but these are only a portion of the Divine Service. The traditional Christian order of service is composed partly of these texts—but there are other elements that are changed every week. The Scripture readings, sermon, prayers, songs, and other elements are constantly changing. In this way, the service provides a balance of the familiar and the changeable. In addition, we have only looked at the words. These texts have been used by countless Christians for centuries. While they have all used the same words, they have not used the same music. Our own worship resources contain a number of different musical settings of these texts. There is no reason for these to be overly repetitious.

It is fairly common for Lutherans to describe these elements as "Lutheran worship." But these are not Lutheran texts, nor are they German texts or even European texts. These classic liturgical texts belong to the whole Church and have been in use for most of the history of the Christian Church. These texts are freely used in other churches. Orthodox, Roman Catholics, Episcopalians and other liturgical churches use the same words that we do. In addition, many churches that do not ordinarily follow this common liturgical structure often use these texts and ideas in songs and other elements of worship. This is true because these are the words of Scripture. This is our common Christian heritage.

Digging Deeper

We've looked at a number of worship texts and the scriptural references behind them, but we've only scratched the surface. Many other liturgical elements as well as many hymns and songs also reflect biblical texts. The Book of Revelation contains a number of references to worship in the life to come (see, for example, Revelation 4–5; 7:9–17; 19:4–10).

There are a number of books on worship that you might find helpful in your continuing study. Consider one of the following, or ask your pastor for other suggestions:

Timothy Maschke, *Gathered Guests: A Guide to Worship in the Lutheran Church*. St. Louis: Concordia, 2009.

James Brauer, *Meaningful Worship: A Guide to the Lutheran Service*. St. Louis: Concordia, 1994.

James Brauer, *Worship, Gottesdienst, Cultus Dei: What the Lutheran Confessions Say about Worship*. St. Louis: Concordia, 2005.

Fred L. Precht, ed., *Lutheran Worship: History and Practice*. St. Louis: Concordia, 1993.

Comparisons

Use of the Lord's Prayer as a model: Anabaptists, Baptists, and some Wesleyans emphasize that Jesus gave the Lord's Prayer as a model and not as a form of prayer for repetition. They encourage spontaneous prayers from the heart rather than repeated prayers.

Formal use of the Lord's Prayer: Most other Christians pray the Lord's Prayer daily or frequently in public worship. The official catechisms of the Eastern Orthodox, Lutheran, Reformed, and Roman Catholic churches contain commentaries on the Lord's Prayer. Repetition is only a problem if people repeat the words without considering what they say. Jesus Himself repeated prayers (see Matthew 26:44).

Prayer with non-Christians: Today, some Christians hold public prayer services with people of other religions. Interreligious services are most popular among Christians who have questioned traditional beliefs about the triune nature of God and do not consider joint services with non-Christians a threat to the Gospel. (In 1964 the papal decree *Lumen Gentium* taught that Christians, Jews, and Muslims all pray to the same Creator.)

Point to Remember

Holy, holy, holy is the Lord of hosts; the whole earth is full of His glory. *Isaiah 6:3*

The Psalms in Worship

The following chart will introduce you to some of the liturgical uses of the psalms from the Old Testament.

RITUAL ACTS	REFERENCES	NOTES
Pilgrimage	Psalms 120–134	Israelites were required to make annual pilgrimages to the sanctuary. Singing psalms was part of the journey.
Procession	Psalm 24:7, 9; 48; 118:19–20; 132	Psalm 132 may have been used as a reenactment of the moving of the ark of the covenant (2 Samuel 6).
Dancing	Psalm 149:3; 150:4. See Exodus 15:20; Judges 21:16–24; 2 Samuel 6:14, 16.	Dance was not an individualistic action, as in modern times, but a liturgical act. (e.g., Moses' anger at the dancing before the golden calf; the Israelites were performing a ritual dance as an act of idol worship.) Israelites probably used ritual dances in their processions to the sanctuary.
Entrance Liturgies	Psalm 15:1–5; 24:3–6	The priests or Levites may have asked the questions found in these psalms. The people may have voiced the responses before entering into the worship area.
Invocation	Psalm 33:1; 111:1; 113:1; 146–150	These psalms seem to have opened a service of praise, prayer, or sacrifice. They invite the congregation to participate with the priests and Levites.
Versicle and Response	Psalm 124; 129; 136	Psalm 124:1 and 129:1 command, "Let Israel now say." This may be a cue from a priest or Levite for the congregation to recite a response.
Choirs	Psalm 4; 5; 6; etc.	Many psalms were written for the "choirmaster."
Ceremonial Washings	Psalm 26:6; 51:7	Washing was a regular part of service at the temple because of the animal sacrifices, but it was also an expression of forgiveness and purity.
Offering	Psalm 66:13–15	The Law of Moses does not prescribe words to accompany the sacrificial acts of the priests. The psalms seem to serve as the "words of institution" for the sacrifices.
Lament/ Fasting	Psalm 44; 60; 74; 79; etc.	In times of national crisis and perhaps also during festivals, Israelites used psalms of lamentation and fasted.

Fourth Maccabees, a Jewish intertestamental book, remarks that the psalms were used in the home (18:9–10, 15). Parents were responsible for teaching psalms to their children.

Lutheran Summary of Worship

Augsburg Confession XXIV 34

Because the Mass is for the purpose of giving the Sacrament, we have Communion every holy day, and if anyone desires the Sacrament, we also offer it on other days, when it is given to all who ask for it. (*Concordia*, p. 49)

Apology of the Augsburg Confession V (III) 189 [310]

The worship and divine service of the Gospel is to receive gifts from God. On the contrary, the worship of the Law is to offer and present our gifts to God. However, we can offer nothing to God unless we have first been reconciled and born again. This passage, too, brings the greatest comfort, as the chief worship of the Gospel is to desire to receive the forgiveness of sins, grace, and righteousness. (*Concordia*, p. 130)

Apology of the Augsburg Confession XV 51

Still, we teach that freedom should be so controlled that the inexperienced may not be offended and, because of freedom's abuse [Romans 14:13–23], may not become more opposed to the true doctrine of the Gospel. Nothing in customary rites should be changed without a reasonable cause. So to nurture unity, old customs that can be kept without sin or great inconvenience should be kept. (*Concordia*, p. 194)

Large Catechism II 66

Even if [or: Even if we were to concede that] all people outside Christianity—whether heathen, Turks, Jews, or false Christians and hypocrites—believe in and worship only one true God, they still do not know what His mind toward them is and cannot expect any love or blessing from Him. . . . For they do not have the Lord Christ, and, besides, are not illumined and favored by any gifts of the Holy Spirit. (*Concordia*, p. 406)

Large Catechism V 47

"That is true, yet it is not written so that we should never do so. Yes, since He speaks the words 'As often as you drink it,' it is still implied that we should do it often. This is added because He wants to have the Sacrament free. He does not limit it to special times, like the Jewish Passover, which they were obliged to eat only once a year. They could only have it on the fourteenth day of the first full moon in the evening [Exodus 12:6, 18]. They still must not change a day." It is as if He would say by these words, "I institute a Passover or Supper for you. You shall enjoy it not only once a year, just upon this evening, but often, when and where you will, according to everyone's opportunity and necessity, bound to no place or appointed time." (*Concordia*, pp. 436–37)

Formula of Concord Epitome X 5–6

Nevertheless, all frivolity and offense should be avoided in this matter. Special care should be taken to exercise patience toward the weak in faith (1 Corinthians 8:9; Romans 14:13).

We believe, teach, and confess that during a time of persecution, when a plain ‹and steadfast› confession is required of us, we should not yield to the enemies in such matters of adiaphora. . . . For in such a case it is no longer a question about adiaphora. But it concerns the truth of the Gospel, [preserving] Christian liberty, and sanctioning open idolatry. It also concerns the prevention of offense to the weak in the faith. In such a case we have nothing to concede. We should plainly confess and endure what God sends because of that confession, and whatever He allows the enemies of His Word to inflict on us. (*Concordia*, pp. 496–97)

TOPIC EIGHTEEN

End Times[1]

Engaging This Topic

> "Anita, I'm so excited! I just came from the John Thompson Bible Prophecy Conference."
> "Who's John Thompson?"
> "What? *You* haven't heard about Dr. John Thompson, today's leading Bible prophecy expert? I have all his books, and it was such an honor to hear him speak."
> "Really? I guess I don't know that much about Bible prophecy."
> "Let me show you what I've learned about the Book of Revelation . . ."

In *Doomsday: The End of the World—a View through Time*, Russell Chandler describes the research of Jon Stone, a professor of religion who has made a list of books published about the end times. After listing 2,100 titles, Stone realized that only fifty books were written by Roman Catholic or mainline Protestant authors! The other 2,050 titles on his list vividly demonstrate the fascination and obsession that American evangelicals (mostly Baptists, Anabaptists, and Pentecostals) have with the end times.

In contrast to the interests of many American evangelicals, this chapter does not even begin with the end times. It begins with the personal end that each person faces—death. Lutherans have traditionally started their study of the second coming of Christ, His final judgment, and heaven and hell with the topic of death because, until Christ returns, that's how we will enter the end times. This represents a different approach from most Christian teaching. Instead of waiting for the coming reign of Christ, Lutherans focus on living in Christ now through the Holy Spirit's work.

1 This chapter adapted from *The Lutheran Difference: End Times*, copyright © 2001 Concordia Publishing House.

Prophecy Buffs

In recent years, Hal Lindsey's *The Late Great Planet Earth* and Tim LaHaye and Jerry Jenkins's fictional *Left Behind* series have made a narrow focus on the end times immensely popular. In some evangelical congregations, the preaching and teaching focus on virtually no other subject. Prophecy teachers compete to provide the latest theory so they can gain a cut of the end-times market share. As a result, historical perspective gets left behind.

For example, few laypeople who believe in the rapture realize that this doctrine first appeared in the 1830s. It had never been taught among Christians before! A pastor named John Nelson Darby popularized the rapture theory nearly 1,800 years after Christ taught the disciples about His reappearing. Yet today many Christians assume that the rapture doctrine is a long-standing interpretation of the Bible. Although some in the early Church held to millennial views and expected the swift return of Christ and His kingdom, even selling all their possessions to await Christ's coming, this sort of premillennialism is not the "dispensational" kind taught by Darby. Nevertheless, the apostles do not teach millennialism, as indicated by John's response to those expecting the return of Christ before his death (John 21:20–24). Those who follow the apostolic teaching do likewise.

The Lutheran reformers had a different, simpler understanding of the end times and the focus of Christian teaching. The following charts will help you compare and contrast the two most widely held views of the end times.

Dispensational Premillennialism

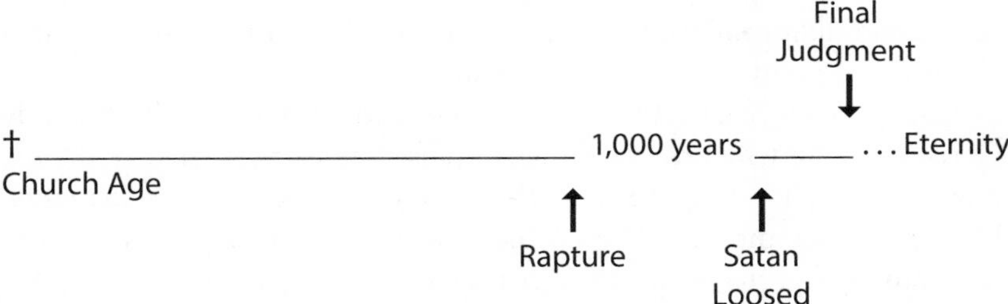

Amillennialism

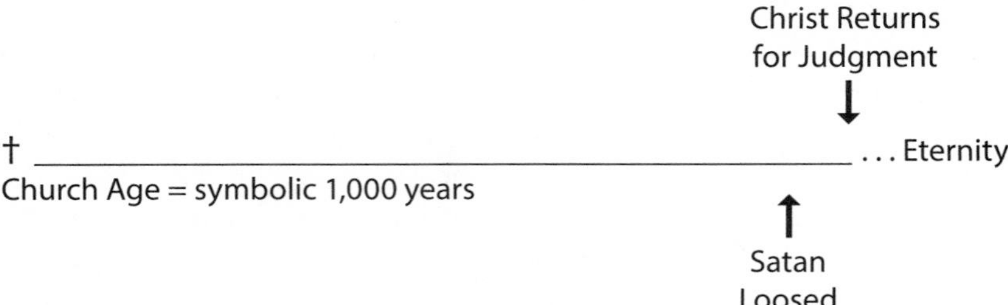

Premillennial and Amillennial

Chart 1 illustrates the commonly held beliefs of a dispensationalist, premillennial understanding of the end times. According to this view, at some point in the future, Christ will return and believers who are alive will meet Him in the air and be taken to heaven. Immediately afterward, a seven-year period of tribulation will commence for those upon the earth. During this tribulation, the Antichrist will appear. Then Christ will return again to establish a politically powerful and glorious kingdom upon earth, which will last 1,000 years. During this time, Satan will be bound and certain martyred saints will be resurrected to reign with Christ on earth. At the conclusion of the 1,000 years, Satan will lead the nations in one last battle against God's people, the battle of Armageddon. Christ will defeat the devil and pronounce final judgment.

According to this schema, Christ will return twice (for the rapture and the second judgment) and raise the dead twice. Then He will establish a glorious and politically powerful kingdom upon earth.

Depicted on chart 2, the alternative view, which aligns itself with early Christianity and Reformation theology, is that Christ's victory on the cross defeated and bound Satan. The reign of Christ, or the *millennium*, has already commenced. During the millennium, which corresponds to the Church Age, the people of Christ reign with Him upon the earth. Yet this is no age of heaven upon earth, because Christ's victorious saints still fight against evil, including what John calls "the spirit of the antichrist." When God has accomplished His gracious purposes in Christ, Satan will be loosed, at which time the full embodiment of rebellion, the Antichrist, will appear. Satan's rebellion will be shortened by Christ's glorious return. Then all the dead will rise for Judgment Day.

This view of the end times, called amillennialism, has only one resurrection of the dead and one return of Christ. It discourages us from hoping for any glorious and politically powerful "heaven upon earth" in the millennium. This view is much simpler than premillennialism and fits with the Bible and early Christian teaching as recorded in the Apostles' Creed.

It goes beyond the scope of this chapter to treat all the significant differences and underlying theological ideas that support these two views. For an in-depth and scholarly treatment of this subject, look to Louis Brighton's commentary on Revelation.[2]

Lutheran Facts

Radical movements periodically arose in the Middle Ages. The Lutheran Reformation helped create a climate in which such groups flourished. While Martin Luther stayed at the Wartburg in 1521–22, his colleague Carlstadt ignited a more radical movement that Luther helped to suppress. In Switzerland, Grebel formed a radical Anabaptist movement in 1522 that Ulrich Zwingli opposed. Grebel's group moved to Moravia and flourished under Hutter. By 1525, the so-called "heavenly prophets," especially Thomas Müntzer, helped to start the bloody Peasants' War.

Many of these radicals used millennialist ideas about the end times that were not based on Scripture to justify either violent actions or sweeping changes in doctrine. Luther opposed the radicals, yet he regretted the bloodshed caused by all parties. He increasingly saw connections between the prophecies in Revelation, the corrupt world, and the pope as Antichrist.

The Mysterious Veil

Vital spark of heavenly flame!
Quit, oh quit this mortal frame!
Trembling, hoping, lingering, flying,
Oh the pain, the bliss of dying!
Cease, fond Nature, cease thy strife
And let me languish into life!
—Alexander Pope, "The Dying Christian to His Soul"

Lutherans begin their study of the end times with a topic that many people hate to discuss: death. The Bible describes death as a veil or a burial shroud (Isaiah 25:7). Sooner or later all people face this mysterious veil. Until Christ reappears, death remains *the* entry point for the end times.

2 *Revelation*, Concordia Commentary (St. Louis: Concordia, 1999).

Lifting the Veil

People die from famine, accidents, disease, and warfare. They die from old age. Properly speaking, these are not the primary causes of death, but what theologians have called the "instrumental" causes of death.

The primary cause of death is sin (Romans 5:12). When Adam and Eve rebelled against God, they died spiritually. Their natural love, trust, and obedience of God were immediately replaced by hatred, fear, and rebellion. They eventually died physically (temporal death) and returned to dust (Genesis 3:17–19). All creation was cursed and subject to death and decay as a result of their sin.

Medical writings describe in great detail what happens to a person at death. Yet all they do is describe what happens to the body. Death is not the end of existence. Rather, death is separation of the soul from the body (Matthew 10:28; Luke 12:20). Jesus shows this by distinguishing between the destruction of the body and of the soul. Also, the Gospel writers describe Jesus' death as the yielding of His spirit (Matthew 27:50).

What happens after death? Hebrews 9:27–28 tells us: "And just as it is appointed for man to die once, and after that comes judgment, so Christ, having been offered once to bear the sins of many, will appear a second time, not to deal with sin but to save those who are eagerly waiting for Him." The Hindu and Buddhist religions variously teach that people are reincarnated after death, living out successive lives in order to achieve enlightenment, and that they ultimately lose their own individuality by joining the life-giving force of the universe in the state of all and nothing (Nirvana). In contrast, the Bible states that people die only once and then face final judgment.

Some believe that all people who die will enjoy a blessed afterlife, that God accepts everyone. However, Proverbs 11:7 describes the death of unbelievers as the loss of all hope.

Christ forgives the sin of believers. Yet in God's description of salvation, there is a "now and not yet" aspect to the lives of believers. That is, God declares them righteous, forgiven children for Christ's sake, yet they still will experience suffering and death. The last enemy of God's people, which Christ will subdue on Judgment Day, is death itself. Paul looks forward to a time when the mortal bodies of believers will be given up for immortal and glorious ones (1 Corinthians 15:50, 53–54).

In contrast to the death of unbelievers, the death of believers is described by God's Word with gentle words: the dead "are asleep" (1 Thessalonians 4:13) and are "blessed" (Revelation 14:13). Far from being the final and irretrievable loss of all that is held dear, the death of believers is a homecoming, the moment when they will be completely released from all sorrow and suffering and glorified with the saints in heaven.

Because we live in the "now and not yet" and because we still face death, we weep at the loss of loved ones, even as we rejoice in the hope of a blessed reunion in heaven. Note well, for example, the emotions of Jesus at the grave of Lazarus. Jesus knew that in a few moments Lazarus would be alive and restored to his family, yet He wept at the suffering of Mary and Martha (John 11:32–36). Similarly, Paul does not tell the Thessalonians to cease their sorrowing. Instead, he emphasizes that in the midst of their sorrow, they have hope (1 Thessalonians 4:13–14).

Facing the Veil

When archaeologists uncover early human burial sites, they frequently find evidence of ritual and belief about an afterlife. For example, early graves often have red ochre (red soil used for making paint) spread about the body as a symbol of blood and life. Whether ancient or modern, every human being must struggle with how to face death.

Death is the great equalizer. Rich and poor, powerful and weak, great and small—all will die. In the final analysis, only shortsighted, foolish, or ignorant people take no thought of the day of their death. We are instead to re-examine our priorities and attitudes about material things, family, work, and goals. Above all, we are to think not only of temporal things but also of eternal things and of our need for Christ.

Mary, a member of our congregation, recently lost a family member in a sudden accident. She cannot help feeling that it was unfair for her loved one to die. She is bitterly depressed. We learn from the Book of Job that from a worldly point of view, suffering and death may seem unfair. Evil, by its very nature, does not operate by just principles. That is, there are no guarantees that "bad" people die young and "good" people live to a ripe old age. So we might well sympathize with Mary when she, like Job, expresses how unfair she thinks it is for a loved one to die unexpectedly and prematurely (Job 1:18–19). But also like Job (19:25–27), Mary can be encouraged to trust Christ as the Redeemer. In the midst of sorrow, God's Word assures her of a blessed reunion in heaven.

Comparisons

Eastern Orthodox: When people die, God judges them immediately. The righteous enter paradise; the unrighteous enter Hades. Orthodox churches reject the idea of purgatory. Based on ancient custom (to prepare people for eternity) they pray for the dead. *The Longer Catechism of the Eastern Church* states: "How have we salvation by Christ's doctrine? When we receive it with all our heart, and walk according to it. . . . How have we salvation by Christ's life? When we imitate it."

Lutheran: Death is a result of the fall and separates body and soul. At death all souls enter heaven or hell depending on their relationship to Jesus Christ. Lutherans differ from other denominations because they emphasize that eternal salvation comes only by God's grace through faith in Christ. Whereas other denominations focus on personal goodness or holiness as preparation for eternity, Lutherans emphasize the holiness and goodness of Christ, the Savior.

Reformed: Death is a result of the fall and separates body and soul. At death all souls enter heaven or hell depending on their predestination to grace. *The Westminster Confession of Faith* states: "[Those who] truly believe in the Lord Jesus and love him in sincerity, and endeavoring to walk in all good conscience before him, may in this life be certainly assured that they are in a state of grace, and may rejoice in the hope of the glory of God" (chapter 18).

Roman Catholic: Death closes the time for accepting or rejecting God's grace. Depending on people's faith and works, they enter one of several states: (1) Unbaptized infants go to limbo; they do not suffer punishment but cannot attain the beatific vision [being in the presence of God, Mary, and all the saints]. (2) The righteous go to purgatory, a step on the way to the beatific vision. In purgatory they make satisfaction for remaining unrighteousness. (3) The Virgin Mary, baptized infants, and some saints directly enter the beatific vision. (4) The utterly wicked go to hell. Roman Catholics pray for the dead to help shorten their time in purgatory. Cf. CCC2 paras. 1006–1037.

Anabaptist: Death is a result of the fall and separates body and soul. The Dordrecht Confession states: "For neither Baptism, Supper, nor church-fellowship, nor any other external ceremony, can, without faith, the new birth, and a change or renewal of life, help or qualify us, that we may please God or receive any consolation or promise of salvation from Him" (article 6).

Baptist: Death is a result of the fall and separates body and soul. Particular Baptists, like the Reformed, teach that all souls enter either heaven or hell depending on their predestination. General Baptists teach that all souls go to heaven or hell depending on whether they have decided to accept Christ. Children who have not reached the age of accountability also go to heaven. "We believe that the blessings of salvation are made free to all by the Gospel; that it is the immediate duty of all to accept them by a cordial, penitent, and obedient faith" (*New Hampshire Baptist Confession*).

Wesleyan: Death is a result of the fall and separates body and soul. At death the soul enters heaven or hell depending on whether it accepted Christ as Savior and led a holy life. John Wesley preached: "But 'without holiness no man shall see the Lord,' [Hebrews 12:14] shall see the face of God in glory. . . . Then, at length, you will see . . . the necessity of holiness in order to glory" (sermon on the new birth).

Liberalism: Death is part of the natural order. There is no place of eternal punishment (hell) for souls after death. At death people escape the wages of sin.

Point to Remember

We believe that Jesus died and rose again, even so, through Jesus, God will bring with Him those who have fallen asleep. *1 Thessalonians 4:14*

Recognize the Signs

Appear, Desire of Nations;
Thine exiles long for home.
Show in the heavens Thy promised sign;
Thou Prince and Savior, come!
—Henry Alford, "Ten Thousand Times Ten Thousand"

Throughout history, Bible readers have associated certain signs with the end of time. For example, Franciscan monks in the Middle Ages feared the coming of the Antichrist and scrutinized the actions of each new emperor or pope, wondering: "Could this one be the Antichrist?"

John and Paul state that, immediately before Christ's second coming, a final rebellion will occur against Him. However, as we read the Book of Revelation, we remember that the primary purpose of its symbols is not to reveal the Antichrist and future world events. Revelation directs our attention to Christ and His glorious victory over all evil. The victory belongs to Christ, and the people of God share in that victory by His grace.

Good and Evil

Many turn immediately to the Book of Revelation for a description of the Antichrist—and find none! Only John's letters use the term *Antichrist.* John makes a number of points in this regard.

While affirming that the Antichrist will indeed come, John states that already many "antichrists" have appeared and that the spirit of the Antichrist is already active in this "last hour" (1 John 2:18). John identifies an antichrist as anyone who "went out from us" (i.e., left Christ's Church, 1 John 2:19) and denied that Jesus is the Christ (1 John 2:22) or that He had come "in the flesh" (1 John 4:2–3; 2 John 7; John is combating an early heresy called *gnosticism*). From these passages we may conclude that

1. the latter days or "end times" already existed in John's day and in fact extend from the day of Pentecost to Judgment Day.
2. throughout these end times the spirit of the Antichrist leads people to deny the person of Christ.
3. the Antichrist is still to come.

Although Paul does not use the term *Antichrist,* he speaks of the "man of lawlessness" who will emerge. In 2 Thessalonians 2:1–12, Paul speaks of a person who will exalt himself above God and will in fact claim to be God (v. 4). Although Paul calls this person the "man of lawlessness" and not the Antichrist, most would see these as different names for the same person. This person will appear immediately before Christ returns (v. 3) and will lead a rebellion against Christ and His people (v. 4). This person is not yet active in power because he is held in check. When God's purposes are accomplished (that is, when the Gospel has been preached to all nations, Matthew 24:14), then the man of lawlessness will be let loose to do the work of Satan (2 Thessalonians 2:9). He will openly reveal himself in opposition to Christ, performing counterfeit miracles that will deceive all who do not love the truth (vv. 9–10). But his rebellion will be short-lived, and he will be destroyed (v. 8).

In Revelation, John saw two beasts summoned by Satan to work evil on earth. The second beast is commonly associated with the Antichrist. In Revelation 13:11–18, John states that this beast, an agent of Satan, has two horns like the lamb but speaks like the dragon. Note the symbolism! In Revelation, *horn* symbolizes power. The person claims to have the power and authority of the Lamb (Christ), but he speaks like the dragon (Satan). He is Satan's agent masquerading as Christ. He is truly a "false christ," which is what *Antichrist* means.

This beast from the earth, like Paul's man of lawlessness, performs miracles to deceive. The man of lawlessness causes all who do not worship

Satan's first agent, the beast from the sea, to be killed. In a travesty of Revelation 7:3, where God places a mark upon His people to show that they belong to Him, this beast forces a mark to be placed on his followers and causes economic hardship for all who do not receive this mark.

John provides clues as to how we might identify the beast. The beast has a mark, the number of his name, 666. In ancient times, letters served as numbers (e.g., a = 1, b = 2). In other words, if one were to take the beast's name, assign a number to every letter according to its order in the alphabet, and then add all those numbers together, the sum would be 666. Since all attempts to identify the beast in this way have failed, many interpret the number symbolically. For example, seven was considered a divine number. So if 777 would be a number of the Holy Trinity, then 666 is a counterfeit of that name. The beast cannot be identified by outward appearance. He appears like a lamb! But his words betray him. He "speaks like the dragon." Just as Christians identify "antichrists" today by their false teachings, they will identify *the* Antichrist by his false words.

Although people give much attention to how the Antichrist will be revealed immediately before the end, both Paul and John state that already God's people fight his spirit. Paul says more about warfare between believers and the powers of darkness in Ephesians 6:10–13. Throughout history, God's people have fought against the forces of evil by His power and grace. Even now we are involved in warfare. Christ gives us the equipment to carry on this fight. Christ's victory on the cross assures us of our victory over sin, death, and the power of Satan.

Although the Antichrist will rage for a time on earth, Revelation 14:9–13 and 20:7–10 maintain that Satan's final rebellion will be short and end in defeat. He, the beasts, and all their followers will be cast into hell.

Discern the Signs

Many people point to certain historical figures as the Antichrist. Some think John in Revelation described Nero Caesar, who persecuted Christians for a short period of time. The Franciscans of the Middle Ages and the reformers stated that the pope exhibited many marks of the Antichrist. During World War II, some people identified Hitler as the Antichrist.

How do these historic people measure against the Bible's description of the Antichrist? Hitler, though truly an evil person, does not fit the description provided by John or Paul. His primary mission was not to rebel against Christ by masquerading as Christ and putting Christians to death. Nero Caesar did indeed persecute Christians. He was responsible for the deaths of Peter and Paul, among others, and his name, in Hebrew and slightly misspelled (!), adds up to 666. Yet though he might properly be thought of as *an* antichrist, he falls short of *the* Antichrist portrayed by the biblical authors. The medieval popes, inasmuch as they held power in the Church and caused people to trust in their own good works rather than Christ, seemed likely candidates. Agreeing with the conclusions of the medieval Franciscans, the Lutheran Confessions state: "Our consciences are excused well enough, for the errors of the kingdom of the pope are clear. Scripture with its entire voice cries out that these errors are a *teaching of demons* [1 Timothy 4:1–3] and of Antichrist" (Tr 42; *Concordia*, p. 301). But the final assault of the Antichrist has not yet appeared.

The spirit of the Antichrist was active in John's day and remains active today. For example, one thinks of the so-called "Jesus Seminar." This group of scholars, many of whom are ordained ministers, maintains that Jesus was only a man and did not rise from the dead. Such people serve the spirit of the Antichrist.

On the cross Jesus defeated Satan and his agents. Christ has given His people the victory. Even though we may suffer for the sake of the Gospel and Christ (as has been true always for the people of God!), we have victory. The proclamation of the Gospel fights against evil. The moment a person comes to faith, Christ's victory snatches that person away from the powers of darkness (Romans 8:31–39). The moment a person dies in the faith, he or she enters glory and celebrates Christ's victory (Revelation 12:10–12).

Comparisons

Symbolism: Most Eastern Orthodox, many Lutherans, many Reformed, many Roman Catholics, and some Wesleyans have interpreted the visions of Revelation symbolically as prophecy. Some sources broadly label traditional Protestant views "historicist" because of the common "historical" arguments that identify the papacy with the Antichrist (1 and 2 John), and the man of sin or man of lawlessness (2 Thessalonians 2), The arguments for this view arose, however, in the medieval period when hermit orders of monks criticized the use of indulgences to enrich the papacy and fund the Crusades. When the monks were persecuted, they concluded that the papacy was under satanic influence. Protestants drew upon a centuries-old criticism when they also referred to the papacy as the Antichrist.

Literalism: Most Anabaptists, Baptists, and some Wesleyans have interpreted the visions of Revelation literally. Some sources also label this as "futurism." The signature aspect of this approach is a linear, literalist interpretation of Revelation.

Historicism: The philosophical approach called *historicism* takes a sequence of events and analyzes it with a system of ideas. Part of that analysis is based on Rationalism, on linear developments of ideas. Another part is based on aesthetics, where certain meanings are seen to be true apart from the flow of time, such as the idea that things evolve to a better state. When applying this and related approaches, theological liberals have not treated Revelation as prophecy. They generally interpret Revelation as a history-bound protest against the Roman Empire. For example, many liberals think the "beast" of Revelation represents the Roman emperor Nero. Some sources merge this view with idealism, with which it shares the view that the Bible should not be taken literally.

Idealism: This view treats most, if not all, of the prophetic language as allegorical descriptions of the continual struggle between good and evil.

Preterism: This group also believes that Revelation speaks about the first century AD. It believes that the early Church did not view Revelation as end-time prophecy. This viewpoint arose in the Counter-Reformation, where we also see some of the roots of historicism and historical-critical thought. This view arose likely as the result of Protestant arguments that the papacy is the persecuting Antichrist.

Point to Remember

Children, it is the last hour, and as you have heard that antichrist is coming, so now many antichrists have come. Therefore we know that it is the last hour. *1 John 2:18*

Love His Appearing

Commending those who love me to His care,
As I hope in their prayers they will commend me,
I look through the help of God to a joyous meeting
With many loved ones gone before.
—"The Creed of Abraham Lincoln"

When Jesus ascended into heaven, angels appeared to His disciples and told them that He would return (Acts 1:10–11). The early Christians lived with this expectation, yet Christ did not return during their lifetime. Today we long for His appearing and the joyous reunion of heaven. All sorts of events are associated with Christ's return, some biblical and others not.

Glorious Appearing

When Christ first came to earth, He was born in humility at Bethlehem. In contrast to His humble birth at Bethlehem, Christ's second coming will be glorious and evident to all. Acts 1:9–11; Matthew 24:29–31; and Revelation 1:7 affirm that He will come in the clouds, attended by His holy angels. All those alive at the time will see Him with their own eyes. Throughout history, individuals have insisted that Christ has already returned. The Jehovah's Witnesses, for example, believe that Christ returned in 1914. But according to Scripture, His return will be an event that no one will miss.

People have often made predictions about Christ's return. Jesus taught emphatically about this event. Although signs provide evidence that Christ will return soon, no one, not even the angels of heaven, knows the exact time (Matthew 24:36, 42–44). On the contrary, Paul states that the day will come like a thief, when people do not expect it (1 Thessalonians 5:1–3). So any prediction about the year of Christ's return does not come from the Bible or Christ. When the Gospel has been proclaimed to all (Matthew 24:14), that is, after the gracious will of God in Christ has accomplished its purpose, Christ will return. Beyond that, nothing more can be stated.

Among the signs that Christ's return is imminent (Matthew 24:33) are the persecution of believers and general apostasy (Matthew 24:4–13). Some interpreters have insisted that the fig tree represents Israel, which reemerged as a nation in 1948, marking the last generation before Christ returns (Matthew 24:32–34). However, a biblical generation (forty years) came and went in 1988, and Christ did not return. The blossoming fig tree is a metaphor, not the sign itself, for Christ's return. In other words, just as a blossoming fig tree tells people that summer is near, so also persecution and apostasy (the "these things" of v. 33) will tell people that Christ's return is near. The disciples' own generation would see these things "begin to happen" (a better translation of the Greek in v. 34). At Christ's return, all the dead will rise and then all people together will stand before Him for judgment (Matthew 25:31–32). The Bible nowhere separates Christ's return from the resurrection of the dead and final judgment. In fact, Paul explicitly states that believers who have died will be among the first to meet Christ at His second coming (1 Thessalonians 4:13–18). As popularized in LaHaye and Jenkins's *Left Behind* series, some people think that Christ will return only for believers alive at that time so they might escape a period of great tribulation upon earth. After that, Christ will establish a glorious earthly millennial kingdom in Jerusalem. They assert that after this millennial kingdom has run its course (a thousand years) and after a final battle (Armageddon), the dead will rise and final judgment will take place.

For unbelievers, Christ's return will be a time of great fear (Isaiah 2:12, 19; Revelation 6:15–17). His return ushers in their final condemnation. LaHaye and Jenkins's teaching is dangerous because it tells people they will have a second chance to repent, after the rapture. But the time to repent is now!

In contrast to the utter terror of unbelievers, believers are called to lift up their heads and rejoice at Christ's return (Luke 21:27–28). His return announces their final deliverance from all evil and suffering and a blessed union with Christ in heaven (Psalm 96:11–13; Revelation 21:2–4). Far from fearing this day, believers in Christ pray for His return to come quickly (Revelation 22:20).

No one knows when Christ will return. How, then, can believers be ready? The Bible compares people who have no faith in Christ and whose worries and desires do not extend beyond this world to people who are drunk and asleep. Christ's unexpected return will indeed take them by surprise (Luke 21:34–36). But those who have faith in Christ's forgiveness are always ready for Christ's return. Although they don't know the time, they expect Christ's return, for they place their hope and trust in Him (1 Thessalonians 5:9–11).

Comforting Presence

Paul compares Christ's coming to the suddenness of a pregnant woman's labor (1 Thessalonians 5:3). Imagine a woman who is completely and utterly surprised when she goes into labor! No, she would not have known the exact time, but surely she would know she was pregnant and that labor was imminent. Christ's return will take many by surprise.

Joe, a fellow Christian and your friend, is worried that he will not be ready for Christ's return. "Jesus is coming like a thief," he says. "What will happen to me if He returns while I am preoccupied with something else or committing a sin?" If Joe assesses his readiness to meet Christ on the basis of his own good behavior, then he has good reason to worry. No person can be ready for Christ's return if his or her own behavior is the standard of readiness. Only the rejection of God's forgiveness in Christ—unbelief—makes a person unprepared for Christ's return. Moreover, if Joe becomes so preoccupied with worldly matters that he no longer cares about forgiveness of sins or comes to hear the Gospel and receive the Sacrament, then he will have good reason to worry. In such a state, a person's faith is at risk. We can tell Joe that the fact he is concerned about his readiness shows his faith is active. A complete unbeliever won't care at all! God has forgiven all sins in Christ. No sin, even one Joe might be committing at the moment of Christ's return, is so "terrible" that it has not already been forgiven at the cross. We can comfort Joe in the fact that God does not desire to catch him by surprise in order to condemn him (1 Thessalonians 5:9).

The Bible often compares Christ's return for His people to a bridegroom coming for His bride. God's people have joy at Christ's return. The joy and fulfillment of attending a wedding on earth are but a small foretaste of the joy and fulfillment of hope believers will have at Christ's return.

Comparisons

At any time: Eastern Orthodox, Lutherans, Roman Catholics, and some Reformed and Wesleyans expect the following signs: apostasy, worldwide preaching of the Gospel, and the appearance of the Antichrist. These churches believe that Christ could return at any time.

Watch for specific signs: Anabaptists and Baptists, with some Wesleyans and Reformed, expect certain identifiable signs: the rapture, seven years of tribulation, the Antichrist, the mass conversion of Jews to Christianity, a thousand-year rule, and a variety of other events based on particular interpretations.

Liberalism: Liberals do not believe Christ will return, since they deny the resurrection of the dead.

Point to Remember

> Now concerning the times and the seasons, brothers, you have no need to have anything written to you. For you yourselves are fully aware that the day of the Lord will come like a thief in the night.
> *1 Thessalonians 5:1–2*

The Millennial Reign

> But peaceful was the night
> Wherein the Prince of Light
> His reign of peace upon the earth began.
> —John Milton, "On the Morning of Christ's Nativity"

Just as people associate the appearance of the Antichrist with the latter days, they also often think of the millennium. Revelation speaks of a thousand-year period when the followers of Christ come to life and reign with Him upon the earth.

We have saved the topic of the millennium until now because it is one of the most controversial. As we look at this subject, it is important to remember the symbolic character of Revelation. For example, the Antichrist is a beast and Satan (a spirit) is a red dragon. Christ (God and man) is a lamb with seven horns and seven eyes!

It is also important to understand how this teaching coincides with God's overall plan of salvation in Christ. A thousand-year reign of Christ is mentioned only in Revelation.

Christ Reigns Now

Millennium is a label attached to the biblical teaching that Christ's people will reign on earth for one thousand years. This teaching is found only in Revelation 20:1–6. Although many other places in the Bible have much to say about the reign of Christ, nowhere else is a thousand-year period connected to it. Having said that, it will become very important for us to let the clear teachings of Scripture about the kingdom of Christ and the reign of God's people help us interpret what Revelation says about the millennium.

In this thousand-year period, Satan is bound in the abyss so that he cannot deceive the nations. Evidence of Christ's rule was manifest during His earthly ministry when He cast out demons. Whereas before Christ's appearing there were comparatively few believers, today millions confess Christ as their Savior. Satan is indeed bound and cannot deceive the nations as he once did.

Take note! Some translations badly garble verse 4, which contains a long sentence in the original Greek. (In an effort to make this text read more like English, the translators divide it into several sentences. For a rendering closer to the Greek, see this passage in the KJV.) Verse 4 describes all God's people from heaven down to earth:

1. those on thrones,
2. the souls of the martyrs, and

3. those who refused the mark of the beast.

A second problem with some translations appears at the end of verse 4. The new life of believers is described as if it were a future event. In fact, more faithful translations show that believers enjoy new life *now* and reign with Christ *now* ("they lived and reigned with Christ" [KJV]).

John states that the "second death" has no power over the people of God, who took part in the "first resurrection" (Revelation 20:6). A few verses later (20:14), he tells us precisely what the second death is—hell. The existence of a second death implies the existence of a first, but John nowhere mentions this. However, in light of what we discovered earlier, the first death is the physical/spiritual death caused by sin. In a like manner, the "first resurrection" implies the existence of a second, also not mentioned elsewhere in Revelation. To complicate matters, John does not give us details concerning what the first resurrection entails. On the basis of this passage, some think there will be two bodily resurrections, yet the rest of Scripture speaks only of one. However, the Bible does speak of people dead in sin rising to new life in Christ (John 5:25; Romans 6:4). This we need to understand as the first resurrection, and the unmentioned second resurrection is the rising of the body at the Last Day. In summary, John states that the second death (hell) has no power over those who take part in the first resurrection (who are given new life in Christ).

John tells us that when Satan is bound, those who sit on thrones to judge for this period are the souls who suffer martyrdom ("beheaded for the testimony of Jesus" [Revelation 20:4]) and who do not worship the beast (the Antichrist). They come to life to reign with Christ in heaven.

At the conclusion of the thousand years, Satan is let loose for a short time, during which he goes out to deceive the nations in such a way that they unite to war against God's people. But just as these nations surround God's people, God's judging fire falls from heaven and Satan, together with his followers, is cast into hell (Revelation 20:7).

John himself states in the first chapter of Revelation that people are made a kingdom through the blood of Christ. Peter also describes believers as a "holy nation." That is, by God's grace in Christ, believers on earth are made part of Christ's kingdom. They claim Christ as their King on earth and look forward to being a part of Christ's glorious kingdom in heaven. Christ rules now in the hearts and minds of His people (Colossians 1).

Peter (1 Peter 2:7–9) and John (Revelation 1:6) link the ideas of kingdom and priesthood together. That is, the authority of believers upon earth in Christ's kingdom of grace is to serve as "priests" to God.

Christ Himself gave this authority to reign to the disciples in Matthew 16:17–19. Christ sent them on His behalf to announce the forgiveness of sins in His name, exercising His authority in the kingdom of grace (Christ's kingdom upon earth). This authority extends to all Christ's disciples. Much erroneous thinking about the millennium arises from unclear thinking about the kingdom of grace and the kingdom of glory. What distinguishes God's people from others is that they become part of the kingdom of grace when they are "born again" through Baptism (John 3:3). In the kingdom of grace, believers still fight against sin and evil on earth and await their final victory over death. The faithful become part of the kingdom of glory after death. In the kingdom of glory, the saints no longer battle evil or are subject to death.

When Satan is loosed in Revelation, he immediately goes out to deceive the nations so that they war against God's people. Therefore, his binding must mean that during the millennium he will not be able to deceive people as he did before the death and resurrection of Christ. The only other place where reference is made to the binding of Satan is in a saying of Jesus (Matthew 12:24–29; Mark 3:23–27; Luke 11:17–22), and here the reference is indirect. In this passage Jesus described His casting out of demons as "binding" the strong man. Jesus' explanation (alongside the image in Revelation) enables us to best interpret Satan's binding as a restriction of his activity. Although he does indeed "prowl around like a roaring lion, seeking someone to devour" (1 Peter 5:8), during the time of the millennium he cannot deceive the nations and lead them in open warfare against God's people as he will after he is loosed.

Millennialists place great emphasis on Jerusalem and the role of the Jewish people during the end times. But millennialists disagree widely. For example, some believe that during the millennium Christ will reign visibly and powerfully upon earth from Israel for a thousand years. That is, the millennium is viewed not only as a spiritual but also as a politically powerful reign of Christ. Accompanying this view is the notion that Jewish people will be part of this kingdom, a heaven upon earth, and that Gentiles will be indirect recipients of the Jewish blessings. Passages such as Isaiah 2:2–5 are used to substantiate this view. But in Isaiah 2:2–5, the "mountain of the house of the Lord" should be understood not as the future and literal raising of the temple mount in Jerusalem, but rather as a figure of speech denoting the reign of God (for which "mountain" is a metaphor), which extends from His covenant of grace (the focus of which was the temple) to all people. The notion that Christ will establish a glorious and politically powerful kingdom on earth contradicts what Jesus says about His kingdom in John 18:36: "My kingdom is not of this world." Alternatively, Scripture makes clear that believers in Christ have been raised to new life (the "first resurrection") and become part of His kingdom. The authority Christians exercise is the authority of Christ to forgive sins. Against this kingdom, the Church, the gates of hell will not prevail (Matthew 16:17–19).

As is so often true in Revelation, the number 1,000 should be interpreted as a symbol for completeness. Many Bible passages use 1,000 in this way. For example, in Psalm 50:10 the cattle on "a thousand hills" belong to God and represent His complete ownership of creation. (For general and symbolic uses of 1,000, see also Deuteronomy 7:9; 32:30; Joshua 23:10; Psalm 84:10; 90:4; 91:7; 105:8; Ecclesiastes 6:6; Isaiah 7:23; 30:17; 60:22; and 2 Peter 3:8. What parent hasn't said, "I've told you a thousand times to pick up your room!")

The complete rule of Christ symbolized by the number 1,000 extends from His first appearance and victory on the cross to the time when He comes again. During this symbolic thousand years, Satan is restricted in his activity so that the Gospel might spread freely to all peoples. At the conclusion of the "thousand years," Satan will be loosed. He will draw the nations into one last battle against Christ's people. But he and his followers will be defeated and condemned to everlasting punishment.

Kingdom Come

For a number of years now, Palestinians and Israelis have lived in the same geographic area. They call the same city, Jerusalem, a spiritual home. For Christians, too, Jerusalem bears significance as the place where Christ was crucified and rose from death.

Susan, a friend at a neighboring community church, insists that Jerusalem will be established as the center of Christ's millennial kingdom. How can we respond to Susan? People like Susan often imagine that God has plans for the Jewish nation irrespective of what Christ accomplished on the cross. Christ reigns now in the midst of and through His people.

In the New Testament, after Christ establishes the Church, the kingdom language begins to disappear from Christian preaching. The disciples understood that Christ's reign is not bound by geography or restricted to one group of people (Israelites; cf. Galatians 3:28: "There is neither Jew nor Greek, there is neither slave nor free, there is neither male nor female, for you are all one in Christ Jesus"). Although Christ intercedes for us at the right hand of the Father, His kingdom is found on earth wherever the Gospel is proclaimed and the Sacraments are rightly administered. In proclaiming Christ's forgiveness, we share Christ with the world.

Comparisons

Amillennialism: Eastern Orthodox, Lutherans, Roman Catholics, and some Reformed and Wesleyans hold that Christ rules now through

His Church. The thousand years of Revelation 20 symbolize the present rule of Christ.

Millennialism: Anabaptists, Baptists, and some Reformed and Wesleyans hold that Christ will establish a literal thousand-year rule on earth. Postmillennialists believe Christ will return after this thousand-year period; premillennialists believe Christ will return before this thousand-year period.

Liberalism: Liberals seek to establish God's kingdom on earth through social justice and peace.

Like most Christians, Lutherans emphasize that no one knows when Christ will return. God's people should focus on proclaiming the Gospel and serving others, not speculate about what cannot be known. Lutherans also emphasize that the created order will continue to decline until Christ returns. We cannot make a heaven on earth!

Point to Remember

Jesus answered, "My kingdom is not of this world." *John 18:36*

Judgment Day

The mighty word of this great Lord
Link body and soul together,
Both of the just and the unjust
To part no more forever.
—Michael Wigglesworth, "The Day of Doom"

As a Puritan, Michael Wigglesworth placed special emphasis on Judgment Day. The title of his poem, "The Day of Doom," shows the anxiety that many Puritans felt about the return of Christ, an anxiety still reflected in people's obsession with the end times today.

We have already learned in previous sections that Christ will return to raise the dead. Then all people will face final judgment. Many in our society would agree that they will stand before God after death and be judged.

Many people believe that as long as the "good" qualities and deeds of a person outweigh the "bad," God will grant entrance into heaven. This view, however, ignores God's holiness and justice. From a worldly point of view, differences indeed exist among the moral qualities of individuals. It appears that some people are not as "bad" as others. But God demands absolute perfection for those who make their own personal behavior the standard by which He will judge them (Matthew 5:48).

Christ, the Judge

By God's power when Christ returns, all the dead will rise and stand before the judgment seat of God. The Bible nowhere separates the second coming of Christ and the resurrection of the dead. On the contrary, they happen in immediate succession with no intervening period of tribulation or millennial kingdom, as some have proposed.

Christians have always maintained that death is not the end of existence. In physical death the soul separates from the body. This has caused people to ask what becomes of the soul separated from the body until they are reunited at the resurrection—the so-called intermediate state of the souls. The Bible shows that the souls of those who die in the faith go immediately to be with Christ in a blessed state. Jesus assured the thief on the cross that "today" he would be in paradise (Luke 23:43). Paul anticipated going to be with the Lord immediately at his death. In Revelation, John sees visions of the souls of the blessed in heaven, praising God and awaiting the final judgment and consummation of all things (Revelation 7:9–17; 6:9–11).

Many have wondered what happens to believers between the day of their death and their resurrection. Scripture teaches that the souls of the departed go immediately to a state of bliss or torment (2 Corinthians 5:8). Nowhere does the Bible support the idea that the souls of people wander about on earth as ghosts or that they have the ability to communicate with the living, either immediately or through mediums. Rather, the Bible connects all such phenomena to demonic activity. If someone asks about the appearance of Samuel to Saul in 1 Samuel 28, we can reply that some theologians commonly interpret this passage either as a trick of Satan or as a truly exceptional event by which God sent Samuel to proclaim His judgment upon Saul. Matthew 27:51–53 shows another exception, by which God illustrated the significance of Jesus' death and resurrection. Concerning the souls of unbelievers, the few references in Scripture lead us to believe that those in torment await their final judgment and condemnation in hell. (See also Luke 16:19–31; 1 Peter 3:19.)

By the power of God, all people will rise in their own physical bodies, being recognizable to themselves and others (Job 19:25–27). It matters not to the divine power of God that bodies over time decay, turn to dust, and are scattered. All will hear the voice of Christ, which will bring the dead to life.

Immediately following the general resurrection of all people comes Judgment Day. Jesus Himself spoke of this event in Matthew 25:31–46. The clear teaching of this parable is that Christ will come to judge all.

People will be judged on the basis of their deeds. The difference between the sheep and the goats is that the sheep are covered by the righteousness of Christ won on the cross. Their sin has been removed from them as far as the east is from the west, and God remembers their sin no more (Psalm 103:12; Jeremiah 31:34). In other words, the difference between the sheep and the goats is not that the sheep are less sinful than the goats. Rather, by faith, the sheep cling to God's forgiveness in Christ. Christ, their judge, sees and remembers only their good deeds when He looks upon them.

Christ will banish unbelievers to everlasting punishment and torment in hell. Christ brings believers into the blessings of eternal life in heaven. If a friend asks us about the relation between judgment passed upon a person at the time of temporal death and the universal judgment of all after the resurrection, we can explain that universal judgment is a public proclamation of the judgment passed at death.

A vast difference exists between the final judgment of believers and unbelievers. There is no "balance" that tips on the side of good deeds that outweigh the bad. All are sinful before God (Romans 3:23). Faith in Christ makes all the difference. When a person comes to faith, she escapes judgment at that moment (John 5:24). At Baptism, Christ's death becomes her death (Romans 6:3–11). Jesus paid for her sins on the cross. No condemnation awaits her (Romans 8:1).

Although the Gospel writers and Paul continually remind people of the final judgment on the Last Day, they also insist that even now we live under God's judgment. Scripture makes clear that already in Christ, God has executed His judgment, for which the Last Day is a public proclamation. He no longer holds their sin against His people. Just as an ambassador is an official representative of an earthly ruler, making official statements at his bequest and on his behalf, so Paul states that he is an ambassador of God. He earnestly desires that people heed the judgment of God in Christ so that their sins are forgiven and by God's grace they receive reconciliation (2 Corinthians 5:16–21).

Reconciled by Christ

Mary and her co-workers are having a discussion about how people get to heaven. "I try to live a good life," Mary says. "I don't hurt anyone. I'm not a criminal. Sure, I haven't always helped people like I could have, but I hope that I have done enough." How can we respond? First, we need to clarify Mary's thinking about good works. From a worldly point of view, differences indeed exist between the good deeds of individuals, such as those of a murderer and a humanitarian, and God does reward the good deeds of unbelievers (their "civil righteousness") with rewards of this world ("civil rewards"). But when it comes to heaven, nothing short of perfection is required. One must depend on Christ alone!

On the Last Day we will all stand before the judgment seat of Christ. But even now we hear Christ's judgment. In the Absolution, the pastor bestows the forgiveness of sins on behalf of Christ. At the Lord's Supper, Christ Himself gives us His body and blood with the bread and wine for our forgiveness. These means prepare us to stand before Christ because they strengthen our faith in His forgiveness.

In 2 Corinthians 5:16–21, Paul expressed how God's judgment in Christ changed his outlook and behavior. He no longer viewed people from a worldly point of view and instead considered himself an ambassador. We, like Paul, should consider how God will use us to call people to repentance and thus, by His grace, bring them to the point where they are ready to stand on Judgment Day clothed in the righteousness of Christ.

Neither Judge nor Jury, but a Witness

God has not called us to condemn other people or to figure out who will make it to heaven. We are witnesses, not a judge or jury. God calls us to speak His Word to the world, proclaiming His judgment of all in Christ. For those in Christ, that judgment is "not guilty." Christ paid the price for sin by His death on the cross and has reconciled God to the world.

Comparisons

Traditional Christians: Christ will bodily raise the dead and finally separate the righteous and the unrighteous.

Liberalism: There is no bodily resurrection or last judgment.

Lutherans also point out that Christ will separate the righteous from the unrighteous on the basis of faith. He will also judge people's works, punishing or rewarding people according to what they have done (the Bible describes degrees of glory and punishment, e.g., 1 Corinthians 3:10–15; Matthew 11:21–24). All the righteous will share the same bliss in heaven.

Point to Remember

For we must all appear before the judgment seat of Christ, so that each one may receive what is due for what he has done in the body, whether good or evil. *2 Corinthians 5:10*

Heaven or Hell?

And the angels, all pallid and wan,
Uprising, unveiling, affirm
That the play is the tragedy, "Man,"
And its hero the Conqueror Worm.
—Edgar Allan Poe, "The Conqueror Worm"

Based on Isaiah 66:24, Poe's "The Conqueror Worm" portrays humankind's end as a tragedy. Gary Larson, in his *Far Side* comics, pictures hell as a place where Beethoven must spend eternity in a room full of accordion players. Many picture heaven as a place where people sport long robes and halos and play harps.

In the previous section, we learned that at the final judgment God will take the righteous to heaven and banish the wicked to hell. Throughout history all sorts of images and ideas have been associated with heaven and hell, many of them fanciful to the point of being ridiculous.

The Christian teaching about heaven and hell is subject to much misunderstanding at the popular and scholarly level. The popular press (Gary Larson is an example) misuse notions of heaven and hell to the extent that many people do not take them seriously. Some deny the existence of hell, just as they deny the existence of Satan.

Tears and Eternity

The Bible nowhere states that hell is a place where devils with pitchforks torment humans. In fact, hell is a place for the devils to suffer torment (Matthew 25:41). Hell is as real as the devils and wicked people who will be tormented there; it is not a fiction and it is more than a "state of mind." Christ Himself emphatically insisted upon the reality of hell. Rather than fixing the location of hell, the Bible tells us—often by using images and metaphors—what hell is like. Thus, in Matthew, Jesus describes it as a "fiery furnace" where there is "weeping and gnashing of teeth" (13:40–43).

Paul, alternatively, describes hell as a place of God's punishment and "eternal destruction," where one is "away from the presence of the Lord" (2 Thessalonians 1:6–10). And John in Revelation speaks of those in hell as drinking the "wine of God's wrath" and suffering everlasting torment (14:9–11).

God's Word describes hell as separation from God, darkness, eternal fire, the gnashing of teeth, and the second death. All these images convey unending torment. Theologians often categorize the torments of hell as both the deprivation of blessings and the addition of suffering. It is the absence of God's care. God is the source of all good things, such as the fruit of the Spirit: love, joy, peace, patience, kindness, goodness, faithfulness, gentleness, and self-control (Galatians 5:22–23). Separation from God describes the complete absence of any such good. The sufferings added to people in hell include inexpressible torments, pains, and tortures of the body and soul.

God casts evildoers into hell. This means all who remain in a state of unbelief in Christ do not stand forgiven and are not clothed in His righteousness. In Revelation, John describes such people as those who ultimately worship the beast (Satan) and receive his mark of ownership (21:6–8).

Some (among them the Roman Catholic Church) think that, after death, unbelievers suffer only for a time until their sins are paid; then they enter heaven. This time is called purgatory. But this is not a biblical teaching. Revelation 14:11; Luke 23:41; and Ephesians 2:8–9 lead to the inescapable conclusion that a believer goes immediately at death to be with the Lord. John in Revelation states that those who suffer in punishment after death do so forever, not for a limited period of time. The thief on the cross, a last-minute believer in Christ (certainly a candidate for purgatory if it existed), was taken immediately into paradise. The teaching that believers must in some measure pay the punishment for their own sins undermines the very foundation of salvation by grace.

As with hell, the Bible does not fix the location of heaven. Scripture does not teach that it is in the sky somewhere or out in space. Neither is it a place where believers will sprout angelic wings and carry around harps. Although the Bible states that the saints in heaven are dressed in white robes (Revelation 7:9), here again the biblical author employs a metaphor to tell us what life in heaven will be like. The white robe is a reminder that the saints in heaven are "clothed" in the righteousness of Christ (Revelation 7:14). Isaiah describes God's glorious heavenly kingdom as a great banquet where God's people feast in His glorious presence (25:6–9). Note the stunning contrast! They feast on God's riches because He swallowed death! Death no longer exists there. In Revelation the glories of God's heavenly kingdom are described as a wedding whereby God unites His people to Christ's glory (21:1–4; 22:3–5). Heaven is an eternal party! When pictured as a city, heaven is a place enlightened by the very glory of God and where the people of God see Him face-to-face. These images convey the bliss that will belong to God's people. Theologians customarily speak of the glory of heaven both as the absence of all things bad—such as sorrow, sin, sickness, and death—and as the addition of perfect blessings in the very presence of God.

John makes clear in Revelation 7:9–17 that those who have washed their robes "white" in the "blood of the Lamb" are fit to stand before God in heaven. This righteousness is granted to a believer at Baptism (Romans 6:1–11).

Hot Topics

One day you hear your co-worker, Curt, say, "I simply cannot believe that a loving God would send people to hell." You might tell Curt that God certainly does not want people to suffer eternal loss and damnation in hell, and therefore He has given His own Son to suffer that loss and damnation on our behalf on the cross. But God's love never comes at the expense of His holy justice. Only the substitutionary death of Christ delivers us from the threat of hell (Romans 3:19–26).

Jesus stated that His followers would endure all sorts of suffering and persecution for the sake of the Gospel. A biblical understanding of heaven and hell will enable us to endure all sorts of trials and tribulations rather than give up our eternal treasure in heaven. What a believer suffers now is trivial compared to the heavenly glory (2 Corinthians 4:17–18).

Lori, a member of your congregation, grieves on the anniversary of her husband's death. "I keep thinking about moments we shared. I just wish we could be together again." What can we say to bring Lori comfort and hope? We can assure her of a reunion with her husband and all God's people in heaven, where they will celebrate together forever in the glory and goodness of God. Isaiah 25 is especially helpful in such a situation. Those blessed moments she had with her husband while he was alive—moments touched by the grace of God—are but a tiny foretaste of the glories awaiting her in heaven, where she and her late husband will banquet together in the glorious presence of God.

Off the Back Burner

At the close of Revelation, John prays, "Come, Lord Jesus" (22:20). His earnest desire, and ours, is to leave this fallen world and to enter heaven.

God delays the reappearance of His Son so that others might hear the Gospel, be saved, and have a place in heaven.

Lutherans often pray, "Come, Lord Jesus. Be our guest," at meals. We can think of this prayer as anticipation of the heavenly banquet and pray for Christ's return. For Lutherans, daily repentance and frequent Communion are preparation for Christ's reappearing.

Comparisons

Orthodox, Lutheran, and the like: Hell is a place of eternal torment for the unrighteous. The new heaven and new earth describe the eternal bliss of heaven.

Roman Catholic: Hell is a place of eternal torment for those who commit mortal sins. It is not the same as purgatory, the place of cleansing suffering for believers. When the kingdom of God comes in its fullness, there will be a new heaven and new earth. Cf. CCC2 paras. 1033–37.

Liberalism: Liberals deny that hell exists. Some believe in a place or state of bliss after death.

Point to Remember

He will wipe every tear from their eyes, and death shall be no more, neither shall there be mourning nor crying nor pain anymore, for the former things have passed away. *Revelation 21:4*

Lutheran Summary of the End Times

Although new twists appear almost daily, the major issues regarding the end times already existed in the sixteenth century at the time of the Lutheran Reformation. Below you will find two examples of how the first Lutherans addressed these issues. The examples will help you understand the Lutheran difference.

Augsburg Confession XVII

Our churches teach that at the end of the world Christ will appear for judgment and will raise all the dead [1 Thessalonians 4:13–5:2]. He will give the godly and elect eternal life and everlasting joys, but He will condemn ungodly people and the devils to be tormented without end [Matthew 25:31–46].

Our churches condemn the Anabaptists, who think that there will be an end to the punishments of condemned men and devils.

Our churches also condemn those who are now spreading certain Jewish opinions, that before the resurrection of the dead the godly shall take possession of the kingdom of the world, the ungodly being everywhere suppressed. (*Concordia*, p. 40)

Large Catechism III 49–58

In the First Petition we prayed about God's honor and name. We prayed that He would prevent the world from adorning its lies and wickedness with God's name, but that He would cause His name to be valued as great and holy both in doctrine and life, so that He may be praised and magnified in us. Here we pray that His kingdom also may come. But just as God's name is holy in itself, and we still pray that it be holy among us, so also His kingdom comes of itself, without our prayer. Yet we still pray that it may come to us, that is, triumph among us and with us, so that we may be a part of those people among whom His name is hallowed and His kingdom prospers.

"But what is God's kingdom?"

Answer, "Nothing other than what we learned in the Creed: God sent His Son, Jesus Christ, our Lord, into the world to redeem and deliver us from the devil's power [1 John 3:8]. He sent Him to bring us to Himself and to govern us as a King of righteousness, life, and salvation against sin, death, and an evil conscience. For this reason He has also given His Holy Spirit, who is to bring these things home to us by His holy Word and to illumine and strengthen us in the faith by His power."

We pray here in the first place that this may happen with us. We pray that His name may be so praised through God's holy Word and a Christian life that we who have accepted it may abide and daily grow in it, and that it may gain approval and acceptance among other people. We pray that it may go forth with power throughout the world [2 Thessalonians 3:1]. We pray that many may find entrance into the kingdom of grace [John 3:5], be made partakers of redemption [Colossians 1:12–14], and be led to it by the Holy Spirit [Romans 8:14], so that we may all together remain forever in the one kingdom now begun.

For the coming of God's kingdom to us happens in two ways: (a) here in time through the Word and faith [Matthew 13]; and (b) in eternity forever through revelation [Luke 19:11; 1 Peter 1:4–5]. Now we pray for both these things. We pray that the kingdom may come to those who are not yet in it, and, by daily growth that it may come to us who have received it, both now and hereafter in eternal life. All this is nothing other than saying, "Dear Father, we pray, give us first Your Word, so that the Gospel may be preached properly throughout the world. Second, may the Gospel be received in faith and work and live in us, so that through the Word and the Holy Spirit's power [Romans 15:18–19], Your kingdom may triumph among us. And we pray that the devil's kingdom be put down [Luke 11:17–20], so that he may have no right or power over us [Luke 10:17–19; Colossians 1], until at last his power may be utterly destroyed. So sin, death, and hell shall be exterminated [Revelation 20:13–14]. Then we may live forever in perfect righteousness and blessedness" [Ephesians 4:12–13].

From this you see that we do not pray here for a crust of bread or a temporal, perishable good. Instead, we pray for an eternal inestimable treasure and everything that God Himself possesses. This is far too great for any human heart to think about desiring, if God had not Himself commanded us to pray for the same. But because He is God, He also claims the honor of giving much more and more abundantly than anyone can understand [Ephesians 3:20]. He is like an eternal, unfailing fountain. The more it pours forth and overflows, the more it continues to give. God desires nothing more seriously from us than that we ask Him for much and great things. In fact, He is angry if we do not ask and pray confidently [Hebrews 4:16].

It's like a time when the richest and most mighty emperor would tell a poor beggar to ask whatever he might desire. The emperor was ready to give great royal presents. But the fool would only beg for a dish of gruel. That man would rightly be considered a rogue and a scoundrel, who treated the command of his Imperial Majesty like a joke and a game and was not worthy of coming into his presence. In the same way, it is a great shame and dishonor to God if we—to whom He offers and pledges so many inexpressible treasures—despise the treasures or do not have the confidence to receive them, but hardly dare to pray for a piece of bread.

All this is the fault of shameful unbelief that does not even look to God for enough decent food to satisfy the stomach. How much less does such unbelief expect to receive eternal treasures from God without doubt? Therefore, we must strengthen ourselves against such doubt and let this be our first prayer. Then, indeed, we shall have everything else in abundance, as Christ teaches, "Seek first the kingdom of God and His righteousness, and all these things will be added to you" [Matthew 6:33]. For how could He allow us to suffer lack and to be desperate for temporal things when He promises to give us what is eternal and never perishes [1 Peter 1:4]? (*Concordia*, pp. 414–15)

The Church of the Lutheran Reformation

by Conrad Bergendoff

Summarized and Updated by Edward A. Engelbrecht

CHAPTER ONE

Rediscovery of the Gospel

Editor's note: The Lutheran Church sprang up and distinguished itself within Western Christian history. For the sake of brevity, we begin our summary with the story of Martin Luther and the causes of the Reformation rather than earlier Christian history. Yet, as the Apostles' Creed teaches us, there is only one Holy Christian Church. As a result, Lutherans trace their history to the believers of the Old and New Testaments as well as to the ancient and medieval eras. For example, the great ecumenical creeds and councils belong to Lutheran heritage as does the ancient liturgical tradition. For the depth of this background, we refer readers to our general Church history, The Church from Age to Age. *We likewise recommend that you read Conrad Bergendoff's complete book* The Church of the Lutheran Reformation, *which is summarized and updated below.*

The story of the Christian Church is one of repeated attempts at reformation. For every living organism grows. But growth can be in different directions, and the Church is always tempted to develop away from its true goal. Then it must be recalled from its false tendency and set on its rightful path. The life and work of Martin Luther achieved such a turn in the Church of the sixteenth century.

Whole libraries have been written on Luther. He has been examined from all angles and by all types of scholars—friendly, hostile, neutral. He has been hailed as a hero of Christendom and condemned as a disrupter of the Church. But our aim is not an evaluation of all the results of Luther's words and deeds. The history of the Church is something more than the story of great individuals, however influential. It is the greatness of Luther's contribution that he pointed to sources of spiritual life beyond himself and in his own experience witnessed to the truth by which the Church lives.

Luther's Early Life and Education

The home Martin Luther was born into on November 10, 1483, was probably a typical German household of the lower middle class. When Luther was less than a year old, the family moved from Eisleben to Mansfeld, where his father leased a smelting furnace. His parents were dutiful members of the town church. The father, however, wanted Martin to become a lawyer, for law was the way to preferment in the rising economic level of the German communities, and Hans and his wife Margarete had ambitions for this son. He was sent to a Latin school in Magdeburg at the age of 14, then to Eisenach, and to the University of Erfurt in 1501. Erfurt had a law school where a student could learn both the law of the church—canon law—and the law of the state. Luther finished his bachelor and master of arts studies and in 1505 was ready to begin the course in law.

In the Erfurt Monastery

Then in July 1505, a radical change in plans took place. Luther forsook his law studies and entered a monastery in Erfurt. We can only guess at what lay behind this decision. We do know that two weeks earlier he had become terrified in a storm when lightning struck close to him. He said that he then vowed to enter a monastery. The Augustinian Hermits were not—despite the name—hermits, but they did carefully regulate the hours of common prayer, work, begging, and meditation. They were friars who belonged to the Observant branch of the Augustinian order, tolerating no laxness in the life of the members. After a year's novitiate, Luther became a member of the order and prepared for the priesthood. He was ordained in the Erfurt Cathedral in April 1507.

In 1510, the order sent Luther and another monk to Rome on business having to do with the order's provincial administration. Luther attended mass after mass at the Roman altars, even climbing the *Scala Santa* on his knees. Later he expressed his astonishment over the carelessness of the clergy in their ministration and his disappointment at not having found what might be expected in the capital of Christendom.

Lecturer at the University of Wittenberg

Johann Staupitz, vicar of the Augustinian order, recognized the talents of the young monk and directed him into studies at the university that might prepare him to teach. In 1512, Luther became a doctor of theology. Staupitz held a professorship at the newly founded University of Wittenberg, a position he found a burden along with his administrative duties. He appointed Luther to take his place at the university.

Luther's first course in the University of Wittenberg was on the Psalms. We now know that Luther had studied the Scriptures in the Erfurt monastery and that he had a good acquaintance with them long before he began to teach. In 1513–17, he lectured on the Psalms, Romans, Galatians, and Hebrews.

Righteousness by Faith

Luther had already learned something about righteousness by faith in his work on the Psalms. Although it is impossible to date this event, it is clear that the climax of Luther's decade-long spiritual struggle was the discovery of the Gospel as "the power of God for salvation to everyone who has faith" and of the "righteousness of God" as a righteousness given by God to the believer for the sake of Jesus Christ. All his intense efforts to merit the love of God by the works that the penitential system of the church had prescribed had proved vain. He could not attain the conviction that he had done enough, although he had tested all the ways of the medieval sacramental system—confession, penance, absolution, celibacy, poverty, obedience, ordination, pilgrimage. God still seemed a wrathful face. However, Luther learned to interpret the royal passages of the Psalms as descriptions of Christ. This led him to understand the work of Christ as opposed to his own works. Christ became the face of God—a loving face, the face of One who sacrificed Himself for us. Forgiveness of sins became a reality in Christ, in whom alone was salvation.

The Ninety-five Theses against Indulgences

In the Early Church, Confession and Absolution were the means by which the sinner received the benefits of the redemption in Christ. To prevent misunderstanding of the promise of forgiveness, confession had to be followed by deeds confirming the penitent's earnestness. This might be a deed of charity, a work of discipline, or a gift, any of which would be required before the absolution and would constitute a satisfaction for the temporal consequence of the sin—only God could take away the guilt of the sin. In the development of the practice of confession, a distinction was made between mortal and venial sins, and a whole classification of sins resulted, each of which had its proper penalty. When the practice became a sacrament enjoined on all members of the Church, the priest in the parish and the bishop and the pope, in more important cases, claimed that they were God's representatives in assessing transgressions and imposing penalties. It was taught that confession and contrition could not be altogether complete and that some penalties would carry over into purgatory. In fact the hierarchy held the keys of the kingdom of God. They could close the Kingdom to high or low, and the pope could excommunicate kings or emperors and close the doors of churches under ban. Since absolution was necessary for the sacraments, the Church had the power to withhold the Means of Grace from any dissident member.

Another side of the matter was the translation of penalties into money payments. Not only venial sins could be pardoned by appropriate gifts, but even mortal sins had their price. The Church could take from its treasury of good deeds built up by the works of saints who had earned more than needed for their own salvation and add them to the donations of the penitent who wanted to care for the penalties of purgatory for himself or dear ones.

Once started, the system of indulgences could be used for other purposes. By the purchase of an indulgence the individual would receive credit on his score of penalties, shortening his stay in purgatory. Through the sale of such indulgences the pope in 1500—a jubilee year—found a way of financing the construction of St. Peter's Basilica in Rome. Princes and bishops might cooperate in the distribution of indulgences and agree on the division of income for their own purposes. For example, Luther's prince had used the system to raise money for the University of Wittenberg. This had brought protests from Luther.

In 1517, the archbishopric of Mainz was for sale. Albert of Hohenzollern bought it for 10,000 ducats, which he had to borrow. The pope allowed Albert to sell indulgences in his three bishoprics, half of the proceeds to be retained by the young archbishop, the other half to go to the building fund of St. Peter's. Tetzel, a Dominican monk, was in charge of the operation. He proclaimed that the indulgence effected the forgiveness of sins and the liberation of friends and family from purgatory. It was this brazen abuse of a sacrament of the Church that drove Luther to issue the Ninety-five Theses, which, on October 31, 1517, he nailed on the door of the Castle Church in Wittenberg as on a bulletin board, inviting discussion and debate.

In the theses Luther expressed his belief that the pope was uninformed of what was going on. But Luther was concerned more about the glory of God than the reputation of the pope. In fact, he argued that the pope can only remit penalties imposed by canon law or for violations of papal decrees. The pope could also declare that God has forgiven the guilt of a repentant sinner, which any priest could also do after confession. But he has no power from God to impose penalties in His name, nor has he any jurisdiction over souls in purgatory. He may only pray for them.

The theses were immediately printed and soon appeared in the cities, the universities, and the parishes throughout Europe. It has been estimated that within the next two years no fewer than a quarter of a million copies of Luther's writings in German were distributed in the church. The monk of Wittenberg had called for an academic debate; he created a controversy in which all of both church and state participated. The only adequate explanation of the rapidity of the spread of these propositions throughout Europe, everywhere raising discussion, approval, or opposition, is that Luther had touched a sensitive nerve in the church of his day.

Excommunication from Rome

In Rome, Leo X had on June 15, 1520, issued a bull, or decree, threatening the excommunication of Luther. It gave Luther sixty days to recant. On December 10, Luther gathered a group of friends, proceeded to a city gate of Wittenberg, and burned a copy of the papal document along with books of papal decrees and canon law. The pope's sentence had suggested that the writings of the heretic should be burned. This was Luther's reply. The actual excommunication was formulated in Rome early in January 1521 and was brought to Germany by John Eck, a professor at Ingolstadt who opposed Luther. In April it was to be presented to a meeting of the imperial diet at Worms, where, according to custom, the excommunication would be followed by the ban of the empire, making it unlawful for anyone to give food, shelter, or assistance to the fugitive. Luther's prince, Frederick the Wise, insisted that Luther be heard and condemned on Scriptural grounds. He gave Luther a promise of safe conduct to Worms and succeeded in getting him an opportunity to appear before the emperor himself. It was here that Luther dared tell the highest official of the empire:

> Unless I am convicted by Scripture and plain reason—I do not accept the authority of popes and councils, for they have contradicted each other—my conscience is captive to the Word of God; I cannot and I will not recant anything, for to go against conscience is neither right nor safe. God help me. Amen.

Despite his heroic stand, Luther was convicted and put under the ban. Charles V, a pious ruler, pledged himself to rid his domains of the heresy promulgated by Luther and his adherents. Yet Luther still had the protection and help of his prince, Elector Frederick. From Worms Luther was spirited away and brought to Frederick's castle at Wartburg. Here for the moment he was secure, and while enemies abroad raged at his writings, Luther could go on making reforms. Both pope and emperor were to find that forces far beyond their power to control had been released.

CHAPTER TWO

Steps toward Reform

The protest against error and evils is a frequent part of the story of mankind. But only to a few has it been given to build up a better structure on the ruins of what has been torn down. Had Luther's task been only to discern and criticize the unscriptural teachings and practices of the Medieval Church, his name might soon have been forgotten. His great constructive deeds, however, proved of permanent worth to the Western Church and affected its future course and character.

The Bible for Everyone

In the enforced quiet of the Wartburg Castle, Luther turned to study, prayer, and writing. Among the results was the translation of the Bible into German, one of his great achievements. Besides the translation Luther provided prefaces for practically all the books, for groups of books, and for each of the Testaments. In these the people found the core of his teaching and thereby received an education in the Bible. Not only was the language new and direct, but Luther had gradually discarded the traditional fourfold interpretation of Scripture—the literal, the allegorical, the moral, the anagogical (prophetic)—and insisted on the simple, literal sense of what was written. He could and did revert at times to the other uses, but the basic meaning was in the literal sense, which any reader should be able to understand. The Bible was the supreme authority for the Christian. Therefore one should be clear and sure about its meaning. From the Bible the Church heard the Word of God, received the promise given to faith, and experienced the fellowship of the Spirit.

In 1523, Luther issued a German language ritual for Baptism, omitting acts that he felt did not belong in an evangelical Sacrament. Later in the same year he recommended an evangelical revision of the Mass—a most important proposal because hitherto the Mass had been the principal observance of the Christian congregation and embodied the teaching of the Medieval Church. The Mass was considered a sacrifice that the priest renewed on each altar as an offering to God for the merit of the believers. The very saying of the Mass was effective before God, and therefore the presence of the congregation was not necessary. Hence the practice of private masses developed, with the notion that the person who gave a gift to have masses said might earn grace for himself or for those he named. This custom Luther utterly opposed. But he saw in the other parts of the Mass a chance for the education and worship of the congregation, and so he urged the retention of the elements that did not suggest sacrifice. The Lord's Supper was a gift to the congregation, not a good deed of the worshiper.

The *Formula missae* of 1523 indicates how conservative Luther was in retaining the historic forms of congregational worship. Though willing to root out every vestige of false doctrine, Luther was averse to radical changes in historic forms of worship. The preaching should be in the vernacular—and this, according to Luther, was the heart of every assembly of Christians—but the ancient forms of prayer and praise were in Latin, and he knew how difficult it was to translate these. Especially the parts carried by the choir, he felt, could be learned in Latin. But his instinct for popular participation inclined him to use more German. He wanted the congregation to sing; therefore German hymns must be provided. When he failed to prevail on others to write hymns, he began to do so himself. The publication in 1524 of his little book of *Eight Hymns* initiated a long and noble history of hymn writing in which some of his own contributions were memorable. "A Mighty Fortress" first appeared in a Wittenberg hymnbook of 1528.

A Peasant Rebellion

Events were already showing that forces being unleashed by Luther's defiance of the papal power would go further than Luther himself. Thomas Müntzer and Andreas Karlstadt were but two of many who saw in a religious reform an opportunity for social and political changes. The peasants of Germany and Switzerland found in Luther's preaching encouragement for their demands on their feudal lords. In some circles, the yearning for economic improvement was mixed with a martial temper of the Old Testament against the foes of God's people, and the coming of the millennium was to right both religious and economic wrongs.

In the Peasant Rebellion, Luther witnessed with dismay the unwarranted use of his teachings. He had not advocated rebellion against the constituted authorities of the state. Luther was not a social reformer and despite his peasant ancestry hardly understood the plight of the lower classes. When we speak of the demarcation of reform we must acknowledge Luther's limitations. He was intent on a reform of the Church as the bearer of the Gospel.

Visitation in the Parishes

While the leaders of reform were engaged in clarifying their positions on theological questions, very important issues in the parishes demanded attention. The followers of Karlstadt had disrupted the traditional forms of worship. Those with Anabaptist leanings questioned the Sacraments, which were at the heart of medieval devotion. Confession and Absolution by the priesthood was challenged by Luther's doctrine of the right of every Christian to confess to a fellow Christian and be forgiven. Monks left monasteries without making provision for the maintenance of their property or for their functions as teachers in schools. In the main, the parish priests were slow to change their allegiance to their bishops; the preachers of reform came rather from the ranks of the monasteries. But parishioners were restless and bewildered. The bishops had exercised a certain discipline, and the ecclesiastical courts had regulated marriage laws. Now these courts were spurned. The new preachers needed supervision, support, and education. Who would take the place of the officials of the old order?

In his own territory each prince exercised governmental powers. Society was still feudal in character, and on their estates the nobles ruled over their lands and the people. Luther had already turned to them in his *Open Letter to the German Nobility*, calling on them to assume responsibilities that the "spiritual estate" (the hierarchy) had wrongly assumed and unjustly discharged. For several years the Elector John, who had ruled Saxony after his brother Frederick died in 1525, had been urged to undertake a comprehensive reordering of conditions in his province. Finally in 1527, a "visitation" began. In place of the bishop a team of four—two jurists, two theologians—was appointed by the elector to go from parish to parish. They were to make an inventory of church property, examine the clergy, and give instructions as to the conduct of the pastor and the congregation. Provision should be made for the salary of the clergy. The schools should be regulated in regard to teachers and curriculum. Melanchthon drew up the instructions for the visitation; Luther wrote a preface to the articles. The model was later followed in other territories.

The "Loci" and the Catechisms

Among the duties of the visitors was the investigation of the faith of the preachers. In a time of turmoil and controversy, how should one determine the true Gospel that the Church was sent to proclaim? As one of the visitors, Melanchthon was best prepared to give an answer. Already in 1521, he had published a little textbook on the theology taught by the Church of the Reformation. Because it treated each doctrine as a separate topic or place, it was called *Loci* (places). Questions on predestination and the freedom of the will, however, were still debated. Even during the visitation Melanchthon and the Lutheran pastor Johann Agricola could not agree on the relationship of the Law to the teaching of the Gospel, and Luther had to intervene. The need in the churches led Luther to compose two of his most effective and educational works—the Small and Large Catechisms. The two catechisms were produced about the same time, 1528–29; the shorter one was intended for the housefather who should be responsible for the religious instruction of his household. Before the father of the family could do so, he himself would first have to learn from the pastor. In the preface to the Small Catechism Luther exhorted the parish pastor to consider it a primary duty to instruct his people.

From Worms to Augsburg

For a decade the reform movement in Germany was able to carry on. The Edict of Worms, which outlawed and excommunicated Luther, did not stop him due to an unforeseen political situation in imperial affairs. Yet the threat hung over the entire realm for years. Therefore sporadic attempts were made to bring together the forces that opposed the old order. But alliances were complicated by imperial ambitions, by the Peasants' War, and by the lack of agreement among reformers who met at Marburg (1529). Also it was not agreed what exactly was the faith that needed defending. In Brandenburg and Nürnberg, a series of articles had been drawn up, about 1525, known as the Ansbach Articles, which, it was hoped, would define the main doctrines concerned in the reform of church and state. Before the debate at Marburg, leaders in Nürnberg and Saxony had formulated in 1529 another list in the so-called Schwabach Articles. The Marburg conference failed to unify the German and Swiss reformers, but it tended to consolidate the Lutherans so that they realized they would have to stand together when the imperial diet should finally call them to account for their actions.

The summons to a diet where the religious question might be discussed and decided came from Emperor Charles in January 1530. The princes and cities were to be at Augsburg in April. Realizing the importance of the coming diet, the Lutherans prepared their case by preparing the Augsburg Confession, written by Melanchthon. The document was presented to and read before the diet on June 25, 1530. Since he was outlawed by the Edict of Worms, Luther could not come to Augsburg. But he stayed at the nearby Coburg Castle and kept in close touch with the theologians and Saxon officials at the diet. His letters and writings of these days, including an exposition of Psalm 119, reveal his distrust of human power but unconquerable faith in his Lord.

Melanchthon was intent on showing that what had happened since Worms was not heretical. In the Church were grievous abuses that needed reform, and the Church of Rome should be as anxious as the reformers to see these wrongs corrected. Luther felt that Melanchthon treaded softly in presenting the issues, and it was clear that Melanchthon was emphasizing the agreement in doctrine with traditional teachings. At the same time Melanchthon warded off suspicion that the Lutherans were in sympathy with the excesses of the "enthusiasts" or of those who used religious doctrine as an excuse for rebellion. Though relatively brief and sketchy, the articles of the Confession became the charter of the Church of the Lutheran Reformation and for centuries has remained the standard around which a reformed part of Christendom gathers. The Roman theologians at Augsburg replied with a Confutation, and Melanchthon in turn responded with a defense, or Apology, of the Augsburg Confession. The foundation for the Lutheran Confessions was thereby laid at Augsburg.

Before his death, Luther composed a series of doctrinal articles called the Smalcald Articles (1537). In the Augsburg Confession, the Apology, the Smalcald Articles, and the Small and Large Catechisms, the Church of the Lutheran Reformation in Germany had a wealth of material that, along with Melanchthon's *Loci* and Luther's voluminous writings, made it a theologically conscious community. It was necessary for this church to know where it stood, for it had rejected a tradition that in many cases was no longer understood, and it had parted company with a highly organized and powerful hierarchical organization that had, in the eyes of the people, equated itself with the kingdom of God on earth.

CHAPTER THREE

Breakup of Church and State

To gain a fuller appreciation for the changes involved in the Reformation, it is helpful to know more about politics in that era. When Charles V became emperor in 1519, he was under the spell of the first Charles—Charlemagne. He thought that Europe could be one and in partnership with a pope holding sway over a universal Church. That dream had persisted through seven centuries and had been a controlling factor in the Christianizing and civilizing of all the European lands. But while the papacy had gathered strength and, since the days of Gregory VII, had extended its power into every corner of Europe, the empire had vainly tried to exercise sovereignty over lands that were intent on becoming independent nations.

Problems of the Empire

The nineteen-year-old emperor was heir to half of Europe. But such an inheritance also meant involvement in practically all the affairs of Europe so that at every step he would be met by some alliance or other of his opponents. Although the emperor nominally was protector of the church, the pope distrusted the universal pretensions of the empire, and in trying to keep Charles out of Italy, the pope time and again turned to France, Charles's perpetual foe. The German princes wanted no restrictions on their power and had a long list of complaints against both pope and emperor. Only if Charles gave them promises would the Germans allow him the imperial name.

Such was the emperor before whom Luther appeared at Worms in 1521 and from whom Elector Frederick of Saxony was willing to shield Luther. Charles was devout and determined to restore the unity of the church. He was urged on by the pope, Hadrian VI, who demanded the enforcement of the Edict of Worms against Luther. But Charles was not free to act as he wished. The imperial chamber refused to put down evangelical truth without a free and general council, which should be called within a year. When the papal legate objected, the chamber presented him with a list of over a hundred grievances of the German states against the papacy. These *Gravamina* give us a picture of the issues at stake. They include indulgences and dispensations, marriage laws and other legal abuses, bans and interdicts, papal levies in the form of annates and incorporations and new tithes, the extravagances of festivals and pilgrimages, the conduct of priests and monks. Until these conditions were corrected, the German princes were not willing to enforce the edict.

Formation of Alliances

Meanwhile the papal legate had succeeded in stemming the spread of reform in the dominions of Ferdinand of Austria, the brother of Charles, and of the dukes of Bavaria. Catholic princes formed the League of Dessau in 1525, and Protestant princes countered in 1526 with the League of Torgau. Hereby the empire was divided and a fateful schism appeared in German history. At the Diet of Spires in 1526, the emperor could only recognize reality and allow the policy of "whose the territory, his the religion" (*cuius regio eius religio*); in other words, the religion of a province was that of its ruler. For the first time, the Lutherans had some legal rights on which to depend in making reforms. It also meant a control of the church by the secular authority, though this was equally true of both opposing ecclesiastical forces.

In 1531, the Lutherans formed the Smalcald League for their defense. The emperor pinned his hopes on a church council that might settle matters. However, such a council would have to be called by the head of the church, and the pope's political problems were inextricably tangled up with his religious purposes. Charles had other concerns than the papal demands for extirpation of heresy.

The Victory of Charles and the Interim

By diplomacy and force, Emperor Charles improved his position by 1544. For example, a victory over the French gave him the opportunity to bind the French king to aid him against both the Turks and the Protestants and to support the council. The Lutheran movement in Cologne was stopped by the deposition of Herman, the archbishop who had been friendly to it. Then in 1545, the council Charles sought opened at Trent.

The Lutheran cause seemed precarious. It had been winning ground during the truce granted reluctantly by the annual diets and the emperor, but the Smalcald League was not unified. In February 1546, Luther died. Although sickness had weakened him in his later years, he had remained the symbol of the Reformation. His death left the field open for theological differences, and his strong, clear voice no longer rallied divided followers.

At the Diet of Regensburg in 1546, Charles's attitude toward the Lutherans hardened. He refused the request of the Germans for a national council and demanded that the religious reforms be referred to the council then assembling at Trent. A treaty with the pope brought a promise of troops and money. Preparations for attack had been under way, and before the Smalcald League was fully aware of the danger, Charles had overwhelmed their forces. Both Philip of Hesse and the Elector John Frederick were taken prisoner. Duke Maurice of Saxony joined Ferdinand of Austria in the war—the duke was rewarded by the transfer of the elector's title from the defeated John.

Exasperated with papal procedures, the emperor attempted a settlement on his own at the Diet of Augsburg in 1548. The Interim, as the name denotes, was a temporary measure, but its purpose was to allay the religious controversy that was splitting the empire. It proposed measures of reform for clergy, education, and church through visitation and provincial synods. While the cup in Communion and the marriage of priests were conceded to the Protestants, the definition of dogmatic points and the retention of most of the customary ceremonies and festivals made the plan unacceptable. In fact neither party was satisfied. The Romanists objected to a secular authority's interference in religious matters. The Protestants saw no fundamental change in the matters they considered essential. But the emperor was adamant. With the aid of Spanish troops, the Interim was imposed wherever he had power. Though unsuccessful, the Augsburg Interim was another example of the contemporary opinion that the secular power had a responsibility to seek unity in religious matters. There was no difference between Charles's protectorate over the church and the influence that the Protestant princes felt it incumbent on themselves to exert in order to secure peace in their provinces.

While the Roman council was suspended, Paul III died in 1549. The new pope, Julius III, yielded to the emperor and returned the council to Trent. The Germans were to be made to attend and to submit to decisions when reached. In 1552, the Protestants were allowed to state their case. They demanded a free and thorough discussion of the articles in dispute and a ratification of the legal decisions already made in their favor. The Saxon and Württemberg theologians presented separate statements. But the council would not dispute with those who were already adjudged heretics and who would not in advance bind themselves to future resolutions. Charles saw that it was hopeless to expect agreement to be reached by a papal council.

Lutheran Victories at Passau and Augsburg

In the Smalcald War, the emperor had not thought it worthwhile to press the siege of the northern German cities. Even within the conquered territories the Interim had kept alive the flame of rebellion. In 1550, Albert of Prussia, John Albert of Mecklenburg, and Hans of Küstrin (Kostrzyn) formed an alliance to defend Protestantism. The show of force was sufficient to frighten Charles, who released John Frederick and Philip and approved a declaration in 1552 that the peace of the empire was not to be broken for matters of conscience in religious issues. This agreement at Passau between Maurice and Ferdinand of Austria and other princes signaled a weariness on every hand and a desire for peace.

The Peace of Augsburg (1555) therefore marks a significant date in Western history. It was a compromise dictated by the realities of the situation. It did not solve all questions, but it established a new principle according to which further settlements would be made. The unity of Europe was a fiction both in church and empire, and the Peace of Augsburg recognized the fact. Instead of imposing the fiction, the rulers allowed Catholics and Protestants to live together under certain conditions. Freedom of religion was not yet achieved for individuals apart from their political situation. On both sides the medieval tradition of "one state, one religion" persisted, but the significant change was the admission that an external unity could not be enforced on all Christians. Church and state had broken up into churches and states.

Chapter five will continue the story of how the Lutheran Church was organized. However, before continuing that history, it is necessary to describe the spread of the Reformation beyond Germany.

CHAPTER FOUR

The Church Anew, beyond Germany

Bohemia

Bohemia had attempted a reformation a century before Luther, but it ended when the Council of Constance approved the martyrdom of John Hus. The cup of the Lord's Supper became the symbol of the Bohemian Utraquists who defied the Roman hierarchy after Hus's death, contenting themselves with a consistory without a bishop ordained by Rome. But in 1467, another branch of Bohemian Christians—the Brethren—formed their own church, electing bishops by lot.

A Prague Interim of 1549 was no more successful than that of Augsburg, but it united the Lutherans and the conservative Utraquists in the demand that authorities respect the century-old compact by which Bohemian reformers were tolerated by Rome, though separated from it. Unfortunately, the Utraquists and the Brethren could not agree on the Augsburg Confession; instead Protestants in the region drew up the *Confessio Bohemica*, which they presented at a diet. By the end of the sixteenth century, the nobles and burghers of Bohemia and Moravia were predominantly evangelical.

Hungary

In Hungary, the Protestants had some freedom since most of the country was under the Turks, who in the decisive battle of Mohács in 1526 wiped out the nobility. Lutheran teaching had spread among the German settlers in Hungary and also to the Slovaks in the north, the Slovenes in the south, and the Magyars in between. Buda, a former German city on an ancient Roman site, was the official residence of the Turkish governor and also had a German court under Margrave George, who favored the Lutherans. In Pressburg, where a remnant of the old faith and state remained, the

Evangelicals were tolerated in the suburbs of the city. As a rule, the Germans and Slavs were Lutherans, the Magyars Calvinists.

Farther south in Carniola, Primus Truber made Laibach a center for Lutheran preaching until he was forced to flee persecution by a Roman bishop and an Austrian prince. But in Nürnberg and Württemberg, where he found refuge, he pursued a remarkable career in giving his people a Slovenian religious literature. In Lutheran history, the name of Matthias Flacius the "Illyrican" reminds us of evangelical steadfastness in southeastern Europe, for this formidable champion of strict doctrine was a native of these regions.

Poland

Poland, through its connection with Lithuania on the east, had long known that the Orthodox Church, which was not bound to Rome, gave both bread and wine in the Sacrament and did not demand celibacy of all its clergy. From the west had come the persecuted Brethren of Bohemia, whose simple life and organization impressed the Poles. As a result, a tradition of tolerance existed even before Lutheran and Calvinistic teachings reached the land. Lutheranism spread rapidly among the German citizens of the towns and the nobility of old Poland, and they engaged evangelical preachers. Polish students went to Wittenberg and came back as leaders. In Lithuania the Radziwill family was the leader of a Calvinist movement and built a large stone church in Vilna. The clergy were encouraged in further studies, and a school was established in Radziejow. In Poland the Gorka family was Lutheran. Three sons attended Wittenberg, and close contact was established with the leaders in East Prussia. Yet the Roman Church was deeply entrenched in the country. It controlled large estates, and its clergy came from wealthy, aristocratic families.

Riga, Latvia, Estonia

Northward along the Baltic was the region that the Teutonic Knights had ruled until Poland broke their power. Catholic bishops had their seats in Riga, Pilten, Pernau, and Dorpat. Half-Christianized peasants inhabited rude villages. German tradesmen were influential in the few, small cities. Johann Lohmüller, a councilman in Riga, corresponded with Luther as early as 1522; there was preaching of Lutheran doctrine in his church a year earlier. Luther replied by letter in 1523, and in the following year, dedicated a psalm exposition to "the dear friends in Christ in Riga and Livonia." He reminded the council of its threefold responsibility—support of the pastor, ordering of instruction of children, and care of the poor. He wrote again in 1525, emphasizing the importance of concord in the congregation and of congregational worship. The new order in Riga became the example followed farther north as Lutheran preaching reached Latvia and Estonia, together then called Livonia.

Denmark

Christian II was king of Denmark and of the union with Sweden. His rule was unpopular in Sweden. At home he was confiscating the indulgence income for his own use while persuading the pope to place the ban on the Swedish Sture family. When the archbishopric of Lund became vacant, the king opposed the pope's candidate—a cardinal who already held three bishoprics—and appeased the pope by an annual money payment. However, Christian II felt the reform movement might be useful to him. His laws indicated a desire for economic and religious reform, but his methods were inconsistent with his purposes.

Through his uncle, Elector Frederick, Christian II negotiated with Wittenberg, which sent Martin Reinhart and then Karlstadt to Copenhagen, though with little result. The Carmelite monk Paulus Heliae proved more influential. Yet he clashed with the king when it became apparent that Christian II was most concerned about keeping church money from going to Rome and curtailing the wealth and power of the bishops. Then the king's attempt to break the resistance of Sweden by murdering the leaders in the "Stockholm Bloodbath" cost him his crown. His own council forced him into exile in 1523. He fled to Saxony, spent some time in Wittenberg, and was present at Augsburg in 1530, where he swore fealty to the old faith and was promised help by the emperor to regain his throne. A vain attempt at invasion of Norway led to his imprisonment by Frederick, the new king.

The Danish nobles, who in 1523 elected Frederick I as king, wanted a national church independent, as the French, from the papacy. Some like Mogens Gjoe were religiously convinced by Lutheranism, and others saw in the transfer of church property a gain for themselves. The burghers in the cities were favorable to the reform. Frederick was ready to protect the preaching of the Gospel. His daughter was married to Albert of Brandenburg, who made Prussia Lutheran. His son Christian was duke of Schleswig-Holstein, where he brought Lutheran theologians to preach and teach. Through the Haderslev Ordinance of 1528, he made his land the first Lutheran province in the north.

The spiritual leader of the Danish Reformation was Hans Tausen. In 1521, he became professor of theology at Copenhagen but left after King Christian II's flight and spent two years at Wittenberg with Luther (1522–24). On Tausen's homecoming to Antvorskov, he preached a Lutheran sermon during Holy Week 1525, for which his prior put him in a dungeon. When the prior sent him to the prior at Viborg (Finland), it was the prior instead of Tausen who changed his stand. A seminary was established for the training of pastors. Tausen also enjoyed the protection of Frederick, who in 1526 named him as chaplain.

King Frederick's stand at the Diet of Odense in 1526 revealed his sympathy for the new order. When criticized for his position, he defended the preaching of the Gospel. He won the friendship of the new archbishop of Lund, and his council agreed that henceforth the confirmation of bishops should be sought from Lund, not Rome.

Norway and Iceland

Norway's dependence on Denmark and the Hanseatic League stood in the way of its growth. Quarrels among the ruling class and the effects of the Black Death further reduced it to a secondary role in the Scandinavian Union. The course of the reform followed closely that of Denmark. Frederick I permitted Lutheran preaching in Bergen, a Hanseatic city, around 1525. When Denmark adopted its new ordinance, its provisions were applied also in Norway; the old bishops were deposed and new superintendents elected, the church's property was confiscated, and the clergy made dependent on state grants. Danish superintendents, teachers, and officials brought in the Danish liturgy, Bible, and hymnals. Popular resistance was limited to revolts against the removal of images and relics from the churches. It would require years to change the religious instruction of the nation, but the foundation was laid in these years for a close relationship between Lutheranism in Norway and Denmark.

Similarly, Iceland received the new forms of church life from Denmark. The two Roman bishops were forcibly removed from office. One was deported to Denmark, the other was executed in Holar in 1550. An Icelandic New Testament was printed in Copenhagen in 1540. The deepening of a religious consciousness consonant with Reformation teaching occurred in Iceland, as in Denmark and Norway, in a later period.

Sweden

In Sweden, too, the disintegration of the traditional Roman power was related to political events. The hated Danish rule, which had culminated in the Stockholm Massacre, called forth a popular uprising among nobility and a strong, independent peasantry. In 1523, Gustavus Vasa emerged as the leader and was elected king after he had driven the Danes out of Sweden. Intent on building up a strong monarchy, the king had to settle accounts with the hierarchy that often had been in collusion with the Danish crown. The church owned almost half the wealth of the country, and men such as Bishop Brask of Linköping wielded both secular and spiritual power. Gustavus found help in another direction.

Olavus Petri, after studies in the monastic school of his home city Örebro and at Uppsala, had gone to Leipzig and then Wittenberg. He seems to have been in Wittenberg at the time of the Ninety-five Theses, for he received his bachelor's degree there in 1516 and his master's in 1518. His later writings show the influence of Luther's teaching of grace, the Bible, and the need of the vernacular. He had learned of Luther's challenge of the supremacy of the papacy, and, like Luther, Olavus came to consider the papacy nonessential to the unity of the Church. On his return to Sweden, he became chancellor to Matthias the bishop of Strengnäs, and a close friend of the archdeacon, Laurentius Andreae, who also had studied abroad and had witnessed the conflict of pope and secular authorities. Bishop Matthias was among the victims of the massacre, but Olavus stayed on and soon attracted attention by his sermons against the Mass, monks, confession, and the worship of the saints. After his coronation in Strengnäs, Gustavus took Laurentius along to Stockholm as his chancellor and there installed Olavus as pastor of the city church and secretary of the city council. Half the townsmen were Germans, and a German pastor preached to them.

In late 1523, relations with the papacy ceased. Christ, Gustavus asserted, was the supreme pontiff. Taxes were levied on the churches, and troops were quartered in monasteries. Bishop Brask tried to resist, but in vain. The king encouraged Lutheran preaching and literature, even commanding a New Testament translation. The character of the Reformation in Sweden was determined to a great extent by the varied literature produced by Olavus.

The progress of the royal program was impeded by a series of rebellions both in the north and in the south, but by the time of the Diet of Västeras in 1527, Gustavus had established his supremacy. Evangelical bishops replaced the conservative ones as vacancies occurred. A brother of Olavus, Laurentius Petri, was named the new archbishop—the former one had fled—and he officiated at the marriage of the king to a German Protestant princess in 1531. The relations of king and reformers were often strained in the following years. Olavus did not hesitate to criticize Gustavus and his excessive measures. Olavus and Laurentius were even threatened with death sentences. Both Olavus and Laurentius died in 1552, the king in 1560. During their lifetime, Sweden had passed from a Danish and Roman dependency to an independent nation with a firmly established evangelical church.

Finland

Reform in Finland, a province of Sweden, stood in close relationship to that of the Swedish Church. Through his lieutenants, Gustavus insured for the royal treasury the income of such church property as he believed was beyond the needs of the church. Martin Skytte, the bishop of Abo (Turku) from 1528 to 1550, was a former Dominican monk from Sigtuna. A humanist and a moderate Romanist, he encouraged young men to go to Wittenberg to study, with the result that several of them became the leaders of the evangelical reform in Finland. Foremost among them was Michael Agricola, who earned a recommendation from Luther. Lutheran in his teaching, he also displayed interest in mysticism, in the early pagan religion of his homeland, and in the spiritualism of Schwenkfeld. His theology was a blend of humanism and the evangelical faith, tolerant of both the old practices and the various expressions of the new.

When Agricola was made bishop of Abo, a second diocese was established at Viborg (Viipuri) near the Russian border. A native of Viborg, Paul Juusten, who also had been at Wittenberg in 1543–46 through Bishop Skytte's patronage, was made rector of the cathedral school at Abo and in 1554 the first bishop of Viborg, later transferring to Abo. What Olavus Petri and Laurentius Andreae did for the spiritual nurture of the people of Sweden during the transition from a Roman to an evangelical community, Agricola and Juusten accomplished in Finland.

CHAPTER FIVE

The Constitution of the Lutheran Church

Having surveyed the development and spread of the Reformation, this chapter returns to the earlier theme of reorganization in church life and practice. Luther opposed the age-old hierarchical Church of Rome on fundamental points of doctrine and organization. The necessary consequence for the followers of the reformers was to build a new organization and to restate the message of the Church. Theologians played a significant part, but since the refashioning of Christ's Church involved the vast property and power of the medieval bishoprics and monasteries as well as the maintenance of education and public order, the participation of the magistrates was inevitable. The Lutheran Church that gradually took shape resulted from the interaction and cooperation between theological teachers and administrators on the one hand, and princes and city leaders on the other. By the end of the century the new forms were firmly fixed.

Melanchthon

Second only to Luther in the reformation of the Church stood Philip Melanchthon. Related on his mother's side to the great Hebrew scholar Reuchlin and drawn through his education to Erasmus, the foremost humanist of the day, Melanchthon became a classical scholar of great distinction. Reuchlin recommended him as professor of Greek and Hebrew at the new university in Wittenberg. Melanchthon's biblical learning and humanistic spirit earned him the admiration of Luther, who proved himself a loyal friend through the many years they labored together at Wittenberg.

Melanchthon was a careful, cautious scholar. He lacked Luther's depth, emotional power, and personal experience of faith. Yet he agreed with Luther's concept of the Word as the final authority and tried to explain the contents of faith in clear and convincing style. In 1521, he produced the first theological textbook of the Reformation, the *Theological Commonplaces* (*Loci Communes*). As the events around him revealed the various ways the Reformation might go, Melanchthon became apprehensive. The Zwickau prophets and the Peasants' War caused him to stress the necessity of order and obedience to government. He hoped a reform in the papal church would heal the divisions already evident, and even at Augsburg in 1530, when he drew up the Confession and the Apology, he thought in terms of reconciliation and restoration of unity. Scholars are still divided as to the real position of Melanchthon on several points of doctrine because it is hard to distinguish between his own thought and his official statements as spokesman of the Lutherans.

Melanchthon functioned as the schoolteacher of the Reformation. Despite his deficiencies as a leader, he rendered incalculable service at a critical period in the history of the Church. His pen framed the Augustana and the Apology, which gave the new movement solid ground to stand on in the battle. His textbook of theology, in many and enlarged editions, became the theology of generations of pastors and teachers. His methods became standard in the schools of Germany and beyond, and his reforms reshaped universities—Wittenberg, Leipzig, Tübingen, Greifswald, Rostock, Heidelberg, Marburg, Königsberg. His interest in the natural sciences gave them new importance, and his devotion to Aristotle was lifelong. It is impossible to conceive of the Reformation without Luther, but it is hard to imagine how the spiritual power of Luther's teaching would have been conserved and channeled into permanent and fructifying streams of influence without the mental clarity of Melanchthon.

Corpus Doctrinae

As noted earlier, the Peace of Augsburg in 1555 guaranteed legal toleration for the Lutheran churches, which were identified by their adherence to the Augsburg Confession of 1530. But in the twenty-five years that had elapsed many questions had arisen to which theologians gave different answers. Who decided the right answer? As long as Luther lived, his personal authority could be appealed to, but after his death controversy arose as to what he would have held. Melanchthon died in 1560, and a second generation came on the scene. Thus in the quarter century following the Peace of Augsburg the churches of the Augsburg Confession gradually reached sufficient agreement to embody their teachings in a commonly accepted document called the Formula of Concord, included in the Book of Concord. Since the Book of Concord has served as the basic theological foundation of the Lutheran Church during the succeeding centuries, we note the particular problems to which it offered the solution.

Three theological questions had begun to agitate the leaders of the various territorial churches. They were connected with the great issues that Luther had raised in his criticism of the papal church and medieval theology. One issue was a cluster of questions about justification. We have seen how this was at the heart of Luther's teaching; man is justified, or declared righteous, not by any merit or works of his own but by the work of Christ whose grace he receives in faith. Out of this statement some questions emerged: Is man fallen in sin totally corrupt? Can he do anything of his own will to come to faith? When God declares a believer righteous, is it because of his faith or because Christ already dwells within him? Do good works play any part in justification? Is the Christian still under the Law? All these points somehow relate to the central doctrine of justification. A second significant source of difference was the doctrine of the Lord's Supper. The Lutherans rejected the Roman theory of the Supper as a sacrifice and of a change of bread and wine into the body and blood of Christ, but they also refused to endorse the Zwinglian idea of the Supper as a memorial feast with no real presence of Christ. This led to questions of how Christ is present in the Supper and to a renewed study of the old problem of the relationship of the divine and human natures in Christ. The third grouping of controversial points dealt with *adiaphora*, or matters in which Christians may have freedom, especially the question of ceremonies and usages that had been raised by the Interim.

After Luther's death, the peril of division among the Lutheran churches was evident as parties began to form and attack one another. One party was led by Matthias Flacius and assumed to speak for Luther. It was called the "genuine" or "authentic" (*Gnesio*) Lutheran group. Another followed the spirit of Melanchthon, though claiming to be no less Lutheran. They were called "Philippists." The parties did not agree on all matters among themselves, but in general they were unified enough not to cause serious ruptures. Sometimes their quarrels had to be stopped by the authorities. Indeed it was the secular rulers who were most intent on finding a basis of unity. This was achieved through the Formula of Concord.

The Book of Concord and Its Acceptance

The Formula asserted that the three Ecumenical Creeds, the Augsburg Confession, the Apology, the Smalcald Articles, and the Catechisms of Luther were the basic confessions of the Lutherans. With the Formula, these were now brought together in one volume as the Book of Concord and published in a German text in June 1580, the fiftieth anniversary of the Augsburg Confession. A Latin text followed in 1584, written by Lukas Osiander and corrected first by Nicholas Selnecker and then by Martin Chemnitz. The introduction to the Formula became the introduction for the whole book. An appendix containing a series of quotations from the

Fathers was designed to show the connection between the Concordia and the theology of the Early Church.

Not all the territories that subscribed to the 1530 confession set their names to the document of 1580. A new generation had come on the scene, and new alignments had been created in the crowded years. While the Formula united many Lutheran provinces and cities, it alienated those who favored reconciliation with the Calvinists.

Outside Germany, Lutheran countries were not at first concerned. The arguments had been among German theologians, and the Formula was a solution for them. Denmark and Norway had adopted an ordinance in 1537 that made the Gospel the basis of preaching; in 1574 the Augsburg Confession was recognized as a confessional norm. The Church Law of 1683 specified the Scriptures, the three Ecumenical Symbols, the Augustana, and the Small Catechism as the confessional standard. At the Council of Uppsala in 1593, Sweden adopted the Augustana and the three Ecumenical Symbols. In the Church Law of 1686, Sweden bound all inhabitants to the Scriptures, the three ancient creeds, and the Augustana as this was "explained in the so-called Book of Concord." Both in Sweden and in Finland the orthodox party had urged the adoption of the Formula, and in practice the Book of Concord had been considered the norm for preaching since the Manual of 1614. A royal decree in 1663, adopted by the diet in 1664, prepared the way for the Church Law regarding the Book of Concord.

As the Roman Church had its decrees and canons of Trent, so the Lutherans now had their standard of teaching. The nature and scope of the norm had been determined by the religious discussions of the years since 1517. The authors of the Formula emphasized that the document answered the questions that had been raised among the reformers. It was proof of the fact that they had not departed from what was declared at the Diet of Augsburg. The Augsburg Confession defined the differences between the Lutherans and the papal church. The Book of Concord set forth the statement of agreement within the Lutheran Church. Sadly, intrigue and violence would soon test the biblically-based peace and unity the Lutherans achieved through the Book of Concord.

CHAPTER SIX

The Appeal to Arms

When in 1619 the election of an emperor took place on the death of Matthias, three of the electors were Protestant. Frederick III of the Palatinate was a Calvinist. His province had turned from Catholicism in 1546, but in the bitter strife between Lutherans and Calvinists, the latter emerged victorious and in 1563 adopted the Heidelberg Catechism, a moderately Calvinistic confession. Elector Frederick IV became fearful of the advances of the Austrian and Bavarian leaders and of the Catholic League that Maximilian of Bavaria had organized in 1609. He attempted a counter league of Protestants, but since Saxony refused to join, it became mainly a Calvinist alliance. Brandenburg was an important fortress of Lutheranism but in 1614 its ruler, Elector John Sigismund, turned Calvinist. He changed the religious status of his territory and adopted a policy of toleration of dissent.

Only John George of Saxony was Lutheran and also elector. He was looked upon as a leader of the Lutheran cause, for his land was stronger than Hesse, Württemberg, and Anhalt to the south, or Brunswick, Mecklenburg, and Holstein to the north. But he disliked change and was content to live by the Augsburg arrangements. Respect for the law of the empire was fundamental with him, and so he would follow a properly elected Catholic emperor. If he could hold Saxony to its usual course, he would not consider it his duty to defend Lutheranism elsewhere. His fondness for drink made him hard to deal with, but the emperor could count on his loyalty to the imperial constitution.

The Thirty Years' War

As Protestants everywhere feared, the Hapsburg ruler Ferdinand II, who had been elected king of Bohemia in 1617, was chosen emperor in 1619. Bohemia was ripe for revolt against the Hapsburgs, and rather than accept the new ruler, the Protestants of Prague threw his deputies out of the council windows. Instead of Ferdinand they invited the Calvinist elector of the Palatinate, Frederick V, to be their king. Their revolt began the

Thirty Years' War, in which all of Europe become involved before settling the religious question.

Ferdinand's army gained the upper hand. At "the peak of the Catholic tide," Ferdinand issued in 1629 the Edict of Restitution. By it the Calvinists were to have no legal rights, all lands acquired by the Protestants since the Peace of Passau in 1552 would go back to the Roman Church, and the emperor's will was to transcend any previous legal decisions. Ferdinand meant to establish himself as emperor and ruler of a Roman Catholic Europe as defined before the Peace of Augsburg. The power to enforce his decree lay in Albrecht Wallenstein's army.

But at last the Hapsburg dynasty had overplayed itself. Even the Catholic princes feared their arrogant new general, Wallenstein, and his marauding troops who lived off the plunder of lands they traversed. The princes concerned with the constitution of the empire resisted Ferdinand's reckless violation of their rights. It was a bad time for Ferdinand to ask that his son be declared his successor, and even the dismissal of Wallenstein failed to win this goal. The Edict of Restitution, however, had proved effective enough to rouse the neutral Protestants to active opposition. Hope for the Protestant cause now depended on the north—the king of Sweden.

Gustavus Adolphus

In the century since Gustavus Vasa inaugurated a new era, Sweden had extended its power beyond Finland by winning new lands at the expense of Russia. On the breakup of the Teutonic Knights, Sweden had gained Estonia in 1561. The war with Poland over Sigismund's claim to the Swedish crown moved from Sweden to the shores of the Baltic. Gustavus Adolphus (b. 1594) secured from Russia all the lands along the Gulf of Finland, but in the contest with Poland he met the resistance of Protestant burghers of Riga and Danzig, who saw their commerce threatened. The Swedish king was a brother-in-law of the elector of Brandenburg who, technically a vassal of Poland, was unwilling to become embroiled in a war between a Protestant relation and a Catholic overlord. Yet Gustavus, with reluctant aid from Denmark, held his own and was more than a match for Wallenstein in the port city of Stralsund.

In 1630, at the low point of Protestant power in Europe, Gustavus Adolphus decided to enter the German scene. He came too late to prevent the Count of Tilly, commander of the Catholic League forces, from destroying Magdeburg, but that fearful catastrophe finally brought Frederick William of Brandenburg and John George of Saxony to Gustavus's side. At Breitenfeld, a few miles from Leipzig, the military genius of the Swedish army overcame the great Tilly in September 1631. The Protestant cause was saved.

From Breitenfeld Gustavus moved south in a triumphant march, spending the winter at Mainz. In the spring he entered Bavaria and would have gone on to Vienna after the death of Tilly at the battle of Lech, but the frantic emperor recalled Wallenstein, and at Lützen the "deliverer" from Sweden lost his own life in November 1632. The Swedish army carried on under Chancellor Axel Oxenstierna until his defeat at Nordlingen in 1634. Wallenstein was assassinated and the command of the Catholic armies passed to the young heirs of Austria and Spain. Despite the general desire for peace and the projected peace at Prague in 1635, which would have restored the situation of 1627, the war went on for more than a decade longer.

Devastation and Peace

The devastation of Germany, Bohemia, and Austria was indescribable. For two decades cities were plundered, the countrysides ravaged, populations scattered; tens of thousands died of plague, hunger, and wounds of war.

It is difficult to assess the religious character of religious wars. Although there were pastors who labored heroically to minister to decimated congregations—also religious books and hymns date from this period—war is not religious, and every church suffered. The mixture of political and religious motives in the rulers cannot be accurately estimated. At times Lutherans fought Lutherans under Catholic rulers; at other times Catholic leaders and generals easily transferred to the Protestant side. The exemplary discipline of the Swedish army did not survive Gustavus, and a mercenary spirit permeated all the military forces. Political rulers were never sure of their generals, who might easily be bribed.

Only one permanent gain came out of the eventual peace. People everywhere perceived that religion was not a proper cause for warfare. The Treaty of Westphalia (1648) finally gave legal recognition to Calvinism. It allowed Protestants to retain all they held on January 1, 1624.

Lutheran Lands

The settlement after the war prefigured the limits of the Lutheran Church. The Roman Church prevailed in the south, where Austria and Bavaria would block advance of the Lutheran Church, and on the west the power of France forbade its expansion. After the revocation of the Edict of Nantes in 1685 and the expulsion of several hundred thousand Huguenots, France was again Roman Catholic. The Swiss Cantons and the Netherlands were divided between the Calvinists and the Catholics. England developed its own forms of Protestantism in which after Archbishop Cranmer's time Lutheran influence was slight. Central Germany and Scandinavia remained the hearth of the Church of the Lutheran Reformation, though divided into fragmentary units.

For a brief period Sweden maintained its role as a European power, enlarging its domain at the expense of Denmark, which lost its three provinces in southern Sweden, and of Norway, which gave up a border province to the victorious neighbor. And for a while Lutheranism followed the Swedish conquests around the Baltic: Estonia, Latvia, and Courland were taken from Poland; Karelia, Ingria, and Keksholm were acquired from Russia. But the meteoric career of Charles XII of Sweden ended in disaster, and Sweden lost its Baltic possessions. The Russian absolutism of Peter the Great—even in his control of the church—and the Roman Catholicism of Poland left little room for Protestantism in the east. Only in the Prussian territory regained from Sweden and expanded by the partition of Poland did Lutheranism find protection.

At the beginning of the eighteenth century, the Lutheran Church found itself established in Scandinavia and northern and central Germany. Lutheranism and Calvinism had won equal rights with the Church of Rome; but unlike Rome, neither the Reformed nor the Lutherans had a single capital. As yet they depended on secular authority for external power—no less than the Roman dioceses. All that bound the Lutherans together was a common faith expressed in a simple manner in Luther's Catechism and more fully in the Book of Concord. In Denmark, Norway, Sweden-Finland, and in all the German territories, secular authorities regulated the church by comprehensive ordinances that spelled out the worship, education, discipline, and pastoral care of the congregations. Orthodoxy could be rigid, but it achieved a definiteness and singleness of purpose that preserved the Church in perilous days.

CHAPTER SEVEN

The Universal Priesthood and Pietism

The devastation of the Thirty Years' War was spiritual as well as physical. In congregations the contrast between orthodoxy as it was taught and the actual spiritual condition of the people deeply disturbed earnest souls, both clerical and lay. Faithful preachers strongly criticized the formal devotions of the church member whose life was a denial of his faith. Drunkenness, sexual license, material greed, ever-present vices, were multiplied by the breakup of family and community relationships while armies ravaged the countryside. Congregations were leaderless, pastors poorly educated, schools closed or deteriorated. The scholastic debates in the universities were of little interest or edification to the average layman.

Devotional Literature

Many spiritually concerned people found comfort in a type of literature outside the orthodox dogmatics. Long before the Reformation, a mystical literature had flourished whose content reflected the writings of Augustine, Bernard of Clairvaux, Johannes Tauler, Thomas à Kempis, and other medieval German and Dutch authors. This literature continued to have a place in Lutheran circles, especially through popular prayer books and books of devotion. Johann Arndt, a Lutheran pastor in Germany (1555–1621), combined this stress on a mystical union with Christ and on Lutheran teaching in his *Four Books on True Christianity* (1606). This book spread rapidly, was soon translated into other languages, and profoundly influenced the evangelical churches. It called for a practical Christianity—the true faith as opposed to mere assent to a system of articles of faith.

Spener and Franke

Philipp Jacob Spener (1635–1705) had been affected early in his life by Arndt's *True Christianity* and the writings of the Puritan Richard Baxter. Following Spener's studies at the University of Strasbourg, he visited

Geneva, where the discipline of the Calvinist congregation impressed him greatly. At Frankfort he became senior pastor in 1666 and attempted to raise the level of congregational life in the Lutheran churches.

Of greater importance was Spener's practice of arranging small gatherings of interested members for the reading of the Bible and doctrinal literature and for discussion of the religious life. In 1675, he published a book that made him famous and started a movement that spread throughout the Lutheran Church. It was the *Pia desideria* (Devout Desires). In this book Spener voiced his criticism of the low estate of the church. He called for better preaching, improved education and discipline of pastors, less polemics, and more edifying sermons. He appealed to the spiritual priesthood of believers, calling on the laity to witness to the faith by the quality of their lives. He believed the teaching of smaller groups would get closer to the people and their needs, thus defending his conventicles. In short, Spener desired an emphasis on sanctification that would balance the orthodox teaching of justification.

Never popular in his pastorates, Spener nevertheless exerted profound influence through his personal friendships, a huge correspondence, and able followers. In Dresden and Berlin he found men who carried his ideas still further and even saved them from consequences he came to fear. His most successful disciple was August Hermann Francke (1663–1727), who had come under Spener's spell as a student and who was a member of Bible study groups while a teacher at Leipzig. Francke himself had experienced a sudden conversion; he made this a model of Christian experience. Conversion, further, seemed to him a prerequisite of theological leadership, more important than the objective study of theology. Accordingly Francke incurred the hostility of the orthodox leader, the younger Johann Carpzov at Leipzig, and was forced to leave first Leipzig, then Erfurt. But through Spener he found a place at Halle, and this he made a great center of Pietism.

Pietism in Germany

At Glaucha, near Halle, Francke demonstrated his powers as preacher and spiritual advisor. Sin and grace was his constant theme in sermons, catechization, prayer services, and private confession. Content was more important to him than form—what he sought was conversion and edification. At the university in Halle he defended himself and like-minded colleagues, such as Joachim Lange. To the orthodox it seemed that the extreme emphasis on conversion and individual experience meant a decline in the significance of the church and the clergy. Christianity became a private matter; the church became a collection of like-minded people with common religious experiences. The aversion to the world characteristic of many Pietists looked like a renunciation of learning and culture, a disregard of beauty in nature and art, and a denial of responsibility for a social and economic order. Introspection, the keeping of diaries, and interest in emotional satisfaction all looked like the emergence of a new type of piety.

Francke, full of confidence and unconcerned about opposition, showed the fruits of his faith in the institutions he founded at Halle such as the "Waisenhaus" (home and school for orphans). On graduation the children went to the far corners of the world bearing the Gospel in the form they had learned it at Halle. The priesthood of believers had found expression—here the laity were not objects of the ministry of the church but active subjects in it.

The spread of the Pietistic Movement in the first half of the eighteenth century bears witness not only to the inherent energy of its members but also to its relationship to the orthodoxy then dominant in the churches of the Reformation. Many princes were attracted to Spener and Francke, for they saw the need of improved conditions in their churches and schools and preferred Spener's and Francke's programs to the theological controversies that divided the people.

Pietism in Denmark, Norway, Iceland

Frederick IV of Denmark, though himself loose in life and morals, welcomed friends of the Pietistic Movement. Through his court preacher, R. J. Lütkens, the king not only gave status to pietistic preachers in the churches of Denmark and Schleswig but also had his name associated with the beginning of overseas missions by the Lutheran Church, for from Halle he secured the pioneer missionaries to the Danish possessions in India. To his reign also belongs the beginning of missionary work in Norwegian Lappland through the Pietist Thomas von Westen. In far-off Greenland a mission was established by Hans Egede and his sons, though this Norwegian pastor counted himself among the orthodox. In Denmark itself leaders in state and church were themselves Pietists or friendly to them. An orphan home modeled after Halle cared for children but also served as a center for the printing of Bibles, hymnbooks, and devotional materials. Pietist interest in education contributed to the establishment of hundreds of new schools—though it was not possible to reach the goal of a school in every parish—to facilitate the reading of religious literature by all.

In two areas are names of enduring significance. The first was Eric Pontoppidan, court preacher in Copenhagen and later bishop of Bergen in Norway. His exposition of Luther's Small Catechism, entitled *Truth unto Righteousness*, proved to be for many generations a national reader in

Denmark and Norway. Comparable to Pontoppidan's influence was that of a hymnwriter, Hans Adolf Brorson, bishop of Ribe. A lyric poet, he sang of the inner experiences of the believer in a way that made him the classic hymnist of Danish-Norwegian Christendom.

Sweden and Finland

Pietism in Sweden followed a unique course. Although Spener's royal acquaintances and well-wishers included Queen Ulrika Eleonora of Sweden, theologian J. F. Mayer (a most violent anti-Pietist) affected the early policy of the government toward the innovators. Yet Pietism got through the walls raised against it by the leaders of church and state.

Over a dozen Swedish students were at Halle in 1694, among them Nils Grubb, who later made his parish in Umea a Pietist center. The German congregation in Karlskrona offered another port of entry. In Stockholm a group of laymen, among them government officials, were meeting with returning Halle students, and on Wednesday and Friday evenings they engaged in Bible study, prayer, hymn singing, and discussion of the spiritual life. They were in correspondence with Francke, who assured them that he wanted no new doctrine but only that the true doctrine express itself in good works.

But the revival in Sweden received new force from an unusual direction. After the defeat of Charles XII at Poltova, more than thirty thousand Swedish prisoners were quartered in Russia, mainly in Siberia. Children of orthodoxy, these lonely exiles sought comfort in religion. In Siberia a Pietist, Josiah Cederhielm, served as leader. In Tobolsk a school was organized and attracted even Russian youth. When finally in 1724, the last prisoner had been released, it was found that hardly five thousand had survived to return home. Among them were ardent Pietists who carried the message of faith active in works back to their parishes.

Pietists were willing to make alliance with governments in their opposition to orthodoxy. However, to the Swedish Lutheran no less than to the French Catholic of the seventeenth century, it was inconceivable that a nation could survive if differences in faith were allowed. When the Pietists threatened the unity of the church, orthodoxy called on the government to forbid private gatherings in the Conventicle Act of 1721. Through the bishops of the dioceses the church retained a uniformity of practice that drove the movement underground except where a bishop such as Andrew Rydelius in Lund was sympathetic. For there were, even among the leaders, those who desired some of the changes for which Pietism clamored.

Finnish as well as Swedish soldiers followed Charles XII to his victories and his defeats. They, too, returning from Russia, called for a more spiritual life in the congregations. In the cataclysm of war, laymen had to be put into vacant parishes, but this exercise of the universal priesthood was unfortunate because these men were ill prepared for the ministry and hard to remove from the parishes after the war. In its early phases Pietism in Finland blended with orthodoxy to produce a milder form of conservatism.

Pietism in Eastern Europe

While under the Swedish government, the churches of Estonia and Latvia felt the force of orthodoxy as maintained by the Swedish bishops. But Ernest Glück, awakened by Spener's writings, enjoyed the encouragement of the sympathetic general superintendent Johann Fischer in translating the Bible into Latvian by 1689 and the support of the Swedish government in its publication. An Estonian translation was made about the same time, but it was not until 1715 that an Estonian New Testament was printed. The entire Bible was available in 1739. Meanwhile, Charles XII had met defeat, and Estonia and Latvia were brought under Russian rule. Peter the Great allowed the churches many privileges as he put them under the control of a governor in Moscow. Indeed Pietism had greater freedom than under Swedish orthodoxy. In 1736, a former student of Francke, Jacob Benjamin Fischer, was the general superintendent of Latvia. Literature and schoolteachers from Halle contributed to the development of the religious life in the Baltic provinces as they broke ties with Sweden.

In Poland, Bohemia, and Hungary, the Hapsburgs were engaged in eradicating all Lutheranism in the period of the spread of Pietism. But on the edge of their domains, fronting Turkish-held territories, Slovaks and Magyars kept in touch with centers of the evangelical world. John Burius was ministering around Pressburg (Bratislava). His son was in contact with Jena and Halle. The eminent historian and geographer Mattias Bel had studied at Halle. He and the Slovak superintendent Daniel Krman made available for the Slovak Lutherans an edition of the Bohemian Brethren-sponsored Kralice Bible that was used into the twentieth century. Pastor Elias Milec wrote pietistic literature in his native Slovak language. A name of honor in this region was that of the Magyar nobleman Georg Bárány who had studied at Halle and was ordained in 1711. His ministry extended to Germans and Magyars, Lutherans and Reformed. His educational interests brought the rite of confirmation and Halle pedagogy to Hungarian churches. It was from this corner of the European world that the Pietism of Spener and Francke was to be challenged and both orthodoxy and Pietism were to be influenced.

Zinzendorf

In Silesia, which had escaped the fate of Bohemia and Hungary by being transferred to Saxony, a colony of Bohemian Brethren found a refuge on the estate of Nikolaus Ludwig Zinzendorf (1700–60). Zinzendorf was of a Lutheran family in Dresden and educated at Halle. Unlike Francke, he did not stress the necessity of penitence but rejoiced in a personal love of Jesus, which for him was the supreme teaching of Scripture. He thought of this love as actually being present in all churches whatever their other differences, and bringing them together was his consuming ambition. The colony of Herrnhut was to be the center of a worldwide community from which he would go in all directions, even to America, and his diaspora emissaries would go, two by two, wherever they could awaken faith in the beloved Jesus. Lutherans, Reformed, Brethren—all were in Herrnhut, and the Moravian, or Herrnhut, congregation was to include them all. The peculiar preaching of Zinzendorf's disciples followed his concentration on the wounds of Christ, the blood of the Lamb, and the redemption of the world. In 1748, Zinzendorf visited German immigrants in America, where Muhlenberg publicly denied him the name Lutheran. During his lifetime Zinzendorf sent out over two hundred missionaries. Their influence was widely felt.

The movement eventuated in a new church of the "Unity of the Brethren" with representative congregations both in Europe and in America. The emotional extravagances of the movement burst into full flower in Herrnhut, causing a reaction that threatened its survival. A more sober Zinzendorf salvaged his plans, but the dream of a new church of the Lamb throughout the earth had vanished.

Radical Pietism

Pietism had in fact stirred into life other latent forces that confused the Church in its judgment of the program of Spener and Francke. By the time of Zinzendorf's death the movement had lost momentum in Lutheran lands, and the radical element of Pietism had drifted away from the Church to new ideas of the times. But the orthodoxy of a previous century was also gone. In indirect ways the currents started by Spener had penetrated all Lutheran lands and continued to produce results in theology and practice.

Fruits of Pietism

Willingly or unwillingly, the leaders of the churches in Lutheran lands had conceded the validity of much of pietistic criticism. The movement had pointed to the unworthy character of many pastors and the uninspired routine of their labors. It had asked for better pastoral care, better sermons, better teaching in the parish schools. It had demanded a Christian activity as a sign of Christian life. The extent of devotional material in the hands of the laity was amazing, and the conventicles centered on the study of Scripture.

Many and salutary as the fruits were, it must be admitted that Pietism's intense concentration on the religious experience of the individual limited the application of the Word of God. The gap between the Church and the world, caused by the development of a secular culture and state, was widened by the withdrawal of Pietist conventicles into their own associations as they waited for the end of the world.

The Western world, which orthodoxy had tried to hold together by encompassing all the estates of society within a religious system, fell apart. The new theories of the state, grounding human government on natural law newly separated from theology, gave man the right to order secular affairs by his own reason. The churches would be left to their own devices. And since the religious experiences of Pietists cut across confessional lines, a fellowship of Christians of various confessions was possible. In state and church a new spirit of toleration was growing—to have profound effects on both.

CHAPTER EIGHT

New Ideas of Man and Society

The intellectual revolution made the latter half of the eighteenth century a period of confusion and religious decline in Europe. The training of the clergy suffered, a large part receiving little university training. The dominant interest in economics, agriculture, and commerce made the pastor's position one of community leadership in secular affairs and public health. In the rural regions the pastor was subject to the demands of a people less and less interested in Church and Sacraments. The festive rites were turned into social events—Baptisms, confirmations, marriages, burials transferred from the sanctuary to the homes. For all the talk about reason, the times showed an astounding interest in the secret societies, especially Masonry. The liturgical life of the church was at a low ebb. In general the cultured class looked condescendingly on the ministry. A rising interest in philanthropic programs—the care of the sick, the poor, and the prisoners—ran parallel to rather than through the churches. Indifference marked the age as much as tolerance, and government regulation of the church was taken for granted. But even this had its limits, as the attempts of Frederick of Prussia to enforce either union or conformity in Brandenburg demonstrated.

Rationalism and Biblical Faith

The gradual adoption of reason as authoritative was considered an enlightening of man in his search for truth and gave to the movement the name of the Enlightenment, in contrast to the enlightening orthodoxy attributed to the Holy Spirit. In reaction to the new fashion of thought, German theologians such as Christian Wolff and Johann Semler conceded the place of reason, and the term "neology" was applied to this school of thought. But as the more radical teachers such as Hermann Reimarus, author of the *Wolfenbütler Fragmente*, discarded much of traditional theology, conservative teachers advanced the claims of revelation in matters beyond reason. The term "supranaturalists" described people who insisted that the Scriptures brought to mankind what the mind of man could not contrive and urged that there is a truth above the natural with which reason can deal.

Underneath the superficiality, the materialism, and the skepticism of the age of reason, there were, however, currents of biblical faith and true religion. As the churches became tools of secular governments and societies of like-minded individuals, men and women still found enlightenment and strength in obedience to the call of God in Word and Sacrament.

The Enlightenment in Denmark

From Christian Wolff's lectures at Halle, Danish students brought the ideas of the Enlightenment back to Denmark. Some of them had already been spread in broader circles by writings of Pontoppidan. His interest in nature, with its proofs of design only a provident God could have created, had opened the eyes of many to the mysteries of the world around them. With G. W. Leibniz and Wolff, he held to a God-given revelation, but reason, too, was a gift by which to appreciate what was revealed. Students at the University of Copenhagen heard the same message from Rosenstand-Goiske. The atonement was necessary, he held, because of the distance between the ideal and the actual. A common trait in all these influential thinkers was their belief that they were combating the agnostic tendency of Deism. They were using the weapons of reason against those whose reason had driven them to unbelief.

The effect of the new movement on the life of the Church can be traced in the careers of N. E. Balle and Christian Bastholm. Balle was a supranaturalist who hoped to retain the old while adopting the new. His doctrinal textbook of 1791 followed an orthodox outline, but the major emphasis was on the moral virtues. Bastholm, the most admired preacher of his generation and author of a textbook on preaching, expressed in 1785 his views on the nature of worship in a proposed liturgy. The service should be short, interesting, moving. Material from the Old Testament or confessional dogmatics should be omitted. Only hymns of praise ought to be sung. The Lord's Supper should not be a part of the service but a separate action, and in rural districts a sermon could be replaced by catechization.

Church attendance declined generally, and the closing decade of the eighteenth century was one of spiritual poverty. While the status of the clergy fell, their efforts in the economic improvement of the land must be acknowledged. It may seem strange that they should teach their parishioners how to raise potatoes, vaccinate against smallpox, and care for their livestock, but the clergy were ministers of the states through whom the foundation of Danish prosperity was being laid. In 1788, the peasants won freedom, and in 1792, Denmark became the first nation to forbid slavery in its colonies.

The Enlightenment in Norway and Iceland

The political union of Norway and Denmark was matched by similar religious developments, though Norway's distance from the centers of rationalism saved it from the more radical tendencies. The positive elements of the Enlightenment served Norway in promoting its own self-consciousness. Foremost among its representatives were bishops. John Ernest Gunnerus, bishop of Trondheim, was Wolffian in his desire to defend Christianity. Natural religion and morality were inadequate to meet human sin. The atonement was necessary, as was a revelation of God beyond the ability of reason. His cultural leadership was evident also in the organization in 1760 of a literary-scientific society in Trondheim.

Peder Hansen, bishop of Kristiansand, went beyond Gunnerus and followed closely in the steps of Bastholm. Neither miracles nor the Bible itself impressed reason, but the teachings of Jesus had an immediate effect. The Old Testament had no religious value; the New Testament was written in accommodation to the cultural level of its times. The Sacraments had meaning only for the untutored. Nordahl Brun, bishop of Bergen, remained more orthodox, though he attempted to explain miracles in accord with reason. The period was marked by an increasing attention to education and the care of the sick, especially by Hansen. Bishop Gunnerus agitated for a university in Norway, but the time was not yet ripe.

Interest in native history, flora, and fauna also characterized the church in Iceland. The two bishop Jonssons, Finnur the father and Hannes the son, explored the origins, the language, and the history of Iceland. The *History of the Icelandic Church* by Finnur Jonsson became fundamental. A jurist, Magnus Stephensen, succeeded despite opposition to get a new hymnbook in the spirit of the Enlightenment adopted in 1801, and Balle's doctrinal text was introduced. In 1802, both of the old Iceland bishoprics were united and moved to Reykjavik.

The Enlightenment in Sweden

The seventeenth century had been one of martial glory for Sweden; in the eighteenth century its heroes were intellectual. More than in any other Lutheran land, the Church of the Reformation was able to maintain its freedom and develop in a way that conserved old as well as adapted new qualities.

Olof von Dalin's satire of both orthodox and pietistic characteristics set a tone, but his supranaturalism saved him from the excesses of rationalism. An even greater influence was Emanuel Swedenborg. Son of the orthodox but tolerant Bishop Jesper Svedberg of Skara, Emanuel developed interests in many directions. In England he studied Newton, empiricism, and mysticism; in Germany, Wolff and rationalism. The Bible remained central in his thought, which spiraled upward from a natural to a spiritual and divine height, using allegory and "correspondence" to create the contents of *True Religion*, published in London in 1772. The resultant new rationalistic and mystic religion denied such fundamental doctrines as the Trinity and the atonement, but did include a final judgment and eternal life in which the ethical life of man found its justification.

The period between Charles XII (d. 1718) and Gustavus III (crowned 1771) was one in which the estates rather than the king ruled. As an estate of the realm, the clergy were involved in the politics of the contending parties, and their fortunes rose or fell with their party. The strength of the bishops saved the church from the subservience the German churches suffered under their governments. Voltaire had followers in Sweden, and caricature of the church went beyond Holberg and Dalin. But when Sweden in 1766 passed the first European ordinance for the freedom of the press, there was a reservation against antireligious literature. As in Germany and Denmark, the literary circles fostered skepticism or a vague Deism, but the majority of the population were in rural parishes of a different spirit.

Even in Stockholm the pietistic preaching of Anders Rutstrom and Peter Murbeck drew crowds. But for most Christians the spiritual guide was the postil of Anders Nohrborg. After only a few years of ministry in Stockholm, Nohrborg died in 1767 at the age of 42. But he left a collection of sermons that were read for the next century. Following an "order of salvation" (an orthodox program filled with pietistic ardor), Nohrborg produced a book of spiritual instruction and edification that did more to keep faith alive than any neological defense.

Indicative of the meeting of the old and the new was the career of Anders Knös. Knös was a biblical Pietist of the Arndt type. Yet he gave to justification a nonorthodox interpretation, stressing what happens in man rather than God's act of forgiveness.

The Enlightenment in Finland

Finland, like Norway, felt fewer effects from Enlightenment rationalism. A new interest in nature characterized the Scandinavian countries. The pastors in Finland, as elsewhere, were leaders in welfare programs of their communities and as owners of land gave time to economic and health conditions of the peasantry. Parsonages were the centers of learning, and a good standard of living was common among the higher clergy, who were often found with officials and the military in the membership of lodges, the first of which was established in Finland in 1756. As in Sweden, Pietist groups maintained themselves. Nohrborg was widely read. Finnish revivals crossed over into northern Sweden. Characteristic of the revivals in Finland was their lay leadership that lived on biblical and devotional literature and was little affected by the currents of speculation in higher intellectual altitudes.

CHAPTER NINE

Mission and Migration

The charge sometimes made that in the sixteenth, seventeenth, and eighteenth centuries the Church of the Reformation showed no interest in missions is no longer considered valid, for the Reformation itself was a tremendous mission effort opposed by formidable forces. Not only did the Reformation mean a reinterpretation of the work of the Church, but in many regions it brought a deepened sense of the Christian faith to people whose conversion from paganism had been very superficial. Nor should it be forgotten that in the sixteenth century knowledge about the people of the earth was still limited. A survey of the continents by Philipp Nicolai in 1599 actually seemed to imply that the message of Christ had penetrated everywhere. The missionary journeys of the Jesuits, who had reached India, Japan, China, and the new world, were known. In Asia travelers found remnants of older Christian communities that seemed to confirm the idea that the apostles had fulfilled the commission of bringing the Word to all nations.

Roman Catholic and Protestant Missions

That the Jesuits rather than the Evangelicals carried the message of Christ to newly found continents has an obvious explanation. Because they fought for their very existence, the followers of Luther and Calvin had neither men nor means to explore foreign lands. Furthermore, the discovery of new continents came before the Reformation, and the hemispheres were divided by the pope between Spain and Portugal. The Reformation took place in Europe, in countries without sea power or hemmed in by Catholic powers.

Governments were involved in missions. Jesuit missionaries followed Portuguese sailors and Spanish and French soldiers. In the evangelical countries the administration of the churches was in the hands of government officials—a missionary project would have to be a state undertaking. Since the king felt a responsibility for the church, he sought to expand the church as his domain expanded. And so the early Lutheran missions were a church and state venture.

Swedish Missions—Lappland and on the Delaware

In Sweden, Gustavus Vasa already before 1560 had been interested in work among the Lapps, and his successors laid the obligation on Swedish pastors along the coast of the Baltic to make regular visits to these nomads. We may consider the missions among Lapps and Finns as the Christianization of regions hitherto pagan. And although the governments had political reasons for their concern, it is to their credit that ecclesiastical matters were an integral part of their programs.

How natural a part the church played is exemplified in the first Lutheran venture into the New World. When the Swedish colony was settled on the banks of the Delaware in 1638, clergymen came along. For example, Johan Campanius, who was there from 1643 to 1648, took time to learn the language of the Indians around the Delaware and translated Luther's Small Catechism into their language, though it did not appear in print until 1696 in Stockholm.

Lutheran Migration to North America

While the Church of Sweden was sending ministers to the church on the Delaware, the Lutheran consistory at Amsterdam was receiving communications from Lutherans on the Hudson. Thus Lutherans were among their colonists on the Hudson, in Manhattan, and in Albany. Not until the English took over the Dutch power in New York in 1664 could Lutheran pastors gain entrance to the city.

There were Germans in Pennsylvania and New York who had left the desolated regions of their mother country after the Thirty Years' War. The ravages of the French along the Rhine drove many out of the Palatinate. They fled to the New World via London, where the German court preachers and Queen Anne sought to help them. Most influential of the emigrant pastors or missionaries from Europe was Henry Melchior Muhlenberg. In their desolation, German Lutherans in Pennsylvania had written to Halle for help. Francke and the court preacher in London, Frederick Ziegenhagen, at length responded by sending Muhlenberg, who was known to Francke and trusted by him since his days at Halle. Muhlenberg, mildly pietistic but orthodox in his faith, soon established himself as the leader, greatly aided by the close cooperation of the Lutherans in the region.

Danish Missions in India and West Indies

While Sweden and Germany were aiding, in different ways, to establish evangelical churches on the continent of North America, Denmark was writing a unique chapter in missions elsewhere. In London a German court preacher was instrumental in gaining government support for German emigrants. In Copenhagen another German preacher at court acted as an intermediary in a missionary cause. King Frederick IV of Denmark was concerned about his colony in India, and though the trading company was less interested, the king asked court pastor Julius Lütkens to find men willing to serve Tranquebar, that faraway place on the southeast coast of India. The Berlin pastors nominated Bartholomew Ziegenbalg and Heinrich Plütschau, who met with Francke's endorsement. They were ordained in Copenhagen, and in July 1706, they landed at Tranquebar. Because of the careful preparation of catechumens for membership, growth was slow. At the time of Ziegenbalg's death in 1719, there were some 250 Christians.

Most famous of the missionaries was the gifted Christian F. Schwartz. He was trained at Halle and spent forty-eight years in India. He mastered the language of the Tamil people and knew their religions and customs. The English made him chaplain in Trichinopoly. He served their church but retained his status as a Lutheran pastor. The Indian raja trusted him even to the point of sharing power with him. He won the respect of everyone with whom he associated. Churches were built and schools organized both for the English and the natives. When the Church of Sweden later joined the society on the field, the modern Tamil Evangelical Lutheran Church grew up, thus preserving a bond with the original Tranquebar mission.

The Copenhagen Mission Board also sponsored Thomas von Westen's work among the Lapps and of Hans Egede's mission in Greenland. Again it was a combination of orthodoxy and Pietism that assumed responsibilities for the carrying of the Gospel to foreign lands. Nor should the foundation of the church in the Danish West Indies be overlooked, where at St. Thomas the Frederick Lutheran Church dates from 1666—a church still in existence.

Eastern Europe—Hungary

Mission and migration characterize the history of the Lutherans on the eastern borders of Europe. The vicissitudes of war and politics constantly affected the peoples' religious institutions as well as their welfare and survival. The changing currents swirled around the foundations of Austria, Prussia, and Russia; in their wake, names of territories and populations emerged and disappeared along with their churches.

Hungary, like ancient Gaul, was divided into three parts after the Turkish victory of 1526. The conquered territory was ruled from Buda, and the evangelical churches were allowed considerable freedom in local parishes but forbidden wider relationships. The tolerance of this island in Islam was widely known and refugees came from persecuted areas. Lutherans, Calvinists, Socinians, Orthodox, and Roman Catholics managed to live peaceably together. Despite some losses to the Reformed and the Unitarians, the Siebenburg or Transylvanian Lutherans held their own. Their orthodoxy made these Lutherans suspicious of Pietists and Moravians, but their own reasonableness tempered their aversion to rationalism.

Changes followed when the Turks were finally driven out around 1700. Roman bishops and Jesuits wanted the reclaimed territory to return to pre-Turkish conditions and everywhere harassed the Evangelicals. Rebellion was fruitless, for the leaders were charged with treason. Only the need for settlers in the new lands led the authorities to grant religious privileges to those who would come.

Austria

The Hapsburg power had also stretched northward. Bohemia, Moravia, and Silesia were unwilling subjects ever since the Brethren, the followers of Hus, had fought for a century against the claims of Rome before Luther endorsed their cause. Both nobles and people embraced the evangelical doctrine. But with the Hapsburg dedication to the Counter-Reformation, a new era began. The result was the beginning of the Thirty Years' War. The troops of Wallenstein successfully resisted Gustavus Adolphus, and the Peace of Westphalia left the Catholics victorious.

After two hundred years, the government at Vienna realized the futility of exterminating Protestantism. The climate of the Enlightenment had nourished also a new spirit of tolerance. State records were still in the hands of the parish priest of the Roman Church and Roman bishops were to supervise the evangelical clergy. The Evangelicals were to declare their faith publicly by registering with the authorities.

Under Joseph II's Edict of Tolerance (1782), Moravian Brethren registered as Lutherans (the Brethren were not given legal status by the edict). In Bohemia they declared themselves mostly as Calvinists. Separate organizations divided Lutherans and Calvinists, though before the edict they had much in common as persecuted groups.

Prussia

As Austria had added country to country and made itself an exponent of Roman Catholicism, so Prussia enlarged itself and emerged as a leader in Protestantism. Saxony had been the staunch defender of Luther and orthodox Lutheranism, but when August II, the Saxon elector, became a Roman Catholic and accepted the Polish throne in 1697, his influence as a Lutheran leader was lost. The elector of Brandenburg gradually acquired surrounding provinces—in the west, lands on the Rhine; in the east, Prussia; in the north, Pomerania—and established the Hohenzollern family on a throne, first at Königsberg, then at Berlin. The Hohenzollerns were Calvinists and welcomed immigrants of other countries to the new Prussian possessions.

Poland

To the north and east lay a region that tried in vain to preserve identity and independence and whose fate affected the destiny of large numbers of Lutherans. Poland had become a name for a degree of unity that characterized the relations of northern Slavic tribes on the border of the East and the West. Lithuanians and Poles were ruled by magnates who treated the peasants on their vast estates as serfs. Calvinism was widely accepted, but Lutherans, Bohemian Brethren, and Socinians had been welcomed and a charter of privileges accorded the signers of the Sandomir Consensus of 1570. When the Napoleonic wars were over, the Congress of Vienna arranged boundaries in Europe, and Poland was divided up between Russia, Prussia, and Austria.

In the Polish lands that fell to Prussia, the German state church made arrangements for schools and churches. A provincial consistory of Posen operated under the Berlin authorities. Even the plan for a Prussian Union applied to the new territory despite opposition that led some to emigrate.

Russian Lands

Quite different was the fate of the churches under Russian rule. After an initial attempt by Russia to govern the Protestants through a common consistory in Warsaw, the supervision was moved to Petrograd. Czar Nicholas gave the Reformed and the Lutherans each a consistory, though around 1865 the Reformed counted less than 10,000, the Lutherans over 235,000, of whom 90 percent were Germans. The large number of Germans in Russian Poland was due to immigration, for the Russians invited and encouraged artisans for the growing industrial centers and farmers for open lands. Polish Lutheranism came to be associated with the Germans, and its fate was intertwined with them. In the old East Prussia the Masurian Poles combined with Lutheran immigrants from the Baltic countries, but a Lithuanian nationalism still dominated.

With Peter the Great, Russia started its advance toward the west. Peter's founding of a new capital was in a region where Finnish Lutheran churches had long been organized. Peter was willing to let them continue to exercise a relative autonomy. Baltic provinces added a couple million people—most of them Lutheran—to the czar's lands. In addition a large number of German immigrants had come in Peter's time to build up St. Petersburg and its trade, and another large immigration in Catherine's reign settled on the banks of the Volga to till the vacant fields.

A Missionary Church

Our survey of missions and migration has swung full circle from Lappland on the one side of the Baltic to the Russian provinces on the other side. It discloses a ceaseless expansion toward the frontiers of the age and a Christian witness by the Lutheran countries to other lands and nations. Sweden and Norwegian emissaries carried the Gospel to Lapps and Finns, to Greenland, and to the Delaware River in America. The Danish government together with Halle missionaries began the Protestant movement in missions on the east coast of India. With prayer and men, German consistories followed the mounting immigration to the eastern shores of North America. On the troubled eastern border of Europe, Lutheran churches arose in migrations and movements of people in Slovenia, Slovakia, Hungary, Austria, Bohemia, Moravia, Silesia, and Poland. Older churches and new ones found themselves under Russian autocracy. Despite the difficulties on all these fronts, the Lutheran doctrines of sin and grace, Law and Gospel, Word and Sacrament were planted in all these regions. Some feared that the revolutions of the time that trusted in man and the structures of society meant the end of Christianity. The result, however, was quite the contrary. The Church of the Lutheran Reformation was spreading seed that would bear rich fruit in many climates.

CHAPTER TEN

The Quest for Freedom

The close of the eighteenth century marked the beginning of a new period in the history of Western civilization. A century that had seen the rise of French culture to dominance in Europe ended with the French Revolution. This great explosion overthrew old political dynasties and the secular power of the Roman Church and initiated an age of democracy. It had been preceded by the Revolution of the American Colonies, which also proclaimed a government of, by, and for the people. In Europe the dream soon turned into the dictatorship of Napoleon, who shook the continent, but after him France again asserted in 1830, 1848, and 1870 a popular sovereignty that had repercussions in all of Western Europe. The new idea of the state as a secular power left open the question of who was to possess its power. The age of royal absolutism as well as of church dominion was gone. A dying aristocracy tried to hold power that a rising middle class in the cities was taking from it. All the while, a muttering could be heard in the new class of industrial workers. In their name, a third revolution in the next century proclaimed in Russia the might of an organized proletariat, which again would fall into the grip of a dictatorship.

No less revolutionary was the cultural transformation. The Deism of England gave way to skepticism and, after Darwin, to a purely secular and materialistic explanation of man and society. Philosophy, no more than politics and literature, had no responsibility to the Church. While these philosophical battles were being waged in the high places of the universities, scholars were examining the Bible as any other human book. Freed from traditional views of the meaning and the authority of Scripture, they stressed its human side. Some of the critical biblical scholars, such as Johann Semler, were themselves professed Christians and thought they were serving the Church. In reality they were reinterpreting Scripture in the light of the rationalism of the day. They read God's revelation in the mirror of their own depths and reflected their own ideas in explaining it.

The Prussian Union

To the religious dilemma of the Church of the Reformation in Germany was added the ambiguous situation in which the organized churches found themselves, not the least in Prussia. The relationship of church to governments produced strange results as governments changed. Saxony, the defender of Luther, was still a strong Lutheran province, but its king was Roman Catholic. The rulers in Prussia had a long Calvinist tradition, yet Prussia was now becoming the centralizing power in a new German Empire. It had long been tolerant of both Lutherans and Reformed under a common administration. The king, Frederick William III, in the year of the three-hundredth anniversary of the Reformation on his own authority proclaimed a union of the two churches. He did not merge them or change their confessions, but he wanted them considered as one communion, and he hoped they might celebrate the Sacrament together. He looked on himself as a liturgical scholar and prepared an Agenda, or order of worship, which he tried to impose on the union in 1821. In the face of opposition the Agenda was allowed as an alternative form. As Prussia incorporated other territories in Pomerania and Westphalia, he tried in 1830 to bring their churches into the union. But the confessional Lutheran Church resisted. A general superintendent, with separate consistories for either Reformed or Lutheran communions, was allowed in the provinces. For a while these superintendents bore the title of bishop, and the Prussian superintendent was archbishop. When Frederick William IV tried to expand the episcopal system rather than allow greater freedom through lay representation in synods, he placed the superintendents directly under himself, thus increasing his power over the churches.

Opposition to Union

Nassau, Rhine-Bavaria, and Baden followed the example of Prussia. While the respective confessions were acknowledged, they lost their normative value in the declaration that the Bible alone was to be the basis of teaching and preaching. On the other hand the union called forth strong protests and a determination on the part of convinced Lutherans not to allow the loss of their identity. As a commemoration of 1517, Claus Harms of Kiel in 1817 issued ninety-five theses containing a ringing denunciation of the rationalism that pervaded Lutheran churches.

When Silesian Lutherans began to organize an independent church, the government would not give it legal standing but looked on it as a sect. In 1841, however, they were allowed to organize as the Evangelical Lutheran Church in Prussia, with Breslau as center. The role of the pastor in the new independent church soon became an issue that resulted in a division and a new synod called Immanuel. One dissident group chose to immigrate to America under Pastor John Grabau and formed with him the Buffalo Synod. Meanwhile in Saxony a large and well-organized group expressed protest against a unionistic spirit by following their pastor, Martin Stephan, to the state of Missouri in 1839. Other Saxon congregations sympathized with Pastor Friedrich Brunn in Nassau, who with his congregation left the state church in 1877 and helped establish the Synod of the Evangelical Lutheran Free Church of Saxony and Other States. The synod included congregations from Rhenish Prussia, Hanover, and Pomerania. In 1908, it merged with the Hermannsburg Free Church.

The war with Denmark in 1864 brought Schleswig-Holstein under Prussian dominion, and after the war with Austria, the regions of Hanover, Electoral Hesse, Nassau, and Frankfort were added to Prussia. Hanover firmly resisted becoming a part of the church union. Leaders such as Ludwig A. Petri and Karl J. Spitta gave depth to the Lutheran consciousness of the province, the former through administrative measures, the latter through his sermons and hymns. Within the Prussian Union many Lutherans were dissatisfied with the vague creedal stand of their church government. In Pomerania Theodor Kliefoth wielded great power as a strong confessional administrator. In Prussia the jurist F. J. Stahl and the journalist E. W. Hengstenberg argued for a clear distinction between church and secular government and for finding the church's identity in its confessions. Hengstenberg's *Evangelische Zeitung* openly opposed the attitude of the secular press of Berlin.

Württemberg

While Prussia was consolidating a new Germany in the north, the southern provinces kept their ancient independence until 1870. From this quarter the new awakening of Lutheranism would receive significant leadership. It had developed a strong, biblically oriented, pietistic character. Some Pietists reacted vigorously against such changes and emigrated to Russia and America rather than conform. However, the rationalistic spirit was never radical and showed itself rather in the improving of schools and congregational life. *The Life of Jesus* by the Tübingen scholar David F. Strauss parted the confessional Lutherans from the nominal Pietists, and from this event came—as elsewhere—a tendency to consider the confessional Lutherans as the true exponents of Christianity.

One of the leaders in the Württemberg church was to prove highly influential. This was Johann T. Beck, who turned to the Bible as the center of a theological system. Not the confessional writings but the Scriptures as the Word of God were his concern. Here he found the kingdom of God as a central theme. Both justification and sanctification could be treated fully from this point of view. A new biblical theology thus came into being, with wide influence in the Lutheran Church. Especially influential was his theory that only when Christ is in us can we understand Scripture.

Bavaria

Even more than Württemberg, the province of Bavaria became a stronghold of confessional Lutheranism. Theology, they maintained, was not completed in the sixteenth century but could be developed in the light of later study. Bavaria was heavily Roman Catholic, and the Lutherans had to defend themselves against Rome rather than a union. They tended to give weight to the experience of the individual by following the views of the influential Reformed theologian Friedrich Schleiermacher (1768–1834). They sought an inner certitude as well as an assurance of the objective validity of the creed. Near Nürnberg, at Neuendettelsau, Wilhelm Loehe developed a deeper understanding of the life of the Lutheran congregation as he made it a center of liturgical renewal and practical service. His efforts extended to America, where he sent a large number of ministers to work among German immigrants.

Lay Movements

Throughout the century a new force found its way into churches, vitally affecting their nature. It came from England and Switzerland in the form of voluntary societies whose members hoped to further the cause of the kingdom of God. Similar groups soon sprang up in Germany. The Basel Missionary Society combined Lutherans and Reformed who began by supporting the Church Missionary Society. A confessional Lutheran Berlin Missionary Society dates from 1824. Another Lutheran society arose in Dresden in 1836, and in 1840 it took over part of the Danish India Mission from the Church Missionary Society. On the initiative of Pastor Louis Harms, a society was organized in his parish in Hermannsburg, and Johannes Gossner founded a society in Berlin, bearing his name.

Out of the same interest for evangelization and ministry came the Inner Mission movement. Industrialization was shifting population from rural regions to cities. Crowded living conditions, poverty, sickness, and juvenile delinquency were accompaniments of the new social order. Neither state nor church seemed ready to meet the pressing needs of working classes who were without roots in the community. Few new churches were built, and clergy were neither sufficient nor well trained. In this situation individual Christians rallied volunteers to create new agencies.

These voluntary groups tended to bring the Lutherans and the Reformed together, awakening the concern of conservatives. At first they opposed the movement because of dislike both of unionism and of the lay leadership. Loehe was able to build an Inner Mission of his own on strictly Lutheran principles, but this was rarely possible. Therefore, because of the desperate need of the population, Lutherans gradually formed joint endeavors with the Reformed and gave their sincere support. Yet where possible they preferred their own organization. Thus in rivalry with the Gustav Adolf Society for aid to German Protestants outside Germany, the confessional Lutherans built up their own "chests of God." In certain cases the official church assumed responsibility for new work. The consistory of Hanover provided some men for the Lutherans in America and for a long period supported congregations in Capetown, Africa. But in the main the consistories were satisfied to carry on routine duties, unaware that the Inner Mission was itself a protest against the rigidity and clerical dominance of the church-state arrangement.

The Lutherans, who sought a clearer definition of what Christ's Church really is, saw that once the state had thrown off its guise of protector, the Church would need a foundation of its own. If religion was not to dissipate in a general mood of philanthropy, it needed a Gospel rooted in the truth of God as revealed to mankind. The kingdom of God was more than an optimistic secular society. Therefore they clung to the Confessions of the Church. As it was, Western civilization was following an illusion of progress while progressing on a path that brought it to the brink of disaster—the World War of 1914–18. Romanticism and realism had created no ideal world of humanity.

How closely knit the countries of Lutheranism had become and how common their problems were is apparent as we trace the story of the Scandinavian churches in the nineteenth century.

The Danish Church

As in Germany so in Denmark a divergence appeared between those who were led by romantic literature to an idealistic view of man and those who saw in philosophy a challenge to a sterner ethical life. A deep stream of Pietism ran through the Danish Church. Pastors cooperated in the revivals that flared up in different sections of the country. But the laity were the real force. They resisted the effort of the church to impose new hymnbooks and worship forms they considered rationalistic.

But something of all these elements—romanticism, rationalism, biblicism, Pietism, activism—merged in the many-sided leader who put his stamp on Christianity in Denmark, Nikolai F. Grundtvig. Central in his thinking was the Sacrament of Baptism and the Apostles' Creed, which had been repeated down through the generations as the true succession of the Church. The Creed and the Lord's Prayer he considered living words of Jesus which, rather than the Bible, held the communion of saints together and which opened up the meaning of the Bible. Grundtvig's ideas in some degree influenced all the Church in Denmark.

The mildly rationalistic administration of the Danish Church had to bear not only Grundtvig's attacks but also those of Søren Kierkegaard. His proclamation, however, was of a different kind. Kierkegaard aimed his darts at a worldly Christianity that seemed to deny the truth of Jesus Christ. In fact he was opposing the whole system of philosophic idealism while making a leap of faith into a kind of purity of life and thinking beyond the ability of the unlearned layman.

In Denmark, as in Germany, the church had been unable to cope with a mobile population. In Copenhagen there were fifty to sixty thousand people to a parish. The slums were being filled by laborers who called religion capitalistic. Economic conditions were unfavorable.

Hans L. Martensen, as a former professor of theology, had exerted definite influence on a theological generation by his works on dogmatics and ethics. He continued a mediating tradition, accepting much of Grundtvig except his view of the Sacraments and hoping to keep the intellectual class in the church.

The remarkable achievement of the Danish Church was to keep all movements within a common framework. Probably nowhere in the Lutheran churches did laymen have so much to do with church affairs as did the followers of Grundtvig and the members of the Inner Mission in Denmark. No great emphasis was placed on confessionalism, but all parties considered themselves faithful to an orthodoxy that had been deeply colored by pietistic experience.

The Church in Sweden

The Napoleonic wars brought change to all the Scandinavian countries. Denmark lost Norway, which gained its own government but was related to Sweden through a personal union with the Swedish royal house. Sweden in turn lost Finland when Russia gained suzerainty and placed it with the Baltic countries under a governor in Moscow.

A French prince became king of Sweden, and his house of Bernadotte soon identified itself with the Swedish people. The constitution of 1809 reasserted the Lutheran faith as the faith of king and nation, though freedom of religion was extended, especially through a greater freedom of the press.

Neither rationalism nor romanticism made deep inroads on the religious temper of Sweden in the first half of the century. In general the educated classes were interested in the Church. A Swedish Bible Society was begun in 1810, and tract and Bible distribution became common. Yet the strength of the Church lay in a widespread revivalism that carried on in various forms in different parts of the country. In central and southern Sweden popular revival preachers attracted the ordinary parishioners in large numbers. The deplorable extent of drunkenness made temperance an element in their preaching. In some regions a dormant Moravian tradition came to life. But more generally the harvest was one of seeds sown by older Swedish devotional books. A more militant revivalism grew up in northern Sweden. They were dissatisfied with the new church books, for these seemed too rationalistic.

After the revolutionary events of 1848 in France and Germany, a wave of conservatism swept Europe. A new series of revivals excited Swedish Church people. As mission societies—aimed at home reform as well as foreign service—multiplied, the National Evangelical Foundation attempted to keep the ferment within the church. The Conventicle Act of 1721 still stood, but it was widely circumvented. Liberal forces finally forced the repeal of the hated act in 1858. As in Denmark and Norway so also in Sweden some societies even held their own Communion services, first under a pastor, then with lay leaders.

Within the church tension had grown between a high church party with its center in Lund and a low church party led from Uppsala. The Lund faculty held that the ministry in its office of Word and Sacrament was transmitted through episcopal ordination. The Uppsala theologians looked with sympathy on lay participation in the organization and work of the church.

The seventies and eighties were difficult decades. American Unitarianism was reflected in the religious philosophy of C. J. Boström, Pontus Vikner, and Viktor Rydberg. August Strindberg introduced a line of antichurch writers such as Ellen Key, Georg Brandes, and Karl Hjalmar Branting. The laboring class was indifferent when not hostile. The state church suffered severe losses to the Free Churches. Thousands of serious-minded church people immigrated to America.

Through strong episcopal leadership the Church of Sweden held its own and gained even more independence from the state at the same time as the state was unwilling to lose the stabilizing contribution of the church. But the unreadiness of the hierarchy to incorporate lay activity into the leadership of the church marked its leaders in the public mind as aristocratic and conservative. The clergy remained highly cultured leaders of worship in churches not attended by the populace. Yet there was a loyalty to the Lutheran Confessions and the liturgy, coupled with an awareness of the intellectual problems of the century, winning for the Church a respect not given to individual groups living on meager revival fare. On a deeper level, the orthodoxy of the official church was pietistic, as was apparent in its hymns, preaching, devotional literature, and religious poetry. The National Evangelical Foundation represented an active lay loyalty, and after 1909, a number of "Bible faithful" pastors and laymen emphasized the authority of Scripture within the missions of the Church at home and abroad. For all its difficulties, Lutheranism in Sweden retained a unique unity of thought and purpose in the family of Lutheran national churches during the revolutionary nineteenth century.

The Church in Norway and Iceland

Freed from Denmark, Norway turned to the task of building a national culture and a state under a constitutional government. Shortly before its separation from Denmark, it had received its own university. Here the theological professors S. B. Hersleb and S. J. Stenersen upheld confessional standards and trained pastors in a biblical tradition. The bishops in Norway were supranaturalists in their theology, with a considerable interest in Grundtvig.

But the main theological figure was an unschooled peasant, Hans Nielsen Hauge—unschooled, that is, in university disciplines but at home in the Bible, the Catechism, Arndt, Pontoppidan, and Kingo. Moral seriousness made him critical of the looseness of the clergy. At the age of 25, he began to speak to people about the Word and the will of God. He had an unusual ability in manual arts and commercial ventures that made him doubly impressive as he taught peasants and small business men the skill of both material and spiritual life. He organized followers and engaged in the business of shipping, milling—even distilling. However, his meetings were still unlawful because of the Conventicle Act, and authorities questioned his accounting procedures. Opposition from both church and state led to his imprisonment, and from 1804 to 1809, he was confined in Oslo. Long, drawn-out examinations did not free him until finally in 1814, when his health was broken. Martyrdom made him a national figure. He gave to the common people a serious, moralistic view of Lutheranism, but he also encouraged them to take an interest in their government. The state church was still his home, and he asked his following to be loyal to it. In Norway as in Sweden the lay movement was responsible for much of the newer forms of activity. There were temperance societies and a mission to returning sailors. A Deaconess Home was founded on the model of Kaiserswerth.

As elsewhere, both the intellectual and the working class were moved by antichurch forces.

Hauge's revivalistic views penetrated all religious forms in nineteenth-century Norway. Unlike the revivalism of Carl Olof Rosenian, which separated from the Church of Sweden, the Norwegian revivals were almost entirely within the Church. In this respect Norway resembled Denmark. The isolated position of Norway saved it from the more violent cultural and social revolutions on the continent. Nationalism, too, united the people even if they disagreed on religious policies. Consequently Norway possessed a more homogeneous life than was possible in either Denmark or Sweden.

Although Denmark lost Norway, it retained Iceland. The middle line views of the court preachers Jacob Mynster and Hans Martensen prevailed against both rationalism and Grundtvig. The education of the ministry was greatly strengthened by the establishment of a theological college in Reykjavik in 1847, which became the theological department when a university was founded in 1911. Observers of religious life in Iceland have remarked on an emphasis on the providence of God in preaching and an interest in spiritualism. Controversy between the conservative and more liberal parties gradually gave way to more united efforts in meeting the challenge of a secular generation. Iceland and Denmark had a common king from 1918 until Iceland declared itself a republic in 1944.

The Church in Finland

It was the fate of Finland to fall under Russian rule in 1809. Yet its independent government and church structure were respected by the Moscow authorities represented by a governor general. The new church law of 1869 abolished the Conventicle Act, declared lay work legal, and afforded freedom for other denominations. The same law separated the school system from control by the church, but the Lutheran Church remained the national church and was granted its own convocation to decide religious matters. Distinctive of Finnish Lutheranism were its revivals.

Theologically the leadership of the church followed J. T. Beck of Tübingen. Meanwhile the church had to defend itself against increased Russian influences, which Finnish nationalism also tried to counter, and at the turn of the century, Marxism infected the radical labor class. An apologetic for the Christian faith was put into contemporary terms by Bishops H. Rabergh and Georg O. Rosenquist. Revivalism, Swedish-Finnish tensions, Russian Orthodoxy, Free Church movements, and an antireligious culture combined to create complex problems for the Finnish Church in the century of Russian rule.

CHAPTER ELEVEN

New Plantings on Five Continents

While the cold light of rationalism seemed to overlay the landscape of Christendom after the middle of the eighteenth century, new shoots of activity appeared in many parts of the Church. The universities were alive with speculation concerning the nature and source of the Christian faith. Governments were trying to bend the congregations and the ministry to political purposes. But deep in the ranks of believing Christians, springs of new energy were breaking forth.

The Missionary Movement

The movement coincided with the era of colonization by the new maritime powers of Europe. Holland and England took the places of Spain and Portugal in gaining new territories in Asia, Africa, and the islands of the South Seas. North and South America were shaped by influences of the Old World. The original Danish-Halle mission in Tranquebar, India, exercised a peculiar attraction. Some of the new efforts centered there, but gradually the whole world became the concern of Protestant missions, and missions of Lutheran churches extended to the ends of the earth.

As noted earlier, the early mission societies grew up on ground prepared by Pietism, not least by the Moravian Brethren, whose genius was a missionary one. The impulse crossed confessional boundaries, often taking on subjective tones of individuals rather than expressing the voice of churches. In Germany the self-conscious confessional Lutheran churches made the Leipzig Society their missionary agency. At its founding in 1836, it was made a branch of the Basel Society and was situated in Dresden, but moved to Leipzig in 1848. Its director, Karl Graul, was recognized as a leader in the theory and practice of missions and himself spent four years in India. He cherished the hope of uniting all Lutheran churches in his organization. Though only partially successful, his missionary journal, *Evangelisch-Lutherisches Missionsblatt*, reached far and wide. The society succeeded in obtaining much of the old Tamil field in India and thus continued the century-old Danish mission as the center of its field. After Germany entered the circle of colonial powers the Leipzig missionaries began work in eastern Africa. Here progress was rapid in Tanzania, especially in the Kilimanjaro region, where by 1913 almost half of the children were in mission schools and the Christians numbered a considerable part of the population.

The insistence of the Leipzig leaders on a higher education of missionaries was not shared by another conservative German Lutheran mission, that of Hermannsburg. Its originator, Pastor Louis Harms, had joined in the activities of the North German Missionary Society but disapproved of its lax doctrinal position. Believing that a group of Christians living among natives would testify most effectively to the Gospel, he sent a colony to Africa in 1865. The experiences of the mission necessitated a change to more conventional methods. Besides work in Africa, Leipzig sent workers to the Telugu area of India, Persia, and Australia.

A third center of positive Lutheranism in Germany grew up in the neighborhood of Nürnberg at Neuendettelsau. Here Wilhelm Loehe developed a colony that reflected his own firm, devotional, and missionary Lutheranism on a confessional basis. Loehe began a deaconess institute in Neuendettelsau, and he and his friends organized a society, published literature, and gathered funds for workers that were trained and sent first to North America, then to the Ukraine, Australia, and Brazil.

The confessional concern was strong also in the Breklum Society in Schleswig-Holstein, another group that had left the North German Society. And the Free Church of Hanover, which had separated from the State Church, held to an independent course abroad as well as at home. The Breklum Society operated in India; the Hanover Free Church operated in Natal and Transvaal, both in South Africa.

Scandinavian Missions

The same pattern of missionary societies of varying churchly character meets us in Scandinavia. Danish interest in the India mission had declined to the point that the old Tamil field was given over partly to English societies, partly to the Leipzig Society. Pastor B. Falk Rönne managed to revive efforts for the Greenland mission by the formation of a Danish Missionary Society in 1821. Later it began anew afield in India under missionary Carl Ochs, who left the Leipzig Society because of its policy in regard to the caste system. The Grundtvig party was not missionary in character, and the Danish Missionary Society came under the control of the Inner Mission. Societies were organized for fields in the Sudan, Japan, and the Near East. A "Society for the Propagation of the Gospel among the Danes in America" was formed in 1869. To coordinate the programs of these various agencies, a Danish Missionary Council was set up in Copenhagen in 1912.

In Norway the romantic figure of H. P. Schroeder, who in 1834 was directed to the Zulus by Robert Moffatt, dominated the early years of missions in that country, and until 1873, he had the support of the Norwegian Missionary Society that was begun in 1842 by most of the elements of the church, including the Moravian Brethren. In addition to the Zulu field in Natal, the Norwegian Society carried on an extensive and successful program in Madagascar after 1866. Another more low church group, which did not ordain its preachers either at home or on its foreign field, was the Norwegian Lutheran China Society begun in 1891. In 1901, the older Norwegian Missionary Society added China to its fields.

From 1835, the Swedish Missionary Society, besides aiding missionary endeavors among the Lapps, served as an agent for gathering mission funds from parochial societies and distributing these among older societies. As the confessional movement gained ground, there was a desire for a distinctive Lutheran society. This brought about the formation of the Lund Missionary Society in 1845. Its first venture was directed toward China, but of its pioneers, one missionary was murdered, and the other had to return for health reasons. The society then entered into negotiations with Leipzig, resulting in a long period of cooperation. The Swedish missionaries worked on the India field with considerable support from their own country but under the direction of the German authorities. The Lund Society merged with the Swedish Society in 1855. The resultant society was absorbed by the Church of Sweden in 1876. Greater independence from Leipzig was granted the Swedish workers after the turn of the century. In 1914, a separation was caused by the war.

The Evangelical National Foundation, originally conceived of as an inner mission movement, expanded in 1855 into a society sending missionaries to Ethiopia and Eritrea and starting a seamen's mission with its first station in Constantinople.

The Finnish Missionary Society, begun in 1859 as an independent agency enjoying church support, took up a field in Amboland, Africa. The Lutheran Gospel Association, similar to the Swedish Evangelical National Foundation, dates from 1873. Since 1900, it has had a field in Japan.

Thus from the early 1800s up to the outbreak of World War I, Lutheran missionary societies in every Lutheran land had carried the Gospel to India, from Bengal to Tranquebar, to Madagascar, Borneo, Sumatra, New Guinea, to Japan and China, to Arabia and Persia, and in Africa, from Ethiopia in the north to Transvaal in the south.

The American Field—The General Synod

From his arrival in 1742, Muhlenberg had steadily forged the German Lutherans in the American colonies into a new fellowship of faith. As the frontier moved westward, missionaries of the Pennsylvania Synod followed into Ohio, where a separate synod was organized in 1818.

The older Lutheran synods were challenged by fresh immigrations from Europe that had other answers for the problems of the Church on both sides of the Atlantic. The need for a unifying agency to guide the confused Lutherans in the older colonies, now states of the union, inspired the organization of the General Synod in 1820.

Loehe's Missionaries and the Missouri Synod

Moved by missionary literature, Friedrich K. D. Wyneken of the Church of Hanover, educated at Göttingen and Halle, came to Baltimore in 1838 to work among fellow countrymen. He was employed by the Ministerium of Pennsylvania as a missionary, settling at Fort Wayne, Indiana. His appeals to Germany for help stressed the motive of loyalty and obligation to the faith and the Church. One of his messages was read by Wilhelm Loehe in Neuendettelsau, who at once took up the cause for the brethren in America. The first two workers were sent in 1842.

The Saxon immigration, deceived by Stephan in Missouri, produced a remarkable leader in C. F. W. Walther. Coming from a long line of pastors, Walther had graduated from Leipzig University. His faith in the Word was firm. His experiences in the colony drove him to lay the foundations of his faith in the Bible and to determine his relationship to the Church. He came to the conclusion that the Gospel, the Sacraments, and the Keys are God's gifts to a congregation faithful to the Scriptures and that such a congregation needed neither the ties with the homeland nor its ministry to be a true church. In 1844, he started a journal, *Der Lutheraner*, which won readers in America and Europe and on new mission fields. Here was a call to a definite position in the evangelical faith and a proclamation of the Gospel as the true treasure of the Church.

The Loehe groups joined with Walther's Missouri congregations and in 1846 at Fort Wayne, Indiana, formed a new Synod: the Evangelical Lutheran Synod of Missouri, Ohio, and Other States. Already, however, tension regarding church polity was developing between Loehe and Walther. When Loehe discontinued aid to the Fort Wayne seminary, Wyneken and Walther went to Germany to confer with the Neuendettelsau pastor. The conversations were polite, but no change was effected on either side.

The Iowa Synod

Despite Loehe's differences with some of his own men in America, he continued to minister wherever possible. In 1853, a score of persons moved to Dubuque. They were joined the following years by others from Neuendettelsau. Foremost among the newcomers were the brothers Siegmund and Gottfried Fritschel, who for decades were leaders in the new synod, the Evangelical Lutheran Synod of Iowa and Other States, organized in 1854.

Until 1925, the Iowa Synod benefited by recruits from the society in Neuendettelsau. A majority of the Texas Synod joined Iowa in 1895. This synod had its beginnings in 1850, when the Chrischona Institute near Basel sent missionaries to organize congregations among German settlers.

The Buffalo Synod

The doctrine of the ministry involved the Missouri Synod in controversy also with another German immigrant body. We have noted that because of resistance to the Prussian Union, John A. A. Grabau in 1839 led a Lutheran group from Prussia and settled in Buffalo and Milwaukee. In 1845, four pastors and ten congregations organized the Buffalo Synod. When some of his people joined Missouri congregations, Grabau protested their acceptance. Grabau as well as Walther visited Loehe and sought German support. Grabau found himself closer to Loehe's position, but Lutheran conferences in Leipzig and Bavaria counseled moderation and peace. In 1866, a majority of the pastors left Grabau for the Missouri Synod, and after Grabau's death in 1879, the remainder of the Buffalo Synod moved toward a more congregational polity. Eventually it was to find fellowship with the Iowa and Ohio synods.

Inasmuch as there was little communication between the various Lutheran bodies in Europe, it is not surprising that immigrant groups in the United States would at first keep to themselves. In addition, the walls of language created an isolation that endured into a second generation. For most of the nineteenth century, the Scandinavian Lutherans built up individual synodical units.

Norwegian Synods

Immigrants from Norway carried with them divisions or tendencies of the homeland. Elling Eielsen brought the Haugean lay movement to America with its emphasis on small gatherings for devotional purposes. He and like-minded countrymen in 1846 in Wisconsin organized The Evangelical Lutheran Church in America (known as Eielsen Synod), but its loose ties and individualism prevented its growth. When a decade later it sought to achieve more solidarity and discipline, it encountered losses, and a repeated attempt in 1876 resulted in a new body—Hauge's Norwegian Evangelical Lutheran Synod in America.

The conservative Church of Norway ministry was represented by able pastors from Norway—H. A. Stub, H. A. Preus, U. V. Koren, and Laurentius Larsen—who formed the Norwegian Lutheran Synod in 1853. This synod was attracted to Walther. When the predestination controversy broke out, the Norwegian Lutheran Synod was divided by an "Anti-Missouri Brotherhood," which in 1890 merged with the Augustana and Conference Norwegians into the United Norwegian Lutheran Church of America, representing about one half of the number of Norwegian Lutheran church members in America.

The Augustana Synod and Danish Synods

The missionary societies of Norway and Sweden included America in their work. In Illinois, Swedish pastors were dissatisfied with the theology of the General Synod and after a few years in the Synod of Northern Illinois organized their own body—the Augustana Synod.

Denmark had a separate missionary society for aid to Danes in America and in 1871 sent out men who, a year later in Wisconsin, laid the foundations for the Danish Evangelical Lutheran Church in America. This body was Grundtvigian in character. Danes who were sympathetic with the Danish Inner Mission separated in 1894 to form the Danish Evangelical Church of North America. So, the Danish divisions among the followers of Grundtvig and the Inner Mission in the Church of Denmark were reflected among Danish Lutherans in the United States.

Finnish and Icelandic Synods

Likewise the Finnish Missionary Society looked on America as a field. In 1888, J. K. Nikander was called for work in the United States. His efforts resulted in the foundation of the Suomi Synod in 1890, uniting congregations of Finns especially in northern Michigan, Minnesota, the Dakotas, and Oregon. Several of its pastors came from the African field of the Finnish Missionary Society. Another Finnish immigrant element, the National Evangelical Lutheran Church, organized in 1898, aligned itself with the Missouri Synod and joined it in 1964.

Small though its population, Iceland sent considerable numbers of its people to America, settling principally in the northwestern states and

Canada. In 1885, the Icelandic Synod was formed, mainly of rural churches. A large congregation grew up in Winnipeg.

The Slovak Synod

Lutherans emigrated also from Slovakia, but the church itself took no measures to care for the faraway brethren. A quarter of a century elapsed before a Slovak Evangelical Lutheran Synod was created in 1902 in Pennsylvania. Its contacts were mainly with the Missouri Synod, and in 1908, the synod joined the Synodical Conference.

Americanization and Movements toward Unity

Each of the immigrant groups was preoccupied with its own affairs, conserving and preserving much of its spiritual heritage while seeking to find a new home in a strange land. Their attitude toward fellow Lutherans was one of questioning and caution. Gradually they found kindred spirits. In the first generation loyalty to church was expressed in a European tongue, and often a second generation grew up in an imported atmosphere as far as church life was concerned. The Pennsylvania and Ohio Germans as well as later immigrants hoped German would remain a living language in America. Also the Scandinavian churches were still using their fathers' languages into the twentieth century. Nor were the earliest attempts to translate Lutheranism into English encouraging examples.

Samuel S. Schmucker in 1855 proposed a "Definite Platform" for a spineless Lutheranism; his own church repudiated him. Confessionalism, even in the older eastern synods, was the real legacy of Muhlenberg. When the anti-unionism of the German confessional churches took root in the Midwest, opportunities for broader unions developed.

The decade from 1865 to 1875 marks a watershed in the history of the Lutheran churches in America. For in that decade the Ministerium of Pennsylvania broke with the General Synod and led in the formation of the General Council. The council gathered under its banner numerous other synods.

In 1872 a federation of conservative Lutheran synods formed, which was titled the Synodical Conference, with the Missouri synod as its largest member. However, doctrinal disputes, especially concerning the interpretation of the doctrine of predestination, led to the withdrawal of the Norwegian and the Ohio synods from the conference. In the General Council a long-standing issue was the policy of pulpit and altar fellowship (Galesburg Rule). In this development the General Synod was deeply affected; its own progress drew it ever closer to a conservative position.

Between 1820 and 1920, over five million Germans and more than two million Scandinavians came to the United States. Only a part of these, of course, were Lutherans, though most of the Scandinavians were nominally so, and the Lutheran Church lost thousands in the process of migration. But the inner unity in these various groupings of synods was a remarkable phenomenon, and the planting of the Lutheran churches on the new continent is a story both of sacrifice and of loyalty, often of heroism, and always of grace.

American Overseas Missions

Since the American churches were themselves the fruit of missionary endeavor, they soon joined older societies in bringing the Gospel to other lands or pioneered on new fields. As an early project of the General Synod, it constituted a missionary society in 1837. The General Synod of the South at first cooperated with the General Synod in India but after 1892 had its own field in Japan. The General Council added a Japanese mission in 1908. The Missouri Synod began a mission of its own in India in 1894.

Thus all of the larger bodies had joined in world missions. But also the smaller and independent synods displayed sacrificial interest. Even the smallest of Lutheran bodies had a part in the missionary movement, for the Church of the Lutheran Brethren was represented in China and the Icelandic Synod in Japan.

South America

Immigration flowed also to South America, but here missionary aid came mainly from the northern continent. Early in the nineteenth century the Missouri Synod began gathering scattered German settlements into congregations—Brazil in 1901 and Argentina in 1913. Some pastoral activity was carried on in Buenos Aires, but not until the formation of The United Lutheran Church in America was an intensive ministry begun among the Slovak, German, and Hungarian Lutherans in this metropolis. Since 1666, Danish Lutheran pastors had been active on the Virgin Islands, which passed into the control of the United States in 1917. On the north coast of South America Dutch Lutheran pastors had established the church in 1743. In 1918, The United Lutheran Church assumed responsibility for the British Guiana ministry among South Americans and blacks. On Puerto Rico the Augustana Synod began a mission after the Spanish-American War of 1898.

Australia

Quite different is the record in Australia. The Prussian Union, which drove Stephan and Grabau to North America, led A. L. Kavel to emigrate in 1838 with his followers to Adelaide. Other groups joined, one of them under Pastor G. D. Fritsche. Doctrinal and practical issues arose to divide the immigrants, so that Kavel became the head of the Immanuel Synod and Fritsche head of the Evangelical Lutheran Synod of Australia. Mergers followed. Thus, in 1910, the Evangelical Lutheran Church Union was formed. Another combined group used the name of the Evangelical Lutheran General Synod.

Mission and Unity

From a period when the life of the Church seemed stifled by a rationalistic view of the world and the governments looked on the churches as necessary police and pedagogical forces of society, came the mighty missionary movement in the evangelical churches of northern Europe. In the Lutheran Church the force of the impulse not only created new agencies of inner mission work but expressed itself also in a new independence and self-government of the church, making the Confessions of the Church the standard of preaching, teaching, and discipline. It refused to conform to contemporary culture that went from rationalism through romanticism to secularism, materialism, and atheism. The preaching of the Gospel at home and to the ends of the earth took on an aggressiveness and a boldness hitherto unknown in the Church of the Reformation. And on foreign fields even more than at home, the various branches of the church came into contact with one another and into a form of cooperation that proved immeasurably significant when the world of the nineteenth century was shaken to its foundations by the world wars of the next century.

CHAPTER TWELVE

The Shaking of the Foundations

The year 1914 ended an era in Western civilization. The unified Germany that had grown up around Prussia found itself in increasing difficulty with its neighbors—Russia, France, and England. When war finally broke out, the flames spread throughout the world engulfing Turkey, Japan, Italy, and the United States. The old order was shaken to its foundations by four years of destruction. When peace was restored, the ancient structures of empires and boundaries of nations were gone. Germany was left to rebuild its government and institutions, but its possessions on the eastern edge of Europe were lost to Russia and its colonies over the earth divided among the victors. The Church of the Lutheran Reformation suffered severely in Europe, but in America a new force had developed that radically altered the situation of Lutheranism in the postwar world.

Years of Crises

What centuries of effort had failed to effect, the disaster of the war in Germany did produce—the separation of church and state. The new German constitution of 1919 proclaimed freedom of religion and of religious association. Yet the separation was not complete. The power of tradition was evident in the regulation that the state would still collect the tax for churches from citizens willing to support them. But since the state no longer exercised any administrative control in the churches, they were forced to self-govern. Synods became the usual form, and a number of the provincial churches adopted the title of "bishop" for the chief officer. In 1922, the twenty-eight provincial churches, the Landeskirchen, organized a Federation of Evangelical Churches.

The 1917 quadricentennial of the Reformation had been eclipsed by the war, but a new interest in Luther was advanced by the writings of Karl Holl. The collection of Luther's works in the Weimar Edition was also delayed by war, but new and more popular reprintings of Luther's works were issued as soon as publication was possible. Not only the Church, however, was interested in Luther. In search of means for raising the morale of a dejected nation, political demagogues proclaimed Luther a national hero who could again give Germany an exalted position in Western culture.

The Church and Hitler

While the theologians wrote about a "theology of crisis," an even greater crisis was fashioned for the churches. The spirit of despair, born of resentment against the Treaty of Versailles, of frustration amid quarreling victors, and of economic depression and social readjustment, found a voice in Adolf Hitler. But the German Church League, the Thuringian German Christians, and the Christian German Movement, while varying in their hatred of the Jews and in their desire to rid the church of Judaism and its Old Testament, agreed that for them the Christian Church was a German church. They could echo Hitler's challenge that the German nation and the German church should be characterized by German soil and German blood. They called for one German church instead of a score and more of provincial churches. This Nazi vision of the church would honor Luther while it opposed the Jews, the Marxists, the pacifists, and the internationalists. Confessionally minded Lutherans and other Christians opposed the movement. For example, in 1932 Hermann Sasse was one of the first theologians to publish criticism of the "Aryan Paragraph" in the Nazi political platform, which ultimately led to his isolation even from his fellow faculty members at Erlangen. A group of pastors under Hans Asmussen issued the "Altona Statement," declaring that the Church lives by the Word and its message cannot be dictated by the state. General Superintendent Otto Dibelius of Berlin fearlessly denounced the aims of the German Christians. The Federation of Evangelical Churches now tried to agree on a new constitution. When a new church constitution was ready, elections were held. Hitler himself, newly appointed as Chancellor on January 30, 1933, came to the aid of the German Christian Movement, with the result that they gained control of the church federation. Pastors were forbidden to speak on controversial subjects. Thus the German churches were supposed to be unified—by a political party.

During the same month that Ludwig Müller became Reichsbischof (Reich Bishop), a Pastors' Emergency League came into being under the leadership of Martin Niemoller. Within a few months its membership grew to more than four thousand. These pastors claimed that they were bound only by Scripture and their confessions in their preaching. They pledged aid to one another. In May 1934, there was a synod at Barmen, where eighteen provincial churches were represented by 139 delegates, of whom fifty-three were laymen. Here a "Theological Declaration Concerning the

Present Situation" was adopted, along with an address by the leader, Hans Asmussen.

The synod hoped that the Reformed and Lutheran churches would cooperate as one—a hope not realized. While Lutherans were active in the movement, there was a difference between their attitude and that of the Reformed. The latter, influenced by Barth, wanted a more complete break with the state, while the former were not ready to give the Barmen Declaration a place alongside the Confessions of the Lutheran Church.

Dietrich Bonhoeffer

The most important Lutheran theologian in recent history was Dietrich Bonhoeffer. Born February 4, 1906, Bonhoeffer was executed by the Nazis on April 9, 1945, in the concentration camp at Flossenbürg, Germany. Although he made important literary contributions in the area of theology, Bonhoeffer is most celebrated for his opposition to the National Socialist regime prior to and during World War II. To express his opposition, Bonhoeffer joined the "Confessing Church" (Bekennende Kirche), which stood against the "German Christians" (Deutsche Christen) who supported Hitler's regime and were led by Reichsbischof Ludwig Müller.

A significant trademark of Bonhoeffer's theology is its push toward practice. He rejected intellectualism that is solely devoted to discussion and that lacks a matching praxis. Theology and faith must become concrete in action because the Church exists for the sake of the world. Unless faith acts, it cannot be considered faith at all. However, with his push into the practice of faith, Bonhoeffer went beyond other contemporary theologians such as Karl Barth. For example, Bonhoeffer had no problem opening his classes with prayer—a rather unusual practice in his time. In fact, prayer is a trademark of his theology. Prayer and practice belong together, and this became an important aspect of the life at the seminary in Finkenwalde.

It is important to note that Bonhoeffer's discussion of grace, justification, and sanctification must be understood in connection to his Christology. Otherwise, if his emphasis on discipleship were to be separated from Christ, Bonhoeffer would be misunderstood as pietistic, a perfectionist, or even synergistic in his approach. Bonhoeffer's theology of discipleship was influenced by Søren Kierkegaard's (1813–55) serious plea for authentic faith. Furthermore, Bonhoeffer affirms the humanity and the incarnational aspect of Christology. Christ can serve as God's mediator only because He became human. Only the Son of God, the God-man, the One who was crucified, can call one into discipleship. Only because of Christ's crucifixion and death as historic events is it possible to heed His call to discipleship. Here Bonhoeffer reveals his Lutheran theological lineage as he advocates a theology of the cross because it points to an event in history, specifically to the crucifixion of Jesus Christ. Bonhoeffer also picked up Luther's doctrine of vocation. Like Luther, Bonhoeffer rejected escapism from the world; instead, discipleship must become manifest in this world. The vocation one pursues in this world is, according to Bonhoeffer, Christologically motivated. Thus it would be wrong to divide the world from the Church or to believe that each has nothing to do with the other. Discipleship connects the spiritual and the worldly realms. Given Bonhoeffer's emphasis on active discipleship, one can see how his life would have ended in conflict with the Nazi regime.

Lutherans on Eastern Borders

The peace after World War I changed the eastern borders of Germany and affected the Lutheran churches that had been a part of that region. The states on this eastern border of Europe were torn by internal conflicts—Slavs against Magyars, Magyars against Austrians, and both Slavs and Magyars against Germans. Freedom came to national communities with the breakup of the Austro-Hungarian Empire, but between World Wars I and II tensions between various groups and the Germans had injurious effects on church organizations. Yet loyalty to Luther's Catechism, the Augsburg Confession, Lutheran hymnody, liturgy, and devotional literature survived the secular divisions. The scarcity of pastors called forth lay leadership in the many small groups created by particular loyalties. World War II again shook the fragile ecclesiastical combinations that independence had brought into being.

Lutherans in Baltic Lands

The collapse of one empire afforded independence in eastern and southeastern Europe, and the end of another brought a moment of freedom to northeastern states. For in its death the Russian Empire relaxed its grip on the Baltic provinces and on the Lutherans within Russia, though a more fearful tyranny was in the making. When the Bolsheviks ended the war with Germany, independence was temporarily allowed Estonia, Latvia, and Finland. The Estonian Church at once reorganized itself into district synods in which the parishes were represented.

The state deposed the bishop in 1939, and with the renewal of war between Russia and Germany, the heavy hand of Russian influence fell on church and nation. Russia's eventual victory drove eighty thousand people into emigration. Half of the clergy scattered to Sweden, Germany, Canada, and Australia. In 1945, only seventy-seven clergymen remained of the 250 who five years earlier had ministered to a church of 900,000 members.

The development in Latvia was not much different, except that here relationships between Latvians and Germans disturbed the peace of the church. A strong romantic movement inspired a Lettish renaissance. The Latvian university at Riga boasted eleven faculties and eight thousand students. The church was drawn into this movement, but more for its sanction of national festivals than for its spiritual contribution. The state interfered with church affairs. After twenty years of freedom, war would again bring Russian domination, this time as a Communist dictatorship.

When the czardom ended, there were over 1.5 million Lutherans in Russia. An Evangelical Lutheran General Synod of Russia had been organized in 1923. After 1929, the Communists instituted a policy of persecution. The seminary was closed in 1931 and most of the pastors were imprisoned or exiled. Lithuania, too, became a free republic in 1918. German, Latvian, and Lithuanian Lutherans each organized their own synod and looked forward to state recognition of their church. But World War II almost completed the elimination of Lutheranism in Lithuania, which World War I started by separating it from older churches.

Finland joined the group of free states in 1917. It had been able to retain a church structure under Russian rule and new forms were unnecessary. It had solved, too, its Swedish relationships without the animosity characterizing Latvian and German associations. Marxism made approaches to the working class difficult. Yet the strong revival spirit of Finnish Christendom prevailed, continuing the pietistic character of the preceding century.

The Scandinavian Churches

The other northern nations—Sweden, Denmark, Norway—succeeded in staying out of World War I, but their churches took a leading part in extending aid to the stricken regions after the war. Sweden celebrated the quadricentennial of the Reformation by preparing a new translation of the Bible.

Vital intellectual work was produced in all these countries. Danish writers renewed interest in both Grundtvig and Kierkegaard and called attention to the books of Holl and Barth. They attempted to relate the Gospel to social needs of the day. Intellectuals in both Denmark and Norway were represented in the membership of the "Oxford," or Moral Re-Armament, movement.

In 1925, Archbishop Nathan Söderblom (1866–1931) assembled in Stockholm the first ecumenical gathering of modern times, an outgrowth of the 1910 Edinburgh Missionary Conference. The Christian Life and Work movement that he headed merged later with the Anglican-sponsored Faith and Order movement to create in 1948 the World Council of Churches. Of all Lutheran leaders in the years after World War I, Söderblom's name ranks first.

Despite leadership, scholarship, improvement of places and ways of worship, and modern means of communication, attendance at Scandinavian church services and at Holy Communion remained small. The ties between church and school slowly dissolved. The churches in Scandinavia retained inherited privileges, but their influence steadily declined among a religiously indifferent population. Terms such as "post-Christian world" were heard. The atom bombs that closed the tragedy of World War II cast vast shadows over the world. Lutherans of Europe looked hopefully across the Atlantic to their brethren in the New World.

Mergers in American Lutheranism

The Lutherans of the United States began a new chapter. The nineteenth century was one of increasing immigration, especially into the midwestern and western states, while the older Lutheran settlements in the east and south sought to keep their identity in the multidenominational environment of a country where all religions had equal freedom. From the first a conviction grew that Lutherans should achieve some kind of unity despite their varied European backgrounds. We have seen how combinations were gradually effected in the General Synod, the General Council, and the Synodical Conference. But the new century saw even more movement toward further unification.

Two major mergers occurred during World War I. In 1917, the quadricentennial year of the Reformation, Norwegian bodies formed The Norwegian Lutheran Church in America, its half-million members representing 92 percent of Norwegian Lutherans in America.

The following year a still larger merger brought together the oldest Lutheran organizations in the United States. While separate in the General Council, the General Synod, and the General Synod of the South, the Lutherans in the eastern and southern states had drawn together in missionary cooperation at home and abroad. A new church, The United Lutheran Church in America, was constituted in 1918.

Another significant merger followed in 1919. The synods of Wisconsin, Michigan, and Minnesota had been formed mainly out of German congregations. In 1917, they merged into one church, which concentrated the education of its pastors at Wauwatosa and later at Thiensville, Wisconsin. Now known as the Wisconsin Evangelical Lutheran Synod, it was the second largest component of the Synodical Conference.

Thus a large part of American Lutheranism had come together in doctrinal and organizational union in the course of three years. But the process continued. The postwar period saw a rapid increase in the use of English in the Lutheran churches. As the walls of separation crumbled, the various language groups recognized their similarity in doctrine, and in the expansion of their activities, they met one another on many fronts. The year of the quadricentennial of the Augsburg Confession witnessed another intersynodical commitment. In 1930, the Joint Synod of Ohio, the Iowa Synod, and the Buffalo Synod merged in the American Lutheran Church.

American Lutheran Conferences

Meanwhile The Norwegian Lutheran Church in America, the Augustana Church, the United Danish Church, and the Lutheran Free Church began to recognize how alike their mission and message were. In the same year as the American Lutheran Church was born, it joined with these other bodies in an association for edification, fellowship, and discussion of common programs, known as the American Lutheran Conference.

In 1917, The Lutheran Church—Missouri Synod passed the million mark in its baptized membership, and in 1944 the 1.5 million figure. In North America the Missouri Synod had pulpit and altar fellowship with the other members of the Synodical Conference, namely, the Joint Synod of Wisconsin and Other States, the small Norwegian Synod, and the Slovak Synod.

The National Lutheran Council

Most far reaching of the unifying forces in American Lutheranism was the National Lutheran Council. Its inception dates from the 1917 quadricentennial of the Reformation and the rudely interrupting events of America's entrance into World War I. The drafting of hundreds of thousands of Lutheran young men into war camps called for a ministry to them by their churches.

In September 1918, the National Lutheran Council came into being, its constitution ratified by the United Lutheran Church, Augustana, the Norwegian Lutheran Church, the Lutheran Free Church, the Joint Synod of Ohio, the Iowa Synod, the Buffalo Synod, the United Danish Church, the Icelandic Synod, and later the Suomi Synod. The council was an agency of these bodies, speaking for them in matters involving the government and representing them to the nation.

The council's most dramatic program was the part it played in relief work and service to the cause of foreign missions in the years following World War I. The name of Lauritz Larsen is gratefully recalled as the early leader in the program of the council both at home and abroad. Early in 1919, commissioners were sent to Europe, who reported on the disasters that had befallen Lutherans in war-torn countries and distributed aid from American churches.

In 1923, the first world gathering of Lutherans took place in Eisenach. Much of the burden of supporting weak churches fell on the National Lutheran Council of the United States, whose funds were deeply cut by years of economic depression. When the third meeting of the World Convention was held in Paris in 1935, the German churches were feeling the effects of their government's control over finances, shutting off communication with their mission fields. Again the council came to the rescue. Scandinavian churches played a great part in the relief measures adopted by the convention. Soon after the war the council helped set up the Lutheran Foreign Missions Conference to consider the needs of Lutheran fields throughout the world.

Lutherans in Asia

India, the oldest of missionary areas, exemplified the trend toward less dependence on European and American societies, though the world disorder caused by the wars of the nations slowed the movement.

The Japan Evangelical Lutheran Church, organized in 1922, was the fruit of work by the United Synod of the South, the United Evangelical Lutheran Church of the United States (Danish), and the Lutheran Gospel Association of Finland. In 1925, a seminary was located in Tokyo.

The Batak Mission, which recalls the achievements of Ludwig Nommensen, had grown to 100,000 members by the time of World War I. It was constituted a church in 1930. Lay leadership played a prominent part, and schools and medical stations went hand in hand with evangelistic work. But war, occupation by the Japanese, and political struggles slowed the desired development of the young church.

A tragic ending came to an extensive and intensive Chinese mission. Dedicated services of missionaries from Scandinavia, Germany, and the United States in the Honan and Hupeh provinces had resulted in a Lutheran Church of China in which sixteen synods had produced a common liturgy, hymnbooks, and a theological seminary. The Missouri Synod had begun prosperous work in Shanghai and Hankow, founding a seminary in the latter city in 1922. The United Lutheran Church had assumed responsibility for the Berlin Mission in Shantung in 1925. All of these fields were lost to the West after 1938 when the Communist regime followed the Japanese invasion.

Lutherans in Africa

Every section of the Lutheran world became interested in Africa, though here, too, World War I played havoc with courageous beginnings. The Leipzig Mission in Tanzania was cared for by the Augustana Church until 1926, when the latter took up its own work to the west in Iramba, central Tanzania. When World War II broke out, 172 German missionaries had to leave. Again Augustana, with the help of Swedish societies, assumed the duties of missionaries of the Leipzig, Bethel, and Berlin societies. A Swedish society, Bible-True Friends, had started work in Ethiopia and Eritrea in 1911; in 1948, they entered Kenya. The Danish Missionary Society and American Lutherans were in Sudan after 1913, while the American Lutheran Church continued earlier Norwegian projects in Madagascar. In South Africa the Berlin Society had begun as early as 1834. Cooperation in Natal and Zululand began in 1912 between Berlin, Norwegian, and Swedish societies and was extended by the association of an American Mission in 1928, of the Hermannsburg Mission in 1938, and of the old Schroeder Mission in 1938. In the Cape region, German immigrants formed congregations and organized a German Evangelical Lutheran Church of South Africa affiliated with the Church of Hanover. The Church of Sweden had an old mission in Rhodesia; and the Finnish Missionary Society had a mission in Ovamboland, ordaining the first native pastors in 1935. German immigrants made up the congregations that in 1926 formed the German Evangelical Lutheran Church in South-West Africa, while Rhenish missionaries worked among natives and formed a synod and established a seminary in 1938. On the west coast the United Lutheran Church inherited the mission in Liberia. The Synodical Conference began work in Nigeria in 1936.

Lutherans in South America

South America combined characteristics of both a mission field and diaspora work. Through the work of the Missouri Synod, a church of over 100,000 members was built up in Brazil (the Evangelical Lutheran Church of Brazil) and Argentina (the Argentina Evangelical Lutheran Church), and the Missouri Synod incorporated them as districts into the North American organization. In Argentina schools were begun in Buenos Aires and Obera. In Brazil a college and a seminary were established in Porto Alegre for the training of pastors, including those using Portuguese. The

General Synod of the United States laid the foundations of what became in 1948 the United Evangelical Lutheran Church of Argentina. It served both immigrants from many countries (Estonian, English, German, Hungarian, Latvian, Slovak) and Spanish-speaking natives. The German synods of Brazil, which had depended on help from the German Evangelical Church after World War I, soon found that the home church could do little. In 1949, they formed the Synodal Federation of the Evangelical Church of the Lutheran Confession in Brazil, establishing their own theological seminary. The La Plata Synod in Brazil, the German-speaking Evangelical Lutheran Church in Bolivia, the Evangelical Lutheran Church in Chile, and the German-speaking Evangelical congregations in Mexico all related themselves to the Foreign Office of the Evangelical Church in Germany and were thus, in a sense, daughter churches of a foreign body. By the time of World War II there were about a half-million members in the Lutheran communities in Latin America.

Lutherans in Australia

Australia more than South America moved in the direction of confessional unity among both the older and the newer immigrants. Gradually the synods that represented the unionistic tendencies of the Basel missions were guided by Neuendettelsau and Hermannsburg missionaries toward a more confessional position.

The Evangelical Lutheran Church Union and the Evangelical Lutheran General Synod merged in 1921 to form the United Evangelical Lutheran Church. A movement then began to bring together the new body and the older, Missouri-related, Evangelical Lutheran Synod, since 1941 known as The Evangelical Lutheran Church of Australia. After years of negotiation a union was created in 1965.

The convulsion of world war with its consequent destruction, exile, and emigration after 1914 affected every part of the Lutheran Church. For Germany it meant a revolution in the relations of church and state. For the churches the old boundaries between East and West were erased and new associations formed. The Scandinavian and American churches suffered least materially, but the spiritual life of all peoples underwent great changes. Most hopeful was the response of these churches to the needs of the afflicted. Out of the throes of the time was born the Lutheran World Convention, whose role in world Lutheranism remains to be recorded as we trace events since 1945.

CHAPTER THIRTEEN

Global Lutheran Fellowships

To understand the effects of the twentieth century ecumenical movement upon the Lutheran Church, more background is necessary. In the middle of the nineteenth century a combination of forces gave increasing vigor to a renewal of the identity of the Church of the Lutheran Reformation in Germany. The skepticism of philosophy made religious minds critical of its relationship to theology. The amalgamation of the territories of Germany into Bismarck's empire tended to bring the various interest groups closer together. The social problems faced by the Church called forth the Inner Mission and challenged the love as well as the faith of established church bodies. In 1832, the memorial of the death of Gustavus Adolphus was widely observed—from it grew the Gustav Adolf Society to aid diaspora congregations in other lands. A revived Roman Catholic Church added urgency to the restoration of a self-conscious Lutheran communion.

Interestingly, the plight of the pastorless Lutherans in America played a part in the confessional renewal of the Lutheran Church. In coming together to help these brethren in the faith, leaders found fellowship and support for a genuine faith. The event above others that made some kind of confessional stand imperative was the Prussian Union, which began in 1817.

The General Lutheran Conference

When the Evangelical Conference, sometimes called the Eisenach Conference, was organized in 1852 to embrace Protestant groups in Germany and Austria, many Lutherans declined participation and met separately the following year. They differed greatly on the policies to be followed if the church was to have greater freedom from the state.

In 1868, it was possible to convene the first all-Lutheran gathering, and so a General Lutheran Conference was organized at Hanover. The conference had no legislative power. It aimed at developing the positive nature of Lutheranism and defending the Church against unionism, Roman Catholicism, and secularism. Until the end of the century the conference was a German assembly. In 1901, it moved across German boundaries to Lund, Sweden, and then to other Scandinavian locations. Because the conference structure permitted the membership of Union churches, the stricter Lutheran members withdrew in 1907 and organized a separate body, the Lutheran Bund, or Alliance.

The Evangelical Federation

The Evangelical Conference meanwhile sought to include in its membership all German Protestants. After World War I its members were elected by the churches and thus spoke for them. In 1922 the Kirchenbund, or German Evangelical Church Federation, developed since the troubled conditions following the war made Protestant consensus desirable in matters related to secular authorities.

The Lutheran World Convention

After World War I, the National Lutheran Council of America approached the General Lutheran Conference. In earlier times they had fraternal correspondence and exchanged visitors between the conference and the General Council of the Evangelical Lutheran Church in North America. But the postwar situation suggested common action by Lutherans in many parts of the world. The conference and the National Lutheran Council called together in 1923 the Lutheran World Convention in Eisenach. The Lutheran World Convention held its second meeting in Copenhagen in 1929.

In the preceding chapter we saw how the Evangelical Federation was taken over by the Hitler regime and how independent theologians like Sasse and the Barmen group challenged its jurisdiction. World War II involved the German churches in resistance to Hitler, and once more the Lutherans of the world were divided by military powers. As soon as communication again was possible, the American section of the Lutheran World Convention sent representatives to Europe. The magnitude of the task assumed by the National Lutheran Council of the United States led in 1945 to an organization of a separate agency—Lutheran World Relief.

The Lutheran World Federation

The experience of three decades of war, depression, and international disorder finally persuaded Lutherans that to meet the changes of the day a world body should represent the whole church both to its members throughout the world and to political powers that were unaware of the effects of their decisions on spiritual communities. The Lutheran World Federation was born at Lund, Sweden, in the summer of 1947 and organized the larger, more liberal Lutheran churches. By the time of the Second Assembly at Hanover, Germany, in 1952, it was clear that the federation's activities could be grouped under three main departments—theology, world service, and world missions.

After 1948, the Lutheran World Federation, in conjunction with the German churches, turned its attention to finding homes in other lands for the many displaced persons. The uniting power of the Lutheran World Federation was evident when it drew together isolated communities of Lutherans whom historical circumstances had separated from their brethren such as those in France and Holland.

The VELKD and the EKD

The years after 1945 were years of consolidation and concentration for almost all Lutheran churches in various lands. In 1948, the greater number of the Lutheran churches in Germany realized a long-cherished desire for unity by the formation of the United Evangelical Lutheran Church of Germany (Vereinigte Evangelisch-Lutherische Kirche Deutschlands [VELKD]). Although some of the member bodies were bisected by the Iron Curtain that divided West and East Germany, around twenty million baptized members made up this first union of German Lutherans since the Reformation. The VELKD sought to unify as much as possible the activities of these churches. Among its firstfruits were new liturgical forms for worship and ministerial acts. The Free Churches did not join, continuing their objection to the former General Conference, namely, that the state churches included Reformed or United parishes.

At the same time as the United Church came into existence, most of the Protestant bodies in Germany joined in establishing anew the German Evangelical Church Union (Evangelische Kirche in Deutschland [EKD]). To the internal problems of German Lutheranism were added the profound questions of the future of the churches in Communist-held lands.

Minority Churches in the East

When the end of the war left all eastern borderlands in Russian hands, a radical change resulted in Lutheran constituencies. The thirteen million Germans who left their former homes as a consequence of the Potsdam Agreement of 1945 authorizing population transfers meant a mass evacuation of churches, parishes, and institutions. What had been German territory or Baltic free states now became Russian controlled territory with new boundaries: Poland, Czechoslovakia, Hungary, Yugoslavia. Of the Germans still in Poland a decade after the Potsdam Agreement, no fewer than 300,000 returned to Germany when the Red Cross in 1955 arranged for permission to leave so families might be reunited, and another 70,000 asked for a similar privilege. This meant the end of the German Lutheran Church there—only the Polish part remained. Its 100,000 members experienced harassment both from the Communist Russian authorities and the Roman Catholic authorities who had again made Poland a Roman stronghold.

Czechoslovakia proved more friendly to its Protestant population, assuming responsibility for the economic needs of parishes and theological seminaries.

The course of the Lutheran Church in Hungary was determined by vacillations in the policy of a Communist government. Sweden and the National Lutheran Council of the United States gave substantial help to reconstruct the church. The repression of the dissident political elements meant a pressure also on the Lutheran clergy to conform to the rule of the all-powerful state.

Yugoslavia combined numerous districts and faiths—Serbia, Croatia, Bosnia, Herzegovina; and Orthodox, Reformed, Lutheran, Roman Catholic. The upheavals of two world wars, including the departure of 100,000 Germans after 1945, left only small Lutheran churches in what was once territory of Austria or Hungary.

All these churches suffered persecution under the Communist regime that tolerated them even as it sought to extirpate them. In East Germany the old Lutheran churches fought heroically against terrific odds. Especially difficult were the prohibitions against instruction of youth and the obstacles to theological training. In Romania Pastor Richard Wurmbrand, first ordained as an Anglican but as a Lutheran after World War II, was arrested on his way to conduct church services in 1948. He was released in 1956, though warned not to preach. After serving in the underground church, he was arrested again in 1959. He eventually wrote the widely read *Tortured for Christ* and other books about persecution, later founding the international organization, Voice of the Martyrs.

Contacts across the borders of east and west became extremely rare. Similar conditions prevailed in Latvia and Estonia, where the attempt of those who remained to conserve the church were critically judged by fellow Lutherans in exiled churches. In 1956, the Lutheran World Federation reviewed its program of aid to minority churches in a conference in Austria, and continuing help flowed through World Service. A second minority churches' conference in 1962 in Yugoslavia enabled the federation to learn where it could be of greatest help.

Lutheran churches played a role in the eventual collapse of Communism in Eastern Europe. For example, in the 1980s St. Nikolai Evangelical Lutheran Church in Leipzig began hosting a weekly prayer vigil for peace. The vigils grew to include thousands of participants, becoming a haven for those who opposed the Communist state. In October 1989, the state attacked protesters in Leipzig, but they gathered en masse to St. Nikolai's prayer vigil on October 9. As an established gathering, it served as a refuge for peaceful protest. Following the vigil that week, seventy thousand protestors marched unopposed through the streets of Leipzig, demonstrating to the East German state the strength of the opposition. A month later, citizens in Berlin were able to tear down the wall separating East and West Germany, which has become the enduring symbol of the collapse of Communism in the twentieth century.

Scandinavian Churches

The Scandinavian countries assumed a large share of the program of the Lutheran World Federation. This agency was instrumental in reconciling the people of Norway and Denmark with their former occupying powers, and together with the churches of Germany they bound up the wounds of war. Ordination of women caused considerable discussion. The secularization of schools did not crowd out religious instruction, though the time allowed for it was reduced. The relationship of church and state was not satisfactorily solved. In Sweden both parliament and the bishops studied what might happen if the Church of Sweden were to be disestablished. The Icelandic Parliament in 1957 gave the church its own council. Lively contacts with other churches kept these countries in the forefront of the ecumenical movement, though the Norwegian Missionary Council voted against the World Council of Churches decision to incorporate the International Missionary Council and thus retained its independence. The attendance at worship services in all these countries remained low, giving rise to concern over the paganization of popular life.

Further Mergers in the USA

The post-World War II period witnessed further unification among the Lutheran churches in America. The member bodies of the American Lutheran Conference determined that there were no great differences in faith or practice among themselves and therefore desired a more organic union.

Thus in less than fifty years the majority of the many different nationalistic synods coalesced into three large bodies, namely, the Lutheran

Church in America with some three million baptized members, the Synodical Conference with almost as many, and The American Lutheran Church, which was somewhat smaller. Each of these groups included Canadian districts or divisions that had grown up in affiliation with bodies in the United States.

Differences within the Synodical Conference caused the Wisconsin Synod and the Evangelical Lutheran [Norwegian] Synod to withdraw in 1963, leaving the Missouri Synod and the Synod of Evangelical Lutheran Churches as sole members. In its steady growth, the Missouri Synod found itself more involved with other Lutheran churches, both during and after World War II. The LCMS had followed the assemblies of the Lutheran World Federation in the capacity of an observer. Formation by these churches of the Lutheran Council in the United States of America (LCUSA) at Cleveland, Ohio, November 16, 1966, brought practically all Lutherans in the United States and Canada into a cooperative organization.

In the latter half of the twentieth century, two significant events occurred in American Lutheran churches. The first was the 1974 walkout of the majority of professors from Concordia Seminary, St. Louis. This happened because the LCMS elected more conservative leadership in the 1960s and 1970s, while the seminary faculty remained committed to liberalizing theological trends and efforts toward pan-Lutheran unity in America. In 1970, the LCMS president, Rev. Dr. J. A. O. Preus, appointed a fact-finding committee to investigate the teachings of the St. Louis seminary professors. Ultimately, the seminary faculty majority responded by boarding the entrance to the seminary and walking off campus in a union-style protest. They became convinced that the majority of the synod would support the soundness of their teaching and their academic freedom by withdrawing from the LCMS. However, only about 3.7 percent of the synod's membership followed the faculty majority, forming a separate synod named the Association of Evangelical Lutheran Churches in 1976.

In 1988, the Association of Evangelical Lutheran Churches (AELC), the Lutheran Church in America (LCA), and The American Lutheran Church (ALC) organized to form the Evangelical Lutheran Church in America (ELCA), the largest Lutheran body in America. Since the merging bodies held to liberal theological positions, including the ordination of women as pastors, the LCMS and other conservative churches did not participate in the merger. Subsequent debate over ordination of actively homosexual ministers caused some divisions in the ELCA, especially after their 2009 Churchwide Assembly. In the two years following, the ELCA experienced a greater than 10 percent decline as more conservative members left to organize other church bodies.

Autonomy and Fellowship

In the world of modern communications the Lutherans of Europe and America came closer to the younger churches of other continents. Both the destruction of the world wars and subsequent rebuilding directed the development of Lutherans around the world. A few examples will illustrate what happened in the missionary areas.

The Ethiopian Evangelical Church Mekane Yesus in 1958 merged the former missions of the Swedish Evangelical Mission Society, the Hermannsburg Society, the Norwegian Lutheran Society, the Icelandic, the Danish, and the American Lutheran agencies into one native church. In Tanzania the seven churches that had grown out of the labors of missionaries from almost all the European and American churches united in 1964 to form the Evangelical Lutheran Church in Tanzania. The various mission churches of southeast Africa, with one exception, united in 1960 in the Evangelical Lutheran Church in Southern Africa, Southeastern Region. The Northern and Southern Transvaal synods merged into the Evangelical Lutheran Church (Transvaal Region) in 1962.

The Communist victory in China drove missionaries of all churches out of the country. They scattered far and wide. Many went to Japan where new churches were founded by missionaries of the Missouri Synod, the Wisconsin Synod, and Norwegian bodies. Older missions of the Japanese Evangelical Lutheran Church were reinforced by new forces from the Augustana and Suomi churches and from the Danish Society. Chinese refugees on Taiwan began to build a church in 1951.

After World War II, the Missouri Synod also began work in the Philippines, Korea, Hong Kong, and New Guinea. In New Guinea the Evangelical Lutheran Church of Australia extended its field, and the old mission of the Neuendettelsau Society, taken over by the American Lutheran Church because of war conditions, organized itself in 1956 into the Evangelical Lutheran Church of New Guinea. This church and the Batak Church in Indonesia became the largest of all Lutheran mission churches. The Batak Church drew up a confession of faith in 1951 that satisfied the conditions of membership in the Lutheran World Federation.

As the missions grew into congregations and congregations made up churches that related themselves to the older communions of the Lutheran Reformation, the younger churches found themselves faced with questions of relationships to other Christians in their own vicinity. (For example, this problem became acute on the oldest Protestant missionary field, India, when Congregationalists, Presbyterians, Methodists, and Anglicans formed the Church of South India in 1947.) Slowly the Lutheran mission churches became autonomous and chose their own leadership. Inspired not only by Swedish example but by Anglican orders and by native needs, some of the Lutheran mission churches adopted the title of *bishop* for their highest office; in other churches the term *president* prevailed. In all of them the synod became the legislative organ, with an executive council or diocesan chapter as an intermediary between the synod and its head. This became the form also on other fields, in Africa and Asia.

What held together these many different kinds of churches around the world? The one common denominator was a Christian faith. Its simplest and most universal expression was found in Luther's Small Catechism that opened the doors to the Scriptures, which have everywhere been accepted as the foundation of the faith and its complete revelation. For the Lutheran of every color and climate, the hymnbook expressed the meaning of the faith for his own life. For the pastor and teacher, the Augsburg Confession and the entire Book of Concord provided the interpretation of Scripture in the preaching and teaching ministry. Out of faith given in the Word and Sacrament, which constituted the contents and spirit of worship and the guidance of thought and action, came the prayer to live and to work in obedience to the Christ revealed in the Word. In the fellowship of the congregation of believers near and far, the Lutheran Christian saw his purpose in life and fulfilled his calling as a member of the Body of Christ. He experienced and confessed the grace of God in Jesus Christ through the Spirit living in His Church.

CHAPTER FOURTEEN

Ecumenical Efforts and the Future Lutheran Church

Luther's purpose was to restore to the Medieval Church its original character. Over the centuries Rome had introduced innovations that obscured the real nature of the one, holy, catholic, and apostolic Church. These novelties in the Mass, the hierarchy, and the papacy, insofar as they were contrary to Scripture, had to be eradicated. The real mission of the Church was to proclaim the Gospel and to administer the Sacraments. Not the initiation of a new church, therefore, but a reaffirmation of the Church of the Word was the genius of the Lutheran Reformation. However, once Word and Sacrament ministry was reestablished, a different matter arose: how does the Church of the Lutheran Reformation relate to other churches? Since the beginning of the twentieth century, this question has predominated.

National Christian Councils and the World Council of Churches

In general the practice of the Lutheran churches everywhere has been to require agreement in doctrine as a condition for participation in the Lord's Supper. But there has been a growing willingness to enter into cooperation with other Protestant churches in meeting common problems of the times. Regional or national associations have been organized on every continent, and Lutherans have participated in many of them.

The greater mobility of populations, the many emigrations, and the improvement of communications hastened a consolidation of Christendom as it faced the complex social problems of the nineteenth century. The Edinburgh Missionary Conference of 1910 became a watershed in Christian history. From that date streams of church life began to flow in the direction of ecumenicity. Although the consequences of World War I proved devastating, they made more urgent the call for common action by Christians. Lutherans responded to the challenge.

Confessions and Ecumenicity

In joining ecumenical endeavors, Lutheran churches have insisted on their confessional character. The World Council, they have helped make clear, cannot be a church but a meeting of churches that possess the basic unity provided through Baptism into Christ. The Church is not a judge over the Gospel but a servant of the Gospel, and its service is the proclamation of the Word to the world. The Gospel creates the Church by the Spirit, and its unity is in the witness it bears to Christ, its Head and Lord.

Lutherans and Vatican Council II (1962–65)

Despite the course of the papal church after Trent, there were some who hoped for reconciliation between Rome and Wittenberg. Spinola, a Roman bishop of Dalmatia, traveled far and wide in the latter part of the seventeenth century visiting Lutheran princes and theologians in the hope of finding a formula for union—but in vain. What mellowing there may have been between Lutherans and Romanists was due to a general spirit of tolerance engendered by the philosophy of rationalism. As governments became theologically neutral, the masses tended toward indifference to the claims of theologians.

For papal power the French Revolution was a catastrophe, to be followed by the liberation of Italy from the temporal rule of the Vatican. At the Vatican Council in 1870, the pope's faithful followers declared him infallible when he speaks *ex cathedra*, that is, when as supreme head of the church he proclaims a doctrine for the whole church. The adoration of Mary and the development of Mariology reached their culmination in 1950 when the dogma of the Assumption of the Virgin Mary to the throne of heaven was promulgated. This decree and that of papal infallibility separated the Roman Church even farther from the churches of the Reformation, justifying their protest against doctrines not based on Scripture.

The remarkable change that Pope John XXIII inaugurated when he called together the bishops of the Roman Church to chart a changed course in the modern world included an approach to Protestants as "separated brethren," an important step toward reversing the four-hundred-year condemnation of the churches of the Reformation. The losses that the Roman Church suffered through war and communism may have influenced the papal call for new measures. The advance, too, of the ecumenical movement by the participation of the Orthodox Church created a challenge to the Church of Rome. The council made ecumenical relations one of its greatest emphases. In 1925, the pope had snubbed the Stockholm Conference, but in 1961, official Roman observers attended the New Delhi meeting of the World Council. The pope even asked for forgiveness of the sins that his church may have committed against the churches of the "separated brethren."

Lutherans welcomed these unexpected approaches from Rome. Already during and after the war years, friendly discussions had taken place between Roman and Lutheran theologians, such as those arranged by Prof. Edmund Schlink of Heidelberg. The Lutheran World Federation encouraged the conversations with Roman representatives.

Lutherans have appreciated the respect newly accorded them and have readily admitted sins of unbrotherliness on their side. Yet there are no plans for a "return to Rome," to which they have been invited.

Late Twentieth Century Movements and Mergers

Since World War II, the emphases on mission and ecumenical relations have continued to influence Lutheran thought and practice. Theological problems arose in the efforts of the World Council of Churches, which began to undermine Christianity's exclusive claim of salvation through Jesus Christ as well as its reliance upon the Holy Scriptures to guide the doctrine and practice of the Church. In response, American evangelicals sought a renewed emphasis on faithful confession of Christ. For example, Billy Graham called for a world congress on evangelism, which met at Berlin in 1966. This gave rise to the Lausanne Movement (1974) with which conservative and mission-minded Lutherans have sympathized.

Several important ecumenical agreements developed in Europe and North America. Many Lutheran and Reformed churches in Europe agreed upon the Leuenberg Concord (1973), which brought them into fellowship. To avoid the sixteenth-century arguments that prevented Lutheran and Reformed Christians from agreeing during the Reformation, their concord emphasized the consequences of the Lord's Supper rather than the mode of Christ's presence in the Supper. In other words, they focused on what the Supper does rather than what the Supper is. (A similar agreement was reached among Lutheran and Reformed churches in North America in 2000.) The 1991 Meissen Agreement brought about intercommunion between German churches and Anglican churches. A parallel agreement, the 1992 Porvoo Communion, established fellowship relations between Anglican churches and Lutheran churches of Scandinavia and the Baltics. More recently, the Community of Protestant Churches now represents a fellowship of about one hundred churches, with Lutheran state churches among them. Their fellowship is based on the Leuenberg Concord. Although these many mergers represent important historical developments, they mask the greatest developments affecting Protestant churches in Europe: rapid decline in membership, in participation, and in sound doctrine. For example, less than 20 percent of professed Lutherans in Europe attend church annually. The mergers gloss over theological issues between the traditions, creating fellowship that does not agree with the Lutheran Confessions.

The most recent meetings of the LWF have focused on important social issues such as the spread of HIV, poverty, and the perils of refugees. These are common causes for older Lutheran churches in Europe and North America as well as the younger Lutheran churches in the global south (South America, Africa, and southern Asia), which are experiencing significant growth. The planned 2017 LWF Assembly will focus on Lutheran and Roman Catholic relations while observing the five hundredth anniversary of the Reformation.

Confessional Renewal

A hopeful sign for global Lutheranism is the rising influence of the Lutheran churches in South America, Africa, and southern Asia. These churches tend to be more doctrinally conservative in their theology and practice than the European and North American churches that planted them as mission churches in centuries past. Many of them also have healing services and exorcisms to address the spiritual needs in their communities. In fact, some of the younger churches have begun to send missionaries back to Europe in an effort to re-evangelize that part of the world. For example, in 2005, Kenyan Lutheran Bishop Walter Obare Omwanza caused a stir when he consecrated Pastor Arne Olsson as a bishop for a conservative Lutheran group in Sweden. Olsson's group opposed the liberal theology and practice of the Church of Sweden but found ready support from the Kenyan church. Events like this are likely to repeat themselves as the mission churches exercise their growing concern to lead global Lutheranism faithfully.

In 1993, confessionally minded Lutheran churches formed the International Lutheran Council, a worldwide association committed to the Holy Scriptures and the Lutheran Confessions. Although this organization is much smaller than the Lutheran World Federation, the growing Lutheran churches of the global south, as well as those in former soviet countries, are increasingly drawn to the ILC because of shared values and concerns.

EPILOGUE

The Church of the Lutheran Reformation came into a world where ancient empires were disintegrating, new continents were being explored, and a new learning was revealing secrets of the earth and the heavens. Today, again, new nations replace old kingdoms, a mysterious universe of space is being discovered, and revolutions are taking place in the minds of men of all races and nations while the Spirit of God seeks to proclaim anew the unmerited grace of God in Jesus Christ, the Alpha and the Omega of the world. To that end, the biblical teachings of justification, Law and Gospel, the true body and blood of Christ in the Sacrament, and the theology of the cross remain essential; these inheritances of the Lutheran Church continue to inspire new life and hope in Christ.

Glossary

abortifacient. Any substance that induces an abortion. RU-486 (mifepristone) may be the most controversial abortifacient. A possible side effect of "the pill" is that, in addition to prohibiting pregnancy, it may also act as an abortifacient.

abortion. Any deliberate act to terminate a pregnancy by destroying human life. In 1973, abortion (within certain parameters) was legalized in all states by the U.S. Supreme Court (*Roe v. Wade*).

Absolution (v. *absolve*). To set free from sin. This Latin term was used by theologians as a translation of the biblical word *aphiemi*, "to set free, cancel, or forgive." By virtue of his office, in the name and stead of Christ, a pastor absolves those who have confessed their sins, affirmed their faith in Christ, and promised to amend their lives (Matthew 16:19; 18:18; John 20:19–23). The Lutheran Church retains private Confession and Absolution as "the very voice of the Gospel," declaring that it would be impious to abolish it (AC XI; Ap XI 2; SA III VIII; SC V). Absolution may be called a Sacrament (Ap XIII 4).

actual sin. Sins committed by a person in distinction from original sin. *See* **original sin.**

adiaphora. From the Greek, meaning "indifferent things." Church rites neither commanded nor forbidden by God (e.g., making the sign of the cross, bowing during the Gloria Patri). Church rites cease being indifferent when by their use or disuse they compromise the confession of faith (FC Ep X; FC SD X).

adultery. Generally defined, adultery is consensual sexual intercourse by a married person with someone other than his or her legal spouse. However, all sexual activity outside of heterosexual marriage falls under the condemnation of the Sixth Commandment.

agnostic. The belief that we can know only about physical things or beings and not about spiritual or supernatural things or beings, such as God.

altar call. An invitation to come forward after a sermon and commit oneself to following Christ. The altar call became an important part of repentance in revivalism in the 1800s.

amillennialism. The doctrine that the thousand-year reign of Christ mentioned in Revelation 20 should not be taken literally. It symbolizes the reign of Christ from His first appearing to His reappearing at the end of time.

angel. In Hebrew and Greek, the word *angel* means "messenger." In the Bible the word sometimes refers to human messengers. For the purposes of this book, an angel is a bodiless (noncorporeal) spiritual being created by God to serve Him and those who believe in Him. Angels possess superhuman strength and sometimes take on the appearance of human men. Evil angels are commonly called demons. *See* **demon.**

angel of the Lord. The phrase *angel of the Lord* appears more than forty times in the Old Testament. Where the angel of the Lord receives divine worship and performs divine acts, Luther and most older Lutheran commentators understood this to mean the preincarnate Son of God.

annulment. A legal declaration that a marriage is null and void.

Antichrist. Based on 1 John 2:18; 4:3, the Antichrist is one who opposes the teachings of Christ. The term is also used to describe "the lawless one" (2 Thessalonians 2:8) or beast of the earth (Revelation 13:11), a deceptive religious leader who will emerge at the end of time.

antinomianism. The belief that Christians are free from many, if not all, of the constraints of moral law.

Apocrypha. A collection of noncanonical books written during the intertestamental period. Luther's 1534 Bible included the Apocrypha between the Old and New Testaments with this remark: "Apocrypha: These books are not held equal to the Sacred Scriptures, and yet are useful and good for reading."

apostasy. Falling away from faith in Christ. The Bible warns that before Christ's reappearing, many will fall away (1 Timothy 4:1).

archangel. The word *archangel* appears only in 1 Thessalonians 4:16 and Jude 9. In the latter verse, *archangel* refers only to the archangel Michael. Daniel 10:21 and 12:1 also refer to Michael as a "prince" or a "great prince," which seems to indicate that only he serves in this capacity.

ark of the covenant. The golden chest God ordered Moses to have made (Exodus 25:9–30). It held the Ten Commandments, Aaron's rod, and a pot of manna. The lid of the ark was called the mercy seat, over which were crafted two artistic representations of cherubim.

atonement. From an old French term meaning "at-one-ment." (Greek: *katallage* [Romans 5:11]; often otherwise "reconciliation" [Romans 5:10; 2 Corinthians 5:19].) The term properly reflects a mutual exchange, or a drawing together of parties previously separated. God's action in Christ to forgive sin in order to restore the relationship between Himself and His fallen creatures. *See also* **mercy seat; propitiation.**

Baptism. From the Greek word meaning "to immerse" or "to wash." Many religions have religious washings. But Christian Baptism applies water "in the name of the Father and of the Son and of the Holy Spirit" as described by Jesus (Matthew 28:19). In Baptism, God washes away the person's sins and welcomes that person as a member of His kingdom. Through water joined to God's Word, the Holy Spirit puts to death our sinful nature, connects us to Christ in His death and resurrection, and gives us new spiritual birth as God's children.

beast. According to Revelation 13:11, a deceptive religious leader who will emerge at the end of time. *See also* **Antichrist.**

bishop (Greek: *episkospos*, "overseer"). Used in the New Testament for those who governed and directed the Christian communities. The New Testament does not distinguish between bishops and presbyters (Acts 14:23; 20:17, 28). The Lutheran Symbols recognized the rank of bishops and described their true function as preaching the Gospel, administering the Sacraments, and using the Keys (AC XXVIII; Ap XXVIII; Tr 60–82; SA II IV 9; III 10).

call. The mechanism whereby a man is chosen for a specific area of pastoral work. The call specifies who, what, and where.

calling. *See* **vocation.**

canon (Greek: *kanon*, "rule"or "standard"). May refer to (a) particular dogmatic formulations approved by Church councils; (b) the authoritative list of the books of the Bible; or (c) the unchanging high point of the Mass containing the Words of Institution and certain prayers.

catechism. From the Greek word meaning "oral instruction," used by St. Paul in Galatians 6:6. A catechism is a book, usually in question-and-answer format, containing basic instruction.

charismatics. From the Greek word *charismata*, meaning "gift." Charismatics share the belief of Pentecostals that God "baptizes" people with the Holy Spirit today by bestowing miraculous gifts/abilities, such as speaking in tongues, prophesying, and healing.

cherubim (singular: *cherub*). Angelic beings that according to archaeological evidence were represented pictorially as winged creatures having a human head and a lion's body (not as the winged chubby babies often depicted in Western art).

Christ. The Greek term for Messiah.

civil union. A civil status similar to marriage that allows same-sex persons (and, in some states and nations, opposite-sex couples) access to benefits traditionally reserved for heterosexual married couples.

close(d) Communion. The ancient practice of only communing members of congregations that have official fellowship with one another. Exceptions may be made in cases of pastoral care. In North America, the Eastern Orthodox Church, Roman Catholics, The Lutheran Church—Missouri Synod, the Wisconsin Evangelical Lutheran Synod, the Evangelical Lutheran Synod, the Association of Reformed Presbyterian Churches, and conservative Anabaptist churches practice close(d) Communion. *See* **open Communion.**

Communion. To take part in something, to share something. "Communion" or "participation" translates the Greek word for fellowship, *koinonia*. In the Lord's Supper, communicants partake of the body and blood of Christ and are made members of His Body, the Church (1 Corinthians 10:16–17).

consistory. An administrative board consisting mainly of clergy, often attached to a regional bishop/district president.

contraception. Any action, device, or medication used to prevent a woman from becoming pregnant. Some contraceptives are prescribed to alleviate specific conditions or to regulate menstruation. Prior to the 1930 Lambeth Conference of Anglican bishops, most Protestant churches (including Lutheran) condemned contraception. In 1965, the U.S. Supreme Court struck down a state law prohibiting contraception for heterosexual married couples (*Griswold v. Connecticut*), virtually legalizing contraception for this country.

contrition. To feel sorrow for one's sins.

corporate worship. People worshiping together in a group (*corporate* comes from the Latin word *corpus*, "body").

covenant. A formal, binding agreement between two or more parties promising the fulfillment of some act. In the Bible, covenants with

God are generally associated with God's initiation of the covenant, His promise of some action associated with the covenant, and the shedding of blood. By virtue of His cross, the Lord's Supper is the "New Covenant" for the forgiveness of sins (Matthew 26:26–28; Mark 14:22–24; Luke 22:19–20; 1 Corinthians 11:23–26). *See also* **atonement; testament.**

creed. From the Latin word *credo*, "I believe." Creeds are summary confessions of faith used by the majority of Christians. When they developed, most people could not read and needed a memorable rule of faith.

Darwinian evolution. Sometimes referred to as organic evolution or macroevolution. This view is currently represented by "neo-Darwinism" and maintains, as corollary theories, that a spiritual realm does not exist (philosophical materialism) and that everything exists by natural causes alone (naturalism). Modern science is proving some Darwinian beliefs less and less tenable.

deacon. Traditionally, an assistant to a bishop or overseer (see Philippians 1:1). The traditional work of a deacon was to assist in the Divine Service and to care for the poor and needy. Deacons also brought Holy Communion to the shut-ins.

Deism. Created by English philosophers in the seventeenth century, this system of "natural religion" is based on points of doctrine attributed to all religions: (1) God exists; (2) He should be worshiped; (3) worship is connected to morality; (4) people should repent of sin; and (5) God will judge people in the world to come.

demon. Evil, fallen angels or spirits. *See also* **angel.**

demonic possession. Control by a demon. The demon-possessed man at Gadara (Luke 8:26–39) displayed the following characteristics: (1) he recognized Jesus' identity as the Son of God, (2) had supernatural strength, and (3) the presence of Christ caused the demons inside of this man to prefer inhabiting the swine.

devil. Term meaning "accuser." Usually a descriptive name of Satan but also used in the plural to refer to evil angels or demons.

Didache. Literally, "the teaching." An ancient document, perhaps originally Jewish, written to prepare converts for Baptism and congregational life. Parts of it may have been written in the first century AD.

Divine Service. A translation of a German term for worship, *Gottesdienst.*

divorce. Dissolution of marriage or the ending of marriage before the death of either spouse.

doctrine. The Latin word for "teaching."

elder. Term derived from the Old (Exodus 3:16) and New Testaments (Luke 7:3), the Greek word *presbyteros*, "elder," is a synonym for *episkopos*, "bishop" (Acts 20:17, 28), "ruler" (1 Timothy 5:17), and "pastor" (1 Peter 5:1–4). Large congregations had a number of presbyters or elders (James 5:14; Acts 15:4, 6, 23; 20:17, 28; 21:18). At least some elders preached and taught (1 Timothy 5:17).

elect. From the Latin for "to choose." Even before He created the world, God chose ("elected") those whom He will save in Christ. The doctrine of election is a comforting doctrine to all who trust in Christ for salvation. *See* **predestination.**

election. From the Latin word "to choose." The teaching that God chose to save His people even before He created the world. *See* **predestination.**

Essenes. A Jewish sect from the time of Christ that emphasized simplicity, purity, sacred meals, and fixed times of prayer. The community that produced the Dead Sea Scrolls was probably Essene.

Eucharist (Greek: *eucharistesas*, "when He had given thanks," [1 Corinthians 11:24]). The Breaking of Bread (Matthew 26:26; 1 Corinthians 10:16), Holy Communion (1 Corinthians 10:16–17), the Lord's Table (1 Corinthians 10:21), the Lord's Supper (1 Corinthians 11:20), the Mass.

evangelical (Greek: *euangelion*, "good news"). Term meaning "loyal to the Gospel of Jesus Christ." The Lutheran Reformation was evangelical because it emphasized the doctrine of Christ's atonement for sin.

evangelicals. In North America, *evangelical* describes Protestant churches that emphasize Christ's atonement for sin as well as mission work. They generally stem from the Reformed, Baptist, and Wesleyan denominational families.

evolution. A worldview that originated in ancient Greece, not with Charles Darwin. This worldview teaches that the universe is eternal, that man is advancing, and that there is no personal God. Thus man defines the unifying concept of existence, the meaning and the purpose of life. *See also* **macroevolution; microevolution.**

***ex nihilo*.** Latin: "from nothing." When we speak of God creating the universe *ex nihilo*, we mean that He created everything that exists, both the seen and the unseen, from nothing.

external Word. An expression used by Luther to describe the Bible and biblical teaching. Luther contrasted the external Word with the internal word or feelings sought by people who believed that the Spirit guided them directly, apart from the Bible.

***filioque*.** Literally, "and the Son." This Latin word was added to the Nicene Creed in the West to emphasize that the Holy Spirit proceeds from the Father and the Son. The Eastern churches have never accepted this statement, insisting that the Spirit proceeds only from the Father.

first (civil) use of the Law. The Law is a curb to restrain sin and disorder, designed to allow life in community to continue.

foreknowledge. The teaching that God knows everything before it happens, including who will believe and who will not believe.

forensic justification. The central way the Bible speaks of our justification before God is in a forensic, or judicial, way. God declares us sinners righteous in His sight through faith in His Son, Jesus Christ.

fornication. Sexual activity between two unmarried persons.

fundamentalism. A reactionary movement against liberalism and modernism that focuses on certain cardinal tenets of the Christian faith—biblical inerrancy among them—often to the exclusion of other beliefs. Liberal Christians often accuse those believing in biblical inerrancy of being "fundamentalists."

Gloria in Excelsis. Latin for "Glory in the highest" to God, sung by the angels (Luke 2:14). The Gloria is sung in the liturgy to praise God for salvation through Jesus.

Gnosticism. From the Greek *gnosis*, "knowledge." Specifically, a late first- and early second-century AD Christian heretical sect that replaced the pure Gospel of Christ with a demand for secret knowledge. Gnostics claimed the only way to salvation was for the spirit to be liberated from the material order, which was considered evil. Gnostics denied Christ taking on human flesh. Today, Gnosticism appears in a variety of forms that militate against God's creation, including militant feminism, homosexual activism, laws that undermine male/female marriage, rejection of the Sacraments, and the like.

God's image. *See* **image of God.**

godparent. A traditional term for a baptismal sponsor, a person who makes required professions and promises in the name of an infant or convert presented for Christian Baptism. A baptismal sponsor should encourage and support the newly baptized person in the Christian faith.

good works. God's love works through us to serve our neighbor. In faith, we cooperate with God's gracious will to care for our neighbor.

Gospel. The message of Christ's death and resurrection for the forgiveness of sins, eternal life, and salvation. The Holy Spirit works through the Gospel in Word and Sacrament to create and sustain faith and to empower good works. The Gospel is found in both the Old and New Testaments.

Gospel reductionism. Using the Gospel to suggest considerable latitude in faith and life not explicitly detailed in the Gospel. Associated with liberal Christianity, Gospel reductionism is closely aligned with antinomianism and partial inspiration.

grace. Properly, God's goodwill and favor in and through Jesus Christ, toward sinners, who can plead no merit or worthiness. Scripture also refers to grace in the sense of a gift God gives to people.

grail. An old French term for the dish or cup used by Jesus during the Last Supper. Many medieval romantic stories surround this grail and attribute special powers to it. In contrast, the early Christians focused on Jesus' body and blood in the Lord's Supper and their power to heal or judge (1 Corinthians 11:27–31).

guardian angel. An angel with responsibility for one of God's children (Psalm 91:11; Matthew 18:10; Acts 12:15).

historical-critical method. An approach to the study of the Scriptures shaped by Enlightenment presuppositions regarding history and the accessibility of historical events to the interpreter. Those who practiced this method more often than not denied the divine character of the Scriptures.

holy. Set apart for a divine purpose (e.g., Holy Scripture is set apart from all other types of writing). The Holy Spirit makes Christians holy. *See* **sanctification.**

hours of prayer. Set times and customs of prayer rooted in early Christian practice: Matins, Lauds, Prime, Terce, Sext, None, Vespers, Compline. (Matins and Lauds were combined in some traditions.) Lutheran hymnals often contain services for Matins (morning service) and Vespers (evening service).

image of God (*imago Dei*). The knowledge of God and holiness of the will, man's original righteousness that was present before the fall (Colossians 3:10; Ephesians 4:24). This image was lost through sin (Romans 1:23). Without original righteousness, God's concreated gifts of human rationality, creativity, and the like are not properly called "the image of

God." Yet by the Holy Spirit, who works through the Gospel in Word and Sacraments, the image of God is being restored in believers as they are being conformed to the image of Christ (Romans 8:29; 2 Corinthians 3:18; Colossians 3:10). This image is to be restored fully in believers only at Christ's second coming.

inerrancy. The teaching that the Bible, as originally inspired by the Holy Spirit and recorded by the prophets, apostles, and evangelists, did not contain errors. Churches teaching biblical inerrancy recognize that scribes and translators may have erred in copying the Bible over the centuries.

infant Communion. Giving Communion to infants, practiced by the Eastern Orthodox Church and now some Protestants. The practice was common in medieval times.

inspiration. Guidance by a spirit. In many religions the term describes a trancelike state of spirit possession. In Christianity the term usually describes the guidance of God's Holy Spirit provided to the prophets and the writers of the Bible (plenary inspiration). *See* **verbal inspiration.**

intercession. Prayer offered on behalf of another person.

intermediate state of souls. Roman Catholics teach that upon death, a person's soul may go to limbo or purgatory rather than directly to heaven or hell. Others teach the soul of a dead person rests in the ground until the resurrection ("soul sleep"). The Bible describes heaven and hell—at times using other terms (paradise, Abraham's bosom, Hades, Gehenna, etc.)—but does not teach about an intermediate state of souls (e.g., Luke 23:40–43).

Judaizers. A group in the Early Church that wished to impose Jewish practices such as circumcision on the Gentiles. Judaizers viewed obedience to the Old Testament Law as necessary for salvation.

justification. God declares sinners to be just or righteous for Christ's sake; that is, God has imputed or charged our sins to Christ and He imputes or credits Christ's righteousness to us.

Keys. The peculiar, special, unique spiritual authority given by Christ to the whole Church to forgive the sins of repentant sinners but to withhold forgiveness from the unrepentant as long as they do not repent (John 20:22–23; Matthew 16:19; 18:15–20; Revelation 1:18). In particular, the Office of the Keys (administered by pastors [AC V] by the call of the Church [AC XIV]) is the office Christ has given to His

Church. The Christian congregation, by the command of Christ, calls pastors to carry out the Office of the Keys publicly in His name and on behalf of the congregation. The pastoral office is a divine institution (Ephesians 4:11; Acts 20:28; 1 Corinthians 4:1; 2 Corinthians 2:10). As Martin Luther said, "God is superabundantly generous in His grace: First, through the spoken Word, by which the forgiveness of sins is preached in the whole world. This is the particular office of the Gospel. Second, through Baptism. Third, through the Holy Sacrament of the Altar. Fourth, through the Power of the Keys. Also through the mutual conversation and consolation of the brethren, 'Where two or three are gathered' (Matthew 18:[20]) and other such verses, especially Romans 1:12" (SA III IV).

kingdom of God. God's rule over the universe, in particular through the Church. Millennialists look for a political rule of Christ on earth. Amillennialists associate the kingdom of God with the Church.

Kyrie. Greek for "Lord." The Kyrie is a prayer based on biblical pleas for God's help (e.g., Mark 10:47).

Law. God's will as recorded in His Word, which shows people how they should live (e.g., the Ten Commandments) and condemns their sins. The preaching of the Law is the cause of contrition or genuine sorrow over sin. The Law must precede the Gospel, otherwise sinners will be confirmed in unrepentance. Like the Gospel, the Law is found in both the Old and New Testaments.

lectionary. From the Latin word for "reading." A collection of texts for public reading.

legalism. Legalism can be (1) seeking salvation from God through obedience to God's commands; (2) emphasizing the Law so that the Gospel's proper role is depreciated or excluded; (3) overstressing the letter, but not the spirit, of the Law.

liberation theology. Political and social teaching encouraged through churchly language (e.g., "salvation" means liberation from oppression by the wealthy).

Lord's Table. An early Christian name for the Lord's Supper, growing out of the Passover, during which the family shared a meal around a table (1 Corinthians 10:21). The altar in today's churches was originally a household table. *See also* **Passover.**

macroevolution. Evolution occurring above the species level, as theorized in contemporary paleontology and evolutionary biology.

Manichaeism. An early third-century AD rival to Christianity that taught a form of dualism between Light and Darkness, each ruled by a king. The current creation was the result of Darkness attempting to overcome Light. It partially succeeded. Man is to recognize this dualistic paradigm and, with the help of great human prophets and teachers, learn to overcome Darkness. Manichaeism, of course, denies that God's creation was "very good" and thus denies the true God.

marriage. Historically, a publicly recognized, lifelong relationship of two opposite-sex individuals who are not too closely related. Marriage is entered into for the purpose of mutual support, sexual intimacy, and the bearing and nurturing of children. Jesus affirmed the biblical basis for traditional marriage, the lifelong one-flesh union of husband and wife (Matthew 19:4–6).

Means of Grace. The means by which God gives us the forgiveness, life, and salvation won by the death and resurrection of Christ: the Gospel, Absolution, Baptism, and the Lord's Supper.

mercy seat. The lid, or cover, of the ark of the covenant; place of the ritual of propitiation performed by the high priest. Paul uses the Greek word for mercy seat, *hilasterion*, to refer to Jesus (Romans 3:25). *See also* **atonement; propitiation.**

Messiah. A Hebrew word meaning "anointed one"—that is, one chosen by God for a special purpose.

microevolution. Observable, small-scale changes within a species, that is, at or below the species level. Bacteria that become resistant to antibiotics are an example of microevolution.

millennium. Literally, a thousand-year period of time. In the Bible the number 1,000 is often used symbolically; for example, "the cattle on a thousand hills" (Psalm 50:10) represents all creation.

ministry. Used in both a wide and narrow sense. In the wide sense, any area of service; in the narrow sense, the Office of the Holy Ministry.

mode of Baptism. The manner in which water is applied in Baptism: immersion, pouring (affusion), or sprinkling.

neighbor. The person my circumstances and gifts call me to serve.

Nunc Dimittis. From the Latin for "now dismiss," the opening words of Simeon's song in Luke 2:29. The Nunc Dimittis is sung after the congregation receives the Lord's Supper.

Offertory. A song accompanying the collecting of the offering.

office. 1. Particular position or area of responsibility with certain prescribed duties. 2. Any number of religious services (i.e., a "choir office").

Office of the Keys. *See* **Keys.**

Old Earth (Progressive) Creationism. Some Christians view this as a variation of theistic evolution, but this assertion is probably going too far. Old Earth Creationism maintains "special creation," the belief that God created directly and miraculously *ex nihilo*, out of nothing. Some Christians are challenged by Old Earth Creationism because it proffers that God created the universe at certain intervals within millions or billions of years. However, some Christians hold this view in light of scientific evidence that seems to indicate an older earth. The problem with Old Earth Creationism is that it seems to insert contemporary scientific theories into the biblical text.

open Communion. Some denominations, influenced especially by the ecumenical movement of the nineteenth century, commune people without regard to belief or denominational membership (some expect that a person will be baptized before they receive the Lord's Supper). *See also* **close(d) Communion.**

ordinance. Literally, something ordered or commanded.

ordination. The ratification or confirmation of the call through prayer, the Word of God, and the laying on of hands. Ordination formally and publicly places a person in office.

original sin. The corruption and guilt all people have inherited from Adam and Eve. Original sin causes a person to commit "actual" sins. *See also* **actual sin.**

partial inspiration. Theologically liberal Christians hold different views of the Bible's inspiration. Some assert that the Bible is God's Word but contains factual errors. Others say that the Holy Spirit helps people determine which parts of the Bible to follow. Others maintain that the Bible is but one of many testimonies to God's Word, including writings of other religions. Still others hold that only those verses in the Bible specifically dealing with the Gospel are inspired. *See* **Gospel reductionism.**

participation. *See* **Communion.**

Passover. The ancient celebration of how God delivered Israel from Egypt (Exodus 12:21–51; Matthew 26:1–30).

penance. In Eastern Orthodoxy and Roman Catholicism, the actions assigned by the priest as an aid to repentance and amendment of life.

perfectionism. The belief that Christians can attain perfect sinlessness in this life. The teaching is popular in the Wesleyan and Anabaptist traditions. Roman Catholics have taught a form of perfectionism to describe the holiness of the saints.

Platonism. The fourth-century-BC Greek philosopher Plato's doctrine of objective and eternal "ideas" and "forms." For Plato, God, or the "Demiurge," is highly impersonal and fashions the things of this world (which is considered eternal) according to the model of the Forms.

polemical (Greek: *polemos*, "battle"). Controversial discussions or arguments involving attack and/or refutation.

postmillennialism. The doctrine that Christ will return after His Church rules politically on earth for a thousand years. This view was extremely popular early in U.S. history, but few churches still hold this view.

prayer. A request or petition for benefits or mercies. More broadly, prayer refers to worship and devotion.

predestination. The act of God whereby He chose those who will be saved in Christ (the "elect"). Calvinists/Presbyterians teach the unbiblical doctrine of double predestination, maintaining that, in addition to the elect, God also chose the remainder of humanity for damnation. *See* **elect.**

premillennialism. The doctrine that Christ will return to establish a thousand-year political rule on earth. This view was taught by John Nelson Darby in the nineteenth century and is popularized today through the writings of Hal Lindsey and Tim LaHaye.

presbyter. *See* **elder.**

priest. In the Old Testament, a Levitical minister of the tabernacle or temple who offered sacrifices on behalf of Israel. In the New Testament, any baptized believer in Christ. Luther and the reformers frequently used the word *priest* to refer to pastors, following medieval usage. This sometimes creates confusion when reading Luther or the Lutheran Confessions.

priesthood. An order of priests. Priests are never isolated as individuals.

propitiation (Greek: *hilasterion*, "atonement"). Hebrews 9:5 translates this word as "mercy seat." The Hebrew equivalent (*kapporeth* [Exodus 25:17]) means the cover or lid of the ark of the covenant on which the high priest once a year would sprinkle blood to propitiate, or make atonement for, the sins of the people. This was a type of the propitiatory sacrifice of Christ on the cross. *See also* **atonement.**

rapture. A doctrine introduced around 1830 by John Nelson Darby, which states that before the millennium, Christ will take up to heaven all Christians living on earth so that they will not suffer tribulation.

rationalism. A philosophical movement that is often hostile to Christianity, especially the Bible's teachings about miracles and faith. Rationalists decide what is true on the basis of human reason rather than Holy Scripture.

regeneration. From a Latin word meaning "rebirth." The act of divine grace by which the sinner is delivered from the power of darkness and transferred into the kingdom of Christ (Colossians 1:13).

reincarnation. A Hindu and Buddhist belief that people who die are born into another body and life, depending on how well they lived. Do not confuse this teaching with the Christian teaching about the incarnation of Jesus.

repentance. In a wide sense, change from a rebellious state to one of harmony with God's will, from trusting in human merit to trusting in Christ's merit. Embraces contrition and justifying faith; sometimes the fruit of repentance are included (Ap XII 28). In the narrow sense, faith and fruit are not included.The means to repentance is God's Word (see Jeremiah 31:18; Acts 5:31). Sometimes taken as an equivalent to penance and penitence.

revivalism. A movement that attempts to assist the conversion of people by stirring up, or "reviving," faith through emotional and persuasive appeals. Revivalism emerged as a method of conversion in American Protestantism. Revivalists emphasize that people need to choose or decide for their own salvation.

Sacrament. From the Latin *sacramentum*; "something to be kept sacred." A Sacrament is a sacred act instituted by God in which God Himself has joined His Word of promise to a visible element and by which He offers, gives, and seals the forgiveness of sins earned by Christ. By this definition, there are two Sacraments: Holy Baptism and the Lord's Supper. Sometimes Holy Absolution is counted as a third Sacrament, even though it has no divinely instituted element (LC IV 74; Ap XIII 4). In Ancient and Medieval Church usage, the term had various meanings: (1) a secret; (2) the Gospel revelation; (3) a mystery; (4) a means of giving, and receiving, grace (e.g., Baptism and Holy Communion); (5) the Office of the Holy Ministry. According to Luther, the chief Sacrament is Christ Himself (WA 6:97).

sacramental presence. Refers to the presence of Jesus' body and blood in, with, and under the bread and wine of the Lord's Supper. Jesus' presence for the forgiveness of sins (Matthew 26:28) differs from His presence in the universe as Lord of creation (Matthew 28:20).

saint. In Scripture, this word refers to believers on earth (Acts 9:32; Romans 1:7) and in heaven (Matthew 27:52). Throughout Church history, it has been used to designate one set apart as especially holy (e.g., St. Paul, St. Francis of Assisi). The Lutheran Reformation rejected prayers and devotions to saints. In Lutheran usage, "saint" is used only for those who were called such before the Reformation.

sanctification. The spiritual growth that follows justification by grace through faith in Christ. Sanctification is God's work through His Means of Grace: Word and Sacraments.

Sanctus. Latin for "holy," from the song of the seraphim in Isaiah 6:2–6.

satisfaction. In Roman Catholicism, amendment for one's sins.

self-examination. Repentance in preparation for receiving Communion.

seraphim (singular: *seraph*). Angelic beings, each possessing faces, feet, and three pairs of wings. Seraphim are mentioned only in Isaiah 6:2–6, where they fly above God's throne, singing praises to Him.

sinful nature. Our human nature, after the fall, is thoroughly corrupted by sin, making us God's enemies and lovers of ourselves.

Son of God. A divine title meaning that Jesus shares the same nature or substance as the heavenly Father, just as a boy shares the same nature or substance as his father.

Son of Man. An Aramaic expression meaning "a person." The prophet Daniel made this a title for the Messiah (Daniel 7:13–14).

speaking in tongues. A Semitic expression used in the Bible to mean "speaking in foreign languages." See Nehemiah 13:24; Isaiah 28:11; and Acts 2:4.

sponsor. *See* **godparent.**

stewards. Servants who administer something on behalf of another. In 1 Corinthians 4:1, Paul describes ministers as stewards of God's mysteries.

syncretism. *See* **unionism and syncretism.**

testament. (1) A covenant between God and human beings. (2) A will or expression of someone's desire as to the disposal of personal property upon death. Jesus called the Lord's Supper the "new testament" that declared His will for His disciples: He took away their sins by His sacrificial death and resurrection (Matthew 26:27–28; Luke 22:20). *See also* **atonement; covenant; propitiation.**

theistic evolution. This perspective finds faith in God and macroevolution compatible and understands that while God is behind the physical universe, He employed Darwinian evolution to bring it into existence. God is the spiritual presence behind the natural processes we observe. God's work of creation described in the Bible is symbolic for what we call evolution, macroevolution being God's instrument for bringing the "creation" into being.

Theotokos. Greek for "God-bearer." A title for the Virgin Mary, emphasizing that she gave birth to the Son of God, not simply a typical human baby.

transubstantiation (Latin: "the change of one substance to another"). In Roman Church teaching, the material substance or basic reality of the bread and wine in the Eucharist are changed by the action of the priest into the body and blood of Jesus Christ. However, the outward appearance, color, taste, dimension, and so on are not affected by this change.

trespasses. Sins; actions that go beyond the boundaries of God's Law.

tribulation. Literally, distress or suffering. Based on Revelation 7:14 and other passages, millennialists anticipate a seven-year tribulation as part of end-time events. Amillennialists read these passages as describing the suffering that Christians currently experience.

two kingdoms. God's "left hand" kingdom governs temporal matters and all our dealings with others here on earth. God's "right hand" kingdom governs our hearts by His grace through faith in Christ.

unionism and syncretism. From the Greek word for "union" or "federation" (*syncretism*). Broadly defined, unionism and syncretism refer to the mixture, or mingling, of incompatible religious teachings within the contexts of worship and joint work. For example, Christians and Muslims cannot, if they wish to remain faithful to their respective traditions, worship together. Such an activity would be "syncretistic."

veneration of angels. The veneration, or worship, of angels is condemned by Scripture (Colossians 2:18; Revelation 22:8–9). Lutherans honor but do not worship or pray to angels.

verbal inspiration. The Holy Spirit guided the prophets, evangelists, and apostles in writing the books of the Bible, inspiring their very words while using their particular styles of expression. Conservative Christian churches hold that the Bible's words are God's Word and that the original manuscripts of Scripture were without error (*see* **inerrancy**), but some mistakes may have entered the text as it was copied, edited, or translated over the centuries.

vocation. From the Latin word for "calling." (1) A person's occupation, or duties, before God. For example, a person may serve as a husband, a father, and an engineer. (a) As a new person in Christ, one is called to serve one's neighbor freely, out of gratitude for Christ's salvation and without the compulsion of the Law. (b) In the family, husband and wife, mother and father, and children all have distinct vocations that bind the family together. The family is the basis for every other community, including civil society and the Church. (c) In the Church (Christ's Body), the pastor is called to stand in the place of Christ, calling the congregation to Confession, announcing Absolution, proclaiming God's Word, and administering the Sacraments. Each member of the congregation is called by his or her distinctive gifts and opportunities to serve and make contributions that build up the Body of Christ. (d) In the state (civil order), each person's vocation contributes to, and depends on, other vocations needed for society to function. (e) As part of humanity's design, all are called to be stewards, though men and women are called to complementary roles of husband and wife, father and mother. (2) With reference to God's own triune nature, the Father calls the Son to be obedient and rewards His humiliation with exaltation. The Spirit is called to proceed from the Father and the Son to convict the world of sin and draw mankind to saving faith.

will. After the fall, humanity is able to exercise free will in temporal matters. However, in spiritual matters, we are spiritually dead (Romans 8:6–7; Ephesians 2:1) and can neither cooperate with nor make a decision to follow God. Our salvation, the forgiveness of our sins, the cleansing of our souls, and the turning of our will toward God is solely the work of the Holy Spirit (1 Corinthians 12:3; 2 Timothy 1:9) through the Gospel. *See* **Gospel.**

Young Earth (Recent) Creationism. While an increasing number of legitimate scientists are supporting this view (the Creation Research Society, the Geo-science Research Institute, and the Institute for Creation Research), the majority of scientists hold that empirical data rule against the earth being relatively young (around 6,000 years old). However, scientific data can be interpreted in different ways. The strength of Young Earth or Recent Creationism is that it appears faithful to God's Word.

Scripture Index

In the following index, page numbers that appear below a book of the Bible indicate discussions of that particular book of Holy Scripture.

Old Testament

Genesis

2 Corinthians

Galatians

Colossians

1 Thessalonians

2 Thessalonians

1 Timothy

Church Life / Theology / Systematic Theology

12-4443
ISBN 13: 978-0-7586-4673-6